THE HORIZON HISTORY OF THE

BRITISH EMPIRE

Helmet of the Household Cavalry.

THE HORIZON HISTORY OF THE

BRITISH EMPIRE

Editor
STEPHEN W. SEARS

**Published by American Heritage Publishing Co., Inc.,
in association with BBC-TV/Time-Life Books**
Book trade distribution by McGraw-Hill Book Company

THE HORIZON HISTORY OF THE
BRITISH EMPIRE

Editor: Stephen W. Sears   *Designer:* Scott Chelius   *Copy Editor:* Brenda Bennerup

AMERICAN HERITAGE PUBLISHING CO., INC.,
A SUBSIDIARY OF McGRAW-HILL, INC.

President and Publisher: Paul Gottlieb   *Editor-in-Chief:* Joseph J. Thorndike
Senior Editor, Book Division: Alvin M. Josephy, Jr.   *Editorial Art Director:* Murray Belsky
General Manager, Book Division: Kenneth W. Leish

This work is based on material originally produced by Time-Life Books in association with the broadcast of the television series *The British Empire* by BBC-TV.

Library of Congress Cataloging in Publication Data: page 500

Introduction

Nowhere in history's record of imperial endeavour is there anything to compare to the British Empire. It was unique. In size it was paramount, ruling the largest area and the most people. Its acquisition was the most haphazard, its holdings the most varied, its motives and benefits the most mixed. It rose, flourished, and declined in less than four centuries, and its effects upon modern history are almost incalculable.

The tale begins in the reign of Elizabeth I and ends in the reign of Elizabeth II. Its earliest manifestation, the so-called first British Empire, consisted primarily of footholds in North America, the West Indies, and India, and resulted in imperial contests with Spain and France. The demise of the first Empire may be dated precisely—October 19, 1781, when Lord Cornwallis's redcoats grounded their muskets at Yorktown. Almost immediately the foundations of a second and more formidable world-wide Empire were laid. Its essential starting point was military triumph over France, notably the victories of Nelson at Trafalgar and Wellington at Waterloo.

Thus began, in 1815, the Pax Britannica, a century free of major war (but not imperial warfare) thanks primarily to the Royal Navy's control of the seven seas. Behind this intimidating shield 19th-Century Britain shrugged off the loss of the American colonies and expanded spectacularly round the globe. By the end of the century London was the "new Rome" and nearly a quarter of the earth's land area was labelled with the imperial red. In remarking the celebration of Queen Victoria's sixtieth year on the throne in 1897, *The Times* of London unblushingly proclaimed that she ruled "the mightiest and most beneficial Empire ever known in the annals of mankind."

The "mightiest" it undoubtedly was; the "most beneficial" is a judgement debated then and since. The motives of imperialism were as diverse as everything else about the Empire. Sometimes it was trade and profit, as in India. Military security raised the Union Jack in South Africa; a dumping ground for an unwanted population was the rationale for the convict settlements in Australia. International rivalry led the British into Afghanistan, and the quest for geographic knowledge led Captain Cook into the Pacific. Zealous missionaries and abolitionists were in the lead in Africa, opium entrepreneurs behind the economic penetration of China.

However they got there and for whatever reasons, Englishmen invariably had the urge to justify their presence in Higher Terms. Stamford Raffles, one of the most noted of the free-lance imperialists and the founder of Singapore, put it this way: "Let it still be the boast of Britain to write her name in characters of light; let her not be remembered as the tempest whose course was desolate, but as the gale of spring reviving the slumbering seeds of mind and calling them to life from the winter of ignorance and oppression. If the time shall come when her empire shall have passed away, these monuments will endure when her triumphs shall have become an empty name."

Of course the time did come when the Empire passed away. The world wars of the 20th Century demolished the Pax Britannica and left the mother country economically debilitated. The sunset of Empire was abrupt. The end came not without conflict, yet compared to past empires the British Empire may be said to have died peacefully in bed. That is one of its enduring monuments, one of the many that remain to mark its passage across history.

Some 30 authors—historians, journalists, political scientists, specialists all—detail this epic tale in the following pages, which draw upon materials assembled by BBC-TV and Time-Life Books for a series of television programs and magazines about the Empire.

Contents

Prologue
JUBILEE DAY

At midday on Tuesday, June 22, 1897, Queen Victoria of England, Defender of the Faith, Empress of India, ruler of the British Dominions beyond the Seas, arrived at St. Paul's Cathedral to thank God for the existence of the greatest Empire ever known.

The representatives of an imperial caste awaited her there. Bishops of the Church of England fluttered hymnsheets and remembered half a century of Christian effort—the suppression of slavery, the conversion of heathen tribes, mission stations from Niger to Labrador. Generals and admirals blazed with medals and remembered half a century of satisfactory campaigning—in India or in Egypt, against Ashanti tribesmen or Maori chiefs, up Burmese backwaters or Manitoba creeks. There were aged proconsuls of Empire, bronzed or emaciated by tropical lifetimes and attended by faded wives in lacy hats. There were scholars in the gowns of Oxford and Cambridge, the twin powerhouses of British ideology. There were poets, musicians, and propagandists, whose transcendental theme of the day was the splendour of imperial Britain.

Two celebrated soldiers commanded the guards of honour. On the south side of the cathedral steps, upon a brown charger, was Field-Marshal Lord Wolseley, Commander-in-Chief of the British Army, hero of the Red River expedition in Canada, the Ashanti War in the Gold Coast, Tel-el-Kebir in Egypt, and many another imperial war, looking after 45 years of more or less constant campaigning, a fairly melancholy 64. On the north side, upon the grey Arab which had carried him victoriously to the relief of Kandahar in 1880, was Field-

Marshal Lord Roberts, veteran of two Afghan Wars, the Indian Mutiny, and the Abyssinian expedition, whose sweet, simple nature and unfailing courage made him the idol of the private soldier.

Behind these allegorical marshals, soldiers from every part of the Queen's Empire honoured the royal presence. The Chinese from Hong Kong wore wide coolie hats. The Zaptiehs, Turkish military policemen from Cyprus, wore fezzes. The Jamaicans wore white gaiters and gold-embroidered jackets. There were Dyaks from Borneo, and Sikhs from India, and Canadian Hussars, and Sierra Leone gunners, and Australian cavalrymen, and British Guiana police, and Maltese, and South Africans, and a troop of jangling Bengal Lancers. One of the Maori riflemen weighed 392 pounds. One of the Dyaks had taken, "in his former occupation," 13 human heads. The officers of the Indian Imperial Service Corps were all princes. The cavalrymen from New South Wales were all giants, with an average height of five feet ten and a half inches and an average chest of 38 inches. And Captain Ames of the 2nd Life Guards, at six foot eight inches the tallest man in the British Army, was the princeliest and most gigantic of all, mounted on his charger and wearing his monstrous plumed helmet of burnished steel.

Satraps from many parts of the Queen's dominions had converged upon London that day: tributary bigwigs of every colour, religion, costume, and deportment, prime ministers of the self-governing colonies, maharajahs and nawabs and hereditary chiefs, governors of distant possessions, military leaders from far commands. There were representa-

tives from other respectful powers: the Dowager Empress of Germany (the Queen's eldest daughter); Crown Prince Franz Ferdinand of Austria-Hungary (whose assassination at Sarajevo in 1914 was to begin the Great War); 23 assorted princesses, a scattering of grand dukes and duchesses, and 40 Indian potentates; Monsignor Cesare Sambucetti, the Papal Nuncio, improbably sharing a carriage with Chang Yen Huan, the Chinese Ambassador; General Nelson A. Miles, Commander-in-Chief of the U.S. Army; Count Ferdinand von Zeppelin, inventor and builder of the rigid airship.

Since the firing of the celebratory guns in Hyde Park that morning, all London had waited in grand expectancy—the greatest of capitals on a climactic day in its history. The excuse for this grandiloquent jamboree was the Queen's Diamond Jubilee— 60 years upon the throne—but its theme was the splendour of Empire. The British Empire had reached its high noon, and on this day of days the people waved their Jubilee flags as exuberantly in imperial fervour as in royalist devotion.

Vast crowds had applauded Victoria in her procession as she made her way from Buckingham Palace to St. Paul's in a plain open landau, beneath a parasol of white lace. On Constitution Hill an army of civil servants, released for the day from their red tape and dockets, discreetly waved pocket handkerchiefs. At a balcony window on Ludgate Hill survivors of the Charge of the Light Brigade, 43 years before, had assembled to offer their now frail allegiance. Around St. Paul's itself the windows of the City offices were crammed with sightseers and festooned with ban-

Pensioned veterans from the Royal Hospital at Chelsea raise a frail but gallant cheer for Queen and Country as the Diamond Jubilee procession passes by.

9

ners. On their roofs gay pavilions had been erected, on their balconies company directors and opulent wives looked down with a proprietary condescension upon the scene below.

At street level the Cockney poor yelled and sang their loyalty, hoisting cheerful, grubby children upon their shoulders and following the parade along the pavements. One man darted into the road outside the Royal Courts of Justice, grabbed a shoe cast off by one of the horses, and triumphantly waved it above his head with a cry of "Jubilee luck!" Several girls wore blouses made from Union Jacks. Guns boomed, bands blared, a million Union Jacks flew, voices from the crowd shouted "Go it, old girl!" or "Three Cheers for India!"

And there, at the centre of it all, wrote the *Daily Mail's* reporter, "was a little plain flushed old lady . . . so very quiet, so very grave, so unmistakably and every inch a lady and a Queen. All in black, a silver streak under the black bonnet, a simple white sunshade, sitting quite still, with the corners of her mouth drawn right down, as if she were trying not to cry. . . . So very quiet, so very grave . . . almost pathetic if you will, that small black figure in the middle of those shining cavaliers, but also very glorious."

At St. Paul's, Victoria was greeted by her own dear Albert Edward (the future Edward VII), mounted, feathered, and carrying a marshal's baton, and by a squadron of miscellaneous nobility assembled on horseback in the cathedral square. There was a fanfare of trumpets, and as the Archbishop of Canterbury raised his prayerbook for the thanksgiving service, two scarlet-coated military bands struck up a ringing hymn.

The Queen was 78 years old, and it had been suggested that her carriage might actually be hauled inside St. Paul's on ramps up the great steps. This dramatic expedient was abandoned; instead the service was held outside, the Queen remaining in her seat. It did not matter. The accumulated history of a thousand years gave dignity to her portly presence. The power, wealth, beauty, gusto, and arrogance of Empire swirled about her

carriage. As the hymns of praise rang out that day, to the thump of the regimental bands and the swell of the great organ inside the cathedral, not merely a congregation, nor even a kingdom, but a quarter of the world figuratively sang its loyalty too— giving patriotic thanks to a God who seemed, despite His alien origins, to have given ample proof that He was thoroughly British.

By 1897 the British had proved themselves the most gifted, resolute, and formidable people of their day. Their long military supremacy, throughout the years of Victoria's reign, had given the world a general peace—the Pax Britannica—of unprecedented length: small wars there had been by the dozen, but none of those dominating international conflicts that have always been the norms of history. A dazzling list of heroes and geniuses had, within the past century, brought lustre to the national reputation: in war, Nelson and Wellington; in letters, Shelley, Keats, Byron, Tennyson, Dickens; in art, Turner and Constable; in science, Darwin, Faraday, Lister; in politics, Palmerston, Gladstone, Disraeli. It had truly been an age of giants, and during its mid-Victorian climax Britain was respected as perhaps no other power had ever been. Her manners, tastes, and values were copied or adopted everywhere. Her products, technicians, ships, and expatriate eccentrics were ubiquitous. Her prestige was terrific. Her self-esteem was limitless.

Now, at the end of this triumphant century, suddenly Empire was all the rage. It was a vulgar conception, fostered by vulgar means, and it thrived upon the gaudy, brassy atmosphere of *fin de siècle*. The new Penny Press, preaching to a huge, newly literate audience, seized upon Empire as a popular circulation-builder. A hazy movement called the "New Imperialism" translated the enthusiasm into politics.

In the 1895 general election the Conservatives had won handsomely on a boldly imperialist platform. The Prime Minister was the sagacious Lord Salisbury, who saw the Empire as a colossal diplomatic stake, and the

Colonial Secretary was the business-like Joseph Chamberlain, "Pushful Joe," who saw it as an immense undeveloped property. These two had arranged the great parade of Jubilee not merely as a tribute to 60 years of queenly rule, but specifically as a grand slam of imperialism—a crowning expression of the achievements, the ideals, the forces, the satisfactions of empire-building. "England without an Empire!" Chamberlain had once exclaimed, "Can you conceive it? England in that case would not be the England we love." In the summer of 1897 the vast majority of the British people flamboyantly agreed with him.

It was a universal craze. The *Daily Mail*, organ of the masses, was rampantly imperialist; but so was *The Times*, the mouthpiece of the ruling classes. "Imperialism in the air," wrote the Socialist Beatrice Webb in her diary that June. "All classes drunk with sightseeing and hysterical loyalty." In the drabbest slums of Glasgow and London's East End, the Diamond Jubilee was greeted with fervent if inebriated enthusiasm. In the most sluggish rural enclaves the yokels built their celebratory beacons. The Queen-Empress herself, after 60 years of fluctuating popularity, had achieved an almost sacred status; she was a kind of fetish-figure for the simpler British, her emotional excesses forgotten, her long withdrawal into sulky widowhood forgiven, even her mortality ignored, so hard was it to imagine a Britain without her plump and pouch-eyed sovereignty.

During previous moments of patriotic apogee the British had generally celebrated the continued immunity of their island state, delivered once more from the designs of foreign tyrants. Now they were honouring something different: the expansion of England, the possession of lands and territories flung across continents, the responsibilities of global power, the distribution of ideas and techniques, the unrivalled success of an Empire upon which, as the souvenir plates proclaimed, "the sun never sets."

In Britain then only a few radical thinkers, advanced economists, Irishmen, and wild poets objected to the idea of Empire. Morally and politically it was generally accepted that Britons had a perfect right to impose their rule upon less fortunate foreigners: anyway, if they did not, other Western powers certainly would. Nevertheless, Empire meant very different things to different classes and professions.

To poor people Empire was largely a consolation—circuses to their lack of bread. England was "two nations" still, as Disraeli had observed. The slums of London were still horrific; the industrial cities of the Midlands and the North were among the saddest of man's artifacts; the countryside, which looked so idyllic to visiting foreigners, hid horrifying extremes of hedonism and despair. But if life was harsh in tenement and hovel, at least outside the flag flew, the rhythms of jingo drummed through the music-halls, and black potentates made obeisance to the Queen. Patriotism, not religion, was the opiate of this proletariat, and at this particular moment of history patriotism was interpreted in terms of imperial glory.

For the hundreds of thousands of Britons who had overtaken their parents by learning to read, the concept of Empire was a dramatic revelation. From office desk or schoolroom blackboard they caught a glimpse of thrilling new horizons—exotic indeed, but in a sense their own. High adventure was a passion of the time, exploited incessantly in sixpenny novel and pulp magazine, and Empire marvellously satisfied its devotees. A world of melodrama, space, and opportunity seemed to lie at an Englishman's feet, and though one might not actually chuck one's job that morning and take passage to the colonies to fight the Zulus or prospect for gold, still it was grand to know that a chap could if he wanted to. As the *Daily Mail* crowed in its Jubilee edition: "We send a boy here and a boy there, and the boy takes hold of the savages of the part he comes to and teaches them to march and shoot as he tells them, to obey him and believe him and die for him and the Queen . . . and each one of us—you and I, and that man in his shirt-sleeves at the corner—is a working part of this world-shaping force."

To a substantial minority of the upper middle classes, Empire was a credit balance. Innumerable British firms, in the 1890s, based their fortunes upon the imperial trade. Cotton merchants in Lancashire, coffee men in Bristol, dynasties of India merchants, speculators in gold, rubber, or cocoa, shipowners, railway-builders—all had found their paths to affluence smoothed by the fact that so much of the world was British. Trade often did follow the flag, and the expansion of England had contributed very comfortably to the well-being of those company directors and their ladies, feather-boa'd and complacent in their bowers above St. Paul's.

Upper bourgeois Britons of another kind—professional men, younger sons, soldiers—looked upon the Empire as an employment exchange. John Stuart Mill once called it "a vast system of unemployment relief for the upper classes." To many educated English, Scottish, and Anglo-Irish families an imperial career was a natural alternative to the Church, the law, or the armed forces at home. They were not generally aristocrats who looked for fulfilment in Africa or Asia. For the most part the imperial career men were sons of the lesser gentry, trained to the British public school ideals of grit, stiff upper lip, comradeship, good humour, and a realistic degree of tolerance. Their background might have been specifically designed for the production of an imperial elite, and consistently for two or three generations they had gone off by P. & O. or Union Castle, with their spinepads for the prevention of sunstroke, their cricket-bags for the maintenance of tradition, their champagne for the sustaining of morale, and their Books of Common Prayer for the elevation of pagans. They were bred to Empire, in a gentlemanly way, and took its existence easily for granted.

And to many of the men who governed England, the statesmen, the greatest of the financiers, the senior civil servants, Empire was a historical instrument, and that imperial festival was a declaration of state. The possession of Empire was a counterweight to the greater size and richer national resources of countries like Germany, Russia, and the United States. It was the means of preserving Britain's greatness, upheld till then chiefly by ingenuity, courage, and good luck. The politician Charles Dilke had coined the phrase "Greater Britain" to define the white overseas possessions of the Crown—Canada, Australia, New Zealand, the South African colonies. The New Imperialists gave an extra meaning to the phrase. They pictured the entire Empire, black, white, or brown, as a single political force, a super-state, potential if not actual, capable of standing up to the new continental powers, maintaining the influence of the Mother Country, and keeping its more fortunate citizens comfortable and rich.

Such were, for the British in their islands, the various meanings of Empire and of Jubilee: entertainment, fillip, profit, opportunity, defiance. To the Queen herself, as she returned to the palace that evening through London's demonstrative streets, it was all delight and grateful emotion. "How kind they are to me!" she kept saying, the tears welling into her eyes. "How kind they are!" By nightfall her personal message to the Empire, distributed across the world by the miracle of the electric telegraph, had reached all but the most hideously inaccessible of her possessions. It was a message of Roman simplicity. "From my heart," it said, "I thank my beloved people. May God bless them."

"I thank my beloved people." This was the imperial touch, for when Her Majesty spoke of "her people" she was referring to nearly 400 million subjects living in all five continents, honouring a thousand religions, speaking a thousand languages—people of every race, culture, stage of development: occupying mud huts in the Australian outback, caves in the Kalahari Desert, exquisite manor houses in Nova Scotia; savages who did not know the use of money, Boers like Biblical patriarchs, Hindu princes of porcelain sensibility, ancillary kings, colonial magnates, Mediterranean noblemen, dung-smeared wizards, cannibals, Confucian scholars, Eskimos, Arabs—such a variety of peoples as had never before, in the whole history of human affairs, owed their allegiance to a single suzerain.

Queen Victoria's Empire embraced nearly a quarter of the earth's land mass, and a quarter of its population. The overseas Empire was 90 times larger than the little Mother Country, and during Victoria's own reign it had expanded from some two million square miles to more than 11 million. The more rabid of the imperial activists saw almost no limit to its future expansion. Cecil Rhodes, the South African empire-builder, was already dreaming of colonizing the solar system. "I would annex the planets if I could," he said. "I often think of that."

There had never been an empire remotely like it before. It was strewn in colossal muddle across the hemispheres, so that the map of the world was splodged untidily and apparently illogically with the imperial red. Though the whole of it looked to London for its supreme authority, and to the Queen for its unifying symbol, still it consisted in effect of two separate empires, differing not only racially and climatically, but historically too.

On the one hand was the Western Empire—Western, that is, in a cultural sense. This consisted for the most part of English settlements overseas, together with old plantation colonies having a substantial white ruling class. Ranging from the enormous Dominion of Canada to petty islands in the Caribbean, this scattered group of possessions really could be called "Greater Britain." Its territories shared an ethnic origin with the British at home, its people spoke the same language and honoured the same values, its predominant culture was English, and its politics were mostly democratic. The great white colonies were self-governing in their domestic affairs; even some of the lesser possessions, like Barbados or the Bahamas, had old traditions of parliamentary government. It was not too fanciful to suppose that if the power at the centre maintained its dynamism, all might one day be linked in a federal structure of equals, looking to London as a central exchange and regulator.

The Eastern Empire was something else. This was Empire of an older kind—despotic, racialist, with white men on top and coloured men below. Its fulcrum and its exemplar was India, which had been conquered by swashbucklers and opportunists, but was now governed with a frigid rectitude. From India the British had extended their power all over south Asia, up the China Sea to Hong Kong, westward to Aden and the Persian Gulf, all down the east coast of Africa. Throughout these immense territories only a handful of Britons lived —administrators, military men, merchants, a few planters. Nowhere was there even a flicker of self-government.

Both these empires, of Orient and Occident, were vaguely familiar to the British at home. Millions of English families had a cousin in Australia or an uncle in British Columbia; hundreds of thousands of soldiers had done their time on tropical stations. If Australia and New Zealand were considered part of the family, India had been British for so long that it had become a kind of domesticized prodigy—a phoenix in the house. What gave a new flare to the imperialism of the 1890s was the emergence of a third empire: Empire in Africa.

Africa, the last unexploited continent, was the true backcloth of the Jubilee drama. It was there that the new lands were to be settled, the gold found, the contemporary savages humbled or converted. The British had been active in Africa for generations—as settlers in the south, elsewhere as explorers, missionaries, traders, and suppressors of slavery. But it was only in the 1880s and 1890s that the African continent became the focus of their imperial obsession.

Africa gave a brutal punch to the apogee of Empire. There was a feeling at once shady and dashing to the imperial goings-on out there. A mixed bag of speculators represented British interests in South Africa; and the ferment which then seized the continent, which gave gusto to the New Imperialism, revolved not so much around patriotism, or duty, or even the needs of commerce and strategy, but simply around the lust for wealth.

It was a tainted sort of imperialism.

The British public did not care. The heroes of the day were by no means all gentlemen in the old sense— Chamberlain himself, the impresario of Empire, was a Birmingham screw-manufacturer. If the great African adventure seemed dubious to the fastidious, to many more Britons it was only a revival of Elizabethan enterprise. Drake and Hawkins had scarcely behaved like gentlemen when they went raiding on the Spanish Main. If the Victorian buccaneers of Africa broke a rule now and then, singed an alien beard or even indulged in an occasional act of piracy, they were only honouring lusty old British traditions.

There was certainly nothing fusty to the idea of Empire. Joe Chamberlain himself set the tone of the New Imperialism when he talked of the British Empire as an estate—a national asset, to be developed by the best technical and managerial techniques as he had developed his screw factory in Birmingham. It is true that it was in a sense a development agency, distributing the skills of the industrial West through many backward countries, and even reviving stagnant cultures; but it was also a pageant, a trading device, an article of faith. The techniques developed by the British to hold this vast conglomeration together were at once mysterious and severly practical.

The first instrument of their supremacy was the Crown. Victoria was the pivot around which that gigantic structure orbited. She was the Great White Queen, the mystic figurehead of Empire, remote and half-divine. Her plinthed, throned, and porticoed statues were everywhere, and her cult was inescapable. Tribesmen of Assam sacrificed goats to her. Saskatchewan Indians of the Canadian prairie called her "Great Mother." Ladies of Melbourne or Singapore were thrilled to curtsey to her nephews, sons-in-law, or distant cousins.

This mystique of monarchy permeated the mechanism of Empire. Colonial governors were anointed, as it were, with the royal unction: with their flag-staffed palaces, their

Resplendent colonial officers of contingents from every corner of the Empire, in London for the Jubilee, posed for a group portrait before the parade.

ceremonial costumes, their elegant aides, their gracious garden-parties, their crested carriages, their majestic protocol, and their enormously superior wives, they stood, however long the range, diffused by the royal radiance. Symbols of the monarchy were stamped across the Empire like talismans: crowns, flags, regimental crests, lions and unicorns, mottoes in medieval French, uniforms of stunning ostentation, orders of chivalry and nobility, Silversmiths by Appointment, the insignia of the Royal Mail. The idea of imperial dominion was charged with primitive emotion, and the Victorian monarchy provided a necessary element of ritual magic.

More down to earth was a second instrument of supremacy, the rule of law. Throughout the disparate scattered realms of Empire, a pattern of justice generally prevailed—not merely legal justice, but a sense of balance, restraint, compromise. The rules were British rules, and they presupposed a common set of values among governors and governed, yet a powerful binding force of Empire was a sense of fair play backed by utter conviction. The motives of imperial expansion were innumerable, and often contradictory, but the Victorian concept of duty was among the most potent. Men were willing, in the 1890s, to dedicate their lives to the administration of the British Empire, mostly without hope of fame or wealth. They did so because they were convinced that the Empire was useful and benevolent to the world at large. This certainty, expressed above all in the rule of law, gave the Empire a kind of ideology, or at least an intellectual purpose and integrity.

But no mystery of kingship, no high-minded hierarchy or order, could have held the Empire together without a third fundamental tool of authority: armed force. Like all other empires, the British Empire was based upon warlike power. It had been conquered by the sword and it was held by the sword—or more pertinently, by the battleship. The Royal Navy was the ultimate guarantor of Jubilee, and in its arrogant and sometimes peculiar grandeur the Empire was most accurately reflected. This was a sea empire. Command of the sea gave it, in effect, internal lines of communication. Admiral Mahan, the American naval historian, discussing the influence of British sea power earlier in the century, had described Britain's "distant, storm-beaten ships" standing between Napoleon and the dominion of the world. If he had been writing of *fin de siècle*, he might have envisaged those fleets standing guard in harbours across the world, patrolling the sea routes of every ocean, paddling up the Irrawaddy or edging through North Sea mists, ensuring that the Empire remained inviolate.

At last the celebration of the Queen's Empire came to a close, and Jubilee Day ended with bonfires, pealing bells, banquets, and sentimental toasts, and the world did not begrudge the old Queen its admiration. Even *Le Figaro* in Paris, not usually sympathetic to perfidious Albion, allowed that Rome had been equalled at last, if not surpassed; while the New York *Times* went so far as to declare the United States "a part, and a great part, of the Greater Britain which seems so plainly destined to dominate this planet."

Of course they did not exactly mean it. The Diamond Jubilee, like the British Empire itself, was comfortably swathed in half-truth, blarney, and red serge. It was an oddly homely occasion; as Mark Twain wrote, all the braggadocio was really "no more than embroidery" to the presence of the Queen-Empress herself, a plain lady in her late seventies, sustained by stays and fortified by a taste for Scotch. There was indulgence in the air. Bygones were momentarily forgotten. Blemishes were temporarily overlooked. On such a day, when flags flew and champagne bubbled and bands puffed and the grand old lady, "tired" but marvellously "pleased," wiped away her tears, who would have the heart to do otherwise?

—*James Morris*

Chapter One
BIRTH OF EMPIRE

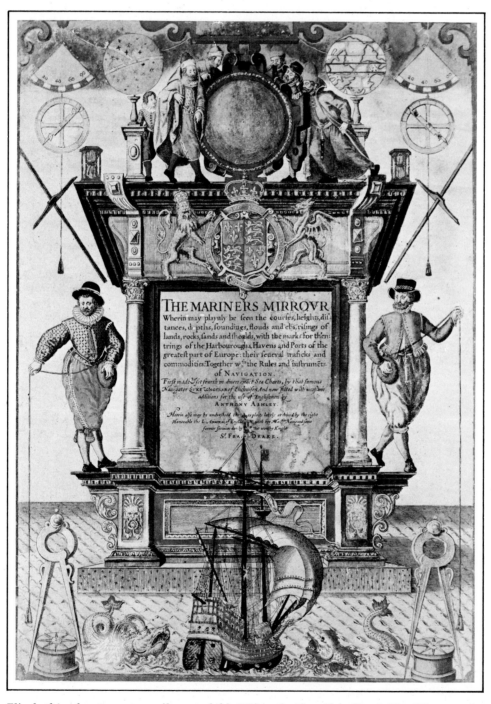

Elizabeth's adventuresome sailors used this 1588 navigational handbook. The title page pictures two Tudor seamen taking soundings amidst measuring devices and navigation aids.

I. A Bold Band of Explorers

Whosoever commands the sea commands the trade; whosoever commands the trade of the world commands the riches of the world, and consequently the world itself." This was first voiced by Sir Walter Raleigh but it had been fully understood by Spanish and Portuguese mariners long before.

Englishmen were latecomers to the sea that lapped their island kingdom. Iberian merchants, not London shopkeepers, first responded to the historic voyages by Columbus, da Gama, and Magellan that between 1492 and 1519 revolutionized men's minds and changed their ideas about the earth, geographically enlarging its circumference by 5,000 miles and revealing the New World of the Americas. The "green sea of darkness" which had been western Europe's prison was transformed into a high-road for expansion; the seaports of the Atlantic became windows to the Far East as shipwright and navigator set about testing what poets had dreamed of: a sea route to Cathay and its fabled wealth.

But the New World, rich in gold and politically ripe for the picking, proved to be a greater attraction than the legendary Ming Treasury. Spain and Portugal proceeded to carve up the newly discovered lands between them. In the early years of the 16th Century, Portugal turned the Indian Ocean into a private lake and the Malabar coast of India into a closed trading preserve. Territorial expansion took Spain slightly longer. Not until the 1540s was the New World safe for commercial and cultural exploitation by Seville merchants and Andalusian priests.

In 1494 His Holiness the Pope was persuaded in the Treaty of Tordesillas to exercise his divine mandate and apportion the world between those most Catholic sovereigns, Ferdinand and Isabella of Spain, and John II of Portugal, on a line a thousand miles west of the Azores. To the Iberian it was obvious that the Lord, considerably aided by Albuquerque, Balboa, Cortés, Pizarro, and the other *conquistadores,* had always intended that neither the New World nor the South-West Passage to Cathay should be plagued by northerners. Spaniards and Portuguese calmly accepted that the profits of world empire belonged to them—"so Catholic, so firm, so true."

Until the mid-16th Century the Spanish and Portuguese seemed to have nothing to fear from the British, at least. Despite their insular location, they were strangely blind to the wonders of the deep. The lure of the nautical unknown, of the pot of gold to be found just over the horizon which persuaded Spaniards by the thousands to undertake their hazardous voyages, exercised no such magic in the north.

The one man in England who was caught up in the dream of discovery was not even a native, but a Venetian merchant who had settled in Bristol. In 1497, two months before da Gama set out on the journey that took him from Lisbon to Calicut, John Cabot sailed west in search of the lands of the Dragon Throne. What he found was the barren rock-ribbed coast of Cape Breton Island, off the coast of Canada. In three more voyages his record was no better—unfriendly sightings of Greenland, Labrador, Newfoundland, and New England, a wildcat, a brace of barbaric Eskimos brought back to London as curiosities, but no Asia and no civilization rich in gold and spices. Bristol merchants were content to concentrate on the safe and profitable business of supervising their cloth exports to Antwerp, Calais, and Cadiz.

On the surface it is surprising that Englishmen did not earlier go down to the sea in ships, and that Columbus's recital of the wonders he had found—"the greatest event since the creation of the world"—did not fire the Anglo-Saxon mind. The island kingdom was more politically unified than Spain, was larger in population than Portugal, and early Tudor sovereigns were just as interested in ships and trade as John II of Portugal or Ferdinand and Isabella of Spain.

Henry VIII, like his father, was not unreceptive to the possibility of new markets for English wool, and during the 1520s he backed a number of abortive efforts to discover a North-West Passage which would bring China within reach of London merchants. Leadership, motive, and economic means were all there, but except for a handful of dreamers, Englishmen were content to remain in their chimney-corners. Time and circumstance were not yet right. The kingdom's political efforts during most of Henry VIII's reign were still directed toward the slaying of a medieval dragon—the conquest of the lost provinces of France. Economic energy remained landlocked in raising sheep, carding wool, weaving cloth, and mining tin. European merchants beat a path to English ports; there was no need to search further afield for new markets or for English navigators to chart the currents of the Channel, let alone the Baltic or the South Atlantic. Spiritual drive, at least for the time being, was also turned inward as the King's matrimonial affairs dragged

The Amazing Dr. Dee

Among the founders of the British Empire, none was more bizzare than the brilliant Welsh intellectual John Dee. Mathematician and sorcerer, astronomer and alchemist, geographer and astrologer, he was acknowledged as England's greatest authority on the mathematics of navigation. Elizabethan sea dogs hungrily devoured his maps, handbooks, and navigational essays.

But Dee's geography was essentially speculative. He was a firm believer in the fabled Southern Continent said to lie in the Pacific to counterbalance the weight of the northern landmasses, and he staunchly supported the theory that there were navigable North-East and North-West Passages to China.

The Doctor was, however, more than a theorist and scientist: he also had a credulous faith in the powers of alchemy and sorcery. For years he struggled to transform base metals into gold and to discover the elixir of life. Like most of her countrymen, Elizabeth took such powers seriously: she appointed Dee Royal Adviser on Mystic Secrets and loved to visit him in his Thames-side house at Mortlake to discuss astrology.

Tragically, his contributions to English expansion were soon forgotten and he died in abject poverty, aged 81, still mesmerized by the gobbledegook of medieval "science." Yet in one way he was the greatest visionary of Tudor England. Long before it became a reality, he was talking confidently about a "British Empire" and hustling off navigators to claim it.

the realm into a religious division.

But within a generation, as the Elizabethan era took shape, apathy turned into unprecedented naval daring. Political, economic, and religious dynamism coalesced and turned outward, producing a breed of adventurer just as ruthless, just as greedy, just as spiritually arrogant as any *conquistador*. In part the metamorphosis was simply the product of malice—why should Spain and Portugal harvest the riches of the East and West? In part it was an offshoot of Protestant zeal—surely the Lord had not intended the entire earth to be Catholic? In part it stemmed from the spectre of economic ruin as the wool trade moved from boom to bust. And in part the transformation was itself a hallucination, a marvellous affliction of the mind which turned the horrors of ocean travel into the romance of discovery. Whatever the explanation, it was not long before Elizabeth's brave seafarers were setting out "to seek new worlds, for gold, for praise, for glory."

In 1550 the English wool industry faced disaster as export figures fell by 35 per cent. London merchants began to look over the top of the world to the Orient, where even in the 16th Century it was argued that China's teeming millions would be England's economic salvation.

The economic remedy was apparent; the proper path was not so easily discerned. Some favoured the northwest, others the north-east route to Cathay. The Cabots—both John and his son Sebastian—had discovered that the westward route consisted of endless miles of icy water and smothering fog. The experts, therefore, favoured the opposite direction: north into the Norwegian Sea, east round the North Cape of Norway into the Barents Sea, and then (the geographers predicted) a warmer trip into temperate waters down the northern coast of China.

Realizing that no single individual had either the economic means to risk such a venture or the international prestige to impress the Celestial Court of China, London merchants in 1553 joined under royal patent to form a joint-stock company. Sebas-

tian Cabot was elected first Governor and the new enterprise was given the optimistic name of the "Company of Merchant Adventurers of England for the Discovery of Lands Unknown."

"Unknown" was indeed the operative word, for instead of finding the Son of Heaven, the explorers ran across Ivan the Terrible of Russia. Three vessels set out in May, 1553, under the command of Sir Hugh Willoughby with Richard Chancellor as chief pilot. Only Chancellor in the *Edward Bonaventure* returned. Sir Hugh and the crews of the *Good Hope* and the *Confidence* froze to death in the Arctic winter on the barren coast of Lapland. The *Bonaventure* had been luckier; despite freezing spray and screaming winds she made her way into the White Sea and the domain of the Tsar of all the Russias. Chancellor journeyed cross-country by sled to Moscow, where he was lavishly and drunkenly entertained by Ivan, and he reached an understanding with the Prince of Muscovy. But Richard Chancellor never lived to profit from his efforts—he was drowned when the *Bonaventure* was wrecked on its second return trip from Russia.

The search for a link with Cathay continued. Company agent Anthony Jenkinson journeyed in 1558–59 from Moscow to the Caspian and thence worked his way to Bokhara, but the silk caravans which had trekked 3,000 miles to China in the days of Kublai Khan had long since ceased, and anarchy prevailed throughout Turkestan. Jenkinson headed next into Persia, where he hoped to establish a link with the Orient through Persian middlemen. Prospects of trade with the Far East proved disappointing, but London merchants were soon exchanging English woollens for ornate Persian carpets.

Frustrated by land, the Merchant Adventurers, who soon acquired the name of the "Muscovy Company," continued their search by sea. Stephen Borough in the *Searchthrift,* a tiny pinnace manned by a crew of eight, managed to push his way into the Kara Sea in quest of Cape Tabin, a promontory whose existence was predicted with certainty by Dr. John Dee—mathematician and geographer and unswerving believer in magic—but which always remained lost in the impenetrable fog and ice of the Arctic. If only Tabin could be rounded, then, according to the experts, the Siberian coast sloped south-east to China and the sailing would be easy. Borough's attempt was so harrowing that it was not until 1580 that Arthur Pet and Charles Jackman responded again to Dr. Dee's continued urging to challenge the Kara Sea. Pet made it back, but Jackman and all his crew disappeared without trace.

If not north-east, then north-west. If Cape Tabin proved elusive in the Siberian cold, perhaps Cabot's Straits and the Broken Lands just north of Hudson Bay would prove more attainable.

With stimulus provided by the ambitions of a rather unsavoury master-mariner and ex-pirate by the name of Martin Frobisher, three small ships, weighing only 60 tons in all, were fitted out to test Dr. Dee's theories that a link between the Atlantic and Pacific existed somewhere north of latitude 60°. On June 8, 1576, the *Gabriel,* the *Michael,* and a ten-ton pinnace sailed past Greenwich Palace and headed north-west for the Greenland coast.

At first it appeared as if Frobisher would follow Chancellor to a watery grave, for the pinnace sank with all hands in a raging storm and the *Michael* conveyed itself "privily away" and ran for home, reporting that Frobisher in the *Gabriel* has been "cast away." Frobisher, however, was not so easily disposed of. He might have little understanding of the theories that had inspired his voyage, but a broken topmast and a leaking ship could not stop an old pirate from adding his name to the growing geography of the day. He sailed on and discovered "Frobisher's Straits." The name had to be changed to "Frobisher's Bay" when it was discerned that the stretch of water led only to the interior of Baffin Island, but the captain was convinced that he had succeeded in his mission. After all, the area was populated by a race of slant-eyed Mongolian people who seemed friendly, and certainly the climate was cold enough to warrant

a great number of English woollens.

And so Martin Frobisher returned to London with the good news of his discovery, one kidnapped native to prove his claim, and a small piece of black rock. Not everyone aboard the *Gabriel* had been so fortunate; five of the crew placed too much faith in the friendliness of the shy and childish Eskimos and were eaten for their confidence. The trip, however, was proclaimed a triumph, especially when it was rumoured that the bit of black rock was gold ore.

The next year merchant-shipowner Michael Lok and Frobisher had no trouble raising money and the short-lived Company of Cathay was founded —not so much in the expectation that China was just over the north-western horizon as that gold was to be had in the Arctic regions. Even the Queen took the bait and invested over £2,000 in two voyages which brought back 1,500 tons of rock, all of which turned out to be iron pyrites and quartz. Elizabeth burnt her fingers; Lok ended up in debtor's prison; Frobisher was once again called a pirate and a rascal; and the fabled riches of Cathay remained as far away as ever.

Dreamers like the Cabots, vendors of black magic like Dr. Dee, and crude opportunists like Frobisher all had been called by the North-West Passage and had been turned back by cold and ice. Now came the turn of a new type, the "scientific navigator." John Davis was the author of two books—*The World's Hydrographical Description,* a defence of the Passage, and *The Seaman's Secrets,* a handbook of navigation—and he was a leader and organizer of dedication and intellectual calibre.

Davis's appearance on the oceanic scene was symptomatic of the fact that the energy and commitment which under the early Tudors had been directed towards the solution of domestic problems was now turned to the greater world without. Three generations earlier Englishmen had been novices in navigation—even as late as 1576 Martin Frobisher was sailing more by guts and good luck than by triangulation and exact compass bearings—but by 1580 Elizabethans were among the best sailors in the

world and John Davis was in part responsible.

There were other symptoms, too, of the new outward urge in Davis's expedition. A century before, a great cloth magnate, Thomas Paycocke of Coggeshall, had donated the proceeds of his trade to found no more than a chantry to sing Masses for his commercial soul; now William Sanderson, of London, invested the profits of his fishmongering to buy Davis two fragile ships—the *Sunshine* and the *Moonshine*—to carry him over the top of the earth. Once English Protestantism had been on the defensive; now the Queen's own Principal Secretary, Sir Francis Walsingham, was urging Davis to "attempt that which God

Martin Frobisher, out of favour when the North-West Passage eluded him, won knighthood fighting the Armada.

17

The goblet given Drake by his Queen. It opened on a hinge at the equator.

Himself hath appointed to be performed"—the spreading of the light of the Gospel into the Arctic unknown.

Three times, in 1585, 1586, and 1587, Davis sought to "see the end of this business," and he reached latitude 73° north, farther than any Englishman had penetrated. He gave his name to Davis Strait and christened the northernmost point that he reached on the Greenland coast "Sanderson's Hope," but no matter how far he went, open water extended farther northward. We know today that Cabot, Davis, and Dee were correct in theory; the polar route runs from Baffin Bay into the Arctic Ocean and out again through the Bering Strait, but it takes an atomic submarine or a powerful ice-breaking oil-tanker to do it, not a 50-ton cockleshell.

Though the East India Company would send George Waymouth in 1602 into Arctic waters, and eight years later Henry Hudson discovered at the cost of his life the true geography of Hudson Bay, the quest for Cathay in northern latitudes really ended with John Davis's third endeavour of 1587. There was no fourth or fifth trip; the very dynamism that had sent Davis to the top of the globe now prevented him from seeing the business finished, for England was headed for a showdown with Spain.

Meanwhile, as the Muscovy Company's sailors fought their way to a standstill in the Arctic wastes, others were tackling different routes to the East with more success: overland through the Middle East, south-east round the Cape of Good Hope, and south-west round Cape Horn.

Of all the voyages which at this time jolted England out of her insularity, Francis Drake's epic and piratical circumnavigation of the globe via the Horn was the most awe-inspiring. Drake's achievement, even more than the victory over the Armada, clearly demonstrated that the oceans were no longer closed Iberian preserves but open to all strong enough to sail them.

The expedition was pure magic. It began on December 13, 1577, and lasted nearly three years. On September 6, 1578, Drake in the *Golden Hind* sailed out of the windswept Strait of Magellan, headed up the South Amer-

ican coast "liberating" the treasures of Spain as he went, travelled as far north as British Columbia in search of the entrance to the North-West Passage, doubled back to California, and on June 17, 1579, took formal possession of the shores near San Francisco Bay for his Queen. Four months later he was in the Philippines, and on November 3 he anchored off the most valuable real estate in the world, the spice islands of the Moluccas where the precious clove grew. Soon the indefatigable captain was delighting the Sultan of Ternate with Elizabethan music and had persuaded him to place the entire spice trade in English hands.

The *Golden Hind* took on a cargo of six tons of cloves, which were fetching five shillings a pound on the European market, and 11 months and a shipwreck later Drake sailed into Plymouth Harbour. It was not the New Albion of California which impressed Elizabeth when Drake finally arrived home but those East Indian cloves, and when she rewarded her captain with a silver goblet she had the cup engraved with a picture of Sir Francis being received by the Sultan of Ternate. At last an Englishman had tapped the treasures of the Indies and approached Cathay.

The Pacific route proved to be an eternity. Just the passage through the Strait of Magellan was a desperate feat. But Drake, even after he had jettisoned half the cargo to save his ship, had made a 4,700 per cent profit, which was more than enough to blind anyone to the horrors of the Horn.

The second alternative to the northern path to the Orient—by way of the eastern Mediterranean—was the oldest and shortest tie between East and West but tortuous beyond description. Chinese silk and East Indian spices were gathered at Indian ports on the Malabar coast; thence they were carried in clumsy ocean-going *baghlas* to the entrance of the Persian Gulf and reshipped by frail coastal vessels to Basra, where the precious cargo was again unloaded and transported by camel caravan to Aleppo and finally to the port of Tripoli. From the bazaars of the Levant they found their way via Italian middlemen to every city of Europe. The risks were incalculable but such was the value of the cloves and nutmeg, silks and sandalwood that a handsome profit was realized if only one shipment in six got through.

During the 1570s, with Iberian naval power still dominating the ocean routes, London merchants had turned to the Levant as the only practical link to the Orient. Special trading rights were secured from the Turkish Sultan by time-honoured means: egregious flattery and the gift of a mechanical clock of extraordinary ingenuity. By 1579 the Levant Company was in business. Despite Muslim piracy and Spanish naval guns in the Mediterranean, it was soon a thriving financial success.

Elizabethans, as usual, were greedy and not content with a transshipment trade in which the real profits went to Turkish and Venetian entrepreneurs, so in 1583 John Newberry and five colleagues journeyed from Aleppo to Baghdad and Basra in an effort to trade directly with the Orient. From Basra, Newberry and three others sailed on to India where, after adventures which belong more to *The Arabian Nights* than to real life, three of the travellers found themselves at the court of the great Akbar to whom they presented the ornate and wordy greetings of their Queen. William Leeds, an expert in fine jewels, was induced to remain at Agra. Ralph Fitch headed farther east into the Ganges delta, trading the whole way. Newberry, convinced that only a sea route round the Cape of Good Hope could successfully tap the riches of India, started home to report his findings, only to vanish somewhere in the barren expanse of central Asia. Fitch kept going, studying commercial possibilities in Siam and Burma, spying on Portuguese trading posts in the East Indies, and eventually retracing his steps to Aleppo. He returned home in April, 1591, after eight years of wandering to discover his estates probated and a memorial service long since offered for his perambulating soul.

The confidence, the sublime arrogance that could lead Thomas Cavendish to assume that the oceans of the world belonged to his Queen led other Elizabethans to imagine a new England beyond the sea, a plantation complete with women and children to sing the Lord's praises.

Of all the maritime powers of the 16th Century only England succeeded in planting living replicas of herself in the wilderness. Castilians by the thousands went forth to conquer, convert, even to marry and settle in the New World, but they carved out a subjugated empire, not a new Spain. Frenchmen crossed the ocean to hunt, trap, and negotiate with the Canadian Indians, but they returned to their Gallic paradise as soon as they could. Only the English created a new England, settled not by subjects of the Crown resolved to live beyond the seas but by pioneers and builders in a land of new promise.

The changeover from woollens to men as England's most valuable export did not come easily. In a way, it was a confession that the search for Cathay had failed and that Elizabethans would have to look elsewhere "for gold, for praise, for glory." Englishmen had to be taught a new vision, and that was the achievement of three men, Richard Hakluyt, Sir Humphrey Gilbert, and Sir Walter Raleigh.

Never was a triumvirate so incongruous. Hakluyt was a Hertfordshire cleric and scholar whose maritime experience included nothing more exciting than a Channel crossing but whose delight in "cosmographie" was so prodigious that he edited 1,700,000 words' worth of travel stories; Gilbert was a West Country squire who fancied himself the instrument of God's ultimate design on earth; and Raleigh was a brilliant courtier whose rapier tongue gave "the lie" even to the court which sustained him and whose scornful genius antagonized everyone save the Queen. But the three were alike in their determination to discover a new kind of Cathay—an El Dorado which could be all things to all men, whether they were plunderers or settlers, adventurers or dreamers.

Sir Humphrey Gilbert, that worthy Devonshire worker in the Lord's vineyard, was the first to be sacrificed to the vision of a new nation. In 1583 he

Apostle of Empire

While acting as chaplain to the English embassy in Paris in 1583, Richard Hakluyt found that the English were held in contempt on the Continent for their "sluggish security." Incensed, he set about his major work: to record every voyage of exploration and settlement undertaken by Englishmen as a way of pushing them on to yet greater achievements. To this end he read everything he could lay his hands on. He had works translated and translated others himself. The first edition of *The Principall Navigations*—700,000 words—appeared in 1589. But in the next decade English explorers proved so ambitious that it was soon out of date. Nothing daunted, Hakluyt added another million words, and the second edition appeared at the end of the century.

It remains a unique work, a combination of pithy narrative, history, diplomacy, and economics, welded together by a towering historical vision. To Hakluyt we owe practically everything we know about many English voyages. The magic of his descriptions transmutes the grim, sordid tales of freezing and cannibalism into the pure gold of high adventure. His arguments, too, were persuasive to Elizabethan readers. Colonies, he said, would "vent" England's excess population. They would be sources of untold wealth. They would be strategically vital in time of war.

His was a heroic, optimistic vision—yet over the next three centuries his dreams were more than fulfilled and his work remained the epic inspiration he had intended it to be.

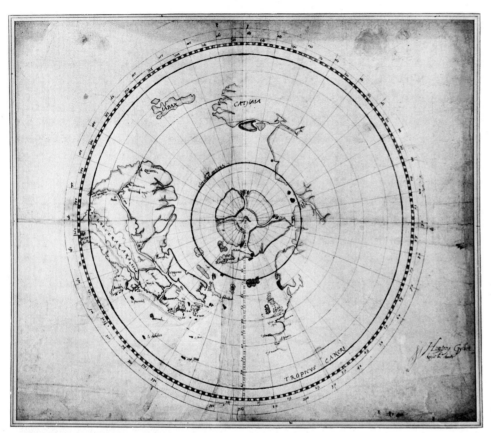

This polar map was drawn in 1582 by Dr. Dee for Sir Humphrey Gilbert. Exercising speculative geography, Dee was convinced of the existence of an easy sea passage through North America (left) to Japan and China (labeled "Cathaia," top).

sailed for Newfoundland with five ships and 260 colonists to establish a bridgehead on the other side of the ocean. The entire venture was a study in contrast: detailed, long-range, practical planning versus petty selfishness, maddening over-confidence, and fatal irresponsibility. On board were shipwrights and carpenters, blacksmiths and miners. There were toys for the "allurement of the savages," an official historian, even a ship's poet who wrote *The Embarkation Ode*.

Two days out the trouble began: the best ship of the flotilla deserted and beat back to home. Then the crew of the *Swallow* locked their captain in his cabin and indulged in a week of pirating among the barks and fishing skiffs off the Grand Banks. After seven weeks the fleet reached St. John's, where 36 fishing vessels of various nationalities were drying their catch. Sir Humphrey immediately declared himself Governor and took posses-

sion of the whole island in the name of the Queen. His authority, alas, extended no farther than his voice, and despite a splendid proclamation announcing that all religious services were to be Church of England, that English justice would henceforth prevail, and that anyone dishonouring Elizabeth's name would lose his ears, the colony disintegrated the moment Englishmen set foot ashore. They mutinied, they stole, they deserted, and they demanded to be sent home when it became clear that there was cod aplenty but no gold—or any other precious metal—to be found.

Sir Humphrey, however, would not give up. He sent the sick, the mutinous, and the disenchanted home on the *Swallow* and headed his three remaining ships towards Nova Scotia in search of new lands and a more permanent abode. Off Cape Race the ultimate disaster occurred. The *Delight* was driven ashore and 100 colonists with all the fleet's provisions

were lost. God's hand was evident, and there was nothing left except to creep home, the expedition a total failure and Sir Humphrey close to bankruptcy.

From the start Gilbert had proved an impossible commander—mulish, impetuous, complacently self-confident—but those very qualities now transformed ignominious failure into immortal legend. Disdaining to leave the overcrowded and cramped ten-ton *Squirrel* for the larger and safer *Golden Hind,* Sir Humphrey deliberately courted disaster, preferring "the wind of a vain report to the weight of his own life." Nemesis overtook him and in a September storm the *Squirrel* was "devoured and swallowed up in the sea." That extraordinary man, part fool, part fanatic, part hero, had followed his own words to the end: "We are as near to heaven by sea as by land."

Colonization ran in the blood, and the following year Gilbert's half-brother, Sir Walter Raleigh, took up where Sir Humphrey had left off.

As in everything he did, Raleigh set about the business with magnificent style, and in 1584 he received one of those delightfully optimistic documents from his Sovereign empowering him to "discover barbarous countries" and "occupy and enjoy the same forever." After a year of reconnaissance to locate a site far enough north to be safe from the Spanish, Sir Walter was ready to set sail.

Raleigh sought to lead the expedition in person but at the last moment had to relinquish command to his daredevil cousin, Sir Richard Grenville, who convoyed 108 adventurers in ten small ships to the Carolina coast.

The colonists made an impressive group: Sir Richard himself, the seaman who would soon make naval history with a gallant single-ship fight against an entire Spanish flotilla; Thomas Cavendish, the future circumnavigator of the earth; John White, artist and observer; Thomas Hariot, botanist, mathematician, author. But gentlemen adventurers, naval heroes, water-colourists, and scientists were not sufficient to sustain a colony.

Grenville's expedition suffered from all the failings that had plagued Gilbert—opportunism, lack of discipline, light-hearted disregard for the realities of successful colonization. They were at first "well entertayned by the Savages," but shortly after their arrival Grenville committed an act of folly which shattered the friendly relations with the Indians. A silver cup had disappeared. Grenville assumed it had been stolen by the Indians and laid waste one of their villages. Soon afterwards he sailed for home, promising to return with a new batch of recruits.

The settlers were left on their own. Shortage of food, the prospect of back-breaking labour, and fear of the Indians reduced the tiny social organism to a mob of hysterical men. They never seemed able to feed themselves properly, and their initial good reception led them to place far too much reliance on continuing Indian goodwill. Disillusion on both sides led to increasing bitterness and finally to a pre-emptive British attack on an Indian village. Had war continued the British would have had no hope, but providentially, a week after the attack, a sail was sighted. It was not the return of Grenville—he had delayed to do a little buccaneering on the way—but a chance visit by Drake, who offered the settlers passage to the Old World. All but 15 bolted for home.

Sir Walter had lost a fortune, but he and Grenville had received a valuable warning: the launching of a living organism takes more than promotional literature and the dream of Empire; it involves money, organization, and above all, men and women with the conviction and staying power to work the rich soil and create a new way of life 3,000 miles from home. Recruiting was all important, and on his second attempt Raleigh offered 150 pioneers 500 acres apiece and a voice in their own government if they dared leave the safety of their firesides and establish a settlement in the New World. The colonists, under the governorship of John White, arrived at Roanoke Island in July, 1587, and found nothing except the bones of one of the 15 volunteers left behind after the flight of the first settlers. Nevertheless, the pioneers elected to make their new home on the ruins of the old one.

The decision was fatal, for the Indians had neither forgiven nor forgotten the brutality and high-handedness of the earlier colonists. White tried to arrange a meeting with the Indians to patch up their differences. The Indians did not arrive. His patience at an end, White assaulted an Indian village. Soon nerves began to falter, and the settlers insisted that White return to England with a frantic appeal for more spades, more axes, more seeds, and more of the necessities of civilization which might save them from extinction.

When White reached London in 1587, he found the kingdom on the verge of war with Spain. Raleigh had invested £40,000 and was nearly bankrupt, and it took months to find new capital and supplies. When Grenville finally succeeded in gathering together a relief party, news of the Armada's sailing arrived, and all Her Majesty's vessels were commandeered for the defence of the realm. Nor did the end of the emergency resolve the matter, for Raleigh had been forced to yield part of his control to a joint-stock company of merchants, who were mortally slow in assembling a second relief party.

Four years after he sailed away, White again set foot on Roanoke Island. He returned on August 18, 1591, after dark. "We let fall our Grapnel neere the shore, & sounded with a trumpet a Call, & afterwardes many familiar English tunes of Songs, and called to them friendly; but had no answere." There never was an answer. Every last soul had vanished in one of history's greatest mysteries.

On a tree was carved the enigmatic message CRO in "fine Romane letters." Inland White and his men found the overgrown ruins of the settlers' fort and houses. On a post by the entrance to the village was carved the word "Croatoan." On the shore they found five chests, previously buried by the settlers, now dug up and broken open.

Had the settlers gone to live with the Indians, had they been massacred by them, or had something else happened? All that survived of the Lost Colony was the legend of a breed of white-faced, blue-eyed Indians somewhere in the interior.

At the cost of martyrdom for the 89 men, 17 women, and 11 children of the Roanoke settlement, two more essential lessons had been learned. First, colonization was too expensive for a single patron; it needed the same kind of group financing and unofficial state support given the Muscovy Company and the East India Company. Second, El Dorado was a figment. There was no way to a quick profit, only back-breaking investment in a new nation. As Francis Bacon said, the founding of colonies was like the planting of trees: "you must make account to lose almost twenty years' profit, and expect your recompense in the end."

—*Lacey Baldwin Smith*

In John White's map of about 1585, Chesapeake Bay is at top, Hatteras at right, and Roanoke Island at centre.

II. Showdown with Spain

News of England's staunchly aggressive attitude was confirmed by Alvarez de la Quadra, Spanish Ambassador in London. He was greatly disturbed; nothing he could say or threaten seemed to have the least effect upon Elizabeth of England or her councillors. The English, against both God and reason, were claiming the "right to go to all lands or provinces belonging to friendly states without exception."

The Ambassador's words went to the core of the forthcoming struggle between the two kingdoms. Spain saw her Empire as a closed mercantile preserve, sanctified by the Pope and delivered into Spanish hands by God Himself for the purpose of bringing Catholic light to the heathen multitude and striking down the enemies of the true faith wherever they might be found. The heretic English, on the other hand, argued that commercially the Lord was neutral; no pontifical proclamation could partition the earth, for the sea lanes were open to all.

King Philip II of Spain held that a foreign trader was a brigand and any country that transgressed his imperial laws an enemy. Elizabeth, who as the half-sister of his dead wife, Mary, might have been expected to show more deference, pointed out that those laws were Spanish, not English. Only if the two monarchs were at open war could her brother-in-law treat merchantmen as pirates.

Whether simple economic rivalry between a defensive, monopolistic Spain and an aggressive, free-enterprise England would alone have generated sufficient hatred and misunderstanding to have led to war is problematical. Add, however, religious hysteria and a spectacular shift in the European balance of power, and a showdown was unavoidable.

Throughout the 1560s imperial Spain stood at the pinnacle of her political, military, economic, and spiritual power. Philip's crowns were world-wide and his resources seemingly endless. He was Lord of Burgundy, Archduke of Milan, King of Naples, and monarch of an empire stretching from the Philippines to the Caribbean, from the Strait of Magellan to the coast of California. The annual profits of world conquest had swelled to a golden torrent of £16,890,000; Spanish soldiers were the finest on the Continent; and Philip himself was the acknowledged leader of a resurgent Catholicism bent on destroying the monster of heresy.

Power, however overwhelming, has its limitations, and for all his royal titles and treasure fleets, Philip was more a paper titan than a solid economic and political giant. Though diplomatically Spanish prestige was unrivalled, her economic strength was a façade. The riches of the Potosi silver mines remained in Spain only long enough to inflate the currency before finding their way into the money-bags of beer-drinking Flemish merchants who supplied the Empire with most of the sinews of war—pitch and lumber and hemp for the navy, saltpetre and tin for the artillery, and the Friday diet of dried fish for the army. Technologically the world was passing Spain by. The shipwrights of Cadiz and Seville continued to build clumsy galleons—floating fortresses garrisoned by soldiers—instead of swift manœuvrable ship-destroying vessels manned by sailors. The navy continued to depend upon giant galleasses with banks of oars and manacled slaves, which worked well enough in the Mediterranean but were ill-suited to defend the sea lanes of world Empire. Even spiritually Spain was withering. As *conquistadores* gave way to bureaucrats, innovation was stifled under piles of administrative orders and conformity became a greater virtue than efficiency.

Nowhere was Spain's weakness so dramatically displayed as in the Netherlands, seemingly the jewel of Philip's Empire but actually torn by religious and political strife. The more Spanish arms sought to enforce orthodoxy by edicts written in blood, the more Dutch nationalism and heresy flourished. By 1566 Spain had a full-scale revolt on her hands which consumed the profits of Empire even faster than the treasure fleets could carry them to Seville.

Then there was England, a kingdom of heretics which gave aid and comfort to Philip's Dutch rebels and, as Ambassador Quadra lamented, was set upon testing the strength of Spanish imperial regulations throughout the New World. In earlier decades England's commercial incursions into Portuguese and Spanish monopolies had been small apologetic affairs without official support. But by the 1560s the nation once land-oriented had turned to the sea, marking the shoals and currents of the Channel, gaining navigational experience, and planning ships of revolutionary design. Within 18 years of Elizabeth's succession the *Revenge* was launched, a 500-ton galleon designed not to carry troops but to be an engine of war, nimble, durable, and dangerous.

It was predictable that upstart Elizabethans in their sleek new ships would eventually clash with Spain. The first Englishman to do so was John Hawkins, the man most responsible for building the new navy.

All Spanish colonial trade was geared to the sailing dates of the great treasure *flota* that sailed early each spring from Seville for Martinique. There it split—half going to the Isthmus of Panama, half to Mexico—to rejoin during the late summer at Havana for the long trip home via the Azores. Outward-bound, Philip's ships carried taffetas and silks, Andalusian wine and the Toledo steel the colonists so prized; on the return trip they transported West Indian sugar, Mexican hides, Peruvian silver, and the spices of the Orient shipped first across the Pacific and then hauled overland from the west coast of South America. Except when the fleet was actually in West Indian waters, there was almost no naval defence. Philip was long on decrees but short on warships, and the Caribbean was at the mercy of French pirates, Dutch interlopers, and, Mr. Hawkins hoped, English slave-runners.

Slavery stood at the root of this new English enterprise. Although the West Indian economy was dependent on Negro labour, the official duty on imported blacks was so high that Spanish customs officials winked at the flourishing black market in slaves. It was a sordid business, but extremely lucrative for the individuals of many nations who indulged in it, and in 1562 that was the aspect of the venture that interested the investors in Hawkins's first voyage. After a short stop-off on the coast of Senegal to gather his human cargo, Hawkins sailed for the island of Hispaniola and bartered 300 black men for sugar, hides, and gold. One hundred and five slaves had to be given outright to the Spanish officials at San Domingo to induce them to overlook trifling commercial irregularities, but even so the profits were spectacular.

Most of the Privy Council bought shares in John Hawkins's second voyage, and the Queen herself presented a floating fossil incongruously christened the *Jesus of Lübeck* as her contribution to the slave trade. Clearly, merchant Hawkins of Plymouth considered himself an instrument of international policy in the Queen's service.

Despite Spanish threats, his fleet of three vessels sailed in October, 1564, on a venture almost as successful as the first. Spanish officials, it is true, demanded higher bribes, the colonists were more hesitant to buy for fear of government reprisal, and investors had to make do with a paltry 60 per cent return on their money, but what the expedition may have lost in profits it made up in experience. Never before had an English fleet anchored off the Spanish Main or Devonshire sailors tasted a potato. For the first time Englishmen watched the natives of Florida smoking a "kind of dried herb," and the Royal Navy learned about that convenient contrivance, the hammock.

Had the Queen and John Hawkins quit when they were ahead, history might have been very different, but the third and final expedition in 1567 ended in a débâcle, the consequences of which led to the Armada 21 years later. Philip had given orders that imperial regulations were to be rigorously enforced and that Hawkins and his crew were to be treated as pirates, to be destroyed by fair means or foul.

After slave-raiding along the African coast, Hawkins shipped over 300 blacks to the Caribbean, and all went well until the moment of return to England. Then, in September, 1568, the antiquated *Jesus of Lübeck* nearly foundered in a tropical storm and the

Spain's King Philip II, "Philip the Prudent," sat for portraitist Sanchez Coello a decade before the Armada.

entire expedition had to seek safety at San Juan de Ulua, the Mexican port of disembarkation for the *flota* from Seville. As Hawkins was repairing his flagship, Philip's new Viceroy, Don Martin Enriquez, arrived with the treasure fleet. On a written promise from the Viceroy that the English would not be molested, Hawkins reluctantly made room in the crowded port for Enriquez's fleet.

What ensued was, depending on one's perspective, either foul treachery or sensible opportunism designed to teach brigands and heretics a lesson. Seizing his chance when Hawkins was at the dinner table, and utilizing his overwhelming manpower, Enriquez led a surprise attack against the English squadron. For the first time Spanish and English ships fought it out, and only Captain Hawkins in the *Minion* and young Francis Drake in the 50-ton *Judith* escaped.

Spain's commercial monopoly had been dramatically defended and the English interlopers repelled, but the results of the Battle of San Juan de Ulua were more than Philip had bargained for. Two men were now bent on revenge. If John Hawkins was to be

treated as a pirate, he would act as a pirate. He had, he reported, lost £28,000 as a consequence of Enriquez's treachery, and he was determined that every blood-smeared penny should be paid back with interest. As for Francis Drake, before San Juan de Ulua he had been a junior sea captain of no importance; now he became *El Draque*—"The Dragon"—a fanatic set upon punishing Philip for the perfidy of his Viceroy.

Another dimension was thus added to the cold war which Elizabeth and Philip had been waging for years. Both monarchs, however, shied away from hot war, for neither was ready for a showdown. Philip had his hands full in the Netherlands and had yet to crush Muslim sea power in the Mediterranean. Elizabeth always backed away from any decision as irrevocable as war; moreover, her northern shires were in open revolt, her naval wall of great new galleons was still a dream in Hawkins's imagination, and no decision had been made about Mary of Scotland, who remained in England as a dangerous and unwanted visitor-cum-prisoner. Messrs. Hawkins and Drake, however, had no cause to be so circumspect, and for the next decade they waged their own small-scale war against Spain.

In 1570 and again in 1571 Hawkins sent Drake into Spanish Caribbean waters to reconnoitre and plan their revenge. Private enterprise, no matter how well organized, could not handle Philip's great galleons clustered together in the yearly treasure *flota*; to have done so would have taken official support and full-scale war. On the other hand, there was no reason why a carefully planned expedition could not launch a surprise attack against the two treasure depots of Nombre de Dios and Panama, and with luck even seize the Isthmus itself, thereby cutting the waist-line of Philip's Empire. It was a mad project, but behind the ruddy cheeks and tub-like profile of Captain Francis Drake there resided a crusader, greedy for gold and adventure but even greedier for revenge upon the enemies of the Lord. Consequently, Francis Drake, with two of his brothers and 71 men in two small craft, sailed forth on May

24, 1572, to inflict God's punishment on the world's mightiest Empire.

Drake sailed directly to a prepared secret anchorage near the southern base of the Isthmus where he put together four small pinnaces for a swift night attack on Nombre de Dios. The assault was a military success but a financial flop—not an ingot of gold was found, for the treasure-houses were full only when the *flota* was in harbour. Then followed a year of frustration as Drake waited in hiding for the arrival of the treasure fleet. This time he planned an overland attack through the dense jungles of Darien to seize the mule-trains carrying the gold and silver of Peru and the silks of the Orient from Panama.

In February, 1573, his carefully planned ambush was prematurely sprung by an English sailor filled with brandy, and all the marauders got for their efforts were unmanageable bales of cheap cloth. Two weeks later, at the elventh hour, English luck finally turned. On the very outskirts of Nombre de Dios they captured a mule-train rich in gold and silver, and Drake sailed away, his "voyage made."

Twenty thousand pounds in gold and silver locked in English sea chests did a great deal to make Drake welcome at Plymouth, but the Queen, officially at least, was not pleased. For the moment, she was bent on peaceful relations with her brother-in-law and had no intentions of openly countenancing piracy in Spanish waters. Moreover, her instincts to shy away from piracy were correct: for the next four years scarcely a single English raid on the Spanish Main was successful.

When in the year 1577 Elizabeth gave official support to Drake's prayer to sail in an English ship upon "the great south sea," in theory the voyage had unobjectionable aims. But no one doubted what the English planned, and according to Drake the Queen told him privately that she "would gladly be revenged on the King of Spain for divers injuries." Drake's circumnavigation of the globe was a buccaneer's daydream come true. Off the western coast of Panama he and Hawkins were amply revenged when the *Golden Hind* encountered the

Cacafuego, a treasure ship containing "thirteen chests full of reals of plate, four score pound weight of gold, and six and twenty tons of silver."

By now both sides had reluctantly concluded that only war could resolve a controversy which was rapidly assuming epic proportions. From the Catholic perspective of Madrid it was clear that the English she-dragon had to be destroyed, for she was nurturing rebellious and heretical subjects in the Netherlands and sanctioning piracy on the high seas. In London it was apparent that God's chosen people could not save the Protestant elect from the Duke of Parma's disciplined Spanish troops in the Lowlands unless Philip and his Catholic horde were crushed.

In 1583 Philip committed one of the few heedless deeds in his otherwise prudent life. Faced with a disastrous failure of the Spanish wheat crop, he asked London merchants to send relief supplies. Then he confiscated every last English ship. Spanish treachery, however, was greater than Spanish efficiency; one vessel escaped and, through one of those extraordinary accidents of history, the Governor of Bilbao who had organized the seizure was captured and carried off to England. In his boot was discovered Philip's personal order to confiscate the grain ships and evidence that he intended to use those same vessels in a great Armada to fulfil "God's obvious design"—the punishment of Elizabeth of England, that "incestuous bastard, begotten and born in sin."

Retaliation was swift and deadly. In 1585 a joint-stock military expedition was organized against the nerve-centre of Philip's Empire, the Caribbean. Twenty-nine ships and 2,300 men sailed under Drake's command. Two colonial capitals were the objectives—San Domingo, the administrative heart of the West Indies, and Cartagena, the seemingly impregnable capital of the Spanish Main. San Domingo fell in a brilliant amphibious assault, and Drake managed to extract £7,000 in ransom.

Cartagena gave way more to hysteria within than Englishmen without, and was ransomed back for £25,000.

There was glory and praise sufficient for all but profit for none. Some £32,000 in ransom, 240 brass cannon, and a dozen or so church bells scarcely made the enterprise an economic success, and shareholders had to settle for 15 shillings on the pound. The international effect, however, was more heartening. The Bank of Seville went bankrupt and the Duke of Parma's Spanish troops in the Netherlands went unpaid.

Cold war had flared into hot war but then just as quickly subsided. Elizabeth preferred to wage war inexpensively, and she thought she could gain more by seeking to corrupt Parma with an offer of a princely title and an independent kingdom than by cutting off his financial resources. As for Philip, he was content for the time being to let matters slide. His every waking hour was dedicated to the appointed task of destroying England, but the Royal Bureaucrat who laboured so diligently in the Lord's filing-system needed time; not a bolt of canvas, not a sack of grain, not a length of hemp could be purchased for God's Armada unless authorized in Madrid. Spain's greatest admiral and naval hero, the Marquis of Santa Cruz, had estimated that a fleet of 510 sail, 40 galleys, six galleasses, 30,000 sailors, and 60,000 soldiers with provisions for eight months would be required to destroy English maritime power.

Such a fleet, though worthy of the cause on which the kingdom was embarking, was organizationally and economically impossible. Philip knew his own strength and settled for an Armada of 130 ships, 19,290 soldiers, 8,350 sailors, and 2,080 galley-slaves. The King understood that there could be little hope of destroying English sea power, but it did not seem too much to expect that naval supremacy could be maintained long enough to convoy Parma's troops from Dunkirk to the Thames estuary and gain a military victory.

In fact this was utterly impossible. Spanish ocean-going galleons were simply too deep for the shallow waters off Dunkirk. Parma pleaded for time to seize a deep-water port. But for Philip's unimaginative mind, there

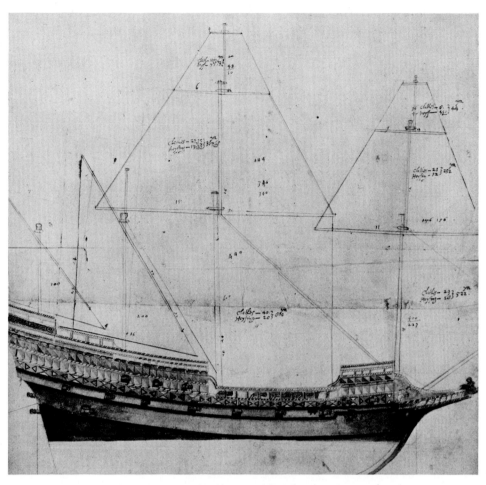

The revolutionary features of Hawkins's new warships are evident in a shipwright's plan of 1586. The lofty sterncastle has been reduced to modest proportions, and the central "pit" for soldiery planked over to provide an additional gun deck.

half of which were being made ready for the Armada, were scuttled and burnt in sight of the castle of Cadiz. As Philip said, "the loss was not very great" for the main fleet was at Lisbon, but "the daring of the attempt was very great indeed," and to make it more destructive Drake swept up the Iberian coast looting and burning as he went. Then to add to the injury, as well as to the pocket-books of English investors, Drake sailed on to the Azores where he encountered the *San Felippe,* a lumbering treasure carrack from the East, her cargo valued at £114,000, enough to pay for the entire expedition twice over. Elizabeth as was her due took £40,000; Drake received £17,000, and London merchant-investors successfully demanded another £40,000.

Elizabeth had need of her money. Drake may have delayed Philip but he had not stopped the Armada, and from 1587 on the Queen had to keep her fleet on more or less constant war footing, a matter of £12,000 a month. At that price even Gloriana was impatient for war.

Her fleet, in fact, was superior in numbers to Philip's. The English force, when fully mobilized, totaled over 200 sail, including 18 deadly galleons of Hawkins's revolutionary design.

These new vessels marked a radical change in the tactics of naval warfare. Longer, lower, and lighter than the battleships of the Armada, they were purely gun platforms, and with them their captains could outmanœuvre and outsail any Spaniard. It was the aim of the English to sink ships, not conduct a land war at sea as if the enemy was some fortress to be scaled and sacked.

By May, 1588, Philip's Armada was finally ready. It was an awesome sight. At stage centre were 20 Portuguese and Castilian galleons, great awkward floating fortresses with high fore and stern castles from which musketeers delivered their fire and their grapnels to hold fast an enemy ship. There were also four 50-gun Italian galleasses, their oars manned by slaves. The second line of battle consisted of 40 merchantmen and carracks, big and rugged and some as formidable

Text Continued on Page 32

was no other way of achieving "God's obvious design." Every other possibility had been thoroughly inspected and dismissed. God could, therefore, be depended upon to sustain the faithful and give them victory, regardless of the odds.

It was a terrible blow to Spanish naval morale when Santa Cruz, "the never-vanquished," suddenly died of typhus fever, but it was an even greater blow to the Duke of Medina Sidonia to be appointed Captain-General of the Ocean Sea in place of the old mariner. The Duke was invariably seasick and confessed that he knew far more about gardening than war. He did not hesitate to voice his doubts about both the enterprise and his own military qualifications, but Philip reassured him: "If you fail, you fail, but the cause being the

cause of God, you will not fail. Take heart and sail as soon as possible."

Philip had ordered "sail as soon as possible," but in his haste he failed to reckon with the English in his time schedule, for even before Medina Sidonia had taken command of the fleet, *El Draque* struck again. He struck not at Lisbon, which was far too well protected, but at Cadiz, where a portion of the Armada was being fitted out. The English attack in April, 1587, was another of those joint-stock company ventures designed to destroy the enemy and to make a profit in the process. Elizabeth provided four ships, Drake three, the Lord Admiral Howard one, and the Levant Company seven "to impeach the purpose of the Spanish fleet."

As with everything Drake did, the results were spectacular—65 vessels,

THE GREAT ARMADA

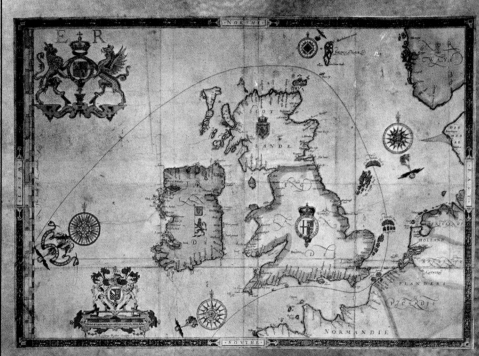

When the Spanish Armada sailed in 1588, it was the most massive naval force the world had ever seen. But its stately vessels were no more than cumbersome floating castles, from which soldiers – who outnumbered sailors two to one – were expected to board enemy vessels. To crush the highly manœuvrable, well-sailored British fleet, negotiate the treacherous shoals of the Dutch coast, and then pick up additional troops with which to invade England would indeed have demanded the divine support on which King Philip counted. None was granted despite the flags inscribed "Arise, Lord, and vindicate your cause." Within ten days, the gale-battered Spaniards were staggering homeward, following the route in the map above, one of a series done in England to record the battle.

A contemporary painting shows English ships (with the red-cross flag of St. George) in the mêlée of battle with the Spanish fleet.

The First Sight of the Spanish Leviathans

The threat of Spanish invasion terrified the nation. Though the English fleet was strong, everyone was aware of the rottenness of home defences – English cities were unwalled and ungarrisoned, and English yeomen had grown soft and fat during decades of peace. Worst of all, there was the fear that a Catholic fifth column might aid the Spaniards.

In the event, the English Catholics were more patriotic than popish. Along with their Protestant countrymen, they barricaded ports, placed guns at strategic points and set up a chain of warning beacons and bonfires along the coastline.

On July 30, 1588, the Spanish Armada, neatly assembled off Lizard Point in Cornwall, was sighted by some of Drake's vessels scouting out of Plymouth. According to legend, Drake himself was playing bowls with Charles Howard, the Lord Admiral, when he heard the news. "There is plenty of time to finish the game," he remarked, "and to thrash the Spaniards too." The story may or may not be true – it was first recorded 40 years later – but it epitomizes English confidence.

The English fleet put out of port the same evening, and the first skirmish the next morning achieved little: the wary English stayed out of range of the Spanish cannon, but themselves inflicted little damage. It was a pattern often repeated in the next few days, as the Armada continued its stately progress in unbroken formation up the Channel.

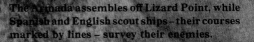

The Armada assembles off Lizard Point, while Spanish and English scout ships – their courses marked by lines – survey their enemies.

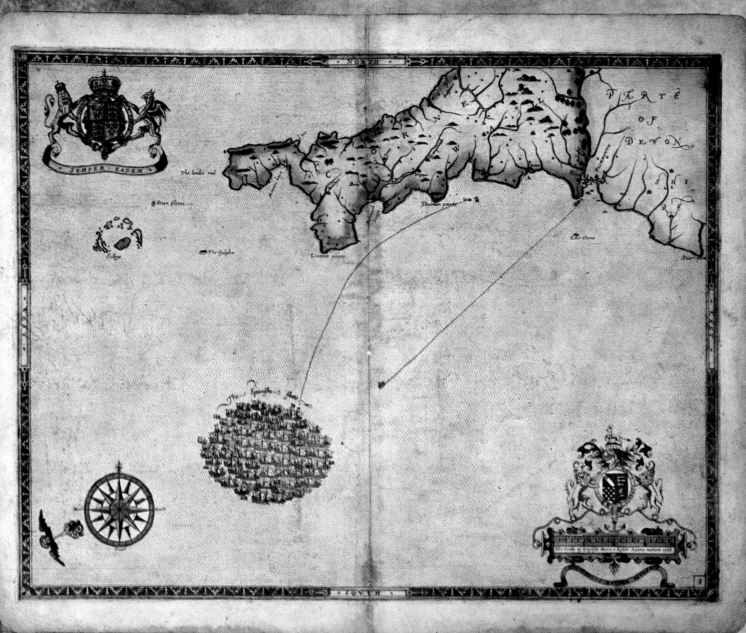

The English fleet cautiously wends its way out of Plymouth to harass the Spanish, now formed in a perfect crescent.

The melancholy inexperienced Duke of Medina Sidonia was the Armada's reluctant leader.

Charles Howard, English Lord Admiral, had a bubbling enthusiasm for his task.

After a minor clash (left), the tight Spanish crescent heads up-Channel again, pursued by the English (right).

Hell-burners of Calais

"Their force was wonderful great and strong, yet we pluck their feathers little by little." So wrote Lord Admiral Howard of the Armada's floating fortresses, as they moved up past the Isle of Wight.

Luck, more than good tactics, came to the aid of the British in the early stages of the battle. The Spanish *Rosario*, broke her bowsprit and a mast, and fell prey to Drake's waiting ships; and the *San Salvador* suddenly and inexplicably exploded in full sight of the Armada, pitching hundreds of men into the sea.

After a week of running battle, Spanish morale, sapped by the days of inconclusive fighting, was dangerously low. On the night of August 7, as the Spaniards lay anchored off Calais, Lord Admiral Howard sent in fireships, and the Spaniards, terror-stricken at the onslaught by the flaming, pitch-encrusted hulks, slipped their cables and scattered in panic. The next day's battle ended the threat of invasion, and the remaining Spanish ships fled into the mists of the North Sea towards the treacherous crags of Scotland and Ireland.

Drake became the envy of all when he seized the *Rosario* and all her spoils, the richest prize taken by the English.

With their fireships, stacke

ith double-loaded cannon which fired at random in the intense heat, the English at last broke the tightly packed ranks of the Armada.

as the galleons. Serving the purposes of modern-day destroyers were 34 pinnaces. Such was the fighting strength of the Armada. It was a fleet so impressive that Charles Howard, Elizabeth's Lord Admiral, considered it the greatest the world had ever seen.

Yet the odds lay with the Lord Admiral. Not only were Hawkins's men-of-war superior to anything Medina Sidonia could throw against them, but the English had armed their warships with more numerous and longer-ranged guns than the Spanish. Their high-velocity nine-pounders had an effective range of a half-mile, while Medina Sidonia's heavier 30-pounders had a range of only a quarter-mile. Finally, the Elizabethan Navy was fighting in home waters, close to supplies, while the Spanish were a thousand miles from their main base at Lisbon. The Spanish captains who sailed in God's service were fully aware of the risks, and they acknowledged that only divine interference could possibly rectify the military imbalance. "We are sailing against England," said one, "in the confident hope of a miracle" which will send "some strange freak of weather" or will deprive "the English of their wits."

The opening phases of the contest (as seen in the accompanying portfolio) began as the two fleets sighted each other on July 30 off the Cornish coast. The next morning the startled Spanish found a squadron of Howard's warships holding the weather gauge. Demonstrating their superior sailing qualities, they had slipped from Plymouth Harbour and captured the advantage of position; it was an advatage they would never lose. Medina Sidonia's only choice was to take up a defensive crescent formation.

For the next week the Armada moved slowly and majestically up the Channel towards Calais. Wary of the timber-smashing power of the enemy 30-pounders, Howard and Drake were content to snipe away at long range and collect their forces. When the Spanish anchored off Calais on August 6, the contest seemed a stand-off.

But in fact the Armada was doomed.

God had not furnished the necessary miracle: word came from the Duke of Parma, 30 miles away at Dunkirk, that light Dutch "flyboats" had his army bottled up in the shallow harbour, and there was no way his troops could reach the deep-draft Spanish galleons. Aboard the Armada's ships, stores were spoiling, water barrels were leaking, and ammunition was running low. Contrary winds and the growing English fleet prevented a retreat down-Channel. Then the distraught Spaniards were further unnerved by the sight of blazing fireships drifting towards them. Most of the Spanish captains fled.

Somehow Medina Sidonia got his ships reassembled, but off Gravelines Howard took the offensive. His nimble ships closed in for punishing broadsides, then skipped away out of range of grapnels and boarding parties. The slaughter grew terrible, and Spanish decks literally ran with blood. The frustrated Spaniards challenged their tormentors to board and fight

A period painting on wood commemorates the victory over the Armada. Spanish ships burn in the background as Elizabeth (on the white horse) rides to Tilbury to review militia massed to repel the Duke of Parma's invasion.

steel-to-steel as tradition called for. Their answer was another volley of murderous broadsides.

Howard broke off the action at last as his own stocks ran low, but for the Armada the ordeal had only begun. The contrary winds continued to drive it northward, into the cold and foggy North Sea. The only hope for home now was a 2,500-mile circuit of the British Isles. Thirst, hunger, and weather were the enemies, and they were more terrible than even Elizabeth's galleons. Ship after ship ran onto the rocks of the Scottish or Irish coasts; on one five-mile stretch of Donegal Bay, reported an Irishmen, lay "eleven hundred dead bodies of men, which the sea had driven upon the shore." Superhuman stamina and seamanship finally brought 66 surviving ships to their home ports, but half of them never sailed again, and two-thirds of their crewmen were dead within a month of disease or dysentery.

Philip would not condemn Medina Sidonia for the debacle. It had been, after all, God's will. "In God's actions," the King said, "reputation is neither lost nor gained."

The defeat of the Armada constituted an absolute, if temporary, upset of the balance of naval power. In time the balance would return; Elizabethans would grow old, domestic controversy would engulf the kingdom, and Spain would learn to defend her treasure fleets with 40 great galleons, half of which were built on the English model, and to transport her riches in fast, new frigates able to outfight or outrun anything in the Queen's Navy. But for the next ten years God was all English and the Elizabethans continued to achieve wonders.

Almost every summer an English squadron went forth to intercept the treasure *flota* as it approached the Azores, and in 1592 the 1,600-ton seven-deck Portuguese carrack *Madre de Dios,* valued at £150,000—more than Elizabeth realized in an entire year out of her regular peacetime revenues—was captured. A syndicate of London merchants did even better. They banded together and turned to privateering in lieu of legitimate trade,

averaging annually between £150,000 and £300,000 in "liberated" Spanish hides, sugar, and spices.

In 1596 Elizabeth decided on a direct attack on Cadiz. Over 100 vessels, 17 of them the Queen's own galleons, and 6,000 men under the joint command of Lord Admiral Howard and the Earl of Essex, with Raleigh as Vice-Admiral, sailed from Plymouth. For once, honour, histrionics, profit, and obedience coincided, and the expedition was the most spectacular success of the Elizabethan Age.

By the sheerest good luck, the entire West Indian treasure fleet was at anchor as the English sailed into Cadiz, and only four huge galleons and a small squadron of row galleys had been left to protect them. Within hours two of the galleons had been captured and two had exploded, and English troops were wading ashore with Essex in their lead beating time on his drum. The victory was staggering: four of Philip's largest galleons, 15 great merchantmen, and a raft of lesser craft destroyed or captured; 120,000 ducats extracted in ransom money and the President of the Contratacion of Seville carried off to London in the expectation that he was worth at least another 100,000; and Cadiz stripped of everything English sailors could carry away with them— bedding, silk gowns, jewellery, church bells, furniture, tapestries, expensive clerical vestments.

Cadiz was the climax. Thereafter the war ground to its costly, inconclusive end. As the new century approached, each side learned new ways —Spain to share the Caribbean trade, England to concentrate on colonization as being, in the long run, more profitable than war and buccaneering. The process took time, and far into the 17th Century men remembered the good old days of those joint-stock company ventures when the Queen and her London merchants had each made £40,000. Though the spirit changed and a new dynasty sat upon the Tudor throne, the old arrogance, the aggressive economic and military self-confidence so characteristic of Drake and Hawkins never totally disappeared.

—*Lacey Baldwin Smith*

Gloriana

She gave her name to a spectacular age, and was herself spectacular: a brilliant, enigmatic Goddess-Queen, Gloriana, a unique and unpredictable combination of play-acting, ruthlessness, and vacilation.

Elizabeth I was a vulgar extrovert who swore "great mouthfilling oaths" and threw slippers at her ministers in her rages— yet to disarm masculine opposition she would not hesitate to claim with emotion the "frail substance" of a woman. She surrounded her court with a veil of pomp, bestowing on her servants glory but little power. Politically she was hard-headed, dedicated to the detailed business of good and economic government. As her faithful and exceedingly devious adviser, William Cecil, remarked, "She is more than a man, and in truth sometimes less than a woman."

But above all, to the despair of her ministers, she hated to commit herself. She prevaricated over the choice of a husband, turning her many proposals to her own diplomatic advantage. In handling her two great problems of statecraft—Mary of Scotland and Philip of Spain—her approach was equally effective.

When Mary fled hostile Scotland for England and made her claim to the Tudor throne, Elizabeth promptly imprisoned her. And there Mary remained for 19 years, spinning her intrigues. Only when she was convinced that her people were united behind her did Gloriana act, ordering Mary beheaded in 1587. In a like manner she avoided a direct confrontation with Philip for 30 years, and when it came England was strong enough to win.

III. Footholds in a New World

Those asleep at dawn aboard *Susan Constant, Godspeed,* and *Discovery* were roused by shouts and the thump of feet running across the decks. All who could—some were too ill to lift themselves—rushed to join their companions. Clambering onto deck cargo and into rigging, they sighted along the outstretched arms that gestured towards the western horizon. There: land! Virginia!

It was May 6, 1607. They had reached at last "Earth's only paradise," where, it was said, grapes grew finer and larger than in Europe, iron and copper abounded, and the soil was "the goodliest under the cope of heaven." But they had not come for soil, nor grapes, nor even copper. They were not farmers with families. There were few labourers—and no women—among them. Most were gentlemen-adventurers and their servants. They were here for gold.

Without the prospect of finding gold or silver the Virginia Company probably would not have sent them, nor would they have wanted to come. The grim fate of Raleigh's earlier effort at Roanoke was certainly no encouragement. Already storms and sickness had charged a toll of lives for the passage. Of the 120 who had left England six months before, 16 were dead, including Edward Brooks, who perished from the heat when "his fat melted within him." Only gold could make such perils worthwhile.

Up the placid James River they chose a site on which to settle. It was low and damp, close to a swamp teeming with pestilence-carrying insects and hemmed by dense woods offering cover to hostile aborigines. They built a fort, naming it after King James, and began their search for gold. They would find none, and within a single year two-thirds of them would be dead. But they had founded the first permanent English foothold in North America. It was a beginning.

The Jamestown settlers were adventurers, but they could not have known the magnitude of the great adventure they initiated. In the wake of the *Susan Constant* there followed a great movement of humanity. An island-nation off the coast of Europe stretched itself across an ocean and, despite appalling difficulties, peopled a giant continent—a whole new English-speaking world that would be rich and populous and powerful.

There were to be two English Americas, whose economic, political, and social differences endured long after they were in theory unified. Thirteen years later, far to the north, the ship *Mayflower* made a landfall on the low, sandy shore of Cape Cod. Some of the passengers fell to their knees and blessed God for bringing them "over ye vast and furious ocean." Others were not so grateful; they had bargained to go to the Virginia Company's territory and found themselves confronting instead the coast of New England, a land of hostile climate and infertile soil. They suspected, perhaps correctly, that this was not by accident but design—the work of the "Pilgrims" who now lifted their voices in prayers of thanksgiving.

There were 51 Pilgrims among the 101 passengers. These separatist Puritans rejected the Established English Church as being tainted by popery and had come to America to establish a New Zion of their own. But James refused to guarantee their religious freedom in the New World, and there had been rumours they would not be welcomed in Virginia. The "strangers" among them grumbled their suspicion that the Puritan "saints" had given Providence a helping hand in causing their arrival at this wild, empty place.

Somehow the Pilgrim leaders won the confidence of the non-Puritans and persuaded most of them to sign a covenant pledging "all due Submission and Obedience" to such "just and equall lawes" as would be enacted for the general good of the colony. This agreement was necessary to replace the patent from the Virginia Company, invalid outside its territory, but the significance of the Mayflower Compact was to be greater than that. It established a precedent in English America: government based on consent of the governed.

To call America in those early years of colonizing "Earth's only paradise" was a mockery. Jamestown settlers by the score died of disease and starvation, and the survivors were reduced to feeding on corpses. It was hardly better in Massachusetts. The building of Plymouth slowed almost to a halt as saints and strangers alike began to die, sometimes two or three a day. By the spring of 1621 more than half the original company was dead.

Why did they take such an appalling gamble? Certainly few were deceived by the Virginia Company's blatantly false advertisements, which extolled the wonders of the new land and neglected to mention the hardships. The Spanish Ambassador in London told of three condemned English felons who were given the choice of going to Virginia or hanging. Two accepted transportation, but the third vehemently insisted he would rather die, and did. Yet Englishmen in increasing numbers were drawn across the Atlantic, or were pushed. During the Great Migration of 1630 to 1643, some 65,000 left their homeland to seek their fortunes in North America and the West Indies.

Historians have set forth a number of explanations for this exodus, some citing national economic and political aims as the prinicpal factors, others saying that social and individual motives were most important. It seems likely that all these theories have some validity: no single impulse, but an interworking of many, carried English stock across the sea and planted it in America.

A feeling of nationalism was one factor. After defeating the Armada, Britons wanted to beat the old rival at her own game of colonization and stake their claims to the New World. The spreading of Christianity was also a motive, one that was given prominent place in the original Virginia charter. Captain John Smith's contention that "reducing heathen people to civility and true religion" took precedence over "gaining provinces" was a widely held belief—or a widely touted one, anyway. It is probably fair to say that this show of crusading zeal was mainly lip-service and, like anti-Spanish patriotism, of minor importance. The true national motive was economic.

Spain had realized fabulous sums in gold and silver from Peru and Mexico. The Virginia Company was so certain that England could do the same from Virginia—a notion not nearly as fanciful then as it seems to us today—that two goldsmiths were included in the first lot of settlers. At Jamestown there were, reported Smith, "no talks, no hope, nor worke, but dig gold, wash gold, refine gold, load gold." Alas, the shipload of ore that the colonists sent home with great anticipation turned out to be iron pyrites, fool's gold.

Despite this and other prospecting disappointments, precious metals continued to encourage colonization indirectly. Like other major powers, England subscribed to mercantilism as the way to build a wealthy and self-sufficient nation. She must sell more abroad than she bought, so the balance of payments could be accumulated in gold and silver in London's coffers. Colonies were integral to this system, since they sold to the mother country raw materials she would otherwise have to buy from rivals.

The colonies, too, would serve as a captive market for goods manufactured at home. During the 16th Century, Europe's supply of hard money —gold and silver—had increased threefold, and England's flourishing merchants had managed to grab their share of it. Now they were eager to invest this capital in the expansion of Empire. The Crown also had a vested interest in overseas growth, since its income would be increased by duties on trade between England and the colonies. There is ample cause, therefore, for saying that the nation's wealth, and her ambitions to be yet wealthier, were of prime importance in the planting and development of the colonies.

But that can be, at most, only half the story. Scores of thousands of men, women, and children did not yank their roots from English soil and subject themselves to a gruelling journey and an uncertain future because it suited a grand economic design. Tenant-farmers and artisans, the bulk of the migrants, were surely less moved by schemes emanating from Whitehall or the City than by their own personal needs and desires.

While more personal, many of their motives derived from these same economic factors, which tended to

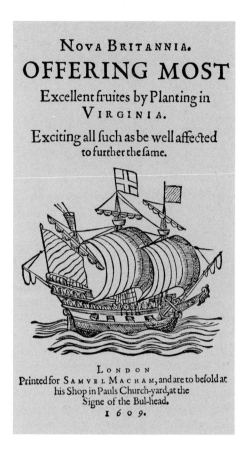

While Jamestown settlers starved, the Virginia Company issued immigrant tracts (above) promising good food, "mountains making a sensible proffer of hidden treasure," and "very loving" Indians. Far more realistic was John Smith's *Generall Historie* (below).

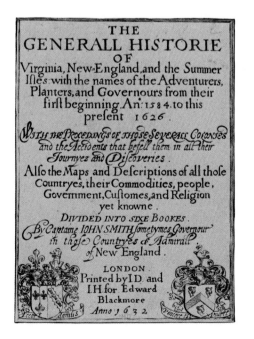

operate on poor people in a negative fashion. The increase in trade and money supply caused inflation and a tremendous rise in the standard of living of the upper classes. While prices climbed spectacularly, working men's wages, which in England were fixed by the landed gentry acting as magistrates, remained low. If a man refused to work for the wages prescribed, he could be jailed or forcibly bound over to a master. In rural areas poverty was made more acute by rapid expansion in the wool industry. As more and more land was dedicated to sheep-raising, fewer and fewer acres required farm workers. Under the near-feudal tenantry system, landlords simply turned unwanted families onto the roads and by-ways.

Poverty and economic depression led to a generally accepted feeling that Great Britain was overpopulated. That this was not in fact true is inconsequential (the problem was one of wealth distribution, not population, and by the end of the 17th Century the country was bemoaning a *shortage* of manpower). Whether or not they could see the real cause, English working men could not escape the depressingly evident effects. Puritan John Winthrop said that man, "the most precious of all creatures, here is more vile and base than the earth we tread upon." Thus it was that some Englishmen went in search of dignity to a land where men, because there were fewer of them, would be more highly valued, and where they could not only buttress that dignity but feed themselves and their families from the produce of freehold property of their own.

Many who were not so inspired were sent to America anyway, frequently with one-inch holes burned in their ears for the crime of not having a job. Richard Hakluyt had spoken of "venting" England's population through emigration to solve the problem of widespread pauperism. Hundreds of homeless children were swept up from the streets and handed over to the Virginia Company as bonded servants, and prisoners, some incarcerated for stealing less than a shilling (stealing more than a shilling invoked the death penalty), were added to the

The social strata that produced so many colonists for America is pictured in these water-colours done in London by Michael Van Meer about 1620. From left: a carter and porter, a water man and his dog, and a farm family.

tide of humanity flowing towards America.

There was another, very important, motivation. While England may not have taken seriously her proclaimed purpose of disseminating the Gospels, religion did become in another way one of the crucial pressures that propelled Englishmen to the New World —for many who settled in New England, probably the most crucial, for their emigration was as much involved with politics as with faith, since the two were inextricably entwined.

Official treatment of Puritans and other minority religious groups, especially under the direction of the dreaded Archbishop Laud, was brutally repressive, and certainly provided cause for leaving the country. For writing a pamphlet criticizing the Church of England one Alexander Leighton was fined £10,000, pilloried, whipped, had both his ears cut off, his nose slit, his face branded, and was imprisoned for life. Such persecution was not rare. It can hardly be entirely coincidental that when this particular sentence was pronounced

on Leighton in 1630, ships bearing thousands of Puritan emigrants were nearing the New England coast of America.

Whatever the motivations for emigration, by the mid-17th Century the American colonies were going concerns. Tobacco had proved the salvation of Virginia. Here was something from the New World that men with money could appreciate. Sixteen pounds of tobacco had as much value as a good horse. A new class of settlers began to arrive: men with capital who could amass the large tracts of land necessary and who could afford the labour to clear it of trees. They imported hordes of bonded servants— some of whom had contracted to work for 21 years before they could gain their freedom—and were granted amounts of land that varied according to the number of workers they brought in.

As early as 1619 it was decided that the colony was ready for partial self-government, and the House of Burgesses, modelled after the Commons, was formed. In 1619, too, the first cargo of what would become in the years ahead an important and bitterly contested trade arrived in Virginia: 20 black slaves.

Maryland and South Carolina followed similar patterns of development, although not achieving their neighbor's prosperity. North Carolina,

with its numerous relatively small holdings, was an exception to the basic settlement pattern of the southern colonies, but on the whole, southern English America—warm in climate, aristocratic in rule, with a largely plantation-based economy— had more in common with the British West Indies than with the "nation" coming of age in New England.

The intertwining of politics and faith that had sent so many to New England continued to operate after they arrived. Massachusetts Bay, the Bible Commonwealth, attracted more than its share of strong-willed individuals. The Puritan faithful managed to dispose of such as Thomas Morton—who welcomed at his home at Merry Mount "all the scum of the country" to drink beer and brandy and even dance around a maypole— by burning down his house and hoisting him by block and tackle, protesting all the way, aboard ship for England. But others, Roger Williams, Anne Hutchinson, Thomas Hooker among them, were not so easily handled; banished, they established colonies or settlements of their own.

Although founded on bitter differences, these "spin-off" colonies— with the exception of Rhode Island, regarded by the others as the black sheep of the New England family— co-operated with Massachusetts when facing common problems. In 1643

they created the New England Confederation, a league that settled border disputes, dealt with hostile Indians, held the line against encroachments from the Dutch to the south and the French to the north, and schemed, unsuccessfully, to bring about the collapse of Rhode Island.

Life in New England was not all religion and politics. The Puritans had another consuming interest: work. This was fortunate. Only a people conscience-bound to the Protestant work ethic could have extracted livelihoods from this hilly, rocky land, which after much coaxing would yield a bare existence. Anything beyond that had to be derived from other sources.

New Englanders answered this challenge with diligence. Most farmed and had another livelihood besides. They were as well manufacturers, traders, fishermen. Immediately after finishing his house in Boston, John Winthrop began building a coastal trading vessel. Before long, New England's fishing and trading boats could be found at work all along the coast of North America and plying the waters of the West Indies.

In colonizing North America, Great Britain followed no systematic master plan. While the South was being settled according to the schemes of profit-motivated companies or in-

dividuals, and while the North was expanding on a pattern determined largely by unorthodox religious and political impulses, England neglected the area between. Into this gap, in some ways the most promising part of the American seaboard, moved the Dutch.

In the 1640s, after 80 years of arduous struggle with Spain and Portugal, the Netherlands emerged as Europe's greatest trading nation, with more ships carrying more goods than any other country, including England. With the same unbending determination that made them masters of the Spice Islands of the East, the Dutch moved on the New World. The main offensive was carried by the Dutch West India Company, a quasi-official organization with its own naval and military forces.

New Netherlands was less a true settlement colony than a trading centre. There was no self-government and the leadership imposed from Holland was generally inept and unpopular. By the 1660s the population was less than 2,000, almost a third of which was English.

But New Amsterdam, at the mouth of the Hudson River and the only important settlement in New Netherlands, was a natural centre for commerce, the finest on the whole eastern seaboard. The British particularly resented the Dutch intrusion because

New Amsterdam drew trade from British colonies to the north and south, offering European goods at favourable prices. Fierce European commercial rivalry led to a series of wars between the two countries in the mid-17th Century. During this period (although not, as it happened, during a declared war) Charles II seized a chance to consolidate British control of the North American coast and, probably not incidentally, benefit the depleted royal treasury. He repeated a previously stated claim that New Netherlands was in reality British territory. In 1664 he sent a squadron to substantiate this assertion.

Peter Stuyvesant, the Dutch Governor, was determined to resist. Not so the phlegmatic, business-minded burghers of New Amsterdam. They decided the proffered terms respecting property rights were generous indeed, and concluded that a future under English rule looked promising. New Amsterdam surrendered without a shot being fired.

Idealism was the inspiration behind two of the most interesting colonial experiments in the New World. In the case of Pennsylvania, the story began prosaically enough—a matter of Charles II discharging an old obligation to a faithful servant, Admiral William Penn. Then the Admiral's son, also named William, became involved.

William the younger had rejected the cachet of his aristocratic birth and Oxford education to become a Quaker, causing his father much distress. Young Penn, who had previously spent some time in the Tower for an anti-Anglican pamphlet, was arrested in 1670 for addressing an "unlawful and tumultuous" assembly in Gracechurch Street. His disputation in court inspired the magistrates to label him impertinent, saucy, pestilent, and troublesome. The jury found him guilty only of "speaking in Gracechurch Street," which caused the court to threaten to have a juryman's nose cut and Penn staked to the ground if they did not return a "proper" verdict. The jurors then found him not guilty and were themselves promptly sent to prison.

Troublesome though he was to the Establishment, because of his father's services Penn was granted in 1681 the area which became Pennsylvania, where he proposed to undertake a "Holy Experiment." The Duke of York threw in Delaware and the Quakers purchased the rights to New Jersey, part of the former Dutch colony. The King insisted on including "Penn" in the name of the colony as a tribute to his old friend. Fearing charges of vanity from his co-religionists, the younger Penn tried unsuccessfully to bribe a royal clerk to drop the idea.

The founder of Pennsylvania was one of the great early American idealists. He devised a "Frame of Government" in 1682 which set forth "the good of the people" as the purpose of government. "Governments rather depend on men," he wrote, "than men upon governments." He avoided bloodshed by contracting a series of solemn treaties with the Indians in his territory. He set up a representative legislature and personally planned the colony's capital, Philadelphia, and the launching of a campaign to attract immigrants.

His Quaker followers shared his idealism. Some 10,000 had experienced the horrors of English prisons (Quakers suffered the same disfavour in England as did Puritans). They opposed slavery and the death penalty and stressed humanitarian public services. But when Penn returned to

England—in all he spent only four years in his colony—there erupted behind him an interminable series of factional struggles. One basic problem was the refusal of the pacifist Quaker-dominated assembly to provide money for protecting the German and Scotch-Irish settlers on the vulnerable frontier. While not all their humanitarian goals were realized, the Quakers prospered in their productive, easily cultivated land, and Philadelphia became a centre of culture as well as of trade.

The British Empire in America was more than a hundred years old when the last colony, Georgia, was founded. It was conceived both as a buffer against encroachment from Spanish Florida and as a Utopian social experiment, and was mainly the work of one man, James Edward Oglethorpe.

Oglethorpe's humanitarian instincts made him—like Penn—an anachronism in a callous age. Having headed a Parliamentary investigation into the evils of English prisons, Oglethorpe was distraught about the plight of good men and women locked away in those brutal, disease-ridden holes for crimes no worse than being in debt. He proposed that they would make excellent colonists.

Georgia was carved from the southern part of Carolina and granted to Oglethorpe and a group of friends, who were to hold the charter for 21 years, after which it would revert to to Crown. At the request of these trustees, the charter specified that they would gain no profit from the new colony; Georgia was not to be a commercial proposition. Parliament granted £10,000 to help transport and establish the settlers. Trustees and other benefactors provided the remainder of the necessary financing. Supported by private benevolence, the colony did not have to impose taxes and therefore had no need for a representative assembly to levy taxes. Since Georgia was planned as a paternalistic settlement for unfortunate settlers, there seemed no reason to allot them any responsibility for their own welfare.

Oglethorpe personally led the first colonists to Georgia in early 1733. They called him "Father" because he

ruled them as a benign dictator. But his well-intended laws restrained the growth of the province. Seeking to avoid the concentration of land-holding common in Virginia, Carolina, and Maryland, he limited each family's holding to 50 acres, which could not be sold nor forfeited for debts. Slavery was forbidden. But because of these restrictions, Georgia's rice could not compete in price with that produced on the larger, more efficient slave-based plantations to the north.

Considering the auspices under which the colony was founded, it is sad to note that most of the settlers were small-minded conformists. Lacking the generosity and tolerance of an Oglethorpe, they wanted nothing better than to live like rich Carolina planters. So the Georgians became unhappy about Oglethorpe's paternalism. They drank despite his prohibition of liquor and began to "hire" slaves—for life. The land policy was gradually eroded until 50 acres were allowed for each member of a family, and estates became transferable. By 1752, when disillusioned trustees handed over the colony to the Crown, Georgia was becoming much like any other southern American province.

The outward-moving edge of English civilization had for decades been colliding with expanding French settlements to the west in the Mississippi Valley and to the north in Canada. These clashes were growing in frequency and violence. It was evident that soon the two empires would be locked in a decisive struggle for domination of the continent.

Perhaps less apparent at the time, but more important in the long run, was the potential for conflict that was growing within the Empire itself. From the beginning, Englishmen in America had moved toward control of their own lives and affairs—sometimes slowly, often haltingly, but rarely taking as many steps back as they took forward. Cromwell's Revolution had been welcomed in many parts of the New World, and when England returned to the old system of royal authority, some colonies were loath to do so. From the Restoration the paths of England and English America began to diverge.

Far to the north, Englishmen and Frenchmen scrambled for footholds in the immense wilderness of Canada —and had been doing so since Tudor days.

Although the English voyager John Cabot had been the first to reach "New Found Land" in 1497, the French were not shy about exploiting what he discovered offshore: one of the world's most bountiful fisheries. An abundant supply from France of cheap salt for preserving their catches gave French fishermen an advantage. This commercial handicap nudged the British into a historically important step. Forced ashore to dry their harvests of cod, they established a base— the first of any European nation—on the coast of what is now Canada.

Still, it was France that most persistently probed the wonders of the new continent. In 1535 Jacques Cartier, drawn by Iroquois tales of gold, jewels, and furs, sailed up the St. Lawrence River to a place the Indians called Kebec. He stayed only one winter and found neither gold nor jewels, but furs there were aplenty, and furs were enough to arouse commercial interest.

Demand for furs grew, for fashion dictated that stylish gentlemen should wear high-crowned felt hats made from beaver skins. But the supply, dependent on migratory Indians, was irregular. Traders at first worked only the coastal regions. Then, in 1608, a wise, devout, and patriotic Frenchman, Samuel de Champlain, led a company of fur traders back to Cartier's Quebec and built a settlement. He brought in missionaries and craftsmen, made alliances with the Indians, and through long years of arduous struggle managed to put both his colony and its trade on a permanent basis. Champlain died in 1634; it was almost entirely because of his work that New France survived.

New France's development was very different from that of the British colonies to the south. The products of the farmers contending with the St. Lawrence Valley's short growing season were minuscule compared with that of Virginia's sprawling, sun-favoured plantations. The few small communities—Quebec, Montreal, Trois-Rivières—were mere villages measured against New England's bustling towns. In 1666 there were only 3,418 people in all of New France; British America had passed the 50,000 mark a quarter of a century earlier. Canada was not primarily a country of settlers, but of fur traders and adventurers.

Ironically, a pair of these hardy French frontiersmen were responsible for bringing the British into the north. The Sieur de Groseillers and his brother-in-law, Pierre Radisson, spent years exploring the great forests round Hudson Bay and trying to persuade their government to establish direct trade with the Indians there. Repeatedly rebuffed—their reward for arriving at Quebec in canoes crammed with high-quality skins was a fine for illegal trading—Groseillers and Radisson journeyed to England in an effort to promote their scheme.

In 1668 Messrs. "Gooseberry and Radishes," as their new British sponsors were wont to call them, led a party of Englishmen to those far north shores where they soon amassed a shipment of furs worth £90,000. Delighted, Charles II granted a royal charter to the "Company of Adventurers of England tradeing into Hudson's Bay" and almost casually assigned the new company control of the area watered by rivers emptying into the Bay—a domain that turned out to be one and a half million square miles, ten times the size of the British Isles.

The Hudson's Bay Company had little interest in governing this vast territory, but exploited its trading franchise with vigour and speed, qualities made necessary by the short period the Bay was navigable each year. Ships carrying weapons, trinkets, and utensils for the Indians left England in June, reached the Bay just after the summer sun had cleared it of ice, hurriedly took on their return cargoes of furs, and sailed for home before the autumn freeze took hold. From the beginning the enterprise was successful for the English and painful for the French, whose Indian

In a gesture typical of his respect for the Indians, James Oglethorpe took a local Yamacraw chief, his wife, and several warriors to England with him for a stay of four months. They met the colony's trustees (as shown here) and George II.

suppliers began diverting the flow of furs northward.

French Canadians smarted from the geopolitical sting as much as from the commercial competition, for they now felt squeezed between expanding British presences both north and south. Chafing at this pressure, New France looked inland. New territories that could be gained and exploited by French explorers, missionaries, soldiers, and traders to the north-west and south-west might enable France to meet the British commercial challenge peacefully. If not, if the conflict escalated from trade to arms, she would control the area vital to military and economic power in the interior of the continent.

On the far side of Lake Superior Frenchmen formed alliances with Indians and regained for Montreal some of the trade lost to Hudson Bay. In 1682 Robert Cavelier, Sieur de La Salle reached the Gulf of Mexico via the Mississippi River; in that same year, having turned his coat once again, Pierre Radisson led a French company to Hudson Bay. This rapid territorial growth, buttressed by strategically placed forts, was remarkable for such a small colony. It was also less than prudent.

New France was totally committing itself to the economically fickle fur trade and the westward expansion necessary to sustain it, an undertaking for which its population and financial resources were insufficient. Considering the British challenge it would have to answer, New France was spreading itself too thin on the ground. A Governor of Montreal succinctly described the seriousness of the impending confrontation. "It would be difficult," he wrote, "for our colony or theirs to subsist other than through the destruction of one by the other." He was correct; the future of the continent would be determined by arms.

Far to the south in the sunny Caribbean, the contest for empire was even more competitive. For in the 17th and especially in the 18th Century, the islands of the West Indies were the richest jewels in Europe's imperial crowns.

The first Englishman to challenge Spain's claim to the Caribbean (a claim blessed by the Pope in the 1494 Treaty of Tordesillas) was Sir Thomas Warner, a bluff Suffolk squire who had once served in James I's personal bodyguard. In 1624 Sir Thomas, his family, and 14 others landed on the golden beach of St. Christopher (or St. Kitts, as they soon called it) in the Leeward Islands.

Practical and determined, they worked with a will, and by March, 1625, when the ship *Hopewell* arrived from Virginia, they had a consignment of 7,000 pounds of tobacco— the major West Indian crop before the coming of sugar—to send home in her. Warner himself returned to whip up more recruits and to seek the protection of the Crown for what he hoped would be a thriving new colony.

He was successful on both counts. Suitable settlers came forward and on September 13, 1625, Charles I issued Warner the first Letters Patent granted for a West Indian island. It gave Warner the authority he wanted not only in St. Kitts but in neighbouring Nevis, Montserrat, and Barbados, where opportunities seemed equally good.

Although St. Kitts was the first English settlement in the Caribbean, a more important acquisition—and one destined never to be disturbed by invaders from another European country—was Barbados. The most easterly of the West Indian islands, Barbados is almost encircled by coral reefs and for the most part very flat. Claimed by England in 1605, the island was not settled until 1627 when an expedition backed by Sir William Courteen landed there.

Courteen, the son of a London cloth-dealer, was a wealthy man and lent large sums of money to the habitually impecunious James I and his son, Charles I, for which he was never repaid. In recompense certain rights in Barbados were granted him and by 1628 he had sent some 1,600 settlers to the island. They hoped to make their fortune by cultivating small estates of tobacco, cotton, indigo, or dye-wood with indentured labour from England.

Courteen was never troubled by foreign encroachments, but English invaders were another matter: it turned out that the Stuart kings had no qualms about giving the same gift more than once. In 1627 the Earl of Carlisle, a courtier and royal favourite, was granted semi-feudal rights as "Lord Proprietor of the Caribees" in all the inhabited West Indies. Though the Earl never visited his domains, his agents forcibly ejected the Courteen group.

Within a decade Carlisle had on his hands a veritable treasure-trove, for in the 1630s Dutch settlers on other islands introduced sugar from Brazil, and altered the whole West Indian economy.

Sugar was introduced in Barbados in 1640, and it meant the beginning of the end for the small-scale planters. Unlike tobacco, which could be profitably cultivated by small-holders on 50 acres, sugar required much more capital, estates of over 500 acres, skilled management, complicated milling machinery—and an ample supply of labour, soon to be supplied by slaves from Africa. The small planters could afford neither the investment in machinery nor the price of land, driven up as the vision of sugar-based wealth attracted the rich.

As Barbados, Antigua, St. Kitts, Nevis, and Montserrat sprouted sugar cane and began to flourish, it was the merchant and the shipowner and the rich planter who reaped most benefit. The less affluent either disappeared or remained as managers and wage-earners. Some took to buccaneering, making a handsome living plundering the French and Spanish.

Soon there arrived white servants of a different kind: the transportees. To relieve the pressure on British gaols, riff-raff, prisoners, and debtors were shipped off, a hundred or so a year, to what was almost white slavery on the large plantations, where they worked side by side with the Negroes. The chief difference between white and black was that in most cases the white man's term of servitude was set by the authority who transported him. The black was enslaved for life. After Cromwell's victory in the Civil War in 1649, political dissidents were also sentenced to transportation to the West Indies. They were soon joined by 7,000 Scotsmen taken prisoner

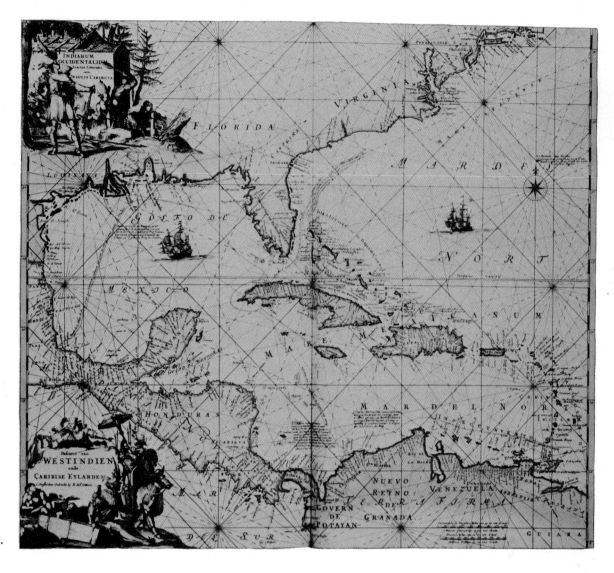

When this 1690 map of the West Indies was drawn, piracy was controlled, sugar was planted, and a Golden Age was beginning. Cuba is at centre; next to it is Hispaniola, below it, Jamaica; at right, the Leeward and Windward Islands.

after the Battle of Worcester in 1651.

Cromwell's outlook was Elizabethan. He longed to continue the process of increasing the New World Empire, a task which in his view the Stuarts had shamefully neglected. He saw no reason why Puritan England and Protestant Holland should not divide the world between them, as once the Catholic Spaniards and Portuguese had done. Brazil and the Far East should be the Dutch portion; America and the Caribbean should be England's. It was a visionary concept. But the Dutch were not impressed, and the proud Spaniards sneered at the notion of any concessions to England.

Cromwell was not deterred. But as he planned an assault on Spanish Hispaniola in 1655, he made the mistake of underestimating his opponents, believing that Spain's American system was so rotten that it would fall at a touch. The admiral chosen for this "Western Design" was William Penn, father of the future founder of Pennsylvania. He was an experienced man who would have done well enough had he been better equipped, and had a sounder choice of general been made than the fumbling Robert Venables. The attack on Hispaniola was driven off with heavy loss.

After this fiasco, the joint commanders decided to invade Jamaica—only weakly held by the Spanish—rather than return home ignominiously, and in this they were successful. Hollow victory though it may have been, the seizure of Jamaica made England the area's second most powerful nation.

Jamaica became best known as the island of the buccaneers or, as they were more respectably known, privateers. These ferocious types came chiefly from France and England, and since Spain did not recognize the claims of either power in the Caribbean, local governors issued them Letters of Marque authorizing acts of war against the Spanish—indeed, against any of their sovereign's enemies. Sir Henry Morgan and William Dampier were only the most notorious of the scores of privateers who despoiled the Spanish Main.

Spain finally recognized English claims in the area in the 1670 Treaty of Madrid, and the arrival of the first Royal Navy squadron at Jamaica in 1685 marked the end of organized free-booting—although sporadic attacks on Spanish towns and shipping continued for a number of years.

Under the Jolly Roger

Henry Morgan has come to represent the archetypal buccaneer. Of humble and obscure Welsh origins he is said to have been kidnapped as a boy and shipped off to Barbados to be an indentured servant. He soon escaped to Tortuga, where French pirates taught him his trade.

Port Royal in Jamaica became his base. He was a natural leader, and his exploits against the Spaniards rivalled in daring—and cruelty—those of Drake a century earlier. Even among his fellow ruffians he had a reputation for unmatched ferocity, habitually torturing captives with fire to gain information.

Soon after Spain recognized British claims in the West Indies in the Treaty of Madrid, Morgan (supposedly in ignorance of the Treaty) raided Panama and sacked it thoroughly. Summoned to England for an explanation, he was not only acquitted but found himself a popular hero. People were glad to listen to the accounts of a man who, it seemed, could rival the feats of the Elizabethans. He was actually knighted and returned to Jamaica as Lieutenant-Governor.

Until his death in 1688 Morgan lived in splendour on his hoarded spoils, but his habitual drunkenness and towering rages became intolerable; in 1683 he was stripped of all public offices. Yet his legend is still pervasive in Jamaica, and there is a sad little rhyme about him:

You was a great one, Morgan,
You was a King uncrowned
When you was under canvas
But now you're underground!

By the 18th Century Caribbean settlers were enjoying a Golden Age, the rich building enormous wealth on the basis of "King Sugar" and slavery.

The slave trade is acknowledged as one of the greatest atrocities in recorded history. An equal atrocity were the conditions of life—if they could be called that—of slaves in the islands. In Barbados in 1763, for example, the slave population stood at 70,000. Over the next eight years 35,000 more were imported, yet the slave population rose to only 74,000—in those eight years, 31,000 slaves died on the island. A complete turn-over of the slave population every twenty years or so was not considered unusual by West Indian planters.

Economically, this mortality rate could be borne because the profits from sugar were so vast. In the 18th Century Jamaica was the mother country's most important colony; in the 1770s one-twelfth of Britain's annual imports, amounting to more than £1,000,000, came from there, and the British West Indies as a whole supplied a quarter of the imports.

The richer settlers, the "Plantocracy," grew ever more powerful. The Crown allowed them a greater measure of self-government than was to be found in the French and Spanish islands. But although they made vast fortunes and enjoyed wide powers in the West Indies, the planters loved to return to England. At home they were usually able to buy seats in the corrupt House of Commons, where they could represent the "West India Interest" to best advantage—and some of the advantages were very great indeed. The Plantocracy's wealth was apt to be paraded ostentatiously like that of the "Nabobs," the East India Company traders who did well in India and returned to unload their fortunes and inflate prices. In *The West Indian*, a play then popular in London, a servant philosophizes: "He's very rich, and that's sufficient. They say he has rum and sugar enough belonging to him to make all the water in the Thames into punch!"

Although the large proprietor lived in state in the West Indies, his life had certain inherent disadvantages. The islands, like islands everywhere, tended to generate a claustrophobic atmosphere, rather like highly organized factories. In the bright hot sun the planter dreamed of the dappled English woodlands, the green shires, the thrill of the chase, London clubs and coffee-houses where he could hobnob with friends and enjoy intelligent conversation away from the potentially explosive situation of his slave-run estates.

His lands usually consisted of cane-fields, provision-grounds, and wood-lands. A planter liked to have at least 200 to 300 acres of his estate planted in cane. The provision-grounds were used by the slaves for growing root crops and vegetables for food. Woodlands supplied lumber and firewood. Pasture was sometimes available for cattle. Each estate had its own mill and boiling-house, and many had a distillery for making rum. Not far from these factory buildings were the small houses occupied by managers and supervisors.

Set apart from the estate buildings were the slave quarters. These might be small individual huts with thatched roofs, or long barracks. The number of slaves depended, roughly, on the number of acres of cane-land to be cultivated, but a population of one adult slave per acre was generally thought sufficient.

Conditions varied greatly from island to island, but in most cases the Plantocracy and their white managers needed the security of firearms. Sometimes slaves revolted—there were 13 revolts in the British West Indies in the 18th Century—and were heavily suppressed, in the worst cases with the help of the nearest military garrison.

These rich and turbulent lands inevitably became pawns in the struggle for world Empire. As Spain's grip on the Caribbean weakened, Britain and France wrestled for control of the trade with the Spanish colonies, and then for territorial advantage against each other. It was a contest primarily waged by navies, and ever more frequently as the 18th Century progressed these emerald seas and glittering isles echoed to the thunder of broadsides.

—*Jim Hicks, Oliver Warner*

At a plantation on Antigua, bundles of freshly cut sugar cane are delivered to a wind-driven crusher by slaves. The cane juice was then piped to the boiling-house, whose fires were stoked by the crushed stalks, and turned into crystallized sugar and molasses.

IV. The Wealth of the Indies

With the Armada beaten back and the situation with Spain "stabilized," English adventurers again turned their eyes towards the East. On December 31, 1600, Elizabeth's Great Seal was affixed to the charter of the East India Company. On its face merely royal assent to a mercantile enterprise, the charter was in fact to lead to the establishment of the British Empire in India. But there was no thought of Empire in the minds of the London merchants who formed themselves into a company. Their aim was to tap the wealth of the Indies not by conquest but by sea trade—in gems, in indigo, in camphor and sulphur, above all in spices.

The trade with the Indies had been pioneered in the late 15th Century by the Portuguese, who were set on breaking the Muslim monopoly of the overland spice trade. Sailing round Africa to India, the Portuguese spread their trading settlements to the Spice Islands—the Moluccas—and themselves became monopolists. At Lisbon the merchants of Europe were forced to pay whatever the Portuguese chose to ask.

The demand for spices remained high for a simple but compelling reason. From autumn to spring the Elizabethans—at least, those who could afford it—ate a great deal of salt meat. Even when fresh meat reappeared on their tables in summer it was poor in quality and taste. Moreover, in order to protect the fishing industry a law had been passed requiring fish to be eaten on two days in every week. Such pallid food could only be enlivened with spices.

All had been well until 1580. Up to that time the Dutch, who handled most of the spice trade in northern Europe, had been able to collect their supplies at Lisbon. But in that year Spain annexed Portugal, and the Dutch, then in rebellion against their Spanish overlords, were no longer able to buy at the Portuguese capital. Spices were still available through middlemen, but prices rose so sharply that the Dutch decided to fit out a fleet and attempt to deal directly with the producers in the East Indies. The Dutch fleet set out in 1595, returning two and a half years later with a large cargo of spices and other exotic merchandise. The Portuguese monopoly, so long the dominant influence in the European spice trade, was broken.

The English, also denied access to the market at Lisbon, were less adventurous but by no means idle. Drake's profitable stopover in the spice islands on his round-the-world voyage had confirmed the rich potential of direct trade with the Indies. The first English expedition to pursue that trade set sail in 1591, but it was a fiasco, a sad log of mutiny, shipwreck, piracy, Portuguese attacks, and starvation. Only one captain, James Lancaster, and twelve of his men made it home, without ships or profit. A second attempt four years later was an even greater disaster. But avarice and adventure overrode news of failure. The East India Company planned its first expedition with care, and turned to the veteran Lancaster to lead it.

Lancaster made sail in 1601 for Sumatra. He carried with him in his five little ships £30,000 in gold and silver coin, iron and tin and lead, and a large supply of the famous English broadcloth. Also aboard were costly presents and a letter from Elizabeth. Leaving a number of merchants behind in Sumatra to "settle a factory" (as trading stations were then described), Lancaster set out for home in 1603 with a cargo of spices worth more than a million pounds. All the ships returned safely, Lancaster was knighted, and the Company authorized a second voyage.

The merchants Lancaster left behind in the East Indies established their station not in Sumatra but at Bantam in Java. They found it difficult to sell their English goods, particularly the heavy broadcloth, which was left rotting in the warehouses. But they learned quickly that there was a large demand in the islands for the fine cotton cloth of India. It was decided in London, on their advice, that the third voyage of the Company's ships should touch on the west coast of India to acquire some of this cloth.

On August 24, 1608, the first English ship to reach an Indian port anchored off the town of Surat, about 170 miles north of present-day Bombay. The choice of Surat was made for several reasons, the most compelling, in the words of a contemporary traveller, being that it was "a city of great trade in all classes of merchandise." In addition, Surat happened not to be under the control of the Portuguese, who still considered the Indian trade their exclusive monopoly.

William Hawkins, commander of the Company fleet, was received politely enough by the local authorities, but they were not very helpful. For permission to trade, they said, Hawkins must apply to the Governor at Cambay, a hundred miles to the north. When Hawkins's messenger returned from Cambay, he brought with him permission for the English to sell the goods they had brought—but also the unwelcome news that only the Emperor himself could grant the right to set up a trading establishment. Hawkins had no alternative. He would have to go to Agra, the capital, himself.

He already knew something of the Mughal Emperor, Jahangir, and his vast dominions. Travellers had reported the great wealth and power of the Empire which then controlled most of northern India and was still expanding toward the independent Hindu states of the south. Ralph Fitch, the peripatetic Englishman who had traversed much of India late in the previous century, described the Mughal capital of Agra as "much greater than London and very populous." The Emperor's stables contained "1,000 elephants, 30,000 horses," and all kinds of exotic animals, "very strange to see." As for the markets, Fitch reported, they were "a great resort of merchants from Persia and out of India, and very much merchandise of silk and cloth and of precious stones, both rubies, diamonds, and pearls." Hawkins would have to tread carefully, for what had he to offer so rich a monarch?

To Hawkins's relief, he was well received in the Mughal capital, where he seems to have caught the Emperor's fancy, at least temporarily. Perhaps this was because he could speak Turkish, the language of the original Mughal conquerors and still used by the imperial family in Agra. He was invited to stay at court and was offered a woman from the palace. Insisting only that she be a Christian, Hawkins accepted and was given an Armenian girl—whom he later married. He was also made a court official and was awarded a large salary. He found himself, in fact, "in great favour . . . to the grief of all mine enemies."

However, these enemies—"Jesuits and Portugalls," he called them—"slept not, but by all means sought my overthrow; and, to say the truth, the Muhammadands near the King envied much that a Christian should be so nigh unto him." Portuguese opposition, imperial vacillation, and Hawkins's own tactlessness soon soured matters. Privileges were granted, then cancelled. Hawkins, an arrogant man who never understood

the subtleties of diplomacy, appeared at court smelling of liquor on one of the rare occasions when the hard-drinking Emperor was trying to give it up, and this brought him a public reprimand and a quick loss of prestige. He and his Armenian wife left Agra for England in November, 1611.

One thing at least was clear—the English would not be able to trade at Surat until they decisively defeated the Portuguese, thus showing the Emperor they were a power to reckon with. The following year a Portuguese fleet attacked two English vessels, the *Red Dragon* and the *Ozeander*, off Surat. The *Dragon* upped anchor, sailed between two enemy vessels, and loosed off a broadside at each. She then drove three other galleons onto a sandbank, while the speedy

Ozeander so "danced the hay" about the others "that they durst not show a man on the decks." This was the first of a series of defeats in minor actions that were finally to end Portuguese dominance.

The English victories impressed the Governor of Surat and, through him, the court at Agra. Though powerful on land, the Mughal Empire was weak at sea—indeed the Emperor regarded naval warfare as a degrading pastime suitable only for Europeans—and Portuguese influence at court was a direct consequence of that weakness. To the considerable annoyance of the "Jesuits and Portugalls," the English were allowed to set up a trading factory at Surat in 1613.

This gain was rapidly reinforced by the dispatch of the first British

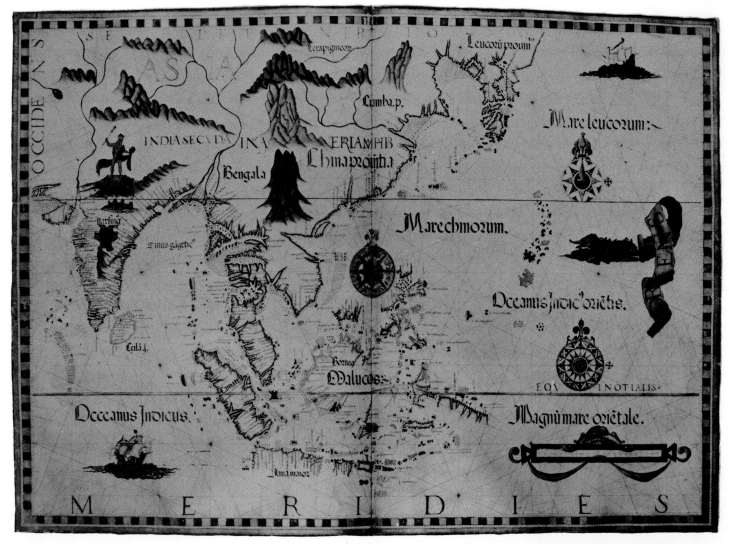

A decorative map from a 16th-Century atlas delineates with considerable detail the coast of South-East Asia and the Moluccas, or Spice Islands. The Malay Peninsula, Sumatra, Java, and Borneo are readily identifiable thanks to the travels of the Portuguese.

Ambassador, Sir Thomas Roe, a courtier who the Company's merchants hoped would "breed regard" for the English and win for them a formal trade treaty.

Roe, a big man with a loud voice who sported an immaculate moustache and goatee, refused to be intimidated by Indian officials and etiquette. He was Ambassador from the court of King James himself, not some rough merchant, even if he was also working for Company interests. At Agra, invited to meet the Emperor, he refused to make the traditional gesture of touching the floor with his forehead. He stepped into the enclosure round the Emperor, reserved for the highest nobles, and demanded a chair to sit on. The courtiers were horrified. He did not get the chair, but he did succeed in bending court etiquette a fraction: "I was desired as a courtesy to ease myself against a pillar covered with silver that held up his canopy."

Roe found the Mughal court a mixture of brutality and refinement. Emperor Jahangir was casual and drunken and occasionally viciously cruel. Yet the arts flourished under his patronage and he was curious about the outside world. His first question to an ambassador always concerned the presents he had brought. Though the Company did send Jahangir a coach and four, it could scarcely rival the munificence of rajahs who gave their ruler trains of jewel-laden elephants.

Roe's unbending sense of his own importance as Ambassador impressed the court. "One Portugal will beat three Hindus," Jahangir was reported to have said, "and one Englishman three Portugals." When he left Agra in November, 1618, Roe took with him a letter from Jahangir to King James assuring him of "good usage" for the English and an agreement granting favourable conditions for English trade at Surat.

Regardless of the fact that they might be gaining ground in India, the English were losing it in their original market, the Spice Islands. In Europe the English and Dutch were allies against Spain and Portugal, but in Asia they were rivals. The Dutch, in greater force and with better ships, dominated the seas, chasing and sinking their allies whenever they could. In the islands they were coercing local rulers into granting monopolies, setting up forts, and using armed force to make the inhabitants trade with them rather than the English.

It was war, Roe warned. "You must speedily look to this maggot," he wrote home. But little was done. A treaty of mutual defence, which in theory provided for the sharing of

A Portuguese amphibious assault on the East India Company trading-post at Surat (top), from a 17th-Century manuscript.

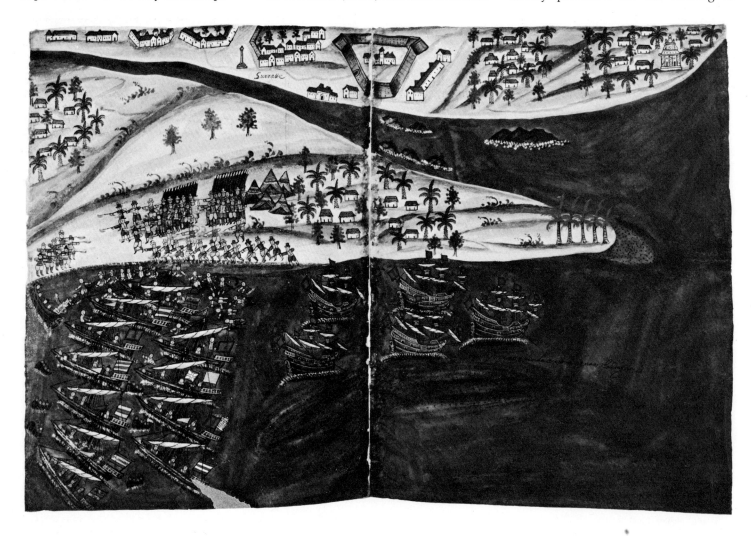

trade, was signed between England and Holland in 1619, but it had little effect on the situation in the East, where the Dutch were determined to drive the English from the Spice Islands. The result was the Amboyna Massacre—without which there might never have been a British Empire in India.

Amboyna, in the Moluccas, was the principal Dutch centre for the spice trade. The town was protected by a strong fort and manned by a large garrison of troops. The English in Amboyna—some 20 men, none of them soldiers—ran a small factory. Yet these few traders, together with a dozen Japanese, were accused of conspiring to expel the Dutch. A Japanese was tortured and "confessed"—"having endured pretty long," the Dutch admitted—that the Japanese planned to take the fort, and under further torture he implicated the English. In February, 1623, ten Englishmen and nine Japanese were executed for conspiring to assassinate the Dutch Governor. In London, Company demands for reprisals came to nothing, and the half-century after the massacre saw the Dutch only increase their pressure. By 1682 the last two English trading stations in the East Indies, on Sumatra and Java, had fallen. The East India Company would not return to the islands for decades.

The spectacular profits the merchants anticipated from the spice trade were thus denied them. Like it or not, they were forced to follow Roe's advice, given even before the Amboyna Massacre. "Let this be received as a rule," he said, "that, if you will profit, seek it at sea, and in quiet trade. . . ." The "quiet trade" would have to be carried on in India, the only solid English foothold in the East.

The Indian trade began to grow only after 1634, when a lasting peace was made with Portugal. One measure of growth was the Company's entry into the coffee and tea trade (England's first coffee house was opened in Oxford in 1649). By the 1640s the number of Company trading stations in India had grown to 25, most of them scattered along the Malabar coast.

If there were many problems to plague the Company in the mid-17th Century, the average employee in India nevertheless managed to live in considerable comfort. At Surat the head merchant—the "President"—was in charge of all the trading stations in western India and Persia. His salary was £500 a year and there were extra allowances to enable him to maintain the kind of appearances necessary to impress the Indians. When he went out he rode in a palanquin preceded by armed soldiers, flag-men, mace-bearers, and a servant carrying a large ostrich-feather fan. The factory was a large house of stone and timber, the lower floors used for trading and storing goods, the upper story containing the living quarters. Near at hand were other buildings, a bath-house, and a chapel.

The English, most of them Puritans who combined business with an ostentatious piety, began their day at dawn with prayers and closed it, at about eight or nine in the evening, with additional addresses to the Deity. On Sunday there were two services, which all the English were expected to attend to hear a suitable sermon by the President or the chaplain.

The Company's employees were very low-paid, but fortunately there

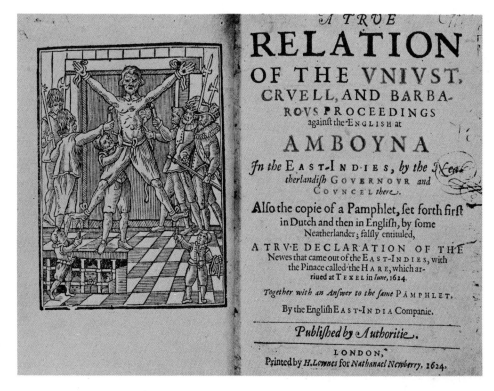

The Company account of the Amboyna Massacre was printed with a graphic frontispiece of Dutch torturers at work.

was a custom among the Indian traders of presenting the English with valuable presents once a year which, as one visitor put it, "prevent the necessity of any great annual expence, and happily contribute towards giving them a life of delight and ease." The daily routine began after morning prayers when the factory gates were opened and the Indian brokers and traders streamed in. Everything depended on the broker. He was "interpreter, head bookkeeper, head secretary, the supplier of cash, and cash-keeper." He conducted "all the trade of his master, to whom, unless pretty well acquainted with the country languages, it is difficult for any of the natives to obtain access."

The brokers arranged all purchases, negotiated with the weavers of the fine cloth for which the area was famous, and saw that there were regular supplies of cotton yarn.

At midday the gates were closed and the English—except for the President, who ate in his own rooms—made for the dining hall. On the table were plates and cups of silver. A

An allegorical painting from the 17th Century is revealing of Indian attitudes towards the foreign interlopers. Seated on an hour-glass throne, Mughal Emperor Jahangir has a learned discourse with one of his sages while, at lower left, James I of England and Turkey's Sultan cool their heels waiting for an audience.

servant brought round a silver jug and basin for washing while Indian, Portuguese, and English cooks waited to present their national dishes "so as to please the curiosity of every palate." There would be a wide variety of curries and plenty of chutneys and sauces. Fowls stewed in butter and stuffed with almonds and raisins would be washed down with "generous Shiraz wine and arrack punch." On Sundays and holidays the menu was even larger and more splendid, with venison, peacocks, apricots, plums, and cherries, European wines, and bottled beer. Sixteen main dishes and a vast amount of alcohol were the rule, and it is little wonder that the English retired afterwards for a siesta until the gates were once again opened for trade at four o'clock. At six the day's business ended, to be followed by "an hour or two with a cold collation and bottle of wine."

No one was allowed outside the factory after supper without permission. This was to keep the younger men away from prostitutes and from brawling in the town. As there were no Englishwomen in the factory, however, breakouts were not infrequent. To help employees with their moral uplift, the Company supplied a quantity of "improving books." These do not seem to have been too effective, and the Company was finally forced to order the President to send back to England anyone who could not resist "drunkenness . . . fornication and uncleanness."

But behind the pleasures of factory life and the slowly expanding trade figures lay a harsher reality: times were precarious between 1630 and 1660. In India a famine in 1630 killed thousands, among them weavers on whose products the Company so heavily relied. The hinterland, constantly fought over by princely rivals for power, was too disturbed for the safe transit of goods, and the small British coastal ships were in continual danger from pirates. In 1653 the appointment of the tyrannical Aurangzeb, the Emperor's son, as Viceroy of the southern regions known as the Deccan brought oppression and pillage to the foreign merchants. Levies and customs dues were arbitrarily fixed and extorted. Bribes grew heavier and threats more constant.

At home the situation was no less critical. When the Civil War broke out in 1642, the East India Company was squeezed between opposing factions. The King seized the Company's supplies of pepper, a commodity of enormous value; Parliament requisitioned guns meant for the Company's ships. The Puritan victory brought no respite. During Cromwell's Commonwealth the Company's very existence was threatened time and again. For three years the Dutch, at war with England over Cromwell's attempt to forbid any imports into English territory except those brought by English ships, attacked Company vessels.

When in 1657 the despairing Company finally threatened to withdraw from the East altogether, Cromwell issued it a fresh charter. The Restoration in 1660 brought yet another charter, from Charles II. Under its terms the Company had the right to coin money, wage war with its own army, and exercise jurisdiction over English subjects in India. Armed with these rights, the Company would eventually be able to march forward to Empire in the East.

Conflicts at home might be resolved, but India itself remained in turmoil. The Mughal Empire was still slowly expanding under Aurangzeb, who seized the throne in 1658. It took him nearly 50 years to conquer the southern kingdoms, in the process creating confusion and chaos. Even in the older, settled imperial dominions there was a breakdown of law and order. The Company's trading caravans were often looted and its agents murdered.

In this unstable situation, the English began to look for a site on which to build a fort. At Surat they felt exposed. But where could they go? Fortunately, a royal marriage came to their rescue. In 1662 Charles II married a Portuguese princess, Catherine of Braganza. Part of her dowry was the Portuguese settlement on the island of Bombay, which in 1665 became English. Crown rule, however, was too expensive for Charles's liking. In 1668, in exchange for a loan, he leased Bombay to the East India Company at an annual rental of £10.

The Company's new Governor, Gerald Aungier, immediately began to fortify Bombay to ensure its safety as the new Company headquarters. The Dutch were attacking Portuguese stations on the Malabar coast in their endeavour to capture a world monopoly in pepper, and it seemed likely that the English would be next. The French, founding their own East India Company in 1664, had begun to establish factories on the same coast. Perhaps they too would in time pose a serious threat. What was needed, Aungier believed, was positive decision and action. "Justice and respect," he wrote to his employers in London, "is quite laid aside; the name of the Honourable Company and the English nation through our long, patient suffering of wrong is become slighted; our complaints, remonstrances, paper protests and threatenings, are laughed at. . . . The times now require you to manage your general commerce with your sword in your hand."

The autocratic Sir Josiah Child, the Company's director in London, appeared to agree. It was the duty of the East India Company, he said, to proceed to lay "the foundations of a large well-guarded sure English dominion in India for all time to come." Events, he said, were forcing the Company "into a sovereign state in India."

By the turn of the century Child's prediction was coming true. The Company now had four major territorial possessions (as distinct from agencies or trading stations): Bombay on the west coast, Calcutta in Bengal, Fort St. George in Madras, and Fort St. David at Cuddalore on the southeastern, or Coromandel, coast. The latter had been acquired by a method highly appealing to the British. When the local Maratha chiefs sold Cuddalore, they included the surrounding land "within ye randome shott of a piece of ordnance." The English sent to Madras for the gun with the longest range and instructed that "it lyes in the gunner's art to load and fire it to the best advantage." This demarcation by artillery was made in September, 1690, and the nearby villages are known to this day as *Gundu Gramam*, or "cannonball villages."

The Company largely owed its grip on Bengal to a remarkable figure, the "honest Mr. Charnock." A rough, ill-educated man, Job Charnock had spent nearly all his life in India and had become almost an Indian himself. As Company agent in Bengal, he founded the city of Calcutta on what had been a malarial swamp. He ruled there "more absolutely than a *Rajah*" and, despite a salary that only ranged between £20 and £40 a year, lived in a style that was Orientally opulent— at apparently no cost to his reputation for honesty.

Madras, to the south, was the first of the Company's possessions to receive a charter from England to form itself into a municipality. Elihu Yale, Governor of Madras from 1687 until 1692, applied anti-piracy laws with great severity against Indians and English alike. There is a story that he hanged his own English groom on a charge of piracy; the actual crime consisted of the servant's having taken his master's horse and stayed away for two nights. In later life, having made a fortune in private trade, the Boston-born Yale achieved more lasting fame by making a donation of £562 to a new college in Connecticut which promptly took his name.

Despite a variety of difficulties and despite the Company's relatively low profit margin, by 1700 the English had solidly staked their claim in India. They lived well and enjoyed the luxuries India had to offer and in general behaved as if they were there to stay. There seemed to be as yet no challenge from the great rival-to-be, France. One Englisman dismissed the French settlement at Chandernagore in Bengal as merely a few houses and "a pretty little church to hear Mass in, which is the chief business of the French in Bengal." He was very wrong. French commercial enterprise was on the increase and as the Mughal Empire slowly fell apart in the first half of the 18th Century, the Europeans were drawn into the vortex. To ensure their own survival, the merchants were about to transform themselves into generals and princes.

—*Michael Edwardes*

THE EAST INDIA COMPANY

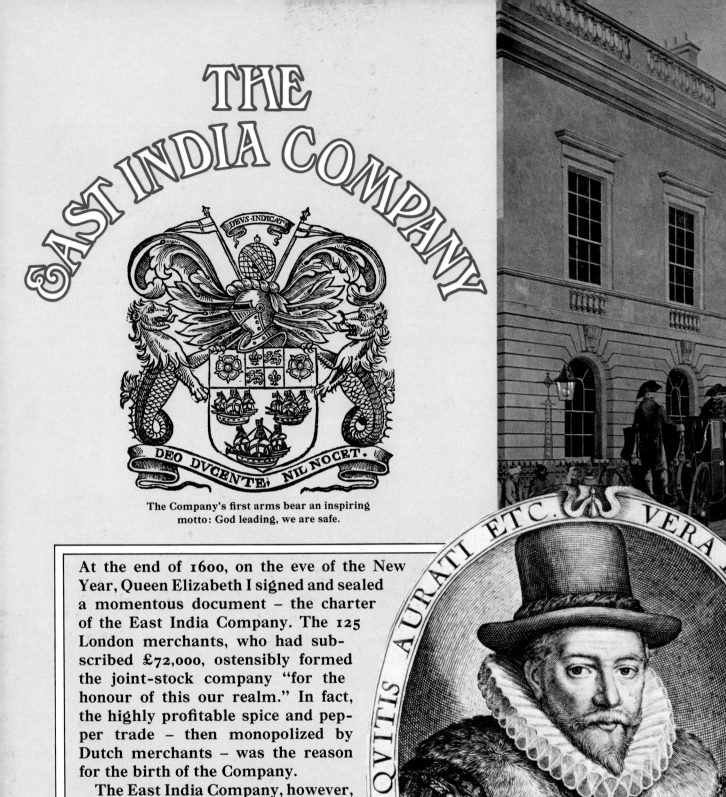

The Company's first arms bear an inspiring
motto: God leading, we are safe.

At the end of 1600, on the eve of the New
Year, Queen Elizabeth I signed and sealed
a momentous document – the charter
of the East India Company. The 125
London merchants, who had subscribed £72,000, ostensibly formed
the joint-stock company "for the
honour of this our realm." In fact,
the highly profitable spice and pepper trade – then monopolized by
Dutch merchants – was the reason
for the birth of the Company.

The East India Company, however,
was not just a business concern – it
was the curtain-raiser for Britain's
Indian Empire. Within two centuries
the Company, with its own army and
navy, ruled India from its London base.

Sir Thomas Smyth, whose diplomatic
and business connections with Russia
and Virginia had given him a knowledge
of international trade, became the first
Governor of the East India Company in 1600.

Two ensigns of the Royal East India Volunteer
– the Company's private army – kneel as
chaplain consecrates the regimental Colours in 179

East India House in Leadenhall Street (left), built in 1648, was the Company's first permanent headquarters. It had outgrown its first office – three rooms in Sir Thomas Smyth's home – and its second in the slightly larger Crosby House. Now a thriving concern, the Company could afford spacious premises, with a large and elegant Court Room (below) where shareholders held tumultuous meetings.

Vignettes of Life in India

Although the hand-painted and printed fabrics of India came to be among the most valuable imports of the East India Company, at first they met with a cool reception. As late as 1643, the directors were sadly commenting that the coloured cottons "serve more to content and pleasure our friends than for any profit that ariseth from the sales." But the directors were capable merchants and they ordered designs to suit English taste, desiring "more white ground" instead of "the sad red grounds which are not so well accepted here."

In response to the demand for Anglicized calicoes, the Indian artists employed to paint the fabrics took inspiration from the merchants they saw in the coastal towns, and portrayed Englishmen in their various activities – driving hard bargains with the natives, relaxing, being entertained and chatting about business. Details from one such fabric are shown here. The new-look calicoes were so enthusiastically received that soon the directors were sending out sample sketches of Englishmen in their home settings for the Indian artists to copy. The results were successful beyond their fondest hopes: a huge demand developed at home in London and the provinces for curtains and dresses, hangings and waistcoats and tablecloths made of these fabrics.

Two European merchants, one in gaily flower-sprigged trousers, raise their hats in a cordial gesture in their portraits by an Indian artist on this hand-painted fabric.

The life of the East is re-created by tiny brush strokes on this fabric. Indians cluster round a flagpole outside the elaborately ornamented, impressionistic trading-factory, in which two English merchants pass the time by chatting about business matters.

The skilful Indian artist caught the aloof expression of this European, who – like an Indian prince – reclines luxuriously in a palanquin.

Exotic Indian instruments, including the long-stemmed sitar and the resonant drum called a "tabla," accompany a group of singers and dancers who entertained the merchants in their leisure-hours.

A soldier – perhaps a forerunner of the private Company troops formally constituted in the 18th Century – parades dutifully with sword over his shoulder.

Building the Great Spice Fleet

Ships to carry the silks and spices of the Orient were the most urgent requirement of the East India Company, and in 1609 it opened a dockyard at Deptford. To one contemporary historian this marked the start of the "increase of great ships in England" that followed the triumph of the island's sailors over the Armada.

The first vessel built was the hopefully named *Trades' Increase*, closely followed by the *Peppercorn*. At 1,293 tons, the *Trades' Increase* was the largest ship ever constructed in England. Its launching was a great social event: King James I and other guests were given a sumptuous feast on dishes and silver that had been brought back by the Company.

Despite its auspicious beginning, the *Trades' Increase* was clumsy and unwieldy, and she came to a sad end at Bantam in Java where she burned to the waterline. At the end of the 1620s, the Company turned from building its own ships to chartering private vessels built to the Company's specifications. The long line of magnificent East Indiamen that followed became world-renowned in the next two centuries for the regularity with which they delivered their cargoes of muslin, silks, spices and tea.

The Money brothers, like many other officials of the East India Company, built ships designed for the Company's needs. To prevent this practice, which led to corruption, directors were banned in 1708 from chartering their own vessels to the Company.

Paintings of majestic East Indiamen from three angles, like this mid-18th-Century work, were frequently commissioned by proud captains.

nder the bored eyes of stevedores, bundles
nd packages mysteriously inscribed in Indian
haracters rest on the London dock after being
nloaded from East Indiamen. Horse-drawn
arts wait to carry the cargoes to warehouses.

Chapter Two
THE FRENCH CHALLENGE

Nelson's mighty *Victory*, 104 guns, had become the symbol of the Royal Navy's dominance during the age of sail. Beyond her is another of Nelson's commands, the 74-gun *Captain*.

I. Warfare in the Wilderness

For a century and a quarter, from about 1690 until 1815, the great powers were so often at war that their conflicts sometimes seemed to run together into one continuous struggle. Alliances formed, shifted, broke up, and reformed with bewildering complexity. Regardless of their allies, however, Britain and France remained bitter opponents throughout. They fought on the Continent and at sea and for colonial advantage round the world—in Canada, in the Caribbean, in India, in America. By the time Britain finally mastered the challenge, the Empire had undergone a major reshaping.

In North America the first French challenge required four wars—all of them on-the-spot versions of European conflicts—and more than 70 years to settle. The fighting began in 1689 with King William's War, eight bloody years of inter-colonial raids and retaliations which ended encouragingly for the French. The Treaty of Ryswick in 1697 gave the Canadians most of the British posts on Hudson Bay, and the French held Acadia, the province on the Atlantic seaboard later renamed Nova Scotia. It was all the encouragement the French were to get. With the next war, that of the Spanish Succession, the tide began running the other way. New France only narrowly avoided total defeat. In the Treaty of Utrecht in 1713 the Hudson's Bay Company regained its forts and the French were compelled to cede the provinces of Newfoundland and Acadia to Britain.

Fatigued by the contest, both sides backed off to recuperate and North America enjoyed a generation of peace, during which New France readied herself for the inevitable resumption of conflict. New forts went up to guard the frontier to the south. On Cape Breton Island in the Gulf of St. Lawrence the biggest shore defence in all America slowly took shape: Louisbourg. Ill-conceived and badly built, a monument to administrative fiddles and shoddy workmanship, the massive stone fortress was formidable only in appearance and cost.

The French had better results building up their commercial strength during this period. Pierre la Verendrye tramped through the swamps and forests of the north-west for 12 years, opening new routes that siphoned into Montreal much of the fur trade that had been going to Hudson Bay. This development was more valuable to the French, and more galling to the English, than a dozen Louisbourgs.

When fighting resumed with the War of the Austrian Succession in 1744, France's policy was to seek victory in Europe while simply holding on to her American possessions. Without reinforcements from France this latter task was difficult, especially in the case of Louisbourg. A well planned expedition led by William Pepperell, a Maine fish merchant, made this abundantly clear in 1745. With the aid of the Royal Navy, the New England volunteers dealt "the severest blow that could have been given to the Enemy, and in the tenderest part," by capturing Louisbourg at small cost.

France did better in Europe, and in the Treaty of Aix-la-Chapelle in 1748 regained Louisbourg, much to the indignation of Britain's colonists. At most, Aix-la-Chapelle was regarded as a truce. The main event was yet to come.

The French began strengthening Louisbourg as soon as they got it back. The British, in turn, built a naval base at Halifax and planted their own settlers among the Frenchmen of Nova Scotia. These French Acadians, humble farmers for the most part, were considered a threat by their British masters despite their protestations of neutrality. Later, when war began, they were forcibly expelled in an episode which for years was the stuff of legend and verse. Six thousand were uprooted from the land of their ancestors, separated from friends and often from families, and shipped off to less vulnerable corners of the Empire. Many ultimately made their way to French Louisiana, where they founded a tropical version of their lost Acadia.

By the time the Acadians were deported, New France and British America were at war in the Ohio Valley, which both nations claimed. The French reinforced their claim in 1753, sending 2,200 Canadian soldiers to build and man Fort le Boeuf near Lake Erie. Soon after it was completed, the young militia officer George Washington arrived at its gates with a letter from the Governor of Virginia, Robert Dinwiddie. Dinwiddie, in no uncertain terms, demanded to know why the French were on land "so notoriously known to be the property of the crown of Great Britain."

"They told me," Washington reported back to his Governor, "that it was their absolute design to take possession of the Ohio, and by G— they would do it." Dinwiddie was not impressed. He sent the young officer back to the Ohio Country with about 150 colonial militiamen.

The French, meanwhile, had captured a half-finished outpost being built by a British party on the site of modern Pittsburgh, completed it, and

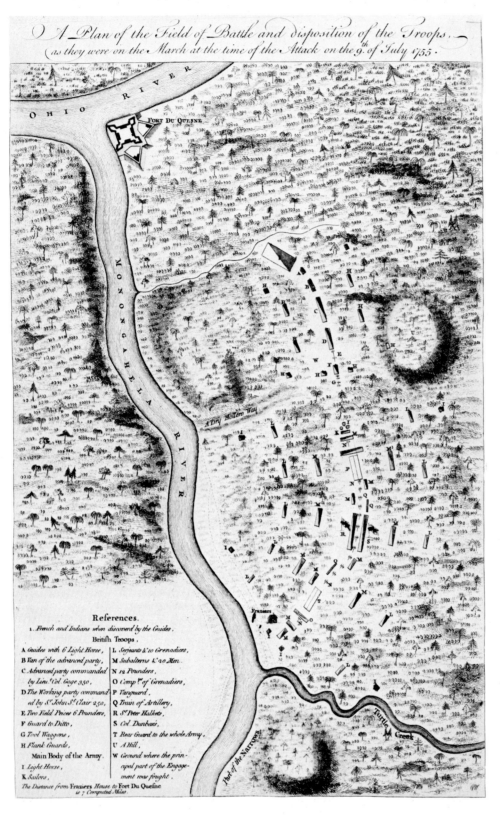

As indicated in this engraved plan, Braddock's army was stretched over some four miles as it approached Fort Duquesne (top left) on July 9, 1755. The head of the column, an advance guard and a working party, absorbed the first blows of the French and Indians. The worst fighting took place as the main body came up.

named it Fort Duquesne. When Washington arrived to evict these interlopers, his Virginians were surrounded in their hastily dug defences and forced to surrender. The French allowed their captives to go home to Virginia, but this generosity did not assuage offended British sensibilities. From a backwoods border clash fought by colonial militia, the Ohio question was promoted to an imperial crisis. George II announced to Parliament that he would defend his American possessions, and sent Major-General Edward Braddock with two regiments of regulars to expel the trespassers.

Braddock, a 60-year-old veteran of the Coldstream Guards and a military traditionalist, had precious little combat experience. But he did have confidence. "These savages," he said of the Frenchmen's Indian allies, "may be a formidable enemy to raw American militia, but upon the King's regular and disciplined troops they can make no impression." Behind fluttering banners and beating drums, his redcoats were a smart, martial sight as they marched towards Fort Duquesne.

The French-Indian force numbered less than a third of Braddock's 1,400 men, but the British never had a chance to count them. Braddock's close-ranked column met the enemy near Fort Duquesne on the afternoon of July 9, 1755. After the opening volley, the French and Indians faded into the heavy woods on either side of the British column and poured a torrent of musket balls into the hapless redcoats.

Unable to see the enemy marksmen, the British began firing wildly in all directions, hitting many of their own comrades. Braddock, shot through the lungs, died muttering "Who would have thought it?" Two-thirds of his expedition fell in the slaughter.

Braddock's march was one thrust in a four-pronged British offensive that was meant to end with the conquest of Canada. The British also failed to penetrate French defences either at Fort Niagara on Lake Ontario or farther east along the Lake Champlain-Richelieu River route to the St. Lawrence. Only in Acadia, where two French forts surrendered, did Britain achieve her initial objectives. The two great empires, although neither officially acknowledged it yet, were at war once more, and so far New France was putting up a remarkably good show for a country of 90,000 defying a neighbour 15 times as big.

Britain officially declared war on France in May, 1756, the start in Europe of the Seven Years' War, known in America as the French and Indian War. Little happened until December when William Pitt became Prime Minister. Pitt the Elder has been called the only Prime Minister in the history of Britain who purposefully and successfully made war an instrument of imperial policy. Whether or not he deserves that less than wholly flattering distinction, he certainly understood the importance of strategy and initiative to national aims.

The three previous Anglo-French wars had been decided, ultimately, on the battlefields of Europe. Pitt determined to go this time directly for the prizes themselves: French colonies and the control of sea routes leading to them. The future of New France would be settled in North America, and not by volunteer armies and colonial militia but by all the military and naval power that Britain could bring to bear on that sector of the world-wide conflict.

It was because of one man, the Marquis de Montcalm, that French arms continued to prevail in America for a year after Pitt took office. Montcalm was probably the greatest commander of the Seven Years' War on either side. He also had the greatest problems. One was his mistrust of and lack of sympathy for the Canadians, which they returned in kind. On his arrival he was surprised to learn that they actually spoke passable French. He preferred to rely on his French regulars.

Montcalm also faced trouble from the men with whom he shared authority in the colony: Pierre de Vaudreuil, the first Canadian-born Governor—in effect a viceroy—and François Bigot, the *intendant* or chief administrator. Vaudreuil was jealous of Mont-

calm and frequently interfered with his command. In turn, the French General seems to have regarded Vaudreuil as a nuisance. "Youth must learn," Montcalm sighed when the 61-year-old Governor toured a defensive position. "As he had never in his life seen either an army or an earthwork, these things struck him as being as novel as they were entertaining."

Bigot, the *intendant,* was no more than an amusing crook. He headed a syndicate that bought surplus stores from the French Crown cheap and sold them back at ridiculously inflated prices. "What a country, what a country," lamented Montcalm, "where knaves grow rich and honest men are ruined." Still, he had to get along with the *intendant* in order to fight the war, and besides, Bigot was an intelligent raconteur whose famed table and vivacious mistress could lend some brightness to the long, grim Canadian winter.

Montcalm's greatest problem was the Royal Navy. Twice as large as

The grimly illustrated title page of an eyewitness account of the Fort William Henry massacre, printed in 1760.

France's, it was rapidly gaining control of the Atlantic. This meant that Montcalm's command—a few thousand French regulars and about 9,000 Canadian militia, very small in comparison to British manpower in America—could not expect a steady flow of reinforcements. He realized that eventually the French fleets would be blocked at home, the entrance to the St. Lawrence would fall to the British, and that his force at Quebec would have to face the enemy alone.

Montcalm's glory derives mainly from the fact that he refused to let these considerations lock him into a defensive posture until it was absolutely necessary.

There were three invasion routes the British could take to pierce the Canadian heartland. One was the St. Lawrence itself. Another was up Lake Champlain and the Richelieu River. The third was in the west, through the lower Great Lakes. Instead of waiting behind his forts for the British, Montcalm marched out to push his enemy back. He struck first—and hard—in the west.

On August 10, 1756, Colonel James Mercer, who commanded the important British base at Oswego on Lake Ontario, awoke to find 3,300 Frenchmen and Canadians outside his walls. Four days later he was killed by French fire and the fort surrendered. The next summer Montcalm moved 8,000 against Fort William Henry near Lake George. The siege began on August 3. Six days later, having learned no help was coming, the British surrendered. Montcalm admonished his Indians to treat the prisoners humanely, but his orders were violated. "They killed and scalp'd all the sick and wounded before our faces," testified one Anglo-American soldier. The next day the Indians attacked the column of prisoners, and before Montcalm's regulars could restore order with fixed bayonets, at least 200 of the captives, including "Officers, privates, Women, and Children," were dead and several hundred others carried off for future ransoming. New Yorkers began destroying boats, bridges, and roads to block Montcalm's expected advance towards Albany.

The French fortress of Louisbourg is in the foreground of this detail of a manuscript map of the English attack in 1758. At upper centre is a satellite battery taken by the invaders. The ships afire at centre are French.

But he was not going to Albany. Facing transport and supply problems and knowing his Canadian auxiliaries wanted to go home for the harvest, he fell back on Fort Ticonderoga, where Lake George flows into Lake Champlain.

Montcalm should have moved. By the next year it was too late, as Pitt's men and Pitt's policies at last took hold and robbed Montcalm of his initiative. Probably the most important of those men was James Wolfe, a tempermental and chronically ill (besides a generally frail constitution, he suffered from "rheumatism and gravel"), bold and devoted soldier. Wolfe was aware of his own reputation for moodiness and stormy outbursts. "Better be a savage of some use," he said, "than a gentle, amorous

puppy, obnoxious to all the world." His superiors suffered his rudeness to gain the benefit of his courage and imagination. The Duke of Newcastle told George II that Pitt's new general was insane. "Mad is he?" responded the King. "Then I hope he will bite some others of my generals."

On June 1, 1758, 200 British vessels, including 23 ships of the line and carrying 13,000 troops, appeared off Louisbourg. Lord Jeffrey Amherst was in charge of the show, but the 32-year-old Wolfe, making his debut in the American war, stole it. It was Wolfe, armed only with a cane, who leapt into the surf under a shower of French fire and bullied his men ashore after several previous attempts to establish a beachhead had failed. It was Wolfe who directed the movement of British

artillery through the siege that followed, closer and closer to the fortress with ever more devastating effect, until the desperate French were plugging the holes in the walls with hogsheads of tea. On July 26 Louisbourg capitulated. The St. Lawrence was unlocked.

But the man who had as much as anyone turned the key went back to England in a pique because Amherst decided it was too late to press on to Quebec that year. "If you will attempt to cut up New France by the roots," Wolfe told him impatiently before departing, "I will come back with pleasure to assist."

The year was not altogether Britain's. At Ticonderoga Montcalm scored a splendid victory over an army of 15,000 trying to force its way to the St. Lawrence. James Abercromby lost almost 2,000 men, the French less than 400. "What a day for France!" wrote Montcalm. "Ah . . . what soldiers are ours! I never saw the like. Why were they not at Louisbourg?"

Why were they not also, he might later have asked, in the west, where the French lost Forts Frontenac and Duquesne? The triumph at Ticonderoga was glorious enough, but the eventuality Montcalm had forseen for the last two years was now reality: New France was confined to the St. Lawrence Valley and it was only a matter of time before the enemy struck at its heart.

Before a year was up Wolfe kept his promise and returned "to cut up New France by the roots." While the mercurial Wolfe was without doubt the hero of the Seven Years' War, it is worth recalling the well-worn adage that Britain's real army was her navy.

British sea power had isolated Montcalm from the reinforcements he needed. It had invalidated the presence of a French fleet at Louisbourg. Now the Royal Navy had carried Wolfe and his army of 10,000 into the heart of the North American land mass, sailing up the treacherous St. Lawrence on a course charted by a promising young naval officer named James Cook.

Once before Quebec, Wolfe, who was even more ill than usual, showed less than his normal impatience to conclude the issue. Perhaps he believed the fortifications to be stronger than they actually were. If so, his conviction was not shared by the French commander. After surveying his defences, Montcalm had dispatched his aide Louis de Bougainville to ask for reinforcements in Paris. The hardpressed French treasury had no money to spare for Canada. "When a house is on fire," said the Minister, Berryer, "one doesn't bother about the stables." "At least, Monsieur," replied Bougainville rather acidly, "one could not accuse you of talking like a horse."

Wolfe bombarded the town throughout July. Houses that survived the fire collapsed under the sheer weight of cannon balls. In the lower town, 150 dwellings were destroyed in one night of incendiary shelling. To destroy a town, however, was not to conquer it, as Wolfe found when he lost 400 men in late July while attempting to make a landing on the French side of the river.

He knew he had to act before the autumn freeze forced his expedition out of the St. Lawrence, but professed he did not know what to do. In early September he wrote to Pitt that he had "such a Choice of Difficulties, that I own myself at a loss how to determine." Wolfe as well as his disappointed officers knew that his depression and indecision were caused by his physical afflictions. "I know perfectly well you cannot cure my complaint," he told his surgeon about this time, "but patch me up so that I may be able to do my duty for the next few days, and I shall be content."

Shortly afterwards, Wolfe broke camp and moved a large part of his force upstream. An attempt to scale the towering cliffs and reach the Plains of Abraham above the town seemed unlikely, but Wolfe kept his plans to himself.

About 4 a.m. on September 13, a French sentry near the Anse au Foulon, one of the few places where a steep, tortuous path climbed up the formidable wall, heard a sound from the darkened river. "Qui vive?" he challenged. "France," came the quiet reply.

"Why don't you speak louder?" persisted the sentry.

"Be quiet. We will be heard," answered the commanding voice, in excellent French. Sensing he was dealing with an officer, the sentry kept his silence. The voice from the dark was indeed an officer's, that of a Highlander named Simon Gray who was in the leading boat of a flotilla carrying almost 5,000 British soldiers. A few minutes later Wolfe stepped on to the shingled beach of the Anse du Foulon. He was honest with his men. "I don't think we can by any means get up here," he said, "but we must use our best endeavour." He was too pessimistic: his advance guard had already crept to the top and silenced the small body of French troops on the summit.

William Pitt the Elder, architect of grand strategy in the Seven Years' War, was painted (above) about 1766 by a follower of the portraitist Richard Brompton. The mezzotint below of James Wolfe celebrated his victory at Quebec.

At sunrise two hours later, Montcalm was astounded to see a red-clad British army assembling on the Plains of Abraham. The war that had begun with a skirmish in thick forest was about to be decided on a field that was practically a parade ground. Here regular soldiers were better suited than irregulars, and Montcalm's army of 4,500 consisted mainly of the latter. But he did not hesitate. "If we give the enemy time to dig in," he said, ordering his men from their trenches, "we shall never be able to attack him with the few troops we have."

The formal British ranks held their fire until the French were within 40 paces, then dispensed two volleys in such precise unison that they were said to sound like two cannon shots. The Frenchmen who were left standing turned and fled. Wolfe, personally leading the counter-charge, was hit three times. From where he lay on the ground he calmly issued an order to cut off the French retreat. He then turned on his side, said "Now, God be praised, I will die in peace," and did so. Montcalm, covered with blood from his own wounds, rode with dignity back into the walled city before dying. The generals were two of some 1,200 casualties in this critical battle that had lasted less than half an hour.

Another year elapsed before a British army of 18,000 compelled the surrender of Montreal and completed the conquest of Canada. Great Britain could take her time; she was riding a world-wide ground-swell of victory In Germany the French were being beaten back. At sea the Royal Navy achieved decisive victories in the Bay of Biscay, the Mediterranean, and the Caribbean. In India Clive had the French on the run. In the West Indies Guadeloupe had already surrendered and other French sugar islands were to follow—costing France a fifth of her overseas trade, whereas in Canada she lost only a twentieth of it. Spain's late and injudicious entry into the war only provided more prizes—Havana in the west and Manila in the east—for English arms. When the European powers finally sat down at the conference table, Great Britain held all the winning cards.

— Jim Hicks

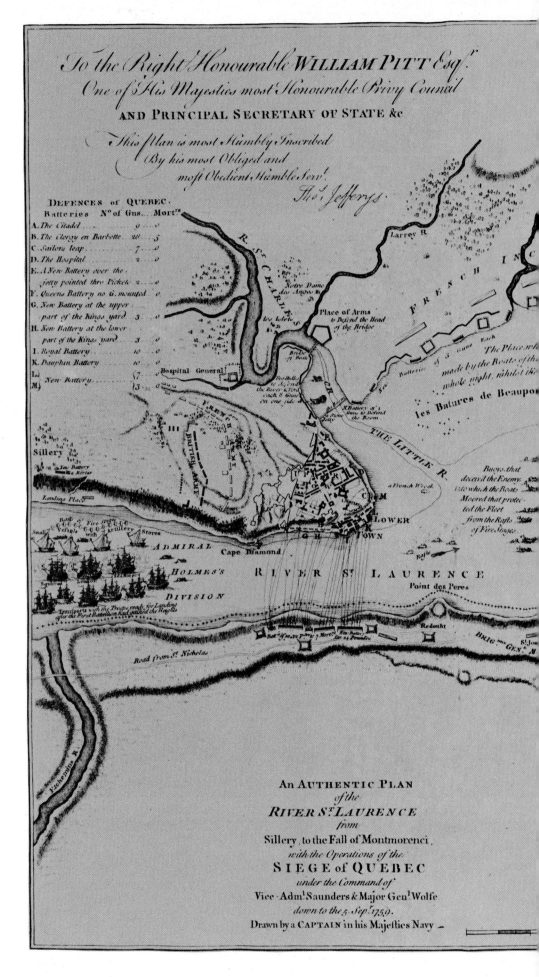

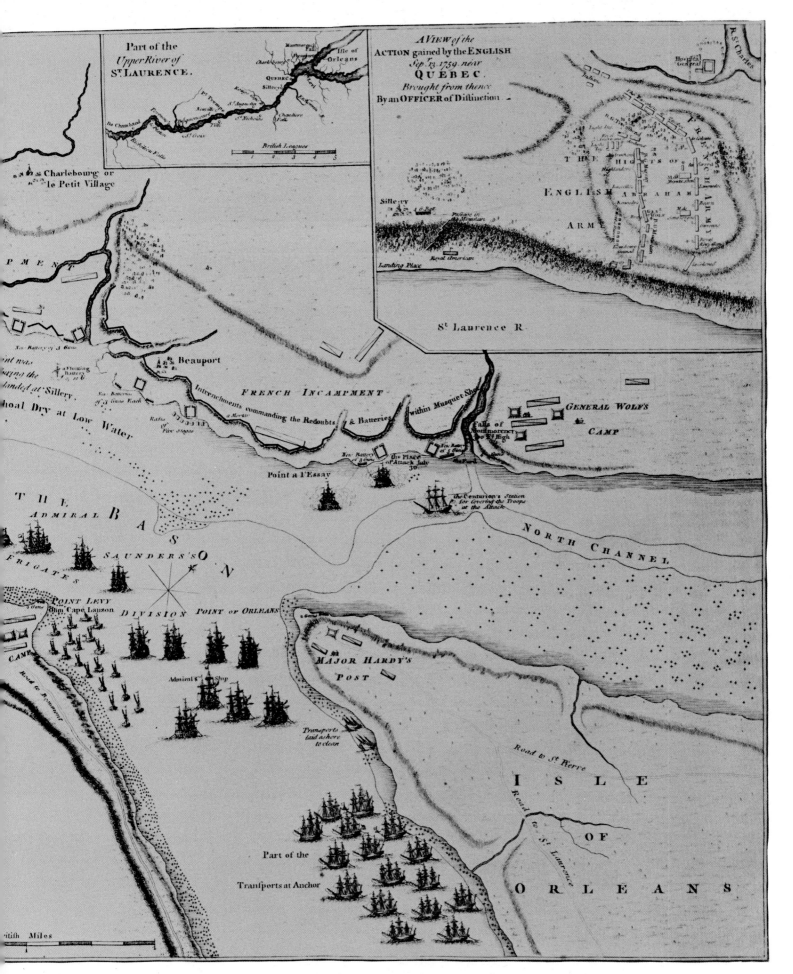

A plan of the campaign against Quebec, drawn by Thomas Jefferys of the Royal Navy. British artillery batters the city, at left. At far left is the flotilla that carried Wolfe to his landing upstream. The inset details the battle on the Plains of Abraham.

II. The Contest for India

The French had arrived on the Indian scene in 1664 in the form of Louis XIV's Compagnie des Indes Orientales, one more of the means by which the Sun King intended to enlarge his glory. Louis, however, proceeded to treat his East India Company like a poor relation, and for years it teetered along precariously.

Its chief posts were at Pondicherry, 85 miles down the eastern Coromandel coast from the British at Madras, and at Chandernagore in Bengal, 16 miles from the English settlement at Calcutta. Until about 1720 relations between the British and French companies were reasonably cordial. But trade and international politics could not be long separated. Concerned over increasing French competition, the directors in London asked if the government would send a fleet to sweep French vessels from the Indian seas.

In 1744, when the War of the Austrian Succession broke out, the government obliged. A blow at France in India was almost as good as a blow against France in Europe or at Louisbourg in Canada, and the East India Company commerce, which brought in more than 10 per cent of Britain's public revenue, was worth protecting.

So the English dispatched six vessels which en route captured four French ships. It was not much—but it was enough to incense the French Governor, Joseph-François Dupleix, who was waiting for just such an excuse to drive the British from India.

Long before Dupleix was appointed to take charge of France's possessions in India in 1742, he had dreamed of creating a French Empire in the East. He believed he could achieve his ambitions within the tangled skein of Indian politics by intrigue, for which he had talent amounting almost to genius. Over the years he had acquired considerable knowledge of the realities of local politics and set up an intelligence network covering all the important Indian courts.

His was a complex game, for no Indian ruler, other than the Emperor himself, had absolute powers to withhold or grant authority. Each ruler owed allegiance to a higher power. Thus both the English in Madras and the French in Pondicherry were dependent on the Nawab of the Carnatic province, who himself owed allegiance to the ruler of Hyderabad. With the death of the last of the great Mughal emperors, Aurangzeb, in 1707, this chain of allegiances, often only nominal, began to collapse. This was the weakness which Dupleix sought to exploit.

He first turned his attention to the British in Madras. In 1746 he won over the Nawab by promising him the town if the French were victorious. Then his army, strengthened by a fleet from home, bombarded Madras. One shell burst open liquor stocks, and the British garrison decided to drown its sorrows instead of fighting. After three days it surrendered.

Dupleix, with bewildering duplicity, then turned his small European force against his Indian ally. The two French cannon ripped through the Nawab's 10,000 undisciplined troops and routed them. It was a demonstration of the enormous superiority of well-handled guns over cavalry, of musket and bayonet over badly tempered sword and pike. Native India, apparently, was ripe for the taking.

Peace in Europe interrupted Dupleix's scheme—the Treaty of Aix-la-Chapelle handed Madras back to Britain—but did not deter him for long. He proceeded to install his own

The Marquis Dupleix, the moving force behind France's imperial dreams in India.

nominee as Governor of defeated Carnatic, a success so easily achieved that he looked farther afield, to Hyderabad itself. Taking advantage of a regal dispute over the succession and supported by a body of French troops under a brilliant soldier, Charles de Bussy, Dupleix placed his own man on the Hyderabad throne.

Dupleix's objective was simple: to surround Madras with French-controlled territory and squeeze out the English. In self-defence the English took up the same game and decided to replace the French puppet in Carnatic with a puppet of their own. The difficulty was that the only likely candidate, the son of the deposed Nawab, was under siege by a Franco-Indian force in the rock fortress of Trichinopoly, 200 miles away. The solution to this dilemma came from the fertile imagination of a captain in the Company's army, Robert Clive.

The Company had come to expect bold, risky thinking from Clive. Back in Shropshire this son of an impoverished squire had early proved difficult, and at 18 he was shipped off to India. He arrived in Madras in 1744 as a clerk in the Company's service. He was virtually penniless and without friends. He disliked his job, and was so quick to take offence at anything he believed affected his honour that he was left alone by most of his colleagues, who feared his temper.

In despair, Clive attempted suicide, but after his pistol misfired twice in succession he was reported to have said "Well, I am reserved for something." Release from his tedious and constricting life came with the French attack on Madras in 1746. He was transferred to military duties, and with the rest of the garrison was taken prisoner. He escaped by blacking his face and putting on Indian clothes and made his way 100 miles south to Fort St. David, the Company's last outpost on the Coromandel coast. There his outbursts of temper convinced some that he was mad. Others, observing his quick thinking and vigourous action, saw a natural guerrilla leader. Both opinions were right. Clive would often retire into what his contemporaries called "melancholy," only to

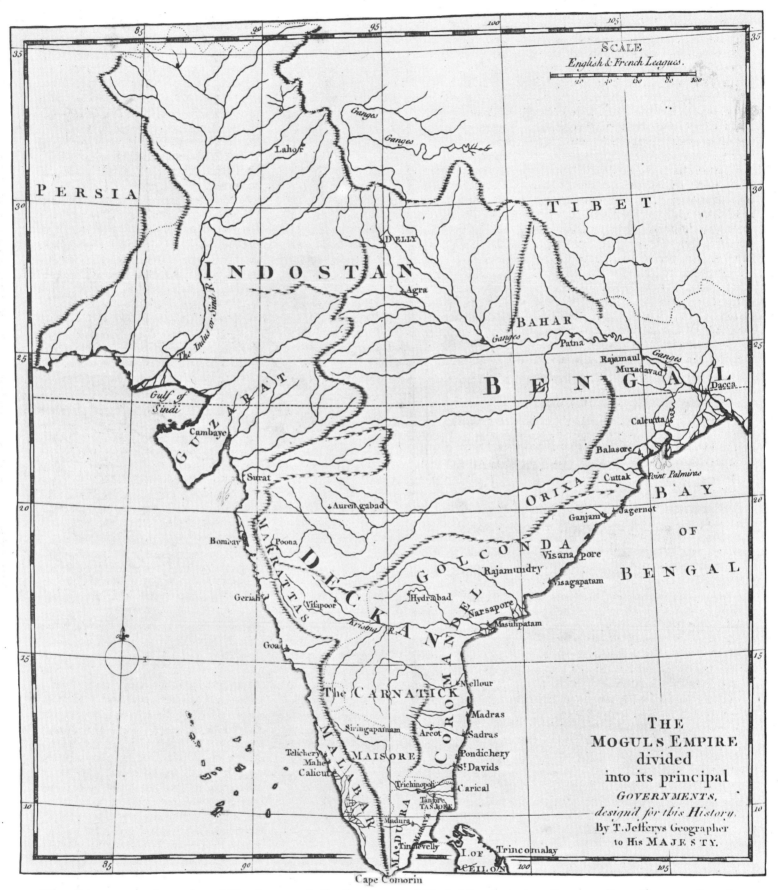

SCALE
English & French Leagues
20 40 60 80 100

PERSIA

TIBET

INDOSTAN

Lahor

Ganges

Ganges

D'ELLY

Agra

BAHAR

The Indus or Sind R.

Ganges

Patna

Rajamaul

Muxadavad

Dacca

BENGAL

Gulf of Sindi

Calcutta

Cambaye

GUZARAT

Balasore

Surat

ORIXA

Cuttak

Point Palmiras

BAY

Aurengabad

Ganjam

Jagernot

Bombay

Poona

GOLCONDA

Visanapore

OF

MARATTAS

Visagapatam

BENGAL

Geriah

DECKAN

Vifipoor

Hydrabad

Rajamundry

Narsapore

Goa

Kristna R.

Masulipatam

COROMANDEL

Nellour

The CARNATICK

Madras

Siringapatnam

Arcot

Sadras

Telichery

Mahe

MAISORE

Pondichery

Calicut

St Davids

MALABAR

Trichinopoli

Carical

Tanore
TANJORE

Madura

THE
MOGULS EMPIRE
divided
into its principal
GOVERNMENTS,
design'd for this History,
By T. Jefferys Geographer
to His MAJESTY.

Tinnevelly

I. OF
CEILON

Trincomalay

Cape Comorin

When this map was drawn for a 1761 volume on India, the once-great Mughal Empire was on the wane, its southern provinces torn by intrigue and rebellion. Poised to pick up the pieces were the Europeans in their trading outposts scattered along the coasts.

65

emerge decisive, bold, and bursting with frenetic energy.

To divert the enemy from its siege of Trichinopoly, Clive determined to go for a sensitive spot in Dupleix's little empire—Arcot, capital of the French puppet governor of Carnatic. Ignoring a monsoon, his tiny British force made straight for the city, marching, according to an eyewitness, "unconcerned through a violent storm of thunder, lightning, and rain." This feat so impressed the Indian garrison of Arcot that it fled headlong.

Finally brought to a halt and braced by the French, the native army took heart again and turned back to lay siege to Clive in Arcot. He held out 53 days, making repeated sorties to sting the besiegers. Finally help arrived, the siege was broken, and Clive marched on to consolidate his victory. Trichinopoly was relieved and the British proceeded with their puppet-making. His policy in ruins, Dupleix was ordered home.

News of the ending of the siege and the victory spread rapidly. It was not only the Indians who found Clive's activities instructive. The English, too, learned a lesson. When the Governor of Madras wrote to his employers in London, he pointed out that the military weakness of the Indian princes was now plain—"and 'tis certain any European nation resolved to war on them with a tolerable force may overrun the whole country."

It had become plain, in short, that the collapse of the Mughal Empire was creating a power vacuum in India. The English in Madras and the French in Hyderabad gathered strength for the contest. But before making their next move, the British faced a new crisis, this one at Calcutta, the East India Company's base in Bengal.

All had gone reasonably well in Bengal until 1756. The Nawab, an able and strong-minded ruler, had kept everyone in order, including the Europeans. When the English began to dig a moat round Fort William at Calcutta in 1743, he had ordered them to stop. "You are merchants," he told them. "What need have you of a fortress?" But after 1748, when the French and the English were preparing for their next war, the Governor in Cal-

cutta was ordered to fortify his post in defiance of the Nawab. Their spirit inflamed by Clive's victories in the south, the English, always naïve about Indian politics, became insolent and belligerent as well. Though technically the Nawab's tenants, they acted as if they had sovereign rights, even giving sanctuary to persons accused of crimes in the Nawab's territory. Then, in April, 1756, the old Nawab died.

The new Nawab, Suraj-ud-daula, was weak and unstable—and headstrong. He ordered the Company's Governor in Calcutta, Roger Drake, to cease fortifying Fort William. Drake arrogantly answered that if the Nawab wanted the moat around the fort filled in, he could do so with the heads of his own subjects. Suraj-ud-daula, still shaky on his new throne, could hardly ignore such an affront to his authority.

His first act was to threaten the English by blockading their branch agencies and interrupting traffic on the rivers. Then he seized a fortified settlement a few miles from his capital. The English there were taken prisoner but treated well.

The Nawab's aim was to put pressure on Governor Drake. But the English would not believe that he merely wanted to negotiate. There were rumours of conspiracies. Spies reported that the French were behind everything.

Drake was convinced that Calcutta could hold off any attack long enough for reinforcements to come from Madras. Even the French believed that the Nawab could not defeat the English and declined an invitation to assist him. The Nawab's army was large but, with the exception of a party of French artillerymen, unimpressive. The French reported to their superiors at Pondicherry their view of the Nawab's troops: "Nothing is more pitiable than the way in which they are mounted and supplied. People say that they have only clay bullets."

The English would not negotiate, and the Nawab's army moved nearer to Calcutta. On June 15, 1756, it reached the River Hugli, which runs through the city. Thoroughly alarmed,

the English then fled into Fort William.

Chaos and indecision went with them. No plan of defence had been prepared, and there was no military officer in the throng competent to prepare one. Altogether, the English had 515 men—English, Portuguese, and Armenian. Hardly any among them "knew the right from the wrong end" of their matchlocks. Soon the Nawab's men were occupying the houses that surrounded and overlooked the fort. From there they pounded the English with a steady stream of cannon balls.

In the centre of all the chaos, Governor Drake still "imagined from the number of men slain of the enemy a terror might seize them, and that they would decamp." But it was Drake who decamped. On the morning of June 19 a council of war decided to evacuate the Eurasian women and children to ships lying down-river from the fort. The European women had gone aboard the day before. Drake, the military commander, and most of the principal merchants determined to go along with the Eurasians. Panic led to the overloading of the boats, and many capsized. "Most of those who crowded into them were drowned, and such as floated with the tide were either made prisoner or massacred."

As the enemy guns kept up their thunderous barrage, the remaining English inside the fort held a hurried meeting. It was decided to suspend Drake and the other members of the council who had fled; Josiah Holwell, the magistrate, was appointed Governor. There was little Holwell could do. The next day he asked for surrender terms.

Suraj-ud-daula inspected his new possession and promised the prisoners that no harm would come to them. He ordered his troops not to loot. But the calm did not last. Some of the European soldiers got drunk and began to assault passing Indians. When complaints reached the Nawab, he asked if there were not some dungeon where defaulters were customarily locked up. He was told that a part of the barracks, known as the "Black Hole," served that purpose. The name Black Hole seems now to suggest the

Prisoners in the notorious Black Hole of Calcutta struggle for a taste of water; from a contemporary engraving.

horrors to come; in fact, it was the usual term used by the English to describe any garrison lock-up used for confining drunken soldiers, and the name was not abandoned by the army until 1868.

When it was suggested to the Nawab that all the prisoners should be confined there for the night to prevent any from escaping, he agreed. And it is reasonable to suppose that he did not know the Black Hole to be a room only 18 feet long and 14 feet wide, with but two air-holes, both strongly barred.

At 8 p.m., according to Holwell—whose published narrative is the principal source for all accounts of

what happened—146 people were forced into the Black Hole by soldiers with "clubs and drawn scymitars." (Holwell, it now seems, overestimated the number. A careful check of the Europeans surviving the siege—and who thus could have been imprisoned in the Black Hole on the terrible night of June 20, 1756—reveals only 64.)

Holwell stumbled toward the nearest window and grasped the bars. The men who could not get near the windows were pushed to the back of the room. Some climbed onto a sleeping-bench that ran the length of the room. Others, seeking to escape the mounting pressure from behind, scrambled underneath the platform—only to be imprisoned by those who were jammed into the cell after them.

Now a silent, tortured fight for air began. The instant a man sagged for

want of air he was trampled to death. From underneath the sleeping bench came the moans of men rapidly suffocating. In their frenzy some took out their pocket knives and slashed at the legs of their companions who had been pushed against the platform and now unwittingly starved them of air. But it made no difference. The men who were stabbed, pressed solidly against their fellows, could not budge. Not every man collapsed to the floor as he died. In some corners the prisoners were so tightly packed that they remained wedged upright long after they had suffocated.

Holwell clung desperately to his place. "By keeping my face between two of the bars," he recalled, "I obtained air enough to give my lungs easy play, though my perspiration was excessive, and thirst commencing."

Robert Clive of India, painted by Nathaniel Dance against a backdrop of the Battle of Plassey.

Eventually, the men's piteous and insistent cries for water made an old guard take pity on them. The only containers for distributing the precious liquid were hats which were pushed through the bars for the guard to fill. These were almost useless. "Though we brought full hats between the bars, there ensued such violent struggles and frequent contests to get at it that, before it reached the lips of anyone, there would scarcely be a small tea-cup left in them. These supplies, like sprinkling water on fire, only served to feed and raise the flame."

Moreover, it soon dawned on the other guards that they had a novel form of entertainment. "They took care to keep us supplied with water," Holwell wrote, "that they might have the satisfaction of seeing us fight for it and held up lights to the bars that they might lose no part of the inhuman diversion."

By morning, when the prisoners were finally released, only Holwell and 22 others remained alive. Partly as a result of his detailed and harrowing description, the Black Hole of Calcutta grew into one of the great imperial myths. The English historian Thomas Babington Macaulay, writing in 1840, conjured up a gradiloquent, doom-laden vision of Suraj-ud-daula "haunted—as the Greek poet would have said—by the furies of those that cursed him with their last breath in the Black Hole."

The reality was not so straightforward. The Black Hole was not a deliberately planned atrocity: Suraj-ud-daula did not know what his order would accomplish. But even if most people at the time accepted Holwell's version, it was not considered one of the Nawab's major misdeeds. More Europeans had died in the siege itself, and certainly the English in Madras were less concerned with revenge than with a strategic problem: whether to risk sending troops to Calcutta at all while the French were preparing for war. There were rumours that a French fleet of 19 ships of the line with 3,000 troops aboard had sailed for Pondicherry. Which was more urgent—the need to reinstate English prestige in Bengal, the most profitable source of the Company's trade, or the defence of Madras?

News of the fall of Calcutta reached Madras in the middle of August, 1756. The council at Madras decided to take the risk and send men and ships to retake Calcutta, and to entrust the expedition to Robert Clive. Displaying considerable prescience, Clive wrote to his father: "This expedition, if attended with success, may enable me to do great things. It is by far the greatest of my undertakings. I go with great forces and great authority."

These "great forces"—four warships of the Royal Navy, two of the Company's, one fireship, 394 European infantry and artillerymen, and 510 native soldiers—arrived in December. Clive's instructions were to avenge the defeats, ensure reparation for losses, and see that the Company's trading rights were restored. But those were only the basic requirements of the East India Company. Admiral Watson, who commanded the ships of the Royal Navy, had been told that if he thought it practicable he was to seize the French settlement at Chandernagore, whether war between France and Britain had been declared or not. Clive's ambitions were more extensive. He hoped to do in Bengal what the Frenchman de Bussy had done in Hyderabad—erect a state wholly dependent on the good will of an outside power.

Retaking Calcutta was surprisingly easy: the enemy fled after the briefest of bombardments on January 7, 1757. But no real injury had been done to the Nawab. Clive was determined to inflict a humiliating defeat on Suraj-ud-daula, for otherwise the old pattern of threat and squeeze could return.

There was also the matter of reparations. Fort William was in ruins and most of Calcutta had been burned to the ground by the Nawab's men. The French at Chandernagore also remained a potential menace to the English. Even more dangerous to Clive's own ambitions was the possibility that he might be recalled to Madras, for the expedition's orders had been to recover Calcutta and then to return and protect the Coromandel coast. The news had now arrived that

Britain and France were at war in Europe.

What to do next was settled by the Nawab himself, who began to advance on Calcutta. Clive launched a dawn attack on the Indian camp on February 6, 1757. This action was described by Clive as "the warmest service I ever yet was engaged in." The Nawab quickly concluded a peace, promised that the Company's privileges would be restored, and agreed to pay compensation. This satisfied Clive—at least until the French had been crushed.

The position of the French was uncomfortable. They would have liked to help the Nawab against the English, but had chosen neutrality in case the English defeated the Nawab. Then they even tried secretly to assist the English in the hope of winning a mutual non-agression pact, despite the war in Europe.

Events seemed to move slowly through this web of intrigue, of offer and counteroffer, but Clive's determination never wavered. Soon the English were moving against the French. On March 14 the siege of Chandernagore began, to end five days later with the surrender of the French after bitter fighting and heavy losses.

About this time, Clive became aware that there was a conspiracy to overthrow the Nawab. Hindu merchants and bankers concerned about their profits from European trade were at the heart of it, and Clive was approached with requests for co-operation. An elderly general, Mir Jafar, was to be placed on the throne, and there would be large sums of money for everybody out of the state treasury, which was rumoured to hold more than £40 million in gold and jewels. Clive could make a profit for himself and his masters.

The conspiracy came to a head in the renowned, ridiculous Battle of Plassey. Clive's forces numbered less than 3,000, the Nawab's over 50,000, but most of Suraj-ud-daula's troops were commanded by men involved in the conspiracy. The battle on June 23, 1757, which founded the British Empire in India, ended in complete victory at a cost to the British of 63 casualties. Even the losers were poorer by only about 500 men.

There was, however, nothing minor about the consequences of Plassey. Clive was now a kingmaker, and the plunder of Bengal was there for the taking.

He placed Mir Jafar on the throne, and then Clive and the others collected their profits. Though Suraj-ud-daula's treasury turned out not to contain the fabulous sums everyone had believed, they were still substantial. The Company became landlord of some 880 square miles, mostly south of Calcutta, with rents estimated at £150,000. Clive himself received £234,000, the senior English merchants between £8,000 and £50,000 each. Together, the Company and private persons netted more than £3 million, the equivalent today of at least 20 times as much. It was plain to all that engineering a revolution was the most profitable game in the world. A lust for gold inflamed the English, and Bengal was to know no peace until they had bled it white.

Clive took a superior view. Other people were avaricious; he himself had merely accepted his just deserts. "Consider the situation in which the battle of Plassey had placed me," he told a Parliamentary committee which dared in 1772 to criticize his behaviour. "A great prince was dependent on my pleasure; an opulent city lay at my mercy; its richest bankers bid against each other for my smiles; I walked through vaults which were thrown open to me alone, piled on either hand with gold and jewels. Mr. Chairman, at this moment I stand astonished at my own moderation!"

Clive's satisfaction over his success in Bengal was shattered in June, 1758, when news reached Calcutta that Fort St. David at Cuddalore, just south of Pondicherry, had fallen to the French. He was astonished. The fort had recently been strengthened. "Were our enemies supplied with wings to fly into the place?" he demanded. Whatever their method, the French forces in India numbered more than 4,000 soldiers, who had been brought there by a powerful fleet. It was to be a different kind of war this time, against a wholly European force instead of native troops stiffened and directed

Walk-Over at Plassey

At the riverside village of Plassey, 20 miles from the Nawab of Bengal's palace at Murshidabad, there was an extensive plain. As dawn came up, dank and wet, on June 23, 1757, the Nawab's army advanced across this plain towards the mango grove where Clive's East India Company army was encamped. The conspiracy-riddled, 50,000-man Bengal force included a battery of French cannon hauled by oxen and war elephants.

The British formed up to meet the advance, but fire from the French battery drove them back into the grove. Clive kept his troops—two-thirds of which were turbaned native soldiers, or sepoys, braced by a single British regiment, the 39th Foot—sheltered throughout the shelling and they took few casualties.

At midday there was a torrential monsoon downpour, which drenched the Indians' gunpowder. Clive's gunners were more foresighted and threw tarpaulins over their pieces and their ammunition. When the rain stopped they opened fire and inflicted heavy casualties. At 3 p.m. Clive decided to engage his infantry and ordered an advance. The young Nawab began withdrawing his troops on the treacherous advice of his commanders.

Suddenly a panic-stricken rout developed. Judging the moment ripe, the chief conspirator, Mir Jafar, led his troops over to the British side and surrendered. By 5 p.m. Suraj-ud-daula was fleeing on his fastest camel to his palace at Murshidabad, where soon the corridors echoed with the wails of his distraught harem.

by a few European soldiers and artillerymen. Yet Clive would not send reinforcements to Madras. Bengal was all-important; money and resources would be vital, and that province was "an inexhaustible fund of riches."

Although they had captured Fort St. David, the French in the south were not in a strong position. Dupleix's successor, the Comte de Lally, had been ordered not only to attack the English but to clean up the French East India Company itself, which was riddled with corruption and inefficiency. Lally's arrogant attitude aroused resentment in men who were capable of frustrating his plans. He could not even bank on the co-operation of the French Admiral, who, waving aside Lally's protests, sailed away in August, 1758, and did not return until over a year later. Lally was short of funds, of transport, of gunpowder, of shot—and of success. Though he recalled de Bussy to his aid from Hyderabad, his attempt to capture Madras ended ignominiously when the English fleet returned in February, 1759.

One by one the French settlements in the south fell to the English. Lally's army was in open mutiny, and there was no sign of the French fleet. When it did arrive, the English were waiting, and though both sides suffered severely, it was the French Admiral who fled, never to return again. The final end of French hopes came at the Battle of Wandiwash in January, 1760, when Eyre Coote, who had been one of Clive's officers in Bengal, inflicted a decisive defeat. News of this reached Clive when he and his wife were on board the ship that was to take them to England. "Having attacked the French in their entrenchments," the dispatch read, "the latter were totally defeated with the loss of their cannon and baggage, General Lally wounded, and M. de Bussy and Colonel Murphy taken prisoners." As Clive observed, the English succeeded in doing to the French all that the French, under Dupleix, had set out to do to them.

The defeat at Wandiwash was really the end of the French bid for Empire. Pondicherry fell after a long siege in January, 1761, and the English razed the fort to the ground. Peace came at last, two years later in the Treaty of Paris that ended the Seven Years' War, and Lally went back to France to be executed as a scapegoat—"one of those murders," Voltaire commented, "which are committed with the sword of justice."

Relieved of the French threat, the outlook for the East India Company should have been bright. It was, however, very bleak, in large measure because of Clive's recommendations to the directors in London. Acting on what they presumed was the expert knowledge possessed by the hero of Plassey, the directors ended the shipment of the bullion which over the previous 150 years had been used to buy goods for shipment to England. Henceforth the Bengal treasury would be expected not only to finance the purchase of these goods but also to assume the administrative costs of the English settlements in India—to support in fact an English Raj, the Indian word for "kingdom" that was later adopted by the British.

This new policy had a devastating effect on the Company's fortunes, but it was no bar to the feverish activity of Company employees on their own

The role played by the Royal Navy was crucial to mastering the French challenge in India. For example, during the siege of Chandernagore in 1757 these British frigates provided the firepower to crack the French fortifications visible at the left.

behalf. Clive had foreseen this when on the eve of his departure for England he remarked that the only threat to Bengal was that of "venality and corruption." In the five years he was away, those dangers were fully realized.

Among other benefits that had flowed from the victory at Plassey was an edict that gave Company employees—and even their servants, if they could produce a Company pass—the freedom to trade without paying duty. Englishmen could therefore undercut any Indian trader. Many did just that, and made themselves fortunes. Exports—which were arranged through the Company—also brought astronomical profits to shrewd traders: as Company agents, they could fix the purchase price they paid to Indians, and then turn round and fix the price the Company paid to them as individual traders. So, while the Company remained poor and Bengal became poorer, the Company's employees grew richer and richer.

The fortunes to be made by this double-dealing were staggering. William Bolts amassed £90,000—some £2,000,000 in current terms—by the time he returned to England in 1765 after only five years in India, and his case was only one of many. Once home, he joined the growing group of fellow "nabobs"—as those who had earned a fortune in the East were nicknamed—who were becoming notorious for the tasteless flaunting of their wealth. Historian Macaulay described the nabobs as pompous upstarts, childishly eager to be counted among the aristocracy. Their insolent and extravagant manners aroused his ire. "The examples of their large and ill-governed households," he wrote, "corrupted half the servants in the country."

Much more serious was the embarrassment suffered by the directors of the Company when their poor financial results were contrasted with the nabobs' wealth. In an effort to get more revenue from Company operations, the directors once again turned to Clive. In 1765, now ennobled as Lord Clive of Plassey and loaded with other honours, he landed at Calcutta. Although it had been his own greed

that had first opened the floodgates, he was deeply distressed by the iniquity he found. "Corruption, Licentiousness, and a want of Principle seem to have possessed the Minds of all the Civil Servants," he wrote. "They have grown Callous, Rapacious, and Luxurious beyond Conception."

He attacked the problems with his customary drive and force. Every employee of the Company was compelled to sign a covenant prohibiting him from accepting "presents" or engaging in private trade. He abolished some overgenerous army allowances, and then clamped down hard on an attempted mutiny.

Emperor Shah Alam was befriended, and he granted the Company the administration of Bengal in exchange for a regular subsidy. Although the administration remained nominally Indian, with Indian methods and laws, power was exercised by the British through a Company man who was nominated as the Nawab's deputy.

Clive went back to England for the last time in 1767. He had done much to harness the rapacity of individuals, but much remained to be done before corruption would be rooted out and an honest, stable administration installed. Meanwhile, the Company continued to move further and further towards bankruptcy as its stockholders pressed for higher dividends. At the same time that the government was demanding it pay £400,000 per annum into the Treasury, the Company was forced to borrow until, threatened both by financial disaster and the possibility of losing its trading charter, it decided to make a fresh effort at reform in Bengal. To carry it out, Warren Hastings was appointed Governor in 1771 and took up his post in the following year.

Hastings was a man of great experience and of a character unusual among the English in India. As a boy he had been a brilliant scholar, but the unwillingness of his guardian to subsidize his further education forced him to go to work in India at the age of 17. Though prepared to make a profit out of the English victory at Plassey, Hastings refused to join in the indiscriminate plunder of Bengal.

Clive and Hastings could not have been more different. Clive was violent, moody, reckless, active, dominating by sheer force of personality. Hastings was a small man who preferred to dress in a dull-coloured suit, patient, achieving more by careful planning than by unthinking action. Subtle and opaque to the outside world, he pursued his purpose implacably, by diplomacy whenever possible, by bullying, intrigue, and deceit if necessary. But those who suffered from—and resented—his actions were rich and powerful. With ordinary people his rule was popular.

When Hastings arrived in 1772, Bengal was in a state of collapse. The government was "as wild as the Chaos itself," and a terrible famine had left the countryside a desert of untilled fields. The Company had plundered the state. Now nature threatened final ruin to both state and Company. Landowners could not pay their taxes and were jailed, leaving their lands to return to the jungle. In 1771 the tax collectors' accounts listed one-third of the cultivable land as "deserted."

Faced with such a fall in revenue, Hastings was compelled to cut down expenses. Ruthlessly he slashed the subsidies to local rulers, even those who were Company puppets. Among his instructions from London had been an order to abandon the sham of double government, to end the pretence behind which the English hid their rule. He removed the collection of revenue from native administrators and made this the responsibility of a board in Calcutta, which became, in effect, the new capital; English supervisors in the districts executed the board's instructions. Duty-free passes were abolished in 1773 and duties reduced. Tougher laws were introduced to provide stability and stimulate trade.

For two years there was a whirl of activity. Hastings knew what he wanted to do, and did it with little protest or opposition. But events in England would change that.

The Company's affairs were in such a state that, in 1772, after being refused a loan by the Bank of England, the directors turned in desperation to the government. Observing the

The POLITICAL BANDITTI assailing the SAVIOUR of INDIA.

The impeachment trial of Warren Hastings was a sensation of the day, inspiring reams of editorial comment and scores of cartoons. The "political banditti" in this cartoon are (from left) Edmund Burke, Lord North, and Charles James Fox.

contrast between the financial plight of the Company and the riches of its returning employees, Parliament ordered an investigation into its affairs. The subsequent revelations led to the passing of a Regulating Act in 1773. Under it, the old dual government in Bengal disappeared; in its place was a new dual government—that of the Company and the Crown.

By the terms of the Regulating Act, Warren Hastings became Governor-General of all of the Company's territories, with a rather vague authority over Madras and Bombay, which had previously been governed independently. A Council of Four was appointed in which he had only a casting vote.

With the new council came another institution whose effects were even more lasting: A Supreme Court in Calcutta. Hastings dreaded the effect on India of "the complicated system of jurisprudence long the acknowledged and lamented curse of lawyer-ridden England." He determined to protect Indians from what Macaulay defined as a "strange tribunal," con-

sisting of "judges not one of whom spoke the language, or was familiar with the usages, of the millions over whom they claimed boundless authority. Its records were kept in unknown characters; its sentences were pronounced in unknown sounds. . . . All the injustice of former oppressors, Asiatic and Europeans, appeared as a blessing when compared with the justice of the Supreme Court."

Convinced that it was better for Indians to be given justice in terms of the traditional laws of Muslims and Hindus, Hastings ordered translations of Indian law books. The books chosen did not throw much light on current practice, but they did develop an interest in India's past. From this strictly practical beginning emerged English Oriental scholarship. Hastings himself was interested in everything Indian, and with his encouragement and support the Asiatic Society of Bengal was founded in 1785.

Warren Hastings' contribution to the British Raj was to build, upon the foundations laid by Clive, the scaffolding of a sovereign state. Op-

posed by enemies both English and Indian, he succeeded in changing the British from armed traders into established rulers. Much of what he did was tentative, for he sorely lacked men of worth and integrity, but he created in British-controlled Bengal an island of peace surrounded by an India swept by marauding armies.

In 1784 William Pitt the Younger introduced his India Act to limit the expansion of the East India Company's private empire. "It has destroyed all my hopes, both here and at home," wrote Hastings, and he immediately resigned. When he left India in 1785, his enemies were waiting for him.

In the years since Plassey, disaffection with Company rule in India had found ever-more influential spokesmen. The vulgar displays of the nabobs seemed to be proof of the tales of corruption and extortion gaining currency among concerned Englishmen at home. "We are Spaniards in our lust for gold," remarked Horace Walpole, "and Dutch in our delicacy of obtaining it."

It was to be Hastings's misfortune that the whole movement for reform of the English role in India came to a focus in the person of Edmund Burke. The brilliant political philosopher was an unremitting crusader for human liberty, and in Burke's view there was no people more in need of freedom than the Indians. For a government-chartered commercial company to exploit an entire nation purely for profit was to the "member for India" nothing short of an outrage. Even history's most notorious conquerers, he said, left behind some monuments of civilization, even if they be only roads and aqueducts and bridges. "Were we to be driven out of India this day, nothing would remain to tell that it had been possessed during the inglorious period of our dominance, by anything better than the orang-u-tang or the tiger."

Pitt's India Act was to Burke and his followers a hollow reform. Hastings was the most obvious symbol of Company rule, and they began a campaign to dramatize their case by bringing him to impeachment before

Parliament, the highest court in English law. In 1788 they succeeded, and thus began one of the most spectacular, and one of the longest, trials in modern English history.

Heading the prosecution was Burke, seconded by such noted figures as the Whig leader Charles James Fox and the celebrated dramatist Richard Sheridan, author of *The School for Scandal.* Burke's opening statement, one of his more notable oratorical outpourings, set the tone of the trial: "I impeach Warren Hastings, Esquire, of high crimes and misdemeanors. . . . I impeach him in the name of the people of India, whose laws, rights, and liberties he has subverted, whose properties he has destroyed, whose country he has laid waste and desolate. I impeach him in the name of human nature itself. . . ." Hastings, in short, as representative of an entire system of rule, was being charged with crimes against humanity, just as Nazi war criminals were charged after World War II.

The trial dragged on, with long interruptions (the peers of the realm, Macaulay observed, were not going to let jury duty interfere with their partridge shooting), for seven years.

The prosecution's charges were many and sensational, but badly grounded in fact. As Hastings sat patiently through his ordeal, it gradually became clear that, whatever the sins of the East India Company, he personally had made enormous efforts to ameliorate the plight of the Indian people. As he testified, "I gave you all, and you have rewarded me with confiscation, disgrace, and a life of impeachment."

At last, in 1795, he won full acquittal. In the long view a certain rough justice had been achieved, for a new order of things was set afoot in India. But it ended any future role in public life for Warren Hastings. For the remaining 23 years of his life he lived in secluded retirement on a Company pension.

During the years of Hastings' rule, he was faced with periodic outbursts from the French. Allowed to return to Pondicherry by the Treaty of Paris, the French came back nursing hopes of retrieving their position in India. To achieve this they counted on the presence of French advisers and military men at many of the Indian courts. These Frenchmen were adventurers, certainly, but Frenchmen first.

Conflict broke out in 1778 when France declared war in support of the rebellious American colonists. On French instigation, the ruler of Mysore, Haidar Ali, launched a campaign against Madras in 1780; with him was a body of French troops under Lally's son. Though Eyre Coote was able to defeat the immense Mysore armies, his victories were partly offset when Haidar's son, Tipu, destroyed an English force of 2,000 troops, killing 500 and taking the rest prisoner. It was the start of the extraordinary rule of Tipu Sahib, "the Tiger of Mysore," who for 15 years provided the French with their hope that here was one Indian who could crush the English.

It required two major campaigns, involving many thousands of troops and led by two of Britain's most noted soldiers, Charles Cornwallis and Lord Wellesley, before the Tiger of Mysore could be subdued; he died in 1799 in Wellesley's attack on his stronghold at Seringapatam, victim of an English soldier who wanted his gold belt buckle. With him died France's last hopes for Empire in India. The subcontinent's future was firmly in British hands.

— *Michael Edwardes*

Tipu's six-foot wooden tiger is poised to devour a European, to the tune of moans and snarls when a crank is turned.

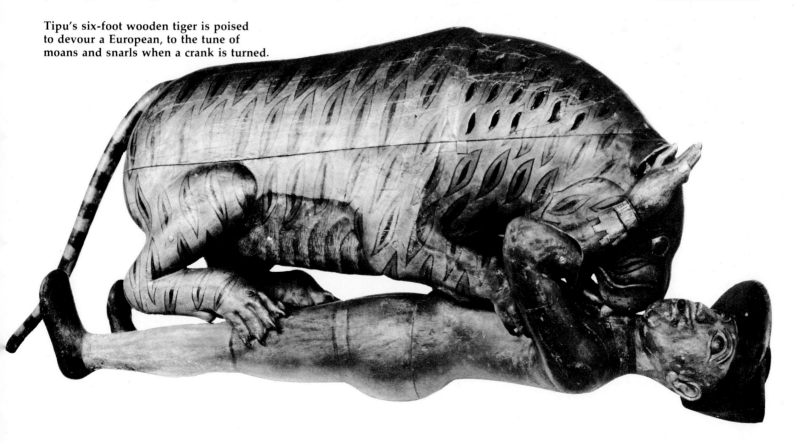

THROUGH INDIAN EYES

During the 18th and early 19th Centuries, prospering officials of the East India Company commissioned Indian artists to paint pictures like the ones seen on these pages. Some of the works were kept as mementoes, others were sent to relatives and friends in England to give them an idea of what life in India was like.

To the artists, the Company men were welcome replacements for their former patrons, the Mughal princes. With techniques refined over the centuries, Indian painters attacked their new subject-matter with vigour. The pictures portray British dress, furniture, architecture and sport, all subtly changed by being viewed through Indian eyes. Some of the works were rapidly executed in the style of street artists. Others were as intricately detailed as the exquisite Persian miniatures that were so beloved by the Mughals. But even in the paintings that meticulously observed the Indian conventions, alien elements crept in, as witness the precisely copied British portraits on the wall of the painting below, which show no trace of Indian style.

An English baby is fed by an Indian wet-nurse, one of the many servants employed to mirror middle-class households in Britain.

Dressed in an Indian kaftan and smoking a hookah – though in a distinctly British interior – a Company official is entertained in his home by a troupe of native musicians.

The wife of a Company official supervises native tailors in her sewing-room. The newly rich British took great pride in their luxurious homes and numerous servants.

An English officer is borne in a palanquin,
then the best transport in India, where
good roads were few and manpower cheap.

Indian jockeys in English riding-habit race
their mounts towards the finishing-post.

Two lawyers argue before a Company official at a murder trial. The accused (left, held by a policeman) beheaded his wife when he learned of her seduction by a Hindu priest (right). The wife's decapitated body, never produced in court, was included by the artist to complete the story. Unfortunately, the outcome of the trial must remain a mystery: the painter did not include this information.

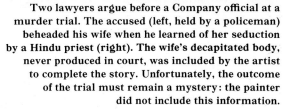

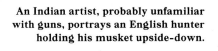

An Indian artist, probably unfamiliar with guns, portrays an English hunter holding his musket upside-down.

III. Rebellion and Global War

Kings no more than commoners are privileged to choose their own exits from life. But the de-departure in 1760 of George II, who died early one morning in his most privy chamber from the strain of trying to relieve his royal person, seemed particularly inappropriate for one whose sceptre represented a British authority that had never been stronger.

Britain's overseas Empire, born in exploration and nurtured with colonization and trade, had been tested in war and confirmed by victory. Englishmen had beaten down the French challenge East and West. British sea power was supreme from Bengal to the Caribbean, from Dakar to North America. George III, only 22 when he succeeded his grandfather, had good cause to tell his subjects as he ascended the throne that he "gloried in the name of Briton." A New England minister exclaimed, "Let us fear God and honour the King, and be peaceable subjects of an easy and happy government."

Even in that hour of bright promise, however, forces were at work which in hardly more than a dozen years would plunge the Empire into civil war, tear from it a great piece of English civilization—great in English wealth, English thought, and Englishmen—and thrust the 13 rebellious American colonies onto their own separate course of history.

George III cannot alone, or even mainly, be blamed for the events which shattered his realm. Most power was Parliament's and Parliament was controlled by an oligarchy made up of conflicting factions. Rich merchants, who believed that what was good for business was good for the nation, pitted their political strength against the landowners, squires who were not "burthened or perplexed by many ideas" but who held strong opinions on one subject: taxes.

A third group, the King's supporters in Parliament, were men who held offices or pensions from the Crown. To stay in power, these politicians had to reconcile the frequently conflicting interests of the merchants and the landowners—and somehow,

somewhere, they had to find money. The interest on the national debt alone was £5 million a year, an astronomical sum for the period, and running an empire was proving a costly business. So it was no surprise that officials searching for additional income should have turned their attention to the North American colonies.

Here, virtually untaxed, was a rich and populous section of the English world. One fifth of all British subjects lived in America. Poverty of the degree common in England was unknown in the New World. American freeholders enjoyed a higher standard of living than their tenant-farmer cousins back home, and the American rich were very rich. In Virginia, wrote an English visitor, "you may really go from house to house living upon Delicatesses, and drinking claret you would not despise at the first tavern in London." Ladies of society paraded in expensive brocaded gowns, a few months behind London's fashions perhaps, but well ahead of English provincial styles.

Only after the Treaty of Paris did English taxpayers learn, to their alarm and astonishment, the cost of victory. Great Britain's public debt averaged £18 per man; that of the colonies, 18 shillings. The average American was paying sixpence a year in taxes; the average Briton had a tax bill 50 times as great.

From the British point of view, the colonies not only appeared capable of contributing to the Empire's purse, but were morally obliged to. Canada, after all, was now British, thus making the colonies secure against further French attacks.

Should they object, there was no reason to expect united opposition. Each colony was jealous of its territory and authority. Squabbles—even near warfare—between neighbouring colonies were commonplace. Southerners were suspicious of New Englanders. Western frontiersmen bitterly resented the political domination of seaboard cities. Class and religious differences were often settled by violence.

British leaders, then, could be excused for presuming that Americans would never unite in opposition to

Westminster. Still, wiser men might have read the danger signals given by American quarrels, might have taken the trouble to inform themselves about American conditions, might have studied more closely the ideas these wildly opinionated American Englishmen were constantly fighting over, and the kind of men doing the fighting.

Many of them, like Thomas Jefferson, consciously and confidently lived by the tenets of an enlightened morality. The success of the Revolution would depend not so much on whether the Americans were right as on whether they were convinced they were right. Jefferson voiced the convictions of many colonists when he wrote to George III, "The great principles of right and wrong are legible to every reader; to pursue them requires not the aid of many counsellors."

Most well-educated Americans—again like Jefferson—studied the works of John Locke, whose *Second Treatise of Government* had provided scholarly justification for Parliament's revolution against James II in 1688. Americans used Locke's ideas to justify their own rebellion—not simply against the King, but against Parliament. Locke wrote that people should not be taxed without their consent, meaning Parliament's consent, for he argued that the Crown possessed only certain specific powers, all others being reserved to the people through their representatives in Parliament. Americans took Locke's words to mean that the colonists had natural rights which Parliament could not violate. This was the basis of the American conviction that Parliament could not tax them without their consent. When Jefferson wrote the Declaration of Independence to justify the Revolution, most of his phrases echoed the thoughts of Locke.

Not all the rebels were philosophers. Some who served from less than idealistic motives served the Revolution nonetheless. In demanding Liberty or Death, Patrick Henry, an ambitious and vainglorious man, was asking for something else as well—fame. Thanks to his particular talent for coining ringing phrases, he won it. There was also that folksy,

All was well between Crown and colonies in 1762 when Boston engraver Nathaniel Hurd paid homage to the new King, George III: "May he live long and happy." Hurd included two other favourites, Pitt and Wolfe, in his tribute.

brilliant, ruthless politician, Sam Adams of Boston. Adams was a believer in the concept of politicking in an atmosphere of rum and tobacco, and his trained mob could take over Boston's streets upon command, terrorizing opposition with tactics a later generation would associate with storm troopers.

It was men like these—idealists, demagogues, in-fighters—who lay in wait for unwary British leaders who would dare to trespass on what the colonists considered to be their rights as Englishmen. Among the first to put his foot over the line set by the colonists was Prime Minister George Grenville.

Crown officers had been trying to suppress the £700,000-a-year smuggling trade which had thrived during the decade of peace. The Americans were already angry about such activities when in 1764 Grenville took

an interest in their cherished rum.

He was concerned not with colonial drinking habits, but colonial trade, of which rum was the lifeblood. New England "floated in a sea of rum" distilled from West Indian molasses. Rum was crucial to the infamous "Triangular Trade" that made many an American fortune. It was shipped to Africa to be exchanged for slaves, who were then transported to the West Indies and traded for more molasses to make more rum.

It also happened to be illegal. Thirty years earlier, to help the British sugar islands in the Caribbean sell their more expensive molasses, the government had put a tax on imports of the syrup from French-held islands. Americans responded by smuggling on such a scale that the British soon gave up trying to collect the duty.

The colonists did not mind, of course, when Grenville proposed to

reduce the tax on foreign molasses from sixpence to threepence a gallon, but they howled when they discovered the government actually planned to enforce the tax levy. The Sugar Act was accompanied by a drive on smuggling. Americans felt that Parliament was unfairly sacrificing them to the interests of the British West Indians, their long-time rivals in the imperial family.

The Sugar Act bore down on a colonial economy already slumping as the war-time boom came to an end. By 1765, two years after the peace treaty with France, unshipped timber lay rotting on wharves. Property values in Rhode Island had dropped by half in two years. "Never," wrote a New Yorker, "was there a time of more general distress and calamity."

At this hardly propitious moment, Parliament passed the Stamp Act. This statute, requiring tax stamps to be affixed to commercial contracts, newspapers, legal documents, university degrees, even tavern licences, seemed almost expressly designed to irritate the most influential colonists. The coals over which Patrick Henry raked King and Parliament were so hot that the speaker of the House of Burgesses accused him of uttering treason. Henry apologized, pulled some notes for proposed resolutions from his pocket, and spoke more treason.

One resolution declared Virginians could be taxed only by their own assembly, and, furthermore, that anyone who said otherwise "shall be deemed an enemy of His Majesty's colony"—heady stuff, since that would most certainly include the King. The assembly approved some of his proposals, although not the wildest ones. As news of these Virginia Resolves swept through the colonies, groups calling themselves "Sons of Liberty" arose to challenge the Stamp Act.

Both the stamps and the stampmasters were soon as popular as smallpox, and it was apparent that resistance extended right through the colonial social structure. For the British, the act's most disastrous effect was the unity it generated. Nine of the colonies sent delegates to a Stamp Act Congress which met in New York in October, 1765. They overcame their differences long enough to petition for repeal and agree on a boycott of British goods. As cancellations of orders flooded London offices, British merchants lost their enthusiasm for George Grenville.

The King was already tired of the Prime Minister's penny-pinching, especially since Grenville had tried to extend his economies to the royal budget. George seized on the opportunity to install the Marquis of Rockingham in Grenville's place. Rockingham knew the Stamp Act had to go, but King and populace alike were in a dudgeon about "American insolence." The merchants, more worried about business than national pride, helped Rockingham by circulating rumours that an army of Englishmen, thrown out of work by the boycott, would march on Parliament. The King reluctantly yielded. The act was repealed.

Americans lit bonfires and danced in the streets to celebrate their "glorious victory over England," ignoring the Declaratory Act, coupled to repeal, which clearly asserted that the colonies were subject to Parliament's rule in "all cases whatsoever." The Patriots, as the radicals were calling themselves, were convinced that their united resistance had defeated Parliament and could do so again.

Trade resumed, and a year later the colonists were delighted when the King replaced Rockingham with William Pitt, who had said he would never try to tax them. Unfortunately, Pitt soon fell victim to gout, and day-to-day control of the country fell into the hands of his Chancellor, the Hon. Charles Townshend. "Champagne Charlie's" wit made him the darling of tavern and drawing-room, and it was said he could deliver brilliant speeches even while he was drunk.

In England debts mounted. Disgruntled squires grew more and more incensed that the colonies had not paid "a single shilling" in taxes and, under Pitt's policy, would not. Townshend, who was reputed to change his political ideas as often as his waistcoats, saw an opportunity. One day in early 1767 he rose in the House and airily declared he had a secret plan for getting money out of the Americans without angering them.

His wondrous scheme, when finally revealed, was nothing other than new duties on various colonial imports, among them tea, paint, glass, and lead. This, he argued, was *external* taxation, and he had it on good authority that the colonies only resented *internal* taxation.

Townshend should have sought better advice. As if the new taxes

With this grim display an editor shut down his paper to protest the Stamp Act.

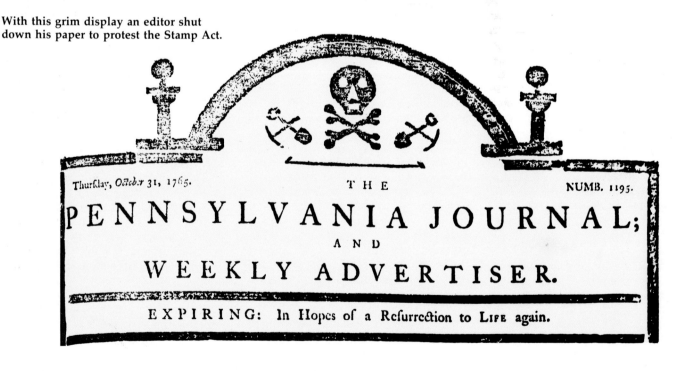

were not enough to cause trouble, Townshend presented another measure certain to rekindle the constitutional crisis. Americans were obliged by the Mutiny Act of 1765 to provide quarters and supplies for British troops when asked. New York was refusing to do so, and Townshend's act had a provision that would suspend the New York assembly until it complied.

New York soon acquiesced and paid for the troops' supplies, but the damage was done. Up and down the colonies Liberty Boys took to the streets, talking once again of "wading thro' seas of blood" to defend their English rights. Sam Adams drafted a protest, not as strong as he would have liked, but, as he put it, "whereas a few of us lead the way . . . we can go no further than we are backed up."

His Massachusetts Circular Letter acknowledged Parliamentary sovereignty, but it insisted that all powers of taxation belonged exclusively to the colonial assemblies. This radical idea was not cordially received by all the colonists, but Lord Hillsborough, British Colonial Secretary, saved the day for Adams. Hillsborough was assigned by the Cabinet to answer the Circular Letter in "kind and lenient" terms. He somehow overlooked the adjectives, telling the colonial assemblies to treat the Circular Letter with "the contempt it deserves," and threatening dissolution for any legislature that dared to approve it.

Here was precisely the spur that the radicals had been looking for. Colonel George Washington, trembling with rage, read Hillsborough's words and declared himself ready to take up arms in defence of America. Colonial assemblies fell over themselves in their rush to endorse the Massachusetts Letter.

Most of the colonies soon subscribed to a Non-Importation Agreement. During 1769 Boston reduced its British imports by half, while New York's fell from £428,000 to £74,000. Discontent reached its highest point in Boston. John Hancock, the wealthiest merchant in the town, followed the general practice of smuggling to avoid taxes. When customs agents seized one of his vessels, the *Liberty,*

it set off a full-fledged riot. The British sent four regiments to occupy Boston. Adams hoped their presence would lead to further trouble.

Thus was established the fever-chart pattern of action and reaction that led towards rebellion. In March, 1770, Adams got his "incident," the Boston Massacre, when a squad of redcoats clashed with a mob and five Bostonians were killed. But the heat from this explosion slowly dissipated as the new ministry under Lord North repealed all the Townshend duties except the tax on tea. The Non-Importation Agreement collapsed.

Rebellion's flame flickered, guttered, and appeared to die. Correspondence between Revolutionary committees fell off as business improved and land rose in value. So calm was the trans-Atlantic relationship that for two years the American colonies were not mentioned once in Parliamentary debate. But if Parliament thought the colonists had dropped their opposition to British authority, it was soon rudely disabused.

In March, 1772, the political temperature bounded upwards again when a band of Rhode Islanders rowed out to His Majesty's revenue cutter *Gaspee,* which had run aground pursuing a smuggler in Narragansett Bay, and burned her to the waterline. A Royal Commission of Inquiry sent to investigate the outrage and bring charges disbanded in disgust when it could find no one in the entire colony of Rhode Island who professed the slightest knowledge of the *Gaspee* affair.

Once more calm returned, but it was an uneasy calm. The next incident, in which Sam Adams again took a hand, began harmlessly enough with Parliament's desire to aid the beleaguered East India Company.

Of the Company's many problems which Warren Hastings was working so assiduously to resolve in far-off Bengal, one was a glut of 18 million pounds of tea in its London warehouses. Although Americans were prodigious tea drinkers, the Company did very poorly in this market. The colonists preferred smuggled Dutch tea, which was cheaper than the Company product, the price of which in-

cluded the Townshend duty. Parliament sought to change this situation by granting the Company a monopoly in America, and letting it sell directly to the colonists through its own agents, eliminating wholesalers on both sides of the Atlantic. A stiff British tea tax was also repealed—but not the Townshend duty. The result was that East India Company tea, duty included, now became cheaper than even smuggled Dutch tea.

It did not take American radicals long to go to the heart of the issue. Not only was a dangerous precedent being set for a trade monopoly, but their cherished rallying cry—"no taxation without representation!"—was in danger of being undercut by the lure of this cheap, high-quality tea: thirst might overcome principle.

In the autumn of 1773, a flotilla loaded with the politically explosive beverage was on the high seas, heading for American ports. Some Company agents to whom it was consigned decided they could do without the business after all and cancelled their orders before the tea was landed. Elsewhere it was locked away by customs men to await calmer days. In Boston, however, the issue was settled in a way that infuriated the British but gave Sam Adams considerable pleasure.

Three vessels carrying 90,000 pounds of tea reached Boston late in November. Soon there was an impasse. The Adams forces refused to let the tea be unloaded, and the Massachusetts Royal Governor, Thomas Hutchinson, refused to let the tea ships depart without the duty being paid. The impasse ended on the night of December 16. A band of Bostonians, thinly disguised as Indians and cheered on by a crowd of 5,000, boarded the ships and dumped the 45 tons of tea, worth some £10,000, into the harbour.

Here was a challenge the British could not ignore. "We must master them," said George III, "or totally leave them to themselves and treat them as aliens." Some Englishmen called for an attack on Boston. Lord North preferred to starve the rebels out. In 1774 Parliament approved his Boston Port Bill, which ordered the city closed to all shipping until it paid for the drowned tea.

Boston's radicals wanted to reply with another trade embargo. To forestall this move, conservative New Yorkers suggested instead an intercolonial congress and the other boycott-weary colonies agreed.

Most Americans still were, if not outright Tories, conservative enough to be alarmed by the radicalism emanating from Boston. The congress was shaping up as a struggle between these moderates and the Patriots, and odds were on the moderates to win. But once again, the King's ministers assisted the radical cause.

Parliament was not yet finished with Massachusetts. Three "Coercive Acts" were passed to impose tighter control on the colony's affairs and on its citizens. These measures, together with the Boston Port Bill, were stigmatized by Patriots as the Intolerable Acts, and so incensed the Bay Colony that British control outside troop-occupied Boston vanished altogether.

While Americans were chewing over this development—what happened to Massachusetts colonists, after all, could happen elsewhere—there arrived from London a copy of another new measure, the Quebec Act.

For the French Canadians of Quebec, the new law was a liberal and welcome one. It restored to them their old French civil law and granted official toleration to their Catholic faith. But this enabled Patriot propagandists to win support by conjuring up visions of the Inquisition at work in Pennsylvania and of decent Protestant churches being "converted into mass houses." The act also extended the boundaries of Quebec to the Ohio River, dashing colonial dreams of expansion in that area and ruining land speculation companies in which influential Americans had invested.

News of the Quebec Act made Americans "ripe for any plan the Congress [might] advise, should it be war itself," and in this atmosphere the delegates gathered in Philadelphia on September 5, 1774. One of their contemporaries called them the "ablest and wealthiest men in America" and most of those who met

The repressive Boston Port Bill that followed the Tea Party inspired this cartoon. Lord North forces a "bitter draught" on an abused America as the Admiralty's Lord Sandwich takes a lecherous peek. France and Spain (left) look on with interest.

in the City of Brotherly Love fitted this description. Pitt himself called it "the most honourable Assembly of Statesmen since those of the ancient Greeks and Romans." A British officer serving in Boston at the time sensed the deep ideological roots of the Revolution; in a letter to his father he said, "The true causes of [the rebellion] are to be found in the nature of mankind; and I think it proceeds from a new nation . . . struggling to throw off that dependency which is so irksome to them." The bullyboys who took to the streets in response to Sam Adams's shrewd propaganda thrusts helped keep the pot a-boil, but the fire would have died down had it not been stoked by the resentment of men of substance who felt threatened by London's latest actions.

In October, 1774, Congress agreed on a Continental Association of the colonies which would institute another boycott of British products. Despite fierce opposition from diehard conservatives, it also pledged united assistance to the Massachusetts colonists should they find themselves fighting a *defensive* war against the British. Most still believed a peaceful settlement was possible, but not all. John Adams, Sam's wealthier and

more conservative cousin, told Patrick Henry that he expected "no redress, but on the contrary, increased resentment and double vengeance. We must fight."

"By God," the Virginian replied, "I am of your opinion."

The Continental Congress broke up, agreeing to meet the following year. When word of its actions reached England, Lord North tried to appease— or at least divide—the colonies by offering some conciliatory propositions. Parliament, he said, would refrain from taxing them directly if colonial assemblies would provide money when requested to do so. It was a classic case of too little too late. The day before North's proposals reached New York, word came from Massachusetts that the cold war had become a hot one.

That first shot fired on Lexington Green early on the morning of April 19, 1775, "the shot heard round the world," changed everything. Lexington killed any chance of Americans accepting North's proposals. Even so, Congress overwhelmingly approved tendering an "Olive Branch" petition to England in July, 1775. While waiting for an answer, it went ahead with war preparations. It was just as well;

the British government, its pride stinging from Lexington and the bloody battle in June at Bunker Hill, rudely rejected the petition. Still, few dared to advocate a complete break with the mother country.

It took a brand-new American, fresh off the boat from Britain, to change their minds. Thomas Paine, ex-corset maker, failed British excise officer, free-thinker, had emigrated to the colonies at the end of 1774. In January, 1776, he published his pamphlet, *Common Sense*, that transformed the American political climate almost literally overnight. In it he labelled George III the "royal brute of Britain" and said the independence of America should have dated from "the first musket that was fired against her."

"We have it in our power," Paine wrote, "to begin the world over again." His words not only electrified the nation; they made it one. It was said that every man in America who could read, read *Common Sense*, and the illiterate had it read to them. After its publication, Britain could only hold its American Empire by force. Probably a third of the colonists still opposed independence, but the cause of these Tories was lost unless the Patriots were beaten on the battlefield.

In March Congress's secret Committee of Correspondence dispatched an envoy to seek French help against the British—assistance which would be crucial in the coming war. In June Thomas Jefferson closeted himself in a Philadelphia carpenter's house to compose the words which—whatever had gone before—would rebuke for ever after cynical assertions that this was a paltry squabble over taxes. He spelled out the "self-evident" truths: that all men are created equal, that they have certain inalienable rights, that governments derive their powers from the consent of the governed.

Congress approved his efforts, and on July 4, 1776, America proclaimed to the world that it was no longer part of the British Empire, but a new nation which would stand and fight to fulfil the aspirations embodied in that Declaration of Independence. The world waited to see if America could make good this promise.

The news of the fighting in Massachusetts came as a shock to the British. Blood had been shed, but George III was not frightened. "When once these rebels have felt a smart blow," he assured the doubters, "they will submit." He would not allow the Empire to be dismantled by an insolent New England rabble, nor would he let the Opposition in Parliament chip away the British Constitution with proposals for appeasement of the rebels. And to those who argued that Britain's strength was in her commerce, not her territories, and that she would gain by freeing the colonies, George sniffed that great events could not be weighed "in the scale of a tradesman behind his counter." Britain would fight for America.

One smart blow: that should do it. It was clearly impossible for England's army to conquer all of that vast land; anyway, Britain did not wish to subjugate the colonies, but to bring them home to Empire. Smash the rebel army and rebellion would vanish with it. But after thirteen years of budget-balancing retrenchment, Britain was ill prepared for war. She had only 7,000 troops in all of North America and few reinforcements to send.

The Americans had no real navy, and sea warfare was expected to be confined to blockade activity, but the British had not enough ships to do even that properly. There were only two ships of the line and some frigates in colonial waters, and the Admiralty was reluctant to spare any of the 20 battleships which were on guard duty at home for fear of sudden French and Spanish intervention.

American strength was an unknown quantity. Some estimated that with a population of two and a half million, the colonies might field several hundred thousand men who, fighting on their own ground, might make a formidable enemy. Others maintained there was nothing to fear militarily from the Americans. General Wolfe, conqueror of Quebec, had called them "the worst soldiers in the universe."

Still, to beat even a weak enemy one must meet him. Armies had to be raised and transported. With luck it took a month to cross the Atlantic; without it, three or four months. The British spent the first year getting ready for a war that had already begun. With clinks and groans and a gnashing of gears, the King's war machine ground into action. Its remarkable inefficiency was offset only by the fact that no competing nation had come up with anything that could beat it—so far. At every level it violated the principle of separating military decisions from political ones. Politicians ran the war and warriors were up to their epaulettes in politics.

The Cabinet planned strategy, sometimes giving too much thought to small detail, and often too little to the grand scheme. The Secretary of State for the Colonies, Lord George Germain, was responsible for the conduct of the armies in the field—despite the fact that he had been cashiered for cowardice at Minden in 1759 and declared "unfit to serve His Majesty in any military capacity whatsoever." To put plans into action, Germain had to grope through a maze of boards, commissions, offices, and departments. He had to find the soldiers, without conscription. Orders had to be issued directly to generals in the field, as the army had no central command. It did not have much of anything. It was transported by the Navy Board, fed by the Treasury (which hired ships for the job), and depended on the Ordnance Board for engineers and artillery.

To make all these components function together was a mammoth and endless task. As shortages were discovered, convoys misdirected, or strategy changed, then ships, men, and supplies had to be set upon new courses—not an easy business when it might take six months for a letter to reach America. As clumsy as it was, the apparatus had been made to work, and work well, by Pitt in the Seven Years' War. Alas for England, she had no Pitt at the helm. The man himself was old, sick, and in the outer darkness of Opposition. The nation lacked leadership.

The Prime Minister, Lord North, certainly failed to provide it. "Upon military matters," he admitted, "I speak ignorantly and therefore without effect." His colleagues heartily agreed. The Earl of Sandwich, First

Lord of the Admiralty, treated North with such contempt that when the Prime Minister had a suggestion for naval action, he cautiously had a third party originate it lest it be rejected out of hand by Sandwich. North talked endlessly of resigning, but the King, who did not know who else he could get without turning to the despised Opposition, told him to "cast off his indecision and bear up"—and to please answer the mail.

The services had no more leadership than the government. Commissions and promotions depended more on family or political connections than on ability. In 1780 there were 23 generals in the House of Commons. It was the best place for a soldier to do his fighting; if the government failed to shower him with patronage and honours he could always sell his vote to the Opposition.

The Cabinet cowered behind collective responsibility. When it was learned, before war with France was declared in 1778, that the French Navy had orders to destroy British shipping, most Cabinet members were out of town. Only the King's angry intervention compelled North to order attacks on French ships without first discussing it with the absent ministers by post.

In fact, while George III had much company in his determination to fight, he sometimes seemed to be alone in his determination to win. When the Cabinet dragged its feet, he summoned it to work in his presence. When a fleet was slow to sail, he personally journeyed to Portsmouth to harry the admirals. "If others will not be active," he sighed, "I must drive." But the age when a king could carry a nation to war on his shoulders was over.

British strategists liked to presume that all would go as planned, and allowed the barest possible margins for mishaps. It was a mistake they made persistently, and they began making it early.

The plan for 1776 was on paper a good one: an expeditionary force to seize New York, then co-operate with a second force striking from Canada down the Hudson Valley. The goal was to isolate New England, where the viper of rebellion had been hatched. Sir William Howe directed the assault on New York. He had the largest force ever seen in America, but moved it as if each of his 25,000 troops was his one and only son. Three times he had Washington's army—and perhaps the end of the rebellion—within his grasp, and three times by caution or indolence let it escape.

The advance from Canada was also infected with caution and sloth, and achieved nothing. The final blow of the campaign was struck not by the British but by Washington, who led his small, ragged, short-rationed force in brazen counterattacks at Trenton and Princeton that did much to restore flagging Patriot morale.

Another year, another distraction. In 1777 it was Philadelphia, seat of the Continental Congress and hive of Loyalists, that lured the British and diverted them from their purpose in the Hudson Valley; by most reckonings this cost them the war. Philadelphia pulled Howe like a magnet. It could be taken, he told London, by his main force while he sent 10,000 men up the Hudson to fulfil the original strategy.

General John Burgoyne, who had politicked his way into command in the north, proposed that the British advance from Canada on two fronts to converge on Albany and there meet Sir William's men coming from the south. London approved both Burgoyne's and Howe's plans, which at that point were not necessarily incompatible. But then Howe changed his mind; he would send only 3,000 men to meet the army from Canada. Finally, he decided to send none at all, but to hold a force ready to "assist" Burgoyne if he needed help. Thus the basic strategy was discarded and British force perilously dispersed.

Burgoyne was already marching into the rebel thickets of upper New York when he discovered that no one was coming to meet him from the south. His "second front" force was routed, leaving his western flank exposed. If he had retreated, Burgoyne later asked Parliament, what would England have thought of him? He was vain, and a habitual gambler. He went forward. The Americans leaped on his line of communications and mauled his army when he tried a last frantic breakthrough. On October 13, 1777, near Saratoga, surrounded, outnumbered, and with no hope of rescue, he surrendered.

The blow struck at Saratoga shook the Empire's foundations and opened cracks in the wall for all to see. The jubilation of the Opposition in Parliament bordered on treason. North tried to resign and Germain and his generals in America plunged into a public orgy of mutual recrimination. France, which had been supporting the rebels secretly, saw at Saratoga the clear indication of Britain's weakness. This was the signal for which Paris had been waiting. The absolute Bourbon monarchy signed a treaty with the anti-monarchical Americans in February, 1778.

After Saratoga transformed civil war to world war, America's importance to British aims and strategy waned before the infinitely greater interest in capturing the West Indies, by value of products the richest region on earth. "Let the dance of rebellion go round," a supporter urged Germain, "while we appropriate the islands." Even the King said he would come to terms with America if he could be sure of conquering the French islands, a victory that would ruin French finances and repay Britain's cost of the war. The Cabinet decided to reduce the effort in the colonies to a holding operation. This was now a sea war.

Britain was little better prepared for a naval conflict than she had been for one on land. She had 41 ships of the line in service to France's 33, but as an island nation she had to keep 30 of these battleships in home waters to fend off invasion and escort merchant convoys. The French ships were free to strike anywhere. Fearing that Spain's navy might also be thrown against her, Britain raced to make up for lost time. Soon ships were being built on "every slip in England" and all commercial shipping was temporarily stopped while the Royal Navy's dreaded press-gangs snatched from the streets the seamen needed to man the new fleet.

But the Navy needed more than ships and sailors; it needed bold men to command them. Too many admirals, like Augustus Keppel, set sail by political winds. Keppel's politics were Opposition, so when he was given command of the nation's main fleet he suspected he was being set up as the sacrificial lamb for the Admiralty's inadequacies, a suspicion that accentuated his natural timidity. After much hesitation he was finally induced to put to sea with 20 ships in June, 1778, but he scurried back to port after two weeks when he learned that 27 French vessels were waiting. He set the terms under which he would sail: a force equal to the French, "ship for ship in the line."

When Keppel finally met the French off Ushant a month later he had the edge, both in ships and firepower, but after an indecisive skirmish the French escaped. The real fighting took place later in England when Keppel and Sir Hugh Palliser, one of his division commanders, blamed each other for the debacle—firing opening salvoes in the Press and closing for action in courts martial and Parliament. The row split the nation and the navy. When Keppel finally won his case in 1779, ecstatic mobs led by Opposition M.P.'s smashed windows in the London houses of Palliser, Germain, and the Prime Minister. While half of England celebrated this great "victory," the French fleet, which remained intact, still menaced the Channel, where it would soon be joined by yet another enemy: the Spanish Navy.

Spain had her own American Empire and no interest in aiding a colonial rebellion, but came into the war in hopes of getting Gibraltar and Minorca from Britain. Her fleet gave England's enemies an overwhelming superiority in numbers, although this was offset somewhat by the Spaniards' less than consummate skill as sailors. "Their ships all sail so badly," groaned a French commodore attached to their fleet, "that they can neither overtake an enemy nor escape from one."

The English also had the 18th-Century equivalent of a secret weapon. In a timely technological breakthrough, they had learned how to sheathe their ships' hulls in copper, which protected them from the fouling by ma-

rine life that slowed down a wooden ship after a few months in the water. "Twenty-five sail of the line, coppered," said an English officer, "will be sufficient to hazard and tease this armada, so as to prevent their effecting anything."

When the combined enemy fleets, 66 ships, appeared off England's south coast in 1779, they achieved little more than a royal proclamation ordering the cows to be driven inland to safer counties. Yet the need to defend home waters severely hamstrung other British efforts. Instead of sweeping up the French islands in the West Indies, Britain was fighting a sea-saw battle there simply to keep control of the sea. Dominica, St. Vincent, and Granada fell to the French in 1778 and 1779. Admiral Samuel Barrington took St. Lucia and held it against a French fleet twice as large as his own—for which he received, he felt, inadequate praise. To show his pique he refused to accept another command.

The Rock of Gibraltar hung like a millstone round the neck of the struggling Empire. Blockaded by the Spanish, it had to be relieved three times by ships badly needed elsewhere.

"We must stretch every nerve," said the King, and stretch they did. The British invaded Spanish Nicaragua and even had plans for an expedition to challenge Spain in the South Pacific when a more urgent crisis, closer to home, demanded their attention.

Holland had refused to stop supplying naval stores to France and Spain. At a crucial Cabinet meeting—during which Lord North and another Minister fell asleep immediately and a third dozed off slowly, dropping his hat to the floor—it was decided to confront the Dutch with an ultimatum. Holland refused the demands and in December, 1780, went to war, adding another 20 battleships to the navies opposing Britain.

A new front was opened in a war that already had more than the British could handle. The Dutch held the Cape of Good Hope and Trincomalee in Ceylon, both vital to control of the Indian Ocean. At the same time that war began with Holland, Haidar Ali, Sultan of Mysore, sent his large, well-disciplined army against British posts on India's east coast. The Eastern Empire, only recently established, was in peril.

A 1777 comment on Britain's plight. France, Spain, and Holland milk the English cow of commerce and America saws off its horns. The British lion cannot be roused and in the background the Howe brothers drowse over a Philadelphia punchbowl.

When the news of Yorktown reached London, the caricaturist Thomas Rowlandson zeroed in on the "State Watchman"—Lord North—who is discovered here by Britannia and George III in the act of "studying plans for the Reduction of America."

Initiative had passed to the enemy. The expedition against Spain's South Seas settlements was cancelled and the force intended for it made for the Cape and the Indian Ocean. But the French reached the Cape first, secured it, and sent a fleet to help Haidar Ali. So the British had to detach yet other precious ships to Indian waters, where they would be kept busy for the remainder of the war.

In November, 1781, British forces seized the Dutch base of Negapatam, the only natural harbour on the southeast coast of India, and two months later captured Trincomalee. The success was short-lived. Bailli de Suffren, a brilliant and uncharacteristically aggressive French admiral, arrived with enough ships to give the French naval superiority. The French took Britain's mainland port of Cuddalore, and in July, 1782, retook Trincomalee.

The nerve had been stretched too thin. Instead of picking off her enemies' colonies, Britain was losing her own. In 1781 the Spanish stormed Pensacola, winning West Florida, and the French took Tobago. The next year three more of Britain's West Indies fell: St. Kitts, Montserrat, and Nevis. In Europe Minorca—its garrison reduced by scurvy to some 800 effectives—finally surrendered to 14,000 Spaniards and Frenchmen.

These diversions had taken the British a long way from America where the war began—and was still going on. Despite the decision to halt offensives in the colonies, the army had a go at the South in 1778 and conquered Georgia. Encouraged, it moved against Charleston in 1780 and won it, with a bag of 7,000 rebels. From Charleston General Charles Cornwallis marched northward in 1781.

The farther he went, the more fierce and resilient was the resistance. For every band of militia he beat, another sprang up like mushrooms in the woods. He groped for the sea. At the James River in Virginia he had to take a defensive position. He chose Yorktown.

Cornwallis was "a good officer, devoted to the service of his country, beloved by the army." The plan, not the man, fixed his army's fate. Now the British force was divided in America—6,000 men at Yorktown and 11,000 at New York—a tenable arrangement if the British Navy controlled the sea between, fatal if it did not.

Admiral Thomas Graves's squadron was cruising off Boston to intercept French supplies. In the West Indies a larger fleet had captured a rich Dutch island, St. Eustatius, and while Admiral George Rodney was counting his £3,000,000 booty, a French fleet led by Comte de Grasse slipped in from Europe, took Tobago, and then set sail for the embattled colonies to the north. Rodney showed up as the French departed, but he said he "was not such a Don Quixote" as to attack 23 ships with his 20. Besides, he was not feeling well. He sent most of his fleet to follow de Grasse northward, but he followed his prize-money to England.

At home, the Channel fleet was once again bending every effort to relieve Gibraltar, which was why de Grasse had been able to leave Europe unmolested. To let the French sail off to America was a conscious choice of a Ministry with too many alternatives. Some of the Gibraltar ships would be sent to America on their return, but it would be too late. Britain had overstretched herself.

And George Washington knew it. "I have never seen a man moved by greater or more sincere joy," said a Frenchman who accompanied the Americans as they dashed south to Yorktown, covering 200 miles in 15 days. Washington had cause for joy; de Grasse had promised to use his ships to trap Cornwallis.

When Graves met the British ships from the West Indies in New York, the penny dropped at last. They hurried south to the Chesapeake and found de Grasse already there, his cruisers blocking Cornwallis's escape by sea. On September 5, 24 French ships came out to fight the 19 British vessels. They fought one day, watched each other for four, and then the French reclaimed their position as the anvil on which Cornwallis was being hammered.

Facing an army of 16,000, backed against waters controlled by a hostile fleet, Cornwallis surrendered. On October 18, 1781, British soldiers walked through a mile-long corridor of Americans and Frenchmen to lay down their arms. Tradition—which has been known to add irony of its own when history fails to provide enough—says that a British band played *The World Turned Upside Down.* When he heard the news in London,

Lord North staggered as if struck by a musket ball. "Oh God," he murmured. "It is all over."

His ministry fell and a new one quested after peace, which was more palatable than expected because of two last-minute victories. Another relief had saved Gibraltar from a tightening Spanish grip and an enemy fleet aimed at Jamaica was defeated by Rodney, now back in the West Indies. That helped to salvage the Empire, but Rodney's failure to pursue the fleeing French and Spanish says something about why it needed salvaging. When a junior officer complained that they might easily have captured 20 ships instead of five, Rodney demurred: "Come, we have done very handsomely as it is."

In the Treaty of Paris in 1783, Britain returned St. Lucia to the French,

agreed to Spain keeping Minorca and Florida, and acknowledged, of course, America's hard-won independence. But Britain successfully rejected rebel claims to Canada, recovered all her own West Indies except Tobago, held Gibraltar, saw to it that the French left the Cape of Good Hope, and won trade rights in the East Indies.

Considering the way the war had gone, it was not a bad settlement, but Britain had lost something which was not written into the treaty—the respect that other nations had accorded her strength. She had fallen, said the Emperor of Austria, "to the rank of a second-rate Power," and would remain there "forever." If he was right about Britain's new position, he was wrong about how long she would be confined to it.

— *Jim Hicks*

IV. Mistress of the Seas

When the House of Commons was told, in December, 1783, that William Pitt the Younger had been named Prime Minister, the members burst into laughter. The Press joined in:
A sight to make surrounding nations stare;
A kingdom trusted to a schoolboy's care.
Pitt was 24 years old.

Despite his youth and some personal faults, he became a great Prime Minister. He drank heavily. His debts at one point compelled him to assign his salary to the banker Thomas Coutts. But he showed a better brain for national finance than any other man in England, and he was scrupulously honest in an era of rampant, casual corruption. Most important of all, he knew precisely what would make Britain great and powerful again: trade.

Europe's diplomatic intrigues were of little interest to him except when they affected Britain's commerce. He preferred to form "an alliance with that more formidable of all Powers, the power of surplus." Knowing trade had to be protected, he made the

Royal Navy an exception to his public economies, building 33 new ships of the line during his first seven years in office.

His revival of Britain was miraculous. Within seven years of her defeat, the "second-rate Power" twice met her old enemies toe-to-toe and twice made them back down. Both of these confrontations involved issues vital to the future of the new Empire Britain was developing in the East to replace the old one which she had lost in America.

In 1787 France supported Dutch republicans who wanted to overthrow the pro-British Prince of Orange. Pitt was alarmed that the Cape of Good Hope and Ceylon, Dutch holdings that lay athwart his trade-routes to the East, might fall into French hands. Pitt was blunt. If France wanted influence in Holland she would have to "fight for it." His Cabinet approved plans to hire Hessian mercenaries and fit out 23 ships of the line to join the 17 then in service. France hesitated, then backed down. She had never intended to intervene, her government said. The possibility of a Dutch revo-

lution dissolved and the security of Britain's Eastern interests was confirmed.

Two years later, Spain tried to enforce her traditional hegemony in the Pacific by seizing British ships and crews at Nootka Sound, on the western shore of what is now Canada. There was more at issue than this tiny outpost established by the East India Company. Spain claimed sovereignty over the entire Pacific, including places she had not settled.

Pitt took personal charge of negotiations, as he had in the Dutch crisis. By May, 1790, 40 ships of the line were being fitted out, and soon 25 of them were at sea. British garrisons in Gibraltar, India, and the Caribbean were reinforced, and the Cabinet opened talks with potential South American revolutionaries about fomenting risings in Spanish colonies there. "The din of war," it was said, "ran through the country like wildfire." This was true power diplomacy, and it worked. Spain withdrew her demands and accepted most of Britain's. She returned the ships and crews, agreed that territory in western America north of her actual settlements was open to other countries, and conceded British rights to navigate and fish in the Pacific.

Pitt tried to keep Britain out of the European war that blew up in the wake of France's Revolution in 1792, although not all Britons shared his distrust of involvement. As France moved on the Netherlands, a 34-year-old naval captain in Norfolk exclaimed happily, "Everything indicated War!" Horatio Nelson's expectations were fulfilled when France declared war on Great Britain and Holland in February, 1793.

If fight England must, then Pitt wanted her to fight at sea where she could strip France of her wealthy colonies. It was the same "blue water" policy his father had followed in the

Seven Years' War, and was politically, economically, and strategically sound for a nation whose army was, in reality, her navy. But George III had his Hanoverian interests, his loathing for the French Revolution, and his place among kings to think of. He prevailed upon Pitt to promise 40,000 men as Britain's contribution to the Flanders campaign then being planned by a coalition of Continental powers against Revolutionary France.

In numbers, Britain's army was contemptible when compared with the half million men bearing arms for France. Britain had only 15,000 soldiers at home and 30,000 scattered about the world. So, as in the American War, she hired Germans. Fourteen thousand of the King's Hanoverian Army were transferred to the

British payroll, and 8,000 Hessian mercenaries were taken on by contract.

The British Navy was still the world's first, although there were only 12 battleships in actual commission. In reserve there were 113 ships of the line waiting to be fitted out, against the French Navy's 76. Within weeks 54 of the British battleships had been commissioned and another 39 were ready for service when needed. Men to sail them was another matter. Naval personnel was down from 110,000 at the end of the American War to only 16,000. Press-gangs began their vigorous and vicious work, but it was months before the ships were adequately manned.

Once again, Britain dispersed her efforts. The early years of war saw her forces capturing and losing Toulon,

Prime Minister William Pitt the Younger addresses the House of Commons in 1793 in a painting by K. A. Hickle. Notables portrayed include Whig leader Charles James Fox (right, front row, in the hat) and at Fox's left, playwright Richard Sheridan.

advancing and retreating with French Royalists, and tramping back and forth across the Lowlands—where the Duke of York's campaigning style taught young Arthur Wellesley, later Duke of Wellington, "how not to do it."

Nor were the West Indies ignored. In a century of struggle with France, 300,000 Englishmen had died in those disease-ridden islands, and this war would contribute more than its share of corpses. Britain captured Martinique, St. Lucia, and Guadeloupe by May, 1794, but French reinforcements and yellow fever eroded the conquests. In San Domingo (Dominican Republic) 7,400 of the 9,000 English soldiers died of the "black vomit" within the space of one year.

Reinforcements were needed everywhere. The King diagnosed the ailment: "The misfortune of our situation is that we have too many objects to attend to and our force consequently must be weak at each place." France supplied the cure. Britain's allies on the Continent were beaten into submission; pushed from Europe, she had to concentrate on enemy colonies overseas.

After the Netherlands fell to the French in 1795, the Prince of Orange fled to England and sent word to his colonies to accept British protection. The Cape of Good Hope resisted, but the British were too strong and the Dutch colonists finally capitulated. Britain then acquired Trincomalee in Ceylon by buying off its garrison of Swiss mercenaries. In 1796 the Dutch colonies of Demerara, Berbice, and Essequibo on the South American mainland were taken; with their exports to Britain of cotton, sugar, and coffee increasing by ten times in three years, they were a prize catch.

One by one, Spain, Prussia, and Austria dropped out of the war against France. The first to go was Spain. In October, 1796, motivated by an inconsolable yearning for Gibraltar, the Spaniards turned their large fleet against England. Fortunately, the Spanish Navy had not improved much since the last war. "The dons may make fine ships," said Nelson, "but they cannot make men."

The British Navy, however, had improved—and now could make men. When a large Spanish fleet sailed from the Mediterranean to join the French in early 1797, Admiral Sir John Jervis was waiting for them off Cape St. Vincent with 15 battleships, one commanded by the still unknown commodore, Nelson. Jervis's Flag Lieutenant counted the Spaniards as they stole forth from a mist. "There are 18 sail of line, Sir John."

"Very well, Sir."

"There are 20 sail of the line, Sir John."

"Very well, Sir."

"There are 27 sail, Sir John, near double our own!"

"If there are 50 sail of the line I will go through them," Jervis replied, and signalled his ships to make for a gap in the Spanish formation.

Having divided the enemy, the British met the Spanish line on a parallel course, pounding each ship with broadsides as it passed. Nelson, whose ship the *Captain* was near the tail of the British line, saw that the main Spanish division was turning, trying to reunite with the others. Without hesitation—and contravening orders for line of battle—he placed the *Captain* directly in the path of the *Santissima Trinidad*, the largest fighting ship in the world. For ten minutes the *Captain* sustained the giant's terrible rain of fire alone, losing her foremast and wheel-post.

When other British ships arrived to take up the duel, Nelson put his crippled vessel alongside the 80-gun *San Nicolas* and led a boarding-party through her stern windows. Finding the three-decker *San Josef* drifting against the other side of his prize, he boarded her under small-arms fire and there received both Spanish captains' swords simultaneously.

Two swords at once! The tale ran through the fleet, the navy, England. The real importance of Cape St. Vincent may have been less that an enemy fleet was beaten than that Nelson was recognized as a champion for the Empire and would thereafter be employed as such.

"In my mind's eye," said Nelson, "I ever saw a radiant orb suspended which beckoned me onwards to renown." His apologists have some-times been loath to allow him his ambition—which is comparable to denying the average man his lungs —by saying he did not *really* mean glory. Of course he did. He lusted for glory and he hated the French with an intense and outspoken hatred. These two passions served him well on a frustrating mission in the Mediterranean in the summer of 1798.

Napoleon sailed from Toulon with 40,000 soldiers and 15 battleships in May, his destination unknown to the English. Without sufficient frigates, which then performed the functions of search planes and radar, Nelson set out to find him. At Malta the French had been and gone, but no one knew where. Nelson guessed it might be Egypt, but that meant sailing east, and any cautious commander would stay to the west in case the French tried to exit to the Atlantic. Nelson sailed east.

The French were not at Alexandria. The day Nelson left Alexandria for the Syrian coast, Napoleon arrived, and a month later was entering Cairo in triumph while Nelson scoured the waters around Sicily. He had missed the big prize—catching Napoleon's army at sea—but the consolation prize would be sufficient. He tried Alexandria again.

Near there on August 1, lying in a two-mile line along the shore of Aboukir Bay, Nelson found the French fleet. It was nearly dark; there was no time to confer with his captains or sound a channel through the shoals. Without pausing, the British line of 13 ships sailed in and opened fire. All that night the British fought by the glow of burning French ships and all the next day fished French sailors from the water. Two French ships were sunk and nine captured; only two escaped. The Battle of the Nile was England's greatest naval victory since the days of the Spanish Armada.

Overnight the Mediterranean became an English sea. Napoleon's army, although intact, was stranded in Egypt. Bonaparte could not march to India—which was his plan—without a fleet behind to supply him. He tried to move up through the Levant but a British naval squadron stopped him at Acre. "If it had not been for you

The Sailor's World

For the men who manned her, a ship like H.M.S. *Victory* was home, the only home they had, and the 20 inches of space that was allotted for each hammock was all that any man could call his own.

A sailor's life was comfortless and boring, due largely to the size of warship crews in the age of sail. The *Victory* carried over 800 men, but a tenth of that number could have sailed her. The rest were only needed in battle—to serve the guns, to board or repel boarders, to repair the damage and attend the wounded.

But battles were rare, and between them the men were kept incessantly busy with jobs, like holystoning the decks, invented just to occupy their hands. Their only lawful pleasure was the rum ration. More than half had either been forced on board by press-gangs or else were thieves and vagabonds sent to the Royal Navy rather than prison in a doubtful act of mercy.

In a tough life, discipline and punishments had to be tougher still. Captains ruled with autocratic power, and crews had no defence against the occasional sadist or tyrant. For fear of desertion shore-leave was very seldom granted; instead cargoes of prostitutes were brought on board in port. Once aboard, crewmen could not expect to set foot on land again until the ship was in need of a major refit, which might be in two years or ten.

And yet, in spite of everything, a mass of unwilling, uneducated men became the proudest, most efficient navy that had ever been seen. Trafalgar was proof of that.

English, I'd have been Emperor of the East," he said later. "But wherever there is water to float a ship we are sure to find you in the way."

By the turn of the century, England had reaped a mighty harvest of her enemies' colonies. Her trade had never been greater. Exports had increased by half since the war began and imports had doubled. But her people were tired of war. Prices had risen faster than wages. A sixth of the population, it was said, was living on charity. The public wanted peace.

Instead it had new enemies. In 1801 a league of Baltic powers—Russia, Sweden, and Denmark—tried to break Britain's relentless blockade of France by challenging her practice of searching their ships. Pitt was determined France would not receive the stores she needed to rebuild her navy. He sent a fleet to assault the Danes at Copenhagen.

Nelson was second in command of the fleet, but led the 12 battleships that met the Danes in what he called the "most terrible" engagement of his career. It was in this battle, on April 2, 1801, that Nelson turned his blind eye to his superior officer's signal to break off the action. "Keep mine for closer battle flying," he ordered. "Nail mine to the mast."

After Nelson's crushing victory, the battered Danes and their intimidated allies yielded. At about the same time an army sent to destroy the French in Egypt was laying siege to Alexandria and marching successfully on Cairo. The war, however, was being lost in England. Pitt had resigned the Prime Ministership.

He had quit over the King's refusal to enfranchise Irish Catholics. When Nelson returned from Denmark, a new Prime Minister, Henry Addington, was eagerly courting peace. Napoleon, although he needed a respite to get more ships, successfully played for time, and Britain yielded more and more of her war-time conquests at the conference table.

In the Peace of Amiens in 1802 Britain agreed to return all the captured French sugar islands, including St. Lucia, highly valued for its strategic position, Tobago, which had been developed with British capital, and Martinique. The French also got back their posts and factories in India and West Africa. To the Dutch were returned the Cape of Good Hope, their holdings in South America, and their West Indian islands, including Cura-çao. In the Mediterranean, Britain gave Minorca to Spain again and withdrew from Elba, the Ionian islands, and Malta. Of all her conquests she retained only Trinidad in the West (formerly Spanish) and Ceylon in the East (formerly Dutch)—the one crucial to control of the Caribbean, the other to the Indian Ocean.

In return, Bonaparte promised to respect frontiers in Europe and withdraw his troops from Egypt, where—unknown in London—the last French garrison was already in the process of surrendering.

The peace that ensued was really only an interval between acts of war. The curtain rose again 18 months later when the British refused to abandon Malta. In Europe the conflict would last until 1815 and Waterloo, but the British Empire was not situated on that Continent, nor could it be won or lost there. The war for Empire would be decided at sea, and much sooner.

One of the sailors on whom that decision would depend, Horatio (now Viscount) Nelson, took command of the Mediterranean fleet in May, 1803, and began an odyssey that was to become an astonishing demonstration of human perseverance. The French Mediterranean fleet was in Toulon, so there Nelson placed himself, and there he stayed for 14 months.

He called that station his "home." It was not a comfortable one. The gales in the Gulf of Lyons exceeded their hostile reputation while Nelson was there. He could have gone to Malta for shelter. "But, if I am to watch the French, I must be at sea; and, if at sea, must have bad weather; and if the ships are not fit to stand bad weather, they are useless." The men were healthy; the introduction of a lemon-juice ration a few years before had eliminated scurvy as a cruise-limiting factor. He trained his crews. He wrote—to the Admiralty, his family, in his diary, and to his beloved mistress Emma Hamilton. He worried mostly about where the French would go if they eluded him. And he waited.

Once, when the main body of Nelson's fleet was a few miles off, Admiral Louis Latouche-Trévill ventured out in pursuit of three ships left on close guard, and then rushed back to safety when the rest of the British appeared. Excited at having teased the lion, Latouche published a letter about it. "You will have seen Latouche's letter," Nelson wrote his brother. "How he chased me and how I ran. I keep it; and if I take him, by God he shall eat it." Latouche escaped that fate by dying, from climbing, it was said, so often up a hill to see if the English were still there that at last his heart gave out.

On March 30, 1805, the long blockade ended: Admiral Pierre Villeneuve slipped out of Toulon, eluded Nelson with the aid of a "French wind," and sailed his squadron to the West Indies. After a fruitless search in the Mediterranean, Nelson pursued the French westward. Once again Villeneuve escaped, recrossed the Atlantic, and in August reached safety in the Spanish port of Cadiz.

To keep the French bottled up, 30 British ships of the line assembled off Cadiz. The flagship *Victory* had been called back to Portsmouth, and Nelson spent a pleasantly domestic three weeks with Emma. On September 28, 1805, the *Victory* was sighted approaching the blockading fleet at Cadiz. "Lord Nelson is arrived," a delighted captain wrote. "A sort of general joy has been the consequence."

All through that summer Napoleon's army had waited in Boulogne with a fleet of boats in readiness to cross the Straits of Dover. In England people prepared for the shock of invasion; nobody, a London newspaper said, could sleep in peace at night. Invasion had been expected, on and off, for seven years, and everyone knew why the blow had not yet fallen: the Royal Navy, so far, had commanded the Channel. In August Napoleon wrote to his admirals: "Come into the Channel, bring our united fleet, and England is ours. If you are only here for 24 hours, all will be over, and six centuries of shame and insult will be avenged."

Nelson was painted by Lemuel Abbott a half dozen years before Trafalgar. He had recently lost his right arm in an exploit against the Spanish.

But his fleet had not come. It was blockaded far to the south by British ships which watched it night and day. In disgust, Napoleon broke up the camps at Boulogne and marched the Grand Army eastward for a land campaign in Austria. He left behind a mandatory order for Villeneuve to attack, whatever the odds against him. "His Majesty counts for nothing the loss of his ships," the orders said, "provided they are lost with glory."

At dawn on October 21, 1805, off Cape Trafalgar in the south of Spain, Napoleon's French and Spanish fleet was sighted, ten miles away against the eastern sky. Men in the British fleet rushed up on deck to look; it was a sight they had longed to see for the past two years. The two fleets prepared themselves for the great battle to come.

All Nelson's captains knew exactly what they had to do. When he took command of the fleet, all of them were invited to dine with him on the *Victory*, and he explained a revolutionary tactical plan. In almost every battle in the past, fleets had manœuvred into parallel lines; when the lines were in range, each ship had fought a duel of gunnery with its nearest opponent. But no day would be long enough, Nelson said, to make this classic movement with the large fleet he had; he proposed to deploy his fleet in two lines. He would lead the first, and cut through the enemy's line about the middle; the other, led by Admiral Cuthbert Collingwood, would cut it near the rear. Both lines would win a victory, he expected, before the enemy's van could make a ponderous and complicated turn in formation and join the battle.

"Something must be left to chance," he wrote to the captains, "nothing is sure in a Sea Fight beyond all others. Shot will carry away the masts and yards of friends as well as foes. But I

Overleaf: As seen here, Trafalgar was an unsubtle slugging match. Nelson's *Victory* (right) and the French *Redoubtable* hammer away at each other.

look with confidence to a Victory. . . . No Captain can do very wrong if he places his Ship alongside that of an Enemy."

Nelson had said he wanted to bring about "a pell-mell battle," and that was what happened. Nothing quite like it had been seen before, and nothing since. The formal lines of battle disappeared. In one square mile of sea, some 60 ships were moving independently, and each of them, all the time, was in range of several enemies. For the captains it was like a deadly game, a mixture of luck and skill—skill in bringing one's own broadside to bear while avoiding the enemy's; luck in the disposition of the clouds of smoke that often hid everything, so that ships, friend or foe, loomed through it at the range of a pistol-shot. Yet the game was played, as it were, in slow motion: probably, once battle was joined, no ship moved at more than one mile an hour, and to turn the great vessels took many minutes.

In this unique situation, the gunners blazed away at any enemy ship that crossed their line of sight, and they were seldom without a target. All the firing was at very close range— a maximum perhaps of 100 or 200 yards, a minimum of a foot or two. Many ships drove their bowsprits into an enemy's rigging and swung until their sides were grinding together. The *Victory* and the French *Redoutable*, thus entangled, drifted down on the English *Téméraire*, and then all three fell aboard the French *Fougueux*—four ships side by side, all facing the same direction as if they were peacefully moored at a quay.

Nelson calmly paced his quarterdeck in the midst of this thunderous chaos. Close action had been joined, and his work was done. It was unthinkable that he should take cover, and almost inevitably a French sharpshooter finally hit him. He was carried below, dying.

By that time the difference in training between the two fleets had begun to tell. After the years of blockade, the British were far better at ship-handling, and in gunnery they could fire three times as fast as the French, and with better aim. In consequence, casualties in the French and Spanish ships were five or sometimes even ten times as many as in their British opponents. There was also a difference in determination. Most of the French and all the Spanish who were dismasted began at once to think of striking their colours. But it simply never crossed the minds of captains of equally battered British ships to do so. Some, by prodigious efforts in the heat of battle, got under way again with patched-together jury-rigs. Some got other ships to tow them, and fought on.

It was this that made Trafalgar a total victory: first Nelson's tactical plan, and then the total, unquestioning confidence he had inspired. While he lay dying down in the dark cockpit of the *Victory* among the other wounded, 19 enemy ships hauled down their flags. Not a single British ship was lost. By four o'clock it was all over. An unknown hand wrote with a pencil in the *Victory's* log: "Partial firing continued until 4:30, when a victory having been reported to the Right Hon. Lord Viscount Nelson, K.B., and Commander-in-Chief, he died of his wound."

Nelson's victory that October afternoon established a supremacy at sea which lasted nearly a century and a half right through the Age of Steam. And that continuous sea supremacy was the essential, stable basis of the British Empire in the 19th Century.

With the world's oceans now be-

longing to Britain, she could select and acquire colonial objectives almost at will. Otherwise insignificant pieces of real estate were seized for strategic reasons in the continuing war with Napoleon. Other colonial holdings, particularly in the French West Indies, were taken for their rich trade potential.

By 1816, after the peace conference, the Union Jack flew over the Cape of Good Hope and Ceylon guarding the lifeline to the East; over Trinidad and St. Lucia and what became British Guiana in the West; and over such scattered outposts as Malta in the Mediterranean, Heligoland in the North Sea, and Mauritius and the Seychelles in the Indian Ocean. And far out in the South Atlantic the desolate islands of Tristan de Cunha and Ascension were annexed simply to be

guardians over the Emperor of the French in exile on St. Helena. When the final French challenge began in 1792, Britain possessed 26 colonies. In 1816 she ruled 43. Her Empire had almost doubled.

There was, too, an added depth to the victory at Trafalgar that went beyond the crushing defeat of Britain's strongest rivals at sea. Supremacy was also a matter of supreme self-confidence. "Remember Nelson": a British admiral flew that signal in one of the last sea battles under sail. And remember Nelson was what the Royal Navy did, all through the years of power—and still does. The standards he set in his lifetime of pride in service and of heroic conduct did not end with his death; they grew and became tradition. After Nelson, to "engage the enemy more closely" was simply what

the navy expected to do, and did without question whatever the odds or the circumstances—and was also what the country confidently expected the navy to do in times of crisis.

No man in modern history had a deeper, more lasting influence on any country's growth. Why was it? What was it that people remembered, and still remember? It was not only success: Wellington won victories as important, but he had no lasting hold on people's hearts. And it was not any kind of moral perfection, for Nelson was no saint. He was a little one-armed man, blind in one eye, not of any very imposing appearance. He was vain, sometimes irritable; unfaithful to his wife; kind, compassionate, understanding; irresistibly lovable—and he was brave.

—*Jim Hicks, David Howarth*

Chapter Three
BEYOND THE RIM OF ASIA

In 1777, before starting for the North Pacific on his third, and final, voyage of exploration, James Cook paused in this idyllic setting to refit his two ships, *Resolution* and *Discovery* (right). The scene is Moorea, in the Society Islands.

I. The Gentle Navigator

Little more than two centuries ago the gigantic world of the southern Pacific was a virtual blank on the maps and in the minds of Europe. Australia and New Zealand had been sighted but their true size was unknown. That these lands—and many Pacific islands as well—were revealed, that so much of the South Pacific became part of the British Empire, was largely due to one man: James Cook.

As a youth Cook had nothing of the sea, still less of the far Pacific, in his sober Yorkshire head. The local schoolmistress found him bright, especially at arithmetic, and he gained an introduction to the Messrs. Walker, a firm of Whitby shipowners whose vessels carried coal from Newcastle to London. In 1746, at the age of 18, Cook signed on as apprentice seaman.

He quickly gained a lasting respect for the rugged Whitby colliers in which he sailed. And as he journeyed up and down the North Sea coasts of England—among the shoaling sands, tricky currents, and ill-lit headlands—he unwittingly received about the best training for exploring unknown shores a man could get.

In 1755 he joined the Royal Navy as a volunteer, having "a mind to try my fortune that way." His timing was good, for shortly afterwards the Seven Years' War broke out and opportunity beckoned. Wolfe's Quebec campaign required that the treacherous reaches of the St. Lawrence be surveyed and marked. Cook was in his element at this work, and the painstaking accuracy of his charting was much admired. In high naval circles heads began to nod approvingly at the mention of his name. One of his captains used the word "genius" in his commendation.

In 1763 the war ended with Britain everywhere triumphant and ready for new undertakings. Hitherto the rivalry between France and Britain had been limited to areas reasonably accessible from Europe. Now, in equally competitive if more peaceable spirit, it spread to the Southern Hemisphere—the unknown infinities of the Pacific and towards the South Pole.

Since early times geographers had speculated about a vast and mysterious continent, *Terra Australis Incognita,* the "Unknown Land of the South." Interest ran high. Defoe placed his *Robinson Crusoe* and Swift his *Gulliver's Travels* in the Pacific, and they proved to be two of the 18th Century's most popular books. If *Terra Australis Incognita* existed, it was quite possibly the home of a large population rich in resources and skilled in manufacture, whose friendship or subjugation would be invaluable to a colonial power.

By 1766 the race was on. Samuel Wallis and Philip Carteret were searching for *Terra Australis* for Britain, and the next year the Chevalier de Bougainville followed for France. Neither expedition achieved much, but Wallis heightened hopes by reporting that southward of Tahiti he had seen mountains rising from the sea. It was an illusion—a line of clouds standing dark against the sunset—but the search now seemed more than ever worthwhile. Paris was known to be planning further efforts. It was essential for Britain to redouble hers.

The scientific bent of the times provided a convenient cloak behind which to hide a determined British expedition. The transit of Venus between the sun and the earth in 1769, an event not due to be repeated for another century, was an opportunity to gather evidence to calculate the earth's distance from the sun, and the Royal Society proposed it be observed from several vantage points, including one in the Pacific. The Admiralty agreed to send a ship for the purpose. Cook would be in command.

Cook urged that his ship should be not a warship but a humble Whitby collier of the type he knew so well. In his view such a vessel, equipped as a floating laboratory, would be ideal for a long oceanic voyage broken by spells of detailed inshore survey work. One of these colliers was purchased, renamed *Endeavour,* and fitted out according to his specifications.

Cook's precise instructions were drafted in two parts. The first dealt with the transit of Venus, which he was to observe from Tahiti. This was for public consumption. The second part was secret. His business at Tahiti finished, he was ordered to head south for 1,500 miles at which latitude—40° south—"there is reason to believe a continent, or land of great extent, may be found."

Previous Pacific exploration had been largely haphazard. As a result, there were long gaps in the outlines of known coasts, and of the relatively few discovered islands, many had been lost again almost as soon as found. No one yet knew whether there was a navigable passage linking the northern Pacific with the Atlantic; no one had ever with certainty seen the east coast of Australia; and it was not clear whether there was a strait between Australia and New Guinea. Above all, no one knew the truth about the Southern Continent.

In search of the truth, the 370-ton *Endeavour* left Plymouth on August 25, 1768. Outward bound she was a happy ship. Cook well understood "the temper and dispossessions of seamen." He was, however, a firm disciplinarian, and in one matter he was remorseless. He was determined to prevent the terrible outbreaks of scurvy that were accepted as the unavoidable cost of long voyages. He was convinced that scurvy resulted from dirty conditions and bad diet. The ship, therefore, was kept scrubbed, ventilated, and fumigated, and the men had to wear clean, warm clothing. And every day he forced down their throats unsalted soups, sauerkraut, and fruit juice.

After dutifully carrying out orders to observe the transit of Venus, Cook steered the *Endeavour* for the underside of the globe to fulfil his secret instructions. (Highlights of this first voyage, and of his later two voyages, appear on the following pages.)

Not content with his six-month circumnavigation of New Zealand, Cook determined to explore the unknown east coast of Australia and to clear up the question of whether the gap now known as Torres Strait between Australia and New Guinea existed.

After a three-week sail through calm warm weather, with the dolphins leaping about the ship "like salmons," the Australian coast was sighted and *Endeavour* began her greatest discovery. Cruising northward, Cook found no harbour for a week. Then a bay opened, and he gently nosed his way in. Here the 18th Century came face to face with Stone Age Aborigines, to the bewilderment of both. Finding the place a naturalist's paradise, the party named it Botany Bay.

Cook sailed on northward, noting but not entering the harbour which was later to be the site of Sydney. A thousand more miles of meticulous recording followed as he moved up the coast, set on solving the problem of the Torres Strait. Tacking gingerly among the fearsome reefs around Cape York, the northernmost tip of Australia, he at length found open water. He had, he said, "settled a doubtful point." Before sailing away he held a little ceremony to take formal possession of Australia. The flag was run up on shore to a brisk salute of musketry.

When he at last sighted the English coast on July 10, 1771, Cook had

revolutionized exploration. Till then it had been a storm-tossed adventure. He had turned it into a controlled, methodical science. His crew, though diminished by tropical disease, remained free from scurvy. And in the botanists' packing-cases were 1,300 new flowers, a massive contribution to the 18th Century's explosion of information.

For his second voyage Cook drafted his own instructions. The *Resolution*, another Whitby collier, would call at Cape Town, then head south to seek out the Southern Continent. If nothing was found he would turn east and circumnavigate the globe as far south as human endurance permitted, retiring northward to winter in less severe climates. If he found land he was to take possession of it. If he did not, then it would be clear to the world that the Southern Continent did not exist in any politically significant latitudes.

No sightings were made south of Cape Town, so Cook turned the *Resolution* eastward as planned, and they fought their way into a forbidding world of gales and ice and pinching cold. By January 18, 1773, he was at lat. 67° S.—farther south than any man had ventured before. Sometimes the fog was so dense that the bows could not be seen from the stern. On clear nights the eerie flicker of the aurora would play so powerfully overhead that the shadows of men on watch fell sharply across the decks. By mid-March they had traversed more than a third of the world's circumference. No land broke the heaving horizons: only icebergs "as high as the dome of St. Paul's." It was time to seek a respite.

A wide-ranging sweep through Equatorial waters restored the strength of the *Resolution*'s crew; then they resumed their "dismal course to the southward." At lat. 71° 10' S. the ship was stopped by solid ice. "It was indeed my opinion," Cook wrote, "that this ice extended quite to the Pole, or perhaps joins to some land to which it has been fixed from the creation." He suspected the proximity of Antarctica, but even if he had found it, at such latitudes it could hold no imperial importance.

He had demolished every shred of evidence for the Southern Continent's existence in the Pacific.

There remained the possibility that it lay in the South Atlantic. He sailed for Cape Horn to find out. Again the searching telescopes revealed no land, no break in the deep-ocean swell. "If I have failed to discover a continent, it is because it does not exist in a navigable sea," he reported.

One nagging question remained to be answered: was there a short route to the Pacific via the Atlantic and northernmost America—that is, a North-West Passage? Those hardy Elizabethan sea dogs—Frobisher, Davis, Hudson, Baffin—had marked the path as far as Hudson Bay. But beyond the map was empty. The Admiralty proposed an expedition to the North Pacific, to search for a channel into Hudson Bay from the western side of the continent.

Cook was now a tired man, and the story of his third voyage reflects it, moving to its sombre climax with the inevitability of Greek tragedy.

With his two little ships, *Resolution* and *Discovery*, he probed the inlets of the mountain-bound coast, rounding the Alaskan Panhandle, piercing the Aleutian chain, struggling on in worsening weather through the strait found by Vitus Bering 50 years before, into the Arctic. There he was stopped by a wall of ice, as he had been in the far south. All that could be heard from ashore was the howling of wolves.

He crossed to the Siberian coast, in vain; no way could be found round the ice. The short summer was ending. He decided to spend the winter investigating the Hawaiian group, and resume the search the next year. His splendid journal stops, significantly, on the day he anchored in Kealakekua Bay. A few weeks later, on February 14, 1779, he was killed by an angry band of natives.

Laid to rest with James Cook were many of the geographical myths of the civilized world. The monument to this "gentle navigator," as diarist Fanny Burney called him, was the map of the Pacific.

—Stuart Legg

ENDEAVOUR, RESOLUTION, DISCOVERY

"Was it not for the pleasure which naturally results to a Man from being the first discoverer," wrote Captain James Cook, "this service would be insupportable." It was a rare moment of self-revelation: for he wrote little of himself in the journals which he kept of his voyages and his personality still remains curiously elusive.

His outward qualities were well known. The steadiness, the determination and thoroughness that guided him in his exploration of the distant places described in the following pages, can readily be seen in his portrait (above) and in his actions. His outward character and achievements are well summarized by the names of his vessels: *Endeavour*, *Resolution*, *Discovery*. But there was more to him than this. Underneath lay an insatiable ambition: he himself said that he sought "not only to go farther than anyone had done before but as far as possible for man to go." This was the quality that gave Cook such a sense of dedication that after leaving New Zealand in April, 1770, he looked, not for the quickest way home, but for "such a rout as might conduce most to the advantage of the Service I am upon."

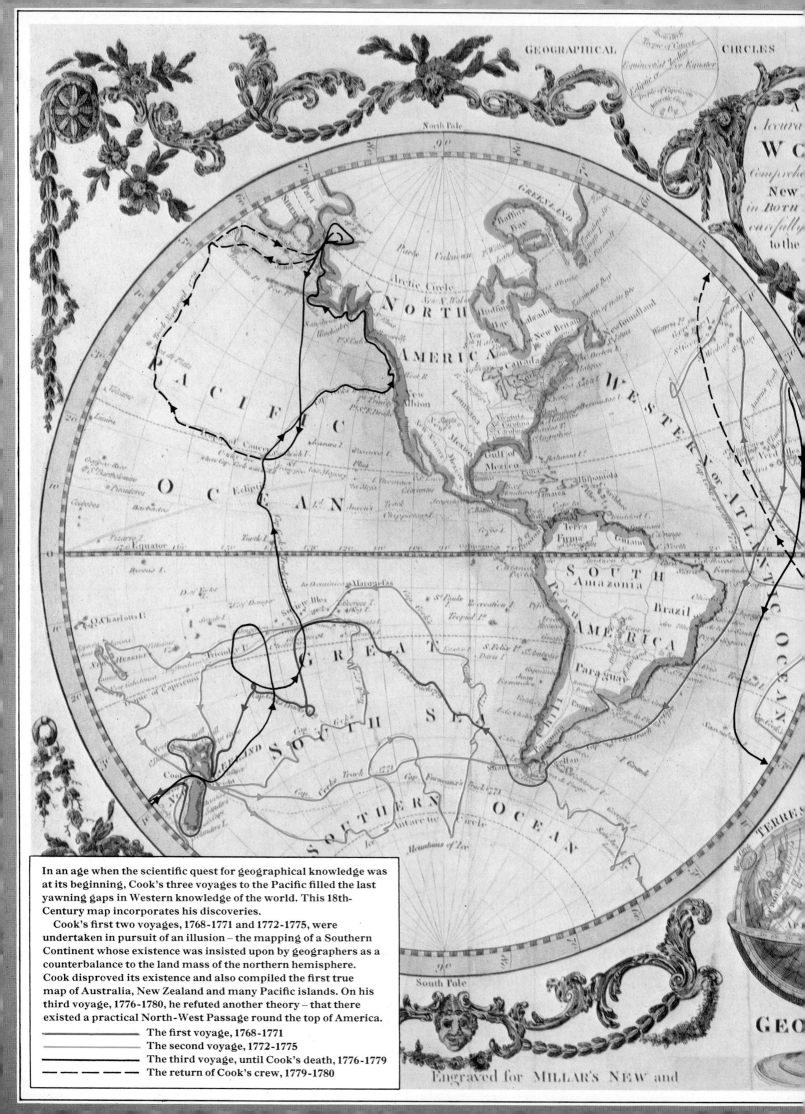

In an age when the scientific quest for geographical knowledge was at its beginning, Cook's three voyages to the Pacific filled the last yawning gaps in Western knowledge of the world. This 18th-Century map incorporates his discoveries.

Cook's first two voyages, 1768-1771 and 1772-1775, were undertaken in pursuit of an illusion – the mapping of a Southern Continent whose existence was insisted upon by geographers as a counterbalance to the land mass of the northern hemisphere. Cook disproved its existence and also compiled the first true map of Australia, New Zealand and many Pacific islands. On his third voyage, 1776-1780, he refuted another theory – that there existed a practical North-West Passage round the top of America.

———————— The first voyage, 1768-1771
———————— The second voyage, 1772-1775
———————— The third voyage, until Cook's death, 1776-1779
– – – – – – The return of Cook's crew, 1779-1780

Engraved for MILLAR's NEW and

The Collapse of a Myth

When Cook left Tahiti during his first voyage, he offered a gallon of rum to the man who first sighted land. Five weeks later, a boy lookout, Nicholas Young, shouted "Land ahead!" and claimed the prize. Could the headland, later named in Nick's honour, be the tip of the conjectural Southern Continent?

By the end of the year Cook had sailed round the northern island and had anchored for repair in "a very snug cove," an inlet that Cook named Queen Charlotte Sound after George III's wife. Cook took possession of all the adjacent lands "in the name and for the use of His Majesty." To complete the ceremony, the Queen was toasted in wine and the empty bottle given to an old native.

Joseph Banks, the *Endeavour*'s naturalist, botanized so assiduously that he soon found no further floral specimens to catalogue, and he was reduced to collecting mosses. Meanwhile, Cook surveyed the area and found that Queen Charlotte Sound opened into a strait which separated two bodies of land. To silence the members of his crew who still insisted that this new land could be an appendage of the fabled Southern Continent, and to complete his charting of New Zealand, Cook sailed round the southern island. By March, 1770, even Banks, a strong believer, had to admit that in this region at least he had seen "the total destruction of our aerial fabric called continent."

The *Endeavour*, Cook's first ship was, like the *Resolution* (above), a Whitby-built vessel. Small, sturdy, and with a shallow draught to venture into uncharted waters, she was chosen by Cook for her similarity to the colliers on which he had once been an apprentice.

Maoris, fishing from small crowded canoes clustered in groups off the coast of New Zealand, used "hooped netts very ingeniously made" of interwoven blades of grass, baited with "fish gutts" to entice the fish.

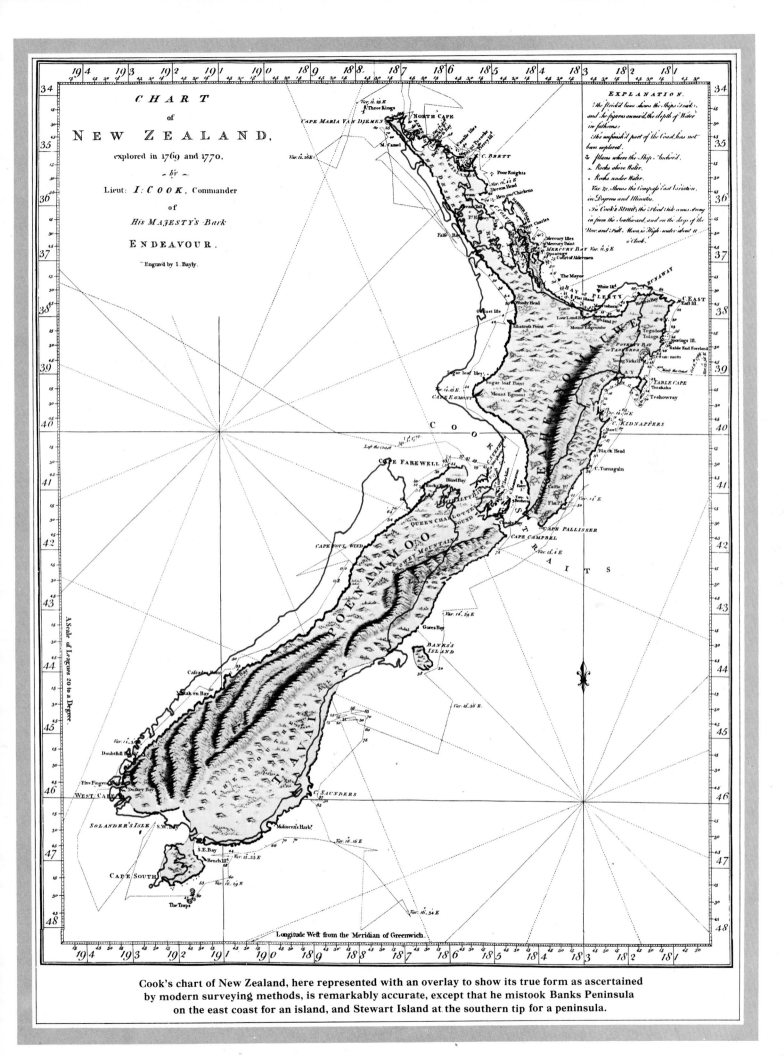

Cook's chart of New Zealand, here represented with an overlay to show its true form as ascertained
by modern surveying methods, is remarkably accurate, except that he mistook Banks Peninsula
on the east coast for an island, and Stewart Island at the southern tip for a peninsula.

103

A Maori chief, standing in the centre of this crowded war-canoe, directs a
man to adjust the sails, while another Maori plays on a pipe in preparation
for a war-dance. An enemy's head, a grisly reminder of their warlike
intentions, dangles from the hand of a warrior.

Expression of the sentiments, by the Hand.
The raising of the hands conjoined, towards heaven, expresses
devotion; Wringing the hands, grief; Throwing them towards heaven, Admiration; Fainting & dejected hands, a-
mazement & despair; Folded hands, Idleness; holding the
fingers indented; musing; holding forth the hands together,
yielding & submision; lifting up the hand & eye to heaven,
calling God to witness; waving the hand from us, Prohibition; extending the right hand to any one; pity, peace,
& safety; scratching the head, thoughtfulness; laying the
hand on the heart, solemn Affirmation; holding up the
Thumb, approbation; laying the fourth finger on the
mouth, bidding silence; giving with the finger & thumb
a giving sparingly; & the fore finger put forth & the rest
contracted, to shew & point at, as much as to say, this is he.

In his methodical scientific manner, Captain Cook carefully
noted in his journal the hand movements of the Maoris,
including finger on lip to signify silence, and recorded
details of their vocabulary, clothing and customs.

Maori patterns of tattooing on
the body were mostly in the form
of spirals drawn with a
sharpened bone dipped in a sooty
liquid and executed, according to
Cook, with "great nicety
and judgement."

Warriors of the Pacific

The artists who went on Cook's voyages – Sidney Parkinson, William Hodges and John Webber – produced memorable paintings of the Maoris, Tahitians and other Pacific islanders, carefully described by Cook in his journals. The Maoris of New Zealand were a "strong raw-boned; well-made active people rather above the common size, of a very dark brown colour with black hair." They were also, on first encounter, insolent and aggressive and were far more interested in war than friendship. Warning volleys fired over their heads only incensed them, and Cook killed several in self-defence.

However, the natives Cook met at Tolago Bay on the east coast of North Island were somewhat more amenable – despite their custom of eating the flesh of enemies killed in battle – and were eager for gifts of Tahitian cloth and glass bottles. Here Cook was able to examine the magnificent, awe-inspiring Maori war-canoes.

Some men and women were persuaded to sing a war-song: "They distorted their faces most hideously," wrote Banks, "rolling their eyes and putting out their tongues. But," he added, "they kept very good time."

This was not a typical encounter. The natives who paddled out in canoes were usually armed and belligerent, ready to hurl stones and abuse. But it soon became apparent, to Banks at least, that their main aim was to display their courage. "We begin to know these people," he wrote more confidently after some months, "and we are much less afraid."

The elaborately symmetrical tattooed swirls on his face, together with the white feathers stuck in his top-knot and heavy ear-ornament, mark out this New Zealand native as a man of importance in his society.

The usually friendly Tahitians are in warlike mood in this painting by William Hodges. A fleet of war-canoes, "very well equipp'd, Man'd and Arm'd" and supervised by dazzlingly clad chiefs, assemble for review in a rehearsal of an attack on the near-by Island of Eimeo.

A Warm Reception on the Friendly Isles

On all three voyages, the Pacific islands offered a welcome respite from the months of ceaseless exploration. The paintings of William Hodges, the artist on Cook's second voyage, captured the exotic qualities of these Pacific outposts.

They were greeted with friendship almost everywhere. The hospitable welcome that awaited Cook's party at the Tonga Islands so impressed Cook that he gave them the alternative name of Friendly Islands. At most islands the weary crew were offered coconuts, fruit and drinks like *kava*, which the natives prepared by chewing roots and spitting the juice into a bowl. Cook was the only one of his crew brave enough to sample this beverage.

In return, apart from the iron nails, beads and other small gifts that Cook distributed, he left sheep, goats and pigs on the Pacific islands at the request of "Farmer" George III. The sheep and goats died, but the pigs survived, multiplying to such an extent that their descendants, known as "Captain Cookers," still roam New Zealand.

This idyllic impression of Tahitian girls swimming in the warm clear waters of Vaitepeha Bay in Tahiti is the work of William Hodges (inset), whose romantic rather than realistic paintings of the South Sea islands furthered the myth popular among Europe's Romantic philosophers of the carefree native living a blissfully happy existence untouched by civilization.

The strange towering monoliths of Easter Island fascinated Cook, like the
great statues elsewhere on the island. He was sure that they were not idols,
but their true origins and purpose have remained a mystery.

A boat from the *Resolution* lands cautiously at Tana in the New Hebrides after a
hostile reception at nearby Eromanga. The natives at Tana proved so friendly that
the brief visit extended to a fortnight, and trade in pigs and coconuts was brisk.

Cook and his officers watch "an extraordinary and barbarous custom" as the Tahitians prepare to offer a human sacrifice for the propitiation of the gods. On the burial-mound in the background is evidence of many other human sacrifices, the victims of which were usually criminals.

Longboats filled with Cook's men pull in to land among the Tongan sailing-boats and canoe

The Luxury of a Sun-warmed Paradise

The South Sea islands, with their palm-lined beaches and clear warm skies, were gladly revisited in 1777 during Cook's third voyage, all the more so because the voyage ahead – to icy regions of the north – would be hard and cheerless.

"I have quitted an easy retirement for an active, perhaps dangerous voyage," Cook had written exuberantly, before he left England. "I embark on as fair a prospect as I can wish."

The aim was to discover a northern sea-route from the Pacific to the Atlantic Ocean. And Cook, once more sailing the *Resolution* – a bad choice for she was feeling her age – was the obvious man for the task.

En route, he stopped at places familiar from previous voyages – the Cook Islands, the Society Islands, Tonga and Tahiti. Uncharacteristically, perhaps because he too was feeling his age, Cook did not press on in his search and spent much of 1777 lingering in these beautiful tropical kingdoms, luxuriating in their timeless atmosphere. For the moment discovery could wait, and he only set off northwards in December.

Tahitian girls, whose elaborately fringed and feathered costumes contrast with the simple dress of their partners, entertain the islanders with stately traditional dances, accompanied by skilled drummers in the background.

the palm-lined harbour of Nomuka Island, where the *Resolution* anchored in April 1777.

Into a "Shattered World" of Ice

The frozen Arctic, which many people still thought concealed a North-West Passage, was the goal of Cook's third journey. As on his second voyage, when he visited the Antarctic, conditions were dismal. The ships drifted slowly through pack-ice, their sails stiff with layers of ice and the men encrusted with frozen snow. Lumps of ice were chipped from the great floes and melted down to drink: "the most expeditious way of watering that I ever met with," commented Cook wryly.

On this voyage, there was at least occasional relief from the monotony of the icy wastes – "like the wreck of a shattered world," as a member of his crew wrote. The men would organize hunting-parties, like this one painted by John Webber (below), to shoot "sea-horses," as they called the solemn-looking walruses, for fresh meat.

When Cook found his way north blocked by ice, his last mission was accomplished. Having disproved the existence of a North-West Passage Cook returned to the warm Pacific islands, where a few months later, his epochal career ended with his murder by natives in Kealakekua Bay, Hawaii.

II. Early Days Down Under

In May, 1787, 11 ships packed with convicts made sail from Portsmouth for Botany Bay in Australia. The great continent that Captain Cook had partially charted and claimed for Britain 17 years earlier was about to be put to imperial use—as a dumping ground for the mother country's criminals.

Years of controversy preceded this decision. Lord Sydney, Secretary of State for the Home Office, had finally promulgated the King's ruling in favour of transportation. Britain's gaols, Sydney said, were so crammed with prisoners that "the greatest danger is apprehended, not only from their escape but from the infectious distempers which may hourly be expected to break out amongst them." The prison hulks on the Thames and at Portsmouth had become monstrous sinks of disease and death.

To many, transportation seemed a reasonable and humane solution. But Botany Bay resembled not at all the garden of Eden conjured up in London newspapers. It was flat, barren, and hostile, and Captain Arthur Phillip, in charge of the expedition and the colony's first Governor, decided that it was altogether unsuitable —even as a dumping ground for London's "sweepings."

Phillip dispatched a ship a few miles north to investigate the harbour which had been sighted, but not charted, by Cook. The report was good, and on January 26, 1788, after a nine-month voyage halfway round the world, the "First Fleet" sailed into what Phillip described as "the finest harbour in the world," an expanse of wonderfully blue, deep water, contained like an inland lake by narrow headlands and fringed with dozens of beautiful little bays and coves.

The fleet moored at Sydney Cove, where Phillip went ashore to inspect the landscape at closer range. He was enthusiastic about what he saw. "I have no doubt that the country will hereafter prove a most valuable acquisition to Great Britain," he noted. There were toasts and a few volleys of musketry as a British flag was unfurled and firmly planted in the virgin ground. It was a pale moment of laboured festivity in an immense, unknown wilderness which Phillip, a 40-year-old half-German whose solemn appearance and pedestrian manner disguised an unusually strong

The prison hulk *York*, anchored at Portsmouth, was notorious for its ferocious discipline and its near-starvation diet. A fresh batch of prisoners is shown arriving. Transportation to penal colonies and settlements was a common sentence; witness the 1826 broadside on the facing page. It was imposed for such crimes as theft, receiving stolen property, and attempted rape.

sense of vision, believed to be "the foundation of an empire."

The next day, in a scene of general confusion described by Watkin Tench, the ubiquitous chronicler of the early years in New South Wales, as "highly picturesque and amusing," Phillip began to discharge his notorious cargo. These 736 men and women, whatever the nature of their crimes, shared a common fate—the terrible sentence of Jeremy Bentham's imaginary judge: "I sentence you, but to what I know not; perhaps to storm and shipwreck, perhaps to infectious disorders, perhaps to famine, perhaps to be devoured by wild beasts. Away—take your chance; perish or prosper, suffer or enjoy; I rid myself of the sight of you."

Were these wretched creatures, most of them old, infirm, or mentally diseased, meant to lay the foundations of an empire, as Phillip seemed sincerely to believe? Or were they merely the first inmates of a new kind of prison from which there was no possible escape?

It is still a matter of debate. Traditionally, historians held the view that Botany Bay was chosen for settlement because its absolute isolation guaranteed the permanent removal of criminal elements from Britain. But some contemporary Australian historians argue that the decision was primarily influenced by the need for a maritime base as a support for the rich British trade with China and throughout the Pacific. It is pointed out that as a convict colony alone, the settlement was unjustifiably expensive (the cost of transportation and the upkeep of minimal living conditions ranged from £27 to £42 per head a year), and that other suggested sites (north-west Canada, Tristan da Cunha, the African Gold Coast, Newfoundland) would have proved equally effective and much more economical. It is certainly a strong possibility that the decision to settle Botany Bay was taken with—in the words of one historian—"the twin hopes of giving England the supplies it needed and ridding England of the people it didn't need."

At the root of the mother country's decision was a skyrocketing crime

AUGUST. 3rd 1825,

SENTENCES
Of all the Prisoners
TRIED AT
Glo'ster
ASSIZES.

F Thos. James, for breaking open the house of John Nicholls, of St, James' Bristol, and stealing shirts, &c.   Death recorded.

Wm, James, for breaking open the house of John Cox, of St. Philip's, Bristol, and stealing 20 lbs. weight of cheese   7 Years Transp.

Arthur Britton, Samuel Crow, and Wm. Crow, for robbing Ann Hicks, on the highway, of 200 guineas in gold   Acquitted

Wm, Williams, for attempting to commit a rape on Hannah Roberts, an infant 10 years of age, at Littledean   3 Years Imp.

George Gwilliam, for intent to commit a rape on Mary Gwilliam, of Stanton, against her will   3 Years Imp.

James Jones, stealing a gelding from J. Calloway, Bristol   Death rec.

James Turner and Thos. Pegler, for robbing J. Underwood on the highway, of a hat   Death rec.

Wm. George, Thos, Parker, and Eliz. Parker, for house-breaking, at Old Sodbury, and stealing a bed quilt   7 Years Transp.

Charles Bence, Henry John, Wm Hill, Doctnr Turner, for a riot, at Pyrton, and assalting several of his Majesty's subjects, particularly J. Coiter— pleaded Guilty: Entered into their own Recognizance,

Robert Hudson, for assaulting Jane Neale, at Stroud, with intent to commit a rape   Two Years Imp.

John Mico, and Robert Shackle, for stealing 2 sacks and 3 casks, from J. Staite, of Bristol   7 Years Transp.

Richard Fowler, for stealing hay, at Winterbourne   12 Months Imp.

John Cosburn, Sam. Watkins, and Richard Kirby, charged with killing and slaying John Richins   Acquitted

George Cooke, for housebreaking at Dursley, and stealing a tea caddy, & other articles   7 Years Transp.

Charles Bessell, Marshall May, and Richard Groves, for breaking open the cellar of A Johnson, nt Baptist Mills, and stealing 2 dozen bottles of wine   Bessell and Groves, Death rec.; May, No Bill.

Sarah Mears, Sarah Orchard, Mary Ann Smith, Resolba Hopkins, and Ellen Wayland, for receiving the above wine, well knowing the same to have been stolen—Mears 14 Years Trans. Orchard, Smith & Wayland Aeq. Hopkins, no bill

Geo. Goode, for killing T. Hawkins, at St. Briavel's   18 months Imp.

Thos. Gardiner, for housebreaking at Chalford, steal. cloth   CONDEM.

Wm. Chivers, for breaking open the house of Fran. Cam, at Iron Acton, and stealing 21 cheeses   Transp. for Life.

Thos. Mills, and Wm. Mills, for breaking open the house of Wm. Cousins, at Wotton-Underedge, and stealing cloth—T. Mills, Evidence; Wm. Mills, CONDEMNED.

Hester James, Stephen Woodward, Job Mills, Wm. Dyer, John Dyer, Wm. Somers, and John S. Vines, for receiving the above cloth, knowing it to have been stolen—Woodward & James, Acq. the others ordered to remain.

Rich. Mee, for stealing a bottle of brandy at Cheltenham   7 Years Tr.

Jas. Hayward. James Kerry, Fred. Clements, and Geo. King, for a burglary in the house of Fanny Newnuryi in Cneltenham, and stealing shoes, &c. Hayward, King's Evidence; Kerry & Clements, Acq. King, DEATH

John Farmer, for attempting to commit an unnatural crime on J. Chappell   Acquitted

Elizabeth Jones, for stealing calico, the property of W. Mumford; also for various other felonies, at Tewkesbury   Transp. for Life

Wm. Evans, and John Denner, for breaking open the cellar of A, Johnson, at Baptist Mills, and stealing 5 dozen bottles of wine   Death rec.

Isaiah John Langstreeth, for stealing tea, at Tewkesbury 7 Yrs. Transp.

H. Bonner, Painter, 4. Unity Street, St. Philip's Pain, Bristol.

rate. In the 1790s Patrick Colquhoun, the metropolitan police magistrate, estimated that there were no less than 105,000 criminals in London (one-eighth of the population). Many of these—beggars, dismissed servants, "profligate, loose, and dissolute characters"—were not criminals at all by modern standards. Nevertheless, there was justification for Colquhoun's bitter complaint that "the vilest and most depraved part of the Community are suffered to deprive us of the privilege of travelling on the Highways, or approaching the Capital after dark, without the risk of being assaulted and robbed, and perhaps even wounded or murdered." He expressed a general fear when he added: "we cannot lie down to rest in our habitations, without the dread of a burglary being committed, our property invaded, and our lives exposed to immense danger before morning."

The growth of crime in Britain ran parallel to the general social upheaval that marked the beginning of the Industrial Revolution. There was a dramatic increase in population, less work, frequent famine, higher prices. Dispossessed rural labourers drifted into the already hopelessly overcrowded towns, where the great ma-

Above, Aborigines with stone axes climb a eucalyptus tree in pursuit of a bat, a lizard, and a squirrel to supplement their diet. The man at the right is poised to hurl a multi-pronged fish spear; behind him a woman fishes from a canoe with a hook and line.

jority lived poverty-stricken in decayed hovels, surroundings in which a life of crime was often the only means of survival.

The only deterrent Parliament could devise to halt violence and crime was an increase in the number of capital offences. In 1688 there were 50 crimes punishable by death, in 1819 nearly 200, ranging from murder, arson, and rape to kidnapping an heiress, sodomy, forgery, house-breaking, picking pockets, stealing goods worth more than five shillings, stealing linen, stealing or maiming or killing horses and cattle and sheep, pulling down houses and churches, destroying turnpikes, cutting down trees in streets and gardens, escaping from transportation, and sending threatening letters.

These measures failed utterly. As before, most crimes remained undetected, and even the public execution of criminals failed as an effective deterrent. Quite the opposite: between 1780 and 1790, when 50 persons a year were publicly executed in London, criminals turned such occasions into festivals of assault and robbery.

The government had long shipped criminals convicted of serious crimes to the Americas, particularly to the West Indies. Nevertheless, English gaols were overflowing. There was

public alarm—a hint of panic—and the decision to ship convicts to Australia was made in an atmosphere of urgency.

The first load of convicts was chosen at random. Little regard was given to farmers or artisans or others with skills that could be utilized by the colony; no regard was given to sex, age, or health. Convicts were simply "the dregs of society": nameless, soulless objects better left unseen.

It was poor material indeed with which to build an empire (if that had ever been the intention), and against the awesome setting of the vast continent into which it was dumped it looked even poorer.

Before anything else, the first white men in Australia had to come to terms with the land. It was unlike anything they had ever seen—and many of the marines who accompanied the "First Fleet" had seen half the world. It seemed cruel, unnatural, incomprehensible; there were few who shared Phillip's early enthusiasm. Most experienced the same shock and sense of disgust as Major Ross, Commandant of Marines: "I do not scruple to pronounce that in the whole world there is not a worse country than what we have yet seen of this," Ross wrote. "All that is contiguous to us is so very barren and forbidding that it may in truth be said here nature is reversed, and if not so, she is nearly worn out. . . ."

This was an understandable, if limited, view, for Australia is certainly a land of extremes. Its core is one gigantic desert: of the total area of nearly 3,000,000 square miles, one fifth is useless and another fifth only barely suitable for sporadic grazing. In the north, in Northern Australia and Queensland, are the tropics—an area of jungle, forest, and swamp covering 40 per cent of the whole country. West of Sydney, behind the "Great Divide," a rugged range that runs the entire length of the continent, lie many thousands of square miles of rich wheat and sheep land—for long the main source of Australia's wealth. To the south, beyond snow-covered mountains, is Victoria, with a lushness and variety of landscape so alien that it might have been transplanted from

some other hemisphere (it was called *Australia Felix*, "happy Australia," by its discoverer, Major Thomas Mitchell). Farther south is the densely forested island of Tasmania. In South Australia only some coastal regions are free of the harsh desert which stretches for more than a thousand miles westward until it is broken by a pocket of fertile country in the corner of Western Australia. Everything else is desert.

"Here nature is reversed," said Major Ross. It was winter in July, summer in January, the one hardly any different from the other; in the bush were birds with wings that could not fly, and strange animals with rabbit-like heads that bounced through the air on great misshapen legs instead of walking; there were birds that sat motionless in the dreary evergreen trees (which were useless for building), seemingly laughing; there was a hardly plausible animal called the platypus, part mammal, part reptile, part bird; and it literally never rained but it poured. The country truly seemed to be one of the Creator's more perverse jokes.

And then there were the Aborigines.

The horror most of the early white settlers experienced in the presence of Aborigines was due partly to a shock of recognition—for the Aborigine was in no way similar to the native peoples Europeans had encountered elsewhere in the Pacific: he was a Caucasian whose ancestors had probably crossed the seas from Asia at some time now lost in pre-history (the Tasmanian Aborigines, a separate race now extinct, may however have come from the Pacific). The mainland Aborigine was, as Alan Moorehead puts it, "a European stone-age man, a living fossil of ourselves as we were in the beginning."

The Aborigines lived an apparently simple and uncomplicated existence. They were a semi-nomadic people: they had no permanent settlements but lived in primitive makeshift huts or lean-tos as they moved from one territory to another in search of food. They had no knowledge of agriculture, and their diet was determined by natural supply—fish, kangaroos, grubs, wild honey, yams. They had few (although very effective) weapons—a spear or boomerang and a club— and even fewer utensils, but the meagre possessions they did have were sacred, and could not be bought by curious white men for a handful of coloured beads.

Despite their apparent simplicity, the Aborigines had an extraordinarily rich and emotional spiritual life. They believed in the existence of a great supernatural being who, in an ancient "dream-time," had awakened their venerated animal ancestors from a deep sleep of non-being into a life of earthly activity. Ancestor worship directed the entire life of the tribe, and the elaborate rituals and ceremonies around which the tribal structure was built were based on ancestral myths and legends. Many of these myths were re-enacted in the *corroboree*, the sacred tribal dances held to celebrate hunts and battles, seasonal changes and events, the arrival of strangers, and as the climax to complex initiation ceremonies.

Charles Darwin saw a *corroboree* when the *Beagle* touched at Australia in 1836: ". . . The dancing consisted in their running either sideways or in Indian file into an open space, and stamping the ground with great force as they marched together. Their heavy footsteps were accompanied with a kind of grunt, by beating their clubs and spears together, and by various gesticulations, such as extending their arms and wriggling their bodies. It was a most rude, barbarous scene, and, to our ideas, without any sort of meaning. . . . Everyone appeared in high spirits, and the group of nearly naked figures, viewed by the light of the blazing fires, all moving in hideous harmony, formed a perfect display of a festival among the lowest barbarians."

Captain Cook had been more discerning. He recognized that the Aborigines had achieved a rare harmony and balance to their lives. "They may appear to some to be the most wretched people on earth," he wrote, "but in reality they are far happier than we Europeans."

The first encounters between white men and the Aborigines were reasonably friendly, since the British government had directed the settlers to "live in amity and kindness with them," and the Aborigines had responded with unexpected cheerfulness. But the more frequent these encounters became, the more the narrow-minded, ill-educated settlers saw of what they considered animal habits and barbarous customs, the more often there was violence.

It became convenient for the authorities not to notice that the Aborigines were "disappearing" from the settled areas. As more and more land was seized by the Crown and given to settlers, the Aborigines were driven back into the interior "as if they were dogs or kangaroos." They were driven away from their sacred totemic shrines and from ancient ceremonial grounds and long-established hunting areas. These grounds were integral to the Aborigines' lives—though they did not claim "ownership"—and it was natural that they should seek to return. Whenever they did they were accused of trespassing or stealing. There were violent clashes, and acts of terrible savagery on both sides. Natives were killed—but they killed back, and the settlers reacted by banding together and sending out expeditions into the bush "to punish the blacks." Carnage was the inevitable result and it continued unchecked for decades until the Myall Creek massacre of 1838, when 28 natives were murdered supposedly in retaliation for an "outrage." Seven men were hanged for the crime after a notorious trial in which the defence, in all good faith, offered the astounding argument, "We were not aware that in killing blacks we were violating the law. . . as it has been so frequently done before."

And, despite the trial and its infamy, it was done again—until the Aborigines were finally pushed out of their ancient territories into the desert. Nobody knows how many there were in Australia when the first white men arrived: perhaps 500,000, perhaps only 150,000; today there are less than 50,000 Aborigines of full blood.

All this came later; in the earliest times it was doubtful whether the colonists would survive at all. Within a few months Phillip's little enterprise was on the verge of collapse.

The livestock brought from England died or disappeared; plants and crops refused to grow; the government provisions began to run desperately low. Scurvy and new, unknown diseases raged through the colony, and almost everyone seemed to be subject to the heavy air of listlessness that hung across the country.

Survival depended almost entirely on the labour of the convicts, but they were too inexperienced and too ill-equipped to be able to cope with anything more than the most primitive forms of gardening and building. Most of them were ill, and all of them were indifferent. "How difficult it is," Phillip wrote, "to make men industrious who have passed their lives in habits of vice and indolence. . . those who have not been brought up to hard work, which are by far the greatest part, bear it badly."

The colony was saved from starvation by the arrival of the "Second Fleet" in 1790—but it was also burdened with another 750 convicts (250 had died on the voyage out), 500 of whom were ill and the rest old or helpless. Again these were the sweepings of London's gaols, and Phillip, who had begged for free settlers to be sent out, protested strongly: "The sending out of the disordered and helpless clears the gaols and may ease the parishes from which they are sent; but, Sir, it is obvious that this settlement, instead of being a Colony which is to support itself, will, if the practice is continued, remain for years a burthen to the mother-country."

But at this stage, Botany Bay—as the colony was known in commemoration of the original intended landing-place—was a gaol first and a colony second as far as the British government was concerned. Another 1,864 convicts were dispatched in 1791 (198 died on the voyage; the rest were for the most part desperately sick on arrival), a year in which the whole white population of Australia (3,433) was at one point living on a weekly ration of two and a half pounds of flour and "bad worm-eaten rice" and two pounds of salt pork.

When convicts arrived in the colony they were assigned directly to the Governor, who then either re-assigned them as labour for settlers or retained them to man government works. As labourers for settlers (military and civil officers and, later, emancipated convicts) the convicts for the most part lived in reasonably humane conditions. But those who lived in government barracks and in the penal settlements on Norfolk Island or at Port Arthur became the victims of brutal tyranny, suffering violence and degradation far worse than anything they had known in England. They were starved, lashed, left to die where they fell, left to rot in the sun.

A convict could, however, be emancipated by the Governor for good conduct, and eventually a system was developed whereby he could be granted a ticket of leave, then a conditional pardon, and finally an absolute pardon before his sentence had been served.

A minority were quick to seize these opportunities, eager to show their worth in whatever fashion—such as the counterfeiter Frazer mentioned by Watkin Tench in his chronicle: "The governor had written to England for a set of locks to be sent for the security of the public stores, which were to be so constructed as to be incapable of being picked. On their arrival his excellency sent for Frazer, and bade him examine them, telling him at the same time that they could not be picked. Frazer laughed and asked for a crooked nail only, to open them all. A nail was brought, and in an instant he verified his assertion."

It was those like Frazer who were responsible for the colony's survival—

the mutineer surgeon Redfern, the Irish rebel surveyor James Meehan, the blackmailer-poet Michael Robinson, the forger-architect Francis Howard Greenway—and who did much to impose character on the young colony. But there were few able to organize, few eager for political control. Though it is still widely believed in Australia that many, even most, of the convicts were "political" prisoners, in fact the total number of "politicals" shipped from England was very small—five "Scottish martyrs" were transported in 1794, and later some Luddites, Derbyshire rioters, conspirators, Chartists, and Trade Unionists, including the six Tolpuddle Martyrs condemned for forming a trade union in 1834. Much later there were many thousands of Irish rebels who, technically, could not be classed as either "politicals" or criminals.

Nevertheless, when Phillip sailed for England in December, 1792, he was confident that the worst problems that had threatened his little colony had been solved: 1,700 acres of land were under cultivation and the results were good, there were a few public buildings and the skeleton of a fine town, much of the "depravity and corruption" that infested the convict barracks was under control. In short, there was a future.

The British government viewed the adventure as a success as well—of a more limited sort. "It was a necessary and essential point of policy to send some of the most incorrigible criminals out of the Kingdom. . . . No cheaper mode of disposing of the con-

victs could be found," Prime Minister William Pitt told the House of Commons, adding with satisfaction that "the chief expence of the colony was already passed and paid."

Phillip was not replaced until 1795, and during the three-year interval between Governors the colony was ruled by a group of completely unscrupulous officers of the garrison, the New South Wales Corps. It was a period of dramatic change that was to have a profound effect on the course of Australian history.

The agricultural system devised for the colony had been essentially "peasant," based on small holdings to be worked by free settlers, officers who had acquired grants, and emancipated convicts. But too many of the early free settlers (of which there were very few) were plainly inadequate for the task. "Some have been people of very suspicious characters, and have narrowly escaped being sent out against their inclinations," wrote one early settler. "Others, low mechanics who have failed in business. . . others, men of dissolute and drunken habits." The ex-convicts were better material, but without capital and with holdings too small for development and hindered by primitive techniques and an unpredictable climate, they soon found themselves hopelessly in debt and at the mercy of speculators and fortune-hunters.

Those who succeeded were those with capital—and the only men with capital in the colony were the officers of the New South Wales Corps, who had instituted a ruthless system of

Australian colonists considered the duck-billed platypus one of the weirder denizens in a land of weird creatures.

monopoly trading which further harassed the struggling settlers. When the settlers went bankrupt—which was almost invariably the case—the officers bought them out, thus acquiring vast estates on the cheap. Thus was the future capitalist economy of the country determined. By 1800 almost the entire colony was under the control of a few officer-farmers and farmer-landlords. They were all-powerful and not particularly ethical in their use of power. Succeeding Governors could not break them.

Their main source of wealth was the import of rum, the "ardent spirits of Bengal." Because of a general shortage of money, rum became hard currency and was used in barter exchange and often as part payment of wages—in a country whose wild consumption of liquor was already

legend, it was more often than not preferred to money. The result was a rapid and disastrous demoralization of the colony's workers. "No one could adequately describe the conditions of riot, dissipation, and depravity that existed among the lowest class of inhabitants," Tench remarked.

From the ranks of the New South Wales Corps came the men who literally built Australia. Pre-eminent among them was John Macarthur, sometimes referred to as the founder of the Australian wool industry, who came to the colony as a lieutenant in 1790.

Macarthur, one of the most controversial figures in Australian history, was both ambitious and enterprising. As a leading member of the officers' "Rum Ring," he was quick to make a fortune and even quicker to put it to use by acquiring good land, which he

farmed successfully. He started breeding sheep in 1795, principally (like other farmers) for mutton. Within five years he was the largest sheepowner in the country, and having imported some Spanish merino rams, he began to turn his attention to producing fine quality wool. While in England in 1801 he showed impressive samples of wool to politicians and manufacturers, managing to convey the impression that he was the only man in Australia capable of supplying it. Macarthur returned to the colony with a grant for a further 5,000 acres of land in order "to extend his flocks to such a degree as may promise to supply a sufficiency of animal food for the Colony as well as a lucrative article for export."

Macarthur's ambition was infectious: when Governor William Bligh —the Captain Bligh against whom the *Bounty* mutineers had rebelled in

The frontier settlement on the shore of Sydney Cove, as it looked in its earliest days. This water-colour drawing and those reproduced on pages 114–15 are by a convict transported to New South Wales in 1792, four years after the colony's founding.

1789—arrived to run the colony in 1806, he was shocked to find that the leading Sydney farmers and financiers were concentrating entirely on the prospective profits of wool-growing while there was a threat of mass starvation. He noted that "habitations and public store-houses were falling into decay; industry was declining; while a pernicious fondness for spirituous liquors was gaining ground." Bligh determined to correct the abuses and check the excesses of those (like Macarthur) "who had grown corpulent in the drunkenness of the Colony."

It was soon clear that the colony was not so big that it could at one time contain two men of such equally explosive temperament. The clash that came was essentially a struggle for power between two extraordinary personalities.

The Governor of New South Wales exercised wide powers, except in the field of law. There existed a court composed of a Judge Advocate and six officers of His Majesty's forces in criminal cases, and a Judge Advocate and two other citizens in civil cases. If the six officers (e.g., members of the New South Wales Corps) or two citizens (e.g., friends of Macarthur) so desired, they could severely hinder and limit government administration. This they did whenever one of Macarthur's numerous legal battles came before the court, or whenever there was a matter that threatened the vital interests of their own ruling military élite.

Bligh never failed to use any opportunity to test his opponent. Finally, when a schooner partly owned by Macarthur violated some port regulation, a warrant was issued for his arrest. In court Macarthur delivered a statement which, according to Bligh, contained "such scurrilous and indecent language mixed with invective, and delivered with so much insolent contempt, that the Judge Advocate threatened to commit him." But the court's six officers openly supported Macarthur and once he was released on bail he had no difficulty persuading them to rebel and depose the Governor. Shortly after sunset on January 26, 1808, in a gaudy little scene "with

A contemporaneous print portrays mutinous troops of the New South Wales Corps dragging Governor William Bligh, one-time captain of the *Bounty*, from his alleged hiding place under his bed. The revolt was known as the Rum Rebellion.

colours flying and music playing," a regiment of the New South Wales Corps, headed by a Lieutenant-Colonel Johnston, marched through the main streets of Sydney to arrest the colony's stormy petrel.

"I have been deeply engaged all this day contending for the liberties of this unhappy colony," Macarthur wrote to his wife, "and I am happy to say I have succeeded. The Tyrant is now no doubt gnashing his teeth with vexation."

Bligh was kept under arrest for nearly a year, and when he was released he was declared an outlaw. He returned to England in 1810—a bitter man with even less faith in his fellows than the little he had possessed before.

The Macarthur rebels looked after the "liberties" of the colony for two years, but Macarthur himself, together with Lieutenant-Colonel Johnston, were called to London to answer for their actions. Johnston was cashiered, and Macarthur was not permitted to return to Australia until 1817.

A new Governor, Lachlan Macquarie, arrived in Sydney in December, 1809. He found the settlement (then with a population of some

10,000) "barely emerging from infantile imbecility . . . the agriculture in a yet languishing state; commerce in its early dawn; revenue unknown; threatened by famine, distracted by faction; the public buildings in a state of dilapidation . . . the population in general depressed by poverty . . . [with] morals in the lowest state of debasement."

Macquarie was intelligent, diligent, and honest, and he brought two fundamental changes to the life of the colony during the 12 years of his governorship. First, by planned building he gave the settlement an air of permanence: a hospital was erected, a church and decent barracks for the convicts were constructed, the mud and brick huts that lined the main streets were replaced by neat, well-designed houses, and better roads and bigger wharves were built. He managed this by properly assigning the increased amount of convict labour (twice as many convicts were shipped to Australia during Macquarie's time than in the previous 21 years) so that it benefited the community as a whole. It was a period of intense growth, and there was a new sense of order and opportunity. As a result, the colony began to attract

Wives for the Aussies

For ladies who were either too ungainly, unattractive, or impecunious to catch husbands in William IV's Britain, Australia was a godsend. It teemed with men starved for female company.

The task of uniting Britain's unfortunate but nubile women with Australia's lusty settlers fell to a philanthropic committee in London which, despite steady ridicule from newspapers and cartoonists, undertook to ship young ladies for a £5 fare and find them jobs in domestic service. All applicants had to produce a certificate of good character from their parish minister. The government contributed a share of their fare.

Despite assurances that every arrangement would be made for their comfort, the voyage to Australia was an ordeal. Racked by sea-sickness and barely sustained on a diet of mouldy biscuit and water, the prospective brides were treated little better than cattle. Arrival in Sydney did nothing to ease their sufferings. Herded into leaking warehouses the weak, ill, and emaciated women could only take on light work.

But the lot of the emigrants improved in 1841 when Caroline Chisolm, a Sydney woman of great energy and compassion, took it upon herself to look after them. She built a hostel and, in the face of considerable hilarity, travelled all over New South Wales in a bullock dray chaperoning young women to respectable households. There, many of them no doubt found the rangy, sunburnt diggers for whom they had endured so much.

more and better qualified free settlers.

At the same time, Macquarie attempted to give purpose to the colony's future by adopting a more humane approach to the convict problem. He was by no means soft; during his rule night-patrols were introduced, the police were re-organized to hound the colony's more dedicated criminals, and he had as many convicts flogged as any of his predecessors. But he believed that some convicts might be reformed if granted clemency, encouragement, and opportunity. He made more land available to emancipated convicts, and many of them became quite successful. And to the horror of Sydney's rigid, closed society, he even admitted "distinguished" ex-convicts—men such as Robinson, Meehan, and Greenway, his architect—to his table.

Macquarie undertook his reforms with the approval of the British government. But his support began to sag dramatically under the weight of mounting criticism, most of which was directed at the "lenient" convict policy (which was blamed for the increase of crime in Britain) and the extravagant public building projects. In 1819 the government sent Commissioner J. T. Bigge to New South Wales and Van Diemen's Land (as Tasmania was then known). His brief was to study all aspects of colonial life (including the "Propriety of admitting into Society Persons who originally came to the Settlement as Convicts"), but in particular he was to study the convict system. He was reminded that "Transportation to New South Wales is intended as a severe Punishment . . . and must be rendered an Object of Terror."

Bigge was openly astonished by what he found. Botany Bay was no longer a gaol (as he believed it should have been) but a healthy colony using convict labour. It was plain that the convicts did not live in terror (as they should have done) but enjoyed good food and lodgings, had easy work (on unnecessary public buildings), and ready access to pleasure. It was a life that could only encourage laziness and debauch. His report recommended harder work, stricter control, fewer pardons, and

more rigid discipline, measures which were adopted in the immediate years to come. But most importantly, he urged that the convicts be taken out of the corrupting atmosphere of the town and made available as labour to the wealthy wool-growers who were settling newly opened territories.

Bigge was quick to recognize that the expanding wool industry could be of great potential benefit to both Britain and Australia, and that it could provide the means whereby the colony could become self-supporting. Of course, it had to remain in the right hands. He recommended that the government make larger grants to settlers with capital, but no land should be given to free settlers without capital, or to "emancipists" who had served their sentences. He was a man dear to John Macarthur's heart—his report was a charter for what Macarthur envisaged as the foundation of a new landed "aristocracy."

And the land was there, virtually for the taking. In 1829 the government laid down boundaries in order to retain control of newly explored areas—whoever crossed the boundaries trespassed and became an outlaw—but the discovery of land had become an adventure in itself.

John Batman's Port Phillip Association settled at Melbourne in 1835. Batman "purchased" land from the Aborigines—100,000 acres of it—for a yearly payment of 100 blankets, 50 knives, 50 tomahawks, scissors, looking-glasses, 20 suits of clothing, and two tons of flour. When the first reports of Major Thomas Mitchell's discoveries in Victoria were made known, settlers flocked to the area; by 1845 most of the available land there was occupied.

South Australia was opened up as an experimental Free Colony (i.e., without convicts) in 1836 following reports of good land by Captain Charles Sturt, who sighted the country in 1830 after an incredible journey down the River Murray. A similar Free Colony had been founded at Swan River in Western Australia in 1829.

By the mid 1830s most of the country between Brisbane and Adelaide had been opened up—but not, as Macarthur dreamed, to a new "aristocracy." It was instead the age of the squatter.

The squatters were entirely new characters on the Australian scene. They came from all classes and backgrounds. Some were the sons of rich colonists, others retired publicans or ex-farm managers; there were many ex-army officers from overseas, and various kinds of professional men looking for new opportunities; there were also large numbers of plain adventurers. They became squatters simply by occupying free land and defying government orders to move.

The British government warned the squatters that it was "as unauthorized an act of presumption for an Australian squatter to drive his flocks into the untrodden wilderness without Her Majesty's express sanction being first obtained, as for a Berkshire farmer to feed his oxen, without rent or licence, in the Queen's demesne of Hampton Court."

But the squatters knew their strength. "Not all the armies of England, not 100,000 soldiers scattered throughout the bush, could drive back our herds," one wrote. "As well might it be attempted to confine the Arabs of the desert within a circle drawn on the sands. . . ." Within a few years the squatters accumulated tremendous force; when the government called them outlaws, it was designating some of the leading citizens of the colony as criminals.

Finally the government bowed to the inevitable and in 1836 recognized them, introducing a squatting licence of £10 a year. By 1840 there were 673 legal squatting stations in New South Wales.

The novelist Anthony Trollope visited one of the larger ones in 1837 and delighted in penning his impressions back home: "The number of sheep at these stations will generally indicate with fair accuracy the mode of life at the head station: 100,000 sheep and upwards require a professed man-cook and a butler to look after them; 40,000 sheep cannot be shorn without a piano; 20,000 is the lowest number that renders napkins at dinner imperative. . . ."

But in reality it was a very hard life. It was not always easy to find a good "run" (land), suitable livestock was difficult to come by, satisfactory labour was scarce (half the population of the stations consisted of convict servants). It was lonely, and with possible attacks from either renegades or natives, often dangerous. There were floods to cope with and often droughts, and there was never anything else to do year after year but an endless round of work—shearing, droving, building.

Many squatters earned huge fortunes and many others failed terribly, but they were all hard workers with immense courage. By the middle of the century they were the backbone of the country's economy. The first load of wool to be commercially exported (in 1821) was 175,400 pounds. In 1830, 2,000,000 pounds were shipped to England; in 1839, 10,000,000; and in 1845, 24,000,000.

They had also become a political force, as the government soon discovered when it attempted to make them pay for their lands. The squatters had long sought security of tenure to the lands which they considered theirs by moral right. But the government price (£1 an acre) was too high, and the demand came at a time of slump when wool prices were down 40 per cent. There was open talk of revolt. The government was surprised to find itself being threatened by British investors and manufacturers (who had been persuaded by the squatters that the colony was on the brink of ruin), and attacked by the Press. It had little alternative but to withdraw its threat to occupy the squatters' lands and to draw up a quick compromise solution to the squatters' claims for security which guaranteed them part-tenure at an acceptable price.

Since the 1820s, humanitarians in Great Britain had been campaigning against convict transportation. By exerting their considerable influence they persuaded the government to set up a committee of investigation. The result was the Report of the Select Committee on Transportation, published in 1838, which was to become a standard history of the life of convicts in New South Wales.

The report concluded that transportation was a form of disguised slavery, and that it corrupted not only the convicts but the society that used them. It found that most of the 75,200 convicts who had been transported up until 1836 had led miserable lives, often subjected to torture and degradation. It calculated that the entire project had so far cost the British government nearly £8,000,000 of public money, and came to the conclusion that transportation did not reform criminals—rather it hardened and brutalized them—and that the thought of exile to Australia could no longer act as a deterrent to crime in Britain when many thousands of assisted immigrants were now flowing into New South Wales to seek better lives.

The enterprise, considered in these terms, could be counted a failure.

Transportation, meanwhile, had become the dominant political issue in the colony. Working-class organizations grouped around the Australian Union Benefit Society (formed in 1838) and composed mainly of immigrants and ex-convicts, sought the end of the policy—not only for humanitarian reasons, but because a continued flow of convicts threatened their own employment. The "exclusives" and the capitalist members of the Patriotic Association—squatters, free settlers, and emancipists—objected strongly to the end of transportation, since it deprived them of their cheap labour.

The report of the Select Committee produced an immediate effect: transportation in 1839 was drastically reduced, and in 1840 it was decided that no more convicts should be sent to New South Wales. Transportation of convicts to the penal settlements at Norfolk Island and Port Arthur continued after 1840, however, though the numbers were greatly reduced. Convicts continued to be shipped to Swan River in Western Australia until as late as 1868 in a desperate attempt to save a floundering colony, but transportation as an idea ended in 1849, when the British—in a test of strength against the Australians—attempted to land a shipload of convicts at Sydney in the hope that it would be accepted as the resumption of normal traffic. The ship was turned back by a public demonstration. Australia was on the way to nationhood.

— *Barry Pree*

A GREEN AND PLEASANT LAND

In the 1830s, as British interest in Australia grew, a colony of free settlers, South Australia, was founded. The first buildings and wharfs of its port, Adelaide, named after William IV's Queen, were erected in 1835 and within a decade the town became a bustling capital city. One man who observed South Australia's burgeoning affluence in the mid-1840s and painted the pictures on these pages was the 22-year-old artist, George Angas, whose father was one of the colony's leading founders. Young Angas's work stands as a fitting tribute to his father's achievement – which settlers themselves also honoured by naming one of the settlements Angaston.

The Mt. Lofty Range, which frowns over Adelaide and the coastal plain, turns from a parched ochre to a brilliant green after the winter rains.

Port Adelaide, with its long wharves and tall warehouses, was the key to South Australia's wealth. Here the colony's silver, copper, wheat and wool flowed out of the harbour and food, machinery and clothing poured in.

A few years after the town was founded Adelaide's
main shopping and business quarter boasted
an avenue of elegant and imposing buildings.

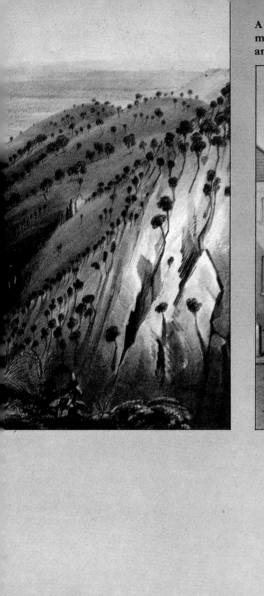

Angaston was, to George Angas, at its loveliest at sunset "when the orange glow lights up the surrounding hills."

The Thrill of the Chase

None of the settlers who arrived in South Australia in the 1840s dawdled long on the quays of Adelaide. Carrying only their hopes and a few possessions they strode off to carve out new lives as farmers and graziers. Soon neat, picturesque settlements mushroomed up among the eucalyptus groves, sheep dotted the landscape, and men began to sow wheat and prospect for minerals.

All work ceased, however, when it was time for the settlers' favourite pastime – kangaroo hunting. With all the abandon of an English hunt, they used packs of greyhounds to run their quarry to earth. Good dogs usually brought down the bounding kangaroos after a dash of two miles or so, but cornered bucks frequently killed their snarling attackers with a vicious blow from their paws or hind legs. Infuriated kangaroos trapped by a water-hole sometimes even seized dogs with their forepaws and held them under the water until they drowned.

se flocks near Adelaide were soon
...aced by swaying fields of wheat which
...de more profitable use of the rich soil.

Panic-stricken kangaroos bound through the scrub of the coastal lowlands, hotly pursued by sleek greyhounds and the rest of the hunt.

THE SEARCH FOR MINERALS in the mountains above Adelaide bore fruit in 1845 when extensive copper deposits were found at Kapunda (below). Within two years, 1,500 tons of the greenish-blue ore had been winched to the surface by horses and shipped to England for smelting. Soon the flourishing mining industry was further enriched by discoveries of silver, lead, iron, marble and opal. By mid-century, South Australia was booming and in 1855 the exertions of her settlers were acknowledged when Britain accorded the vibrant young colony of South Australia self-government – just two decades after the first shaky wooden buildings had gone up at Adelaide.

George Angas, who painted the portfolio on Adelaide, travelled to New Zealand in 1846 to record scenes of Maori life. This is a detail from one of his careful portrait studies. The highly intricate tattoo pattern was characteristic of a tribal chieftain.

III. The Maori Challenge

New Zealand, which the Dutchman Abel Janszoon Tasman sighted in 1642 and which Cook rediscovered in 1769, is almost exactly on the opposite side of the world from Great Britain. It is about the same size, but warmer: subtropical in the far north, temperate in the south. Its two principal islands, about 1,300 miles east of Australia, are very hilly, often mountainous, and have an unusual variety of scenery—lakes, fiords, glaciers, plains, dense forest, endless beaches. Because it was remote from other lands for immense periods of time its native flora and fauna are unique. There are no native mammals except a bat (the Polynesians introduced even the dog and the rat). The multitudes of birds include many flightless species. One, the moa, grew up to ten feet high, but it had been exterminated some time before the arrival of Cook.

The Maori people whom Cook encountered were the most numerous of the Polynesian peoples. In the 18th Century they numbered perhaps 200,000 to 300,000—no one knows. Their ancestors had sailed in canoes to New Zealand from eastern Polynesia at approximately the time of Christ.

Though the Europeans called them savages, the Maoris, unlike the Australian Aborigines, were organized in a way that was fairly easy for Europeans to grasp. They lived in great tribes and subtribes, each with its own territory that was collectively owned by the group, not by individuals. There were chiefs, priests, generals, aristocrats, commoners, slaves. They had not only their tribal territories, with defined boundaries, but much other property as well.

Cook's discoveries elsewhere in the Pacific basin had a profound effect on Europe—perhaps, it was supposed, the "noble savage" of the Romantic imagination lived in Tahiti. But people thought of the inhabitants of New Zealand as rather frightening if unusually intelligent savages. Such news as reached Britain about New Zealand over the next half-century did little to alter that impression.

The Maoris were exceedingly warlike and, on occasion, cannibals. Human flesh was not a regular feature of their diet, however, since it was usually available only after battles. Fighting usually stemmed from land disputes, quarrels over women, or from insults. Most Maori villages were placed near a *pa*, a fortress built on an inaccessible hilltop or promontory and protected with great ditches and palisades of tree trunks. Cook thought that "a small number of resolute men might defend themselves a long time against a vast superior force, arm'd in the manner as these people are." So it later proved, even against European weapons.

Though Cook's annexation of New Zealand was ignored by his government, which had as yet few political ambitions in the area, other European explorers visited it. After the establishment of the Botany Bay convict settlement in Australia, contacts with the Maoris became more frequent. Ships crossed the Tasman Sea from Sydney seeking seal furs and timber for ships' masts and spars. After about 1800, British, French, and American whaling ships began to call to refit and trade with the Maoris.

Considering that they had had neither money nor even a barter system, the Maoris learned to trade with astonishing rapidity, bartering food and timber for nails (which they flattened out to make chisels), fishhooks, axes, and anything red (their favourite colour). As a more exotic payment, the Maoris also lent their women to the sailors.

But with familiarity came trouble. Brutal seamen had no scruples about kidnapping Maori men and women, and they often broke the *tapu*, the prohibitions which protected sacred objects (the word became "taboo" in English). By 1810 relations between Maoris and Europeans had degenerated into sporadic warfare. After the crew of the *Boyd* were killed and eaten, skippers tended to keep away from these dangerous shores.

In 1814 an Anglican parson from Sydney, Samuel Marsden, set up a mission station at the Bay of Islands in northern New Zealand. It was not a success. One early missionary, Thomas Kendall, was in effect converted himself. "I have been so poisoned by the apparent sublimity of their ideas, that I have been almost completely turned from a Christian to a Heathen," Kendall wrote. He was dismissed after he took to sleeping with a Maori girl. Other missionaries had scarcely more effect. The Maoris felt no need of this new religion; in the words of one chief, it was quite unsuited for warriors who were not used to turning the other cheek.

As payment for their services and goods the Maoris increasingly demanded—and often would take nothing but—guns. As a result, their society was torn apart by relentless tribal warfare, the casualties of which were unprecedented. By one estimate, the Maoris lost 65,000 warriors from 1801 to 1840, chiefly after 1820.

Even more devastating were the diseases brought by the white men. The Maoris, like other Polynesians, had lived in isolation from other peoples and from many of the germs, viruses, and bacteria common to the rest of the world. They had developed no immunity or resistance, and were decimated by epidemics of measles, influenza, smallpox, and cholera. Venereal diseases, too, took a heavy toll.

The Maori population was reduced, chiefly through disease, by possibly 40 per cent. Many were disheartened and lost faith in their gods, who seemed to have deserted them, and turned instead to the missionaries. In the late 1820s and in the 1830s tens of thousands of Maoris were converted. They were fast becoming a Christian people.

While the missionaries were tilling their spiritual field, a man who was to have a deeper influence on New Zealand history lay in London's Newgate prison, sentenced for abducting an heiress. Edward Gibbon Wakefield was an unstable visionary with a complex plan for "systematic colonisation." He believed that if land in colonies were sold by the Crown to "capitalist farmers" at a "sufficient price," the revenues would pay the fares of carefully chosen immigrants. The labouring immigrant, eager to acquire land of his own, would have to work for several years to accumulate the price of a farm, thereby keeping the ranks of farm-labourers well filled. The existence of this pool of workers would encourage more capitalist farmers to migrate. With the widespread application of this utopian plan, Wakefield expected to create colonies which reproduced the best features of British society, but without its poverty and urban overcrowding.

Although Wakefield's plan seemed at first original, it was in fact conservative, even reactionary. He aimed at preserving the supposed virtues of pre-industrial England, a largely legendary world of the squire surrounded by his contented, forelock-tugging yokels. Wakefield's scheme was also impractical. What sort of wage could be paid that would be high enough for labourers to become landowners yet low enough to attract capital investment? Wakefield never said. In any event, in 1837 Wakefield set up the New Zealand Company, dedicated to sending numerous settlers to the Antipodes. His plans were opposed by the mission societies in London and, for a time, by the Colonial Office. He was distrusted for his criminal past, and the missions were convinced that European settlement would ruin the Maoris the way that it had damaged—or destroyed—other primitive peoples.

Colonization of a sort had already begun. By 1838 there were about 2,000 European settlers, mostly in the north. They included many deserters from ships, escaped convicts from Australia, and other riff-raff. Lives and property, Maori or European, were far from secure. "Everyone did as he liked," one settler wrote, "except when his neighbours would not let him." Sydney "land sharks" were trying to buy Maori land for next to nothing. It was becoming increasingly clear that something must be done—and done quickly—to bring order to a lawless land.

In 1839 the British government reluctantly decided to take action. A naval officer, Captain William Hobson, was sent to negotiate annexation with the Maoris. His instructions expressed the government's pious hope of preventing that "process of War and Spoliation" which had so often led to the crushing of uncivilized tribes by European settlers. The government also hoped that New Zealand might become a Christian colony, an example to the world of good racial relations.

On February 5, 1840, several hundred Maoris gathered at Waitangi— the Waters of Lamentation—on North Island to discuss annexation. The result was no foregone conclusion. Many of the chieftains who gathered in the marquee set up on the lawn in front of the British Residency wanted a return to a golden Polynesian age before the coming of the disruptive Europeans. But a chief named Tamati Waka Nene won the day with his passionate exhortation to dispense with nostalgia and fear. Christianity, trade, and peace were blessings he would gladly exchange for a pagan past and an anarchic present. "You must preserve our customs, and never permit our lands to be wrested from us," he told Hobson. "Stay then our friend, our father, our governor."

The next day, some 50 chiefs signed the Treaty of Waitangi. Over the next few months it was carried about the country for others to sign. Although many refused, 500 put their names on the document, thereby ceding their sovereignty to the Queen. They were guaranteed in return the possession of their lands and given the rights of British subjects.

The treaty was of dubious legality, for it was not clear whether the Maoris understood what they had done. Their lands, for instance, could now only be sold to the Crown—but Maori land was held in common and before the Europeans arrived there was no system by which it could be sold at all. And Hobson, anxious to prevent settlers from making their own laws, never waited to hear from the South Island chiefs. He formally annexed the whole country on May 21, 1840.

Implementing the treaty was another matter. No one knew how to "protect" a native people from the dangers brought by civilization. By now the first of Wakefield's settlers had arrived. Their aim was not to benefit the Maoris but to benefit themselves—to establish a prosperous white colony.

The first Wakefield settlement was established near the present capital, Wellington, in 1840. Next year further colonies were planted in Nelson, across Cook Strait, and at New Plymouth. In the north Governor Hobson placed his capital at Auckland, on Waitemata Harbour. None of these settlements was very successful at first. In some there was a surplus of labour and unemployment. In a great many there was repeated trouble with the Maoris.

Despite the good, indeed noble, instructions given to Governor Hobson, for decades New Zealand experienced outbreaks of chaos and violence similar to those which darkened the early history of most other colonies.

The first bloodshed took place in 1843 when two Maori chiefs disputed the New Zealand Company's title to land it claimed to have bought from the native owners. Since this formidable pair was known to have slaughtered large numbers of tribal enemies, they were not the sort a sensible man would quarrel with. Nevertheless, Captain Arthur Wakefield, brother of Edward, led a party of armed settlers to arrest the chiefs for obstructing a land survey. Twenty-two Europeans were killed, including the foolhardy Wakefield.

There was more trouble around the new town of Auckland. Conflicts over trade turned several chiefs against the government, which had imposed customs duties, and American traders further incited the Maoris. A large war party cut down the British flagstaff and sacked a township. In the year of skirmishing which followed, the rebels beat British troops several times. On one such occasion, a strongly fortified *pa* was bombarded by artillery, then assaulted by British soldiers, sailors, and marines, who advanced in close formation. One-third of them were killed or wounded. The rest retreated in disorder.

Finally the sporadic warfare of the 1840s died down, and the European settlements began to prosper. The success story in New Zealand, as in Australia, was sheep-raising. Wool was in world-wide demand and could be transported everywhere. It provided the export income needed to

The signing of the Treaty of Waitangi on February 6, 1840, marked Britain's annexation of New Zealand. The first to sign, as shown in this commemorative painting, was the Maori chief Tamati Waka Nene. William Hobson is the central seated figure.

pay for the imports the settlers had to have to survive.

This period of growth coincided with the governorship of George Grey, a brilliant scholar and one of the greatest 19th-Century agents of Empire. Grey was still in his thirties during his first period of office, from 1845 to 1853, but he at once revealed himself as an efficient—and sometimes ruthless—administrator. His intentions towards the Maoris were of the best, and although many settlers regarded him as a tyrant who refused them self-government, among the Maoris he had in these years the prestige of a high chief. He was well suited by origin to protect them: being an Irishman, he had an aversion to anything which even faintly smacked of landlordism.

Grey took many steps to improve the standards of Maori life. He subsidized mission schools and appointed resident magistrates to accustom the Maoris to British concepts of law. He built hospitals and encouraged the tribesmen to take up farming by lending them money to buy equipment. As a result many prospered. Maoris owned much of the coastal shipping; they grew fruit and vegetables and grain which they sold to settlers in the towns and exported to Australia.

Yet in the long term many of these measures were useless. To large numbers of Maoris the government's aim was offensive: it proposed to "elevate" them as a step toward the amalgamation of the two races. The Maori was to abandon his "primitive" culture and

become instead a brown European.

Even the fine British intention of protecting the Maoris from land speculators misfired. The Treaty of Waitangi supposedly empowered only Crown agents to buy land, thus barring land sharks who concluded rapid and illegal deals with an individual rather than with the tribe. Yet as the numbers of settlers grew and the demand for land increased, government land-purchase officers acted like land sharks themselves in their eagerness to make a purchase. One man described how a Crown agent named Robert Parris went to offer his condolences to a Maori widow: "Parris commenced blubbering at some distance and he rubbed noses [the usual Maori greeting] with the widow and the three or four other withered old

Raffles of Singapore

The spirit of the legendary Raffles dominated Britain's 19th-Century Empire in the Far East. Romantic, adventurous, ambitious, individualistic, he turned his unlikely dream of permanent British authority in Southeast Asia into reality. At his chosen base, Singapore, which was in 1819 no more than a mangrove swamp inhabited by a few hundred fishermen, he laid the foundations for a port that within 25 years was to become a bastion of the British Empire.

Thomas Stamford Raffles, the son of a sea captain, joined the East India Company as a clerk in 1795 at the age of 14. Bright and energetic, he rose swiftly through Company ranks and at 24 was on his way to the Far East. When the British "liberated" Java from the Dutch during the Napoleonic Wars, Raffles took over its administration. He endeared himself to the Javanese by uprooting the repressive, feudal Dutch policies and throwing himself into a study

of the island's archaeology, zoology, botany, and literature.

The Congress of Vienna handed Java back to the Dutch, however, so he returned home—to acclaim and rewards, including knighthood. The Queen herself came to inspect his Eastern art.

By 1818 Raffles was back in the Far East promoting a new, bold plan: to slip ashore on a strategically placed island not already occupied by the Dutch and negotiate an agreement with the local ruler to establish a trading post.

In January, 1819, he found what he was looking for off the tip of the Malayan Peninsula. "The island of Sincapore," he wrote, "seems in every respect most peculiarly adapted for our subject. . . . It gives us the command of China and Japan, with Siam and Cambodia, Cochin China, etc., to say nothing of the Islands themselves." On February 6, 1819, in a hastily improvised ceremony, a treaty drawn up by Raffles was stamped with the seal of the Sultan of Johore. Presents were distributed all round, the Union Jack was hoisted, salutes were fired.

What Raffles had immediately grasped was Singapore's dominating position overlooking the narrow Malacca Straits on the major Eastern trade route. He went to work diligently to turn his dream into reality, and when he left Singapore for the last time in 1823 it was an established, fast-growing settlement. Three years later, at age 44, he was dead of brain disease.

Raffles' vision of British economic superiority, his belief in the value of free trade, had at one stroke founded a port that needed no further guidance from him to become "the gateway to the East."

things there. It was worth the trip to see the profile of Parris' mug as he was getting up steam. I suppose he had a 'motive' . . . some hopes of land in that direction."

Such tricks became all too common after Grey's departure in 1853. Indeed the land question was to trigger decades of sporadic warfare between settlers and Maoris that made a mockery of Grey's prophesy of New Zealand as "one harmonious community."

To support their vast sheep ranches the settlers burned the forests and planted grass seed in the ash. The Maoris, on the other hand, used little land for their own crops of *kumara* (sweet potato) and other roots. They relied on the great forests to provide them with their traditional fare of birds and berries and edible plants.

The settlers thought the Maoris were not "using" their lands. The Maoris thought the settlers excessively greedy. When a tribe sold its land it was selling its country, its native land, its collective inheritance, not merely some individually owned transferable asset.

The conflict was sharpened by a growing sense of nationalism on both sides. By 1856 the settlers had been granted "responsible government"— a constitution, a parliament, control of most domestic affairs. Simultaneously, a movement towards unity spread among the various Maori tribes. Only by becoming a separatist nation, their leaders said, could they avoid absorption by the whites.

Fighting waxed and waned through the 1860s. The British found it frustratingly difficult to come to grips with the Maoris. They had no organized army, no lines of communication, no towns which could be attacked. The Maoris would build a palisaded fortress. The troops would attack, often with heavy losses. The Maoris would vanish. Eventually the British worked out the tactic of driving covered trenches towards the *pa*. Although the Maoris ridiculed the trenches, once offering to dig them wherever the British wanted for a shilling a day, this methodical approach prevailed.

In the end, the Maoris' old-fashioned flintlocks, double-barreled shotguns, clubs, and spears were no match for howitzers, Enfield rifles, and grenades, and warfare petered out in the late 1860s. But Maori resistance was not crushed. The king and his followers lived on in the centre of North Island in splendid isolation. Europeans crossed the boundary at their peril—and several who did so were killed. Not until the 1880's, when the Maoris agreed to the construction of a railway, was the "King Country" safe for settlers. The king himself submitted in 1881.

The main result of the war was to break the will of most Maoris to resist land sales. Hereafter land courts, land speculators, and unscrupulous lawyers steadily, remorselessly separated them from their patrimony. This turned them even against the missionaries. These men of God pointed toward Heaven, said the Maoris, and when the natives looked upward their lands were stolen.

By the end of the century they had sold over half their land, most of it their best land, to the settlers. Many had drunk the proceeds, a particularly tragic irony, since the Maoris were among the few people in the world who, when "discovered" by Europeans, had no alcohol or other stimulants. But by the late 19th Century many had acquired an insatiable and deadly thirst, which became one of their major social problems.

It was a sad awakening from the dreams of ideal racial relations in New Zealand. Enough of the ideals survived for the settlers to create, in 1867, four Maori parliamentary electorates. But this, too, was part of the world of the acquisitive, aggressive, hard-working, puritanical white man —a world alien to the Maoris but one which was now the key to the future of New Zealand.

Anthony Trollope was in New Zealand in 1872. He wrote what might have been an epitaph for the Maoris: "There is scope for poetry in their past history. There is room for philanthropy as to their present condition. But in regard to their future—there is hardly a place for hope." Fortunately, the New Zealanders would prove him wrong.

— *Keith Sinclair*

Brooke of Sarawak

At the height of his fame, Raffles of Singapore was a hero to the young, and few worshipped more ardently than a youthful army officer named James Brooke. Inspired by Raffles' articles on the Far East, Brooke developed an ambitious scheme for a British settlement in Borneo. If the idea had been put forward by anyone else it would have been dismissed as the wild dream of a romantic young madman, but Brooke's absolute conviction of its worth was infectious.

Brooke was a true disciple of Raffles: he believed that commercial prosperity could only be guaranteed by territorial possession; and, like Raffles, he believed that "any government instituted for the purpose must be directed to the advancement of the native interests and the development of native resources."

When he arrived in the northern Borneo province of Sarawak in 1838, Brooke found it in chaos, torn by tribal civil wars. He plunged headlong into the turmoil, emerging three adventuresome years later on top of the heap. In 1841, in a long and elaborate ceremony, he was acclaimed the new Rajah of Sarawak.

The odds were against him in this land of few natural resources, but Brooke refused to be discouraged. He welcomed all commerce from anywhere so long as it did not interfere with the interests of the natives. He issued a code of laws and opened roads and waterways and mounted a vigorous campaign against the pirates infesting the area. It was a peculiar, spectacular life, and the "White Rajah" thrived on it. By the 1850s he had brought peace and a measure of order and prosperity to

his private little empire. Sarawak was still poor—it would never become rich—but it had an economic base upon which to build.

Brooke died in 1868, and was succeeded as Rajah by his nephew, Charles. Charles's rule lasted until 1917, during which time Sarawak became a British protectorate. Then his son took up the reins. The Brooke dynasty only came to an end in 1946, when Sarawak became a Crown possession.

Sarawak was the creation of a romantic egoist. Brooke's achievement was carrying out his declared intentions; his motives were inspired by an overwhelming passion for the Orient and an absolute conviction that he had a mission there. The survival of this principality for more than a hundred years, against all odds, in an area where it could hardly have been expected to last one year, remains one of the remarkable monuments to private enterprise and determination on record.

Chapter Four
BRITISH INDIA

Thomas Hickey portrayed a British District Officer with a cross-section of Indian rulers and merchants. The East India Company depended on such officers to collect revenues and act as administrators.

I. A Clash of Cultures

In Warren Hastings's time, the British in India played the role of a foreign conqueror operating a state that differed only in details from any other Indian state. Hastings's successors, however, made changes that cleared the way for something unique in India: a state in which the inhabitants were ruled not only by men of another race but according to principles from another culture and another experience.

The impeachment of Hastings was not just a question of personal enmities. Concern for the public good in India was also involved. Out of the argument and rhetoric slowly emerged certain broad principles about the relationship between Britain and India. The East India Company must not be permitted to exercise irresponsible dominion in India. It might rule, but its employees must be accountable to Parliament. The machinery for this new relationship between Company and Crown, India and Britain, was established by the India Act of 1784, which had driven Hastings to resign.

The Act created two tiers of supervision. In London the Company's affairs would henceforth be watched over by a minister, the President of the Board of Control, and in Calcutta by a Governor-General whose appointment had to be approved by the British government. To emphasize the Governor-General's special position, he would always be an English nobleman—a species, it was thought, untainted by the need for commercial profit and thus above corruption.

The first Governor-General was Lord Cornwallis, a distinguished soldier whose reputation had even survived capitulation at Yorktown in the American War of Independence. He was a great landowner, close to the Prime Minister, his honesty unassailable by the Company or anyone else. He would not only be Governor-General but also Commander-in-Chief; no one before had wielded so much authority. But Cornwallis was a new type of ruler, courteous and incorruptible. "Here there was no broken fortune to be mended," wrote Henry Dundas, the President of the Board of Control, "here there was no avarice to be gratified, here there was no beggarly mushroom kindred to be provided for, no crew of hungry followers gaping to be gorged."

The first task was to clean out corruption, still flourishing despite all that Hastings had tried to do. Company administrators were traders first and rulers afterwards. Cornwallis insisted that private trade must cease and that civil servants be paid a substantial salary to compensate for what they were giving up. A man could remain a trader, and trade, or he could be an official and content himself with a large salary—but he could not be both.

If Englishmen were corrupt they could be reformed or replaced, but to Cornwallis Indians were untrustworthy in civilian roles, though they had fine qualities as fighting men. "Every native of India, I verily believe, is corrupt," he wrote. Indians were dismissed from all posts calling for a salary of over £500 a year. It was the only way, Cornwallis was convinced. "I think it must be universally admitted, that without a large and well-regulated body of Europeans, our hold on these valuable dominions must be very insecure." Indians of quality were thus deprived of the chance to rise in the Company's service—a matter of deep bitterness in the years to come.

Behind all Cornwallis's reforms was his desire to establish the rule of law rather than the arbitrary law of the ruler. The British, following Indian practice, had made no distinction between the authority that made the law and the authority that enforced it. Even those who collected revenue had judicial powers. Cornwallis put an end to this. It was a revolutionary change, and with his reorganization of the courts of law it gave Indians real protection against arbitrary tyranny.

Yet for all these changes, Cornwallis's India retained the age-old features of Indian society. He adapted British institutions to the Indian scene because there were no other alternatives. He did not want to change Indian society; on the contrary, being a good Whig he believed that government should interfere as little as possible in the lives of the people. What he did was designed to protect the people.

Unfortunately, he failed to understand the system he was dealing with. The British, like the Indian rulers they displaced, depended for their income on revenue from the land. In Bengal land revenue was collected by a hereditary class of men known as *zemindars*—agents of the ruler who paid over to him as little as they could, keeping the surplus for themselves. The *zemindar* was not the owner of land—that was assumed to belong to the ruler. Cornwallis, however, assumed that there must be a landowning class, with rights and duties that could be defined. The *zemindars* were therefore regarded as owning the land. Taxes were fixed, and land could be sold for nonpayment. Soon land began to change hands so often that the rural society and its economy were severely shaken, adding to the

Cornwallis as he looked in 1792, during his tenure as India's Governor-General.

oppressed state of the countryside.

It was not only peasants who had to flee the land. Iron-smelters, too, had gone, and charcoal-burners. In large towns factories closed and many of the markets disappeared.

The weavers that remained effectively became slaves. Their bondage originated with the Company in London, which informed Calcutta how much cloth was required. Weavers who failed to deliver were liable to heavy fines. It was hardly surprising that many left the trade.

Cornwallis was responsible for a great deal of economic devastation. Yet he believed he had created an unaggressive state which ruled Indians for their own good along English lines. Though the implications of what he had done were not understood at the time, he had, by consolidating British power over the administration and over ambitious princes in neighbouring states, laid out the foundations for the creations of the Raj.

When he sailed home in 1795 there was for the first time a definable *British* presence in the country. In the early days there had been little sense of racial superiority; the British were patriotic but inoffensive about it. As the century came to a close however, the atmosphere was changing. New men out from England, with new ideas of superiority and new values, contributed to a segregation of the races and a growing contempt among

the British for the manners and morals of those they ruled. As power and stability were added to wealth, the British began to construct great mansions, churches, and government buildings, designed according to the current European fashions. This alien architecture was one of the first British statements to the people they ruled that a new caste, with its own temples and its own customs, now topped all other castes.

The growing size of the British community in India contributed a great deal to its sense of exclusivity. In this increasingly closed society, with its own code of social behaviour, everyone knew everyone else. There was very little to do, for the cares of office took up only a fraction of a civil servant's time. The British lived with all the luxury and vulgarity of the newly rich back home. Behind the elegant facades of their great houses they aped the social life of England, with elaborate rounds of balls and dinner parties. Fortunes were regularly lost and won at cards. Even a man of modest income (by Calcutta standards) would have 60 servants. An army officer on campaign travelled like a prince, with a cook, a valet, a groom, a barber, and 15 or 20 coolies to carry his supplies of wine and brandy and look after his live chickens and goats.

As a Victorian civil servant later put it, the British in India lived in "splendid sloth and languid debauchery." There was a great deal of outward show. "Great men rode about in stagecoaches, with a dozen servants running before and behind them to bawl out their titles; and little men lounged in palanquins or drove a chariot for which they never intended to pay, drawn by horses which they bullied or cajoled out of the stables of wealthy Indians."

The new British attitude was typified by the "grand design" of Lord Wellesley, the Governor-General who arrived in 1798. His purpose was, quite simply, to create an empire in India before the French did. He brought with him the desperate fear of the French Revolution which had caught hold of the British at home. A lone Frenchman at a native court was the advance guard of some great sub-

version. A letter to some French Governor was an indictment of treason. Every mercenary was a threat. Because of this attitude, Wellesley attacked Tipu, the Tiger of Mysore, and destroyed him, and then turned on the Marathas of southern India, the only other native power that seemed to offer a front for French aggression.

Wellesley was recalled before his grand design was complete and he had fully satisfied his "conscientious conviction that no greater blessing can be conferred on the native inhabitants of India than the extension of the British authority, influence, and power." But his protégés took up the burden, and by 1818 the Marathas had been overwhelmed and anarchy quelled. The British Indian state put in Wellesley's charge in 1798 had covered Bengal and Bihar, with dependencies in Madras and Bombay, and contained about 30 million inhabitants. Now it covered almost the entire subcontinent, an area of more than a million square miles, with a population of an estimated 250 million.

India had not been conquered because of any innate superiority of the British (although it became fashionable for Englishmen to think so), but because of its general political malaise. Anarchy had wasted the resources of the country and dissipated the political energy of its people. Nor had Indian leaders grasped the powerful reasons that drove the British to expand. At first it was argued that Napoleon's threat to British interests fully justified the expansion of power that began under Wellesley. But after Waterloo in 1815 it became obvious that the real motive behind the decision to take India was—and always had been—commercial.

The East India Company's trade had become unprofitable. It had been limited to areas of British influence and had centred mainly on cotton and textiles in the north, saltpetre in Bengal, and spices and indigo elsewhere. When the British took over Bengal, Company profits had to be poured back into the state coffers to carry the heavy costs of administration, for which land revenue alone was not sufficient. The Company's real wealth, which by any reckoning was immense, was dependent on China, where tea was paid for by the notorious trade in Indian opium.

British hegemony in India guaranteed the security of this trade and, since the Company had lost its monopoly when its charter came up for renewal in 1813, promised a welcome boost to its prosperity. But the early excitement of conquest subsided quickly when the British paused to take stock. The complexity of the task before them was daunting.

Indian states were highly individualistic, each bound in its own complex traditions. Only Bengal, once a rich and powerful Mughal province, had as yet felt the full impact of British rule; its people, "the soft Bengalees" whose fate began to plague the English conscience, had not yet recovered from the brutal treatment of the Clive era. Elsewhere the old patterns of Indian life remained relatively undisturbed.

In the north-west was the kingdom of the decadent Nawab of Oudh, whose cruel oppression held his people in a condition of apathetic despair. Mysore, in the centre of the predominantly Muslim south, had been tamed, but was still suspicious and sullenly anti-British. In the centre of the subcontinent, the Nizam of Hyderabad governed a state larger than Spain with the diplomatic tact always needed to remain free within a geographical trap. On its borders and throughout the vast wastes of central India were the remaining fragments of the Maratha Confederacy, whose fighting chiefs had once controlled almost half of India, including the glittering old Mughal capital of Delhi. To the north-west, cut off by deserts, Rajputana existed in its traditional feudal isolation. Farther north, held in check by a peace treaty, lay the kingdom of the Punjab, ruled by the religiously militant Sikhs.

Englishmen could discern only one factor common to the various states, and they were to learn by hard experience that it was the primary factor—the all-pervasive power of religion.

The great majority of Indians were Hindus. The ordinary Englishman had no idea what this meant and what he could glean repulsed him. Polytheistic, unorganized, non-dogmatic, Hinduism was a way of life rather than an institutional religion in the Western sense. It was very ancient—some 3,000 years old—and its cults, customs, and mysteries were so embedded in the hearts of its followers that it had become a life in itself, governing all political, social, and emotional behaviour. Its gods and rituals varied according to area and individual tradition; it was elusive, undefinable, sometimes barbarous, sometimes of striking beauty. Its most powerful characteristic was the caste system. The castes govern—then as

Text Continued on Page 141

Cock-fighting was a favourite diversion of the English in India. This scene of opulent confusion was painted in Lucknow in 1790 by John Zoffany (who included himself, seated at upper right, in the canvas) for former Governor Warren Hastings.

137

Every Hindu's class, trade and li[fe]
style was predetermined by whic[h]
ever of the 3,000 castes grouped [in]
four major divisions he was b[orn]
into. An ancient Hindu hymn cl[aims]
that each division – Brahmins, Ksha[t]
triyas, Vaisyas and Sudras – spra[ng]
from the severed bod[y of] Purus[a,]
the primeval mal[e f]orm o[f the]
Creator, Brahma (below). Altho[u]

An astrologer, a member of the Brahmin or
priest caste, sits cross-legged beside his
books. According to legend, the priesthood
was created to instruct mankind, and
occupy the pinnacle of the caste pyramid.

Merchants, like this grain-seller,
traders and money-lenders made
up the Vaisyas, the third of the
four castes. Brahmins and
Kshattriyas tended to dismiss all
Vaisyas as dishonest and miserly.

OF CASTE

ent research has shown that this
ount was probably a forgery per-
rated by the Brahmin priesthood
enhance its own prestige, it was
en by Hindus as a divine injunc-
n to establish a social system
t was uniquely intricate, rigid
stratified. At best it made for
ial stability; at worst it was a justi-
ation for cruelty and oppression.

Armed with a matchlock, this soldier aptly
represents the Kshattriya, or warrior caste.
Holding a secondary position in the social
hierarchy, the fierce Kshattriyas were, according to Hindu tradition, the defenders of India.

A dark-skinned servant massages the
leg of his higher caste master. Superior
only to the casteless "Untouchables,"
servants formed the fourth
caste group, the Sudras, and
lived in unremitting servitude.

now—the entire fabric of the lives of their adherents, and therefore of most of India. Caste determined each man's social function. Loss of caste, which could be incurred by even unintentional infringements of religious law, meant a fate beyond the comprehension of a Westerner, something deeper and more terrible than any Christian concept of Hell.

Next to Hinduism, the most important religion was that of Islam, which had been brought to India by the Mughals. It was monotheistic, and its god was the all-seeing, all-hearing, all-speaking, all-powerful Allah, who controlled the destinies of all men, and whose Will was to be served in all things by all Muslims.

There were also other religions—Jainism, founded in about 600 B.C., with its concept of a universal law, and Buddhism, which had been almost wiped out in India by the Mughals. There were Parsee followers of the Persian prophet Zoroaster; Sikhism, which began in the Punjab in the 15th Century and evolved as religious militantism; and even Christian and Jewish sects of ancient origin.

The power of religion, a power alien to an Englishman, was most noticeable in the Indians' apparently placid acceptance of whatever condition in which they found themselves. Two-thirds of the total population lived on the land, in communal societies in about half a million villages.

It was a precarious living. The landscape was extreme—great mountain ranges fell away to vast plains that were mostly arid; extravagant tropical growth fringed valleys that were either hot and dusty, or hot and wet. Rainfall was unpredictable, and there were monsoons on which millions depended for water but which were frequently of devastating strength, bringing catastrophe and famine in their wake. The Indians seemed to accept everything as being integral to some divine plan. It was a condition that Englishmen—for want of better words—called "eternal" or "timeless."

The effect had been heightened by the recent warfare and anarchy. The scars were everywhere: dry canals, neglected roads, dead livestock, ruined crops, deserted villages. The countryside seemed without life, its land and its people exhausted. Only in a few cities, mostly ports, was there any sign of former commercial prosperity. The once-great textile industry was in decline, partly because of the country's internal disorder but also because machine-made goods from Lancashire had begun to dominate the English market, squeezing out the goods that had been imported from India, and had even begun to invade the native Indian market.

All this—the political, social, and economic condition of 250 million Indians—was to be re-ordered and ruled by a few hundred Englishmen, most of whom were in their twenties, supported by 13,000 British troops.

There were realists among the young administrators who fully understood the delicacy of the situation. Charles Metcalfe was one. "Our domination in India is by conquest," he wrote. "It is naturally disgusting to the inhabitants and can only be maintained by military force. It is our positive duty to render them justice, protect their rights, and to study their happiness. By the performance of this duty, we may allay and keep dormant their innate disaffection. . . . " But in England it was a time of debate. The intellectual ramifications of the American and French revolutions were still being felt and the thinkers of the age were obsessed with the nature of man and his perfectibility. After 1818 they began to focus their attention on India, on making the subcontinent a political laboratory.

The traditional attitude held that India should be ruled along the lines already established by Cornwallis: law and order should be maintained as a solid basis for secure trade, but there should be no radical interference in the social and religious institutions and customs of Indians. To interfere would be to tap a volcano. But there were many men of influence in England who believed that this 18th-Century attitude, devoted as it was to outdated commercial interests, was no longer feasible in the age of the Industrial Revolution, and was in fact even immoral.

The first challenge came from the Evangelical Revival. Its members included powerful figures such as William Wilberforce, the campaigner against slavery, and Charles Grant, chairman of the Company directors. They believed that Indian society was fundamentally wicked and they proposed it be totally Anglicized by means of Christian education. They considered Indian religions to be "one grand abomination," the reason the Indians were "a race of men lamentably base and degenerate." The intentions of the Evangelicals were defined by Wilberforce as "the gradual introduction and establishment of our own principles and opinions; of our laws, institutions, and manners; above all, as the source of every other improvement, of our religion, and consequently of our morals."

On an altogether different level were those who believed that the highest social ideal, the answer to all society's ills, was to achieve the greatest happiness for the greatest number of people. This philosophy, known as "Utilitarianism," attempted to judge every social measure by its "utility" or the degree to which it tended to increase happiness. Its main exponent, Jeremy Bentham, defined happiness only in terms of a lack of hardship. It was a shallow philosophy, but it did provide a useful yardstick in making a practical start to the removal of patent injustices—as one of Bentham's followers, Lord William Bentinck, was to show when he became Governor-General of India in 1828.

Like the Evangelicals, the Utilitarians were convinced of the natural superiority of the West and were contemptuous of Indian customs and culture. But they attributed the sins of the country not to its religions but to the greatest of India's hardships—the inhuman poverty in which the majority of its inhabitants lived. James Mill, a senior official in the East India Company, wrote that poverty was "the effect of bad laws and bad government; and is never characteristic of any people who are governed well." He believed that once the poverty of India was relieved, Indians would begin to tread the path of Western reason and enlightenment.

At a Hindu wedding ceremony the bridegroom, resplendent in exotic headgear and luxurious clothes, frequently eclipsed his heavily veiled bride.

Metcalfe of Delhi

The British had seized India by the sword and ruled it for their own gain, but by the early 19th Century the tide of public opinion had turned against so expensive and degrading a system. Many of the East India Company's officials were eager to give their military and economic dominance a moral, even religious justification. And so a new breed of men came out to India. Some of them were startlingly liberal in outlook and some paternalistic and authoritarian, but they were all linked by one common denominator—an unprecedented dedication to the task of honest administration and reform.

One of the most enlightened was Sir Charles Metcalfe. Ten years after joining the East India Company as a clerk in 1801 he became Resident of Delhi, and astounded his contemporaries by introducing a revolutionary humanitarian penal code. At a time when a thief in England would be hanged for stealing five shillings, Metcalfe abolished all forms of capital punishment and outlawed flogging. He banned both suttee and slavery. On one occasion he impounded all the spears and swords he could find, beat them into plough-shares and pruning-hooks in the best Biblical tradition, and returned them to their astonished owners. He climaxed his Indian career in the mid-1830s with a one-year spell as Acting Governor-General.

Metcalfe went on to serve stints as Governor of Jamaica and then Canada, whose problems, including agitation for self-government, he found a world away from what he had faced in India.

Therein lay the best—and only—security for British interests. Mill's ideas were contained in three great projects for humanitarian (but decidedly authoritarian) reform— a new method of revenue assessment, codification of the law, and the creation of a strong central government responsible for the whole country.

A third group was in a position to bring about direct changes in India. It was composed of men who had been active participants in the British rise to power and who now held important positions in the administration: Thomas Munro, leader of the group, Charles Metcalfe, Mountstuart Elphinstone, and John Malcolm.

The Munro school had great sympathy for the Indians and their culture. It subscribed to the "noble savage" philosophy, which asserted that man's innate goodness, corrupted by society, was still to be found in primitive communities. It sounded a romantic view, yet these four were by no means dreamers; they were experienced and practical administrators who foresaw the dangers of radical change. "The ruling vice of our Government is innovation," Munro believed.

Munro also believed strongly in the involvement of the administration with the people, rather than the simple dictation to them of British principles (of which principles he nevertheless steadfastly approved). He wanted to close the gap between the rulers and the ruled, and he despised fellow countrymen who maintained that Indians were too corrupt to take part in government. "Foreign conquerors have treated the natives with violence and often with great cruelty, but none has treated them with so much scorn as we, none has stigmatized the whole people as unworthy of trust."

He achieved a considerable victory over conservative opinion when, as Governor of Madras, he condemned the Cornwallis revenue system and forced recognition of his own methods. By raising the *zamindars* to landlord status, Cornwallis had dispossessed the peasants of their ancient hereditary rights to the land they cultivated. In Munro's system, the peasant dealt directly with the government and acquired his own proprietary rights to land, and the tax collector regained his former police powers. It was a halfway return to tradition, and it was adopted by the Munro school wherever possible.

But the Utilitarians and Evangelicals were closer than the "romantic" administrators to the seat of power in London, and in 1828 their efforts were rewarded when Lord Bentinck was sent to India as Governor-General. His mandate for reform was a concentrated amalgam of their radical ideals.

Bentinck began with a frontal attack on the social evils of India. This he did in the name of "universal moral law" (that is, British moral law), and it won the unqualified approval of the British public, whose imagination was captured by the exotic details of the campaign. British rule in India now openly took on the character of a moral crusade as its former essentially commercial nature was lost to public view.

Social evils certainly existed in India. One of the worst of these was the custom of killing girl babies to avoid eventual prohibitive marriage settlements. It was a custom of great antiquity practised by "primitive" tribes and some Rajput castes. Rajputs sometimes sold their female children, but in doing so they forever lost their caste. Killing was therefore thought more desirable, and since women were anyway considered to be property, useful or not, it was viewed as a practical convenience.

In Bengal in 1795 the British had declared the practice to be murder and banned it. But it was difficult to enforce this since it meant policing the most private domains of the Indians. Persistent endeavours of British administrators during Bentinck's rule brought the practice under control, but it was a slow process. As late as 1870 the government had to pass another act to ensure that all births were registered and to check that female children remained alive.

Suttee, the self-immolation of widows, was equally offensive to the "universal moral law." Again, it was an extremely ancient custom, practised mainly by higher castes among Hindus. In theory, it was a voluntary act in which a widow

At a Muslim burial it was customary for the shrouded corpse to be borne to the grave on a special litter (foreground). At right is a cemetery caretaker.

elected to join her husband in death by throwing herself on his funeral pyre. The suttee (from *sati*, meaning "virtuous one") was enacted in the ecstatic atmosphere of a religious festival. There had been legendarily spectacular suttees: a Sikh prince had been accompanied in death by ten wives and 300 concubines, and a Rajah of Marwar had been followed in flames by his 64 wives. But even the ordinary village suttee carried great prestige for the family concerned if it was well arranged and executed. It was not only a matter of prestige: a suttee left the dead man's relatives free to divide his property without the interfering claims of a widow.

The practice may originally have been an act of suicide, but with time

it began to verge on murder. An 1818 British report noted, "There are very many reasons for thinking that such an event as a voluntary suttee rarely occurs. The people will not be disappointed of their show; and the entire population of the village will turn out to assist in dragging [the widow] to the bank of the river, and in keeping her on the pile."

Muslims found the practice repulsive, and Mughal rulers had tried to forbid it. A compromise measure was taken in 1812, when suttee became legal only in cases where the act was voluntary and the victim was over 16 years of age and not pregnant. The suttees then came under the supervision of the police.

But the presence of police only gave

the impression of government approval, and the number of suttees increased: 839 cases were reported in Bengal in 1818, more than double the figure for 30 years earlier. Hindus let it be known they would react violently to a complete abolition of suttee. But the pressure in England for abolition was enormous and Bentinck had to risk the consequences. Suttee was declared illegal in 1829. Surprisingly, there was no immediate Indian reaction.

Bentinck's next act of reform not only did not meet with any hostility, it was actually welcomed. This was the move to suppress Thuggee. The Thugs were robber bands who roamed central and northern India and practised ritual murder by strangling their arbitrarily chosen victims with scarves. According to legend, they had been given divine sanction to kill by the goddess Kali, providing they used a strip of cloth and shed no blood. The destruction of life was the prime motive, the profits from robbery the recompense. Although Bentinck ordered the supression of Thuggee in 1829, 20 years would pass before the menace was ended.

One other social problem in India, insidiously more evil than the rest, attracted much less public attention and became therefore more difficult to eradicate. From the beginning there were British administrators who deplored the Indian slave traffic, but they had always been balked at any solution.

Cornwallis tried to limit the traffic by preventing the export of slaves overseas and to parts of India not under British control. But the government was unwilling to take any really drastic action for fear of jeopardizing its relationship with the powerful slave-traders. When Charles Metcalfe banned the resale of slaves in Delhi, he was severely censured for his interference. The government considered his measure one that "his Lordship in Council was not prepared to sanction." Bentinck approached the problem with extreme caution, and he managed to halt the flow of traffic to some degree by stopping the sale of slaves between individual districts. The Charter Act of 1833 stipulated that he

A band of Thugs strangles a traveller in northern India, depicted in a contemporaneous water-colour. It has been estimated that this practice of ritualistic murder claimed perhaps two million victims during the first two centuries of British rule.

was to abolish slavery altogether—when it proved feasible to do so. But apparently it never did. Slavery continued as before and did not become completely illegal until the Crown assumed power in India in 1858.

Bentinck was satisfied that he had cauterized two of the great social cankers of India, and had brought two others under control—and the volcano had not stirred. But a shockwave had been felt. Although the reforms hardly touched Muslims, and only certain castes of Hindus in restricted areas, and at least one reform—the suppression of Thuggee—had been widely popular, they nevertheless produced an over-all effect by establishing the authoritarian presence and power of a Western God.

The authority of British rule was described by a Frenchman, Victor Jacquement, who travelled across India in the 1830s. So impressed was Jacquement with its benefits that he could not understand those who wished to educate Indians: "Some officials say openly that English supremacy in Asia cannot be eternal, and that it is their duty to humanity to prepare India to govern herself by raising the moral and intellectual capacity of its inhabitants. . . . If I thought that the foundation of English schools would hasten the fall of English power, I would certainly close these schools, for . . . no national government would secure them the benefits which they owe to the British government."

But few thought that far ahead. General education in English was, as Bentinck said, to be a "panacea for the regeneration of India."

Indian education had become fossilized. Higher education for Hindus was almost exclusively the privilege of Brahmins, the priestly caste. It was conducted in Sanskrit, a dead language, and was concerned entirely with the study of religious texts. Muslim education was, in theory, available to all Muslims, but it too was conducted in a language (Arabic) not spoken in India, and it was equally esoteric in content. Schools were dependent entirely on communities and individual rulers for the funds they received.

The Charter Act of 1813 had set aside an annual sum of £10,000 for the education of the "Natives of India," but the government had not dictated a policy. Nevertheless, schools teaching Western subjects in English had sprung up, vigorously supported by zealous missionaries determined to convert the Indians via Christian education away from "the degrading and polluting worship of idols." A Committee of Public Instruction was formed in 1823 to shape a policy, and at first it favoured the preservation of Oriental learning. Bentinck lost no time in altering the Committee's course. His arguments in favour of Western education carried the powerful backing of the Evangelical and Utilitarian groups in England, and he found additional support in Ram Mohun Roy, a Bengali reformer who pleaded that Indians be allowed to study "mathematics, natural philosophy, chemistry, anatomy, and other useful sciences, which the natives of Europe have carried to a degree of perfection that has raised them above the inhabitants of other parts of the world."

In 1835 English was made the language of education. The historic resolution stated: "The great object of the British Government ought to be the promotion of European literature and science among the natives of India. . . . "

The first impact of Western science on Indian education was felt in the foundation of the Calcutta Medical College, which sought to correct the disastrous state of public health caused by the decline of the ancient, rigid, superstition-ridden Muslim and Hindu medical systems. A fuller impact came later when Indians trained in Western technology began to construct and administer canals, roads, and railways.

It was also during Bentinck's rule that the Law Commission was formed, headed by the poet-historian-politician Thomas Babington Macaulay. The Law Commission was set up in order to find a uniform legal code, the elusive dream of all British administrators in India.

Under Warren Hastings, district courts—Company institutions—were set up in order to retain the continuity of the Indian system. They were presided over by British judge-magistrates who relied entirely on Indian law officers for interpretation of the questions at hand. These courts were subject in authority to a Supreme Court first set up in Calcutta and later in Madras and Bombay which administered a dual system of British law for the British and customary law based on custom for their Indian subjects.

In the district courts—greatly increased in number by Cornwallis—the "quill-driving lawyers" were successful in correcting many injustices. Cornwallis had modified the Muslim criminal code, and with certain barbarous aspects pruned, it became more humane than that of England. But it was still all very unsatisfactory: there were language barriers, questions of procedure, and the "absurdity and darkness" of the ancient texts.

The courts were too remote and too expensive to have an immediate impact on the Indian masses, and so the subdued chaos in which they existed was allowed to drift—for want of a solution—until Macaulay's Law Commission had formulated a uniform legal code. Incredibly, it took the Commission 30 years to evolve its system of "universal principles." The chaotic procedures that grew up under Hastings and Cornwallis in the late 18th Century remained in practice until 1861. Of all Bentinck's important reforms, the uniform legal code thus took the longest to make its full effects felt.

Bentinck left India in 1835, and with him went the rush to reform. For a decade it was possible to stand back and measure the extraordinary change the British adventure had brought to Indian life.

The material nature of the change was felt most acutely in trade and industry. Until the 1813 Charter Act the East India Company's trading monopoly guaranteed a certain degree of stability. But the Charter Act threw India open to private British enterprise. The result was a sharp decline in Indian industry which depended largely on the export of its textiles. The

The Marquess of Dalhousie, the highly active Governor-General of India, sets a fast pace for his retinue entering Cawnpore in 1852, as sketched by G. F. Atkinson.

goods of the Industrial Revolution came to India, but the Revolution stayed at home.

Many Indians might have looked to the land for an alternative living, but there too the old patterns had disappeared. Because of the continual change of ownership and the competition in growing exotic commercial crops, more land was under cultivation but the peasant derived no benefit from it. The cultivation of commercial crops—opium above all, as well as indigo, jute, and (later) tea—was almost exclusively under the control of Europeans, and the cultivation of indigenous staple crops such as rice and wheat was run by absentee landlords.

Socially, a new Indian middle class had emerged. Some of its members had grown rich by trading with the merchants of continental Europe and America, or by trading in the Indian interior, an area made inaccessible to private British merchants by Company prohibitions. Others had turned to land speculation. They were quick to see that the technological innovations of the British in communications and transport were of great future ad-

vantage to India, and they actively encouraged progress. From them Bentinck drew his recruits for a new-style administration, and they were the first to take hold of the opportunities for Western education and to supply India with a new force of doctors and teachers. They also worked to regenerate the flagging Indian cultural life.

The rise of this new middle class coincided with the arrival in India of the Marquess of Dalhousie, which in 1848 put an abrupt end to the period of tranquillity that had followed Bentinck's departure.

The new Governor-General was the complete reformer, utterly convinced of the superiority of the West in all things. He precipitated a new process of innovation at a time when the people of India had only just begun to gauge the consequences of the reforms of his predecessors. He began the Indian railway system, introduced the telegraph, and pushed the reforms in education to their maximum limit. But his career was capped by a dazzling display of the old imperialism: he annexed eight states in as many years, including the Punjab. Incapable

of believing that Hindus could administer their own states, he put into effect the "doctrine of lapse" which allowed the British to take over states from Hindu princes who had no natural heirs, thus refusing to recognize the Hindu custom of adoption.

The Indian upper classes and the new middle class viewed this situation with growing alarm. They had been slow to grasp the essentially dynamic quality of British rule; it took time to see that the Bentinck regime had gradually undermined some of the most fundamental Indian traditions. But now they understood immediately that Dalhousie was intent on cutting out of India the last vestiges of Indian independence.

Conservatives and traditionalists—and those who would later be labelled Nationalists—began to see the British-Indian relationship in a different light. It had always looked absurd: the great mass of India held by a few pockets of a doll-like British society that was an arrogant reconstruction of England, composed of a handful of civil servants and a few thousand soldiers and their families claustrophobically bound together by anachronistic customs and imported prejudices. Now these isolated groups of "little Englands" began to look monstrous: greedy, racist, ruthless. It was natural that the innovations and inventions of such people should be considered evil. The telegraph, the railways, and the roads were a means of destroying ancient communal life; technological advances in factories were a threat to caste; changes of occupation necessary for survival often meant the eternally damning loss of caste; above all, education in Western principles was considered to be a deliberate corruption of the minds of the young, an attempt to sow seeds of doubt and contempt for traditional authority in the hearts of the country's future leaders.

Everywhere an Indian looked he could see rents in the social, economic, and political fabric of his life. It was clear that the social reforms introduced by the British, and carried out with complete disregard for Indian feeling, had been made not for the future improvement of the Indians' welfare but because Indian customs offended British morality. It was equally clear that the economic reforms had been designed to make Englishmen richer and Indians poorer.

Emerging prophets of nationalism found many eager, fervent supporters. The first important figures were modernizers—Henry Derozio and Ram Mohun Roy.

Derozio was a Portuguese-Indian who had been brought up a Christian. At the age of 17 he joined the Hindu College as a teacher and later became assistant headmaster. In five brief years he exercised an enormous influence over his middle-class pupils. He taught them the radical, sceptical, scientific thought of the West, and his group of young followers, known as "Young Bengal," grew up free-thinking and almost totally Western in outlook, attacking everything in Hinduism that struck them as irrational. It was a staggering legacy for a man who died at the age of 21.

Ram Mohun Roy also favoured Westernization—but not at a cost to Hinduism. A brilliant and prolific writer in Persian, English, and Bengali, he believed that India could and should benefit greatly from Western liberal ideals and Western technology, but he saw no reason for India to renounce her true nature for Western social ideology. He was primarily concerned with reforming Hinduism: he wanted to restore its purity, to break with the elaborate, ritualistic worship of many gods and return instead to the worship of the "Formless True God" of the ancient Hindu texts. This, he hoped, would give back to the Hindu his sense of identity and pride.

Neither Derozio nor Roy had much appeal for the conservative classes who sought an immediate—and anti-Western—solution (although the ideas of both became very important later on in the common fight to get the British out of India). Derozio's ideas seemed too radical, long-ranging, and impractical. Ram Mohun's tightrope ideology offended the traditionalists, since it required drastic reinterpretation of Hindu scripture.

Although there was no single ideology that commanded widespread attention, organized groups with distinctly nationalist feelings began to appear on the Bengal political scene. The most important was the British Indian Association, formed in 1851 to protest against discrimination in law and to establish claims when the East India Company's charter came due for renewal in 1853. Strictly an upper-class organization, it mainly strove for the right to commercial equality and the readmittance of the Indian upper classes into the administration of the country. But on a broader scale the Association spoke for India as a whole. "The British Government," a speaker told the Bombay branch in 1852, "professes to educate the Natives to an equality with Europeans, an object worthy of the age and of Britain. But if Englishmen after educating the Natives to be their equals continue to treat them as their inferiors—if they deny the stimulus of honourable ambition—are they not in effect undoing all they have done, unteaching the Native all that he has been taught, and pursuing a suicidal policy, which will inevitably array all the talent, honour, and intelligence of the country ultimately in irreconcilable hostility to the ruling power?"

It was indeed a suicidal policy.

These ideas reflected the amorphous sense of discontent, puzzlement, and despair of the Indian masses. Support was widespread, and it included the intellectual youth of India who, disillusioned and frustrated by British discrimination and obstinacy, increasingly turned away from pro-Western ideals towards a fiercely proud sense of identity as Indians. (Or rather, as Hindus. Muslims remained comparatively aloof and disinterested in the Westernization trauma.)

By the mid-1850s India was riven with tensions and geared for change. But a change for what? What would come after? What would be lost? Indians felt desperately insecure. It was an explosive situation in which only the smallest spark was needed to ignite the flame of hostility.

— *Michael Edwardes, Barry Pree*

II. Warfare on India's Borders

In the early years of the 19th Century, with India in its increasingly firm grasp, the East India Company began to cast anxious glances at its neighbours. The most immediate threat seemed to come from the east, where Burma, truculent and expansionist, appeared entirely capable of devouring the Bengalese nerve-centre of Anglo-India.

Burma was a highly organized state, the most powerful monarchy in South-East Asia. It had 20 centuries of tradition behind it, a written language rich in ancient literature, and a firmly established Buddhist religion. Against this ancient country the British deployed the technological wonders of 19th-Century warfare.

Although it was the conquests of Arakan and Assam in the late 18th Century that brought Burma to the borders of India and thus face to face with the British Empire, relations between the two powers had been brittle from the time of their first contacts, two centuries earlier. The first Englishman to visit Burma was Ralph Fitch, who arrived in Pegu (Lower Burma) in 1587. Rangoon was then a mere fishing village, but the Shwe Dagon pagoda, the country's greatest Buddhist temple, "all gilded from the foote to the toppe," impressed Fitch as "of a wonderful bignesse" and "the fairest place. . . that is in the world." His tales of the country's own riches and the caravans that brought from China "great store of mastic [a resin used for varnish], gold, silver, and many other things of China work" began to awaken British commerical interest. However, it was not until 1619 that the East India Company established trading stations and started to deal in Burmese tung oil, timber, and ivory.

In 1755 the ruler of Ava (Upper Burma) named Alaungpaya overthrew the Pegu dynasty in the south, which had long ruled the country, and laid the foundations of modern Burma. He considered himself "the Lord of Earth and Air," answerable to none, free to make and break agreements at will—an attitude which made for a relationship of bewildering unpredictability.

A Captain Baker immediately took Alaungpaya gifts of gunpowder, a few muskets, a gilt looking-glass, and some lavender water, and offered him British support. It was refused. Yet two years after this rebuff, in 1757, Alaungpaya reopened the discussion with a letter addressed to George II written on gold leaf studded with rubies and containing an invitation to his court. To the English representative who came in response he gave 24 ears of maize, 18 oranges, five cucumbers, and two grants of land for trading factories. Two years later the British merchants at one of these stations were sitting down to breakfast with the local Burmese Governor when at a signal a band of soldiers rushed into the room. They killed the eight Englishmen present and more than 100 of the Indian employees who manned the station.

Alaungpaya's justification for this outrage was that he had discovered the British were conspiring to overthrow him. When he died in 1760, his successor again invited British traders into Burma. Once more the traders came in, but they continued to complain of harassment. Increasingly Burmese and British interests were coming into conflict.

In 1795, as Burma consolidated her hold on Arakan and Assam, 5,000 Burmese troops invaded British territory in pursuit of Arakanese rebels who had taken refuge there. The Governor-General, Sir John Shore, meekly surrendered the fugitives. In the years that followed there were repeated crises over fugitives, smuggling, and boundaries. The flashpoint came when a king named Bagyidaw ascended to the throne of Ava in 1819.

A low, flat, almost worthless island called Shapuree, in the mouth of the river that separated Burmese territory from that of the Company, became the testing ground for conflicting claims. In 1823 Bagyidaw, claiming that the island had been his property since time immemorial, sent a thousand soldiers to evict the 12 Company sepoys who occupied it. The Burmese soon evacuated the island and the British moved back in, only to leave again, driven away by sleeping sickness.

The fact that nobody actually wanted to stay on Shapuree made no difference. When Lord Amherst, the new Governor-General, made a conciliatory move, the Burmese threatened to invade Bengal. When the Burmese were in a mood to make the island neutral ground, the British refused. Finally, on March 5, 1824, Amherst declared war on Burma.

The news of so remote a conflict was barely noticed at home. In India, however, British soldiers were thrilled. "Never shall I forget the shouts of joy with which we welcomed the intelligence of a war with the Burmese," wrote Ensign F. B. Doveton. "Here would be glory for a young soldier," perhaps even an opportunity to sustain "a flesh wound, in *the easiest possible manner.*"

The Burmese were hardly more realistic. Their commander, Maha Bandula, included in his expeditionary baggage a pair of golden fetters with which to secure Governor-General Amherst when he captured him.

Bandula at first seemed on the verge of making good his promise. His army of 60,000 crossed the Bengalese border and at Ramu, in May, 1824, almost annihilated a smaller British force. Dread and terror spread among the merchants of Calcutta.

Bandula's army soon turned round and marched back into Burma, however, and for a very good reason—Lower Burma had been invaded by the British. Lord Amherst had wisely seen that the Company should not fight in the difficult hill-country of the border areas, but should strike at the heart of Burma, the Irrawaddy River Valley. On May 10, 1824, Sir Archibald Campbell with 11,000 British and sepoy soldiers arrived off Rangoon in a fleet of warships. The next day the troops went ashore, found the city abandoned, and went on a rampage.

The British bivouacked in and around Burma's holiest shrine, the Shwe Dagon pagoda, raising their flag on its lofty, guilded spire. The Burmese, meanwhile, hastily threw up a ring of bamboo forts to hem in the invader. "Stockades sprang up like mushrooms in every direction," wrote Ensign Doveton, "so that, look which way we would, there was ever a pleasing variety from which to pick and choose whenever our general wished to relieve the monotony of the cantonment by the excitement of a sortie."

Not all of these sorties were cause for celebration. When the British moved on the biggest stockade, Kemmendine, defended by 20,000 Burmese, their combined naval and ground attack collapsed ignominiously. The troops reached the stockade's high walls only to discover they had left their scaling ladders behind. During their retreat they suffered battering fire both from their own ships in the river and from their reserve units to the rear, who thought they were the enemy trying to break through. A week later they tried again—this time remembering their ladders—and were victorious.

Defects in planning soon showed up. Campbell had brought neither fresh food nor transport, hoping to find both on arrival. He did not. For the next six months, pelted by monsoon rains in the Irrawaddy Delta, the force was unable to advance upriver toward Ava, the Burmese capital. During the enforced wait malaria and dysentery took a heavy toll. Most of the force went down to the coast where they spent their time conquering Burma's maritime provinces.

While all this was happening, Maha Bandula, far to the north, undertook an epic march. Having heard of the landing at Rangoon, he turned his 60,000 soldiers from Bengal and drove them over the hills of Arakan, a difficult route at the best of times. He did it during the rains, when flooding streams, leeches, and malaria-bearing mosquitoes turned the jungle into a waterlogged nightmare.

Under the protecting guns of the Royal Navy, British regulars launch an amphibious assault on Rangoon in 1824, during the First Burmese War. The troops discovered their ungainly helmets and tight coats to be quite unsuited to warfare in tropical Burma.

By November, 1824, when the rainy season ended, Bandula was threatening the British at Rangoon. Campbell's men may have genuinely welcomed action as an alternative to the punishment of the climate. In six months, 1,200 Europeans and many Indians had died, mainly from disease.

On the night of November 30 the British, now defending Kemmendine, saw the sky up-river begin to glow. Soon a fleet of 100-foot-long fire rafts appeared, floating towards the British ships. "The scene before us was a grand and imposing spectacle; the whole jungle was illuminated, the Golden Pagoda at Rangoon, and everything around us, was as clearly discernible as at noonday," wrote a British officer. Behind the fire rafts,

which British sailors were busily fending off, swarmed boatloads of Burmese warriors. They were joined by others from the jungle in an attack on Kemmendine, but the outnumbered British repulsed them.

On December 3 Bandula failed to take Kemmendine again, and the following day he was repulsed once more. His troops now lay in a wide semicircle round Rangoon.

To convince the enemy that he had either pulled out or lost heart, Campbell ordered his men to keep out of sight and had the artillery reduce its rate of fire to a few desultory rounds a day. Thus Bandula was completely taken by surprise when 1,500 British troops sprang out of their trenches on December 7 and charged. It was a rout.

Campbell estimated that 5,000 Burmese were killed or wounded that day. Bandula managed to rally 20,000 men farther up the Irrawaddy, behind what Sir Archibald called "the most formidable, intrenched, and stockaded works I ever saw," but they were soon dislodged by a British force of only 1,300 men assisted in equal parts by superior artillery and unquestionably magnificent courage.

Campbell continued the pursuit, marching with 2,500 men by land and sending another 1,300 in riverboats. He caught up with Bandula at the village of Danubyu, 50 miles upstream. The British began their attack with an all-night artillery, mortar, and rocket barrage on April 1, 1825. They were still in their trenches the next day when it was learned the enemy had evacuated their stockade. Bandula, while in conference with some of his officers, had been killed by a mortar shell. Although his brother tried to assume command, the death of their great general was too demoralizing for the Burmese soldiers. They fled.

Campbell advanced up the river to Prome, but could not continue to Ava because the rains came again. Meanwhile, British forces had been making progress elsewhere in the large country. They conquered Assam in January, 1825, and by the end of April, Arakan was under their control. The Burmese hastily accepted a one-month armistice to discuss a treaty, but rejected British terms. Fighting would resume when the rains ended.

At Prome the Burmese tried the same tactics they had used at Rangoon, building stockades round the British position. In December, 1825, Campbell's men struck at these forts, clearing out stockade after stockade, until the enemy again sued for peace.

They balked at the British demand that they surrender much of their territory. "The question is not how much you will cede to us," a general on Campbell's staff remarked gravely, "but how much we shall return to you." A draft treaty was signed on January 3, 1826, and the Burmese were given until January 18 to have it approved.

When that date passed with no ratification, Campbell resumed his march. He was 45 miles from Ava, at a town called Yandabo, when two European missionaries, who had been released from a Burmese prison for the purpose, arrived with a treaty and £250,000 in gold and silver as a down payment on the indemnity demanded by the British.

Under the Treaty of Yandabo, which ended the First Anglo-Burmese War, the English got the provinces of Assam, Arakan, and Manipur, all bordering on Bengal, and Tenasserim, a long tongue of land extending south into the Malay Peninsula. In addition, Ava promised to accept a British resident and pay an indemnity of £1,000,000.

The war had cost Great Britain about £13,000,000. Forty thousand men had been employed in it, of whom 15,000 died, mainly from disease. The British left Rangoon when the second instalment of the indemnity was paid in 1827, a move that enabled the Burmese King to save face. He let it be known that the exhausted English had begged for peace, but since they did not have enough money to leave he had magnanimously paid their fares home.

For the next two decades or so, Anglo-Burmese relations were peaceful but increasingly strained. The Burmese remained as proud and uncooperative as ever, much to the dismay of the British resident at the court of Ava. At Rangoon local officials considered English merchants a source of supplementary income to be extracted by any available means.

In 1851 the Burmese Governor of Rangoon falsely charged the masters of two British vessels with murder and made them pay £920 for their

The storming of Rangoon's beautiful Shwe Dagon pagoda assured victory in the Second Burmese War. Astonished British troops found the pagoda covered in pure gold.

freedom. They asked the government of India for compensation. It was over this amount that the Second Anglo-Burmese War began. Lord Dalhousie, the aggressive Indian Governor-General, had just polished off a successful war with the Sikhs and had troops to spare. He decided that the Burmese must be brought to heel.

Seldom has a war grown out of a more inconsequential "incident." Commodore Lambert, whom Dalhousie sent to investigate the case of the two sea captains, was by the Governor-General's own admission a "combustible" sort. Early in 1852 Lambert seized a vessel belonging to the King of Ava, claiming he was "obliged" to do so "in consequence of the insults offered by the Governor of Rangoon." He was referring to the fact that a British delegation, calling unannounced on the official, were turned away because the man was asleep.

The Rangoon Governor tried to open negotiations. Lambert said he would receive him on his frigate. The Governor suggested Lambert should come to him. Lambert refused. The Governor said that if the British attempted to take away the King's ship, he would have to fight. Lambert replied that if so much as a pistol was fired he would level the riverside forts of Rangoon.

And that was what happened. Two ships, *Hermes* and *Fox,* started downriver with the Burmese vessel in tow. Shots were fired from the shore and the two ships answered with devastating effect. Lambert wrote to his headquarters, "I am confident the Government of India will see it was unavoidable and necessary to vindicate the honour of the British flag."

When he got word the next day that the Governor was ready to comply with all British demands, Lambert did not bother answering. It would be war.

Dalhousie admitted that his emissary had acted "in disobedience of his orders," but once fighting had begun he fell back on the familiar need to assert the Company's authority. "We can't afford," he said, "to be shown to the door anywhere in the East." Not ready for a full-scale campaign, he stalled by sending the Burmese King an insulting ultimatum in which the compensation demanded was raised from £920 to £100,000. On April 1, 1852, he declared war on Burma.

General Sir Henry Godwin, with about 8,000 men, easily took Rangoon's chief fort after a furious cannonading. When the British ships opened fire on Rangoon the next day, some Burmese soldiers tried to escape the bombardment by jumping into the river—"as if resolved," wrote an English officer, "on becoming targets for practice."

On April 14 Godwin's men swept some 20,000 Burmese from their main redoubt, the Shwe Dagon pagoda, and the enemy continued to provide entertainment for the British. Recalling the scene, Colonel William F. B. Laurie wrote: "It was amusing to see them chevied through the bushes, across the plain where the artillery was drawn up, by the European soldiers. Crack! crack! crack!—away they ran, as if a legion of evil spirits were after them." Naval guns did "fearful execution" to Rangoon.

By June almost the whole province of Lower Burma was occupied. "But the beasts don't give in," groused Dalhousie. "There is no symptom of submission and I now give up all hope of it." Prome fell to the invaders in October but still, Dalhousie complained, the Burmese would not recognize "their actual inferiority to the British power." The Burmese simply refused to answer the peace proposals, which entailed cession of Lower Burma.

Patience at an end, Dalhousie annexed Lower Burma on December 20, 1852, by simply proclaiming it was "henceforth a portion of the British Territories in the East," and told its people to "submit to the authority of the British Government . . . whose rule was marked by justice and beneficence."

The Times, which was wont to pass judgment on wars in those days the way a theatre critic might now review plays, pronounced the Second Anglo-Burmese War "generally inglorious." One report put British dead at about 3,000. It had cost £1,000,000, more than a thousand times the amount of the claim which began it. By cutting off Burma from the sea the war markedly reduced that nation's ability to challenge British supremacy in South-East Asia, or even to sustain its own independence—which, economically speaking, was being rapidly eroded by the influx of British goods from India.

Despite some guerrilla resistance, Lower Burma was soon organized as a province of India. On the grounds that the Burmese were unreliable, uneducated, and lazy—though their patronizing critics never failed to credit them for being "good-humoured"—the new British overlords imported Sikhs for policemen, Bengali clerks for the lower ranks of the civil service, and Madras coolies for labourers. Lower Burma was turned into British Burma.

While the eastern border of Bengal was being secured against the troublesome Burmese, fear grew in London and Calcutta that another—and far greater—threat was approaching India's North-West Frontier. This menace was the Russian Empire.

By hindsight such fears seem fantastic. Although in the early 19th Century Russia was advancing southward in central Asia, and although some Russian generals may have dreamed of conquering India one day, they were a long way off—some 2,000 miles, and in between lay the inhospitable terrain occupied by the independent kingdoms of Afghanistan and the Punjab.

The fear of Russia grew slowly at first. In the early years of the century the view of sensible military strategists prevailed that, if the threat ever developed, it could best be met on the plains of northern India, near well-established bases, rather than in the wilds of central Asia.

This view was undermined when in 1826 Russia successfully attacked Persia and supplanted Britain as the dominant influence in that country.

After his victory over the Persians, the Russian commander spoke openly of a coming war with England. In London Lord Ellenborough, the minister responsible for the affairs of British India, believed that Russian forces could one day use Afghanistan as a base for an advance into India. He assumed, however, that the Russians would first seek to establish influence with the ruler of Afghanistan and infiltrate the country. So Ellenborough reasoned that the situation in Afghanistan should be closely watched, especially as after almost 20 years of anarchy a new ruler, Dost Muhammad, seemed about to bring peace to the country.

Over the next several years the British watched Dost Muhammad secure the Afghan throne. He seemed to have little to fear from the man he displaced, the inept and dispirited Shah Shuja, who huddled under the protective wing of the Sikh ruler of neighbouring Punjab and hatched flimsy plots to regain power. Then, in 1834, the situation took a different turn when a new ruler succeeded to the throne of Persia.

His ambitions were enlarged by his Russian advisers. In particular, he was encouraged to occupy the town of Herat on the western border of Afghanistan. This was to be the prelude, it was said, to the conquest of other Afghan towns. Naturally, the news was not well received in London, and the British minister at the Persian court was instructed "especially to warn the Persian government against allowing themselves to be pushed on to make war against the Afghans." The Persian reaction of polite indifference added to the sense of unease in London. The Foreign Minister, Lord Palmerston, carefully briefed the new Governor-General, Lord Auckland, before his departure for India. It was clear that great events of some kind were taking place in central Asia and it would be wise for the government of India to know more about them. Officials were instructed to

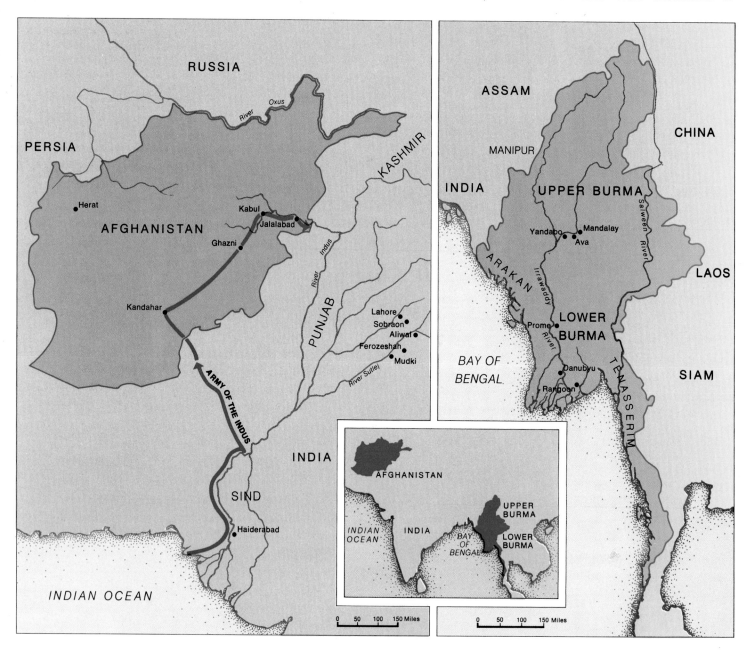

152

collect geographical and political intelligence, including the sending of a British commercial envoy to the Afghan capital at Kabul.

The assignment was given to Alexander Burnes, a former soldier in the East India Company's army, who had a flair for languages and a remarkable record as an explorer. In London Burnes was acknowledged to be the greatest authority on the affairs of central Asia.

Not everyone in India, however, held a high opinion of him, and some of his critics were in a position to influence the Governor-General. In particular there was the ambitious, influential William Hay Macnaghten, head of the Foreign and Political Department.

Like Burnes, Macnaghten had started life as an officer in the Company's army, but had quickly exchanged the sword for the pen. He was a confirmed bureaucrat who avoided the dangers and excitement of travel in harsh India. The contrast between Macnaghten and Burnes was profound—Macnaghten cold, delighting in intrigue for its own sake, "dry as an old nut," as a contemporary put it; and Burnes, an almost Byronic figure, enjoying himself in native dress and with native women, seeing tragedy in the making yet taking no action to avert it.

Burnes's mission to Kabul was not supposed to be political, merely commercial, and he had no authority to offer Dost Muhammad anything. He wrote to Macnaghten for instructions. Dost wanted an alliance, he said, and if he did not get it he would undoubtedly turn to the Persians and the Russians. There was news that a Persian army with Russian advisers was on its way to seize Herat and that a Russian diplomatic envoy would be arriving at Kabul. Macnaghten replied only with a warning to Dost Muhammad not to enter into alliances with any other states.

Burnes took the hint. In trying to persuade the government of India that it must support Dost Muhammad he might be prejudicing his own future. It was obvious that Auckland and his advisers had taken the arrival of the Russian envoy in Kabul as a threat

and decided that British interests could only be protected by violent action.

When Auckland asked for his views, Burnes replied that he still regarded Dost as "a man of undoubted ability: and if half you do for others were done for him . . . he would abandon Persia and Russia tomorrow." But in the same letter he protected his flanks by saying that if the British government was contemplating replacing Dost, it had "only to send Shuja with an agent and two of its regiments, as honorary escort, and an avowal to the Afghans that we have taken up his cause to ensure his being fixed forever on the Throne." It was exactly what Auckland and Macnaghten wanted to hear—and Burnes obviously knew it.

The Persian advance on Herat and the arrival in Kabul of the alleged Russian diplomat set off hysteria in London and Calcutta. The British Ambassador to Russia was instructed to ask for an explanation. The Russians denied knowledge of any agent, and it seems likely that the man who announced himself to Dost Muhammad as an envoy had no official standing whatever. But it hardly mattered. By the time the Russian reply was received, Auckland had already set out to place his own man on the throne of Afghanistan. Here again was the old puppet-ruler game that Clive and his successors had been playing in India with such diligence for generations.

The plan was the sole responsibility of William Macnaghten—or so it was said after his death. Ranjit Singh, ruler of the Punjab, would supply the men, the British would furnish money and advisers, and Shah Shuja would be the figurehead.

A treaty between the three parties was signed in Lahore in June, 1838, but it soon became clear that Ranjit Singh had no intention of using Sikh forces to put Shuja back on his throne. The wily old Sikh saw that Auckland had the bit between his teeth and that the British would fight the battles for him. He was right. In October Auckland issued a manifesto: "His Majesty Shah Shuja will enter Afghanistan surrounded by his own troops

and will be protected by a British army against foreign intervention and factious opposition."

While that army, grandiloquently christened "the Army of the Indus," was being assembled, Auckland looked round to see who could be squeezed to pay for it. No one, it seemed, in British India. His eye fell on Sind, adjoining the Punjab to the south. Its only connection with the British so far was through an 1832 treaty that opened the Indus to commerce—but definitely not to armed vessels or military stores. It was decided to march through Sind and on the way bully the three Amirs of this disunited area into paying for the expedition. The treaty between the Amirs and the British was set aside "while the present exigency lasts."

The "present exigency" need not in fact have lasted at all. In September, after a campaign of incredible inefficiency, the Persians had given up the siege of Herat and marched away, and the supposed Russian envoy had left Kabul. The two ostensible reasons for the venture had disappeared—but too late to change British plans.

The Army of the Indus started its march through Sind in December, 1838, devastating the countryside and looting at will until the Amirs gave in. With the army went William Macnaghten, "Envoy and Minister on the part of the government of India at the court of Shah Shuja."

The Company's army contained only some 9,500 combat troops, but there were over 38,000 camp-followers and 30,000 camels. The army depended for its supplies on Indian contractors, and an army on the move was like a city of tented shops which packed up each morning and reappeared each night. There were no sanitary arrangements, and so among the items delivered to the fighting men were dysentery and cholera.

The commanders of the expedition, Generals Willoughby Cotton and John Keane, were mediocre even by the standards of the time. A further burden was the fact that the two only had authority in military matters. The real command of the expedition lay with Macnaghten and the other "politicals."

An 1834 book on his adventures in central Asia won Alexander Burnes instant fame.

Kandahar, 70 miles inside the border and 300 from Kabul, was taken in April, 1839. Though Macnaghten's despatch to Lord Auckland claimed that Shuja was received with "feelings nearly amounting to adoration," others would not have agreed. Most of the population stayed away from the official installation of Shuja as ruler of Afghanistan. Those chiefs who came forward to support him had mainly been bought with lavish bribes of British gold.

The advance on Kabul and Dost Muhammad continued, leaving General Sir William Nott to hold Kandahar. Cumbersome and diseased, the army took two months to cover the 200 miles to the town of Ghazni. There the reception was different. The walls were defended. It was a month before a storming-party was able to enter the town after blowing the gates. The rest of the army followed and enjoyed itself in an orgy of loot and rape. Not to be outdone by his allies, Shuja had 50 prisoners hacked to death. Even in such a violent country as Afghanistan, this was noted and remembered.

The fall of Ghazni led, at least for the time being, to a withdrawal of support for Dost Muhammad. Macnaghten's generous bribes were so effective that all that remained of Dost's defiance was a row of abandoned cannon across the road to Kabul.

At last, in August, 1839, Shah Shuja and the British reached the undefended walls of Kabul. Preparations were made for a ceremonial entry. Alexander Burnes, who had been generally ignored by Macnaghten, unexpectedly found himself at the moment of Macnaghten's triumph invited to enter the city by the envoy's side.

Surrounded by British bayonets, Shah Shuja, after 30 years of exile, rode through the gates. Resplendent with jewels and mounted upon a white horse, with Macnaghten on one side and Burnes on the other, both in blue and gold dress uniforms, the Shah entered the palace of his ancestors and broke suddenly into "a paroxysm of childish delight."

There were no signs of delight on the faces of his subjects. Macnaghten chose to see respect, but others observed only "stern and scowling looks."

When the news of the installation of his puppet reached Lord Auckland, everyone congratulated him on his great foresight and statesmanship, embroidering their congratulations with balls and galas in his honour. No one in authority appeared to be worried about what to do next. Even the death of Ranjit Singh of the Punjab, the third "partner" in the Afghan enterprise, was noticed only for the horror of his barbaric obsequies, in which four of his widows and a number of female servants were burned alive on his funeral pyre.

In Kabul it was increasingly obvious to Macnaghten that the British could not leave their protégé to himself. Gold had bought some sort of allegiance from many Afghan chiefs, but next to gold they respected power, and it was clear to all that Shah Shuja possessed no power of his own.

The army settled into Kabul and, like occupying forces throughout history, made itself highly unpopular. On other levels, too, the British built up antagonism. The recklessness with

Bureaucrat William Macnaghten, chief planner of the Afghan invasion.

which money was squandered soon drove prices sky-high. The activities of Christian missionaries inflamed Muslim religious fanaticism, as did the soldiers' thoughtless defilement of shrines sacred to the Afghans.

The British politicals were not helping either. General Nott, commanding at Kandahar, caustically remarked that "the conduct of the thousand and one politicals has ruined our cause and bared the throat of every European in this country to the sword and knife of the revengeful Afghan." Nott may have had in mind the actions of one political who destroyed a village of 23 people because "he thought they looked insultingly at him."

One problem at least was solved—that of Dost Muhammad. Although evading all efforts to capture him, he finally decided that in the face of the overwhelming British presence further resistance was useless and that a voluntary submission would leave his honour untarnished—especially as his son would carry on the struggle. On a crisp morning in November, 1840, Macnaghten was on his daily ride outside Kabul when he was hailed by another horseman. Following behind was Dost Muhammad himself, who dismounted, saluted the envoy, and offered his sword. Side by side the two men rode into the city. Dost was sent into India with a recommendation that he be well treated.

Auckland received him graciously and generously, awarding the fallen monarch a substantial pension. Seeing the wealth and luxury of British India for the first time, Dost commented: "I cannot understand why the rulers of so great an empire should have gone across the Indus to deprive me of my poor and barren country." More and more Englishmen—especially those in Afghanistan—were beginning to agree with him.

All through 1841 the storm gathered. Macnaghten was ordered to cancel the subsidies which kept some of the chiefs quiet. Powerful tribes were in revolt, led by Dost Muhammad's son, Akbar Khan. Alexander Burnes, once more ignored by the envoy and living a separate life in his house deep in the city, heard news of rebellion and intrigue. Soldiers were attacked in the city streets, British officers out shooting were stoned by gangs of angry villagers. Rumours abounded of preparations for an attack on the hated foreigners and their puppet.

Yet no attempt was made to protect the British positions. On the contrary, the cantonment they built for themselves was on an open plain outside the city. To make matters worse, a new general had taken command early in 1841 on the retirement of the elderly General Cotton. General Nott, the obvious candidate as his successor, was too independent and outspoken for Macnaghten's liking. The new general, William Elphinstone, was so crippled with rheumatic gout that he was unlikely to resist the envoy's pressures.

For all the rumours of a coming revolt, the rising was a surprise to everyone, including Alexander Burnes. On November 1 there were strong indications that an attack was about to take place on his house. Instead of moving into the military cantonment which, for all its faults, was at least safer than the city, Burnes asked only that his guard be increased. Even at eight o'clock the next morning, with a mob at the gates calling for his death, his urgent message to Macnaghten suggesting that troops be sent into the city also claimed that he could probably deal with the disturbance himself. But the situation was out of control. Burnes, courageous to the last, harangued the mob, offering money in return for safe-conduct, and was greeted with howls for blood. He retreated into the house and waited for help. It never came.

The noise from the city could be heard by Macnaghten and Elphinstone in the cantonment as they argued about what should be done. Only the despised Shah Shuja acted, sending some of his own troops in a hopeless attempt to help Burnes. The mob broke through the mud walls of the house. Attempting to escape disguised as a native, Burnes was recognized and hacked to pieces.

In the cantonment, muddle and inertia still reigned. Seeing that the British were not moving on the city, the mob began to plunder, murder, and rape. Elphinstone's feeble response on that November evening was to write a note to Macnaghten: "We must see what the morning brings, and then think what can be done. . . ."

News of the murder of Burnes and the immobility of the British spread rapidly throughout the country. Garrisons were attacked, columns massacred, and the chiefs began to move on Kabul. On November 13 the Afghans swept down on the cantonment. The charge was eventually thrown back, but the situation was clearly desperate. If the British were to save themselves, it would not be through superior military expertise. There was nothing for it but to make a deal. Forced into negotiation, Macnaghten fell back on his old methods: where guns had failed, gold and intrigue would certainly succeed.

On December 23 Macnaghten set out with a small escort to bargain with Akbar Khan, Dost Muhammad's son. They met on the bank of the Kabul River, just a quarter of a mile from the cantonment. Macnaghten complained that there were too many Afghans crowding in. "They are all in the secret," Akbar answered. According to one who was present, "no sooner were these words uttered than I heard Akbar call out 'Beeger' [seize] and turning round I saw him grasp the envoy's hand with an expression of the most diabolical ferocity."

Macnaghten was immediately shot to death by Akbar. Two of the escorting British officers escaped, but another was cut down. Later Macnaghten's headless corpse was displayed hanging from a pole set up in the Kabul bazaar.

As far as British morale was concerned, this was the last blow. Akbar Khan now dictated a curt treaty. The British were to go at once, leaving all their treasure and most of their artillery.

On January 6, 1842, the once-proud Army of the Indus marched out of Kabul for India. It had 90 miles of snow, freezing temperatures, and high passes to face to reach Jalalabad, where a British garrison was securely dug in, although under siege. If the Afghans proved treacherous, as many feared, there was little hope.

Some 4,500 fighting troops, hundreds of them sick and wounded, a large party of women and children, a vast quantity of baggage, and 12,000 panic-stricken camp-followers straggled out of the cantonment. Even before the rear guard formed up, 50 lay dead. Many camp-followers gave up almost at once, and sat apathetically by the roadside waiting for the relief of death from bullet or knife.

The column made barely six miles the first day. Looking back through the bitter darkness, the British saw their cantonment ablaze. Most of the provisions had been thrown away by terrified servants. The rear guard came in at two o'clock in the morning, having fought through "literally a continuous land of poor wretches, men, women, and children, dead or dying from the cold and wounds, who unable to move entreated their comrades to kill them and put an end to their misery." Next morning the confusion was even worse. There was no order, wrote Lieutenant Vincent Eyre, only a "mingled mob of soldiers, camp-followers, and cattle, preserving not even the faintest semblance of

Lady Sale's Journal

One of the few survivors of the deadly retreat from Kabul was Lady Florentine Sale, the wife of a British general. Somehow she managed to keep up her journal; this is from her entry for the third day:

"At sunrise no order had been issued for the march, and the confusion was fearful. The force was perfectly disorganised, nearly every man paralysed with cold, so as to be scarcely able to hold his musket or move. Many frozen corpses lay on the ground. The Sipahees burnt their caps, accoutrements, and clothes to keep themselves warm. . . . Sturt [her son-in-law] gave those men on duty each one glass to warm and cheer them—a comfort they fully appreciated, as they had long been without what was now become necessary. For myself, whilst I sat for hours on my horse in the cold I felt grateful for a tumbler of sherry, which at any other time would have made me very unlady-like, but now merely warmed me. . . .

"[In the Khurd-Kabul Pass] the ladies were heavily fired on. On one camel were Mrs. Mainwaring and her infant, scarcely three months old. This camel was shot and the unfortunate lady pursued her way on foot . . . with her child in her arms through the deep snow. . . .

"Poor Sturt [who had been shot in the stomach] was laid on the side of a bank, with his wife and myself beside him. Dr. Bryce came and examined Sturt's wound: he dressed it, but I saw by the expression of his countenance that there was no hope. . . ."

that regularity and discipline on which depended our only chance of escape."

At the tail of the column, Afghan looters were at work. Akbar hovered in the distance, holding several score hostages and claiming he would try to ensure the safety of the column, but seemingly unable to control his followers. The second night the thermometer plunged and there was a foot of snow on the ground. Some of the sepoys burned their coats for a few minutes of warmth.

There was worse to come. As the British entered the five-mile Khurd-Kabul Pass, so deep that the winter sun never reached its floor, they came under heavy attack. Three thousand of the refugees were killed that day.

As the survivors settled down for the third night, in the highest and coldest spot, snow began to fall again. There were just four small tents left. Elphinstone had one, two were occupied by a few wives and their children, and the fourth was for the sick—a hopeless gesture in view of the numbers of wounded and frost-bitten.

January 10 saw the grimmest massacre of all. With almost all the sepoys so frost-bitten that they could not load or fire their muskets, the few Europeans were the only troops able to mount any sort of resistance. Even that was hopeless, for the next defile —the Tunghi Tariki Gorge, a bottleneck 50 yards long and just three or four yards wide—was a gruesome death-trap. The straggling mass of refugees was so helpless that the tribesmen no longer wasted valuable ammunition on them, preferring to move in with drawn swords and cut the throats of their victims at leisure. The advance guard struggled through the gorge and waited for the main body. It never came; it had ceased to exist. Nine thousand camp-followers perished. Three thousand remained, with just 450 Europeans to lead them.

As the column descended the far side of the passes out of the snow, the instinct for self-preservation flickered brighter. Led by Brigadier John Shelton, Her Majesty's 44th Regiment rallied to keep the Afghans at bay. After a brief rest, the troops, seek-

ing to escape the encumbering camp-followers, pressed on through the night in an attempt to cover 22 miles and beat the Afghans to the formidable two-mile Jagdalak Defile. In vain: the whole mob followed, drawing the Afghans' fire.

Akbar sent an offer to negotiate. Elphinstone and Shelton were regaled with food, but the troops were in despair, "having seen enough of Afghan treachery to convince them that these repeated negotiations were mere hollow artifices." They were right. Akbar, having apparently done his best to persuade his violent chieftains not to slaughter the remnants of the British force, refused to allow the two commanders to leave his camp.

The troops, with no message from Elphinstone, had no choice but to press on. The end was near: at the summit of the Jagdalak Defile stood a six-foot barrier of prickly holly-oak. The infantry struggled to tear a hole in the stout branches while bullets poured in among them. When they finally succeeded in opening a path they were trampled underfoot as mounted officers rushed for the gap. Of the 3,500 men and women Elphinstone had left behind him, just 20 officers and 45 European soldiers now survived. The dozen or so with horses rode on ahead. The rest, down to 20 muskets and 40 rounds of ammunition, straggled on in scattered groups until at dawn, when they reached Gandamak, the Afghans closed in to finish them off. Just one man escaped.

When the news reached India, Auckland pronounced the disasters "as inexplicable as they are appalling." The defeat was total. The puppet ruler Shuja had been killed soon after the British left Kabul. When the news reached England, the government fell. Auckland was replaced as Governor-General by Lord Ellenborough, who arrived to take over in February, 1842. Auckland had already taken some action. He appointed General Sir George Pollock to command an "Army of Retribution" then assembling. Pollock was a man of experience and decision who had spent 40 years in the Company's forces.

On its retreat from Kabul, the Army of the Indus had to pass through a series of rocky defiles (left) that slowed its pace to a crawl. The column was constantly sniped at and pillaged (below); even the Afghan children, one of the British officers noted, "were seen stabbing at wounded grenadiers."

When Ellenborough arrived he called "for the re-establishment of our military reputation by the infliction of some signal and decisive blow upon the Afghans." One British army went to the relief of Nott, still holding out in Kandahar, another to that of General Robert Sale, besieged at Jalalabad. Ellenborough ordered his generals to retire "by way of Kabul, if they so wished," thus offering them an opportunity to inflict that "signal and decisive blow."

Nott and Pollock, sweeping all before them, moved on the Afghan capital. Nott arrived first, on September 17, and Pollock two days later. There the hostages taken by Akbar were released on the payment of 20,000 rupees to their gaoler. All that was left of the Army of the Indus was 31 officers, 10 women, 11 children, two civilian clerks, and 52 soldiers—all British. Some 16,000 had perished. It was one of the greatest disasters in the history of the Empire.

Nothing remained but revenge. Kabul was almost entirely destroyed, the inhabitants suffering "every kind of disgraceful outrage." In the disillusioned words of one young British officer, "Tears, supplications, were no avail; fierce oaths were the only answer; the musket was deliberately raised, the trigger pulled. . . . In fact we are nothing but hired assassins."

With British military prestige now believed restored, the Army of Retribution retired to India. As it marched through the Punjab it was passed by a small band of horsemen escorting Dost Muhammad back to rule Afghanistan—a suitable epilogue to the whole unhappy affair.

Determined to seal the North-West Frontier, the British turned their attention to the two border states, Sind and the Punjab. The instrument chosen to subdue the Amirs of Sind was General Sir Charles Napier, "a small dark-visaged old man—with a falcon's glance." Technically at least, Napier was merely to ensure that the Amirs remained friendly, but he had no doubts about his real mission. "We have no right to seize Sind," he wrote before leaving to take up his new appointment, "yet we shall do so, and a very advantageous, humane, and useful piece of rascality it will be."

The method was simple. A new treaty was presented to the Amirs. When they demurred, Napier advanced.

On February 17, 1843, Napier won a particularly bloody battle near the main town of Haiderabad. To the Amirs' question of what terms he would give in return for surrender, Napier told them, "Life and nothing more. And I want your decision before twelve o'clock, as I shall by that time have buried my dead, and given my soldiers their breakfasts." The Amirs gave in, recognizing in Napier a man as ruthless as themselves.

These methods led to the formal annexation of Sind to the Company's dominions. Ellenborough issued a grandiloquent proclamation, and Napier received £70,000 in prize-money and the governorship of the new province.

Many high-ranking British officers and administrators made no secret of their belief that the British would soon also annex the Punjab. After the death of Ranjit Singh, the Punjab had fallen into anarchy. When civil war broke out, as the British expected, then would come the opportunity to move in.

General Gough (centre, in the cape) confers with his officers after the Battle of Ferozeshah in the First Sikh War. Having dealt the British heavy losses, the Sikhs burned their camp and left the field.

The opportunity arrived in 1845 when an army of Sikhs swept into British India. Though still torn by anarchy, they were temporarily united by fear of British expansion. The British, eager for control of the vast Punjabi plains, were ready. But the Sikhs proved the Company's toughest native foes; only after four years, and two bitter wars, did they finally submit.

In the first two indecisive engagements at Mudki and Ferozeshah in December, 1845, British losses were staggering. This was largely due to the leadership of Sir Hugh Gough, a 66-year-old Irishman of great charm and extraordinary bravery but also of such incompetence that his only plan of attack was repeated frontal assaults. At Ferozeshah, while the Sikh artillery tore hideous holes in the British ranks, Gough recklessly rode up and down in a white coat to draw the enemy fire. The British were saved from total disaster only by the coming of darkness and the premature withdrawal of the Sikhs.

Two months later, Gough retrieved his reputation with two overwhelming victories: a brilliant cavalry charge at Aliwal and an infantry assault at Sobraon that forced the Sikhs back into the River Sutlej until it was clogged with their shattered bodies. From Sobraon the British marched to the Sikh capital of Lahore.

The peace treaty ending the First Sikh War did not call for annexation, but the state was put into the hands of British officials and the army garrisoned strategic forts and towns.

The Punjab still seethed. In 1848, during the regime of the aggressive Governor-General Dalhousie, a second war broke out. Again Sir Hugh Gough bumbled and fumbled, pitting bayonets against guns and suffering fearful casualties, yet somehow he snatched victory from defeat.

This time there was to be no sharing of power. The Punjab was annexed and those who did not like the fact were warned by Governor John Lawrence, "Will you be governed by the pen or the sword? Choose." After a decade of strife the North-West Frontier was at last secure—at least until the next contest in the "Great Game," as the British liked to call their long-standing imperial rivalry with expansionist Russia.

—*Jim Hicks, Michael Edwardes*

III. The Opium War

Opium has long been woven into the Western literary imagery of Oriental evil. Drugs, secret traps, lizard eyes glittering behind lacquered screens—the fantasies epitomized by Sax Rohmer's Dr. Fu Manchu have struck deep. As a result, most people who know the Opium War of 1839–42 only by name naturally suppose the British waged it to free China from opium: a whiff of grapeshot sterilizing the poppy's fumes, the whole affair in line with Victorian morality.

The truth is something quite different. The British Empire was the world's largest grower, processor, and exporter of opium, and China was its primary market. The English fostered addiction in China, got a virtual monopoly of the drug, and blundered into war largely to defend their profits against an Emperor who was struggling to stamp out the trade. If Her Majesty's Government had no clear-cut opium policy for China, it was at least grimly determined to protect its interests. For opium was the hard political currency of the Far East, and England had made it so.

At the heart of Britain's attitude towards opium was the fact that so much of it was grown in India, its well-being essential to the entire Indian economy. By 1875, for example, the Indian Empire's income (in round figures) was £40 million, the equivalent of £320 million today. Almost a third of that sum came from two English monopolies, salt and opium, originally acquired by the British East India Company; opium's share came to £6.5 million—nearly 17 per cent of India's gross national income. That was as much as England then spent on all public works, education, transport, communications, and administration of justice in the subcontinent. Politically, the British Raj was as addicted to opium as any 20-pipe-a-day coolie. Had China cut off the trade, the economic withdrawal symptoms could well have shaken the the Indian Empire to bits. Hence the Opium War.

"If the Chinese must be poisoned by opium, I would rather they were poisoned for the benefit of our Indian subjects than for the benefit of any other exchequer," Sir George Campbell said in the House of Commons in 1880; he was proclaiming a policy that two generations of imperial administrators had acted on but not so bluntly voiced.

Yet it would caricature history to see the British government as a frock-coated Mafia, degrading China with drugs for bloated profits. One must remember that opium was once the aspirin of Europe. The English took it copiously: in 1840 the average annual intake was slightly over a quarter-ounce per person. Doctors prescribed it for hysteria, travel sickness, toothache, neuralgia, flu, cholera, hay fever, ulcers, and insomnia. King George IV's doctors prescribed opium as a hangover cure; Coleridge wrote *Kubla Khan* on it; Berlioz imbibed, vomited for two hours, and emerged from his experience with the inspiration for the *Symphonie Fantastique*.

The lowliest took it as freely as the most exalted. Opium was used as pain killer and memory-wiper wherever the "dark satanic mills" stood—in Birmingham, Lancashire, Sheffield, Nottingham—and by rural labourers throughout the countryside. The English proletariat took it to escape the atrocious monotony and fatigue of their work. Opium, to reverse Marx,

159

was the religion of the people. Nor did addiction necessarily impede a lifetime of concentrated effort. Clive of India was an addict for 20 years. William Wilberforce, the anti-slavery crusader, took opium every day for 45 years. Children were raised on it. If an infant cried, the Victorians dosed him with soothing tinctures—McMunn's Elixir, Mother Bailey's Quieting Syrup, Batley's Sedative Solution, Godfrey's Cordial—that contained up to half a grain of opium per fluid ounce, and sometimes quieted the child forever.

Thus at the time of the Opium War there could have been few Englishmen who had not taken opium for relief or stimulus. Add to this the lack of public interest in the politics of so remote and exotic a land as China and it is no surprise that the British public, in so far as it knew about China's predicament at all, was quite indifferent to it.

There is a further point. The war must be seen in the context of its time. Just as the Chinese side was ignored by Victorian writers, British grievances have fallen from grace today. Not all of them were the pompous sensitivities of an exploiter-race, and opium was not the sole cause of the war.

Its origins lay far back, within the Chinese Empire itself. In the 18th Century this empire was the largest and oldest in the world. Other Asian nations—Vietnam, Burma, Korea—were tributaries to the Celestial Throne; their ambassadors came regularly to Peking to make the "three kneelings and nine prostrations." For more than 3,000 years the Chinese had dealt with all other states, when they dealt at all, as inferiors.

And so, when English traders arrived in the late 1700s and presented their royal credentials, Chinese officials treated them as ignorant barbarians. The fact that another empire was growing thousands of miles away, stronger, richer, and incomparably better developed in technology, would not have seemed possible to the Emperor. Only he embodied the Will of Heaven.

The Victorians have been rightly castigated for their insensitivity to Chinese forms and customs. But nothing surpassed the arrogant myopia with which China eyed the barbarians. What was there to look at? Why should a superior man study an inferior? What Britain wanted, initially, was an equitable trade relationship with China. To the Emperor there could be no such equity: that would have violated the immutable *tao*, the Way of Heaven.

This attitude is best shown in the Emperor Ch'ien-lung's response to the Macartney mission in 1793. George III, anxious to secure a footing in China, sent Lord George Macartney to Peking to ask for equal representation and free trade, a British trading port, and a permanent embassy in the capital. The British wanted to sell the Chinese their Indian cotton, and to buy tea and silk. Opium was not yet a major issue.

All Macartney got was a letter to take back to George III. There would be no commissioner or embassy in Peking. There was already a trading port, Canton, where barbarians could do business, but even that was a sign of imperial indulgence, for "as your Ambassador can see for himself, we possess all things. I set no value on objects strange or ingenious, and have no use for your country's manufactures. . . . But as the tea, silk, and porcelain which the Celestial Empire produces are absolute necessities to the European nations and to yourselves, we have permitted, as a signal mark of favour, that foreign *hongs* [trading companies] should be established at Canton." Ch'ien-lung consolingly added that he was not offended by these wheedlings from a barbarian king. "I do not forget the lonely remoteness of your island, cut off from the world by intervening wastes of sea, nor do I overlook your excusable ignorance of the usages of our Celestial Empire. . . ."

Macartney had failed; he did not go in low enough. The only way an envoy could approach the Celestial Throne was in supplication, as a vassal. When Lord Amherst tried to visit the Emperor in 1816, he obstinately refused to make the nine prostrations and was sent away without an audience. On the other hand, when an Italian trade mission *did* make the right obeisances, the Emperor promptly claimed Italy as part of the Celestial Empire.

Even before the Macartney mission reached Peking, cartoonist James Gillray accurately predicted the chilly Chinese reception of Macartney and his ingenious gifts.

There was, it seemed, no way of winning.

The most galling truth was that Ch'ien-lung was right about Anglo-Chinese trade. China's economy was self-sufficient. It did not need English goods, but the English needed Chinese tea and silk—though not, as Ch'ien-lung thought, as items of survival, but for the profits that could be made from their resale. Between 1792 and 1809 China's exports were twice her imports. The East India Company shipped £16.5 million in goods to China, and brought back £27 millions' worth—a trade deficit of £10.5 million. This was partly reduced by Company receipts from England in silver bullion—the Chinese merchants liked to be paid in metal. But the net imbalance was still £8 million. How, then, to pay the Chinese for tea and silk? The answer was opium.

Opium was known in China long before the English arrived. Its source, the red poppy known as *Papaver somniferum*, was probably introduced by Arab traders. These singular adventurers were running a trading station in Canton as early as A.D. 300. The drug's early history was predominantly medical. A staple of Greek medicine, it entered the Arab pharmacopœia when the legacy of classical science passed to Arab doctors. By the 10th Century opium was well-known to Chinese doctors and mentioned in every herbal treatise.

There is no early evidence of an addiction problem among Chinese peasants or at the imperial court, and there was no significant vogue for it among the elite of scholar-officials and poets, who preferred to get roaring drunk on rice wine. The use of opium as a widespread, addictive, pleasure-giving indulgence came to China from the West. The Chinese had to learn to *smoke* it.

Opium is a flexible drug that can be taken internally in a variety of ways. These methods all have drawbacks, particularly the fact that a user cannot delicately regulate his dose to his own convenience. The smoker, however, can "tune" his intake precisely. A pipe takes five or six breaths to finish; anything from one to twenty pipes may be consumed according to curiosity or need. The human lung absorbs the narcotic into the blood, and thence to the brain, faster than the stomach or gut, so that the effect comes faster and the smoker knows how far to go. Moreover, the ritual of smoking is pleasant, especially in a formalistic culture like China's.

But the idea of inhaling smoke was unnatural to man until tobacco, a plant unknown in China and Europe, was discovered. Spanish colonists brought it from America to the Philippines, and merchants from Fukien brought it in their junks to China. Soon the habit of mixing opium with tobacco, which originated in the Dutch East Indies, spread to China. The first opium dens were seen on Formosa. From there opium smoking established itself on the mainland.

Dutch and Portuguese traders supplied the opium, most of which they imported from India. In the early 18th Century, when smoking was still largely confined to Formosa, the Portuguese could unload no more than 200 chests a year there—about ten tons. But it so stupefied the Formosan workers and officials that Emperor Yung Ch'eng, thousands of miles away in Peking, could no longer ignore the reports. He issued an edict against opium in 1729. The punishment for smoking was 100 strokes of the bamboo rod and exile to the inland frontier. Keepers of opium dens were to be strangled.

Yung Ch'eng's edict did not work, and the continuing Chinese demand for the drug suggested to the East India Company a way to pay for Chinese tea and silk. At first the trade was erratic. Then, in 1794, the Company dispatched a freighter to Whampoa, 13 miles downriver from Canton, where it remained anchored offshore for a year, selling opium to smugglers. There was some trading at Macao, but for the next 25 years Whampoa was the chief port for the drug. By 1820 the yearly consumption of opium had risen to 4,000 chests, despite a flurry of edicts and threats from Peking. In 1821 the opium merchants withdrew from Macao and Whampoa and set up their trade station under the lee of Lintin Island, at the mouth of the Canton River.

By now a complete shuttle system had developed: large, armed British hulks formed a floating depot of storehouses, receiving cargoes from swift opium clippers and off-loading into "scrambling dragons," fast galleys armed with cannon and grappling-irons, which ferried it "secretly" to the mainland. The Chinese authorities issued regular proclamations, whenever a clipper arrived, warning the foreign devils to sail away before "the dragons of war . . . with their fiery discharges, annihilate all who oppose this edict." Nobody took the least notice of this formal rhetoric.

Most of the opium was ferried 40 miles upriver to Canton itself, the only Chinese city open for foreign trade. Here were crowded along the waterfront the "factories"—the trading stations—of the East India Company and of French, Dutch, and American merchants.

Opium had long grown in India, but the East India Company turned it into an immense industry. No land in the provinces of India, Bihar, and Benares could be sown with poppies without the Company's permission, and not an ounce of opium could leave India without passing through the Company's control. Increasing tracts of land were turned over to opium, and it was the best land: *Papaver somniferum* is a delicate bloom, needing rich soil and constant irrigation. There was of course no comparison between the profits of opium-growing and the margin one might scrape from the same acreage sown with grain. By 1839 India was producing a pound of opium for every ounce that came from its nearest competitor, Turkey.

The soil was ploughed three times and weeded, then scored with a grid of irrigation dykes. Poppy-seeds were sown in November; in March the flower shed its petals and was ready. Its bulbous seedcases were slit with hooked knives or mussel shells. White juice oozed all night from the slit pod and the next day's sun hardened it into a dark sticky gum. This raw opium was scraped off, collected, and delivered to the village officers. The exudation could not be hurried and a farmer might gather no more than an ounce each day. It was finicky, tedious work.

At the Company's depot the opium was pressed into fist-sized cakes, wrapped in a crust of dry poppy-leaves, and packed in mango-wood chests. There was no standard weight. The average chest contained about 125 pounds, rising sometimes to 140 pounds. Since an opium addict was expected to consume up to 40 grains a day, one chest might represent a month's supply for 8,000 addicts. It was estimated that there were somewhere between 10 to 12 million addicts in China by the 1840s.

Significantly, the East India Company always strove to minimize addiction in India. Its directors wrote in 1817 to the Governor of Bengal, expressing the hope that his measures "will tend to restrain the use of this pernicious drug. . . . Were it possible to prevent the use of the drug altogether, except for the purposes of medicine, we would gladly do it in compassion for mankind." In other words, don't drug *our* peasants; they won't work so hard. In the year they penned these nobly unctuous words, the directors sold over 500,000 pounds of opium to the China smugglers.

In the late 1830s it was costing the Company about £15 to produce a chest of opium on its own territory and bring it to Calcutta. There it was auctioned to exporters and smugglers, loaded into the opium clippers, and dispatched to China. Theoretically, the Company's responsibility for the opium ended at the Calcutta wharves, and since its authority emanated from the British government this was a useful moral escape hatch for both. The government, of course, knew about Chinese resentment over the smuggling trade, but it still adopted the Company's opium policy as its own: a House of Commons committee reported in 1831 that "the monopoly of Opium in Bengal supplies the Govt. with a revenue amounting to £981,293 per annum; and the duty amounts to 301¾% on the cost of the article. In the present state of the revenue it does not appear advisable to abandon so important a source of revenue."

From 1800 to 1837, the Company

reaped an average profit of 465 per cent from its opium auctions in Calcutta. But this represented only half of the Indian opium supply going to China. The rest was Malwa opium, produced by Indian firms located outside the area under Company control and auctioned and shipped from Bombay. But the Company got its cut there, too. To reach Bombay from Malwa in the north, the opium had to cross Company territory, and a transit tax was imposed on it. This tax brought profits almost as great as those from growing opium. It began at £20 a chest in the 18th Century, rising to £30 and finally, in 1847, to £43. In 1835 the tax return from Malwa opium was nearly £320,000.

The Company had the independent Indian growers nicely trapped. If Malwa opium went up in price, Company opium would force it off the China market. So the independents had to make do with profits half as large as the Company's (albeit a handsome 200 per cent). Besides, the Chinese dealers preferred the Company's opium to Malwa's: it was finer and purer. English merchants kept stricter quality controls.

In 1830 a missionary at Canton noted the booming trade off Lintin Island: "fear of [the smugglers'] *cannon balls* effectively prevents the Chinese war junks from interfering with them . . . the boats are but seldom interfered with, nor are they likely to be, so long as the *Free Traders* can afford to pay the Mandarins so much better for not fighting, than the Government will for doing their duty." Because so many Cantonese were involved in the opium business as middlemen, dealers, processors, and smokers, the Emperor's commands were impossibly hard for the government officials (most of whom were bribed anyway) to carry out. By now, opium had cancelled out China's favourable trade balance, and the drain it created on her silver reserves threatened inflation.

The English trade superintendent in Canton, Captain Charles Elliot, neither backed nor controlled the opium smugglers. His powers were vague, his ammunition blank. Lord Palmerston, the Foreign Secretary,

had instructed the first Canton superintendent that "It is not desirable that you should encourage such adventures [opium smuggling]; but you must never lose sight of the fact that you have no authority to interfere with or protect them." This waffling directive typified Britain's lack of a coherent opium policy and left Captain Elliot in a dilemma. He feared an opium crisis would ruin *all* British trade with China.

The situation drifted. The imperial Viceroy in Canton, sent to end the trade, became as corruptly involved as the merchants, but to deceive the Emperor he made a great show of rounding up a number of Chinese opium dealers. Irascible memos were arriving from the Vermilion Pencil of the Celestial Throne, proclaiming, among other things, the death penalty for opium smoking. The Viceroy was dashing nervously about, lopping off Chinese heads to mollify the imperial wrath. And an imperial High Commissioner, equipped with plenipotentiary powers to stamp out the opium trade, was on his way south from Peking.

Lin Tse-hsü, the High Commissioner, came with his retinue into Canton in March, 1839. This formidable man had emerged from poverty to become one of the most powerful scholar-officials in imperial China. He was 54 years old, frugal, tough, and wily, and he distrusted barbarians. He told the Canton traders what he was going to do—but then he *did* it, which left the English, used to years of paper threats from Peking, flabbergasted. Lin saw no point in wasting time; worse, he was unbribable. The whites' reaction to him passed from scepticism through incredulity to alarmed respect.

On March 18 Commissioner Lin sent his demand to the English traders. First, all opium in foreign hands was to be handed over for destruction. "There must not be the smallest item concealed or withheld." Second, the barbarians must sign a bond never to import opium again, and recognize that if anyone did he would "suffer the extreme rigour of the law"—decapitation.

Captain Elliot was away in Macao.

Before the Opium War, all of China's foreign trade was funneled through Canton, with the Western traders restricted to their hongs in a narrow waterfront area. An unknown Chinese artist painted the busy scene for an American patron in the 1820s.

When he returned on March 24 he found armed junks stationed at all the Canton quays to prevent barbarians from sailing or disembarking. Soldiers surrounded the foreigners' compound. Lin had decreed that all loading or unloading of goods was to stop, and that craftsmen or servants in British employ were to quit or be prosecuted for conducting "secret relations with foreign countries." Deprived of their cooks and nannies, the English families muddled on, boiling their own eggs and cursing Peking. Elliot realized that he, as trade superintendent, was in Lin's eyes guilty of sheltering the smugglers. The whole foreign community in Canton was hostage for the opium.

So poor Elliot, victim of Whitehall's hypocritical shilly-shallying, armed with no power, and in fact personally opposed to opium smuggling, did the only thing he could: he gave in. He not only agreed to hand over the opium but also committed the government to indemnify the opium traders for their loss.

All the opium in the Canton area—20,283 chests—was soon in Lin's hands. The first part of his task was done. The second, the utter suppression of all future trade, remained. Commissioner Lin sent his new demands to Elliot, who read them with horror. Her Majesty's Government must not only withdraw from the Chinese opium trade, but stop making opium. Any vessel carrying opium in Chinese waters would be confiscated and its officers "be left to suffer death at the hands of the Celestial Court."

The trade superintendent condemned this "monstrous instrument" as something no Englishman could sign. He wrote a dispatch to Palmerston, asking him to reply "to all these unjust violences . . . in the form of a swift and heavy blow unprefaced by one word of written communication." In short, a pre-emptive strike and an undeclared war.

Lin, meanwhile, was destroying the opium. It was melted in a huge vat, disinfected with lime, and sluiced into the Canton estuary. The stench was atrocious.

But all Lin had done was kill the trade at Canton; by October, 1839, more than 15 opium ships were running the drug to Chusan and other ports north and east. Within nine months of Elliot's submission, 8,000 new chests were smuggled into China. It was an unpluggable flow. Nor did Lin manage to stop Chinese consumption. He went so far as to set up a clinic outside Canton where addicts could try to break their habit in voluntary confinement, tapering off with other harmless drugs—a surprisingly modern notion—but there were few volunteers, and the death penalty failed to deter the addicts.

The English were wholly outraged by Lin's brusqueness and his "excessive" demands. Palmerston labeled his methods "unfair," his pressure on the whole British community in Canton a bellicose act that cried out for revenge. He and the Foreign Office prepared for war, but at a leisurely pace. The issue was not even debated in the House of Commons until March 19, 1840, when Lord John Russell announced that the government backed Elliot's plea for gunboats and would send in troops to get (a) reparations for the insult to British subjects in Canton, (b) payment for the 20,283 chests of opium destroyed, and (c) a firm treaty of security for China traders.

But the first actions in the Opium War had in fact been fought seven months before. On September 4, 1839, there was a skirmish between British and Chinese ships in the Canton estuary—the "Battle of Kowloon." The Chinese claimed a resounding victory, but as far as can be determined, nobody won it and hardly

Text Continued on Page 166

163

TRADERS IN OBLIVION

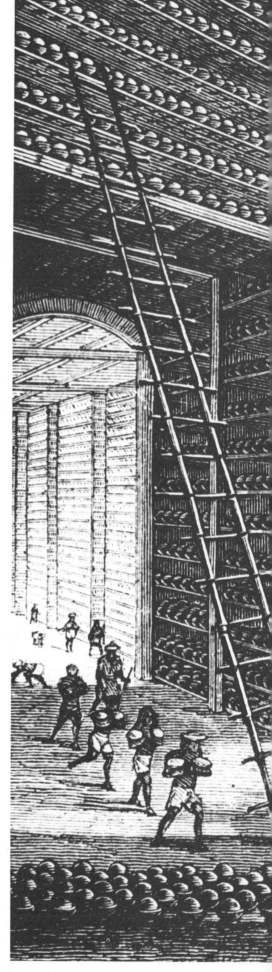

Although the East India Company lost its monopoly of trade in the subcontinent in 1813, its monopoly of the opium traffic made the loss easily bearable. As befitted anything so profitable, the processing of the drug was highly efficient. Some of the steps are illustrated here.

After harvesting, the gummy narcotic was shaped into solid lumps and wrapped carefully in poppy leaves. An expert could produce 100 opium balls a day. After weighing (above left), the two-pound balls were shelved in towering stacking rooms (right) to await shipment. Indian workers continually turned the balls and dusted them with crushed opium petals to keep them free of mildew and insects.

The "foreign mud," as the Chinese called it, was packed into solidly built wooden chests for shipping (above right). The Company's part in the noxious trade ended "officially" when it sold the chests to smugglers in Calcutta.

Upon arrival in China, dealers examined and weighed the opium (below). Finally, it was boiled to remove impurities and mixed with tobacco for the addicts' pipes.

The British fleet devastates the war junks defending Canton in January, 1841. Spearheading the assault was the East India Company's paddlewheeler *Nemesis* (right).

anyone was hurt. On November 3 a more serious engagement took place off Chuenpi, when the warships *Volage* and *Hyacinth*, carrying English refugees from Canton, were set upon by a fleet of war junks. Again, both sides claimed to have won; the evidence is that the Chinese lost. Then, on June 21, 1840, the British expeditionary force arrived.

The gap between the two forces was enormous. The Chinese had no idea of what they were facing, and their generals' contempt for barbarians clouded their never very acute power of strategic planning. One need only "display the celestial terror" and the barbarians would run. If they ran, one adviser told the Emperor, they would trip; and everyone knew that the soldiers were so tightly buttoned in their quaint uniforms that, once down, they could never get up.

Chinese officers even took the English musket for a sign of weakness; the barbarians did not use the bow, thus showing disregard for ritual and precedent. Chinese cities were protected by guns some of which, exquisitely cast in bronze, dated from the early 14th Century. The army was so riddled with graft that gunners in a battery overlooking the Canton estuary were found to be

using a mixture of 30 per cent gunpowder and 70 per cent sand. They had sold the rest to British smugglers. Intelligence reports were useless, for the officers put in fabulously puffed claims of enemy casualties in order to get promotion.

A comic-opera war? Perhaps—but the blood was real. The British expeditionary force—20 warships carrying 4,000 troops, epitomizing Palmerston's gunboat diplomacy—first attacked the port of Ting-hai, on Chusan island. In nine minutes under the broadsides of 15 cruisers, most of Ting-hai was rubble. English troops landed and swept through the town and its outlying farms, looting and raping. The inhabitants, a British diarist noted, "in a thousand instances received great injustice at our hands."

After this, however, the Opium War became a curiously sporadic affair. It was not a matter of large armies battling, breaking, re-forming, and attacking again, but rather of random engagements in slow motion, as between walkers under water.

Finally, on August 20, 1840, the Emperor in Peking got a letter from Lord Palmerston which had been written six months earlier in response to Captain Elliot's report from Canton dated November, 1839—a lapse of

nine months. Palmerston made five main demands. Confiscated opium was to be paid for by the Chinese. The Chinese must communicate with British officials in a "civilized" manner—as equals. The Chinese government must pay the Cantonese guild-merchants' debt to English traders. British war costs must be indemnified. Lastly, a "sufficiently large and properly situated island" must become a permanent Crown possession. The island Palmerston probably had in mind was Chusan. What England eventually got was Hong Kong.

Naturally, the Emperor refused. Exasperated by Lin's failure to suppress the opium trade and blaming him for the diplomatic nightmare which had unleashed the barbarian navy on China, he stripped Lin of his rank and exiled him to the wastes of Turkestan. Another official, Ch'i-shan, was appointed in his place.

But it was clear by now who was on top. On January 7, 1841, the English fleet struck at the main defences of the Canton estuary. These fell and within 24 hours most of the Chinese fleet had been annihilated and the War God's descendant, Admiral Kuan, had asked for a truce.

Canton was at England's mercy, and negotiations on Palmerston's demands began between Captain Elliott and Ch'i-shan. But now a secret dispatch came from the Emperor: Ch'i-shan must break off all parley with the barbarians, for some 4,000 imperial troops were on their way to Canton to cut the English to rags.

This put Ch'i-shan in a suicidal quandary. If he kept negotiating, it would be treason; if he did not, the barbarians would occupy Canton within a few days. He chose the former alternative, and on January 18, 1841, Captain Elliot was given a signed agreement by which the harbour and island of Hong Kong became the property of the British Crown. On hearing this, the Emperor was apoplectic. He confiscated Ch'i-shan's fortune and drove him into exile. Ever hopeful, he then sent a fresh trio of officials to Canton to "destroy the foreigners." Two were his cousins, the third was a stone-deaf septuagenarian general, Yang Feng.

The 20 British warships continued advancing up the estuary, their guns blasting the way for the landing parties which took fort after fort. On March 18 Canton was under fire. The English landed and occupied the wharves and foreign factories. Two days later Yang Feng, faced with a hopeless military situation, obtained a truce. The English demanded, and got, a bribe of £600,000 on the understanding they would spare the city and leave.

Captain Elliot and most of the foreign merchants were quite content with these arrangements. But in London the Company's directors and Palmerston were mortified. Palmerston castigated Elliot for failing to demand a sum that would cover not only compensation for the opium losses but also the whole cost of the campaign. The cession of Hong Kong —"a barren island"—was no substitute for hard cash. "You seem," Palmerston wrote scathingly to Elliot, "to have considered my Instructions were Waste Paper." He then sacked him.

In August, 1841, English troops (reinforced by detachments of the Indian army) began moving north towards Peking, rolling the Chinese back before them and sacking the coastal towns.

Meanwhile, the Chinese planned a counterattack against newly captured Ningpo. As befitted a military adventure, it was planned to take place on the Day of the Tiger (March 10) and at the Hour of the Tiger (between 3 and 5 p.m.). There was little attempt at secrecy: in the morning all the Chinese began to leave the town, drawing their hands across their throats and pointing to the British soldiers.

When the attack came it was, for the Chinese, a tragic failure. Seeing the gate of the city open, 3,500 Chinese rushed forward—straight into a well-laid minefield. British troops rushed around the outside of the walls to shoot down those who fled. Other Chinese who managed to enter the town thronged into a straight street blocked by cannon, which fired point-blank. Soon the dead lay five and six deep. The British clambered over them to harry the remnants of the Emperor's army pell-mell across the countryside.

In May the British moved on northward. In Chapu, south of Shanghai, they were held up briefly by 300 ferocious Tatars, who used a temple as a fortress. The building was set on fire. Rather than submit, many soldiers—and their families—committed suicide by hanging, poisoning, drowning, or slitting their own throats. It was a scene often repeated during the British advance.

Shanghai, at the mouth of the Yangtze, fell to them in June. They turned inland, up the Yangtze, and captured Chinkiang a month later. Chinkiang's prefect, General Hai-lin, burnt himself to death on a pyre of official papers.

With this, Chinese resistance ended. The British sailed into Nanking in August, and their squadron was closely followed up the Yangtze by a fleet of opium vessels. On August 29, 1842, the Treaty of Nanking was signed and the Opium War was over.

The Chinese had little to bargain with and England wrote its own treaty. First, there was payment for the opium Lin had destroyed in 1839—£600,000. When the Chinese protested, imagining that the £600,000 they had already paid in Canton was an opium indemnity, they were unctuously told that considering the time and inconvenience, not to speak of compound interest, £1,200,000 was a fair sum. The final indemnity China had to pay was in fact over £2,000,000.

Canton was opened to foreign (mainly British) trade, and four new "treaty ports" with it: Nanking, Ningpo, Foochow, and Amoy. At all of these England had unrestricted business facilities and full diplomatic equality. Finally, the cession of Hong Kong was made official by the Nanking Treaty.

The one matter not dealt with in the treaty was opium. China, having no power to stop it, tacitly agreed that the trade would go on. In Hong Kong Britain had a legal and immune staging-post for the opium trade. The drug was still *officially* illegal and it suited the British government to keep it so: thus it could meet moral criticism with the sophistry that its responsibility for opium ended at the Calcutta docks, and protect the smugglers with the Royal Navy while virtuously deploring their trade. India's economy prospered mightily. Its exports of opium to China soared from 2,000 tons in 1843 to nearly 5,000 in 1866. By then it was computed by British observers that eight out of ten adult Chinese in Fukien province, and nine out of ten in Canton, smoked the drug.

For the British Empire, the Opium War was a complete success. It vindicated Palmerston's faith in the gunboat. India was much benefited. Through its hold on the treaty ports and Hong Kong, Britain became master of the Far East. For the Chinese Empire, the war was disaster. The last empire of the ancient world, with 4,000 years of accumulated history, had been assailed by barbarians. The Celestial Throne had unfurled its scrolls and orders; the Ineffable Dragon, whose very scales glittering in the smoke could strike men helpless with awe, huffed fire on the round-eyed interlopers—and the only result was total defeat.

China could not face the reality of this humiliation. Its people, and especially its ruling elite, retreated into self-isolation, clinging to their traditional Confucian world-view because they could imagine nothing else. All change would be for the worse, they felt. Thus the Chinese could not grasp the meaning of their loss—which was that Western capitalism, with its immense technological thrust, had made their own culture obsolete.

Nothing, after the Treaty of Nanking, could reverse the collapse of imperial China. And nothing has let the Chinese forget it.

—*Robert Hughes*

Daumier comments on the Opium War.

IV. The Great Mutiny

In the 1850s the British Army introduced a new rifle to replace the venerable old musket affectionately known to generations of soldiers as "Brown Bess." It seemed an inoffensive and sensible step. No longer would soldiers have to fumble with separate packets of bullets and gunpowder to charge their clumsy muzzle-loaders, for with the new Enfield rifle went ammunition that combined bullet and gunpowder in one cartridge. It was welcomed everywhere—except in India. There, to the stunned amazement of Britons, the arrival of the cartridge was the trigger for the Indian Mutiny of 1857—the most horrific explosion of violence in the history of the Empire.

By the mid-1850s the temper of the great subcontinent was tense and uneasy and dangerous. At issue were many of the social reforms of Governor-General Bentinck that dated from the 1830s and were still only half-digested, overlaid with the more rapid-paced changes initiated by a more recent Raj, the Marquess of Dalhousie. This was "culture shock," frightening and unnerving. Further unease came from economic upheavals, widening tax burdens, changes in land-ownership patterns—and losses of special privileges. The discontent of an entire society became focused in just one of its elements: the troops of the Indian army, the sepoys.

Historians have found no evidence that the Mutiny was the result of a single centrally organized and directed conspiracy. The various plans of revolt simply had an underlying similarity of approach—the subversion of the sepoys' loyalty by skilful exploitation of their fears.

The worsening situation was reported to the Governor-General in his marble palace in Calcutta, but none of his advisers seemed to take it seriously. After all, the loyalty of the sepoys was not in doubt in spite of a number of mutinies and near-mutinies in the past.

Previous incidents were mostly the result of sepoy fears that over-zealous British officers were determined to convert them to Christianity by forcing them to violate the tenets of their religions. In 1806 the sepoys of Vellore, in southern India, revolted after they were instructed to trim their beards, wear restyled turbans, and give up caste-marks. In 1824 a sepoy regiment refused to embark for the First Burmese War because travel by sea would render them outcastes. Six of the ringleaders were hanged and hundreds put on hard labour.

The tradition-bound Indian society, conscious that trouble was in the air, turned to traditional magic to protect itself. There was a wide sale of charms against unknown evils. Magical symbols began to appear on walls, and prophecies were heard throughout the land. It was said—by whom, nobody knew—that British rule was coming to an end, and that it would happen on the 100th anniversary of the Battle of Plassey, which had established British rule in Bengal on June 23, 1757.

Resentment increased with feverish speed among the sepoys, especially those of Bengal, which—like Madras and Bombay, the other two major administrative areas of British India—had its own army. Most Bengal sepoys came from Oudh, a province seething with discontent since its annexation by the British the year before. The Oudh sepoys formerly had many privileges, but with annexation those privileges disappeared.

Fear of the British and of their inexplicable actions prepared the sepoys to believe anything. The old order was being destroyed, and it was by no means improbable that the white man intended to destroy the old religion as well. The situation was explosive. The cartridge for the new Enfield rifle was the spark that set it off.

The cartridge contained both gunpowder and a bullet, which was fixed to the base. The top of the cartridge had to be bitten or torn off so that the powder could be poured into the rifle. Then the bullet was rammed home, still inside the cartridge, its passage down the barrel being eased by a coating of grease round the base. Quickly the rumour spread that the grease was made of cow or pig fat. The cow is sacred to the Hindu and the pig is an unclean animal to the Muslim, and so it seemed to the sepoys that here was yet another attempt to break their adherence to religious traditions.

It is difficult for the Western mind to comprehend how such a seemingly insignificant matter could have made such an impression. From the point of view of the sepoys, however, whether Hindu or Muslim, they felt they were being forced into a polluting practice that threatened them with eternal damnation.

It seems highly likely that some of the cartridges were, in fact, greased with pig's or bullock's fat, though the contractors had been instructed to use mutton fat. As early as 1853, when a supply of the new cartridges arrived from England for climate tests, Colonel Henry Tucker, Adjutant-General of the Bengal army, warned that unless "it be known that the grease in these cartridges is not of a nature to offend or interfere with the prejudices of caste" they should not be issued. His warning was ignored. In 1857, when the sepoys' fears became known, there were suggestions that the drill should be revised. The cartridges could be torn, not bitten, and the grease could be made up by the men themselves of oil and wax. But it was too late. The fear of pollution was too firmly fixed.

These fears were easily played upon by those who hoped to persuade the sepoys to turn their guns against the British. There were reports of nocturnal barracks meetings. Mysterious fires broke out and burning arrows were shot into the thatched roofs of officers' bungalows. The telegraph station at a military post near Calcutta was burned down.

The incidents were reported, and the reports were passed up through the chain of authority until they ultimately arrived on the table of the Governor-General. In the highly centralized system of British administration, everything had to be committed to paper and no action could be taken until it had been approved by a higher authority. A flood of paper flowed endlessly towards the Governor-General's office, silting up the channels of communication, stifling all initiative. As one 19th-Century historian of the Mutiny put it: "A letter was written where a blow ought to have been struck."

As the army bureaucracy shuffled

its papers, it no doubt paused to consider how thin it was stretched in northern India. Most of the European troops assigned to Bengal had been moved west to secure the Punjab after its conquest and annexation eight years earlier. At Calcutta there was one British infantry battalion, and another was stationed 400 miles away at Dinapur. One regiment was stationed at Agra and one at Lucknow. Altogether, in Bengal—an area as large as France and Germany combined—the British in East India Company units and the Queen's forces (lent to the Company by the Crown) added up to only four infantry battalions and a few batteries of artillery. In India as a whole, there were about 40,000 Europeans in the Company and royal armies, compared to some 300,000 Indian soldiers.

In March there was a brief flare-up when a native unit refused an issue of the new cartridges. It was disarmed under the guns of a British regiment hastily brought back from Burma. One young sepoy killed two British officers and tried to ignite a revolt, but he was captured and quickly hung.

Concluding that the situation was in hand, the commander-in-chief, General George Anson, saw no reason to alter the usual hot-weather routine of the army. Despite continuing reports of barracks mysteriously going up in flames and of secret meetings among the sepoys, European troops were marched to cooler stations in the foothills of the Himalayas. Officers went on leave. General Anson—who had seen no fighting since the Napoleonic Wars more than 40 years earlier—retired with his staff to the hill-station of Simla, nearly a thousand miles away from the civil government in Calcutta.

As the officers and their families relaxed in the cool of their hill retreats, down on the plains, in the great military cantonment of Meerut 40 miles outside Delhi, trouble was brewing. There, 85 sepoys had refused to accept the new cartridge. They were court-martialled, found guilty of disobedience, and sentenced to varying terms of hard labour. On May 9 the whole garrison was paraded to witness the sentences being put into effect.

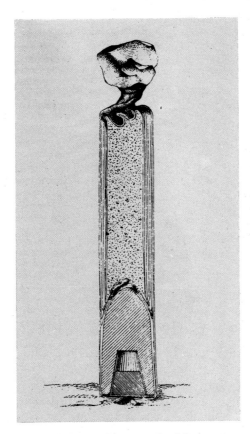

The Enfield cartridge, spark of the great Indian Mutiny, drawn in cross-section.

For a young lieutenant, Hugh Gough, the events of that day were heavy with foreboding. Even the weather underlined the menace. There were dark, low clouds, and a hot dry wind was blowing across the parade ground where some 4,000 men were drawn up to form three sides of a hollow square. On the fourth, open side of the square stood the 85 sepoys. They were clad in their uniforms, but their feet were bare and they carried no weapons. Their comrades, rigid at attention, carried arms, but their ammunition pouches were empty by order. The British troops had the new Enfields loaded with the new cartridges. Gaps in their ranks showed the open mouths of guns; at each breech was a gunner at the ready.

A British officer stepped forward and read from a paper, an Indian officer translating his words into careful Hindustani. When they had finished, a party of British soldiers moved down the file ripping the buttons from the uniforms of the 85 sepoys and the coats from their backs.

Armourers with tools and shackles came forward and began to fit fetters on the condemned men, many of whom had served the British government with perfect loyalty through long years and bloody battles. For a moment it seemed to Lieutenant Gough as if the sepoys would attack the British with their bare hands; but the prisoners were marched off and the tension eased.

That evening a native officer of his own troop came to Gough to warn him that the next day the sepoys would mutiny—all of them, even the cavalry. They would break open the jail and release their comrades. Death was planned for the white soldiers and their families. When Gough informed his superiors, his story was greeted with laughter. When he had been in India a little longer, he was told, he would learn not to take such tales seriously.

The next day was May 10, 1857. About 5 p.m. a rumour spread in Meerut bazaar that British troops were coming to seize the sepoys' arms. An angry mob of villagers surged out to attack the Europeans' bungalows. On the parade ground, sepoys slipped away from white officers desperately trying to control them.

When Gough went out on his veranda an hour later the horizon was a sea of flame. Galloping down to the cavalry lines, he found "a thousand sepoys dancing and leaping frantically about, calling and yelling to each other and blazing away with their muskets in all directions." Meerut was a city of horror. British officers were cut down by their own men. Two officers' wives were murdered.

The suddenness of the attack caught the senior officers off balance. Most were old and had not had to fight since their youth, and they seemed to have no idea what to do. The mutineers were able to break open the jail, release the 85 prisoners, and set off on the road to Delhi, 40 miles away, quite unmolested.

The next day they reached the old imperial capital. Some went to the palace, the great red sandstone fort from which the Mughal emperors had ruled all India before the coming of the British. Inside were men who had waited long for an opportunity to do something against the usurping British. They welcomed the sepoys as liberators, and all the romantic appeal of a once-great native dynasty rising again was grafted on to the confused aims of the mutineers.

There was little the few British officers and civilians in Delhi could do against the three native regiments stationed there and the mutineers from Meerut. The arsenal, one of the largest in India, was inside the city walls and guarded only by native troops. By nightfall of May 11 the Europeans in Delhi were in a bad way. Some escaped, some were prisoners in the palace, but many had been killed either by their own men or when the arsenal was blown up to prevent it from falling into the hands of the mutineers.

On the evening of the next day, May 12, General Anson was host to a Simla dinner party. The wine and the talk were good, and when he was handed a telegram, he set it aside. When the ladies had left the table, he opened the flimsy blue form. It was from Delhi. "We must leave office," it read. "All the bungalows are on fire, burned down by the sepoys of Meerut. They came in this morning. . . . We are off. Goodbye."

The problems of organizing a force for the recapture of Delhi were formidable. Anson, struggling to acquire ammunition, carts, bullocks, clothing, and food, found himself enmeshed in military red tape. The war departments, with their mounds of memoranda establishing precedents and routines for peace-time were totally unprepared for war.

It was early June before the British completed their march to Delhi. With only 600 cavalry and some 2,000 infantry, there was no hope of assaulting the 24-foot walls and beating the 30,000 rebels inside. They settled down to wait for a massive siege-train of guns and ammunition wagons to make its way from the Punjab, 300 miles to the north-west. Already the campaign had claimed Anson, dead of cholera; soon the same disease claimed his successor. The grim summer months passed slowly.

Meanwhile the Mutiny was spreading. Soon after the fall of Delhi to the mutineers, the British communities in two other cities, Lucknow and Cawnpore, in the state of Oudh, were threatened with extinction.

In Oudh, 250 miles south-east of Delhi, the British were faced not only with a military rebellion but with a mass revolt. The recently annexed province was in chaos, the people poverty-stricken, the soldiers of its disbanded army turning to banditry.

When the news of the outbreak at Meerut reached Lucknow, the situation immediately became dangerous. Buildings were set on fire and armed Indians began to gather in the city and to attack European positions. The thin web of British rule was broken. "Every outpost, I fear, has fallen," wrote the commander, Sir Henry Lawrence, on June 12, "and we daily expect to be besieged by the confederated mutineers and their allies." His prediction was accurate. Soon some 3,000 people—British troops and their families, loyal Indians, non-combatants —were under siege in Lawrence's Residency compound by 20,000 rebels.

Forty-two miles away at Cawnpore, another garrison was fighting for its life. In charge was Major-General Sir Hugh Wheeler. A man in his early seventies, he had served in India for 54 years—and none of them had prepared him for what he was now to face. Cawnpore was a large station, with many European and Eurasian families. To protect them Wheeler had only 60 European artillerymen on whom he could rely absolutely.

On the night of June 4 nearly all his sepoys mutinied, burning their barracks and looting. The few who remained loyal joined Wheeler inside his flimsy entrenchments. Behind a rampart four feet high made of loose earth were 240 men and 375 women and children. The sun was at its hottest, and there was little protection from the mutineers' plunging artillery fire except shallow trenches.

The death-roll grew steadily. On June 23, the anniversary of the Battle of Plassey, a great assault was beaten off. But food and water were scarce, and the route to the well was exposed to heavy fire. By June 25 the ammunition was almost gone and there was no sign of relief. Wheeler agreed to surrender. The British were to give up all but their side-arms.

On June 27 what remained of the garrison marched out of their entrenchments. Suddenly, without warning, a shot was heard. Fearful of treachery, the British immediately opened fire. The mutineers replied with grape-shot and ball.

Of those who survived this last battle, the men—60 in number—were killed and the women and children were imprisoned. On July 15, when news reached Cawnpore that the British were approaching the city, all the remaining prisoners were ordered killed. A party of sepoys was detailed to execute the 210 women and children. Apparently unable to bring themselves to commit such cold-blooded murder, they fired high. Butchers were then summoned from the bazaar to finish the job with knives. The next morning the corpses were thrown down a well.

Two days later a British relief force under General Henry Havelock reached Cawnpore. When they entered the town they expected to release the women and children imprisoned there. Instead they found a slaughter-house. "I am not exaggerating," wrote one officer, "when I tell you that the soles of my boots were more than covered with the blood of these poor wretched creatures."

The British left the death room untouched and only partially filled in the well so that they would stand as terrible reminders to new troops from England that their duty was revenge.

At Cawnpore, Brigadier-General James Neill issued an order on July 25 that every captured rebel, whether proved guilty or not, "will be taken down to the house and will be forced to clean up a small portion of the bloodstains. The task will be made as revolting to his feelings as possible. . . . The culprit will be immediately hanged." The Cawnpore murderers, of course, had fled long before.

Neill's ferocity was not exceptional. The British everywhere, enraged by the atrocity, were responding with a reign of terror. They began what one 19th-Century historian of the Mutiny,

J. W. Kaye, called a "Bloody Assize." Indiscriminate lynchings were commonplace. "Volunteer hanging parties," wrote Kaye, "went out into the districts, and amateur executioners were not wanting for the occasion. One gentleman boasted of the numbers he had finished off quite 'in an artistic manner,' with mango trees for gibbets and elephants for drops."

Hanging, however, was usually thought too good for mutineers. When the facilities were available there was a more hideous ritual. With great ceremony the victim was escorted to a parade ground while a military band played some lively air. He was ranged against the muzzle of one of the big guns and strapped into position. Then the band would fall silent and the only sound would be the faint crackle of the portfire as it was lowered to the touch-hole. With a flash and a roar,

an obscene shower of blood and entrails would cover the spectators.

While Neill was engaged in vengeance at Cawnpore, major efforts were being mounted to retake Delhi and Lucknow.

On September 4 the long-awaited siege-train from the Punjab reached the British force outside Delhi. Three days later the first breaching battery was aimed against the city walls. For a week the heavy artillery hammered away. Then, on September 14, the attack opened. Some 5,000 British and Indian troops fought their way through the breached walls under a rain of grape-shot and musketballs. In the furious street fighting that followed, the British captured the city's liquor cellars and drunken troops ran amok in an orgy of vengeance, unable or unwilling to distinguish between mutineers and residents.

After a week of continuous looting and skirmishing the city was won. An officer viewing the ruins wrote: "The demon of destruction seems to have enjoyed a perfect revel." The British had lost nearly 600 dead in the campaign, but a major step in suppressing the Mutiny had been taken.

General Havelock, meanwhile, was fighting his way towards besieged Lucknow. For almost three night-marish months the garrison had held out in the Residency compound under heavy sniper and artillery fire. A shell had killed the commander, Sir Henry Lawrence, and casualties were high among both non-combatants and fighting men.

At least the men of the garrison had their duties. But the women and children were confined to the cellars, and lived a grim life punctuated only by alarms and deaths. The children suf-

A period print offers a comprehensive view of the Cawnpore Massacre. The artist combined the killing of surrendering captives (left) with the slaughter, some two weeks later, of the noncombatants. At right, the bodies are tossed down a canopied well.

The hanging of mutineers, witnessed by their countrymen who remained loyal. Such an execution was especially degrading to Hindus, for the hangman was an outcaste.

fered most. The heat was intense and whenever there was an attack the lights had to be put out and they lay trembling in the darkness, awaiting the outcome.

On September 25, after bloody fighting, Havelock battered his way through to the Residency. "The half-famished garrison," he wrote, "contrived to regale me, not only with beef cutlets, but with mock turtle soup and champagne." But Havelock could do nothing in return. The force he brought to Lucknow was not strong enough to break out again.

Reinforcements, however, were by now arriving in India in ever-increasing numbers. With them came two generals who were to bring the campaign against the mutineers to an end —Sir Colin Campbell and Sir Hugh Rose.

Campbell advanced with 5,000 men on Lucknow, entering the city on November 16. He slowly cleared the city of rebel forces as those in the Residency made preparations for the evacuation. On November 19 the sad remnant of the garrison marched out. Campbell made no attempt to hold the city. He did not have the troops,

and there were more pressing calls. Cawnpore was threatened by a force of some 20,000 men under the command of the best of the rebel generals, Tantia Topi. With Campbell's arrival, the British took the offensive, routed Tantia Topi, and saved the city. Still the campaign dragged on. Not until March, 1858, did Campbell retake Lucknow, and not until May did large-scale operations in the north come to an end.

The fall of the two great centres of the revolt, Delhi and Lucknow, marked the beginning of the end. Civilian leaders of the Mutiny disappeared, some never to be heard of again. Only a few fought on alongside their sepoy followers who—as the British made clear—stood as much chance of death if they surrendered as if they went on fighting to the bitter end.

While Campbell completed his campaign in Oudh, Sir Henry Rose turned on the rebels in central India.

Rose, starting from Bombay, made for Jhansi, which he reached on March 21. When the British launched their assault they were met with strong resistance, but finally they broke

through the walls into the city. No quarter was given, even to women and children. Those rebels who could not escape, wrote an eyewitness, "threw their women and babes down wells and then jumped down themselves." The fighting went on for some days, until the streets were so full of corpses that all the squares were turned into cremation grounds. The British claimed to have killed 5,000 "rebels" in the town, but many must have been innocent citizens.

Rose pushed on, and one by one the rebel forces were defeated and their leaders killed or captured. Peace was officially declared on July 8, 1859. "War is at an end; Rebellion is put down, the Noise of Arms is no longer heard where the enemies of the State have persisted in their last Struggle," proclaimed the Governor-General. The British in the subcontinent and at home began to breathe freely once again.

There had been no real danger that British rule in India would be overthrown. The majority of the native soldiers remained loyal. In fact, without them the British could hardly have suppressed the rebellion. During the attack on Delhi, for example, of 11,200 combatants on the British side no fewer than 7,900 were Indian. Large areas of the country remained unruffled by what the Indians called "the devil's wind."

The British lost about 11,000 men. There are no reliable figures for sepoy or civilian deaths, but many thousands, both guilty and innocent, perished. The scars of the rebellion were there for all to see. Ruined cities, burnt villages, and dead fields ran like a swathe across northern India. In Britain the Mutiny did more than produce a wave of hysteria and a desire for vengeance: it convinced the politicians that the Crown must assume full responsibility from the East India Company for the government of India. This was done by royal proclamation on November 1, 1858.

One of the first problems to be tackled was the reorganization of the army. The Company's white troops were disbanded (and some of the men mutinied in protest). Henceforth there was to be a permanent garrison

A map drawn soon after the Mutiny features the four cities most affected: Meerut, Delhi, Cawnpore, and Lucknow. Other disturbed areas are underlined.

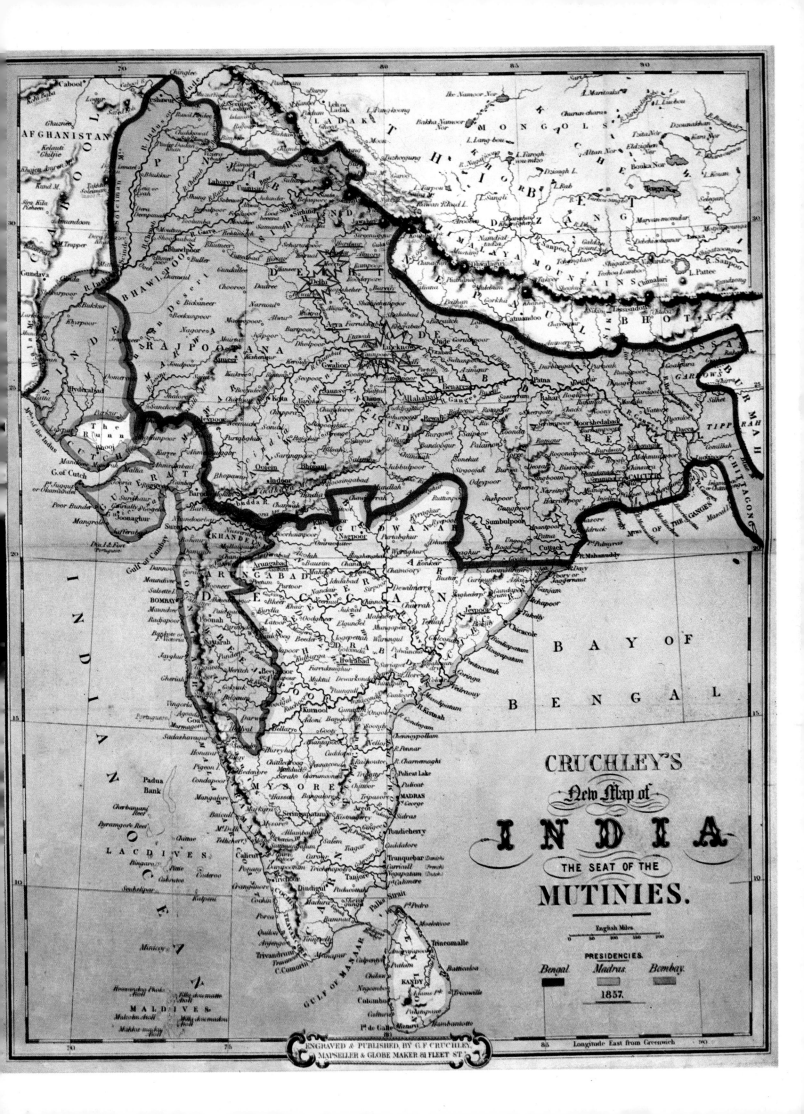

CRUCHLEY'S
New Map of
INDIA
THE SEAT OF THE
MUTINIES.

English Miles

PRESIDENCIES.
Bengal   Madras.   Bombay.

1857.

ENGRAVED & PUBLISHED BY G.F. CRUCHLEY,
MAPSELLER & GLOBE MAKER 81 FLEET ST

of British Army troops; regiments would do tours of duty and then be replaced. The problem of the Indian element in the army was more difficult. Two innovations were made: the proportion of native to British troops was not allowed to exceed two to one; and the artillery was to be almost exclusively in the hands of the Queen's regiments. By 1861 there were about 70,000 British troops to 135,000 native troops, and the British held all the arsenals and forts.

The task of civil reconstruction took many years. The first step was an attempt at reconciliation. The landed princes, who had generally either sided with the British or been neutral, were no longer threatened with annexation. Over the years that followed the Mutiny, every attempt was made to show them that their true interests lay with the British, and everything was done to give them a position—albeit empty of real power—in the new Empire of India. Recognizing that one of the causes of the Mutiny had been the fear that the British intended to make all Indians Christian, Queen Victoria proclaimed categorically that, though "firmly relying ourselves upon the truth of Christianity and acknowledging with gratitude the solace of religion, we disclaim alike the right and the desire to impose our convictions on any other subjects."

What had the revolt been? Was it merely a military mutiny in a part of the army, as the British believed, or a national uprising, as later Indian historians have argued? The truth lies somewhere in between. It was traditional India that had risen against the British, the India that remembered its past, hated the present, and dreaded the future—the future that was now certain to belong to the Westernized Indian, not to soldiers or princes.

—*Michael Edwardes*

Sir Colin Campbell retakes Lucknow in March, 1858, his assault headed by the red-coated Queen's Bays. At right are the 1st King's Dragoon Guards.

Chapter Five
THE DARK CONTINENT

A bull elephant trumpets angrily at the intrusion of explorer David Livingstone's steam launch *Ma Robert*. The painting, of which this is a detail, is the work of Thomas Baines, the artist attached to Livingstone's expedition up the Zambezi in 1858–62.

I. Black Ivory

Ivory was one of the first prized commodities of the Dark Continent to be exploited by Europeans. Before long, however, a product of far greater value was filling the holds of the trading ships that anchored off the pestilential Guinea coast. This was "black ivory"—the enslaved peoples of West Africa.

The Portuguese and Spanish were the first to make slaving pay. Later the French, the Danes, the Swedes, the Brandenburgers, and the Dutch all used and traded slaves. But it was the English who became the most daring, the most efficient, and by far the most prosperous in this most lucrative trade.

England's initial ventures were tentative and brief. Most famous were the slave-trading voyages of that audacious Elizabethan sea-dog John Hawkins. But slaving was not a matter of urgency to England until, following in the wake of earlier European conquerors, she too began to acquire Caribbean colonies.

In 1663 Charles II chartered the Company of Royal Adventurers of England Trading to Africa, and celebrated its founding with a handsome new coin, the guinea, stamped from purest African gold. The new company's very name served notice to foreign rivals that the steaming West African littoral that supplied most of the New World's slaves was now England's hunting-ground as well. And the creation of the company itself signalled the intention to challenge the Spanish, for the Adventurers were required to deliver at least 3,000 African slaves a year to the new sugar islands in the West Indies.

Established slaving nations had already developed the "triangular trade" which England now adopted.

It was a three-legged traffic, each leg profitable: European ships brought manufactured goods to the Guinea coast, where acquisitive local monarchs accepted them in exchange for slaves; the slaves were shipped across the Atlantic—the notorious Middle Passage in the trade—and sold to Caribbean planters; the proceeds went into sugar which was carried back to Europe to buy more trade goods.

To ensure a regular supply of slaves, the Royal Adventurers built a chain of fortified trading posts along the Guinea coast, following the pattern set by the Portuguese and elaborated by the Dutch. The Dutch response was immediate. In 1667 they seized all but one of the English forts. The Company of Royal Adventurers collapsed with a loss of over £120,000. For five years English investors bided their time. Then, in 1672, a second enterprise, the Royal African Company, built new forts and in time controlled the slave coast from Senegal in the north down to Portuguese Angola. By royal charter, only the company's own skippers had the right to carry black cargo.

London might lay down rules, but it was the local monarchs on the Guinea coast who called the tune. To them, the sale of their brothers was neither new or shocking. Africans had sold slaves abroad, along with ivory, ostrich feathers, and ebony, as early as 300 B.C. Their trade with the Arabs was thriving seven centuries before the first white slavers set sail. And they themselves had always taken internal slavery for granted. Prisoners of war were almost invariably made vassals and there were slave-markets in many African towns. Ownership carried obligations to feed, clothe, shelter, and protect, but there was no moral or religious impediment to

slaves being sold. The Europeans took advantage of this, and taught Africans to sell other Africans.

Before the European companies could set up their stockaded trading posts or "factories," scores of which soon dotted the coastline, they had to secure a lease from the local native ruler. This was not a difficult task. The factories were important to the chiefs' prestige and, more significant, they were valued sources of revenue. The chiefs exacted heavy port duties and royal salutes from slaving captains, thus gaining "face" and profit. Autocratic, often irrational, local rulers set the price per slave and permitted none to be loaded aboard until the trade goods were in their hands.

To remain on good terms, the European factors deliberately kept their presence inconspicuous and behaved in an obsequious manner. Pitiable and repugnant at the same time, the men willing to sink into these degrading jobs were the key figures in the whole grisly exchange. Cooped up in the stench of their factories, neighbour to slaves within and contemptuous blacks without, they seldom survived for more than two or three years.

Myths compounded by ignorance tended to create justifications for slavery. It was widely believed that all Africans were cannibals and that they practised appalling brutalities on each other. Slavery, so ran the popular belief, was a distinct step up from the savagery in which Negroes lived. Most Englishmen, therefore, would have considered it eccentric even to question the rights and wrongs of slavery. The Old Testament, after all, provided specific precedents and sanctions. In Genesis Noah curses Canaan, the son of swarthy Ham: "a

servant of servants shall he be unto his brethen."

But some Europeans justified slavery from the opposite side of the religious fence. Many Catholics and Protestants considered it their duty to baptize the heathen, thus conferring a Christian blessing and rendering enslavement almost holy. Boswell, after dutifully recording attacks on slavery by his hero Dr. Johnson, recorded his own pro-slavery views. "To abolish a *status* which in all ages God has sanctioned," he wrote, "would be extreme cruelty to the African savages, a portion of whom it saves from massacre, or intolerable bondage in their own country, and introduces them to a much happier state of life. . . . To abolish the trade would be to shut the gates of mercy on mankind."

There were pragmatists who were more forthright. An 18th-Century economist, Malachy Postlethwayt, put his finger firmly on the underlying realities: "The *Negro-Trade* and the natural Consequences resulting from it, may be justly esteemed an inexhaustable Fund of Wealth and Naval Power to this Nation."

Both government and private enterprise profited handsomely from the start. In the early days of the Royal African Company its stockholders earned dividends as high as 300 per cent. But the monopoly's overhead

was high, too, and by the 1680s the price of slaves delivered had rocketed from £7 to £20 per head. The sugar islanders groaned. Fly-by-night interlopers began carrying West Africans to the Caribbean at cut-rate prices. Under these pressures, the government in 1698 was forced to permit any British skipper to carry slaves, so long as he paid one-tenth of his cargo's value to the Royal African Company. Altogether, company and private skippers delivered some 300,000 slaves to the New World.

Part of the slaving profits came from a curious contract, the *Asiento*, which was sold by the Spanish King and licensed the holder to supply Spain's colonies with blacks. At first it went to individual merchants, later to whichever nation held maritime supremacy. England obtained it in 1713 under the Treaty of Utrecht that ended the War of the Spanish Succession and established her as Europe's leading commercial power. The traders of the newly formed South Sea Company contracted to supply Spanish America with 144,000 slaves over 30 years.

As trade both with Africa and the Americas grew, Bristol, better placed geographically for both runs than London, became the nation's premier slaving port. In the mid-18th Century, Bristol in its turn gave way to Liverpool. The Royal African Company, ailing ever since it lost its monopoly, collapsed, and a consortium of merchants, aided by government subsidies, took over its trading forts. The

newcomers were mostly men of the industrial-minded north, and Liverpool was the natural port for their manufactured goods. By 1797 one Liverpool ship in four was a slaver, and local merchants had captured five-eighths of the English trade and three-sevenths of the trade of all Europe. Liverpool and the industrial hinterland used the profits of slavery to help finance the Industrial Revolution. Merchants invested in great docks, canals, foundries, factories. They underwrote Watt's steam engine, the construction of the Liverpool-London railway, the expansion of the Welsh slate industry.

The lion's share of slaving profits was in the hands of about ten major companies, but virtually everybody dabbled in the business. A contemporary account notes that "Small vessels are fitted out by attorneys, drapers, ropers, grocers, tallow-chandlers, barbers, taylors." Small investors would buy an eighth, a sixteenth, even a thirty-secondth of a venture. Ships' chandlers displayed leg-irons, manacles, thumbscrews, and other essentials of the trade. Jewellers offered silver padlocks for "Blacks and Dogs." Liverpool matrons sauntered about attended by small black boys fancifully dressed in silk costumes and shimmering turbans.

Across the Atlantic, slavery was becoming a major factor in the increasing enmity between England and the Thirteen Colonies. The Yankees had moved into the trade with rum. This was distilled in New England from the molasses the Americans took home in exchange for the wretched "Jamaica quality" fish they sold as slave-fodder in the sugar islands. In 1723 the Yankees shipped a few experimental hogsheads to the Guinea coast. When the New England spirits proved to be to black rulers' taste, there began the second triangular trade—molasses to rum to slaves.

Almost from the start, there were men and nations who felt they owed something to their slaves. In the 17th Century the Spanish enacted a few rudimentary statutes to ease the spiritual and material lot of their chattels. Slaves had to be baptized. They were permitted to marry, and owners were forbidden to separate married couples by sale.

The French, in 1685, introduced the *Code Noire,* which decreed that slaves must be baptized and that they need not work on Sundays or religious holidays. The Black Code set minimum, and minimal, standards for clothing, for the care of the sick and the old, and for food—the protein equivalent of a single smoked herring a day. Marriages between black women and white masters were permitted, provided the master first freed the woman. Their children were born free. The *Code Noire,* however, looked better on paper than it was in practice. In French colonies ill-treatment brought about some of the most vicious of all slave uprisings.

The English produced no such codes. The question of treatment, humane or otherwise, was left to the colonists themselves, whose attitudes ranged from indulgent to savage. The only bill of rights to emerge from London concerned not the rights of the slaves, but the rights of the Caribbean slave-owners. The 1667 "Act to regulate the Negroes on the British plantations" defined blacks as "of wild, barbarous and savage nature" and imposed severe restrictions and punishments.

But the round of repression, insurrection, and repression did not go unchallenged. The same century that saw Englishmen enter the trade also saw a few Englishmen—humanitarians, philosophers, Quakers—begin to oppose it. But anti-slavery senti-

ment did not yet have grass-roots support. Towards the end of the century a number of wealthy colonials retired to England, bringing their domestic slaves with them. Blacks began to be seen in the streets. Sometimes they escaped, and then ordinary people saw them hunted down. Sometimes they were resold, and ordinary people read the advertisements. Some whites began to worry: could the basic tenets of English liberty be ignored on English soil? The question demanded an answer, not only to satisfy the man in the street, but also to satisfy the retired colonials, whose property rights stood in jeopardy.

The legal authorities quarrelled among themselves. One Lord Chief Justice proclaimed that "as soon as a Negroe comes into England, he becomes free." The Court of Common Pleas, however, ruled that a slave remained a slave because he was a heathen. What, then, of those who had been baptized? In 1729 the Law Officers of the Crown decreed that neither residence in England nor baptism limited the master's property rights. The former colonials could rest safe in the knowledge that their slaves were legally theirs.

Their smug security lasted almost half a century. In 1772, in a case brought by a determined young civil servant named Granville Sharp, the Lord Chief Justice, Lord Mansfield, ruled that all slaves in England, whether or not they chose to remain in their old masters' service, were free men.

While Mansfield, spurred on by Sharp, was slaughtering one sacred cow—the slave-owner's property rights—the economist Adam Smith was preparing to demolish another—the hitherto unquestioned monetary contribution that slavery made to the Empire. In 1776 his penetrating analysis of pre-industrial economics, *The Wealth of Nations,* concluded: "The experience of all ages and nations demonstrates that the work done by slaves, though it appears to cost only their maintenance, is in the end the dearest of any."

Not surprisingly, an economist's conclusions about slavery failed to convince any large section of the pub-

lic. That became the goal of the Society for the Abolition of the Slave Trade, founded in 1787 by Granville Sharp and six of his Quaker friends, plus a young idealistic Cambridge student named Thomas Clarkson.

The Society set itself two tasks: to gather and circulate "such information as may tend to the Abolition of the Slave Trade," and to win Parliamentary support. Clarkson undertook the first. The second fell to a moneyed, fashionable, brilliant young Member of Parliament from Hull, William Wilberforce.

William Wilberforce was not the stuff of which reformers are usually made. He had inherited a fortune and was lavishly self-indulgent. After Cambridge he plunged into the drinking and gambling world of high society, though his dissipations were moderate by the standards of the time. He was undersized, frail, and shortsighted, but his social gifts were quite irresistible; he was a brilliant mimic and sang well. And he was courageous.

He was also guilt-ridden about his indulgent life. After months of mental turmoil he announced his conversion to militantly reformist and religious Evangelicalism, then sweeping Britain's lower and middle classes. Soon after, he found the call he had been waiting for—a call above all party interest, irresistible to a true Christian conscience, and one which he believed came directly from God: the fight against slavery.

Wilberforce and Clarkson made a formidable team, although apart from their dogged devotion to abolition they had little in common. Clarkson was massive, unworldly, tongue-tied. Wilberforce was urbane and so beguiling an orator that he was known as "the nightingale of the House." Boswell once heard Wilberforce speak and commented: "I saw what seemed a shrimp mount upon the table, but as I listened, he grew and grew until the shrimp became a whale." Clarkson and Wilberforce worked together much as solicitor and barrister, the one assembling the brief, the other standing in the full glare of publicity before the bar of Parliament and the nation.

An 1828 study of anti-slavery crusader William Wilberforce, by Thomas Lawrence.

Theirs was a long, lonely, frustrating crusade. The West Indian lobby was both powerful and skilful. The French Revolution, raising radicalism to power, drove many Members of Parliament into conservative, anti-reform shells. Yet they fought on, year after weary year. In every session Wilberforce tried to reawaken the issue; in every session Parliament rejected him.

Slowly, however, the mood in the country and in the House began to soften. The French Wars had become a fact of life, no longer the sole national obsession. There was no further reason for Parliament to postpone "irrelevant" legislation. Once more Wilberforce rose in the House to ask leave to present an Abolition Bill. And at last, on March 25, 1807, the bill received the King's Assent. As of January 1, 1808, "all manner of dealing and trading" in slaves in Africa and their transport elsewhere was "utterly abolished, prohibited and declared to be unlawful." Any British subject defying this decree faced a fine of £100; any ship involved was forfeited to the Crown.

Outlawing the trade had been battle enough. Enforcing the law along thousands of miles of fever-coast and in the tempestuous latitudes of the Atlantic was beyond the power of even the Mother of Parliaments. So Westminster turned to the war-worn and overstretched handmaiden of British policy, the Royal Navy. For a half century, as glimpsed in the accompanying portfolio, it pursued the hard and thankless task of blockading African coastlines and capturing suspected slavers.

Wilberforce and the abolitionists had won their first victory after 18 abrasive years. But the ownership of slaves in British territories was still permitted. And within seven years England was to be responsible for the fate of more blacks than ever. Having defeated Napoleon, she acquired many additional slave-owning territories.

The road to emancipation was as tortuous as the road to abolition of the slave trade; it took 25 years after the trade's end to achieve the end of slavery itself. During these years, slave-owning, like slave-trading, came to be widely acknowledged as a social evil, but many Parliamentarians still hesitated to deprive the planters of their labour force. Moreover, it was generally and sincerely felt—by Wilberforce among others—that with the traffic outlawed slaves would be treated more humanely; the planters, knowing they could get no new stock, would feel impelled to safeguard the slaves they already owned. Optimists believed that the institution would simply fade away, with the slaves gradually being transformed into free, hired workers.

As a result, Parliament concentrated on encouraging colonial legislatures to enact amelioration statutes. But the planters viewed all such recommendations as unwarranted interference. The sugar islanders were having trouble enough keeping their heads above water without Whitehall's meddling in their domestic affairs.

Wilberforce, though ailing, led debate after debate. As in the days of the fight to exterminate the trade, abolitionists again stumped the country, pamphleteering and proselytizing. The indefatigable Clarkson, though weakened by a stroke, still continued to organize protest meetings and write tracts.

Once again there was a shift in the public mood. The 1832 Reform Bill vastly extended the voting franchise, and the newly influential middle class supported slavery's abolition. They elected new M.P.'s—men who owed nothing to and would gain nothing from the colonies—who helped push the legislation through.

On July 5, 1833, the bill was introduced that finally freed the slaves throughout the British Dominions (with the exception of India and St. Helena, where slaves were freed by a special act in 1843.) The measure included guarantees of up to £20,000,000 to compensate the planters for their losses.

Wilberforce, now 74, lay dying. "Thank God," he said, "that I should have witnessed a day in which England is willing to give twenty millions sterling for the abolition of slavery." But he did not live to witness the passing of the act to which he had devoted his life. He died on July 29, exactly one month before the measure finally became law.

—*Charlotte and Denis Plimmer*

MISSION OF MERCY

After Britain in 1807
banned slave-trading by her
subjects, international treaties gave her Navy
the right to curb foreign slavers as well as her own.
For 50 years thereafter, British crews risked
their lives along the disease-ridden slave coast
to thwart the men who defied the fragile
web of anti-slaving agreements. One such
mission was undertaken by
H.M.S. *Linnet*, whose voyage in 1852
was recorded in these watercolours
by her Captain, Henry Need.

The *Linnet*, *en route* to slaving waters, puts
out a boat to search for a man overboard.

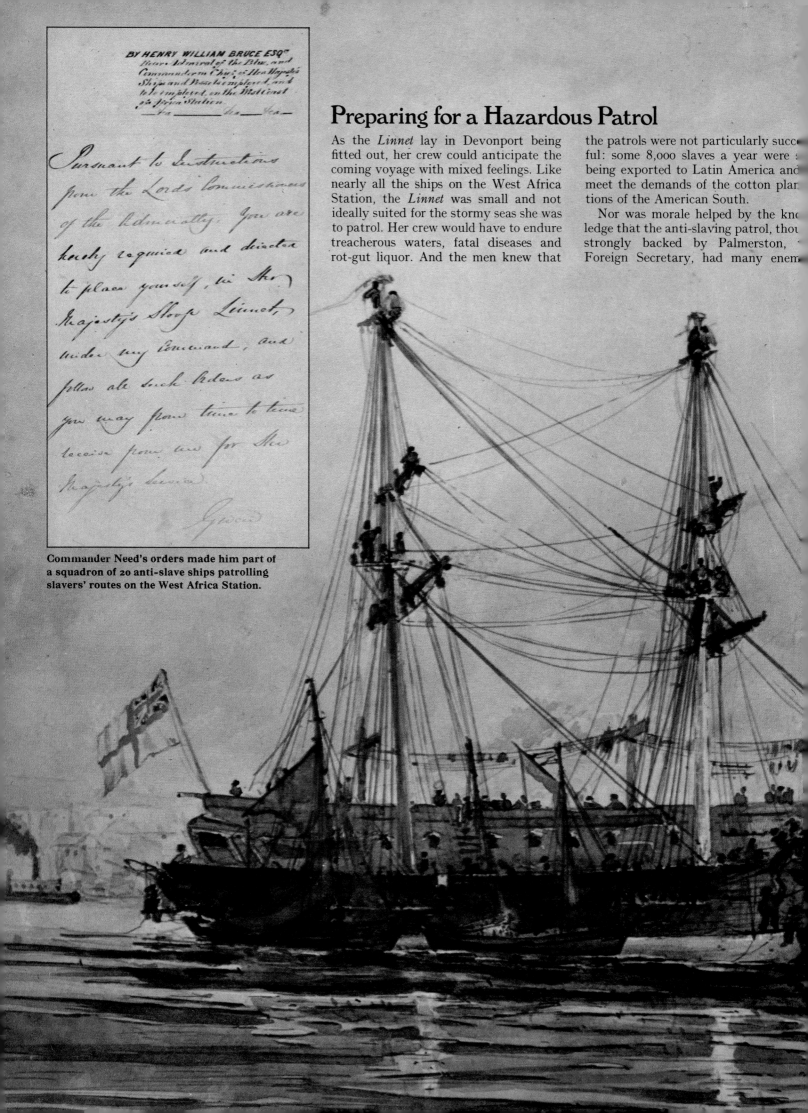

Commander Need's orders made him part of a squadron of 20 anti-slave ships patrolling slavers' routes on the West Africa Station.

Preparing for a Hazardous Patrol

As the *Linnet* lay in Devonport being fitted out, her crew could anticipate the coming voyage with mixed feelings. Like nearly all the ships on the West Africa Station, the *Linnet* was small and not ideally suited for the stormy seas she was to patrol. Her crew would have to endure treacherous waters, fatal diseases and rot-gut liquor. And the men knew that the patrols were not particularly succe[ss]ful: some 8,000 slaves a year were [still] being exported to Latin America and [to] meet the demands of the cotton plan[ta]tions of the American South.

Nor was morale helped by the kno[w]ledge that the anti-slaving patrol, thou[gh] strongly backed by Palmerston, [the] Foreign Secretary, had many enem[ies] ho condemned the deployment of the sentimental squadron" and referred widely to Palmerston's "darling policy." But the *Linnet*'s crew also had much to look forward to: the excitement of the chase and the prospect of promotion and prize-money, for the government had already paid out some £1,300,000 to crews who had made captures.

At Kabenda Bay, a haunt of slavers near the Congo River, African boatmen sell fresh provisions to the *Linnet*'s crew, crying "Hi, Jack! Biggy piggy for hungry belly soldier."

A hundred miles south of the Congo, the *Linnet*'s boat comes ashore at Ambriz, whose deadly liquor knocked sailors unconscious; drunk in the gutters, the tars were easy prey to malaria.

Crewmen swarm over the *Linnet*'s deck and spars, overhauling the intricate web of rigging on the 361-ton ship.

The mosquito-ridden mangrove swamps of the slave coast were known to be rife with malaria and yellow fever. However it was not until 1881 that the mosquito bite was shown to be the cause of both diseases.

Commander Need takes the *Linnet*'s boats up the Pongos River, near Freetown, to search the islands which were a favourite haunt of slave-traders. Here they loaded their newly-purchased merchandise, brought from the interior by negro slave-drivers.

uties and Dangers Inland

e of Commander Need's tasks was to
laver – to agree with local chiefs on
thods of stopping the slave-trade. In
41, some enterprising officers had struck
and and destroyed the slave-factories
ich were the marshalling-yards of the
de. But this destruction of property
voked a legal storm, and the following
ar it became necessary for officers to
clude treaties with native chiefs to
e formal sanction to such actions.

Frequent trips ashore were a real
nger to British crews, for shore leave
ought closer the threat of yellow fever
opularly known as "black vomit"),
laria, dysentery and smallpox. Mor-
lity rates could be appalling: in 1841, for
ample, 46 men died out of 50 who spent
few days up the Pongos River, Sierra
one, where the *Linnet* herself patrolled.
ch disasters only diminished after 1854
en quinine began to be used regularly
a preventive dosage against fever.

The wily Canybar Allee was one of the
many native officials who thrived on the
lucrative trade in "black ivory." For such
canny merchants the only deterrent was
the sight of a British man-of-war.

mmander Need holds a palaver with the King of Ambriz. Though Need represents the
eatest power in the world, he is distinguished from his crewmen only by his officer's
p – an unimpressive sight in comparison with the African chief, gorgeously attired
d sitting under a fine umbrella of the sort Victoria often sent African potentates.

A Slave-Pirate Cornered

On April 30, 1854, Commander Need captured the slaver *Mellidon*. Like all slavers, she was easy to identify by the stench of her cargo and by sharks ominously tracking in her wake. The *Linnet*'s crew did what they could for the slaves and took the *Mellidon* to the nearest "prize court" for condemnation. As for the ship, she was probably burnt or sawn in half at Destruction Bay, Sierra Leone; her slaves were resettled ashore under the watchful eyes of missionaries.

From 1810 to 1864 the Royal Navy rescued some 150,000 slaves en route for the Americas; at best these represented only 10 per cent of the number exported during those years. The end of the West African slave-trade came in the 1860s when other nations passed the necessary laws or enforced existing ones.

The *Linnet*'s boats close in on a quarry for the capture. The preceding chase could have lasted 24 hours or more for, like many other slavers, the *Mellidon* was a fast clipper.

Below the decks of a captured slaver, slaves enjoy conditions of comparative ease during the journey to port where a special court would make their freedom official.

II. Cape Colony

At a summer house in London's Kew Gardens, on a mild spring day in 1795, the Prince of Orange sat worrying over a piece of paper before him. The shock of exile was still fresh and he had not yet fully recovered from a hurried Channel crossing as he fled the invading armies of Revolutionary France. His country was under foreign occupation and no longer even known as the Dutch Republic; the conquering French had rechristened it the Batavian Republic. Now he was being asked to sign away his colonies to Britain to prevent them from falling into French hands. The British were especially interested in the Cape of Good Hope, which commanded the route to their growing Empire in the East. Powerless, the Prince had no option but to sign the agreement and satisfy his hosts.

By that small movement of the pen he did far more than give Britain a base on the route to India. He set in train events which would transform the Cape from the mere victualling-post it had been for 300 years into a nation in its own right. It would be a strange and troubled country, for it lacked the vital element of national unity, being divided from the start between austere Dutch-speaking farmers, incoming British settlers, and a potentially explosive indigenous population.

Though the Portuguese had been first on the spot in 1496, they were intent only on getting silks and spices out of the East. The voyage took six months or more, and since food and water could not be kept fresh it was necessary to have a half-way house to replenish the larder. Portuguese ships anchoring at Table Bay to re-victual would leave letters under large flat stones for homeward-bound ships to pick up and deliver.

When the Portuguese trading empire fell into decline, Dutch merchants took over. To provide for the passing ships, the Dutch East India Company established a little settlement in 1652 under the shadow of Table Mountain. It was intended to be nothing more than a farm to grow vegetables and raise cattle, with a fort to protect it from the local Hottentot tribesmen. Despite the efforts of the Dutch company to limit the settlement, it grew. Children were born and grew up knowing no other country. Thinking of it as theirs, they wanted to govern it themselves. Most were farmers; the Dutch word for "farmer" being *boer*, they came to be known as Boers.

As their numbers grew the Dutch company had increasing trouble with them. The Boers would not accept the fact that they were simply a branch office of a commercial enterprise. They claimed the right to make their own laws and sell their produce to anyone who called at the Cape at prices they themselves would determine. Eventually the company went bankrupt and the Dutch government took over the management of the Cape until the Prince of Orange gave it away.

On June 11, 1795, nine British men-of-war dropped anchor in Simon's Bay and sent ashore a message that they had come to take over until France had been dealt with, after which they would immediately leave. The commanders of the expedition expected no resistance and began lowering boats to disembark their 1,600 troops. But the Boers saw this as a good moment to make a bid for complete independence from further outside intervention. They collected their guns and came down to the beaches to resist the take-over.

So began what could be called the first Boer War; it was certainly the first war fought by these enterprising inhabitants of a new land. From this moment in 1795, the British were regarded as invaders.

After a month of skirmishing, the Boer militiamen realized that they were outclassed by the redcoats and so they dispersed and made their way back to their farms. The British hoisted the Union Jack over the castle in Cape Town and set about convincing the Boers that they bore them no malice and were only temporary residents.

The British gave evidence of their good intentions. They removed many of the restrictions on internal trade previously imposed by the Dutch East India Company, lifted the duty on imports, reduced taxes, and cancelled some crippling monopolies. They then settled down comfortably in the mild climate to watch the sea lanes and to study this peculiar, remote outpost of European civilization.

The settlement consisted of some 16,000 whites of Dutch, German, and French Huguenot extraction. Interspersed in the predominantly agricultural community was a good proportion of skilled artisans. The Huguenots, fleeing from religious persecution in France at the end of the 17th Century, had been a par-

ticularly valuable addition to the culture of the colony and had introduced vineyards, which were to play a large part in the South African economy.

Alongside the Europeans were 17,000 slaves, imported mainly from the Dutch East Indies. Since many were skilled craftsmen, they were able to contribute to the charm and grace of Cape architecture. There were also a few thousand indigenous Hottentots, generally regarded as "an indolent, faithless rabble" whose principal activity was stealing.

The peculiar racial mixture was completed by one more ingredient—the half-caste. It was almost inevitable that this should have happened. The Cape, after all, was the first shore-leave sailors had in a three-month outward-bound voyage.

On the borders of this strange society hovered the Bushmen. They were a small-statured, yellow-skinned people who for thousands of years had had all southern Africa to themselves. Ignorant of metallurgy, they used stone tools and simple weapons and lived in the manner of the late Stone Age. They roamed the land in small family groups, possessing nothing that could not be conveniently carried by each man, never killing more than was needed for their requirements and rarely at odds with each other.

In a time roughly dated as the 10th Century, a Bantu people who were taller than the Bushmen, who knew the use of iron, and most important, who were cattle-owners, began moving south. This invasion continued over the centuries, wave after wave, until in the 17th Century the Bantu came up against the first groups of white cattle-owners. These were Boers probing northward from the Cape. They, too, were looking for greener and more abundant grass.

Squeezed in between were the Bushmen. They were deprived of their food supply as the Boers shot game indiscriminately. When they helped themselves to the white man's cattle, the white man started to shoot them—in fact adding the hunting of Bushmen to his list of recreations. (For Boers, the primitive and vicious Bushmen could not be regarded as part of the human order and so it was perfectly justifiable to hunt him.) In pursuit of survival the Bushmen took themselves off to the west. There in the empty desert wastes of the Kalahari they have somehow managed to survive.

This then was the situation as the British found it—and it did not contribute to their peace of mind. The northward-moving Boers were already in conflict with the southward-moving Bantu. The British suggested that a halt be called to the Boers' advance. They fixed a boundary as the limit of the Cape Colony and requested both Bantu and Boer to respect it as a dividing line.

On paper this was a sensible, pragmatic arrangement. But cows do not respect paper; when they strayed across the border their owners naturally sought to recoup their losses. Border raids by Bantu and Boer were frequent and there was no effective way to prevent them.

Before matters became too heated, the British were relieved of their responsibilities by the Treaty of Amiens in 1802, a peace signed by the warring Continental powers to gain a desperately needed breathing-space in the long Napoleonic Wars. The Cape was handed back to the Dutch.

Dutch control was exercised far more loosely than before, and the Boers began to feel they were on the way to being their own masters. They also began to think of themselves as South Africans rather than as Europeans in southern Africa. Since the word "Boer" did not carry much dignity, they began to emphasize their national identity by styling themselves "Afrikaners."

They had developed a fierce pride in themselves and their accomplishments, and they considered religion their strongest defence against the inimical elements of this barbarous and severe land. The Afrikaners' God was the stern disciplinarian of the Old Testament, the vengeful deity who demanded an eye for an eye and a tooth for a tooth. Their approach to biblical interpretation derived from Calvin, but their version of Calvinism stressed that there was a clear distinction between God's chosen leaders, the Afrikaners, and the black inhabitants, who were destined to be inferior beings. God had so decreed in Genesis; to Afrikaners, it was incontestable that all coloured people were descended from Canaan, and were therefore destined by God to serve.

The Afrikaners' feeling of uniqueness, their unbending religious beliefs, their mastery of the environment and of its people all reinforced their conviction that they had been placed

Cape Town as it looked in 1775, painted by Dutch visitor Johannes Schumacher. At centre is the town fortress; at right is the appropriately named Table Mountain.

The Delights of Cape Town

Most of the English settlers who began to pour into Cape Colony in 1820 were soon disillusioned. Far from being "a succession of parks," as promised, it was a hard land and a dangerous one.

In Cape Town, however, the promise of new prosperity under British rule proved to be quite true. In this lively, cosmopolitan town there was a boom in the latest springed carriages and Parisian confectionery, and smart hotels catered to British Army officers from Bengal or Madras who spent long holidays at the Cape. To the local people the officers' wealth was staggering. They brought with them their own packs of hounds and so many race horses that a barracks had to be converted to stables. They spent £60,000 a year at the Cape, and well-to-do Dutch burghers, considering them "fair game for pillage," made haste to marry their daughters to gentlemen of such means.

The arrival of piano teachers, butlers, seamstresses, and shoemakers from Britain began to smooth the rough edges of a society previously dominated by the Boers. Theatres opened. London styles became all the rage. "Our houses," wrote one Boer, "which so lately were crowded with the heavy Dutch furniture, now have the light elegant appearance of a London residence." Decorative fireplaces were introduced for the burning of coal imported from Newcastle. Drawing room musicales simulated the genteel atmosphere of Jane Austen's England. For some, at least, Cape Town was the answer to their dreams.

in this land for some special purpose, and that any interference with that purpose must necessarily be against the Lord's wishes. It was a reassuring philosophy, but it was soon put to the test. The British, impelled by events in Europe, sailed once more into Simon's Bay in 1806. War had broken out again between France and half of Europe. Napoleon's fleet had been defeated at Trafalgar, but he was still supreme on the Continent and potentially dangerous elsewhere. To forestall any French attempt to seize the Cape and threaten India, the British seized it themselves.

In 1814, with Napoleon defeated and exiled in Elba, the Prince of Orange returned to his own country and demanded his colonies back. But Britain was adamant about keeping the Cape: she was determined never again to be in doubt about access to India. The following year, at the Congress of Vienna, she agreed to buy it. The total payment made to the Dutch was £6,000,000, with the Dutch colonies in South America (which later became British Guiana) thrown in. It looked cheap at the price.

The British statesmen might not have considered it such a bargain had they had a complete picture of the liabilities they were accepting. The Cape's economy was on the point of collapse. Inflation was so rampant that people had to resort to barter. The frontier problem was acute as more and more people trekked away from the problems at the Cape itself to seek a better life in the vast hinterland. The pressure for land was unremitting. Boers took it for granted that an average farmer needed 6,000 acres; each child (and 15 children in a family was no exception) had the same ideal. But they were finding that nothing in this land was as plentiful as it first appeared. The soil was thin and easily exhausted. Droughts occurred every second or third year and might last months.

Rubbing salt into an already festering wound, the British appointed Lord Charles Somerset as Governor, a man with the very highest opinion of himself. He was descended from the Plantagenet kings and was obviously conscious of the fact. Somer-

set descended on the Cape with so large a household staff, so much furniture, and so many horses that two ships were required to transport them. His authority was almost absolute. He was Governor, commander-in-chief, and Judge of the Appeal Court. His only overlord was the Secretary of State in Whitehall, with whom any exchange of letters took at least six months.

Somerset promptly began to interfere in Boer affairs. He clamped down on the Press and forbade "all meetings which might be for the purpose of discussing public measures and political subjects." Worst of all from the Afrikaners' point of view, he decreed that testimony by a black man or a half-caste should have equal weight with that of a white man. This reflected the Evangelical Revival's belief in the equality of all men before God, the popular battle-cry of men like William Wilberforce and other fighters in the campaign against slavery. But in South Africa, where racialist beliefs were as strong as anywhere in the colonial world and where the economy rested heavily on slavery, such attitudes were dynamite—especially when imposed with High Tory arrogance on a proud and obstinate people.

The Afrikaners were suffering from culture shock, the same malady then striking native India, and it was equally painful. Edicts and decrees and laws drove English ways deeper into the developing local culture. English was to be spoken in the schools and the courts and there was even an attempt to install English preachers in the churches. Over 4,000 English settlers were imported. Blacks and half-castes gained a measure of equality in many areas. The last straw for the Afrikaners was the abolition of slavery in the 1830s.

These grievances, along with the ever-lasting need for more land, drove the Afrikaners to consider more seriously than ever before the habitual remedy when their neighbourhood became too crowded or restricted: to pack their wagons and trek in search of freedom. Individuals had been solving their problems in this fashion since the days of Dutch East India

The first English settlers, 4,000 strong, reached South Africa in 1820. As depicted here, they came ashore at Algoa Bay on the east Cape.

Company rule. But never had there been treks by great numbers or for long distances.

In the hinterland there were bound to be places which could support the kind of life they wanted and where the British would have no inclination to follow. Let them keep the Cape. It was already too crowded. The Afrikaners would imitate the Israelites and go in search of a land of milk and honey—up the east coast towards Natal and inland beyond the Orange and Vaal rivers, where generous rainfall made the countryside seem a promised land in comparison with the arid grasslands nearer the Cape.

From 1836 to 1838, the years of the Great Trek, nearly a quarter of the European population of Cape Colony —some 10,000 men, women, and children—took to their wagons to escape British domination. Most were unable to sell their farms and simply abandoned them, together with most of their possessions.

The trekkers moved northeast, their herds of cattle, sheep, and goats trailing along behind. It was truly an exodus. The Voortrekkers, as they came to be known, had no very clear idea of their destination but they trusted blindly in God to lead them. The British watched this mass migration with growing amazement and even awe.

The Great Trek brought forward men whose qualities of leadership set them apart from their fellows. There was Louis Trichardt, a wealthy stockfarmer who had seen this situation coming and had done some exploring of the interior on his own. This knowledge was now invaluable. Andries Potgieter fitted out a train of 50 wagons and provided it with an armed escort of 40 men, which gave him considerable authority in the conduct of affairs. Sarel Cilliers, an ex-elder of the church, had a dominating influence on the spiritual welfare of his group of trekkers (daily service around the wagons was a strict part of the routine). Gerrit Maritz, a wagon-maker and leader of another group, showed the exceptional foresight to pack the only set of law books trekkers had when they endeavoured to set up a separate republic.

The most commanding figure, certainly the legendary embodiment of the Great Trek, was Piet Retief. He summed up the reasons for the Trek in a celebrated manifesto: "We are resolved that wherever we go we shall uphold the just principles of liberty. . . . We shall molest no one, nor take away the smallest possessions of others, but we shall feel justified in defending our possessions and persons against any foe to the utmost of our being.

Once across the Orange River, the Voortrekkers were beyond the farthest reaches of British jurisdiction. A few decided this was far enough and settled down in the flatlands. The others divided into two main groups, one veering eastward towards Natal, and the other pushing north to the next great natural obstacle, the Vaal River.

The Natal party had to surmount the formidable Drakensberg Mountains which seal off the coastal area from the interior. This they achieved after gruelling trial and error and enormous distress for the elderly and the sick, who were strapped into stretchers and carried up and down precipitous slopes. Over a thousand wagons, after being laboriously hauled to the top of the range, were tobogganed down the other side. When the party assembled in the lush coastal land, it thanked God for its safety.

But they were not alone in their promised land, for Natal was dominated by the Zulu nation, soon to become the implacable foe of the Afrikaners.

It was under the leadership of a brilliant chief named Chaka that the Zulus had begun their march to power and nationhood. The first thing Chaka did was throw out traditional military tactics and revolutionize the Zulu army. He subjected his soldiers to rigorous training and iron discipline. He made military service compulsory and organized his army into regiments, each with a distinctive uniform of furs and feathered head-dresses. Chaka equipped his troops with stout stabbing assegais which, like the Roman short-sword, were hefted underhand and compelled close, hand-to-hand fighting. Through rigorous training marches, he produced an infantry that could cover 60 miles a day in a time when European armies considered 15 miles a remarkable day's march.

By the 1820s, however, Chaka was becoming cruelly and capriciously psychotic. Finally his tyranny became too high a price to pay for his genius, and in 1828 he was stabbed to death by his half-brother, Dingane.

At first, the Zulus viewed the Boer trekkers tolerantly and were fascinated by their firearms and horses, neither of which they had seen before. They were prepared to grant concessions of land in exchange for these, and Dingane condescended (with no realization of what he was doing) to make his mark on a piece of paper entitling the trekkers to occupy and farm certain outlying portions of his kingdom. Dingane found the Afrikaners odd and amusing and they looked quite harmless. For a few years peace prevailed. The settlement at Port Natal, soon to be renamed Durban, began to grow, and the Zulu *kraals* (the Boer word for the native villages) also prospered.

But as more and more wagons came over the Drakensberg Mountains Dingane's attitude began to change. He demanded to know how many more were coming. No one could tell him, but his counsellors suggested there might be no end to them and that the Zulu's country would be overrun. Dingane was also beginning to understand that the gun was a far more effective weapon than the spear and that a large number of these people armed with guns might be a more formidable force than his army had encountered before. Perhaps, ran the thinking, it would be wise to stop that possibility from developing by a campaign of annihilation.

The trekkers, however, took precautions. Each night they drew their wagons up into circles—known as *laagers*—and posted sentinels. Dingane had no desire to risk a frontal attack against guns. He would deal more craftily with the situation.

To this end, he summoned Piet Retief to his Great Place, or royal kraal, with a promise that he would turn over a large tract of land for the trekker's use. Retief was warned that this might be a trap, but he thought it worth the personal risk if Dingane was sincere. With half a dozen others he set off. No one was allowed to come armed into the chief's presence, so Retief and his companions dutifully left their weapons outside the camp. Dingane sat and talked amicably with them, and when Retief drew up a paper, he set his mark to it transferring nearly the whole of Natal to the trekkers. Retief pocketed this and rose to go after a suitable exchange of presents to mark the occasion. It was then that Dingane gave a signal. Retief and his little party were clubbed to death.

Immediately large bodies of Zulu troops fanned out from the Great Place to attack the various wagon circles. They moved so quickly and with such stealth that the first laager they fell upon was taken completely by surprise. A fearful massacre of men, women, and children followed, the site of which was thereafter known as Weenen, "place of weeping."

Other scattered groups were slaughtered before the trekkers could rally themselves and check the Zulu army. Nearly 400 Boers perished.

The survivors determined on revenge. On December 16, 1838, under the command of Andries Pretorius, they took their stand on the banks of the Umslatos River. The river protected one flank, and a crescent of tightly grouped wagons with thorn bushes between the wheels covered the other. They then made a solemn convenant with God that if He should give them victory they would build a church to His glory on the site and forever after keep the anniversary as a day of thanksgiving and the sign of His deliverance.

Zulu warriors 11,000 strong attacked the position in successive waves. Crouched behind their wagons, the 460 Afrikaners fired as fast as the guns could be loaded by the women and children. At the end of the day Zulu dead were piled high against the wagon wheels and the river ran red with blood. It was renamed Blood River, and the same name was given to the battle. The Zulu war machine had been broken for the first time. Dingane himself escaped, but when the trekkers entered his Great Place, which they burnt, the body of Piet Retief was found. In his pocket was the document ceding most of Natal to the trekkers.

The Afrikaners set about forming themselves into a republic, with a council and a flag and other trappings of independence. This was no simple task, for they were by no means united in their ideas of what form their government should take. Their strong, individual sense of independence led to many quarrels among their leaders, too many of whom looked for guidance and took advice only from the voice of God.

Left to themselves, no doubt they could have hammered out a workable form of statecraft, but they were not to be granted the luxury of time. Down at the Cape the British had finally come to see the Great Trek as a devastating vote of no confidence in their colonial policy. The rebuff was intensified by the news that the trekkers had formally declared themselves a republic and were offering to open negotiations with Her Majesty's government. Moreover, foreign policy was involved, since the Afrikaners possessed Port Natal, a strategically important harbour on the sea route to India. Secretary of State Lord John Russell, who regarded the whole action as a personal insult to the young Queen Victoria, issued instructions in 1841 to the Governor at the Cape to put Natal under British jurisdiction.

The Governor was Sir George Napier, of whom Wellington thought so highly that when asked to nominate three candidates for a position of command he had simply scribbled "Napier. Napier. Napier." He immediately assembled his troops and

Some notion of the ordeal that faced Voortrekkers crossing the Drakensberg range into Natal can be glimpsed in the sketch at left. Below is the Zulu massacre of trekkers at Weenen.

a small fleet and sailed up the coast to present the necessary papers of annexation. Again the Afrikaners came down to the beaches ready to fight, and again they were outclassed by the redcoats. In 1843 Natal submitted to the rule of the detested British.

The more defiant Natal Afrikaners trekked westward, back over the Drakensberg range to join their fellows beyond the Vaal River. This group, too, had had to fight off an African tribe, the Matabele, in a pitched battle in 1837. After their victory they too declared themselves a republic, the Transvaal. Since they were a thousand miles from Cape Town and had no seaport, the British let them go, and in 1852 recognized the Transvaal Republic. Two years later, a second Boer republic, the Orange Free State, took shape.

All would have been well for these survivors of the Great Trek but for one unforeseen factor which the Good Lord had not chosen to reveal while guiding them to the Promised Land. As they unpacked their wagons and marked out their farms, built their homesteads and churches, and thanked their God for delivering them finally from the British, they were blissfully unaware that beneath their feet lay the world's greatest deposits of gold and diamonds, wealth that would all too soon bring strangers flooding into their newly established homeland.

—David Lytton

III. Exploring West Africa

The exploration of darkest Africa, one of the grand adventures of the 19th Century, had its genesis one June evening in 1788, when there came together at St. Alban's Tavern in London nine of the twelve gentlemen who made up the Saturday's Club.

What the club lacked in numbers it more than made up for in brains and social push. In 18th-Century London the group represented a cutting-edge of scientific inquiry, eager for knowledge, hungry for fact, passionately conscious of a whole wide world awaiting explanation. The gentlemen of the Saturday's Club were convinced that the spirit of the age demanded action.

Their leading member was Sir Joseph Banks, a botanist who had been the chief scientist on Captain Cook's first voyage. A man of much influence in London's dawn of modern science, Banks convinced his fellow members that they should issue a challenging manifesto. "Nothing worthy of research by sea, the Poles themselves excepted, remains to be examined," it asserted, "but by land, the objects of Discovery are still so vast, as to include at least a third of the habitable surface of the earth; for much of Asia, a still larger proportion of America, and almost the whole of Africa, are unvisited and unknown." So wide an ignorance, it concluded, "must be considered as a reproach upon the present age."

The Saturday's Club, deciding to concentrate upon the largest area of contemporary ignorance, formed the "Association for Promoting the Discovery of the Interior Parts of Africa" and laid upon each member a subscription of five guineas a year for three years. From this most modest beginning there came in time a great, many-sided, highly influential enterprise.

To the initial concern with geographical exploration, other driving motives were soon added. High on the list was Britain's growing belief in the virtue of overseas trade—provided of course that the trade was British. Banks sought to persuade colonial administrators, who had far less to do now that the North Americans had so rudely removed themselves from their control, that "whoever colonizes in that part of [West] Africa with spirit will clearly be able to sell colonial products of all kinds in European markets." Let the Old World right the balance lost to Britain by the departure of so much of the New. The administrators listened and hoped that it could be so.

The French Wars unleashed a nationalist rivalry that was to become the spring to power much of the drive for Empire in Africa. More and more, as the years passed, discovery responded to the call of patriotism. When French commerce recovered in the wake of Waterloo, the old questions about geography began to be asked in ways more attractive to practical merchants or to ambitious politicians conscious of the rising waves of anti-foreign fervour. Where lay the regions of inland Africa that would be best for trade? Which were the most useful ports along the coast to seize and hold against malicious rivals?

Other sources of public interest grew in strength as the old century ended and the new began, helping Banks and the African Association find the money and the men they needed. Considerable assistance came from British philanthropists, who wanted to end the slave trade by land as well as by sea. The best way to do this, they thought, was to promote other types of trade. If answers to Africa's geographic puzzles could be found, abolitionists like Wilberforce believed, profit could go hand in hand with charity, and the light of civilization would cast its saving gleam in dark places.

Responding to these incentives, the whole subject of Africa became fashionable. The Dark Continent's mysteries had long provoked curiosity; now they began to evoke romance. It was with several high-flown verses entitled *Timbuctoo*—a name which then and for long afterwards seemed to echo all that was most curious about Africa—that the 19-year-old Alfred Tennyson carried off the Cambridge Chancellor's poetry prize in 1829:

*Wide Africa, doth thy sun
lighten, thy hills unfold a
city as fair
as those which starred the night
o' the older world?
Or is the rumour of thy
Timbuktoo
a dream as frail as those of
ancient time?*

At the outset of the great adventure, however, the primary demand was merely for the facts of geography. The Association's early volunteers might if they wished dilate upon the peoples whom they found, just as they might report upon the lions, elephants, and other amazing fauna they met upon their way, but that was not their main task. What the Association wanted to know was the layout of the land, and it is easy to see why. The map of inland Africa was an almost total blank but for scraps of dubious information inherited from medieval or even Graeco-Roman atlases.

Banks and those who followed him concentrated upon two problems of geography that were judged of central value. These concerned the source and course of two great African rivers, the Niger and the Nile. If those problems could be solved, it was argued, at least a basic skeleton for Africa's inland topography would become available.

Most European geographers of the day believed that the Niger took its rise somewhere in the middle of Africa, possibly in a vast lake which also, if inexplicably, might be the source of the Nile as well. Again following ancient errors, they believed that the Niger flowed westward until it became the Senegal River and so joined its waters with the Atlantic. There were some who questioned this, arguing that the Niger flowed eastward, but they in their turn had no idea where it ended.

Did the Niger perhaps join the Nile? Or possibly another great river, the Congo, of which nothing was known but its lower course and estuary? And where, in any case, did the mainstream of the Nile take its rise? Back in the early 1770s a Scottish nobleman named James Bruce had returned from a long stay in Ethiopia with the claim to have found the source of the Blue Nile in an Ethiopian lake. But the Blue Nile, English savants replied, was not the "true Nile"; besides, Bruce should properly be doubted, for he had written copiously and worse still admiringly of the African peoples among whom he had lived. No reliable scientist, it was thought, would have done that.

All these questions about Africa's major rivers, and many others of the same kind, were to be answered in two major periods of discovery. Between 1797 and 1830 the course and termination of the Niger, and much of the general topography of the countries through which it flowed, were fixed beyond further doubt. The Nile, however, had to wait until the second wave of discovery in mid-century.

The men who marched into Africa on these journeys of discovery were a mixed bag, but they had certain things in common. They were all strong on optimism. It could scarcely have been otherwise, for they plunged into a "darkness" that was practically complete. They seldom had the vaguest notion of where they were going or what, if they ever got there, they would find. Their clothing and equipment was almost always wildly inappropriate. They wore heavy serge, the trousers tight, the jackets long, and boots made for the drawing rooms of Europe or the barrack squares of northern latitudes. They carried far too much baggage or, more often, far too little. They took fearful risks, mainly from the climate. They never had enough money. Several had no money at all.

Up to the 1840s they were all amateurs. Most were "men of no family," as the Victorians would have said. Many were half-pay officers from the lower commissioned ranks for which promotion, at least after the Napoleonic Wars, was next to impossible without private means to buy advancement. Several were doctors hard up for the next week's rent in days before medicine ceased to be a trade and became a respectable profession. Later on it would be said that the British Empire was won on the playing fields of Eton. But its obscure

Land of Myth and Monsters

Until the early 1800s, the Dark Continent was illuminated only fitfully by legends and snippets of knowledge handed down from scribe to scribe over the centuries. Medieval map-makers compensated for their ignorance by peopling the emptiness with brilliant cities, bizarre men, and hideous monsters.

Much of this had mythological origins in the classics. According to Pliny, African fauna included *pegasi*—winged horses with horns—and the terrifying *mantichora,* with its triple row of teeth, human face, lion's body, and its "special taste for human flesh." Solinus spoke of ants "as big as a mastiff" that scraped up "sand of golde which they keepe that no man may fetch it away and if any man adventure, they persue him to death."

The peoples of Africa were believed to be equally strange and equally savage. Pliny records the presence of *Blemmyes*—men who "by report have no head but mouth and eies in their breasts." Their barbarous behaviour was generally attributed to the extreme heat of the Torrid Zone, which inflamed the brain.

These early accounts had their counterparts in the 18th-Century fables of the wealth and splendour of Africa's empires. The greatest magnet of all was mysterious Timbuktu, a city paved with gold, a centre of learning and culture. When René Caillié finally reached Timbuktu in 1828 and reported it "a mass of ill-looking houses built of earth," he was indignantly refuted. The world preferred to cling to its romantic notions.

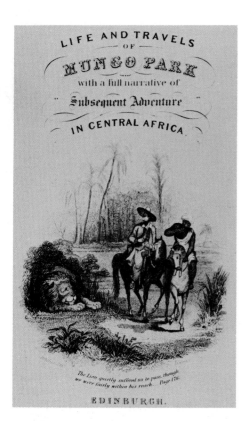

Park lets a sleeping lion lie: the title page illustration from his account.

early victories were scored on the kicked-up grass of academies that any Etonian would have blushed to recognize.

Some volunteered for African exploration because they lacked employment at home. Others went because they were ambitious men offended by the barriers to promotion in a Britain still dominated by aristocratic privilege. A few, and those among the best, answered the call of Christian duty, fervently believing that exploration could somehow help to rescue Africa from pagan misery and damnation. If fame was a spur to many of them, it was a modest fame: social acceptance at home and a "decent competence," a small but sure place in the sun of Britain's rising imperial grandeur.

A few achieved these aims, and one or two were afterwards to figure high among the folk heroes of Britannia's pantheon of glory. Of those who survived, one or two also made money. But not many survived, and the money was never very much.

Even when they contrived to es-

cape death upon their travels, it was rare for the leader of an expedition to get any more than a congratulatory scroll as his reward. Farther down the line, among the servants or enlisted men, the case was sorrier still. By 1840 the number of British servicemen lost trying to establish the truth about the Niger had passed the 150 mark. Even their names are utterly forgotten.

The African Association's first efforts brought only disappointment, for it got off the mark with two false starts. In 1789 it gave the American adventurer John Ledyard the tidy little task of crossing the Sahara from Egypt and then of "traversing from East to West, in the latitude attributed to the Niger, the widest part of the Continent of Africa." Ledyard proceeded to Cairo, but fell ill and died there. The Association persevered. The next year it commissioned a 50-year-old Irishman named Daniel Houghton to try for Timbuktu, this time by way of the Gambia River on the far west coast. Houghton had married a wealthy wife who had scattered her fortune, and seems to have been happy to escape his creditors. Having landed at the mouth of the Gambia, this rather pathetic optimist wrote bravely to his wife that he hoped to reach Timbuktu within a month but she was not to worry "if my silence appears long," He vanished up-river, and his silence proved as long as the grave.

The Association began to be dismayed, fearing that Africa could never be made to yield its secrets. But in 1795 Banks heard of another volunteer from his friend and scientific colleague James Dickson, one of the founders of London's Linnean Society. Dickson had a youthful brother-in-law lately returned from a long voyage to the East Indies and now eager to try his hand at African discovery. After Banks and his friends had seen him, they agreed he would be suitable. They did better than they knew. With Mungo Park they achieved their first big breakthrough.

Park was a man whose early background stood him in peculiarly good stead for the tremendous challenge he undertook. A small-farmer's son

of the Scottish Lowlands, one of a large and penniless family, he was framed in a dour frugality of manners and material expectation. Like others of his kind, he might well have trained for the ministry, and seems to have had a strong inclination in that direction. As it was, he managed to qualify as a medical practitioner, though with much personal sacrifice and no little difficulty.

He had a capacity for penetrating beyond the exotic to the stuff of humankind. "Whatever difference there is between the Negro and the European in the conformation of the nose and the colour of the skin," he concluded after his first journey, "there is none in the genuine sympathies and characteristic feelings of our common nature." Not many later explorers found it possible to utter any such sentiments. But the great imperial century had yet to persuade Europeans of their natural superiority to Africans, and Park had no such notion.

When the Association sent him off in May, 1795, he was 23 years old. His orders were to reach the Niger from the Gambia estuary and find out the truth about its direction of flow and its termination. His material preparations were minimal. His journey was to last two years, but his "baggage was light, consisting chiefly of provisions for two days."

Thus equipped, he left the upper Gambia and rode off into the interior. In the months that followed he suffered fearful troubles and misadventures, but most of these, as he wrote afterwards with a rare generosity, were nobody's fault but his own. He moved across African state borders without meeting formalities or paying dues. He persisted in pushing on when friendly rulers advised him to turn back. His medical training helped to save him, but so did his sense of fun. Africans liked him. The feeling was mutual.

Passing through the state of Bondu, one of three Muslim theocracies founded in the 18th Century but of which nothing was then known in Europe, Park found himself besieged on one occasion by a dozen of the ruler's wives, "most of them young and handsome," who "rallied me with a good deal of gaiety on different subjects, particularly upon the whiteness of my skin, and the prominence of my nose. They insisted that both were artificial. The first, they said, was produced when I was an infant, by dipping me in milk; and they insisted that my nose had been pinched every day till it acquired its present unsightly and unnatural conformity." Park seems to have enjoyed the encounter as much as the ladies.

Nearing the Niger, he entered a country long embroiled in dynastic strife and the coups of ambitious generals. Danger began to gather round him, but his never-failing courage carried him onward to the northeast. On July 20, 1796, he was at last rewarded, and "saw with infinite pleasure the great object of my mission, the long sought for majestic Niger glittering in the sun . . . as broad as the Thames at Westminster, and flowing slowly *to the eastward.*"

If the first part of his great quest was accomplished, there still remained the second. To go on very far eastward following the river, it would be necessary to secure admission to the Bambara kingdom. The king wished him well, and sent him 5,000 cowries "to enable me to purchase provisions in the course of my journey," but refused to admit him.

The king's fears, clearly enough, lay in likely reactions from the local trading community, who would certainly interpret Park's arrival as some kind of future threat to their commercial monopoly. Why otherwise should a white man penetrate their country if it were not to open the road to his fellow countrymen?

This was not the first or last occasion when a white explorer would run into the opposition of an African business community. Park did not blame the king. "He argued probably, as my guide argued: who, when he was told that I had come from a great distance, and through many dangers, to behold the Joliba river [the Niger], naturally inquired, if there were no rivers in my own country, and whether one river was not like another," To the guide it was clear that some other motive must lie behind the making of so exacting a journey.

Helped by the king's cowries, a good currency in that area, Park went on eastward for a time, but was soon obliged to turn back for want of guides or food. Penniless by now (or rather cowrieless) he was in dire straits, and his journey back to the Gambia was long and terrible. When at last he got there, he found no British shipping nor hope of any. In the end he was obliged to go home on a North American slaver via the West Indies.

In London Park was fêted. The African Association had up to now fathered nothing but chaos. Banks proudly showed off his protégé at dinner parties and at breakfast discussions. Park submitted to the adulation with a sullen resignation. Like many explorers after him, he found the transition from the rigours and adventures of the wilderness to the trivialities of society an irritating one. But he had one great consolation: the publication in 1799 of his account was an immediate success, thanks to both its transparent honesty and its brevity. It has become a classic.

Park returned to his medical trade, always hankering after Africa. It was 1805 before he was called on again, this time in very different circumstances.

Now it was no longer only a question of exploration, but also of ousting the French from their footholds on the Gambia. An ambitious expedition was planned. Park had 43 European companions, most of them soldiers, together with carpenters and other artisans who were to build river boats for a voyage down the Niger to its unknown termination.

But everything went wrong. Most of Park's companions died of fever long before the Niger was reached. When the remnants of the party at length reached the river they found hostility everywhere, aroused by local rulers of inland commerce. Near the end of his tether, Park nonetheless held on. "I shall set sail to the East," he wrote London, "with the fixed resolution to discover the termination of the Niger or perish in the attempt."

Painfully he began to build a boat.

This miniature of Mungo Park is a copy of Henry Edridge's portrait from life.

Of four carpenters who had left the Gambia with him, the only one still alive was on his deathbed. Two other European survivors were almost as helpless. With the single remaining able-bodied soldier Park put together a 40-foot craft from discarded Niger canoes found rotting on the bank. It took them 18 days. Then he hoisted the Union Jack, embarked with his four surviving companions, one of whom was no longer in his right mind, and four African servants.

After tracing the river's course for hundreds of miles as it flowed east and south, they came to grief in a clash with natives in what is now north-western Nigeria. All of them died except one African who managed to escape to inform the outside world of Park's fate.

Geographically speaking, Park's was only a half-success. Yet in other ways it proved a triumph. His two journeys were perhaps the most influential of all the early ventures into Africa, if only because Park's heroic courage and endurance set the tone and temper for most of those who followed him. They also set a high mark in personal modesty, not the least of this attractive man's qualities. His account of his first journey reveals a traveller whom people at every level of society could and did admire.

The question remained, where did the Niger end? Banks and his successors turned their attention to the trans-Saharan route. For this approach the city of Tripoli played the part filled on the west coast by the Gambia estuary.

Several parties sent out from Tripoli ended in disaster. But in 1822 there came the great northern breakthrough. Major Dixon Denham, Dr. Walter Oudney, and Captain Hugh Clapperton crossed the Sahara to Lake Chad in a success comparable to Park's first journey. Oudney died, but Denham went on southward to the Shari River beyond Lake Chad and the powerful kingdom of Bornu in what is now north-western Nigeria. Clapperton went eastward to the rich Hausa cities of Kano and Sokoto.

So it was that Denham and Clapperton brought back to England the first modern reports of strong and wealthy states south of the Sahara. At last those at home who had long preached the mission of British trade with inland Africa felt themselves fully justified. The night of ignorance was still fairly black, but dawn seemed on the way. Beyond the desert lay kingdoms and cities with obvious commercial possibilities, if only

sound communications could be established.

These states, moreover, had impressive rulers who appeared amenable to argument. Clapperton, a half-pay naval officer of cheerful disposition but little education, had found Sultan Bello of Sokoto disconcertingly erudite. "He asked me a great many questions about Europe, and our religious distinctions. He was acquainted with the names of some of the more ancient sects, and asked whether we were Nestorians or Socinians."

All this was welcomed in London as gratifying evidence of stability in the inland country where wealth was waiting to be tapped. Besides, Clapperton came back with more than information. He brought from Sultan Bello a letter to George IV that offered friendship. What he required, Bello wrote, was a safe and sure source of guns and ammunition. In exchange he would welcome a British consul, would open the way to his kingdom from the west coast, and would prohibit the coastal export of slaves.

On the last two points the Sultan was offering more than he could de-

liver, but this the British had yet to realize. Eager to exploit a promising relationship, they sent Clapperton back to Africa in 1825. After great labours he got through to Bello's capital of Sokoto, only to fall ill and die. With him was a Cornishman named Richard Lander, just past his 21st birthday, a cheerful easy-going chap "as broad as he was long." Lander's patience and resilience got him back to the coast and ultimately back home, where he turned Clapperton's blunt, earthy journal over to a publisher.

The Colonial Office found Bello to be a sad disappointment, yet officials admitted that someone should be sent back to the scene, if only to discover where the Niger reached the sea.

The job went to Lander. In 1830 he and his brother, John, were landed on the coast at Badagry near what is now the frontier of Dahomey. Their orders, reminiscent of those given to Park long before, were to march inland until they struck the Niger and then "to follow its course, if possible to its termination, wherever that may be." They carried out these orders with a total lack of fuss, bother, or pretension, and within 17 months were back again in England with the certainty that the Niger flowed into the Bight of Biafra.

The key provided by the Landers to the truth about the Niger happened to fit a door on whose threshold British trading interests were firmly established, and where the French were scarcely present. This door to the interior was the great Niger delta system along the coast of the Bights of Biafra and Benin, a coast studded with thriving merchant towns that British traders had long regarded as their own special preserve. Now it was clear that the delta could open the way by river to the lands discovered by Clapperton and others. The impossibly difficult Saharan route could be abandoned.

Eager to encourage profitable "legitimate trade" and thus wean African merchants away from slaving, influential philanthropists added their arguments to those of merchants and officials. The Niger delta should

Major Denham's party reaches a tribal capital near Lake Chad after crossing the Sahara. This illustration from Denham's 1826 account is based on the explorer's sketch.

198

become the chief focus of British effort.

But African opposition to European inland journeys was making itself felt. African traders on the coast had no objection to European monopoly of the sea-borne carrying trade, but they showed a powerful resentment when Europeans offered competition on land—where Africans had their own monopoly. Explorers and missionaries were welcome enough; they did no harm, and possibly might do some good. But traders were another matter. African states turned out their troops, called up their war canoes, fortified their trading towns, bought cannon and muskets, and closed the inland trails. Clashes followed.

Richard Lander, broader of beam than ever and still as optimistic, lost his life in one of these. In 1832 he went back to the west coast for a third time, now as leader of a trading expedition promoted by a newly formed African Inland Commercial Company. Lander and his companions were to go up the Niger in two steamships and establish a trading post in the far interior. He duly took his iron-clad ship as far north as the border of Hausaland, where he was welcomed by a potentate only too happy to deal directly with European suppliers, thus cutting out the coastal middlemen. The coastal middlemen felt less warmly towards the enterprise. They decided they had better act, and in 1834 they attacked Lander and his party. Game to the last though badly wounded, Lander was described by an eye-witness as "cheering on his men" before he drowned.

Two large reconnaissance expeditions—one in 1831–32, the other in 1841—came to the same tragic end. Yet the pressures for inland discovery from the delta were strong enough by now to absorb these shocks. Merchants and missionaries pounded on the doors of the Foreign and Colonial Offices, and the ministers, unable to withstand them, felt obliged to dip into the Treasury. The Treasury justified its spending by pointing to impressive trade and humanitarian statistics. The anti-slaving effort in the delta had greatly reduced the slave trade as shrewd African entrepreneurs moved instead into the booming palm-oil business. This ingredient was vital in the manufacture of soap, and by 1848 exports stood at 25,000 tons annually. Commerce was doing its job; Christianity would quickly follow.

More than Christianity followed. In 1849 the Foreign Office under Palmerston appointed a trader named John Beecroft as Her Britannic Majesty's First Consul for the Bights of Benin and Biafra. A new epoch opened. From then on the process set in motion by the explorers became one of continual British encroachment on the mainland.

One great obstacle remained to be hurdled before the full fruits of exploration could be gathered in—the continuingly high and crippling death-rate of Europeans from disease. The delta's reputation as the white man's grave had become legendary:

> *Beware and take care*
> *of the Bight of Benin:*
> *For one that comes out*
> *There are forty go in.*

But in 1854 Dr. William Balfour Baikie took a large party of Europeans far up the Niger and not one of them died. Quinine was the answer. Others had long suspected its saving virtue. British naval crews, cruising for months on anti-slaving patrols in West African waters, had sometimes used quinine, though more in desperate hope that it might do some good than from any firmly based belief. Baikie made it firm. Though yellow fever continued to take its toll the malaria death-rate began to fall.

Meanwhile, explorers returned to the northern gateway. Starting from Tripoli and heading across the Sahara, successive missions continued to fill in the blanks on the maps of central Africa. Of those who went the route of Denham and Clapperton, none was as successful as a young German scientist, Heinrich Barth, whose expedition of the 1850s, undertaken in British service, proved of a historical and geographical value whose full importance has been realized only in our own time.

Barth was one of the great 19th-Century explorers of Africa. He shared the courage and cool judgement of the best of the amateurs and adven-

An 1852 Heinrich Barth drawing is the source for this lithograph. It shows a royal procession on the way to the palace of the Sultan of Bornu near Lake Chad.

turers, but unlike them he had taken himself through arduous years of scholarly preparation and travel in North Africa. By the time he left for the Sudan in 1849 at age 28, he possessed an intellectual and practical experience that none of the others could claim. And to round it off, he enjoyed good luck. Not only did he persist, he persisted with success.

With another German, Adolf Overweg, and James Richardson, the English leader of the expedition, Barth was sent to investigate the internal African slave trade, and in December, 1849, the trio left Tripoli for Mourzouk. At one point Barth spent 28 hours in the desert without water, keeping himself alive by sucking his own blood. Richardson died on the first leg of the journey and Overweg some 18 months later. Barth pressed on alone, interviewing chiefs, discussing treaties, and compiling detailed reports with meticulous attention to detail. He was once taken for a Turkish spy—because of his habit of writing everything down—and at other times for a rain-maker, a charmwriter, and an angel. His reports on the geography, history, and peoples of the regions he visited constitute the most authoritative documents on 19th-Century north-central Africa.

This single-minded man spent five years in the western Sudan; by 1855, when he returned to England, he knew more about its regions and peoples than any other European would learn for another 30 or 40 years. In the matter of history, for example, it was Barth who first saw a copy of the *Tarikh al-Sudan,* "The Chronicle of the Sudan" (c. 1650), and recognized it for what it was—a major sourcebook of inland West African history. This document lies at the base of most of what is known today about the distant history of those regions.

Park, Clapperton, the Landers, Barth: these were the men, with one or two more, who had climbed the peaks of exploring achievement by the 1850s. But there were others who reached the higher slopes.

Young René Caillié crossed the whole of western Africa during the 1820s, and did it with nobody's help but his own. The gallant Gordon

A beribboned Heinrich Barth posed for a photographer upon his return to England.

Laing was the first European to cross the Sahara north to south (over 2,600 miles); he finally reached fabled Timbuktu, only to be murdered there. In the 1840s great East African journeys of discovery were made by two German missionaries, Johann Krapf and Johann Rebmann. A Portuguese expedition led by Antonio Gamitto succeeded in a memorable journey to the central Congolese grasslands.

Gamitto's journey was a part of a Portuguese effort to build a link across middle Africa between Angola and Mozambique, their holdings on the opposite coasts. Later on, during the rush for colonies, the Portuguese would argue that they had long preceded Britain in these middle African lands and, according to the rules of imperial carve-up, should be awarded their possession. But this was to be one occasion when Lisbon's appetite for colonial glory would go unsatisfied.

By the 1850s the times were changing fast. The outline of imperialist ambition was beginning to take shape in Africa. The men who had explored western and even central Africa had done it in the name of scientific inquiry and possible trading advantage. Those who now began to penetrate eastern Africa, seeking the truth about the origins of the Nile and the countries through which it flowed, came from a Britain deeply concerned with territorial expansion into the African continent.

And as the times changed, so did human attitudes. As one kind of darkness lifted, another intensified. Mental arteries thickened with the conviction of Victorian superiority. Back at the outset of the century, Park had seen no differences between Africans and Europeans in the "characteristic feelings of our common nature." Barth in the 1850s would have echoed that, but by that date Barth was an exception. For the men who clarified the geography of East Africa during the second great period of exploration during the 1850s and 1860s—Burton, Speke, Baker, and their like—there could be no question of any "common nature" between Africans and Europeans. For Burton the mental development of the African ceased when he reached adulthood: "thenceforth he grows backwards, instead of forwards." For Baker, the African mind was "as stagnant as the morass which forms its puny world."

Thus the notion of the white man's civilizing "duty" became a commonplace. Britain in its age of power became racist, though of course with the very best of intentions, and would so remain for almost a century until the imperial power was spent.

It was scarcely the fault of the explorers, for while it is true that exploration opened the way to invasion, very few of the early explorers had any thought of pioneering for an empire. What happened was that the explorers drew the traders behind them, and the traders hauled along the governments, and the governments, thrust on by a public opinion increasingly inflamed by notions of national grandeur, were at last induced to reach out for the fruits of exploration. And so in the years that followed the 1860s, during a dawn that many Africans were to find singularly grey and that none of the explorers had foreseen when bearing back their little lamps, the darkness that hid Africa from Europe's eyes was lifted.

—*Basil Davidson*

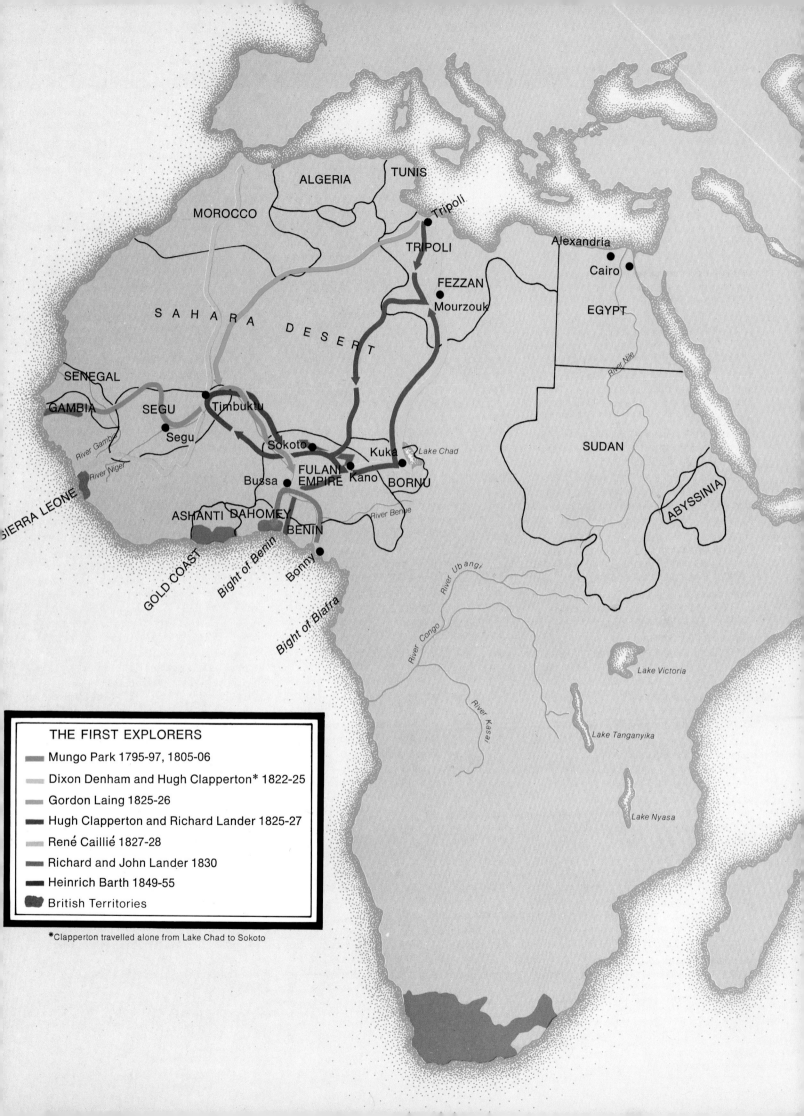

MOROCCO

ALGERIA

TUNIS

Tripoli

TRIPOLI

Alexandria

Cairo

FEZZAN

Mourzouk

EGYPT

S A H A R A D E S E R T

River Nile

SENEGAL

GAMBIA

SEGU

Timbuktu

River Gambia

Segu

River Niger

SUDAN

SIERRA LEONE

Sokoto

Bussa

FULANI EMPIRE

Kano

Kuka

Lake Chad

BORNU

ABYSSINIA

ASHANTI DAHOMEY

BENIN

River Benue

GOLD COAST

Bight of Benin

Bonny

Bight of Biafra

River Ubangi

River Congo

River Kasai

Lake Victoria

Lake Tanganyika

Lake Nyasa

THE FIRST EXPLORERS

- Mungo Park 1795-97, 1805-06
- Dixon Denham and Hugh Clapperton* 1822-25
- Gordon Laing 1825-26
- Hugh Clapperton and Richard Lander 1825-27
- René Caillié 1827-28
- Richard and John Lander 1830
- Heinrich Barth 1849-55
- British Territories

*Clapperton travelled alone from Lake Chad to Sokoto

IV. The Vision of David Livingstone

In 1840, among the probationaries of the London Missionary Society, was a young doctor trained in Glasgow and London who had been provisionally accepted to convert the heathen in China as soon as British guns overcame that government's attempts to keep out opium grown in British India. David Livingston (a final "e" was added later) was the personification of the porridge-and-Bible-raised Scot, self-educated and self-reliant. Hesitant in manner, when drawn out he radiated a strange and compelling charm. There was steel in his nature, which could be put down to ambition and egotism, but which went with a startling power of concentration and endurance.

Livingstone's attention was diverted from China to Africa by Bishop Samuel Wilberforce, the son of the great campaigner against slavery, who was calling a new crusade to halt once and for all the African slave trade. By 1841 Livingstone was working for the Missionary Society in Kuruman, farther north from the Cape than any missionary had been before. He travelled in a Boer wagon, revelling in the new experience which he called "excellent for the health, and agreeable to those who are not fastidious over trifles"—as he never was.

The quarrels of his missionary "brethren" in South Africa disgusted him. He thought them soft and wanted to be away from them, ahead of them. He had been sent to Kuruman as a temporary replacement for the resident missionary, Dr. Robert Moffat, who was away on leave. Without waiting for Dr. Moffat to return, Livingstone pushed north to set up a station on the frontier of the new Boer colony of Transvaal.

He was soon as disgusted with the Boers as he had been with his missionary companions. He was also at odds with the Society over his plan to train black clergy to be left behind to do the routine conversions and pastoral ministration while the pioneer missionary, like St. Augustine, forged farther and farther into the wilderness.

To everybody but Livingstone it was an uninviting prospect. Almost nothing was known to white men of the interior of central Africa—and little to black men either; most tribes were innocent of geographical sense beyond the lie of their hunting-grounds or pasturage. It was thought that the central plateau was an extension of the Kalahari Desert, perhaps even meeting the Sahara somewhere. The sources of the great rivers, the Nile, the Congo, the Zambezi, were unknown. But Livingstone was intrigued by a report of a freshwater lake, Ngami, where there might be a populous place to be won for the Gospel.

It took him six years to reach it, building one mission after another, wresting with the desert and the drought. As he probed north he perfected an art of exploration all his own. He was not the first missionary to see the need to master local languages, but he set about it with unusual zeal, working out his own grammatical analyses. Towards Africans his approach was wholly original—anthropological rather than missionary. He thought of each black man or woman as an individual. He lived his own life, "the imitation of Christ," as an exemplar, but he did not condemn the ways of the tribes. The contrast of cruelty and consideration in African behaviour set him thinking.

He felt at home with the African personality, and his ascendancy was the result of his own will as a person, not as simply a white man. He did not threaten, belabour, or bluster when Africans opposed him. He argued patiently and doggedly in their own tongue. He could not always manage them, but he seems always to have retained their respect.

A clue to that respect may be found in his approach to the members of the African medical profession—those that other white men dismissed as witch doctors. With them he observed the same medical etiquette as he would have done in Harley Street. His skill brought him a large African practice, yet he avoided taking a local doctor's patients. He waited to be consulted.

Livingstone respected African lore. He studied local crafts. He asked the uses of every plant, finding 40 edible roots and 30 fruits in the Kalahari Desert, where he lived on the *tsama* melons that kept the Bushmen alive. Those who followed grumbled that he had described everything. He studied fossils, geology, and, above all, geography and hydrology. Armed with his sextant, compass, chronometers, and nautical almanack, he reckoned longitude and latitude. And throughout he kept precise records in notebooks later transcribed into journals.

These tasks filled his days, developing in him the ability to move with the assurance of an African but with the science and resources of European civilization behind him. He told the directors of the Missionary Society he was prepared to go anywhere for them, provided it was forward.

In 1843 Livingstone thought he should do his duty as a missionary and marry, and considered advertising for a wife. But when he returned to Kuruman and finally met the Moffats he decided to marry their daughter Mary instead. Livingstone's inclusion of his wife in his gruelling expeditions and his separation from his family over the years would draw much criticism. Though his first love letter urged his intended to "let your affection towards Him be much more than towards me," Livingstone later insisted that he had loved her before they married and increasingly afterwards, and there is no record that she felt ill-treated.

She was, after all, a missionary's daughter, and she knew that hardship, even martyrdom, was her lot. She was thin as a lath when they married, and she settled down to infant-school teaching and to the production of five babies in about as many years. She moved with him from station to station, and finally took the family exploring with him.

Livingstone received "with feelings of irrepressible delight" the Society's permission to prospect for a better mission site. In 1844 he set out with traders and hunters, the first white expedition to cross the Kalahari, and finally discovered Lake Ngami. The Royal Geographical Society awarded him £25—"they missed a cypher out," he jested. Politically and geographically it proved a decisive breakthrough, for it revealed beyond the desert a huge area of well-watered country.

The Boers were incensed at Livingstone's intention to educate a cadre of native teachers and his reprobation of their custom of kidnapping African children for domestic slavery. They charged he was arming the natives, and while he was away they attacked the mission, taking special care to destroy his records, books, and scientific instruments. Knowing the Boers' intentions, he had little alternative but to make his wife and children into explorers.

The following year, therefore, he brought the family to Lake Ngami. The children nearly died of thirst on the way; in the swamps their eyes were covered with flies and not a square inch of their skin was without an insect bite—but they survived. Livingstone now encountered his greatest enemies: the anopheles mosquito, carrier of malaria, and the tsetse fly, carrier of the cattle-sickness that made it almost impossible to use animal transport in the middle belt of Africa. Livingstone, his family feverish and shaking round him, resolved to discover the cause of malaria, and over the years wrote much about it and its treatment, but demonstrated only that a tough constitution could survive repeated bouts of it with the aid of quinine.

At Lake Ngami he heard of far richer country, far finer rivers, and a great people, the Makololo, to the north. Ngami was too unhealthy for a mission. They all returned to Kolobeng mission where he had worked earlier. Mary, desperately sick, lost her fifth baby there, and was sent to recover with her parents. They were stunned when they saw the sad condition of their daughter and her children.

Livingstone returned to Ngami and finally, with the help of a hunter, got through to the Makololo country. There he found a river, the Zambezi, that suggested to him that here was a highway into a great, new, unknown, prosperous Africa—where a mission and a colony could be planted.

But his family could not accompany him in the ardours of exploring it, nor could they stay on the edge of the desert where Boers were thirsting for missionary blood. Livingstone told his family they must go back to Scotland and live on charity. When the children asked why they could not return to the only life they knew, he answered, "The mark of Cain is on your foreheads; your father is a missionary." For them henceforth he was a rare stranger, awesomely famous who now and then sent them letters, affectionate but pious, from the "dark Interior" that enveloped him.

By 1853 Livingstone was back among the Makololo and back exploring. The Zambezi rapids turned him back, but he was undeterred. There just *had* to be a way into this great new African world for Christianity and commerce, if only by native jungle paths. With a troop of Makololo attendants, Livingstone started for Portuguese Angola on the west coast.

It was a journey of a thousand miles, first by canoe and portage, then by land through tribes that became increasingly exacting in the tolls they charged, and increasingly hostile as Livingstone encountered the evidence of widespread slave-trading. The trade goods he had brought up by wagon from the Cape ran out so that the Makololo had to surrender their copper bangles and Livingstone his spare clothes and the oxen. Chiefs demanded his rifles, and then his men as slaves. On several occasions he had to threaten to shoot. They were frequently reduced to cassava mush for food. Worst of all, he went down repeatedly with malaria and dysen-

In 1864, following his Zambezi expedition, Livingstone went to London (where this photograph was taken) to raise funds to support a return to central Africa.

tery, spending days and weeks incapacitated in village huts or in his tiny tent.

In his *Missionary Travels* he makes light of these difficulties, treating them almost as amusing mishaps on an invigorating excursion through a veritable Arcadia. It was not bravado. Livingstone was determined to prove white men could travel through Africa. Native hostility, he believed, would pass away when legitimate commerce opened the roads and slaving became unprofitable.

He finally staggered into Portuguese Angola at the River Cuango, then spent weeks in bed in the house of the British slavery commissioner, recovering from total prostration.

When he was on his feet again, he decided, to the amazement of the Portuguese and his British host, to retrace his steps and attempt to reach Mozambique on the east coast, about 2,000 miles away. His Makololo, he said with truth, could not get home

without him. But what weighed as much with Livingstone was that he had not found a really practicable highway to the interior. The idea that the Zambezi provided a way downstream to the east still possessed him.

Meanwhile, he sent his journals and maps to England. They were lost at sea. He rewrote them, then vanished into the jungle on March 1, 1855.

On the journey back he went down with rheumatic fever as well as malaria. But once again he went on, and became the first European to visit "the smoke that thunders"—the great natural phenomenon that he revealed to the Victorian world as "Victoria Falls." Their discovery symbolized the opening up of the whole of central Africa to Europe.

With a new Makololo team, Livingstone started downstream on the Zambezi, mapping every mile of the route, exultation in his heart as the

great river went on and on, picking up tributaries, towards the sea. The going through the mountains was hard, and since war raged between slaving-tribes, he made a natural detour on the western bank. Thus he was utterly ignorant of the impassable rock-strewn Quebrabasa Rapids.

When he finally marched into Portuguese territory, he had completed the *traversa*, the crossing of central Africa, which had only once been done before (by two half-caste traders) and was not done again until 1879. An Englishman had thus achieved what the Portuguese needed to do to lay the foundations for their claim to "own" the whole middle belt of tropical Africa from sea to sea.

Livingstone was swift to emphasize the real importance of his feat. He wrote home: "I have been able to follow up my original plan of opening a way to the sea on either the East or West coast of Africa from a healthy locality in the Interior of the continent. . . . By this fine river flowing through a fine fertile country we have water conveyance to within 1° or 2° of the Makololo, the only impediments I know being one or two rapids (not cataracts) and robbers." It was an over-optimistic assumption.

He returned to a hero's welcome in England. His reception was such, his father-in-law Moffat wrote, as to make "a score of light heads dizzy." From the Queen and Prince Consort downwards, everyone wanted to see and hear him. In 1857, outshining even the news of the Indian Mutiny, Livingstone had achieved something that in his age can only be compared to the first moon walk by the astronauts. His demeanour was modest, his message exhilarating, his devotion matched only by his courage. He was an ideal Victorian hero.

Missionary Travels, the full story of his discoveries, became the season's best-seller. The book drove home a message aimed at two contrasting audiences: businessmen interested in profits, and ardent young churchmen longing for a medieval crusade in a materialist world. He told the businessmen that British enterprise had only to reach

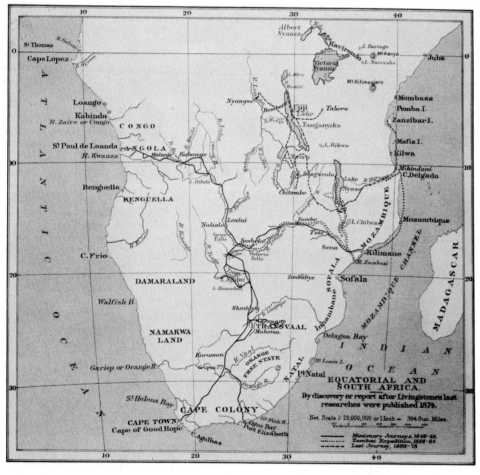

A map made after Livingstone's death traces "by discovery or report" his explorations.

out to possess vast untapped markets and mineral wealth in Africa. Hard-headed men were carried away by the missionary who spoke of the cotton he had found growing, of the seams of coal, the iron. Cotton, Coal, Iron—the three pillars on which Britain was built! They dreamed of fleets of steamers chugging up the Zambezi laden with bales of cloth, and chugging down with bales of raw cotton.

To his university audience he outlined the beckoning new field of apostolic work which, in alliance with the profit motive, would uproot the slave-trade. "I go back to Africa to try to make an open path for commerce and Christianity," he thundered. "Carry out the work I have begun. *I leave it with you.*"

The results were gratifying. Plans were set afoot to establish a universities' mission to Africa. Prime Minister Palmerston advanced Treasury money for an expedition which appealed to his abolitionist principles and his patriotism. At the Admiralty an officer began designing steamers.

Missionary Travels was compulsive reading: it made everything seem so astonishingly simple that one might wonder why the Portuguese were so slow in linking up their opposite-coast colonies—especially as the Doctor said that there was no risk of fever once one got beyond the swampy river mouth. Robert Moffat threw the book aside, calling it "a pack of lies." Others, fever-ridden in Africa, would later do the same.

His new Zambezi expedition totally failed in its objectives, but disillusion took five years, from 1858 through 1862, and it had unlooked-for consequences.

Livingstone by himself could have made the journey and discovered that the Quebrabasa Rapids and gorge made nonsense of his prospectus. But he insisted on proceeding by steamer at the head of a six-man team. The obverse of all his virtues rose to the surface in the hot, smelly, verminous cabin of the asthmatic steamer *Ma Robert*. He became carping, vacillating, suspicious, ungenerous, unforgiving. He gave no encouragement to his team, no credit,

no explanations—and rounded on them for malingering and even for dishonesty. Livingstone always had to have his own way.

At Quebrabasa Livingstone's disastrous assumptions were revealed. The falls were impassable by the *Ma Robert*. He spoke desperately of dynamiting a way through; he claimed that "a steamer of light draught" could get through in flood-tide; but his sense of guilt and failure may be gauged from his cry, "the honours heaped on me were not of my seeking."

Then he decided to explore up the Shire River, a tributary of the Zambezi, but again cataracts held up the *Ma Robert*. Livingstone brought up supplies and went forward overland, discovering Lake Shirwa. There he heard of the mighty "Lake of Stars" beyond it, and determined to win it for himself. On the next stage of the journey upriver they found Lake Nyasa—something at last to justify the Zambezi expedition. Livingstone sent the great news home, and set off by foot to lead the faithful Makololo back to their own country and revisit Victoria Falls.

While he was thus engaged, preparations (inspired by his reports, which had arrived in England) were made to follow up his discovery of Lake Nyasa—on a scale that startled Livingstone after the Quebrabasa débâcle. The government sent out a new steamer to replace the *Ma Robert*. Another steamer was on the way, built in sections to Livingstone's own specification so that it could be dismantled and carried round the Shire cataracts and launched on the lake. One gunboat on the lake, he felt, would end slaving in the area.

It was not to be. There were clashes with slavers. The bishop sent out to begin the Christian colonization of the upper Shire died of malaria. For the explorer there was a personal

tragedy. Mary Livingstone, who had come to join him in his moment of triumph, succumbed to a tropical fever. Livingstone made a last effort to put a steamer on Lake Nyasa, but before it could be dismantled for carrying to the lake he received a letter of recall from London. His team had, in truth, disintegrated, its stamina and morale exhausted.

If the government thought that the Zambezi expedition had failed, the public did not. Livingstone's exploits, despite rumours of dissension and scandals, had made him more of a popular hero than ever. Once again, sitting down to write the story of the adventure, he played down all the miscalculations and tragedies and wrote a tale of stirring effort in the face of great but surmountable obstacles.

What was Livingstone to do next? Sir Roderick Murchison and the Royal Geographical Society opportunely proposed in 1865 that he explore the watershed between Lake Nyasa and the west and ascertain how the great central lakes were fed. Livingstone agreed, though he insisted that he would return to Africa as both a missionary and explorer.

He collected an extraordinarily miscellaneous entourage of Indian sepoys and former slaves, but he proved as incapable of leading this mixed team as he had the British. Instead, it often led him. The natives were mutinous, cruel, and cowardly. The ex-slaves deserted and reported that Livingstone had been killed (which prompted plans for a search-party). The Indians deserted too, and soon Livingstone was reduced to a handful of "hearty native companions" together with porters hired on the way. In 1867 he lost his medicines, and felt he had received his sentence of death.

The little caravan marched to Lake Nyasa, over the Shire Highlands, and

Text Continued on Page 209

Overleaf: While Livingstone's admirers were legion, there was the occasional detractor—none of whom had a more barbed sense of humour than the painter of the water-colours reproduced on the next three pages. During the 1880s an unknown artist assembled his satirical series, from which these six examples are drawn, added burlesque captions, and bound the collection into a single volume (never published) under the title "Scenes in Hot Latitudes." They portray the saga of "Dr. Myth," clad in a red coat and carrying an umbrella, on his dotty search for the source of the Nile. An explanatory commentary appears below the artist's original captions.

"April 1st: Doctor quits Lake Slap Dash Anika at its Northern Extremity and entering the Wishi Washi ascends that River as far as Potti Wotti."

Livingstone inauspiciously chooses April Fool's Day to leave Lake Tanganyika by way of what he thinks is the Nile and lands at a village. In fact, he explored only to the west of Tanganyika, along the Lualaba (the upper Congo), which he did indeed mistake for the Nile.

"Arrived at Potti Wotti, Doctor visits what Pottiwottians assure him is the source of the Wishi Washi, but is convinced this must be the spot reached by Herr Tarry Diddlherr in 1867. Determines to cross Tippi Toppi range and explore the other side. (Bottle has German label, suspects it must therefore be that in R.G.S. map)."

African villagers tell Livingstone that here the Nile has its origin but the Doctor, sceptical, decides that it is only the spot presumed to be the source on the basis of a report made to the Royal Geographical Society by a fictitious German explorer.

"Doctor with boys Mumbo and Jumbo and two hanki panki guides starts up Wishi Washi for Manchew country to visit king Sanguini, who has sent him a most pressing invitation to come and take a chop."

Livingstone and his servants, led by two devious guides, travel to the country of the cannibals to visit their bloodthirsty king.

"Doctor, while fishing for Pickili Wickles below falls of the slope in the Coquilla country, discovers that Puddi Muddi flows into Wishi Washi and not Wishi Washi into Puddi Muddi as suggested by R.G.S. and so marks their map."

Observing a waterfall, Livingstone concludes that the Congo (Puddi-Muddi) flows into the Nile and not the reverse. Neither theory was correct; the rivers are not connected.

"The Doctor having waited in vain for the promised supplies from the R.G.S. is suddenly and unexpectedly cheered by the welcome sounds of 'Hail, Columbia' and by the arrival of the 'Bird of Freedom,' bearing on its outstretched wings New England's pride, with help, succour and the star-spangled banner."

Stanley, arriving vaingloriously on a heavily laden American eagle, rescues Livingstone.

"Upon which the R.G.S. gave a dinner and Doctor Speculum gave a speech. Upon the Doctor's health being proposed, he said it was all bosh and useless to send him any more supplies."

R.G.S. Chairman, "Doctor Speculum" – a pun on the Society's self-indulgent, unfounded speculations about Livingstone's situation – determines to leave Livingstone to his fate.

down into the Valley of Luangwa. He went on to discover Lake Bangweulu and Lake Mweru, and after nearly three years, almost exhausted, arrived in Ujiji, the great Arab slave-centre on Lake Tanganyika.

By then he had become dependent on the Arabs with whose slave-caravans he often marched, walking alongside the weeping captives. His difficulties grew as his trade goods were used up buying guides and porters, and when at last he reached Ujiji he found that the supplies sent up to him had been plundered. He was virtually penniless in the centre of Africa, but remarked how thankful he was for the little tea and coffee that survived and the flannel for his rheumatism.

For two years he held out in the area, making attempt after attempt to reach the Luapula and Lualaba rivers, increasingly obsessed that they formed the source of the Nile. Finally he succeeded, only to witness an appalling massacre of women traders by the Arabs on the banks of the Lualaba. He felt he had been in Hell.

Without medicines, a living skeleton, he trudged slowly back to Ujiji, where he wrote 40 letters, none of which got through, to describe the slave-trade. But five days later, on November 10, 1871, he heard that a white man was approaching, saw the Stars and Stripes advancing through the bush, and beheld a young man who walked briskly but deferentially towards him, raised his cap, and asked, "Dr. Livingstone, I presume?"

The questioner was, of course, Henry Morton Stanley, the encounter the most famous in the history of African exploration. The great Livingstone had been found alive, and the world rejoiced.

Stanley had come up from the bottom of the social ladder. Born in Wales as John Rowlands and rejected by his parents, he was brought up in a harsh, loveless environment. Yet by sheer intelligence and inner drive he drew basic education, self-discipline, and religious faith from his squalid surroundings. He fled to the United States, and in New Orleans he was noticed by a kindly merchant, Henry Morton Stanley, who adopted

him and gave him his name. When the Civil War broke out, young Stanley joined the Confederates, was captured, and readily enlisted on the Union side to escape the horrors of prisoner-of-war camp.

After the war he took to the sea and then to journalism, travelling widely in America and Asia. In 1869 he was on a roving commission for the New York *Herald* when he was called to Paris to receive his instructions to find Livingstone.

When Livingstone realized what Stanley had brought him in the way of supplies, and after Stanley had told him of the world's admiration for him, he cried, "You have brought new life!" Stanley's appearance was a divine dispensation (and so must have been the inspiration of James Gordon Bennett, owner of the *Herald*, who had sent the journalist forth). He began to write up his journals for the American to take back, recuperated with the aid of Stanley's medicines, delicacies, wines, and tin hip-bath, and then proposed they should together explore Lake Tanganyika.

Livingstone's goal was to find a river running out of it that would join with Lake Albert—thus proving that Lake Tanganyika was a mere link in the Nile network which originated, he believed, far to the south. The expedition duly found the expected river—but flowing *into* the lake. Stanley now tried to persuade Livingstone to return to England, but to no avail. He sadly said good-by, leaving a great load of supplies. Then Livingstone set off westward determined to bring off the greatest *coup* of his career. For 18 months he sought his grail, the legendary mountains of Crophi and Mophi, the "Mountains of the Moon" from which the Nile was supposed to spring. He bacame a little sicker, a little weaker as the weeks and months went on. He could not observe the stars to take his position, then he could not walk. His spleen was a knob of blood, his bowels so perforated by dysentery that he could only be carried in fearful pain. On May 1, 1873, in a mud hut, he took a little camomile tea, struggled to his knees against a crude bed, and died, still dressed in tattered serge

jacket and trousers, stained with mud and blood.

He had become perhaps the most eminent and revered person in Great Britain. His discoveries were second to none. He had opened up Africa, he had gone in far deeper and stayed in far longer, reported, observed, mapped, and charted far more extensively than any other explorer. His books were numbered among the great travel volumes of the language.

Yet as a missionary he had failed, for he had turned from teaching to win fame for his travels and explorations. As the liberator of Africa he had failed, for the slave-trade was worse than he had found it and had spread along the routes he pioneered. The Portuguese had outwitted him, the Arabs massacred and enslaved under his eyes. As a husband and father he had failed, his wife dead of fever on an expedition he should not have called her to make in her declining years.

And finally, even as an explorer he had failed, for he had not made that great discovery that was to retrieve all —the discovery of the spot he was sure existed where the Nile rose from four amazing fountains between fabled Crophi and Mophi.

The historic despatch to Lord Russell was already drafted, with gaps left for details: "I have the pleasure of reporting to your Lordship that on the ——I succeeded at last in reaching four remarkable fountains, each of which, at no great distance off becomes a large river. They rise at the base of a swell of land or earthen mound which can scarcely be called a hill, for it seems only about——feet above the general level."

The blanks were never filled in, for Livingstone was, as in saner moments he suspected, in the basin of the Congo and not of the Nile. He had the levels of the Luapula and the lakes all wrong, just as he had had the levels of the Zambezi wrong when he told England that there was an almost canal-smooth river flowing out of a verdant, fertile, mineral-rich land in the centre of Africa. And he was 70 miles off in his reckoning of where he was when he died.

—*Roy Lewis*

V. The Mystery of the Nile

The vision that dominated Livingstone's last years—the Nile springing forth from central Africa's Mountains of the Moon—was as old as Ptolemy. The intervening 1,700 years had only deepened the legend, and the source of the Nile remained one of the world's great geographic mysteries.

In the 1850s the feeling grew, especially among the influential group of men who composed the Royal Geographical Society, that the time was at hand to settle the matter. They were inspired by the travels of two German missionaries, Johann Rebmann and Johann Krapf. They had reported two huge snow-capped mountains on the Equator—Kilimanjaro and Kenya—sights that led them to wonder whether these mountains drained into a huge basin that gave birth to the Nile. They had been assured by Arab ivory traders that there was a vast inland sea extending from about latitude 10° S. north to the Equator. The report of two peaks—the Mountains of the Moon?—and a great lake presented a coincidence with Ptolemy's map that was far too obvious to miss.

A swarthy, stern-looking, moustachioed man of 35 presented himself to the Society and offered to take an expedition and clear up all doubts. He was Lieutenant Richard Burton of the East India Company's Bombay Light Infantry. The Society accepted his offer, sufficient money was raised, and the East India Company granted him a furlough. Burton selected as his companion Lieutenant John Hanning Speke.

To the Society, the qualifications of Burton and Speke seemed perfectly suited to the task. Burton was already known for his bold exploits in dangerous country, and although he had blighted his prospects in the Indian service by his bluntness in dealing with superior officers, he was not yet the frighteningly controversial figure he would become. His linguistic abilities attested in Company examinations, his grasp of Eastern religious and social customs, and his evident valour and resourcefulness made him an obvious leader. Speke seemed almost as suitable. He

was 29 and had had considerable experience in collecting botanical and zoological specimens in the Himalayas. He was also a surveyor.

Although the two personalities were superficially so complementary, they were in fact utterly incompatible, and the history of Nile exploration for the next 25 years would be affected by that fact.

Richard Burton, first son of a retired army officer, had an upbringing unconventional even for the profligate Regency period. Richard and his brother and sister were coached by a series of brow-beaten tutors as the Burton family moved erratically through France and Italy. From this strange education there emerged a faulty classicist but a first-rate swordsman.

Burton believed his mother's story that he was descended morganatically from Louis XIV of France. He developed a taste for wine, women, fighting, gambling, mysticism, daredevilry, and, above all, for languages. Languages were the precious tools with which to satisfy his insatiable curiosity about exotic peoples.

Self-confident, undisciplined, devoid of tact or consideration, Burton was a stormy petrel at Oxford and was sent down without a degree. He then became an officer in the Indian Army, where he rapidly mastered Persian, Afghan, Hindi, Urdu, and Arabic and rendered superlative service as an intelligence officer. But he cut the Company directors to the quick when he told them they were losing touch with their subjects (he sent them a prediction that approximated the date of the Mutiny of 1857), and earned a furious reprimand for criticizing British bayonet drill (though his manual on the subject was adopted after the disasters of the Crimean War). His attempt to abduct a nun in Goa completed his disgrace.

Burton determined to retrieve his reputation by journeying to Mecca, the holy city of the Muslims, which infidels were forbidden to enter on pain of death. He donned an Arab personality so complete that he was able to pass among the most devout Muslims, and his informative and entertaining book, *A Pilgrimage to El*

Medinah and Meccah, made him famous.

John Speke, as fair and charming as Burton was saturnine and sarcastic, came of a Somerset family whose origins went back to the Conquest of 1066. He was a fanatic about personal fitness. Dominated by his mother and sisters, awkward with other women, he had a narcissistic tinge to his make-up that gave a special quality to his ambition for fame and acclaim. At 17 he joined the Indian Army and found action in the Sikh Wars.

In 1849, the fighting over, Speke said he "conceived the idea of exploring central equatorial Africa," for which he prepared himself by mapping Himalayan mountain passes. In 1854 he joined Burton on an expedition in Somalia in East Africa. It went badly, due in part to his fumbling. Nevertheless, two years later Speke was invited by Burton to join his so-called Lakes Expedition to central Africa.

Burton later said that he took Speke "to give him another chance" after his failures in Somalia, and felt he could rely on his toughness and prowess. As for Speke, he was determined to be associated with any Nile discoveries. Perhaps, since he doubted Burton's single-mindedness to see it through, he foresaw an opportunity to advance his own ambitions.

They assembled their party in Zanzibar. It included 36 African porters, ten gun-carrying slaves, four drivers, a posse of Baluchi soldiers to protect them, and four servants. Even this elaborate caravan could not carry all that was needed in the way of provisions, trade goods, camp equipment, ammunition, scientific equipment, medicines, and stores, including an iron boat in seven sections, intended to enable them to explore the great lake that was their goal. A second caravan was organized to bring up the additional stores needed. On June 25, 1857, the march began.

Though Burton and Speke were the first Europeans to make the journey to the "Sea of Ujiji," as Lake Tanganyika was called, the trail had been a caravan-route for decades. The expedition proved to be only nominally under the command of its European

The face of Richard Burton (above), said a friend, was "the most sinister I have ever seen." At right is John Speke, Burton's lieutenant in their search for the Nile's source and his later rival.

leaders. Indiscipline was the rule, theft endemic, and desertions began as soon as the men marched from the coastal strip into hot bush country.

After three weeks they had covered 118 miles (with more than 600 ahead of them) and both men were already so sick they often had to be carried. Listening to rumours of dreaded Ngoni warriors ahead, the Baluchi soldiers mutinied and had to be quelled by an emaciated Burton who faced them down with his revolver.

The travellers' health improved as they reached the savannah country. But Speke and Burton were already on uneasy terms. When his fever developed into delirium, Speke had poured out his resentment at Burton and became so violent that his weapons had to be removed. When he recovered he kept largely to his own tent.

Finally, tattered and emaciated, the two Englishmen walked into Kazeh (today called Tabora) on November 7, 1857. Speke was almost blind with ophthalmia. There they recuperated for three weeks, and there Burton learned from the Arab inhabitants that there was not one but three great lakes or seas: the "Sea of Niassa" (Lake Nyasa) to the south, the "Sea of Ujiji" (Lake Tanganyika) just ahead, and the "Sea of Ukerewe" (Lake Victoria) to the north.

They pushed on hopefully, but Burton became so ill that Speke had to take command temporarily. On December 14 they were in sight of Lake Tanganyika, but Speke could not see it, and Burton, whose legs were paralysed, had to be carried. He gazed at it with "wonder, admiration and delight." Owing to an ear infection, Speke was now nearly deaf as well as half-blind.

The most urgent task was to find what outlets there were from the lake, and thus to decide whether the Nile had its origin here. They set out to explore in canoes—a journey that was agony to both—but were unable to reach the northern end of the lake. But the natives assured them that the river flowed *into*, not out of the lake—which meant Lake Tanganyika could not be the Nile's source.

Even though the relief caravan had arrived, it had been so badly plundered en route that their position appeared to be desperate. Burton decided to return to Zanzibar with news of the discoveries thus far made.

The exhausted men retraced their steps but were forced to halt at Kazeh. Burton was still unable to walk and needed more rest before they could continue. Speke persuaded Burton to allow him to take a small party on a trek to the reputed Sea of Ukerewe to the north. Burton agreed, partly to get some relief from Speke's company, partly because he was contemptuous of Speke's ability to achieve any useful results on his own.

Speke made a successful foray northward, and three weeks later, on August 3, 1858, beheld the huge expanse of Lake Victoria, which he decided in a flash of inspiration was at last the Ptolemaic source of the Nile. "This, I maintain," he wrote later, "was *the* discovery of the Nile." He noted that the lake was "so broad you could not see across it, and so long that nobody knew its length." He hurried back to Burton to announce the great discovery.

Burton received the information coldly. While acknowledging that Speke had found *a* lake, he demanded to know what proof Speke had that it was *the* lake? And of course, in strict geographical logic, Burton was right. But in other respects he was disastrously wrong. His denigration of Speke's achievement further antagonized his companion, while his rejection of Speke's suggestion that they should both go and investigate the lake's true extent was a gross tactical blunder.

The result was that Speke hugged the "discovery" to himself with the solicitude of a mother for its unborn babe, suspecting that Burton would rob him of the major credit. Meanwhile, Burton's growing "scientific" scepticism was fuelled by a suppressed fear that he had made a fatal mistake himself. On the way back to Zanzibar the two men avoided the subject of the Nile, and were soon barely on speaking terms—though when Speke became so ill that he

Hero in Decline

Richard Burton's epic journey to central Africa was his last major expedition. The romantic explorer and adventurer found himself stiffled by a Victorian Establishment outraged by his unrepentant contempt for accepted standards of behaviour and infuriated by his lifelong interest in erotica. Already he had reported on India's homosexual brothels and he was to translate two Eastern love-manuals, the *Kama Sutra* and *The Perfumed Garden*.

The first link in the chain that bound him was forged by his marriage to a fanatical Catholic, Isabel Arundell. She symbolized so much that Burton fought all his life: bigotry, prudery, and a cloying sentimentality that drove him from her for years at a time. Yet the marriage lasted. She adored him, and he seemed to become dependent on her.

After serving in two insultingly minor diplomatic posts, Burton finally gained a top position as Counsel in Damascus. But controversy dogged his every step, and he was recalled by a nervous Foreign Office.

Eventually the Burtons arrived in the diplomatic backwater of Trieste, where he worked hard to finish his remarkable translation of *The Arabian Nights* and was deep into a new translation of *The Perfumed Garden* when he died in 1890. The hysterical Isabel persuaded a priest to receive her husband into the Church he had mocked while alive. To "safeguard" his reputation, she then burned all his unpublished manuscripts and copious journals, leaving much of Burton's character and achievements forever enigmatic.

nearly died, Burton nursed him with solicitude.

Their one point of agreement was that on their return to London they should fit out a new expedition to test Speke's theory, but they quarrelled yet again as soon as they reached the Indian Ocean. By the time they reached Aden to take ship for home, their relationship was merely a polite veneer covering utter hostility. They found a vessel available immediately. Speke seized this piece of good luck. But Burton, in a pattern of behaviour often repeated, overlooked the prompt public presentation of his claim and dallied in Aden for some days on a plea of continuing ill-health. In fact his delay was partly to avoid Speke's presence, now nearly intolerable to his spirit.

Speke promised to say nothing of their discoveries until Burton rejoined him in London. But on the advice of a journalist friend he met aboard ship, as soon as he reached London he went to Sir Roderick Murchison, president of the Royal Geographical Society, to claim the Nile. This caused an immediate sensation and, knowing nothing of the quarrel between Speke and Burton, Murchison said, "Speke, we must send you there again."

When Burton arrived he found that the chance of a lifetime was gone forever—"the ground was completely cut from beneath my feet." Speke had been promised command of the new expedition, and although the Society might have reversed this decision in view of the dispute that now emerged into the open, in fact it had to be confirmed. Burton received the Society's coveted Gold Medal, but Speke was the hero of the hour, the lion of the drawing-rooms with his fresh boyish charm and shyness that was in such pleasant contrast to Burton's uncomfortable erudition and contempt for convention.

Burton's account, *The Lake Regions of Central Africa,* almost ignored Speke, who told his own story with venom in *Blackwood's Magazine*.

After sick-leave in the United States, Burton returned to England to find himself out of fashion and out of money. Thereafter he declined into

the most eccentric member of the consular service, generally given the most unpleasant postings that the Foreign Office had on its books.

For his new expedition to central Africa Speke selected as his companion an old friend, James Grant, who was prepared to accept from Speke the subordinate position that Speke had rebelled against with Burton. The partnership of Speke and Grant would be harmonious, for they shared the same outlook and the same love of hunting and natural history.

The Royal Geographical Society and the Foreign Office worked out a combined operation. Speke and Grant were to go from Zanzibar to Lake Victoria. John Petherick, the British consul in Khartoum and an ivory-trader familiar with the upper reaches of the Nile, would advance southward and rendezvous with Speke's party at the northern end of the lake.

Another traveller had decided independently to advance upon the central African lakes from the north and race Speke and Grant to the source of the Nile, or assist them if they ran out of supplies. This was Samuel Baker, a big-game hunter from Ceylon, who would be accompanied by his beautiful young Hungarian wife, Florence.

In August, 1859, Speke and Grant set out from Zanzibar. They traversed the same route to Kazeh, and Speke declared it to be much easier than Burton had found it—"like marching up the Grant Trunk road in Bengal," he wrote later.

But from Kazeh on it was the familiar story of sickness, desertions, and blackmailing native chiefs. While Grant recuperated from an ulcerous leg, Speke spent several fascinating months at the splendid court of the Buganda kingdom on Lake Victoria. At last, in July, 1862, the explorers moved on—but separately. Speke reserved to himself the discovery of the lake's outlet—the beginning of the Nile—at a place called "the Stones." Speke found "the Stones," which he named Ripon Falls, and tried to descend the Nile by canoe, but was turned back by hostile natives.

The explorers were told of another great lake to the west, Luta Nzige (later named Lake Albert), which received the Nile from Lake Victoria. But they lacked Petherick's reinforcements and could not take advantage of the information. Travelling with an ivory and slave caravan, they reached Gondokoro in the Sudan in February, 1863.

It was not Petherick who met them under the Union Jack but Samuel and Florence Baker. The Bakers' supplies were still ample and Speke and Grant replenished their stocks. When Petherick and his wife arrived soon afterwards, Speke treated them coldly. He started a vendetta by refusing Petherick's help, later insinuating that Petherick had failed to meet him (for all that, Speke was 14 months late) in order to go slave-raiding.

To the Bakers, Speke was all affability. Baker was downcast at being forestalled in the Lake Victoria exploration, but Speke told him that there was still a prize to be won by locating and mapping Luta Nzige. This proposal had the additional advantage that, if Baker was successful, his work would probably strengthen Speke's case to have found the true outlet of the Nile. Speke then sailed down-river in Baker's boats to Khartoum and telegraphed Sir Roderick Murchison that "the Nile is settled!"

But it was far from settled. Speke had a hero's welcome once more in London in June, 1863. Most geographers were inclined to agree that he had substantiated his earlier claim that the Nile rose in a majestic lake, which must be called Lake Victoria just as Africa's greatest waterfall on the Zambezi had been named Victoria Falls by Livingstone. Yet there was a twofold weakness in Speke's case. He had not circumnavigated Lake Victoria, thus failing to prove that his sightings of the northern and southern shores were of the same continuous body of water; and he had not sailed down-river from "the Stones" continuously to a known point on the Nile. Burton publicly denounced Speke's claims.

The whole matter, it was decided, should be debated at the forthcoming meeting in Bath of the British Association for the Advancement of Science. A confrontation there between Speke and Burton was expected. It never took place. Speke had always calmed his nerves by hunting, and so it was at Bath. He went off to shoot partridges and while climbing a wall his gun went off, mortally wounding him. Some at the time thought he had been driven to suicide by Burton's hounding, but the evidence is that it was an accident.

In the meantime, Samuel and Florence Baker were adding further important knowledge, even if it fell short of being conclusive, about the Nile's source. In background Baker was akin to Grant and Speke. He was a practical man whose experience included the creation of an English colony village in Ceylon and the construction of railways. He had considerable means thanks to a family fortune built on West Indian sugar and slavery.

Florence Baker had met her husband-to-be in Budapest, where he was building a railroad. She was a perfect choice for an explorer's wife. His mind turned to Africa and she ac-

companied him as a matter of course. Never did she flinch, and in several crises he owed his life to her cool resources. "Mrs. Baker was not a *screamer*," he wrote appreciatively. "In the moment of suspected danger a touch on my sleeve was considered sufficient warning."

Before they met Speke and Grant in the Sudan, the Bakers had made a thorough exploration of the region between the Atbara River, a tributary of the Nile, and the Ethiopian highlands. Then in March, 1863, following Speke's suggestion, they set off to locate that great lake, Luta Nzige, reported off to the north-west of Lake Victoria.

It was a gruelling experience. Both were weakened by illness. Crossing the Kafu River, Florence became unconscious with what Baker took to be sunstroke followed by brain fever. She was carried in a litter for several marches and finally a grave was dug. But she insisted that, dead or alive, she would reach the lake. She did,

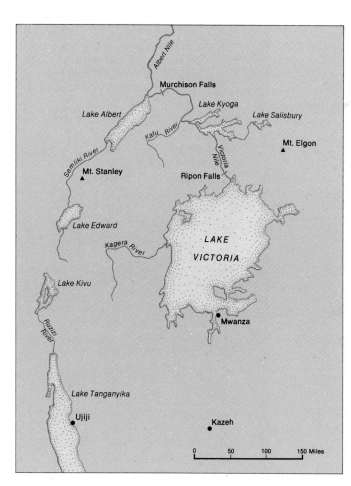

The lakes region of central Africa is shown here. The Nile rises in mountain streams, such as the Kagera, feeding Lake Victoria.

Samuel Baker painted himself setting off on his ox in search of Lake Albert in 1864. Demonstrative Bunyoro warriors (right) try to extort more of the party's supplies.

alive. On March 14, 1864, they beheld it and Baker named it Albert after the late Prince Consort. After invoking the Almighty's blessing they staggered down to the shore. "Here," he exulted, "was the reward of all our labour—for the years of tenacity with which we had toiled through Africa: England had won the sources of the Nile!"

Baker, however, much exaggerated his prize. He was deceived by a haze from the marshes into thinking it continued 100 miles or more. They found both a river flowing into the lake, which Baker correctly assumed came from Lake Victoria, and the Nile flowing out of the lake. They paddled up the inlet river only to be stopped by an awesome cataract which Baker named Murchison Falls. Since they could not go round the waterfall, they could not fully confirm Speke's theory that the Nile rose in Lake Victoria.

On their return to London in 1865 their account of their discoveries somewhat strengthened Speke's case. But their evidence was not regarded as completely conclusive. Baker thought it possible that Lake Albert was the major source, Lake Victoria the minor one.

Within a few months Baker was knighted for his work. It was second-ary to Burton's or Speke's, but he had not used a penny of public money, his bluff manner was acceptable, and his talents as a sportsman were considered highly commendable. He received the Royal Geographical Society's Gold Medal, purchased a country house, and wrote letters to *The Times* on African questions.

When Livingstone's last expedition failed to settle once and for all the Nile question—and in fact raised more questions than it answered—it was left to that upstart American, Henry Morton Stanley, to resolve the matter. That is precisely what Stanley did in 15 years of methodical exploration.

In 1875, financed by the *Daily Telegraph* and the New York *Herald*, he sailed to Zanzibar to organize an expedition to settle whether Livingstone was right about the Lualaba being the Nile—or whether it was really the Congo. On November 12, 1875, the 365-strong party set out, carrying with it the disassembled sections of a boat called the *Lady Alice*. They would be gone for 999 days.

It was an appallingly costly transcontinental march (only Stanley and 82 others survived the disease, the accidents, and the fighting) but an immensely informative one. In Febru-ary, 1876, they reached Lake Victoria, put the *Lady Alice* together, and proceeded to circumnavigate the biggest lake in the world after Lake Superior. The expedition marched south to Lake Tanganyika, which they also circumnavigated in the *Lady Alice*, and found it to be the longest lake in the world.

It remained to discover where the Lualaba flowed, and Stanley prepared to do what Livingstone had not dared —to sail down it and see where it flowed into the sea. Stanley set off downriver, keeping pace with a column marching along the bank. For almost the whole distance they had to fight, either on the river or on the banks. Presently the river curved westward and they felt sure it was the Congo. But the force dwindled steadily from wounds and disease. Above Livingstone Falls Stanley abandoned the river and struck inland, desperate for food but assuring his men that help lay ahead. They reached the sea finally at Banana Point at the mouth of the Congo, 2,000 miles across the continent from Zanzibar.

Both Stanley and his chroniclers ran out of superlatives when evaluating this journey. He was even compared to Columbus, for he had opened up to the world a huge new productive territory, the size of Europe, well served by waterways which could be traversed by steamers launched above the rapids. Stanley wrote his famous book, *Through the Dark Continent*, and began to plan railways and steamer services.

On a second expedition a decade later, undertaken for imperial motives, Stanley added to his laurels by finding the Ruwenzori range, Ptolemy's famous Mountains of the Moon, where the Nile took its rise. Grudgingly Britain acknowledged the "presumptuous Mr. Stanley" as one of the greatest explorers of his day. His last years were marked by renaturalization as a British subject, election to Parliament, and a knighthood.

The river skeleton of the map of Africa was at last complete—the Niger, the Zambezi, the Congo, the Nile. The stage was set for an immense power struggle for Empire in the Dark Continent.

—*Roy Lewis*

Henry Morton Stanley (right, with his faithful gunbearer Kalulu in a studio photographer's jungle) considered himself Livingstone's heir; "may I be selected to succeed him in opening up Africa to the shining light of Christianity!" he wrote in his diary. His equipment included the sectioned canoe above, named for his mentor. Heavy fighting marked Stanley's expeditions. In the scene below, from the *Illustrated London News*, his party is attacked by a flotilla of native war canoes.

Chapter Six
AFRICAN TAKE-OVER

General Sir Garnet Wolseley, Victorian specialist in brushfire warfare from one end of Africa to the other and the "Modern Major-General" in Gilbert and Sullivan's *Pirates of Penzance*.

I. Buckets of Diamonds

To 15-year-old Erasmus Jacobs the glittering stone that caught his eye as he strolled along the bank of the Orange River one day in 1866 was no more than a *mooi klip* —a pretty pebble. Erasmus pocketed it and when he got back to his father's farm near Hope Town in the north of Cape Colony, he gave the bauble to his little sister to add to the collection of stones she played games with.

A few weeks later the Jacobs children were playing with the stones when Schalk van Niekerk, a local divisional councillor, came by. The bright pebble caught his eye. Suspecting it might be a diamond, he asked if he might have it. Shortly afterwards he showed it to a passing peddler, John O'Reilly, who also guessed it might be a diamond because he could scratch his name on glass with it. He paid van Niekerk a few pounds for it, and dispatched it by ordinary mail to the government mineralogist, Dr. Guybon Atherstone, at Grahamstown. Dr. Atherstone promptly replied, "it has blunted even jewellers' files here."

Indeed it was a diamond, of 21¼ carats (about one-eighth of an ounce). Sir Philip Woodhouse, Governor of Cape Colony, bought it for £500 and arranged for it to be displayed at the Paris Exhibition of 1867—a tantalizing foretaste of South Africa's future.

Cape Colony, together with the other British colony of Natal and the two Boer republics, the Orange Free State and the Transvaal, were far from prosperous. A handful of British and Boer farmers struggled to eke out an existence. Cape Colony had a deficit approaching a million pounds and precious little industry that might help reduce it. There was but one short railway line of 63 miles from Cape Town to Wellington and a seven-mile spur from Durban to the coast in Natal. Telegraph lines did not penetrate inland; the main means of communication with the interior was ox-wagon.

The prime importance of the Cape had been as a staging post on the route to India. Now, with the Suez Canal due to open in 1869, providing a short cut to the East, the cost of maintaining a garrison for the Simonstown naval base and Durban seemed out of all proportion to their value. Diamonds would change all that. From a liability South Africa would suddenly become a dazzling asset, one of the richest prizes in the Empire.

Surprisingly, this first South African diamond aroused little excitement. A London firm did dispatch a geologist to the Orange River, but he reported no sign of diamond-producing gravel and concluded that the stone must have arrived there in the crop of an ostrich. He did not venture to speculate where the ostrich might have first eaten the diamond.

The ostrich theory was soon shot down. In 1869 the now-alert Schalk van Niekerk came upon another diamond that had been found near the Orange River by a shepherd boy. The new find was a superb white diamond of 85 carats, which was eventually sold to the Earl of Dudley for £25,000. Colonial Secretary Sir Richard Southey proudly laid it on a table before the Cape Parliament and declared: "Gentlemen, this is the rock on which the future of South Africa will be built." Appropriately, the diamond was named "Star of South Africa."

Suddenly the whole of Cape Colony was talking about nothing but diamonds. There were more finds, not only along the Orange River but in even greater profusion by the Vaal River farther north. The new discoveries were just within the borders of the Transvaal and the Orange Free State. Within weeks everyone seemed headed for the fields, with highly romantic notions of what they would find. "They saw in their lively imaginings," said one contemporary, "fields glittering with diamonds like dewdrops in the waving grass or branches of trees along the Vaal River, and covering the highways and by-ways like hoarfrost."

But for those who made the journey, the on-the-spot reality was far from idyllic. The mining camps that mushroomed at Pneil and Klipdrift along the Vaal could be reached only by a hard 700-mile slog from Cape Town by horseback or ox-drawn wagon, or by a 500-mile mountainous journey from Durban or Port Elizabeth in Natal.

The mining communities, a few hundred tents and corrugated-iron huts, were scorching dust-bowls in summer and dank morasses of mud in winter. Food was high-priced and malaria common. Most diggers had little notion of what a rough diamond looked like, and even less how to find one. They set up tents haphazardly and started groping almost aimlessly in the sand and gravel. If nothing much turned up in a few days, they moved on. The names of the early mining communities—Cawood's Hope, Forlorn Hope, Good Hope, Last Hope—reflect their aspirations and their disappointments.

For every tale of frustration there was one of good luck. One young man was said to have found a diamond on the earth floor of a church when he knelt to pray. "An English gentleman," reported a visitor to the diggings, "having worked a claim for six months and found nothing, went home disgusted, giving away his claim. The man who got it found on the same day a fine diamond of 29½ carats before he had gone six inches deeper than his predecessor."

The eternal hope that beneath the next layer of gravel lay a fortune kept the diggers going during the worst privations. "Men who set out to work in the morning, not knowing where their dinner was to come from, became richer than any member of their family had ever been before it was time for an eleven o'clock snack," reported Charles Payton, a correspondent sent from London.

Until he struck a rich find the digger could live fairly economically, Payton advised. "The digger must do all his own cooking, marketing, and washing. A plain cookery book will be of much assistance to him." The cost of fitting out—a tent, bedding, tools, and planks to make the sorting tables—he estimated at about £30. Monthly expenses would be slightly more than £18, including a claim licence at ten shillings, wages for four native workers of 30 shillings each month, food, and water at threepence a bucket. On top of this was the cost of buying a claim, but the more ruthless diggers simply "jumped" other claims if their owners did not keep up licence payments.

Important new discoveries sustained the excitement. In August, 1870, diamonds were found on a farm some 20 miles south of the early Vaal diggings and a month later more were found nearby. Scarcely were the diggers getting their shacks up there when Cornelius du Plooy, who owned a farm across the way, found a diamond in the plaster he was mixing to decorate his house. He promptly sold out for £2,000 as the diggers came rushing in.

The real prize, however, was the Vooruitzigt farm of two Boer brothers, Johannes and Diedrich De Beer. Diamonds were found there in May, 1871, and then, a couple of months later, in even richer abundance at a little hillock close by. Beneath this

ground, it turned out, were two of the richest diamond deposits ever located in South Africa. They became known as the De Beers mine and the Kimberley mine.

The Kimberleys—both the mine and the town that sprang up nearby—were named for the British Colonial Secretary of the day, who complained he could not spell those Dutch names. During the next 40 years the burrowings of its diggers created the awesome Big Hole, a mile in circumference and the deepest open-pit mine ever dug by man. Today the Big Hole, abandoned and half full of water, is the first stop for every visitor to Kimberley, a memorial to the incredible energy that men expended in dredging up quick wealth.

The De Beers brothers, however, did not wait to see this deep digging; they sold the land they had bought for £50 in 1860 to a Port Elizabeth

DIAMONDS! DIAMONDS!!

ANOTHER DIAMOND FOUND, 83¼ carats!

HOPE TOWN.

The following extra to the *Colesberg Advertiser* reached us on Thursday, and was immediately issued as an extra to the *Cape Argus*:

18th March, 1869, 4·15 p.m.

The whole place, I mean the inhabitants, are in a great state of excitement. Schalk van Niekerk has just come in, and brought with him the largest diamond that has yet been found in South Africa. The gem weighs 83¼ (eighty-three and a half) carats—first water —and is said to be worth between £25,000 and £30,000. Found *in* the Colony, somewhere below the "Kalk." Mr. Niekerk is the gentleman who was the finder of, or who brought to notice, the first diamond, which was sold to the Governor for £500. That brought in by him to-day, he purchased from the Hottentot or Kafir doctor, of whom we heard about a year ago, using it as a charm in his profession. Niekerk gave him 500 sheep, ten head of cattle, and a horse for it. I wonder what that fellow Gregory would say now, were he here. Perhaps in this instance it was also dropped by an ostrich (?)

19th March.

The diamond has just been disposed of to Messrs. Lilienfeld Brothers for £11,200 (Eleven Thousand Two Hundred Pounds Sterling.)

P.S.—This news is confirmed by dispatch from the Civil Commissioner of Hope Town.

A Cape Colony newspaper account of the discovery of the "Star of South Africa."

syndicate for £6,000 and went off to farm quietly elsewhere.

Kimberley, whose population sky-rocketed to over 10,000, quickly took on the lusty, raucous atmosphere common to mining boom towns, with billiard halls and bars, cheap hotels and canteens, a racecourse of sorts, and the usual quota of con men. One Champagne Charlie salted his claim with fake diamonds he had filed down from champagne-bottle bottoms, sold out fast at a profit, and vanished. At Dodd's Bar the whisky and cigars were free to roulette and faro players. Prostitutes profited mightily in a seller's market.

But all told, the South African diamond rush was relatively peaceful, with occasional sprees the chief disturbance. The main problem was illicit diamond buying. Nimble-fingered workers at the diggings pocketed, palmed, or swallowed diamonds when the boss's eye was turned, then sold them on the quiet. In those early days security at the diggings was unknown and there are some estimates that almost half the diamonds found were disposed of through various and sundry under-the-table deals.

By the end of 1871 the South African diggings were yielding at least £50,000 worth of diamonds a week, easily outstripping Brazil, the previous major diamond-producing country. A year later production was six times that of Brazil; by 1880, 20 times. Indeed, the colony became diamond supplier to the world.

This flood of fine stones was just the rejuvenation that the diamond industry was desperately seeking. Brazilian output had been tailing off since 1860, while the demand for diamonds rose every year. Now, with the new flow of stones, there were suddenly barely enough experienced diamond-cutters to cope; their wages in 1871 were 13 times higher than in 1861. The great diamond merchants of Europe sent their representatives post-haste to Kimberley to open buying offices. The colony which a year or so earlier had been of little interest to anyone had become the new El Dorado. "A diamond stood for the making of history, for Empire, and for unbounded wealth," wrote a digger.

Until the diamond discoveries, few politicians either in Cape Colony or in Britain took the two infant Boer republics, the Transvaal and the Orange Free State, very seriously. The Voortrekkers had fled the Cape "to preserve their purity," establishing their farms in isolated communities scattered across the veld; the largest town in the Transvaal, Potchefstroom, had a mere hundred houses. The combined population of both republics was 45,000, compared to 200,000 in Cape Colony. Their coffers were almost permanently empty; the postmaster-general of the Transvaal sometimes had to take his salary in stamps. But the Boers were quite ready to accept poverty and hardship provided the British left them to their own way of life.

They were resentful of intruders, especially foreigners. When an English mineralogist, John Henry Davis, found gold-bearing rock in 1852 on the farm of a cousin of Marthinus Pretorius, President of the Transvaal, he was paid £600 for his samples and asked to leave. Later the Boers appointed their own mineralogist to search for gold and other minerals, but they included in his contract a fearsome clause that if he did discover mineral wealth and mentioned it to any foreign government and "so cause the independence of the Republic to be disturbed or threatened in any way, such action shall be punished with the penalty of death and no extenuating circumstances will be taken into consideration."

Now their isolation evaporated. Klipdrift, one of the first boom towns, was on the fringe of the Transvaal. Just across the Vaal River, in territory claimed by the Orange Free State, was Kimberley. Both republics responded to the challenge, but they lacked the manpower and the resources to make their authority firmly felt in the diamond fields. President Jan Brand of the Orange Free State sent in a magistrate and a handful of police to try to maintain some order at the diggings. President Pretorius of the Transvaal acted more rashly. He declared that he was giving ex-clusive rights to search for diamonds in the Transvaal to a company of three men, in return for a royalty of 6 per cent. The diggers greeted this proposal with derision, promptly declaring their independence as the Klipdrift Republic. Pretorius marched towards Klipdrift with a small commando troop, but at the last moment decided not to challenge the new republic by force.

Now the British authorities began to take an active interest in the diamond rush. Could the weak Boer republics provide the necessary law and order at the mining camps? Many politicians doubted it, especially as the majority of diggers were British and were clamouring for British rule. Furthermore, it seemed inconceivable that Britain should not have a stake in the richest diamond discoveries the world had ever known. The potential wealth from the mines could change the balance of power in southern Africa. Two penniless Boer republics had been no threat to British rule; two wealthy ones might be, especially as they would form a barrier right across to the Kalahari Desert, cutting off direct British access from the Cape to central Africa.

The British began manoeuvring for possession of the diamond fields. The loophole they discovered was that almost all the diamonds were on territory inhabited by the Griqua tribe. Since it had never really mattered before, no one had ever worked out precisely whether this Griqua land belonged to the Boer republics. The British now set up a commission under Robert Keate, the Lieutenant-Governor of Natal, to "arbitrate" the issue. This provoked an anguished plea by President Brand of the Orange Free State that a disinterested foreign power should settle the dispute. Keate's commission loftily refused to give way. The British have never liked to have their disputes settled by foreigners.

Keate's decision was hardly surprising: the Boer republics, he announced, could not rule what was known as West Griqualand. And with equal consistency the Griqua chief was persuaded to ask the British government to annex his land. British commissioners were sent in to establish law and order, and at the beginning of November, 1871, the Union Jack was run up over the diamond fields.

The Orange Free State was later given £90,000 compensation for the loss of West Griqualand, a contemptible sum considering that diamond production there was worth between £2,000,000 and £3,000,000 every year. The Transvaal received nothing at all. The Boers never forgot or forgave the British.

The same month that the British took over the diamond fields, a tall auburn-haired young Englishman in baggy white cricket flannels came trekking over the veld with a bucket and spade, a few volumes of the classics, a Greek lexicon, and a box of cough lozenges. His name was Cecil Rhodes, and he was just 18 and several thousand miles from his father's quiet vicarage at Bishop's Stortford in Hertfordshire.

Rhodes had been brought up in a strict, pious Victorian atmosphere. His father was anxious that Cecil and his four brothers should enter the Church "as a preliminary step in becoming angels." That proposal never matured, for Cecil caught tuberculosis. The doctor recommended an open-air life to restore his health, and he journeyed to South Africa in 1870 to join his eldest brother Herbert, who ran a cotton farm in Natal. Herbert soon left for the diamond fields, but Cecil, with the dedication to succeed that was to mark his career, persevered and brought in a fine cotton crop. Cotton prices, however, were poor. In disgust Rhodes took off to join his brother at the diggings.

He set up his tent at Kimberley and wrote his mother that the place looked like "Stilton cheese." As for the diamonds, they were right on his doorstep. "I found a $17\frac{6}{8}$ carat on Saturday," he wrote home. "It was very slightly off and I hope to get £100 for it. Yesterday, I found a three and a half perfect stone, but glassy, which I sold for £30. . . . I average £100 a week."

While the majority of diggers had no sense of organization and wan-

The Big Hole

When operations began at the Kimberley diamond mine—the Big Hole, as it came to be known—the diggers had only a short walk to reach their claims. But as the level of the diggings went lower and lower, it was necessary to construct inclined roadways to reach them. These soon became so steep that the task of bringing up the blue earth by wheelbarrow turned into a back-breaking job. Also, the ramps frequently collapsed. It was then that a great web of steel cables was spun down to the claims. Along these strands bucketloads of earth were winched by huge windlasses known as horse whims, turned by horses or mules, to the crator's edge.

As Big Hole grew ever deeper, it was a spectacular sight. "The whole face of the vast pit," wrote a visitor, "seemed to be covered by a monstrous cobweb, shining in the moonlight as if every filament was a silver strand." At a depth of 800 feet open-pit mining became impractical, and the shift was made to a complex of side shafts and tunnels. Finally, on August 4, 1914, at a depth of 3,610 feet, operations were suspended as uneconomic.

In the course of 43 years men had removed 25 million tons of earth from the Big Hole and recovered at least 14,500,000 carats—about three tons—of diamonds. Among these stones were three of the world's most famous—the Tiffany, an orange-coloured brilliant of 287.42 carats; the Porter Rhodes, a blue-white octahedron of 153.50 carats; and the Kimberley, which after cutting was a flawless, champagne-coloured diamond of 50.09 carats.

dered aimlessly from claim to claim, Rhodes selected his claims carefully and worked them thoroughly. He would sit on an upturned bucket reading Plutarch's *Lives* while waiting for his African workers to bring up more buckets of yellow gravel for him to sort.

He did not make friends easily; there always seemed a shell round him which few could break. He was big, uncouth, shambling, and dozy. His eyes were a watery blue and his mouth drooped at the corners, giving him a permanently morose expression. He shook hands limply, with two fingers outstretched, and his voice was surprisingly staccato and squeaky. Everyone called him Rhodes, not Cecil, and he even signed letters to his family with an icy C. J. Rhodes. One acquaintance found him "a compound of moody silence and impulsive action. He was hot tempered and even violent at times but in working towards his ends he laid his plans with care and circumspection." He lived very simply, preferring a grilled chop and onions eaten out beneath the stars. He was a compulsive gambler, but had little use for women. Occasionally he went to dances in Kimberley, but always seemed to select the plainest women as his partners.

After a while Rhodes went into partnership with another young Englishman, Charles Rudd, who had been a champion athlete at Harrow and Cambridge before deteriorating health also made him seek an open-air life in South Africa. Rudd proved an ideal partner for the restless Rhodes, who was determined to combine his diamond digging with taking a degree at Oxford. Throughout the eight years that Rhodes spent commuting between Kimberley and Oriel College to complete his degree, Rudd worked on, quietly and competently managing their claims.

As he travelled between the two strangely contrasted worlds of Kimberley and Oxford, Rhodes was beginning to formulate his grand design for the future. He had already amassed a considerable fortune for a young man, but that was just the bare foundation-stone of the wealth he wanted in order to fulfil an emerging dream: making not only Africa, but most of the world, British. At Oxford one evening he invited some friends to dinner and during dessert made a little speech in which he explained that he thought it right for every man, at the beginning of his life, to put an aim before him, and for his part he meant to work for the British Empire. "I contend that we are the first race in the world, and that the more of the world we inhabit, the better it is for the human race. I contend that every acre added to our territory provides for the birth of more of the English race, who otherwise would not be brought into existence. Added to which the absorption of the greater portion of the world under our rule simply means the end of all wars."

As insurance for his dream he wrote a will handing over his entire estate "for the establishment, promotion and development of a Secret Society, the true aim and object whereof shall be the extension of British rule throughout the world." He even hoped that the United States might be brought back into the fold of Empire.

Henceforth his life was dedicated. A fortune in diamonds was one way of underwriting his goals. "I often go and sit on the edge of the De Beers mine," he once said, "and I reckon up the value of the diamonds in the 'blue' and the power conferred by them. Every foot of the blue ground means so much power."

The discovery of this "blue" ground changed the character of the diggings dramatically. The diamond fields in India and Brazil, as well as the early South Africa discoveries along the Orange and Vaal rivers, had been scattered deposits in the sands along the river banks. At Kimberley, therefore, it was assumed that the diamonds were all in the first few feet of yellow topsoil, and diggers scooped out the soil in their small claims with frantic haste, then moved on. The more persistent went down into a flaky blue rock they called "Kimberlite"—and found even more diamonds imbedded there. It turned out that the stones were buried in narrow "pipes" forced up from deep in the earth by volcanic action. Each pipe was but a few hundred feet in diam-

Cecil Rhodes roughs it in the field. Eventually, and inevitably, he was portrayed as "The Colossus of Rhodes" standing astride Africa.

eter and could be excavated properly only by careful scientific techniques.

For a while the diggers stuck to their individual claims, which they could only reach, as the open pits got deeper and deeper, by buckets and trolleys slung from cables. "It is as though you were looking down into a vast bowl," wrote Anthony Trollope after visiting the Big Hole in 1877. "Round the bottom are various marvellous incrustations among which ants are working with all the unusual energy of the ant-tribe."

Rhodes was determined to set this house in order. He already had a profitable sideline, the renting of steam pumps to get water out of flooded claims. Now, he told Rudd, "the time is coming when the small man will have to go. These pits cannot be worked much deeper. We shall have to mine the ground on the largest possible scale. Now is the time to buy."

Rhodes and Rudd concentrated on buying out individual owners at what had been the De Beers farm. They soon owned a major share of the claims and in 1880 formed the De Beers Mining Company Limited, capitalized at £200,000.

Consolidation was taking place at all the mines. In 1881, 12 companies owned the entire Kimberley mine; ten years earlier there had been 1,600 individual claims. By 1885 the four main mines, Kimberley, De Beers, Dorstfontein, and Bultfontein, were controlled by 42 companies (many of them with interlocking boards of directors), with only a sprinkling of private holdings.

As the diamond business became more complex and costly, Rhodes and Rudd turned frequently for advice to Alfred Beit. A nervous little man, Beit had first come to Kimberley in 1875 as a diamond buyer, and he appeared to have the financial wizardry Rhodes needed to consolidate his diamond empire.

When they first met, Rhodes had inquired, "What's your game?"

"I am going to control the whole diamond output before I am much older," replied Beit.

"That's funny," said Rhodes, "I have made up my mind to do the same. We had better join hands."

Beit's flair for diamonds was uncanny. Once, when a man tried to sell him some stolen diamonds, he identified them immediately as stones that had passed through his hands seven years earlier.

Rhodes, Rudd, and Beit had to match wits with other masters of the diamond trade. Francis Baring Gould, who owned a major stake in the Kimberley mine, could count on excellent financial connections in London to support his plans for future ex-

pansion. Another fierce competitor, Joseph B. Robinson (known as "The Buccaneer"), was a quarrelsome and aggressive man who was envious of Rhodes and spent much of his career trying to thwart his every project. Above all, there was Barney Barnato, the irrepressible East End music-hall entertainer and boxer turned diamond magnate.

Barnato, the son of a small London shopkeeper, had left school at 14 and supported himself with a host of odd jobs. At one time or another he had been a pub bouncer, had sold theatre ticket stubs discarded after the first act to gullible bargain hunters, and eventually had done a music-hall turn of his own. He followed the trail to the diggings in 1873. His capital when he arrived consisted of 40 boxes of cigars of doubtful quality. No one wanted his cigars so he turned his hand to any job going, including boxer at the local circus, taking on all comers. Later he became a *kopje walloper*—an itinerant diamond buyer drifting round the fields buying up stones. The legend goes that he picked up an aged pony that knew the route so well that it always stopped at the claims where Barnato might be able to pick up a few stones. Although he lacked any real knowledge of diamonds, he made up for his ignorance with a sunny, genial personality. Diggers were willing to sell to this friendly man because they felt he was one of their own.

Barnato bought four claims in 1876 very near the centre of the Kimberley "pipe." He and his brother worked like demons, digging ever deeper into the blue ground. Soon he was making £2,000 a week, and formed the Barnato Diamond Mining Company.

Like Rhodes, Barnato kept on quietly buying up claims all round. In 1885 he merged his company with Francis Gould's Kimberley Central Mining Company, thus giving him as strong a hold on the Kimberley mine as Rhodes had at De Beers. By then the wealthiest diamond man in South Africa, with an income of £200,000 a year, Barnato was a formidable rival.

Barnato was on the whole content with his holdings and felt there was plenty of room in the business for both Rhodes and himself. Not so Rhodes, who saw his diamond empire merely as a springboard from which to plan the expansion of a great British Empire that would dominate all of Africa. Control of the whole diamond business, now worth £4,000,000 to £5,000,000 a year, would guarantee him the financial resources for this grand design.

Rhodes's belief in the benefits of monopoly were strengthened by the wild fluctuation of diamond prices. He was sure that if one company ran all production, the price of gemstones could be maintained at a high profit level by judicious control of the supply. Rhodes enjoyed pointing out that the whole foundation of the diamond's worth was based on the relationship between men and women; as long as they fell in love the future of the diamond was assured. He calculated that 4 million diamonds were needed every year for engagement rings. He hoped to supply all of them.

Rhodes's ambitious scheme was blocked by the existence of the two companies that together owned the Kimberley mine: Barnato's Kimberley Central and the Compagnie Francais des Mines de Diamant de Cap de Bon Esperance, understandably known simply as the French Company.

In 1887 Rhodes began his bid for control of the French Company. Seeking financial support, he travelled to London and approached N. M. Rothschild and Sons, the aristocrat of merchant banking houses. Rothschild's offered him a loan of £1,000,000, whereupon Rhodes bid £1,400,000 for control of the Compagnie Français. Back in Kimberley, Barnato received a cable warning of the deal and promptly topped Rhodes's offer by £300,000. Rhodes was not unduly perturbed. "You can go on bidding *ad infinitum*," he told Barnato, "but we shall have it in the end."

And he did. A compromise was worked out, whereby Rhodes bought the French Company for £1,400,000, his original offer, and immediately sold it to Barnato for a one-fifth stake in Kimberley Central plus £300,000 in cash.

That seemed to leave Barnato in an even stronger position, for he now owned the French Company and retained four-fifths of Kimberley Central. But the one-fifth share in Kimberley Central was the crucial toe-hold Rhodes needed. He and his associates began buying up all the Central shares they could corral. Barnato fought back, buying shares at absurd prices himself, so that the price soared from £14 to £49. In vain: some of his principal shareholders could not resist Rhodes's supersalesmanship, for in return for their securities he was offering tempting holdings in the new monopoly he proposed to form.

Rhodes tackled Barnato himself by inviting him to lunch at the exclusive Kimberley Club. Barney's East End background had disqualified him for membership, but he was far too shrewd to be won over by Rhodes's hardly subtle manœuvre. After several lunches however, Barnato began to see his rival in a new light. Previously he had felt that Rhodes, with his Oxford degree, was a snob who despised him for his humble beginnings. Now he found him more sympathetic. "The worst of Rhodes," he confessed, "is that when you have been with him for half an hour, you not only agree with him, but you come to believe you have always held his opinion."

It took time, but Rhodes prevailed. The final discussion lasted right through the night, with Barnato sipping rum and hot milk and listening in a daze as Rhodes pulled out maps and expounded his plans for expansion into central Africa. Finally, about 4 a.m., Barnato capitulated. "If it will please him," he told his nephew, "we'll let him have it."

In return for promising to merge Kimberley Central with De Beers, Barnato was guaranteed the largest individual shareholding and a life governorship in the new company. There was a final stumbling-block when a handful of dissident Kimberley Central shareholders challenged the merger in the courts. "They can do anything, My Lord," their counsel told the judge. "I suppose since the time of the East India Company, no company has had such power as this." When the judge agreed, Barnato put his company into voluntary liquidation. On July 18, 1889, Rhodes delivered a cheque for £5,338,650 (the largest sum ever covered by one cheque up to that time) for the assets of Kimberley Central.

Cecil Rhodes, only 35 years old, controlled 90 per cent of the world's diamond output and, with the resources of De Beers Consolidated Mines behind him, the financial power to proceed with his African ambitions. He knew exactly how he wanted to celebrate. "I've always wanted to see a bucketful of diamonds," he remarked. Barnato obligingly had a bucket filled with gems. Rhodes plunged in his hands ecstatically and let the diamonds cascade through his fingers. In the years ahead, possessed by a vision, he would convince himself he could deal with the huge expanses of central Africa as though they, too, could be placed in a bucket for him to possess and fondle.

—*Timothy S. Green*

At top are "horse whim" windlasses that rimmed the Kimberley mine and winched diamond-bearing soil to the surface. At right is a typical individual claim. In the 1877 photograph overleaf, the Kimberley looks like nothing so much as an archaeological "dig" among the pueblos of the American Southwest.

II. Struggle for South Africa

With southern Africa passing from a liability to an asset in the twinkling of a diamond strike, London began to look more closely at the running of this outpost of Empire. The concept of a South African confederation was attractive. By consolidating the ill-assorted clutch of colonies, Boer states, native kingdoms, and territories into one cohesive dominion, the British believed that both the expense of administration and the incessant petty squabbling could be reduced.

The idea found little favour in southern Africa. The stable Cape Colony had no wish to assume the problems of its poor relations, and few of the native kingdoms would willingly pass under European hegemony. Certainly neither of the Boer republics was eager to submit to a British government.

But in 1877 a Natal official sent on a mission to the Transvaal reported that the Boer administration, still stunned by the British takeover of the diamond fields, was enfeebled and in bankruptcy. With bland assurances that it was best for all concerned, the country was promptly annexed by the Crown. Anti-British sentiment among the Boers was further crystallized.

The next year, the government sent Sir Bartle Frere to Cape Colony as Governor, with plenary powers in the other British possessions. Frere was a proconsul of Empire, with a distinguished Indian career behind him. He was noted for his independence and his willingness to assume major responsibilities.

He soon decided that the major obstacle to confederation was the Zulu nation. For 40 years, since their bitter war with the Boer trekkers, the Zulus had remained at peace. Now, however, they were under a new chief, Cetshwayo, who was deeply imbued with the glories of the Zulu past. He maintained a 40,000-man army and issued truculent pronouncements that left his European neighbours uneasy. Cetshwayo apparently had no territorial ambitions, but the native peoples of all southern Africa drew a measure of defiance from his example of armed preparedness. No one was more aware of this than Governor Frere. He determined to pick a preventative war with the Zulus.

Frere began by offering to negotiate a boundary dispute between the Zulus and the Transvaal Boers, hoping both to limit Zulu power and to please the Boers. To his consternation, the commission he set up found in favour of the Zulus. Frere withheld this news until he had collected his troops and then promulgated the commission's recommendation—but coupled it with an ultimatum that ordered Cetshwayo to disband his army. The Governor knew perfectly well that the terms would not be accepted, and when the short period of grace expired, British troops entered Zululand. London was not informed of the ultimatum in time to do anything about it.

Command of the invasion was given to Frederic Thesiger, 2nd Baron Chelmsford, an intelligent, methodical officer well aware of the difficulties of his task. There was no proper target in Zululand, and occupying the entire country was out of the question. The only possible objectives were a smashing defeat of the Zulu army and the capture of the King himself. Since his enemy could easily cover 50 miles a day for days on end (the British might make five miles on a good day), Chelmsford could hardly conduct a chase. He hoped to be attacked so that the massed fire of his troops' modern breech-loading rifles could come into action.

Chelmsford disposed his troops—8,000 regulars, 1,000 mounted volunteers, and 7,000 native troops from Natal—into three columns, which were to enter Zululand separately and converge on the royal kraal at Ulundi. The army creaked into motion in January, 1879. The troops advanced from one strong camp site to the next, always ready to accept the hoped-for attack. Periodically they waited while a slow, vulnerable ox-train moved back to the Natal border to bring up supplies. Over half the force was preoccupied with the commissariat.

Fortunately for the British, Cetshwayo was no grand strategist. He could think of no plan but to assemble the entire Zulu army at Ulundi and then launch a succession of attacks. After each assault, he intended to reassemble the regiments for rest and refitting and then try again. The raw courage of his warriors, his nation's only military asset, would be used until it was either victorious or broken and spent.

Chelmsford and the central column forded the Buffalo River at a crossing called Rorke's Drift, marked by a mission-station at which he left a small reserve force, and started along the track to Ulundi. On January 20 a camp was established in the shadow of Isandhlwana Mountain, on a broad, level plain. It was a strong position, close to wood and water. Two days later Chelmsford set out with half his force to check on a scouting report of Zulu troops in the foothills ahead and to find a new campsite. Once a base was established, the rear half of the force at Isandhlwana would be brought forward.

But the main Zulu force, 20,000 strong, was not in the foothills. It had slipped unseen into a ravine near the Isandhlwana camp. There was a new moon due and the Zulus planned to sit out this inauspicious time and attack the next day, January 23. But when by chance a British scout spotted them squatting in utter silence, they came boiling out of hiding and shook themselves into battle order on the run. Within minutes the Zulu tide was lapping against the British line.

Although the British were defending a large area, they were not worried; their first volleys stopped the Zulus 100 yards away and the entire mass threw themselves down, humming in anger like a gigantic swarm of bees, trying to edge forward against the sustained rifle fire. Their losses were fearful. This was exactly the battle the British wanted. Then, with hardly any warning, the situation changed radically.

The troops began to run short of cartridges. There were half a million rounds in the camp, packed in two wagons, one for each of the two battalions, a quarter of a mile apart. Messengers sent by the camp commander, Colonel Anthony Durnford, and by the other commanders, arrived for replenishment. It took some a long

Cape Colony's Governor Sir Henry Frere pledged to eliminate the "Zulu incubus."

time to get there, for parts of the battle line were more than a mile from the wagons. When they did arrive, some found that they had come to the wrong place: the quartermaster of the 1st Battalion would not issue ammunition to messengers from 2nd Battalion companies, and vice versa. Neither quartermaster would issue any ammunition to the native troops. The men in the line had expended the 50 rounds in their pouches, and the messengers could not keep up the supplies.

Across the battle front the British fire slackened for want of ammunition. The Zulus noticed the change and one of their regiments leaped up, rattling their assegais against their shields and shouting their war cry. The Natal natives, panic-stricken, fled, leaving a gaping hole in the British line. Thousands of maddened Zulus poured into the opening, taking the men from behind as the frontal attack smashed home.

Organized resistance was over in minutes. The few survivors who rallied for a last stand near the wagon park lasted little longer. The six companies of the 2nd Warwickshire died to a man. Several hundred staff officers, mounted volunteers, bands-

men, cooks, grooms, and wagon drivers started down the broken ground to the Buffalo River four miles away, with the Zulus hacking and stabbing at them as they ran. The river was in flood, and most of those who reached the bank died there or in the crossing.

Many who escaped had remarkable tales to tell afterwards. Lieutenant Horace Smith-Dorrien seized a free horse and rode all the way to the river without even being threatened. He learned later that he owed his life—as did several other officers—to the fact that he was wearing a blue patrol jacket. Cetshwayo had told his warriors to kill only soldiers, who could be identified by their red coats. Anyone else, he said, was a civilian and could be safely ignored.

Back in the camp, the orgy of destruction had spent itself. The dead and wounded defenders were disembowelled by the Zulus, who also dispatched their own desperately wounded comrades. They carried off the bodies of their dead (some 2,000) and dragged away the guns. Then, satisfied that they had fulfilled the demands of their great fighting traditions, they streamed away to their kraals. Of the 1,800 men in the camp that morning, perhaps 55 Europeans and some 300 Natal troops survived.

Chelmsford, summoned by a survivor, started back across the plain late in the afternoon. He came up to the camp at dark, scarcely able to credit what had happened, and spent a sleepless night in the midst of the carnage. He was further dismayed by the sound of rifle-fire from the direction of the river. The outpost at Rorke's Drift was under attack.

Chelmsford had left B Company of the 2nd Battalion, 24th Foot, under Lieutenant Gonville Bromhead to guard Rorke's Drift: 80-odd British troops and a company of Natal natives. Another 36 men were hospital patients in a crude farmhouse. The only other building in the mission station was a stone storehouse crammed with bags of meal and crates of biscuits.

Late the previous afternoon two exhausted riders had reached the Drift, where Lieutenant John Chard, Royal Engineers, was working on the

The Zulu War marked the finish of Lord Chelmsford's career as field commander.

river crossing. They gasped out the news of Isandhlwana, and added that a wing of the Zulu army, 4,000 strong, that had taken no part in the battle was heading for the outpost. Chard rushed back to the mission to find that Bromhead, already alerted, was trying to load the sick into wagons for a retreat. Chard, the senior officer, saw that the garrison would never get away in time. They had no choice but to stand and fight.

Using the stored bags and crates, his men ran a low wall around the buildings, incorporating two of the wagons into the back wall to save time. Cross-walls were built as second lines of defence. It was too late to get the sick out of the farmhouse; Chard posted volunteer riflemen in each room.

The Zulus, meanwhile, had forded the fast-flowing Buffalo River by linking arms and charging the current. At the sight of the mission station, they broke into a charge. At the last moment, with the Zulus upon them, the native troops fled, leaving Chard with fewer than 90 hale men to defend his extended ramparts.

The Zulus attacked towards sunset, and the battle lasted until the early morning hours. Wave after

The last stand of the 24th Foot in the Battle of Isandhlwana in 1879. Lacking cartridges due to a monumental logistics blunder, the redcoats had only their bayonets with which to withstand the fierce Zulu charge. They died to the last man in a matter of minutes.

wave of Zulus threw themselves at the makeshift defences. Their attacks forced Chard to abandon the perimeter walls of meal bags and biscuit tins and withdraw behind the second line of defence. This left the hospital building exposed. Zulus dashed forward and flattened themselves against its walls, out of reach of the defenders' fire. While the men inside reloaded, the Zulus threw themselves against the barricaded doors. The front of the building was breached.

Inside, Privates Henry Hook and John Williams retreated through the rooms ahead of the Zulus, dragging the wounded behind them. Finally the Zulus set the roof on fire. The hospital was abandoned. The 11 surviving patients were lifted through a small window and somehow ran or were half-carried over an undefended patch of ground towards the new barricade. Nine of them made it.

The battle surged on in the light of the burning hospital. Gun barrels glowed in the dark, their heat firing off rounds before the defenders had time to pull the trigger. The men lost

all count of the charges and all sense of time. They existed in a slow eternity of noise and smoke and flashes, of straining black faces that rose out of the darkness, danced briefly in the light of the muzzle blasts, and then sank back out of sight. It was after midnight when the rushes began to subside, and after two o'clock in the morning when the last charge was over.

Abandoning direct assault, the Zulus settled down under cover and those with rifles sniped away by the light of the burning hospital. Two hours later the fire finally flickered out, and the shooting died away with it. Darkness and an uneasy silence descended over the battle scene.

As dawn broke, the troops, their eyes reddened, their hands blistered and black with powder, strained to see their enemies. By the smouldering ruins of the hospital, among the scattering bags and tins, 500 Zulu dead were sprawled in the grey light. But the Zulu regiments had gone. Exhaustion had set in: the warriors had not eaten since leaving Ulundi four

days before, and the previous day alone they had run nearly 20 miles to Rorke's Drift and then fought a six-hour battle.

Chelmsford and his men came up soon after to find 15 of the garrison dead and two more dying, and eight wounded. No fewer than 11 of the Rorke's Drift defenders, including Chard and Bromhead, were awarded the Victoria Cross.

The rest of the war was anticlimactic. Chelmsford was back where he started. He sent for replacements and planned a second invasion. Slowly and methodically, leaving nothing to chance, his 17,500-man army made its way towards Ulundi.

The people at home and the government were deeply shocked by news of the Battle of Isandhlwana, one of the worst defeats suffered by imperial troops in the 19th Century. The widely respected General Sir Garnet Wolseley was dispatched to restore order. Before he could take up his new position, however, Lord Chelmsford had his revenge.

On July 4, 1879, a mile and a half

from the royal kraal, Chelmsford's army formed a classic square and braced itself for attack. The 20,000 Zulus gathered in a vast crescent and advanced at a jog to their last great battle.

Not one got within 30 yards of the British lines. A hail of lead from rifles and Gatling machine guns scythed down wave after wave of screaming warriors. "Their noble ardour," wrote a war correspondent, "could not endure in the face of the appliances of civilized warfare." When the fury of the Zulu attack faltered, the 17th Lancers charged out of the square to deliver the final blow. The natives broke into head-long flight, leaving a thousand dead on the battlefield.

Some weeks later, Cetshwayo himself was captured, bringing to an end the Zulu War—and in fact the Zulu nation. In 1887 Zululand was annexed by the Crown, and once-proud warriors became labourers and house-boys on Natal estates.

Ironically, Chelmsford's final triumph over the Zulus created serious trouble in the Transvaal. The Zulu threat had temporarily checked the bitterness of the Boer inhabitants at the British takeover, but now they felt there was no further reason for the British to remain in control. The neighbouring Orange Free State was still independent. Why not they?

One of the leaders rallying support for the re-establishment of the republic was Paul Kruger, an untidy-looking man with hunched shoulders and an extensive, wispy beard, habitually dressed in black and wearing a large, floppy hat. The British considered Kruger a malevolent rabble-raiser, blinded by religious cant. But to his own people he was a noble patriot, struggling for the rights of an oppressed race.

When rumours of a Boer uprising became persistent, Wolseley decided that a visit to Pretoria, the Transvaal capital, was imperative. En route he told the assembled crowds, as if he were speaking to ignorant natives, "So long as the sun shines, the Transvaal will remain British territory." This was by no means the unanimous view in London, but Wolseley, having taken the initiative, received govern-

ment support. The "infernal Boers," as he called them, greeted him at Pretoria with banners and petitions calling for independence. Kruger collected the signatures of 80 per cent of the electorate in support of his demands.

Wolesley began to pull strings to get himself back home, perhaps to the comfort of a peerage. First, however, he disposed of a military problem. The Bapedi tribe, living in a remote corner of the Transvaal, had long maintained an aggressive independence and had, indeed, already undertaken one war against the Boers. Now they threatened again. Wolseley assembled a "Transvaal Field Force" of 1,400 British infantry, 400 colonial horse, and 10,000 friendly Africans. There followed, in his words, "a filthy little war," conducted with typical Wolseley efficiency and flair. The entire Bapedi tribe were all but exterminated.

The Boers were impressed, but they were quick to note that with the Bapedi destroyed, the British presence in the Transvaal was even less necessary than ever. Boer discontent increased. In open defiance, nearly 3,000 men assembled on the veld under the flag of the republic. "I feel I could walk over them easily," Wolseley told his wife. He assured the government that there was little to worry about. He told the Colonial Office that the Boers were prepared "to renounce all further disturbing action, and to return to the peaceful cares of their rural life."

The government was inclined to believe him and at long last, in 1880, he got the order to go home. So anxious was he to get away from this country he detested that he travelled 300 miles in three days, exchanging horses every few miles and galloping most of the way.

In the same year, Gladstone's Liberal government displaced Disraeli and the Conservatives. Gladstone had already described the annexation of the Transvaal as "dishonourable," but in office he found it impossible to extricate Britain from its difficult position. Then he immersed himself in a solution to the Irish problem, which he hoped would be his greatest contribution to political life, and for-

got about South Africa altogether. He was soon to be reminded of it.

In December, 1880, discontent in the Transvaal broke into open disturbance at Potchefstroom. A local magistrate had seized the wagon of a Boer to pay the costs of a legal suit. Just before the wagon was due to be sold at public auction, Piet Cronje, who was to become one of the most famous of the Boer military leaders, and a band of burghers seized it and handed it back to the owner. The Boers used this small act of defiance as the excuse for rebellion, and five days later they proclaimed the Transvaal a republic.

Wolseley's replacement was 45-year-old Major-General Sir George Colley, whose reputation was based on a brilliant career at Sandhurst and the Staff College. He was considered one of the army's leading military academics, but now he confessed to being bewildered. "I cannot conceive," he said, "what can have so suddenly caused the Boers to act as they have." Before Colley could ponder any further, the whole province had risen in arms and the scattered British garrisons in the Transvaal found themselves besieged.

Colley sent a column of redcoats from Natal to Pretoria. It was Christmas week, 1880. The men of the Connaught Rangers marched confidently along the track, the band playing "Kiss Me Mother, Kiss Your Darling Daughter"; then the column was shot to pieces by hidden Boer riflemen. More than half the Connaughts lay dead or wounded on the road; the remainder gave in. The Boers lost two men. In imperial terms there was only one answer to such an outrage against British authority: war.

Sir George's opponents did not seem, at first sight, very impressive. They consisted of irregulars who accepted little discipline. Military decisions were made only after long discussions at which everyone could have a say. What was less well known was that they were expert shots, and that they had an instinctive knowledge of the tactics suitable to their local conditions.

Colley decided to advance into the Transvaal with a column of a thousand men and six field pieces. He travelled up the main route from Natal, through the difficult passes of the Drakensberg range. The Boers watched his progress and dug in at a place called Laing's Nek. Colley decided to take them on. A detachment of British infantry, in perfect line, went forward to dislodge the enemy. The order to fix bayonets was given, then "Charge!" The Boers unloosed a withering fusillade. Nearly all the British officers, their swords glinting in the sunlight, fell at once. Only a few of the troops managed to reach the Boer position. Of 480 men engaged, 150 did not return. The Boers were more formidable than they looked.

General Colley was staggered by this setback. He was in a difficult position, because furious political activity was taking place in London to stop the war before it got out of hand, and he had no idea what the political moves were. It seemed that the Boers were in a strong position and Gladstone, engrossed with Ireland, had no real wish to force a show-down. General Colley decided that a British military victory was essential before a settlement was reached which would leave imperial honour and his own reputation shattered beyond repair.

One hill, Majuba, dominated the Laing's Nek area. From it the Boer lines were clearly visible; if it were taken the enemy might well be obliged to withdraw without firing another shot. On the night of February 26, 1881, Colley assembled his force, about 600 strong. It was a steep climb to the summit of Majuba, through scrub and loose stone, but by dawn all the troops had reached the top. They watched as the Boers moved about below. Colley surveyed the scene with satisfaction. "We could stay here forever," he remarked, and in his confidence gave no order to dig in or to haul up the artillery. The troops lay about resting.

Below, the Boer commander called for volunteers to storm the hill. About 180 Boers began the climb. Colley turned down a suggestion that defences should now be dug. Satisfied that all was well, he lay down and went to sleep.

The Boers advanced slowly, from boulder to boulder, and the British riflemen had the greatest difficulty locating them. To several officers it was plain that marksmanship in the army was sadly lacking. Suddenly the Boers were at the top and in force. The redcoats gathered in defensive positions and Sir George was awakened. Fierce hand-to-hand fighting took place as the British struggled to maintain their positions. Soon they were being picked off one by one by the incredibly accurate Boer riflemen. The British firing was as wild; hardly a Boer was hit.

The British infantry began to withdraw; as one officer put it, "A general funk had become established." Men began to slide down the slope. Boers stood on the edge of the escarpment and picked them off like wild game. A small party remained on the plateau with Sir George. The General, showing great personal bravery, urged them on until he was shot dead. Then the remainder surrendered.

So ended the brief Battle of Majuba Hill. Transvaal farmers had defeated British regulars. The British had lost 93 dead and 133 wounded; the Boers, one dead and five wounded.

Thanks to a newly established cable link, the news was received in London the following day. The British public was astounded and the government furious. How would it affect the peace on which Gladstone was already determined? "I do not like peace before we have retrieved our honour," the Queen wrote. But Gladstone argued that a generous policy on the Transvaal had already been agreed in Cabinet, had been transmitted to the Boers, and a reply was awaited. The defeat should not affect the previously decided policy.

Kruger replied to Gladstone's message in conciliatory tones. He had got what he wanted: British military defeat, and a hint of autonomy. There was no need for Gladstone to change his mind. The Boers agreed to return to their homes and the British agreed not to follow them into the Transvaal. Kruger and his associates were recognized by the British government as the legitimate Boer leaders for the purpose of negotiations.

These negotiations were concluded in August, 1881, and resulted in the Treaty of Pretoria, which recognized the Transvaal's independence but retained for Britain a vaguely defined "suzerainty" and control of the Transvaal's foreign affairs. It was presented in Britain as a liberal, humanitarian measure giving considerable freedom to a former colony, and in South Africa as a great victory for Boer nationalism over stifling British imperialism.

The Opposition was horrified. Conservatives saw the creation of a semi-independent state in the centre of southern Africa as an unacceptable threat to British superiority there. One of the chief Opposition spokesmen, Sir Michael Hicks Beach, a former Colonial Secretary, said of the Liberal government with uncanny prescience: "They have secured not only that peace shall not be lasting, but that it shall be the precursor of infinitely worse trouble than any from which their weak yielding has for the moment delivered them."

The Boer War of 1881 had been a small war, and the Empire was accustomed to small wars. But there was something about this one that made it different. The lion had been humiliated and the Empire threatened in an area where it was expanding rapidly. One day, perhaps, the war would have to be fought again.

A step in that direction came just five years later, thanks to an ironic geological fact. This nation of Boer farmers was growing up over the greatest source of gold the world had ever seen.

Gold had first been discovered in the Transvaal back in the 1850s, not in vast amounts but enough to keep hopeful diggers, many of them English, criss-crossing the area in search of a big find. It was a forbidding part of the country, a line of high ridges rising up to 6,500 feet. This treeless veld, where the wind whipped biting dust into clouds that clogged nose, eyes, and mouth, was known as the Witwatersrand, the "Edge of White Water," after the clear sparkling streams that tumbled down its northern side. To most people it was simply the Rand.

Who actually discovered the Rand

British cavalrymen stare in disbelief as their comrades, routed by sharpshooting Boers, stream down the slopes of Majuba Hill during the 1881 Boer War.

"gold-reef" is still a matter of dispute. There were at least two people involved, George Walker and George Harrison. These two, who emerged briefly into the historical limelight only to vanish again into the shadows, had worked together odd-jobbing for Boer farmers and prospecting when they could. One day in February, 1886—so runs the most widely accepted version of the story—Walker idly broke off a piece of rock while on a stroll to see his friend. When he arrived he crushed the rock with a ploughshare and panned the dust in a borrowed saucepan. There for all to see was a tell-tale streak of gold. They agreed on prospecting rights with the owner of the land, and by June it was clear that the find was a remarkably big one.

Within a few days all the Transvaal knew of the strike. Prospectors quickly discovered further outcrops: the gold-reef extended at least 30 miles. Within a month the government proclaimed the whole area a "public digging" and ordered a site to be chosen for a village. The three officials who were given the job were all named Johann or Johannes, and by mutual agreement they named the patch of land they selected Johannesburg.

All that summer of 1886 ships from every corner of the world arrived at the Cape crammed with fortune-hungry diggers. Business in mules, horses, ox-wagons, and coaches boomed as locals cashed in on the demand for transport for the 350-mile journey inland. Within weeks Johannesburg was a burgeoning township of tents and flimsy wooden buildings set in rough lines on the veld, while a stone's throw away miners hacked trenches into the rocky soil.

They soon found that the gold was not to be easily won. There were no nuggets: the metal was locked into the rock in tiny particles. To get at it at all, the rock had to be laboriously crushed, then washed and sieved. But from the first there were those with money enough to set up massive rock-crushers and apply a system of chemical reactions based on mercury that would separate the gold from the rock-dust.

The trouble and expense of such large-scale operations turned Johannesburg into a theatre for big-time impresarios acting behind the scenes in Kimberley, Cape Town, London, New York, Paris, and Berlin to establish syndicates to tap the treasures of

1.— Enemy coming round hill to attack retreating party.
2.— Enemy in possession of Majuba Mountain doing d.º d.º
3.— Enemy in Dongas & side of hill .... d.º d.º
4.— Our troops retreating down side of hill under heavy fire.
5.— Shell fired from Mount Prospect Camp, about 3 m. distant.
6.— Ledge of rocks.
7.— Hussars Picket & some officers of 60.th Rifles & others looking on at the Battle.
8.— 15.th Hussars retreating.
9.— Falls (small)
10.— Laing's Neck.

the new El Dorado. Among them, not surprisingly, was Cecil Rhodes.

Many dreamed of a trans-African empire: the Germans, who saw it as a possible link between their colonies in South-West and East Africa; the Portuguese, to join Angola to Mozambique; the Boers, now able to expand only in that direction. For Cecil Rhodes, it was crucial for his epic dream of a railway—a highway for economic domination—running on British territory all the way from the Cape to Cairo, 4,000 miles away.

Only one of these plans had real significance and that was Rhodes's. His imagination was wild with schemes for African Empire; "If there be a God," he said once, "I think that what He would like me to do is paint as much of Africa British-red as possible." With the wealth from his Kimberley diamonds and his Rand gold, with growing political power (he became Cape Colony's Prime Minister in 1890), he set out in pursuit of his grandiose dream. Before he was finished, he would precipitate an imperial crisis.

—*Donald Morris, Brian Gardner*

III. From Suez to Khartoum

In the age of the Pharaohs, Jehovah visited ten plagues upon the land of Egypt. Since then Egypt had suffered, almost without intermission, an eleventh plague—vicious government by foreign aggressors. Down the centuries Arabs, Mamelukes, and Turks had successively conquered her, exploited her, lived in extravagance on the misery of her peasant fellaheen.

Britain had no interest in joining the long line of Egypt's alien conquerors. Her vital lifeline to India was the three-month route round the Cape of Good Hope; the Mediterranean was of relatively minor concern. Then, in 1798, Napoleon invaded Egypt. There was the nightmarish possibility that he might make for India through the Middle East. Suddenly Egypt acquired strategic significance.

The British reaction had been violent: Nelson shot the French fleet to shreds in the Battle of the Nile. But in British eyes there remained a long-term threat to the route to India. The lands around the eastern Mediterranean formed part of the moribund Ottoman Empire. Should it collapse, Russia might sweep southward or France eastward, swallowing much of the Arab world and imperilling India. Accordingly, Gibraltar and Malta became first-line naval bases and Britain let it be known that she would tolerate no rival foreign presence in Turkish Egypt.

That country, however, was soon moving along a new course, charted by Mohammed Ali, the "Father of Modern Egypt." Appointed Viceroy by the Turkish Sultan, he was a formidable, colourful scoundrel. Clamping down a ruthless dictatorship, he started industries, introduced large-scale cultivation of long-staple cotton, and began an irrigation system. Above all, he built up an army, which won for him a considerable measure of autonomy from the Sultan.

Mohammed Ali also allowed a British officer, Lieutenant Thomas Waghorn, to organize an overland route between the Mediterranean and the Red Sea. Steamships began to voyage regularly from London to Alexandria, and from Suez to Bombay, with Waghorn's river boats and pack-animals bridging the land barrier between, cutting the journey to India to one month. Britain was well content.

But in 1854 Mohammed Said succeeded to the viceregal throne. Obese, extravagant, jovial, he too was a despot, but with ideas well intentioned and even liberal. His permissive good nature opened the country to an influx of European traders, technicians, experts, and promoters. Among these was Ferdinand de Lesseps, a Frenchman obsessed with a dream: a canal piercing the Isthmus of Suez and providing a new sea route to the East. De Lesseps was a man of extraordinary persuasiveness and perseverance. He talked Said into backing his idea with absurdly generous concessions: large areas of land adjacent to the proposed route of the canal, handsome mineral rights, and free forced labour. The dynamic Frenchman then rushed to and fro between Cairo and the capitals of Europe, expounding his vision, exorcizing doubts, mobilizing support for his projected Suez Canal Company.

Official Britain was opposed to the whole project from the start. In the first place, London was entirely satisfied with the Cape and overland routes to India. In the second, though de Lesseps was a lone wolf, he was French: inevitably his enterprise would once again place an ominous French presence between England and her Empire in the East. At the moment, however, Britain and France were fighting side by side to contain Russia in the Crimea, so efforts to scotch the canal would have to be limited and indirect.

The project staggered through a series of financial crises, and for a time construction ceased. London was jubilant. But somehow de Lesseps persuaded first Said and then his successor, Ismail Pasha, to advance more and more money, mortgaging future dividends and borrowing from Europe's bankers to do so. Finally the arduous, ten-year task of building the canal was finished. On opening day, November 17, 1869, the French imperial yacht, with the Empress Eugénie waving from the bridge, led a procession of 51 ships from Port Said to Suez and back. It was one of the grandiose spectacles of the century.

The Suez Canal was the first stage on Ismail's road to ruin. He spent money like water on lavish living and on public works of every kind: palaces, harbours, bridges, railways, ships. Word spread that Egypt was a splendid field for bankers. At last, in

1875, as the net of foreign bankers, contractors, and agents began to tighten, Ismail had to fall back on his only real assets to raise cash for the interest on his loans. He let it be known that his Suez Canal shares were for sale.

It was then that Prime Minister Benjamin Disraeli stepped in. Already the Canal was changing the pattern of ocean trade; already British shipping was its major user. It was clear that having failed to prevent the Canal, Britain must aim to control it.

Parliament was not in session. The only means of obtaining the money was by a loan. And the only bank able to advance the needed £4 million quickly was the house of Rothschild.

Montague Corry, Disraeli's private secretary, sped to the City and laid the request before Baron Lionel de Rothschild. He needed the money tomorrow, he said, and offered the British government as security. "You shall have it," Rothschild replied.

A few days later Britain stood possessed of 44 per cent of the shares of the Suez Canal Company. It was the point of no return on the road that lead to a series of direct interventions forced upon her by the politics of Empire and by the facts of imperial geography.

The £4 million Disraeli paid to Ismail quickly melted away. The Egyptian foreign debt soared. All along the Nile the *kurbash*—the tax-collector's rhinoceros-hide lash—was busier than ever. But no more could be flogged from the fellaheen. In 1876 debt payments were halted. Egypt was bankrupt.

"Egypt was to be delivered to the children of the north," Jeremiah had prophesied. Now it was coming to pass as European creditors raised their cry. Germany, Austria, Italy, and Turkey were all involved, but the principal concerned powers were Britain and France. Their nationals were owed huge sums, but more important

were imperial factors. Britain had gained virtual control of the Canal's finances, and could not now stand aside from Egypt's future. France was equally concerned, for a different reason: she was building an empire in North Africa, and one day Egypt might be required as its eastern pivot.

Cautiously the two imperial powers came together to press on Ismail a Commission of the Debt—"like a dog and a cat taking a mouse for a walk," as an Egyptian put it. Ismail tried to raise an army to rid the country of the infidel usurers, but the sullen peasants failed to respond. At the demand of Britain and France, the Turkish Sultan deposed Ismail, and in 1879 he sailed away on the royal yacht with all the jewels he could snatch.

With Ismail's departure the British and the French virtually took over the management of Egypt's finances. The new Khedive, Tewfik, found himself in fiscal fetters. But neither power had reckoned with the hitherto muted

In this panoramic aerial view of the Suez Canal (the perspective of which owes something to artistic licence), Suez, the southern terminus, is in the foreground. At upper right is Port Said, on the Mediterranean, and at upper left the sprawling Nile Delta.

voice of the people of the Nile Valley, a voice that now began to speak through the person of Ahmed Bey Arabi.

Arabi, a colonel in the Egyptian Army, was a man of the people, simple, slow-spoken, sincere. He called for an end to the corruption of the Turkish upper class in Egypt and for a halt to foreign interference in the affairs of his impoverished country. He was arrested and brought before a Council of Ministers. But his peasant troops burst in, toppled the Council from their chairs, emptied inkpots over their heads, and chased them out through the windows. Political upheaval followed and alarm seized the creditor nations. The British Press, even the anti-imperialist Gladstone, Liberal Prime Minister, denounced Arabi as a mutineer and a bloodthirsty fanatic. They utterly failed to understand that he was the national spirit of an Egypt becoming, for the first time, articulate.

Diplomatic telegrams flew about Europe. Britain and France drafted a joint note affirming their support of Khedive Tewfik. They requested the Turkish Sultan to send a force and augmented their own naval squadrons in Egyptian waters. Savage rioting broke out in Alexandria in the course of which European diplomats were manhandled and a large number of Christians killed. Arabi, angered by the menacing foreign warships, began to dig emplacements and train his guns seaward. On London's instructions the British admiral called on him to stop. He continued the work. On the morning of July 11, 1882, the British ships opened fire.

All day the bombardment of Alexandria continued. One of those watching from the flagship's bridge was Herbert Kitchener, a tall mustachioed young subaltern on his first visit to Egypt; in the course of events he would play a larger role in Anglo-Egyptian affairs. By 5 p.m. the forts were wrecked. Inside the flaming town infuriated Egyptians ran wild, destroying anything belonging to foreigners. British marines landed to restore order.

The day's events nearly brought down Gladstone's government. He took refuge behind a barrage of verbiage, but at length reluctantly agreed that it was essential to replace anarchy and conflict in Egypt with peace and order. "Failing the cooperation of Europe, this work will be undertaken by the single power of England," he said.

Europe—or rather France—indeed failed to cooperate. She was nervous about the reaction of her neighbours, especially Germany, and at the critical moment the French squadron vanished over the horizon. Britain was left alone to deal with Arabi, to keep the Canal open, and to assure Egypt's future on behalf of her creditors.

The first task was quickly discharged. With 20,000 men General Sir Garnet Wolseley, that hero of imperial campaigning, steamed into the Canal past the gesticulating figure of Ferdinand de Lesseps standing on the quay, horrified at the possibility that his canal might be damaged in the hostilities. A month later British bayonets routed Arabi's forces at Tel-el-Kebir. Britain had wanted neither the Canal nor Egypt; now she had both.

The heaviest burden fell on Evelyn Baring, a member of the famous banking family who had served in the Indian administration. With the modest title of Agent and Consul-General, he would govern Egypt for nearly a quarter of a century. Patient and adroit, Baring proved himself one of the outstanding British imperial proconsuls.

One commitment at least could be avoided. Britain was careful not to annex Egypt. Instead, she would administer through the most suitable Egyptian government until the country could stand on its own feet. Even so, the difficulties facing Baring were acute. He could assure his own authority internally, for he was backed by London and by British occupation forces on the spot. But when Egypt's international liabilities were concerned, he had to take account of all the European creditors; in trying to steer a course which would satisfy all, he inevitably satisfied very few.

France, especially, had no intention of being satisfied. Jealous of Britain's increased power in the Middle East, she reverted to her previous role of irritant and rival. At every turn she demanded to know when the British would implement their intention to leave Egypt.

Baring had hardly been installed when trouble started. Stretching from Wadi Halfa towards the great lakes of Africa, from the Red Sea to the Sahara, lay a vast expanse of desert and scrub threaded by the Upper Nile. This was the huge territory of the Sudan. Its economy, such as it was, rested almost entirely on the sale of ivory and black slaves.

From early times Egypt had pushed southward beyond Wadi Halfa into this wild cruel land for distances corresponding to the ebb and flow of her power. By 1880 some 40,000 Egyptian troops manned posts across the Sudan, enforcing with their guns the rule of a Governor-General in Khartoum. It was an utterly corrupt rule. Soldiers plundered the natives and Egyptian officialdom took its cut from the traffic in human flesh as it passed on its way to the slave markets of Cairo and Constantinople. Everywhere there was poverty and oppression.

In 1881 an obscure man of religion, Mohammed Ahmed el-Sayyid Abdullah, fired a spark into the Sudan tinderbox. He proclaimed himself the long-expected Mahdi—the Guided One of the Prophet—and began preaching. The time had come, he urged, to make an end of the Egyptians and their Turkish overlords, to return to the purity of the true Muslim faith. The Mahdi's fervent eloquence magnetized first the downtrodden local population, then several warlike desert tribes. An Egyptian force sent from Khartoum to arrest him retired in haste. A second one was hacked to pieces. A month before the British bombardment of Alexandria, a larger punitive force met the same fate. The Mahdi's swelling horde of Dervish warriors were beyond Egyptian capacity to counter. In January, 1883, came news that El-Obeid, the provincial capital of Kordofan, with its well-stocked arsenal and treasury, had fallen to the Mahdi. Revolt was mushrooming into civil war.

Britain at first refused to extend her intervention to the Upper Nile. If the Egyptian officials wished to act, that was their affair. The officials determined to make one final supreme effort. A contingent of some 15,000 men —many of them criminals from the gaols—was assembled and placed under Colonel William Hicks, a retired British officer from India. Hicks dutifully struck west from Khartoum into the savage deserts of Kordofan. A few weeks later the Mahdi's main army fell upon his thirsty exhausted men. The disaster was nearly total. Only 300 wounded survivors crawled away into the tamarisk scrub.

The situation in the Sudan was now desperate. Baring laid the choice before London: a British expeditionary force, or total withdrawal. London held to its policy: Egypt must come first, even if it meant—as it did— installing a new government in Cairo that would agree to evacuate the Sudan. But how to get the garrisons out? They were strung out along nearly 2,000 miles of the White and Blue Niles and scattered deep in the interior. The task would require a man of exceptional calibre. At this point

someone in the War Office—it has never been clear who—mentioned the name of Major-General Charles George Gordon.

Gordon was one of the last of the fabled Victorian eccentrics. Short, slight, sunburnt, he seemed to prance on tiptoes everywhere he went, boundless boyish energy shining from his bright blue eyes. He had fought with distinction in the Crimea, but was far too unorthodox for the steady climb to the top in the British Army. Instead he had taken service with other governments, with most of whom he eventually quarrelled. Whatever spare time Gordon's worldly battle allowed was devoted to the Bible and to good works among the poor. He was a brilliant commando officer and at the same time a man of passionate feeling for the underdog. For the task of organizing an abject retreat, of unsparingly abandoning those unable to join it, no one could have been more ill-fitted.

Gordon was no stranger to the Sudan. He had spent nearly six whirl-

wind years there in the service of Ismail Pasha. He first governed the province of Equatoria, where he had mapped the Nile to within 60 miles of its source, driven out the local slave-traders, and forced the Egyptian garrisons into good behaviour. Later he became Governor-General of the entire Sudan. As before, he drove himself to the limit of his strength against the cruelty and corruption around him. In Khartoum his trim white-clad figure, ceaselessly trotting to and fro, red fez above blazing blue eyes, became for the wretched native population the hope of a better day. Out on the camel-tracks he was equally familiar, grappling with slavers, rooting out venal officials, appointing faithful disciples to posts of responsibility.

But doubts and despondency assailed Gordon. He began to despair of the conduct of his Egyptian troops, to doubt whether slavery could ever be eradicated in a Muslim country. On Ismail's removal he had finally resigned. The old sleazy Egyptian regime returned to the Sudan. And Gordon, a bygone hero in his late forties, was on the shelf in England, in virtual retirement.

His appointment in the Sudan crisis was partly due to the aura of romance that still surrounded him. In part it was probably brought about by the more imperially-minded men in Gladstone's entourage, such as Secretary for War Lord Hartington and Garnet Wolseley. The government's orders directed him to go to Khartoum, arrange the evacuation of the Sudan, and attempt nothing further.

Baring was strongly opposed to the choice of Gordon, but at length—to his bitter self-reproach later—he concurred in it. The two men had met earlier during Gordon's spell in the Sudan. Now, in Cairo, they came face to face again. Their comments on each other underlined the gulf between them. Baring, said Gordon, "has a pretentious, grand, patronizing way about him." Gordon, said Baring, "was hot-headed, impulsive, and swayed by his emotions. He knew nothing of the springs of action which move governing bodies."

In the spring of 1884 Khartoum had

A photograph of Charles Gordon, taken when he was Governor-General of the Sudan, is a perfect reflection of his romantic image.

not yet been threatened by the Mahdi's Dervishes. Gordon received a delirious welcome in the city and instantly set about strengthening its morale. Chains were struck from prisoners, bonfires made of debt records, whips and branding-irons from the torture chambers piled up and destroyed.

His energy ablaze, Gordon pelted Baring in Cairo with up to 30 telegrams a day, producing a spate of new ideas for dealing with the emergency, then cancelling them in favour of newer brainwaves. "I have received a fresh batch of telegrams from Gordon," Baring wearily reported to London. "His statements and proposals are hopelessly contradictory." He implored Gordon to think things out calmly, then embody his suggestions in a single message. But it was becoming clear that the furore in Gordon's mind was blurring the stark simplicity of his orders. He was certain that seasoned British and Indian troops could readily rout the Mahdi. And he made an ominous pledge never to leave Khartoum himself until everyone else under his command had had a chance to go.

Then, suddenly, the telegraph line went dead. The tribes between Khartoum and the Egyptian frontier had risen for the Mahdi. It was no longer a question of how to evacuate the Egyptian garrison, but of how to get Gordon himself out.

The grip was tightening, but the city could still breathe. It had 8,000 defenders, six months' food, and a flotilla of steamers on the Nile. Runners could still get through the lines. Gordon himself could easily have slipped out to safety. And now that the outlying garrisons were beyond help it was his duty, in the eyes of the British government, to do so. But nothing was farther from Gordon's mind. The Egyptian soldiers in Khartoum, the bewildered population of the city: these, in the sight of the Lord, were Gordon's personal charges. If he could not take them with him, he would remain to the end.

Spring dragged into summer. The messengers from Khartoum dwindled. All over England the pressure to rescue Gordon rose to insistent levels.

Queen Victoria, as ever, expressed the public's feelings unerringly. "You are bound to try and save him," she stormed at Secretary for War Hartington, who had been all for sending Gordon in the first place. "You have incurred fearful responsibility." Still the government did nothing to mount a rescue. In effect, all through the summer of 1884 a silent battle of wills was raging, across the deserts and the seas, between Gordon in Khartoum, with his deep conviction that to leave his people to their fate would be "the climax of meanness," and Gladstone in London, with his abhorrence of subjecting the Sudan to imperial occupation and his belief that Gordon was trying to blackmail him into ordering it.

Then in late summer Hartington threatened to resign. This would have doomed the government, for in his solid phlegmatic way he reflected the image of John Bull. Gladstone gave in. By the end of September Garnet Wolseley was heading southward from Cairo at the head of a relieving force.

Wolseley's progress up the Nile was painfully slow. Both Major Kitchener, sent ahead to establish contact with Khartoum, and Gordon urged the use of a lighter, swifter flying column. But the expedition continued its steady march. Soon the Nile began its annual fall. The boats carrying ammunition and supplies became more difficult to handle. The pace slowed further.

Daunting news meanwhile reached Gordon in the form of a letter from the Mahdi. He demanded voluntary capitulation; a forced surrender would not be accepted. As the Mahdi moved his armies forward to ring the city, Gordon continued his daily rounds of the defences, encouraging, inspecting, shoring up the shrinking morale. Then he would climb to the roof of the Governor's palace and spend lonely hours with his telescope, watching the Dervish horsemen manœuvring in the nearby desert, straining to see any sign of relief rounding the glinting reachings of the river.

A hundred miles short of the city, Wolseley's advance guard met four

of Gordon's steamers, sent down to provide speedy transport for the first relieving troops. They delivered Gordon's journal—scribbled on waste paper and old telegraph forms—with its urgent final plea: "Now mark this, if the Expeditionary Force does not come in ten days *the town may fall.* I have done my best for the honour of our country. Good bye." But almost simultaneously a runner brought in another message: "Khartoum is alright. Could hold out for years." It had probably been sent to deceive Dervish scouts. But the British commander on the spot acted on it. Three more days were lost in overhauling the river craft and cautiously reconnoitring the country ahead. They waited too long.

The Mahdi, alarmed by Wolseley's approach, had ordered an attack. The Egyptian defenders, weakened beyond further resistance by fear and hunger, collapsed. Six terrible hours of massacre, rape, and loot followed as the shrieking hordes burst through the streets. At the palace, against the Mahdi's orders, Gordon was speared to death, his head cut off, and his body flung into a well.

Two days later, on January 28, 1885, Wolseley's steamers arrived within sight of Khartoum. They could see no flag flying from the Governor's palace, and as they neared the town they ran into a tempest of fire. Wolseley was curtly ordered to return, and his expedition retired in some disorder.

In England a wave of hysterical anger swept the country. Crowds gathered in Downing Street to hoot and hiss at Gladstone. The Queen berated him. He was saved by Russia: choosing the moment of British distraction, the Russians made a lunge towards the Oxus and India. Gladstone loosed the full fury of his oratory upon them and succeeded in diverting public wrath from himself to the Tsar.

The nation's outrage was gradually soothed as Gordon made the imperceptible transition from hero to martyr, a metamorphosis aided by a State service in St. Paul's, the erection of statues, and the manufacture of thousands of commemorative medals, bookmarks, and figurines. Nothing in his life, it seemed, became Gordon like the leaving of it.

But beneath the surface profound national feeling had been lastingly roused. De Lesseps, Arabi, the Mahdi: in remorseless succession they had dragged imperial Britain into the Canal, into Egypt, into the Sudan. Nearly everyone knew that the deepening involvement could not be allowed to end in ignominy.

The reconquest of the Sudan was probably inevitable from the moment of Gordon's death, but in the intervening years other reasons accumulated. The Mahdi died shortly after his famous victim, and reports percolating from the Sudan confirmed that the rule of the Khalifa who succeeded him was vicious and that the slave trade was more active than ever. Influential philanthropic societies in Britain exerted pressure for the eradication of this regime that fostered slavery.

In 1892 Baring became Lord Cromer. It was clear that his labours in Egypt were proving a phenomenal success: the Egyptian budget was in surplus and the revenues were being prudently invested where they could multiply. The country was solvent, merchants were prosperous. As for the fellaheen, forced labour was gone and living was a little more secure. Such civilizing progress, it was urged, should not be confined to Egypt; the Sudan also deserved attention.

Two years later Gladstone finally retired from politics and the Tories who replaced him in 1895 had none of the Grand Old Man's aversion to imperial enterprise. Europe's scramble for colonies in Africa was gathering momentum, and the Tories were quick to point to the danger of leaving a power vacuum on the Upper Nile. And from that scramble came the clinching event that was to set the wheels in motion. On March 1, 1896, the Italian Army, in an attempt to occupy Abyssinia, was crushingly defeated at Adowa. An Italian outpost at Kassala, just within the eastern Sudan, was threatened by the Khalifa's Dervishes. European prestige was at stake, and Italy, with German support, appealed for diversionary help.

Evelyn Baring, Lord Cromer, was a proconsul whose reports had a certain "first chapter of Genesis" flavour to them. Portrait by Sargent.

Twelve days later the British decided to invade the Sudan.

The Sudan expedition of 1896–98 stirred public pride and patriotism as few previous imperial campaigns had done. It coincided with Victoria's Diamond Jubilee; sentiment for Empire was at its zenith and a triumphant advance up the Nile would be the crowning achievement. It would avenge the heroic dead, replace a cruel despotism by benevolent rule, add still another red patch to the map. And Kitchener, the stern silent man of action, whose grim moustaches projected the inflexible purpose of Britain, would be in command.

That stiff, forbidding figure had no intention of disappointing expectation. Surly, frugal, exacting, disliked by his officers for his inordinate ambition, aloof from his men yet revered by them for his unbending will, he was not the man to tarnish his own image by any hint of failure. The troops would be equipped with every modern form of weaponry and supply. Overwhelming artillery would be brought to bear. The firepower of the rifle brigades would be formidably augmented by the new Maxim machine guns.

The objective would be Omdurman, the squalid town across the Nile

from Khartoum that was the Khalifa's capital and the Mahdi's burial place. There would, however, be no undue haste to reach it, for now there was no one awaiting relief.

So Kitchener's juggernaut, efficient and relentless as its master, rolled up the Nile, and in London frock-coated peers and silk-hatted bankers, clerks and cabbies, bootblacks and barmaids devoured the special editions with their telegraphed reports. They read of the only important action fought on the way: the storming of the Emir Mahmud's barricades at Atbara with pipes skirling, fifes shrilling, drums beating; of Kitchener cheered to the echo by men hoisting their helmets on bloody bayonets as he rode along the lines. They read of the climax at Omdurman: of the Khalifa and his generals hurling their 50,000 gleaming spearpoints at the British guns; of the Egyptian brigades wheeling steadily to concentrate their deadly fire; of the 21st Lancers charging, young Winston Churchill with them; of the heaps of half-naked dead piling up before the sputtering Maxims; of the gunboats thundering from the river, Lieutenant David Beatty, a future First Sea Lord, in command of one of them; of the dark hordes fleeing vanquished into the desert. They read of the memorial

Fashoda Crisis

Omdurman was not the end of the campaign for Kitchener. London warned him that a French party under a Captain Jean-Baptiste Marchand had set out from the west coast to reach the Upper Nile. Kitchener was to proceed upstream at once and dislodge any French he found.

Marchand's feat was a *tour de force*. With seven officers and 120 Senegalese he marched through 3,000 miles of unmapped equatorial forest and swamp. In March, 1898, he laid claim to the Upper Nile and raised the Tricolour over a group of mud huts called Fashoda. In due course Kitchener arrived with a powerful force, including artillery and four Maxims.

London seethed with indignation. The reserve fleet was prepared for action. The *Daily Mail* labelled Marchand's force the "scum of the deserts" and *The Times* accused the French of "pretentions which are altogether inadmissible." Paris seemed equally immovable. Premier Declassé said he "would accept war rather than submit." The French popular press responded in kind to the chauvinistic Fleet Street outcries.

But neither side was as set on war as the newspapers implied. Marchand was ordered to withdraw, for there was little real choice. As Declassé admitted, "We have nothing but arguments, and they have the troops." The storm died as quickly as it rose. The two governments soon signed an agreement defining their spheres of interest in Equatorial Africa. And in 1904 Fashoda was renamed Kodok to erase a symbol of humiliation to the French.

service to Gordon, with the massed voices of the soldiers singing his favourite hymn "Abide with Me" and the British and Egyptian flags slowly rising into the azure sky; of Kitchener, who detested all emotion, unable to control his shaking shoulders.

From start to finish it had been a set-piece with a foregone denouement. But in the quieter, more rational months that followed, the hoisting of the two flags side by side took on a lasting significance. Cromer, artist in "the springs which move governing bodies," devised a novel formula for the future governance of the Sudan, a formula that would at once mitigate the burden to Britain of annexation, keep Europe at arm's length, and acknowledge the cooperation which had routed the Khalifa. The conquered land would henceforth be ruled, and its initial development financed, by Britain and Egypt as partners. It would be a condominium—the Anglo-Egyptian Sudan.

Palmerston had defined his attitude towards Egypt by an analogy: "When I travel from London to York, I like to find a comfortable inn on the road. But I do not want to own the house." Having willy nilly become the owner, Britain did much to set the house in order. Cromer gave a long cool sight of virtues of "sea-green incorruptibility." For a nation pinioned by foreign creditors taking advantage of its inexperience, he negotiated a large measure of relief. And for a people critically dependent on water for their prosperity, he set new sights for productivity. His irrigation engineers made possible the doubling of the sugar crop and the trebling of the cotton crop. The giant High Dam at Aswan, completed in 1968, is only an extension of the great system of water storage and control of which Cromer's men laid the foundations.

The Anglo-Egyptian Sudan, ravaged by the slave trade and by Mahdist rule, was set upon a similar road. Its first Governor-General was Lord Kitchener of Khartoum. Cromer, in one of his more masterly understatements, said that Kitchener's methods were "perhaps a little more peremptory than is usual in civil affairs." But he assembled a hand-picked group of young men from British universities and so formed the nucleus of the Sudan Civil Service that came to rival its Indian twin in ability and devotion.

Honest, capable government; solvency; progress in physical development—great gifts of permanent value, especially in the foetid Turko-Egyptian context of the time. But Britain could not bring herself to relax her grip, partly because the Suez Canal she had sought to stop had become vital to her, and partly for fear of seeing her wider work undone. That work inevitably came to reflect the personal beliefs and prejudices of the proconsul who presided over it for so long.

In economic affairs Cromer's outlook was *laissez-faire*. He encouraged foreign investment, but left it to seek profits where it could without reference to the overall benefit of Egypt. As a result, few new industries appeared to offset the country's unbalanced dependence on cotton and sugar, and in any case Europe wanted primary materials rather than industrial competition. In social matters Cromer believed fervently in self-help: under him poverty was largely left to charity, health (except for quarantine enforcement) to private initiative, and education to the recruiting requirements of the government service.

But Egypt's deeper discontent with Cromer's rule stemmed from his perpetuation of Britain's original political misjudgments. In the early days of intervention, she had twice failed to perceive the genuine nature of national feeling astir from below. She mistook national movements—of reform in the case of Arabi, of protest in that of the Mahdi—for mere outbreaks of anarchy and fanaticism. Since she never came to terms with these national aspirations, Britain could never answer the question of when she would leave. The question was finally answered for her by Nasser in 1956. British presence had at last come to be seen as different only in degree, not in kind, from that of the long chain of foreign conquerors that had preceded her.

—*Stuart Legg*

ROUT & REVENGE

The British government unwittingly put a torch to a powder keg when in 1884 it dispatched General Charles Gordon to the sunscorched Sudan, a land considered vital to control of the headwaters of the Nile. Gordon's orders were to rescue Egyptian garrisons being threatened by rebellious desert tribes led by their "messiah," the Mahdi. When against orders Gordon challenged the Mahdi, he was himself besieged in Khartoum and London was in a dilemma. Only after bitter wrangling was a relief column under Garnet Wolseley sent up the Nile towards Khartoum. It arrived too late; as depicted above, when Wolseley's advance guard steamed within sight of the town it was greeted by heavy fire. Gordon was dead and Khartoum had fallen. Back home the demands for revenge were clamourous. The Mahdi had sown the wind; 13 years later his successor reaped the whirlwind when in a famous campaign the Sudan was swept into the British Empire.

The Fall of Khartoum

As Wolseley floundered up the Nile towards Khartoum, Gordon's plight grew more and more desperate. Scarcely a day passed without a furious Dervish assault on some part of the town. In August he lost 800 of his best men in an abortive attempt to lift the siege. Many commanders might have broken under the strain, but Gordon, buoyed up by a burning religious faith, felt confident enough to tell Wolseley in a message smuggled through the lines that he was as safe in Khartoum as in a London drawing-room.

But as the Dervish net grew tighter and tighter around the town, a note of urgency crept into Gordon's messages. In mid-December he warned Wolseley that Khartoum might fall if relief did not arrive by Christmas Eve. Yet somehow the emaciated garrison struggled into the New Year, drawing what nourishment it could out of rats and mice, shoe leather, palm-tree fibre and mimosa gum.

As Wolseley's column battled its way nearer and nearer the town, the British public held its breath. For a while, it seemed Wolseley would be in time. But on January 26, 1885, the Mahdi hurled his men at the exhausted city. They swept the defenders aside and raced for the steps of the palace where Gordon, resplendent in sword and uniform stood awaiting his fate. He made no attempt to defend himself and was speedily hacked to death. When news of the disaster reached England the unfortunate Mr. Gladstone was the most convenient target for the storm of grief and indignation that swept the country.

Punch was so sure Khartoum had been relieved that on February 7, 1885 it depicted Gordon greeting his rescuer, Sir Herbert Stewart (above). But the following week, after learning that the two men were dead, it humbly published an illustration showing a distraught Britannia before the fallen city (below).

Gladstone, a humiliated lion, is soundly kicked for his refusal to come to Gordon's aid until too late. From being the Grand Old Man he became the MOG – Murderer of Gordon.

Gordon, with the calm of a man apparently seeking death, faces the Dervishes. After being speared in his chest, he turned and meekly offered his back.

The Highlanders fired their rifles so
furiously at the battle of Atbara that the guns
grew red hot and had to be swapped for cool
ones from units waiting to go into action.

Many British officers were felled by
sunstroke in the desert glare and had to be
carried by native troops on protected
stretchers until the ill-effects wore off.

The Road to Revenge

For 11 years after Gordon's death Britain
nursed her wounded pride. Then, in 1896,
General Sir Herbert Kitchener was given
an Anglo-Egyptian army of 15,000 men
to smash the Dervishes. He left nothing
to chance. First he secured communications on the Nile with a flotilla of steamers
and gunboats; then he built a railway
across the waterless Nubian desert. From
its terminus he would march on the
Dervish capital at the little town of
Omdurman near Khartoum.

As the line slowly moved forward,
Kitchener imperiously pushed men and
machines to the limit. His chief engineer
once exploded: "You'll break the record
and your own ruddy neck!" Kitchener,
unmoved, pressed harder, determined to
smash the Khalifa, commander of the
Dervishes since the Mahdi's death in 1885.

Victory over Dervish forces at Atbara
on April 8, 1898, opened the road to
Omdurman. But the army had first to
make an exhausting, 200-mile march.
These drawings by the *Daily Graphic*'s
war artist capture the atmosphere of the
trek. At journey's end, the troops were
hot, filthy, fatigued, sullen and grimly
intent on revenge for their hardships.
Kitchener was delighted.

Native girls often took pity on the Sudanese
troops serving with Kitchener's army and
slaked their thirst with refreshing
draughts of water from goatskin bottles.

Cavalrymen watered their horses at the muddy puddles which formed in the sand whenever rain storms swept over the desert. But these were few and far between and horses were usually just as thirsty as their riders.

A native swimmer, employed by the *Daily Graphic*'s artist, carries sketches, wrapped in his turban, to the nearest steamer, always keeping a wary eye open for crocodiles.

1. Mahdi's Tomb.
2. Khartum.
3. Jebel Surgham.
4. Um Mutragar.
5. Dervish Encampment.
6. British Hospital.
7. Camel Corps.
8. Sirdar and Staff.
9. Pennon of Head Quarters.
10. 2nd Rifle Brigade.
11. Lancashire Fusiliers.
12. Northumb. Fusiliers.

OMDURMAN—THE FIRST BATTLE—6.

SEPTEMBER 2nd, 1898.

(IN ORDER THAT THE POSITIONS OF THE DIFFERENT REGIMENTS MAY BE READILY DISTINGUISHED, THE HOME UNIFO

STORY OF THE BATTLE TOLD IN HEADLINES: Reconquest of the Soudan · Sir Herbert Kitchener's brilliant Victory · Gordon's murderers punished · The Khalifa's Army completely annihilated · The highest gift of Generalship · Splendid courage and discipline of British, Soudanese and Egyptian Troops · "A Second Balaclava Charge" · Unparalleled savage daring and heroism

Bloodbath at Omdurman

When dawn rose at Omdurman on September 2, 1898, Kitchener was ready. His infantry, as the contemporary print (left) shows, was in line of battle, supported by artillery and reserves. Then this ruthless and ambitious man waited for the Dervish attack, confident that the outcome of the battle would crown his Egyptian career with a crushing victory.

Suddenly the first Dervish banner appeared in the distant hills. Others bobbed up alongside it, and the throb of war drums drifted on the morning air towards Kitchener's tense troops. As the men watched, a great wave of Dervishes welled up in the heights and rolled down towards the British. Kitchener could hardly believe that the Khalifa would make a frontal assault, but the spear-waving warriors swept on. None of them got closer than 300 yards; the murderous fire of machine-guns, rifles and artillery scythed down wave after wave until a ragged carpet of brown bodies, torn with vermilion wounds, covered the ground. It was more of an execution than a battle.

When the shattered Dervishes fled at midday, they left behind a staggering 11,000 dead, 16,000 wounded and 4,000 prisoners. Kitchener's losses were a mere 48 casualties. For the grievous death of Gordon, Britain had exacted a hideous revenge – and claimed it as a great victory for civilization.

Kitchener, seen as Sirdar (Commander-in-Chief) of the British-run Egyptian Army, became a peer after Omdurman. To complete his victory he destroyed the Mahdi's tomb, exhumed the body, and sent the skull to the London College of Surgeons.

A Quite Magnificent Blunder

The charge of the 21st Lancers at Omdurman shown here added a dash of idiotic heroism to what was otherwise a day of unrelieved butchery. The 21st, whose ranks included 2nd Lieutenant Winston Churchill, was on a prosaic scouting mission when the future Prime Minister spotted what he thought were about 150 Dervishes in a dried-up watercourse. The 300 Lancers broke into a headlong charge.

A horrible shock awaited them. The shallow depression was really a deep ravine, holding not a handful of men but 3,000 warriors, lined up 12 deep. It was impossible for the 21st to rein in their excited horses and so they plunged on, yelling defiantly. Churchill swept through the foe, blazing away with his pistol, and emerged unscathed. His comrades were not so lucky.

In 120 seconds, 70 cavalrymen and 119 horses were killed or wounded. Many of the dead were hacked to pieces by the frenzied Dervishes. The heroism of the troopers against such odds was so great that three of them won Victoria Crosses.

It had all been a terrible mistake. But the heroic blunders of British cavalry have – with the aid of forgiving memory – habitually been transformed into glorious feats. This charge was no exception.

A map dating from 1891 details the extent of European holdings in the Dark Continent. The hatched areas are British; as indicated in the key at left, they range from possessions and protectorates through commercial holdings to spheres of influence.

IV. The Imperial Scramble

In the early 1880s, in the ornate chambers of the Foreign Office in Whitehall, the clerks who registered the correspondence from Africa faced a difficulty both practical and symbolic: under what headings should they file this swiftly growing mass of dispatches? For nine-tenths of Africa there were no archives at all, in sharp contrast to the elaborate filing systems covering the rest of the world. Only dispatches from the British settlements in Cape Colony and Natal had a niche to themselves. Even Egypt, so critical to British interests, had no file of its own. "Turkey," wrote the faceless men, shovelling the latest message from Cairo into their out-trays and thus into the archives of the Ottoman Empire. As far as the filing clerks were concerned, the rest of Africa simply did not exist.

The prevailing view of the Dark Continent was that expressed four decades earlier by James Stephen of the British Colonial Office: "I cannot but think that even if our National resources were far more potent than they at present are, it would be very bad policy to employ in Africa that part of them which is available for Colonisation. . . . If we could acquire the Dominion of the whole of that Continent it would be but a worthless possession."

In support of Mr. Stephen's opinions, querulous missives of complaint penned by consuls and merchants in the 1860s and 1870s from West Africa continued to be tied with red tape and shelved under the general label "The Slave Trade." Weightier correspondence from the eastern seaboard, full of anxious accounts of growing German influence and the expeditions into central Africa sponsored by an assortment of European powers, was often similarly disposed of. Most of what was left was filed under (and sometimes actually sent to) Bombay. The explanation for this odd procedure lay in the fact that Zanzibar, from which most East African correspondence came, was traditionally regarded as a mere outpost of the Indian Raj.

This huge gap in the work of Whitehall was, of course, no more than a mirror to most of the minds and maps of Europe at that time. Europeans had only scraped the fringes of Africa. The British were entrenched in different ways at the two extremities, Egypt and South Africa. In West Africa they had a handful of small commercial settlements from the Gambia to the Niger Delta, and in the east they had installed themselves as the mentor of the Sultan of Zanzibar. The French were in Tunisia and Algeria to the north, in scattered trading colonies from Senegal to Gabon in the west, and in Madagascar and the Comoro Islands in the east. The Portuguese had trading interests on both seaboards that went back three or four centuries into a more glorious past. That was all.

Yet by 1900 only Liberia, Morocco, Libya, and Ethiopia were left unannexed or uncontrolled by some European power. Of those, Liberia was already in the pockets of European money-lenders, Morocco was spared for only another few years before France and Spain gobbled it up between them, and both Libya and Ethiopia would eventually be consumed by the ambition of Italy.

At first sight the motives behind this precipitate scramble into Africa seem puzzling. "I do not exactly know the cause of this sudden revolution," admitted Lord Salisbury in 1891 when, as Foreign Secretary and Prime Minister he had already master-minded the extension of British influence over half the continent in a matter of six years, "but there it is." Certainly no traditional reasons for colonial expansion could account for it. The anti-slavery lobby might inspire many an earnest newspaper and outraged bishop to flights of well-intentioned rhetoric against the continuing slave trade, but no British government was ready to undertake a crusade only on that score against the warring tribes and natural hazards that screened the heart of Africa from the world.

Nor was there much apparent likelihood of trade following the flag over most of Africa. Only in the small west coast colonies and in southern Africa were purely commercial interests important in determining government intervention. In West Africa official action came only after British merchants complained that French rivals were profiting while they were left to struggle on in the painful purity of free trade. In southern Africa the diamond interests and the activities of Cecil Rhodes powerfully assisted a hesitant government towards the declaration of a sphere of interest as far north as the Zambezi.

The fundamental quality of these moves, however, was protective rather than expansive. They expressed a desire to preserve what had already been made rather than an ambition to win new territories for their own sake. So it was, too, with Britain's annexations in the great African scramble: essentially, they were all part of a response to a change in the international atmosphere that posed new threats to British prosperity and power.

The threat to free trade in West Africa was one aspect of this change, for it indicated that Britain's industrial and trading supremacy was no longer absolute. Previously, British merchants could be left to themselves to open new doors and new markets. Now, with the emergence of serious commercial rivals in Germany, France, and (at a distance) the United States, free trade threatened to become a liability. Instead of opening doors, the imperialists sought to close them.

The continuing decay of the Ottoman Empire and the rise of Germany, especially after her victory in the Franco-Prussian War of 1870, brought fresh complexities to the power game. The defence of the new Suez Canal became a paramount British interest; to protect that waterway, vital to the maintenance of the Raj, even the hitherto unknown heartlands of Africa assumed strategic importance.

Thus Britain's part in the scramble for Africa was less a matter of action than of reaction. The initiatives came from elsewhere—the first of them from that notorious royal entrepreneur, King Leopold II of Belgium. A ruler with a crafty, megalomaniac turn of mind, Leopold had long nursed a vision of imperial glory such as his little country could scarcely sustain. Now he saw the unclaimed heart of Africa as the place in which his vision might be fulfilled.

Under the cover of a "scientific" organization called the International

African Association, Leopold proposed to create a commercial empire that would span the continent. With that energetic explorer Henry Morton Stanley as his agent, he staked his claim between 1879 and 1884 to the greater part of the Congo River Basin. When an international conference in Berlin in 1884 recognized Leopold's claim to the Congo, it triggered a series of European claims and counterclaims. The Portuguese revived ancient claims to influence along the Congo. The Germans moved into South-West Africa, Togoland, the Cameroons, and East Africa. The French suddenly saw the possibility of linking their West African possessions with the upper basin of the Congo. And the British were driven to protect their possessions from the other powers.

Disease-ridden West Africa had the most fearsome reputation of any part of the Dark Continent. "When you have made up your mind to go to West Africa," said a veteran of that grim coast, "the very best thing you can do is to get it unmade and go to Scotland instead; but if your intelligence is not strong enough to do so, abstain from exposing yourself to the direct rays of the sun, take four grains of quinine every day . . . and get some introductions to the Wesleyans; they are the only people on the Coast who have got a hearse with feathers."

It was for Sierra Leone, which in 1807 became Britain's first West African colony, that the term "White

Man's Grave" was originally coined. Europeans died there mainly from malaria and yellow fever—or from the "cures" that were nearly as dangerous as the ailments. Blood-letting to "drain away" the fever was common, and leeches were standard in colonial medical kits. On the same principle, salivating was induced by calomel, often at the expense of the victim's teeth, or by quicksilver and mercury, more drastic treatments that inflamed the mouth and sometimes caused the patient to suffocate on his own swollen tongue. Quinine's efficacy was not appreciated until Dr. William Baikie's 1854 expedition up the Niger. After clinging to the edge of West Africa for centuries, the British could at last begin moving inland.

The area seemed to hold little economic attraction: in the 1840s it was noted that there was more trade with the Isle of Skye than with the whole of West Africa. For the most part, this corner of Empire was acquired and developed through the sum of unofficial forces—humanitarians determined to end slavery and spread Christianity; merchants eager for trade, however small its total volume; and individual Britons following their own burning stars of imperial destiny.

Two nations of uncommon strength and political complexity had come to power in the Gold Coast area of West Africa in the 18th Century. Closest to the seaboard, and most heavily engaged in commerce with the Europeans, were the allied Fante tribes.

Farther inland, almost unknown to the white men, was the great empire of the Ashanti, with a tradition of fierce militarism. Recurring warfare between Fante and Ashanti made a shambles of the commerce of the African Company of Merchants. The Company sent four Europeans to negotiate with the Asantehene, the Ashanti king. Nothing lasting resulted from their mission, but they returned from Kumasi with such an amazing report—of a metropolis with broad avenues, of 30,000 parading warriors, of nobles so heavily festooned with gold that they had to rest their weighted arms upon the heads of servants—that no one would believe them.

By 1821 the Gold Coast situation had so deteriorated that the government abolished the Company and took control. Governor Sir Charles Macarthy had an imposing manner and intended to impose it on the Ashanti. Wearing a plumed hat and riding in a carriage drawn by six Africans, Macarthy set out to discipline the haughty savages.

He met them on January 22, 1824, on the banks of the Bonsa River. They were unseen, but the sound of their drums and horns indicated an army of many thousands. He had only 500 men, but was convinced most of the Ashanti were just waiting for a chance to defect. To this end he had his band play "God Save the King." There came back the discordant strains of an Ashanti war hymn. Again the band

In a 1904 special issue on colonialism, a German satirical magazine remarked on the activities of the great powers in Africa. At left, Britons strike a favourable balance of trade; at centre, Frenchmen get acquainted; at right, Germans get things organized.

played the British anthem while Macarthy and his officers stood at attention. After several rounds of this peculiar musical debate the Ashanti came—shooting, not defecting. What ensued was more mêlée than battle. The Ashanti overran the British position, killed Sir Charles, and carried his head in triumph to Kumasi. Thereafter it was borne ceremoniously through the streets of the capital as one of the main attractions of the annual Festival of Yams.

By 1828 Whitehall was so weary of the Gold Coast problem that it agreed to hand the administration back to the merchants. They established what amounted to a British protectorate from the coast to the Ashanti frontier. In 1850 Great Britain bought out local Danish holdings and 20 years later those of the Dutch. Gradually, the Gold Coast was becoming part of the British Empire.

Not, however, as far as the proud Ashanti were concerned. In 1862 they twice defeated British-led armies; a third force could not even find them. This débâcle led to a House of Commons report in 1865 which declared that all further extensions of territory or new treaties with native tribes "would be inexpedient," and urged eventual withdrawal from almost all West African commitments.

There was not that much from which to withdraw. Gambia was a narrow strip of riverside holdings; the blacks of Sierra Leone—freed slaves—huddled close to the coast and Freetown;

and in what is now Nigeria only Lagos was British territory.

The new policy was interpreted by Gold Coast chiefs as a sign of British weakness, a fact which helped to ensure that it would never work. Britain either had to be involved or get out, and whatever the politicians in London said, there were Englishmen on the spot who were determined to stay.

In 1867 a new Asantehene took the Ashanti throne. His name was Kofi Karikari, but before long he was to be known throughout Britain as "King Coffee," the most terrifying and therefore useful bogyman in the Victorian nanny's repertoire. Mere mentions of his ferocity sent a whole generation of English children shivering to their beds. When in 1872 the Dutch ceded to Britain territories that he considered to belong to the Ashanti, King Coffee drained a toast to victory from the skull of Sir Charles Macarthy and sent his armies to do battle. The British government grudgingly accepted that unless it was to abandon its protectorate, it would have to subdue the Ashanti.

Put in charge was that specialist of colonial warfare, General Sir Garnet Wolseley. He was a bold soldier but not a foolish one: he insisted on a leavening of regulars (the Black Watch, the Rifle Brigade, the Royal Welch Fusiliers) for his force of Africans and Indians. Thus reinforced, he marched on Kumasi in January, 1874. Some 20 miles from the capital he found the Ashanti army. The battle was quickly

over. The reckless bravery and antiquated muskets of the Africans were no match for the disciplined firepower of Wolseley's British square. Hundreds of Ashanti fell, including three of their greatest chiefs. The survivors fled. With pipes skirling, the Black Watch swept all before them into Kumasi.

The Ashanti would not stay conquered, however. In 1900 they rose up again, only to be suppressed after a savage campaign of guerrilla warfare. In 1902 the land of the Ashanti was formally annexed to the Crown.

In Nigeria, as in the Gold Coast, businessmen had made British influence a fact before the officials of Empire confirmed it. In the early days Liverpool merchant houses grew rich buying, shipping, and selling human merchandise from the Niger region. After slave-trading was made illegal, they turned their attention to Europe's sudden passion for being clean. The Niger Delta's export of palm oil, a prime ingredient in soap, had escalated to more than 30,000 tons a year by the 1870s.

The man who eventually coerced the guardians of Empire into making Nigeria British was George Taubman Goldie. Like Cecil Rhodes, he was a businessman with imperial ambitions that could not be measured by any yardstick of personal profit.

Goldie's background was more likely to raise Victorian eyebrows than to qualify him for any conventional service to Empire. He studied at the Royal Military Academy, Woolwich, but confessed he was "blind drunk" when he passed his examination and was as explosive as "a gun-powder magazine." Two years later he inherited a fortune and bolted the army to devote himself to gaudy liaisons and a "life of idleness and dissipation." It was probably with a sigh of relief that his family packed him off to Nigeria in 1875 to sort out the difficulties of a company in which they owned an interest.

Not yet 30, he had enough acumen to see the problem: too much competition. He solved it by inducing rival firms to join in forming the United African Company. White traders could then present a solid front and deal

George Goldie, called the "Founder of Nigeria," as he looked in 1898.

Frederick Lugard served as a general trouble-shooter in British Africa.

with Africans on a take-it-or-leave-it basis.

While Goldie was absorbing his rivals, a new challenger entered the arena. The French were acquiring colonies and encouraging private enterprise to move in on British merchants' territory. By 1882 there were 17 French trading stations on the Upper Niger, an area Goldie liked to think of as his own.

He decided the best way to protect the Niger was to gain a royal charter for his company. London was cool to the idea, but he prepared for it anyway. He regularly traded at a loss to force competing French firms to sell out to him. He succeeded, and when the great powers met in Berlin in 1884 to fix African spheres of influence, France and Germany had to agree to British control of the area. London now had administrative responsibility which it did not want to pay for, so Goldie got his charter. His company became the Royal Niger Company. Although the river was supposed to be open to anyone, the Niger Company used its quasi-governmental powers to charge fees and duties that effectually stopped all trade but its own.

Arguments about who owned what in the hinterlands were raging and would continue to rage until the turn of the century. Lord Salisbury, the Foreign Secretary, summed up these disputes nicely after an 1890 agreement with France: "We have been engaged in drawing lines upon maps where no white man's foot has ever trod; we have been giving away mountains and rivers and lakes to each other, only hindered by the small impediment that we never knew exactly where the mountains and rivers and lakes were."

Sometimes these contests shifted dramatically from conference-table maps to the ground itself, where men, not pencils, drew the lines, and force, or threat of force, settled the issue. A notable figure in these confrontations was Frederick Lugard.

If any white man looms larger in Nigeria's history than George Goldie, it is Lugard. He was already famous for his work in East Africa, where he had infuriated the French by leading Britain's intervention in Uganda's religious wars. Lugard hated West Africa, but he was apparently well suited to its rigours. In 1894, during a surprise attack by marauding tribesmen, an arrow pierced his sun helmet and lodged in his head. His men dragged him about the ground by the arrow in their attempts to pull it out, until someone braced his feet on Lugard's shoulders. The arrow—which was extracted with a sizeable piece of his skull attached—was poisoned. He chewed some antidotal roots, led a successful counter-attack, and marched 13 more miles before calling it a day.

France began to expand along the Niger, arguing that occupation was the test of ownership. The British government began to realize its interests needed more protection than a private company could provide. In 1897 Colonial Secretary Joseph Chamberlain asked Lugard to organize a small army that could "go anywhere and do anything." Lugard was to match the French detachment for detachment, occupying a village next to each one of theirs. In May, 1898, James Willcocks led the new West African Frontier Force into French-infested territory.

The campaign had its comic-opera aspects. Where Willcocks first hoisted the Union Jack, a Frenchman arrived with 12 Senegalese soldiers and raised the Tricolour. The two Europeans ceremoniously saluted each other's flag and then began arguing. But there was a deadly serious undercurrent to Chamberlain's chessboard policy. At one village Willcocks's men pushed their way through a barrier of armed Senegalese soldiers. At another French troops with fixed bayonets followed the British for a mile, cursing and spitting at them.

Fearing that an incident on the Niger might plunge Europe into an Anglo-French war—just what Chamberlain wanted them to think—the French finally yielded at the conference table. The Anglo-French agreement of 1898 did not give Britain as much of West Africa as she claimed, but more than she would have had without Chamberlain's daring tactics. In Gambia, Sierra Leone, and the Gold Coast her territory was restricted or reduced. In Nigeria, France retained a station on the navigable portion of the Niger, but Britain kept the richest part of the country. Considering how little the Royal Niger Company had actually occupied—almost nothing away from the river—the settlement was a victory for the English.

Lugard was named High Commissioner of Northern Nigeria. The million square miles he took over on January 1, 1900, was mostly unexplored. There were places where the wheel was unknown and others where old and sophisticated civilizations thrived in great walled cities. Lugard's task in bringing Nigeria the benefits of Empire, and Empire the benefits of Nigeria, would be a colossal one.

Only a tenth of Northern Nigeria was under some semblance of British control. The most challenging job was to bring into line the proud Fulani people. As usual, the Colonial Office did not want him to do anything expensive, expressing the hope that "Col. Lugard will be able to obtain a personal ascendancy which will prevent the necessity for strong measures." Chamberlain, wary of adverse home opinion, put it bluntly: "We must not have another native war."

But they soon had one, which erupted over the murder of a British official. "If the life of a European can be taken with impunity," Lugard stated, "the prestige of the government would be gone, and prestige is another word for self-preservation in a country where millions are ruled by a few score."

In January, 1903, he dispatched a force to teach the Fulani a lesson. It was quick and painful. The British were heavily outnumbered at all times, but their artillery and especially their Maxims more than evened the balance. In three months an old and powerful empire was completely overturned.

Ruling this gigantic territory, Lugard knew, would be more difficult than conquering it. "It is obvious that we cannot in any sense administer it," he said. "We must utilize the existing machinery and endeavour only to improve it." His famous concept of "indirect rule" was not truly new. It was, in fact, as old as the Roman Empire, but with his special application of the idea Lugard became its most noted exponent.

His approach has been criticized on the grounds that it held back the political development of the Africans, keeping them enthralled to old tribal structures. It is true that in some respects it ran counter to British ideals of democracy and equality. Yet he did much with the human material he found.

He appointed the higher ranking native officials and let them, in turn, choose their own headmen—but he insisted the headmen go out and actually administer their districts. He barred European officers from native courts lest it appear that the African judges had "lost all power." In practice, British officers had to play the administrative concerto by ear to strike the delicate balance between African authority and theirs. In sophisticated emirates British residents could truly function as advisers; in small pagan domains they often were, in reality, the local government. When the three Nigerian protectorates— Northern and Southern Nigeria, and Lagos—were united under a single administration in 1911, the man selected to establish this new nation was, naturally, Sir Frederick.

For Britain, India always remained the most important imperial blue chip, and many of London's actions in the partition of Africa were dictated ultimately by the demands of India's defence. For all the advantages western and southern Africa possessed in terms of commerce, mineral wealth, or existing British settlement, they took second place to the virgin uplands of East Africa. There the stark compulsions of imperial strategy resulted in the last great extension of India's protective belt, its *cordon sanitaire*. Already British influence and diplomacy had stretched the *cordon* from Teheran and Constantinople to Cairo and Zanzibar. Now, as new threats began to sap the *cordon*'s strength, Britain had to replace influence by occupation and diplomacy by force and carry India's effective frontiers inland from the East African coast to the shores of Lake Victoria.

For the better part of a century, British imperial influence was wielded over East Africa via the Sultan of Zanzibar. In the 1860s a second British interest in the East African territories was established through the search for the Nile's source. Soon it became part of the conventional wisdom of Empire that whoever controlled Lake Victoria must also dominate Egypt. King Leopold's International African Association sent one expedition after another to central Africa. France tried to obtain special trading concessions. German missionaries, already established in the area that became known as Tanganyika, were joined by German explorers and government agents. The scramble was on.

The British started very slowly. In the early 1880s Gladstone was again in power, and reluctant as he had been to be sucked into Egypt, he was even more perturbed by the thought of tackling the unknown perils of East Africa. A young botanist, Harry Johnston, later to become famous as the founder of British power in Nyasaland, tried to stake a claim on the slopes of Mount Kilimanjaro and wrote glowingly of the prospects for white settlement in the temperate highlands. Others were equally enthusiastic about the fresh air, clear streams, and rolling pastures farther north, in what was later to be known as Kenya.

But Gladstone was moved only to magisterial bafflement. "Terribly have I been puzzled," he wrote, "on finding a group of the soberest men among us to have concocted a scheme such as that touching the mountain country behind Zanzibar with an unrememberable name." Far from being alarmed by reports of German Chancellor Bismarck's interest in the area, he was positively pleased to think someone else might take up the burden of civilizing Africa. "If Germany becomes a colonising power, God speed her," he said. Yet in the long run, by accepting the Egyptian commitment Gladstone had effectively made the choice for East Africa as well; the two could not finally be separated. If Egypt's security was vital to the Empire, then the configuration of the Nile demanded that East Africa ultimately come under British rule.

It was Bismarck who forced the British hand. By 1885 the Germans were comfortably established in East Africa. But the Chancellor was always more interested in making Germany the pivot of Europe than the mistress of an empire. In exchange for British help in stabilizing eastern Europe, he negotiated an agreement that divided East Africa into two sections—Ger-

Delamere of Kenya

Hugh Cholmondeley, third Baron Delamere, was one of the first and most influential of Kenya's white settlers. In common with the young British aristocracy of his day, Delamere was a sportsman and a bit of a rip. When at Eton he haunted the neighbouring Ascot racecourse. With youthful arrogance he once wrecked a boot shop in Windsor High Street and threw the proprietor's stock to the indulgent populace. Along with his title he inherited a sizeable fortune and a hunting stable.

Big game lured Delamere to Africa. On a hunting trip in 1898 he found himself in northern Kenya, viewing with disbelieving joy the cool green slopes of the highlands. Four years later he was back, inspired by the dream of an African Arcadia where the sheep might graze, the huntsmen ride, and the wheatfields spread to the horizon.

The government welcomed him with open arms. In 1903 he was granted 100,000 acres in the Rift Valley. Zebra and wildebeest ran there in thousands, giraffe sauntered beneath the yellow-barked fever trees, and lion hunted by the water-holes. On Lake Naivasha flamingoes rimmed the water's edge with pink. To Delamere it was heaven.

There was a peculiarly romantic and expansive character to this vast holding, compounded of the new frontier and an old feudalism, the dawn of a country and the twilight of a social class. It was as if Delamere, the flamboyant aristocrat, had by himself made white Kenya carefree and nonchalant.

many in the south, Britain in the north.

Now at last the British began to move—though slowly still. Unwilling as ever to spend government money for colonial administration, they granted a charter to the Imperial British East Africa Company. It was an ailing infant from the start, however. In an essentially profitless and lawless territory it could make little impact, and within five years it was bankrupt. By 1895 London was forced to withdraw its charter and declare the northern territories of East Africa a protectorate.

Long before then, however, the logic of imperial strategy had forced the British into unaccustomed paths in Africa. The continued decline of Turkish power and growing fears of a Russian advance into the Near East made Egypt ever-more important to Britain. The security of the Upper Nile was deemed essential; visions of diabolical foreign engineers turning off the waters like a kitchen tap seemed to haunt the Cabinet.

Finally Lord Salisbury declared the entire Nile Valley a British sphere of influence, and between 1889 and 1892 made it stick by intimidating or cajoling all Britain's rivals into mutual definitions of interest throughout the rest of Africa. With Italy he fixed the frontier between British East Africa and the new Italian colony in Somalia. To limit Portugal and her colony in Mozambique he threw Britain's weight behind the creation of a solid block of British territory from southern to central Africa. To the French he made concessions in West Africa in order to hang on to the Nile and the east. With Germany he made his biggest and best deal. He bargained the island of Heligoland in the North Sea, delivered to Germany for a naval base, against a settlement of most of the Anglo-German frontiers in Africa, including recognition of a formal British protectorate in Zanzibar and the removal of all German influence from Uganda. "Fancy sacrificing two African kingdoms for a bath tub in the North Sea!" a German colonizer exclaimed.

As a result of Salisbury's various bargains, the strategy of supremacy on the Nile reigned supreme in London's African policies. All that remained to complete Britain's role in the partition of the continent was for the new policy of occupation, already entrenched in Egypt, to replace the old policy of influence. Once more the goad was provided by the great powers. The Italians in Ethiopia, Leopold in the Congo, and the French in West and Equatorial Africa all began probing towards the no man's land of the Sudan. Still haunted by their nightmare of the Nile being turned off, the British in 1896 sent Kitchener southward from Cairo to Khartoum, ostensibly to revenge the death of Gordon. They also began constructing a railroad from Mombasa on the east coast to Lake Victoria.

The Uganda railway was sold to the electorate at home with customary piety as a means of suppressing the slave trade. But in fact it was built to get British troops into Uganda to forestall foreign threats to the Nile. In the event, the work dragged on painfully and expensively, and critics in London christened it the "Lunatic Line." Not until 1901 did the tracks finally reach Lake Victoria, and another quarter of a century passed before the last stretch to Kampala, on the other side of the lake, was finished—long after the line's original strategic purpose had been buried in the Whitehall archives.

But in the meantime it had acquired other purposes of its own. Once built, it greatly transformed the prospects of the territory, for along with the rails came all those benefits of civilization that the imperialists and humanitarians were united in wishing to bestow upon Darkest Africa. So strategy was turned at last to the ends of commerce, and as the new century opened East Africa became the latest horizon of British colonial settlement. Many had suggested this ever since Harry Johnston first tried to establish himself on the slopes of Kilimanjaro two decades before. Now the dream was a financial necessity. Although the railway generated new trade with the Africans, that alone could never make it a paying proposition or supply the taxes needed to pay for the administration of the territory through which it ran. Only the richer trade that Europeans

An African artist painted this view of the formal reception held on the occasion of the arrival of a new British Governor in East Africa.

engaged in could do that, and the British government accordingly bent its efforts to encourage white settlement.

Kenya was opened to white settlement with the exploitation of virgin land as the primary aim. Uganda, on the other hand, was designated an exclusively African country, where white ownership of land was prohibited and the progress of the native inhabitants was paramount, however slowly achieved. At the time this division appeared fair enough. Uganda was richer than Kenya and had a more highly developed African society, but it was physically less suited to white colonization. In Kenya Gladstone's "unrememberable" mountain country continued to tempt adventurous and visionary white men looking for new frontiers to conquer. Thus the legal separation of the two seemed to follow the laws of nature as well as the demands of colonial budgets. Humanitarians and imperialists alike declared themselves satisfied.

Even so, what with the tsetse-fly, the lions, the terrain, and the Equatorial storms, farming in Kenya was apt to prove a quick way to bankruptcy. In its anxiety to fill the unprofitable spaces, the government was forced to offer highly favourable terms to potential settlers. This readiness to hand out huge areas of land at bargain prices—or at virtually no cost at all—was characteristic of Kenya in its early years.

On the whole, they were the halcyon years. Gradually the corrugated iron shanties gave way to stone-walled country houses with half-timbered Elizabethan-style façades overlooking terraces and formal gardens. The highlands had begun to develop the relaxed life style that was soon to win the region the nickname of "the happy valley."

Sport thrived: Kenya's first cricket match was held in Nairobi in 1899, and tennis, soccer, and golf soon followed. The icy streams of the Aberdare mountains were stocked with New Zealand trout, and fly-fishing became all the rage. And on many a frosty morning the uplands echoed to the tinny blare of a hunting horn as yelping hounds gave chase to a jackal.

The game was plentiful, the skies were wide, and nobody cared if the trains didn't run on time. Indeed, it was established practice that if a passenger saw a lion anywhere near the track he would stop the train and organize a quick safari. When Theodore Roosevelt visited Kenya in 1910 he rode on the cow-catcher for hours at a time roaring with delight at the sight of some of the finest game in Africa.

The slave trade was ended, the Nile was secure, prosperity was advancing, and the Raj was supreme. The world in Kenya seemed young and fresh. But of course it could not last. By and by poorer emigrants arrived. Dour Afrikaners trekked in from the south to lay claim to the latest version of their Promised Land, and the wives and the civil servants came to extend the long arm of England, Home, and Duty along the railway line, imposing new restrictions upon Arcadian freedom. And what the future held was unimaginable.

—*Jim Hicks, David Holden*

THE LUNATIC LINE

The planners of British East Africa's Uganda railway were confident that the nearly 600 miles from Mombasa on the coast to Lake Victoria could be traversed in four years. But the debilitating coastal climate, the mountainous terrain, the tangled thorn bush infested with tsetse-fly played havoc with this optimism. In the first two years only 100 miles of track were laid, and the next 200 miles progressed little faster. Lions and rhinos terrorized the construction crews inching their way forward.

In Parliament it was christened the "Lunatic Line." The Foreign Office ordered the project's chief engineer to redouble his efforts to reach Lake Victoria. To raise the apparent rate of progress he resorted to short cuts and temporary viaducts and bridges. But there was no avoiding the Kikuyu Escarpment and the deep cleft called Great Rift Valley. Slowly, painfully they were breached. In 1901 the first train reached the lake, a year behind schedule. By 1903, after the temporary works were replaced by permanent structures, London had £5 million sunk in the Lunatic Line.

UGANDA RAILWAY.

THE HIGHLANDS OF
BRITISH EAST AFRICA
AS A
WINTER HOME FOR ARISTOCRATS

HAS BECOME A FASHION.

SPORTSMEN in search of BIG GAME make it a hobby.

STUDENTS of NATURAL HISTORY revel in this FIELD of
NATURE'S own MAKING.

UGANDA RAILWAY, BRITISH EAST AFRICA.
ARRIVAL OF THE FIRST COOK'S EXCURSION, AND THE RESULT OF CAREFULLY PRESERVING THE BIG GAME.

UGANDA RAILWAY Observation Cars
pass through the Greatest Natural
GAME PRESERVE in the WORLD.

For reliable information, etc., address:
PUBLICITY DEPT., UGANDA RAILWAY.
DEWAR HOUSE, HAYMARKET, S.W.

The Uganda line's builders imported
32,000 Indian coolies as labourers;
on the facing page is one such crew,
posing with a well-shaded British
surveyor. Special angled platforms
carrying supplies (above) were
lowered into the deep Rift Valley.
The light-hearted poster at left
records the historic day when
the first Cook's excursion arrived.

257

Above is one of the inclined tracks used to get equipment and supplies down into the Great Rift Valley. When trains finally began to chuff along the Lunatic Line (right), they hauled not troops as originally intended but instead settlers and goods for Kenya and Uganda.

258

Chapter Seven
IMPERIAL HIGH NOON

Victoria was the supreme symbol of Britain's 19th-Century imperial grandeur. This shows her in 1876, when she became Empress of India; the ivory throne was the gift of an Indian prince.

I. Canada Makes Good

While English explorers and proconsuls daubed imperial red across the map of Africa, the older British colonies were undergoing evolutionary changes. When the high noon of the Empire arrived in the 1890s there was revealed a new pattern of relationships between colonies and Crown.

Showing the way was British North America. Wolfe's crushing victory over the French on the Plains of Abraham had breathed life into British Canada, but the lusty infant had ahead of it a century and a half of often painful growth.

The American Revolution had a profound effect on Canada. On the one hand the boundary that war-weary Britain conceded to the victorious Americans sliced right through what had been Quebec and deprived the St. Lawrence province of half the great inland territory her explorers and soldiers had won a century before. But a second consequence was entirely beneficial. This was the resettlement of persecuted British Americans who had remained loyal to the Crown during the war. The British government felt duty-bound to move some 40,000 of them to safety in the north, and the King showed his gratitude by allowing the Loyalists and their descendants to append to their name the letters "U.E.," for United Empire.

Most of them, about 30,000, went to Nova Scotia, where they built new towns for themselves and opened new lands for farming. Some 10,000 made their way up the St. Lawrence and began clearing the formidable forests of western Quebec. Their arrival increased the population of these two regions by 50 per cent.

They were farmers, builders, tradesmen, and artisans, and their coming transformed the formerly French provinces from mere fur-trading and fishing establishments to true settlement colonies. In addition to skills and tools, they brought with them their British, basically democratic, political ideas. They were monarchists, else they would not be there, but they were also English, and would not happily tolerate the authoritarian institutions left behind by the French.

Parliament accommodated them with the Constitutional Act of 1791. This ended the conciliar system, which had governed Quebec since the days of Champlain, and substituted what passed in those days for representative government. At the same time, Parliament sought to forestall antagonism between nationalities by splitting Quebec into two provinces. Lower Canada, which included the cities of Montreal and Quebec, was largely inhabited by French Canadians. Upper Canada, beyond the Ottawa River, was almost entirely peopled by British.

During the War of 1812 expansionist-minded American "War Hawks" attempted to snatch up British America, but thanks in large measure to their own bumbling they gained nothing but a stand-off. With peace came new people by the hundreds of thousands to fill the open spaces. The series of economic depressions after the Napoleonic Wars inspired a migration of British people such as had not been seen since the settlement of the American colonies 200 years before. Between 1825 and 1850 the population of Nova Scotia jumped from 104,000 to 277,000, that of New Brunswick increased from 74,000 to 194,000, and that of Upper Canada, astonishingly, rose fivefold, from 158,000 to 791,000.

Canada was changing very fast socially and economically, but the government was not keeping pace. By the 1791 Constitution Upper and Lower Canada each had a governmental structure that superficially resembled Britain's. But in both provinces legislative councils answered to the British Governor and thus to the British Crown. The elected representatives did not control their own government.

The challenge came from two fronts: the reform-minded immigrants of Upper Canada, and the French Catholics of Lower Canada. The two movements were quite different. The immigrants —labourers, frontiersmen, Nonconformists—had little in common with the radicals of the neighbouring province, other than frustration. In Lower Canada it was the older residents, the French Catholics, who were unhappy. In many ways, these *Patriotes* were more conservative than radical. They would never challenge their Church nor the feudal landholding system, but they too could rail against a government controlled by an English-speaking, Protestant oligarchy.

Lower Canada's leading reformer was a well-born seminary-educated French-Canadian lawyer named Louis-Joseph Papineau. This distinguished orator and cultivated gentleman had been a power in Lower Canada's politics since 1815. By contrast, William Lyon Mackenzie, who suddenly jumped from an obscure newspaper job to leadership of Upper Canada's reformers, was a small, excitable, unimposing figure, completely self-taught, whose mind stirred with violent antagonism towards privilege.

Both groups found the established machinery of government unresponsive to the democratic will. When in 1834 a financial depression was added to the accumulated disappointments

As sketched by a British officer, the regulars (left) made short work of the Papineau insurgents, crushing the 1837 rebellion. The scene is St. Eustache, near Montreal.

of reformers in both provinces, rebellion began to simmer near the surface.

In Montreal the military commander, Sir John Colborne, who had delivered the decisive counter-attack at Waterloo, was not caught unawares. When in 1837 an English radical named Nelson proclaimed a republic, Colborne's troops captured him with hardly any fighting. Papineau, the supposed leader of the rebellion, fled ignominiously over the border. Meanwhile, in Upper Canada a band of rebellious farmers, headed by Mackenzie, threatened Toronto for two days, but they were dispersed in half an hour once a loyalist force was raised. Mackenzie and other radicals also fled to the United States.

The rebellions had ended within weeks, but it was an embarrassing way for the Empire to mark Victoria's first year on the throne; Britain's Whig government wisely decided to examine the situation which had provoked them. The Earl of Durham was sent to North America to investigate.

The report Durham laid before Parliament nine months later has been called the "Magna Carta of the Second British Empire" because it outlined a new kind of relationship between Britain and her colonies— one that hopefully would avoid the sort of problem that led to the American Revolution.

Durham recommended, in effect, that Canada's French population should be submerged in a sea of Britons and thus eventually Anglicized. His first thought was for a federal union of all the provinces, but realizing this was perhaps too visionary he plumped for the unification of Upper and Lower Canada as a start. This part of his report was promptly implemented. The new Province of Canada came into being in 1841. Unification was only half of Durham's prescribed remedy for the ills of British North America. His report embodied another major recommendation as well, but neither Canadian conservatives nor the government at home much liked it.

It called for *responsible* government in the colonies. Though the system operating in the provinces looked on the surface like a copy of Britain's own governmental structure, Durham recognized that the analogy was false. The ultimate power in Great Britain lay with Parliament. But the governments in the Canadian colonies were in reality appointed by and answerable to London, not to the elected

representatives of the colonists. This was the cause of the frustration that led to the rebellions. Durham's scheme was for a truly Parliamentary-style system wherein the executive was responsible to the elected assembly. It would be, in domestic matters at least, self-government.

This, said Durham, would ensure against unrest in the future. But neither the provincial Tories, who knew themselves to be outnumbered by reformers, nor the British government, which said there was no point in having colonies if you did not rule them, were attracted to the idea. It was rejected.

Economics can command what politics will not countenance. Over the next decade the captains of Britain's Industrial Revolution, who viewed colonial obligations as an encumbrance to commerce, moved the country nearer and nearer to free trade. The last vestiges of support for the old Mercantilist system disappeared. The Corn Law, which gave Canadian grain an advantage on British markets, was repealed in 1846. The Navigation Acts went in 1849.

With the end of economic rationalization for the Old Colonial System came the end of support for the system itself. If there was no commercial advantage to be had from Empire, why pay for running it? A new Whig government decided to implement Durham's plan for responsible self-government in North America after all. In a sense, Britain was declaring herself independent from her North American colonies.

In 1850 hardly anyone could have foreseen the area making up modern Canada as a united country. Settlements, colonies, and provinces were separated by vast distances and by local concerns; the forces that were one day to impose unity were weak and disjointed.

The oldest colony, Newfoundland, rode the Atlantic like a great ship anchored off the coast, looking eastward to the sea from which its people harvested their fish and to Europe where they sold their catch. To Newfoundlanders, other British North Americans were potential competitors, as were the despised Americans and

French. Newfoundland imported some wheat from the Province of Canada—a small area then, in comparison to the vast country that was soon to bear the same name—but was convinced that nothing could be gained from a closer relationship.

The Maritime Provinces—Nova Scotia, New Brunswick, and Prince Edward Island—also turned their backs, geographically and culturally, on Canada. Proud of their famous seamanship, their conservative tradition, and their superior education, the Maritimers looked down on the less-refined society to the west. During the winter, when the St. Lawrence was frozen, Halifax on the Atlantic and Montreal 500 miles away might as well have been on separate planets, so impassable were the woodlands between them. The Maritime region's natural commercial centre, in fact, should have been Boston, but the long memories of Loyalist families kept the Maritimes bound to London and Empire. Only a railroad could bind them to Canada.

The most populous colony, Canada, was not even united within itself. Instead of merging into the English population, the French-speaking *Canadiens* were fiercely resolved to protect their language and culture. They were outnumbered—less than a million to 1.5 million British Canadians—but they maintained their political identity. In order for the provincial government to function at all, the two nationalities had to support strange and strained coalitions. Ten of these precarious administrations came and went between 1854 and 1864. And while the businessmen of Montreal and Toronto may have yearned to be tied to the British Atlantic coast by rails, their only year-round outlet to the sea was the Grand Trunk Railway, opened in 1853, terminating at Portland, Maine.

To the north and west were the immense territories of the Hudson's Bay Company, almost unpopulated but for Indians, a few traders, and the Métis, a people of mixed French and Indian origin who made up the Red River Colony in present-day Manitoba. Here was a potentially rich agricultural region, but there was no way to make use of it without a railway. In this area as in eastern Canada, geography directed the paths of commerce southward to the United States. The Hudson's Bay Company, for example, communicated with its colony via St. Paul, Minnesota, rather than through the bay after which it was named.

Finally, beyond the Rocky Mountains, lay Britain's Pacific provinces, originally controlled by the Hudson's Bay Company. Vancouver Island was made a Crown colony in 1849 to secure its naval base. After the discovery of gold on the Fraser River drew prospectors to British Columbia in 1858, it, too, was given colonial status. Vancouver was united with mainland British Columbia in 1866. British Columbia was more remote from Canada or Nova Scotia than was Europe. The only practical way to get there was by sea, all the way round Cape Horn. The colony's natural commerical centre was San Francisco.

Some British North Americans, of course, sensed that the legacy of potential nationhood they had inherited upon the breakdown of the Old Colonial System could only be fully realized through some kind of union. But the difficulties seemed insurmountable. For the moment the colonies had enough to do adjusting their economies to their new independent situations. The loss of their preferential markets in Britain had left them floundering. They did not regain their footing until 1854, when a Reciprocity Treaty with the United States provided new buyers for their lumber and grain.

While few colonists were interested in political union during the 1850s, many saw the value of closer economic ties if the colonies could only be united by rail. Some even dared to dream of a line stretching all the way across the plains to the Pacific. A dream it was: in 1850 there were only 66 miles of track in British North America. Ten years later there were 2,000 miles. The Grand Trunk Railway's intercolonial line now reached from Lake Huron tantalizingly close to its goal, Halifax. There it halted. The Grand Trunk was in desperate financial trouble, and so was the provincial government of Canada, which had guaranteed the loans the company had raised.

Radical Jack

Lord Durham is chiefly remembered as the author of the report that laid the foundations of a united, self-governing Canada. But Durham was not just a successful colonial administrator; he was a man quite out of the ordinary.

When he came of age in 1813 life stretched before him like a glittering highway. With his dazzling good looks he charmed his way through countless Regency drawing rooms. He inherited vast properties and collieries that earned immense profits; "£40,000 a year was the sort of income a man could jog along on," he remarked light-heartedly. His integrity was absolute, his ambition enormous. The Prime Ministership seemed well within his grasp.

Instead he was a traitor to his class. In the political ferment after the French Revolution he became a champion of electoral reform. As Lord Privy Seal in the Cabinet of his father-in-law, Earl Grey, he drafted the First Reform Bill. Durham's passion for the oppressed was genuine, but his arrogant insistence on far-reaching democratic remedies antagonized fellow aristocrats. They labelled him "Radical Jack" and edged him out of politics. He was not yet 40.

In subsequent years Whig leaders kept him abroad as much as possible, sending him twice on diplomatic missions to Russia before dispatching him to the troubled Canadian colonies. There his report recommending representative government for Canada, when it was barely a reality in Britain, was the most radical colonial paper ever presented to Parliament.

At this point an adroit English financial operator named Edward W. Watkin arrived on the scene. Neatly manipulating the logic of the situation, he transformed what appeared to be a barrier to colonial unity—the inability to finish the line—into a positive force for federation. Sent out by Baring Brothers, Canada's London bankers, to reorganize the Grand Trunk, Watkin soon perceived that if a railway, once built, could unite the provinces, then the provinces, once united, could build a railway.

Between 1861 and 1863 he developed a scheme for extending the line from coast to coast, a plan that created much excitement among colonial politicians and businessmen and at the same time raised the hopes of the railroad's anxious London creditors. He pointed out that no one province by itself had the financial resources to back so titanic a project. Obviously some kind of federation would be necessary.

Watkin's proposal, appealing as it did to the desire for financial reward for investors rather than to any idealistic motives, revived discussion of union both in the colonies and in London. The British government, which liked the railway plan, hesitated over the political implications, but Watkin and his associates at Baring pushed ahead, using all their influence.

Meanwhile, the colonies were getting a strong—if unfriendly—shove towards union from their gigantic neighbour to the south. The United States had been threatening to revoke the Reciprocity Treaty, on which the prosperity of the colonies depended, ever since Canadian tariffs on manufactured imports had gone up in the late 1850s. Clearly audible beneath the diplomatic exchanges were mutterings of "Manifest Destiny," that magical phrase used by Americans to mean that God and history intended them eventually to occupy all North America. The outbreak of the Civil War increased the tension. The North's seizure of the British ship

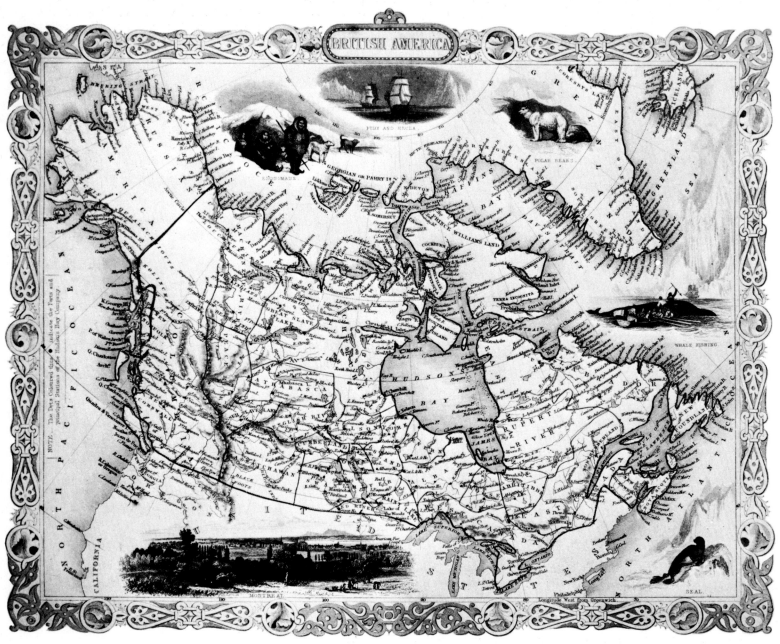

Trent at the end of 1861 raised war alarms. When British troops were rushed to defend the Canadian frontier, the fact that they had to be transported from Halifax by sledge over snow-covered trails was a powerful argument for the completion of a railway.

War fever abated but enmity continued, especially when Washington announced that the Reciprocity Treaty would not be renewed at the expiration of its ten-year period. In 1863 the British Cabinet, urged on by London financiers interested in Watkin's project, reversed its position and advocated federation. And in 1864, weary of political confusion and deadlock, the province of Canada's leaders—Conservative John A. Macdonald, reformer George Brown, and *Canadien* Georges Cartier—agreed to set aside their traditional antagonisms, form a coalition government, and seek federation.

They found a ready-made platform from which to launch their campaign: the three Maritime Provinces had agreed to a meeting to discuss a possible regional federation. Macdonald's group sent polite letters asking if they could attend to discuss a plan for wider union, and the Maritimers consented.

After two months of frantic preparation, Macdonald, Cartier, Brown, and A. T. Galt, a long-time advocate of federation, steamed down the St. Lawrence on the Canadian government ship *Queen Victoria* to Prince Edward Island. The welcome they received at Charlottetown on September 1, 1864, must have made them anxious for the fate of their bold proposals. One lone provincial official, handling the oars himself, rowed out to meet them. His explanation was hardly reassuring: the Nova Scotians, New Brunswickers, and his own government were at the circus.

All during the sessions the Canadians hammered away at the Maritime delegates on the advantages of a united British North America. Talk progressed to the specific sort of union that Macdonald envisaged. He wanted a powerful central government in order to "avoid the mistakes of our neighbours," a pointed reference to the American Civil War. "If

we can only attain that object—a vigorous general government—we shall not be New Brunswickers, nor Nova Scotians, nor Canadians, but British Americans, under the sway of the British sovereign."

The last phrase was important. There was no question of cutting the imperial ties. Macdonald called for "a great British Monarchy, in connection with the British Empire, and under the British Queen."

A conference of all British North American colonies convened at Quebec in October to discuss union in greater detail. In less than three weeks the conference passed a series of 72 resolutions—the Quebec Resolutions—which covered every aspect of government in such detail that, if Parliament and the provincial legislatures approved them, little more than a change of title on the first page would transform these declarations into a constitution.

To the dismay of the scheme's advocates, it was not to be that simple. In 1865 the voters of New Brunswick threw out their government for its advocacy of federation. Prince Edward Island rejected the scheme. Newfoundland's legislature decided in 1866 to bide its time for a while; it was to bide it for 83 years. Only in Canada did federation win approval.

Neither London, now positively eager for a colonial union to which it could shift some of the expenses of North American defence, nor the railway-builders and their bankers would let a little thing like provincial public opinion stand in their way. For all the financial and political pressure they applied, however, it was the Americans who pushed the recalcitrant colonists into the fold.

With the end of the Civil War the United States possessed the world's largest army, a fact which added weight to the remarks made by Secretary of State William H. Seward: "I know that Nature designs this whole continent, not merely these thirty-six states, to be, sooner or later, within the magic circle of the American Union." In 1866 Congress terminated the Reciprocity Treaty.

That was enough. In London in

December, 1866, delegates from New Brunswick (which had restored the pro-federation party to power), Nova Scotia, and Canada approved a revision of the scheme. Their London Resolutions were written into law as the British North America Act, which in March of 1867 was approved by Parliament as apathetically, said Macdonald with umbrage, as "a private bill uniting two or three English parishes." The Act provided the strong central government Macdonald wanted. It broke the province of Canada once again into its original French and English components, now called Quebec and Ontario. It required the new federal government to move immediately to complete the intercolonial railway. And it provided for the later entry into the union of other British North American colonies.

Finally, the new nation's name. It would be Canada, but what kind of Canada? Macdonald, underscoring his loyalty to the Crown, wished to call it the "Kingdom of Canada," but it was feared this might offend the "republican susceptibilities of the Yankees." S. L. Tilley of New Brunswick, it was said, was handed the solution by the Almighty during the London Conference when he attended a service in Westminster Abbey and heard the 72nd Psalm: "He shall have dominion also from sea to sea, and from the river unto the ends of the earth."

Thus the Act directed that the provinces "shall form and be one dominion." On July 1, 1867, the Dominion of Canada was born.

"We are all merely provincial politicians at present," said John Macdonald, the Dominion's first Prime Minister. "Perhaps by and by some of us will rise to the level of national statesmen." His critics would have said that he at least would never achieve such heights. Perhaps so: he had learned his politics in the old province of Canada where it was a notable achievement simply to stay in office, and he knew well the stratagems of ruse, surprise, and compromise on which survival depended. Yet he had already confounded those who judged him a party hack by his masterful management of federation. He

British North America in 1851. At right, Newfoundland, the Maritimes, and Canada; at centre, Hudson's Bay Company lands; at left, the Pacific provinces.

had been knighted for his role as the union's chief architect. Now he was ready to belie his carefree, often boyish, and sometimes downright dissolute behaviour by accepting the responsibility for guiding, defending, and—God, Parliament, and the Hudson's Bay Company willing—enlarging his new nation.

"We hope to close our session this week," the Prime Minister wrote in June of 1869, "and a very momentous session it has been. We have quietly and almost without observation annexed all the territory between here and the Rocky Mountains." The Hudson's Bay Company was being compelled to surrender both Rupert's Land and its rights in the North-West Territory to the Crown, which would then hand them over to Canada. The Company was to receive £300,000, would retain 45,000 acres round its forts, and could claim up to one-twentieth of the remaining fertile land.

While this enormous property transaction was being speedily arranged, no one bothered to ask the Métis, the French-Indian inhabitants of the region, their opinion or even to inform them what was happening. They were understandably alarmed when Canadian surveyors began sighting their transits across the Red River homesteads they had been cultivating for years. When William McDougall, the newly appointed Governor of the territory, arrived at the border town of Pembina on October 21, 1869, he found the road blocked by a barricade and 40 armed horsemen.

The man who assumed leadership of the rebellion was 25-year-old Louis Riel. He had studied classics at the College of Montreal and had a quick temper, a taste for popular adulation, and an intense patriotism bordering on mental unbalance. Riel gathered about him some 500 armed and disciplined Métis guerrillas. On November 2 they took over Fort Garry, the Hudson's Bay Company headquarters and strategic centre of the colony.

It was a blow for Macdonald. If Canada could not install a governor in a new territory its weakness "would

John A. Macdonald, the chief architect of Dominion, was called Canada's Disraeli.

be painfully exhibited, not only to the people of Red River, but to the people and Government of the United States." But his opportunism did not fail him. He found a bolt-hole.

"We have thrown the responsibility on the Imperial Government," he wrote to the beleaguered McDougall in December. On the first day of that month Canada was to pay the Hudson's Bay Company its £300,000 and the Colonial Office was to proclaim the transfer of the territory of Canada. But a careful reading of the contract indicated to Macdonald's law-trained eye that nothing *compelled* Canada to take delivery at any particular time. A week before the deadline, like a suspicious prospective house purchaser, Macdonald cabled London: "Canada cannot accept North-West until peaceable possession can be given."

Lord Granville, the Colonial Secretary, was astonished. "Government by Company has become impossible," he cabled. "Government by Canada only alternative and ought to be established promptly." But Macdonald was not about to put the Dominion at the mercy of some rebels and "their Yankee wire-pullers." Granville finally conceded that the territory re-

mained the problem of the Company and the imperial government in London.

Politically it was still a big problem for Macdonald. Sympathy for the Métis ran strong among French Canadians, who demanded peaceful negotiations with the rebels. Then, in March, 1870, Riel executed a young English Canadian, Thomas Scott, who had been involved in two attempts to overthrow his provisional government. Now Macdonald's task was doubly difficult. Ontario's English Canadians howled for tough reprisals; there almost certainly would have to be a military expedition.

Macdonald again climbed onto his tightrope. He would yield to Red River's demands to be taken into the Dominion as a federal province rather than a non-self-governing territory, but he would send troops as well.

The strain of the crisis told on the Prime Minister. Shortly before troops led by that epitome of British generalship, Garnet Wolseley, departed for Red River, Macdonald went on one of his famous drinking bouts, swaying through the House of Commons bar and lurching in and out of Ottawa's hotels for an entire weekend. "Bad news," the word spread, "Sir John A. has broken out again." But on Monday he was in the House explaining the bill that would make Red River, to be called Manitoba, a province. Although bleary-eyed, he was convincing. The measure passed.

Wolseley's expedition included a strong complement of British regulars to impress the United States with the Empire's continued commitment to Canada. When they arrived at Fort Garry on August 24, after a brutally hard march, there was no fight. Riel had disbanded his army and prepared his government for a peaceful transfer of power. He slipped out the back gate when the troops arrived at the front, crossed the U.S. border, and became a school teacher. But Canada had not seen the last of him.

In the years of peace that followed, Macdonald began to realize some of his ambitions for the young country. The creation of Manitoba and the acquisition of the North-West Territories was followed by British Columbia's entry into the Dominion in 1871 and Prince Edward Island's in 1873. The prophetic psalm had been fulfilled; Canada now stretched from sea to sea.

Although a new treaty with America eased the tension between the two nations and ended the threats to Canada's territory, the most pressing unfinished piece of business remained the transcontinental railway. The line from Halifax to the Great Lakes was under way and would be completed in 1876. But Canada now reached to the Pacific. Not until 1880 was the nation's economy healthy enough to get on with the railroad. A contract was awarded to the Canadian Pacific Railway Company.

The company's president was George Stephen, president of a Montreal bank. Stephen needed an engineer of exceptional talent, will, and experience to drive the line across the continent. He selected an American, William Cornelius Van Horne. "Van Horne can do it," a friend told Stephen, "but he will take all authority he gets and more; so define how much you want him to have." Stephen made him general manager with wide authority.

On first inspection the contract appeared extremely generous. The company would get 25 million acres along the line, a subsidy of $25,000,000, and the 700 miles of railway already built. The deal soon turned out to be not so good after all. The project was a money-eater from the start. To pierce the rugged, barren geological formation called the Pre-Cambrian Shield north of Lake Superior, Van Horne employed every known technique and invented some new ones. Where rock could not be levelled down, he levelled up, filling whole gorges with crushed stone to carry the rails. He imported a rapid track-laying machine from America, but still he needed 12,000 men and 5,000 horses to complete the section. The cash subsidy which had seemed so large was quickly used up.

"Stephen did more work and worked harder than I did," Van Horne said later. "I had only to build the road, but Stephen had to find the money." It was hard to come by. By 1884 the company was near bankrupt-

cy. Stephen had no choice but to ask the government for a loan— $22,500,000, almost as much as the original subsidy and astronomical for a country with such a small population. But Macdonald wanted the railway and Canada needed it: the loan was made.

The infusion kept construction going only a year before Stephen was compelled to ask for more money. This time Macdonald hesitated. His government was having trouble enough riding out an economic depression. He was not sure it could afford the political embarrassment of bailing out the Canadian Pacific again. Ever the patient opportunist, he stalled— and then opportunity came. As so often happened during his long career, it appeared in the form of another problem, this time an old one come back to haunt him. Louis Riel was in Canada again, and the Métis had risen.

To escape the unfamiliar civilization that provincial status had imposed on Manitoba, many of the Métis had moved west to Saskatchewan. Now civilization caught up with them again. The buffalo had disappeared, farmers were moving in, and those harbingers of dispossession, the surveyors, had come on the scene, marking out the line for the railway across

their homesteads. Early in 1885 Riel organized a rebel provisional government.

Perhaps Riel did not realize how much the North-West had changed since his 1869–70 rebellion. One new element made it particularly different —the North-West Mounted Police, established in 1873 to extend Canadian law and authority to the western plains. The rebels would not necessarily be defeated by the thinly spread Mounties, but their presence meant that Riel could not control the country without a clash, and a clash would surely bring a strong response from Ottawa.

The clash took place near Duck Lake on March 26, 1885, when a dozen Mounties and soldiers were killed in a shoot-out with the rebels. Macdonald heard of the Duck Lake incident by wire the day after it occurred. He wanted to get a large military force into the area quickly. The unfinished railway was the obvious means. Could the quelling of the rebellion help the railway?

Van Horne was thinking the same thoughts. The troops would have to march over stretches where no tracks yet existed, but it could be done. He already had engines waiting with steam up and commissary arrangements underway before receiving

An English cartoon entitled "The Emigrant's Welcome to Canada" jibes at what the Dominion had to offer the new settler—who, in any case, appears unprepared.

orders to move 5,000 Canadian militiamen to Saskatchewan. Within a week the first of three striking columns detrained and marched towards Batoche, Riel's headquarters. In 1870 it had taken Garnet Wolseley three months to reach Red River. There was sharp skirmishing, but with such overwhelming force on the scene so quickly the government soon triumphed. Riel gave himself up on May 15.

The House of Commons knew the victory had been the railway's as much as the militia's. It approved Macdonald's proposal for the Canadian Pacific to issue $35,000,000 in new stock, $20,000,000 of it to be guaranteed by the government.

In July Riel was convicted of high treason and sentenced to death. French Canada clamoured for remission of his sentence. Many thought he was insane and should be locked away in an asylum. Riel was examined by doctors, who reported that he was capable of distinguishing right from wrong, then the legal definition of sanity. That was good enough for Macdonald. "He shall die," he said, "though every dog in Quebec bark in his favour." On November 7, 1885, at a place called Craigellachie, the last spike of the transcontinental railway was driven home. Canada was no longer a "geographical expression." Nine days later, at the police barracks in Regina, Louis Riel was hanged.

Canada had expanded to fill the whole width of the continent, the rails that provided an east-west axis were there, and the high tariff wall that inhibited the flow of goods from—and thus dependence on—the United States was still firm. But something was not working.

Economic depression seemed to have settled in to stay forever. The wheels of industry in the East turned more and more slowly and the prairies in the West stayed empty of farmers. Racial and religious ill-will abounded. In 1891, seizing on the growing discontent, the opposition Liberal Party announced that it was ready to try another course of action. Under the leadership of Wilfrid Laurier it committed itself to a policy of unrestricted reciprocity with the United States. If approved by the electorate, this would be an abrupt and dramatic shift from the direction in which Macdonald had so long led the nation.

Macdonald rose to meet his last great challenge. If Laurier won, he said, Canada would pivot as if a giant hand had turned the top half of the North American continent by 90 degrees. With unrestricted reciprocity there would be little need for the east-west Canadian Pacific railway; the flow of goods would be principally north-south. Canada's own economic identity would be lost as she fragmented into a satellite held fast to the U.S. by the power of commercial gravity—a prelude to annexation. So Macdonald told the Canadian people during the campaign of 1891, and the people believed him. They put Macdonald's Conservatives back into the House they had ruled, with one short hiatus, since 1867. But the founder of the nation was shattered by the hard fight. Macdonald collapsed a week before the election, never recovered sufficiently to take office, and died six months later at the age of 76. His epitaph cited his allegiance to Empire: "A British subject I was born, a British subject I will die."

If the Conservative victory actually saved the nation from some awful fate, it did not seem to improve the fate it was already suffering. The business slump continued and racial antagonism became more acrimonious. In the next election, in 1896, the Conservatives were turned out. The new Liberal government did not mention its now-discarded programme for free trade with the States. Canada's basic policies remained unchanged. But the state of the nation changed remarkably. Under the leadership of Wilfrid Laurier, her first French-speaking Prime Minister, Canada enjoyed the most prosperous decade in her short history.

A prime factor in the new prosperity was immigration. Canada had been steadily losing people to the United States, drawn south by the greater opportunities available there. Now, suddenly, people came to Canada—and stayed. They stampeded on to the western plains to claim free homesteads at the remarkable rate of 300,000 a year. When gold was discovered in the Klondike in 1897, thousands struggled farther west through mountain wastes to seek their fortunes. The westward rush of immigrants compelled the creation in 1905 of two new provinces, Alberta and Saskatchewan. Europe's demands for grain increased; wheat prices climbed; freight costs went down. Canada boomed.

The economic revival gave Canadians new confidence—enough confidence to begin asking themselves who they were. *Were* they Canadians? What about the "British subject I was born?" These questions were influenced by the old French vs. English struggle, but they were not primarily about that; they were also questions about the nation's constitution. French-born Laurier proudly represented Canada at Queen Victoria's Diamond Jubilee and frankly admitted that he enjoyed dealing in imperial affairs, but he found it impossible to say "when nation ended and Empire began."

The issue was not an idle one. Canada could regulate her tariffs, control her immigration, raise and manage her own armed forces. On the other hand, she could not treat with a foreign power, not even her next-door neighbour, without going through London.

As to what her role should be and what powers and responsibilities she should have, no convincing answers immediately emerged. There was a general desire to remain in the Empire, but no clear-cut consensus on particular questions.

Probably the best hints to Canada's future were in the nation's instinctive responses, her impulsive acts. One such instinct was demonstrated in 1914. After the years of wrangling over sharing imperial defence, when Britain and Germany went to war Canada immediately committed herself. More than a twentieth of her entire population, 600,000 men, enlisted to fight, and 50,000 of them remained in Europe, buried. The old bond still held firm.

—*Jim Hicks*

At top, the last spike of the Canadian Pacific is driven home on November 7, 1885. Below is a rough and ready hostelry in the Klondike gold fields.

II. Australia and New Zealand Come of Age

Among the 100,000 prospectors of all nationalities who flocked to California after gold was discovered there in 1848 was one Edward Hammond Hargraves, from New South Wales, Australia. A few months at the California diggings convinced Hargraves that he had seen the same geological features, indicating rich alluvial deposits of gold, in his homeland. He packed his tools and sought the next boat back. "There's no gold in the country you're going to," scoffed another digger as Hargraves departed, "and if there is, that darned Queen of yours won't let you touch it."

"There's as much gold in the country I'm going to as there is in California," Hargraves snapped back. "And her Gracious Majesty the Queen, God bless her, will appoint me one of her Gold Commissioners." Hargraves proved to be a prophet. Within a matter of weeks of landing in Sydney in early 1851 he discovered alluvial gold on a tributary of the Macquarie River near Bathurst.

Actually Hargraves was not the first man to find gold, but earlier reports in the 1820s and 1830s had been hushed up, for no one in authority was anxious for a colony that was primarily a convict settlement to become the centre of a gold rush. Hargraves, however, had a flair for self-promotion. He hurried with the news of his discovery to Deas Thomson, the Colonial Secretary of New South Wales. "If this is gold country, Mr. Hargraves, it will stop the home government from sending us any more convicts," Thomson reasoned. "But it comes as a clap of thunder, and we are scarcely prepared to credit it."

Thousands were. "A complete mental madness appears to have seized every member of the community," the Bathurst *Free Press* reported. "There has been a universal rush to the diggings." Hargraves, basking in the glory of discovery, was duly made a gold-field commissioner, received a £10,000 reward, and was given a life pension.

The gold had been found on Crown land and the authorities quickly established a system whereby prospective diggers had to buy licences costing 30 shillings per month. Soon 4,000 men were at work, mostly on the Turon, a tributary of the Macquarie. It was a strange scene, according to an early visitor: "As we topped a ridge, my companion suddenly said, 'Stop and listen.' I pulled up my horse and heard as I imagined the rushing of some mighty cataract. 'It's the cradles,' said he; and so it was—the grating of the gravel or rubble on the metal sifters of five hundred [miner's cradles]. . . . There was no pause or the slightest variation in the cadence as it floated up to us on the still air."

That first year the New South Wales strike yielded about £350,000 worth of gold. The prospect, said William Charles Wentworth, a leading New South Wales politician, was for "an era which must in a very few years precipitate us from a colony into a nation." The transportation of convicts to the colony had already stopped in 1842; now gold could tempt the genuine immigrant who had been reluctant to venture before.

The New South Wales gold was merely a prologue. The fledgling colony of Victoria, which had only been separated from New South Wales in 1849 and was anxious to make its name, offered a reward of £200 to anyone finding gold within 200 miles of Melbourne; in August, 1851, as if on cue, gold was discovered at Ballarat, just 60 miles from the capital. More was found at nearby Bendigo Creek a couple of months later. These discoveries made the New South Wales strike pale by comparison. Over the next 15 years Victoria yielded more than 30 million ounces worth £124 million—one-third of the world's gold output in that time. The gold transformed Victoria from a struggling pastoral settlement into one of the best known colonies in the British Empire.

The first news of the discoveries reached England, along with £800 worth of gold, aboard the *Thomas Arbuthnot,* whose captain reported that "The colony is completely paralysed. Every man and boy who is able to lift a shovel is off . . . to the diggings." *The Times* fanned the excitement: "Deposits have been found that beat Sydney and even California. . . . Such supply, so abundant, so accessible and so wide-spread, cannot soon be exhausted, the only limit to production at the present being the want of hands." Everyone scrambled to catch the next boat. Charles Dickens, surveying the chaos in London's shipping offices, saw "legions of bankers' clerks, merchants' lads, embryo secretaries, and incipient cashiers . . . beg of hard-hearted ship-brokers to grant them the favour of a berth on their last-advertised, teak-built, poop-decked, copper-bottomed, double-fastened, fast-sailing, surgeon-carrying emigrant ship."

Quite apart from the flood of immigrants, which trebled Australia's population within a decade, general trade with "down under" soared as merchants in Sydney and Melbourne placed unprecedented orders. British exports to Australia jumped 500 per cent between 1851 and 1853.

The diggers were a wildly assorted lot. "There were merchants, cabmen, magistrates and convicts," a visitor noted, "tailors, cooks, coachmen and lawyers' clerks and their masters, doctors of physic and music, aldermen, an ADC on leave, scavengers, sailors, a real live lord on his travels—all levelled by community of pursuit. . . ." Regardless of the hard life, most of them stuck it out and a few were handsomely rewarded, for the alluvial diggings in Victoria were studded with some of the biggest nuggets ever found. The largest, called the Welcome Stranger, weighed 2,284 oz. and fetched £9,534.

Wherever the diggers stampeded, they were invariably a democratic bunch, working together as "mates" with no regard for class or privilege. "The distinction of class you find laid aside," one of them wrote. "The highly educated Oxonian is associated with the illiterate labourer from Wilts or Somerset; the descendants of those who sit in 'lordly halls' has a mate in the reformed prisoner of Millbank or Pentonville. . . . Everything is in fact the perfect realization of a great republic."

They were also considerably more orderly than the rip-roaring California Forty-Niners. Though there were thieves and murderers among them, most were God-fearing men who managed to settle their disputes in boxing matches. In 1852 the police commissioners at Bendigo could supervise 100,000 men with only three constables, two carbines, and a sword. This tranquillity was due in large part to the prohibition of liquor throughout the diggings.

By the golden fifties the Australian colonies were beginning to develop their own character. Henry Parkes, whose towering frame and booming voice would dominate New South Wales politics for the next generation, told the assembly in Sydney in 1858 that "In principle this country is essentially democratic, and the differences of grade, so far as it goes amongst us, would be laughed at by men in the Mother Country." Class differences were indeed less than in the old country, but would they remain so? Many settlers feared that the system of landlordism and poverty they

had escaped at home—the "repulsive features of the social system of the Dark Ages," as Parkes phrased it—would be repeated here.

Despite such fears, reactionary social attitudes were never a real danger in Australia. Wealth was too quickly acquired to confer nobility, and there were many other interests—banking and shipping, for example—to dilute the aspirations of property owners. There were no demands for revolution, merely a demand for equality and shared privilege. In the 1850s nearly a quarter of the new immigrants were skilled tradesmen and professional people who created a heady atmosphere of individual freedom, expansion, and social mobility. Political devolution rapidly followed. In 1855 four of the colonies—New South Wales, Victoria, South Australia, and Tasmania—were given self-government on local issues, although

London retained jurisdiction over foreign questions.

The prosperity brought by gold stimulated the economy of the colonies, especially Victoria, at a remarkable rate. Victoria's population rose from 97,000 in 1851 to over 500,000 a decade later. Apart from producing a third of the world's gold, Victoria supplied a sixth of Britain's wool. Melbourne mushroomed from a village into a city of 140,000 people, lit by gaslight, with a university, a public library, and an opera house seating 4,000.

For all her meteoric expansion, however, Australia was still a string of individual colonies perched round the eastern and southern rim of an enormous and only barely explored continent. The colonies were parochial in outlook. New South Wales was for free trade, Victoria next door was fiercely protectionist. Each levied

Englishman Samuel Gill sketched a family working their claim in the gold fields of Victoria. The digger wields his pick, his wife rocks a cradle to separate out the nuggets, the son carries water to the cradle, and the daughter shovels in the pay-dirt.

271

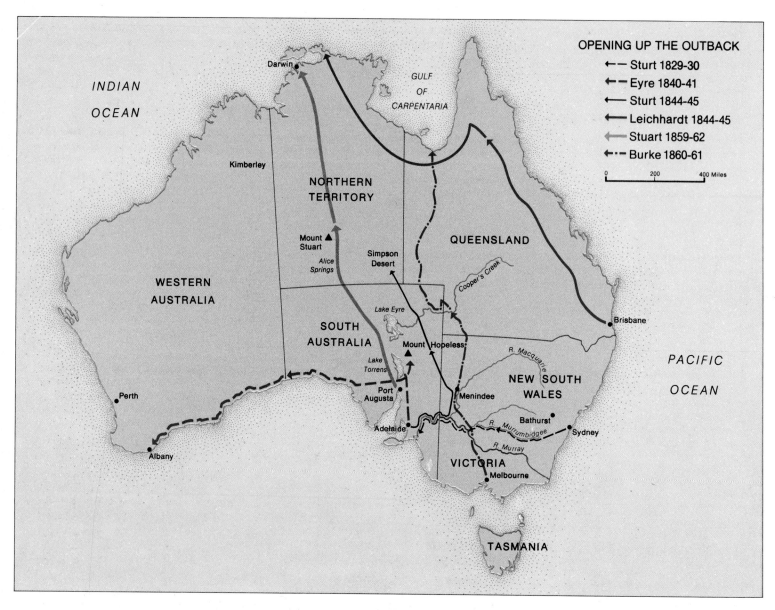

INDIAN OCEAN

Darwin

GULF OF CARPENTARIA

Kimberley

NORTHERN TERRITORY

Mount Stuart ▲

Alice Springs

Simpson Desert

QUEENSLAND

WESTERN AUSTRALIA

Cooper's Creek

Lake Eyre

SOUTH AUSTRALIA

Mount Hopeless ▲

Lake Torrens

Brisbane

PACIFIC OCEAN

R. Macquarie

NEW SOUTH WALES

Perth

Port Augusta

Meninclee

Bathurst

Adelaide

R. Murrumbidgee

Sydney

Albany

R. Murray

VICTORIA

Melbourne

TASMANIA

---

its own customs duties on goods arriving from the others. Local politics was hardly sophisticated. "The curse of Australian politics," said Sir John Young, Governor of New South Wales in the 1860s, "is that there are no parties in the strict sense of the term, but merely cliques or groups." Legislative assemblies frequently broke up in turmoil as members accused each other of drunkenness, favouritism, or corruption.

Australia faced another generation of such parochialism before it emerged as a cohesive nation. After the flush of the 1850s, the next decade saw dwindling immigration, unemployment in the cities, and declining prosperity in the gold fields. The carefree digger

suddenly found he had either to become a mundane wage-earner working for a mining company or try his hand at farming, about which he knew nothing.

The main achievement of the 1860s was the final exploration of the continent. The great battles in Australia's history were fought against the elements—the deserts, the scorching sun, the sheer vastness of the land. The heroes were the explorers, the Livingstones and Stanleys of Australia, who pitted their wills and wits against the "ghastly blank" of central Australia.

Since the earliest days the lands beyond the Blue Mountains, part of the forbidding Great Dividing Range that stretches for 3,000 miles the length of

Australia's eastern coast, took hold of the imagination of the new settlers. Perhaps behind the mountains lay great rivers providing an easy route towards China, or fields as soft and gentle as those of southern England, or some fabulously rich El Dorado. Was the interior a vast desert? Or did it contain an inland sea to rival the Mediterranean?

Explorers and surveyors and adventurers pushed steadily inland, and wherever they went the "overlanders" —free settlers and ex-convicts driving their flocks before them—followed in quick pursuit, pouring by the hundreds into the valleys and plains in search of a "good run" of land.

The inexorable push to the west

took the explorers ever closer, they believed, to the edge of the green inland sea. No one was so utterly convinced of the existence of this sea as Captain Charles Sturt. Born in India in 1795, Sturt had served with distinction in Canada, France, and Ireland before sailing for New South Wales in 1826 in charge of a convict guard. He was a tall, gaunt young man with a sensitive appearance and manner. Like few newcomers before him, he quickly acquired an appreciation of Australia's landscape and native people, its strange animals and plants. He was the natural choice to lead an expedition that in 1829 sought to find a solution to "the problem of the rivers."

In the preceding three years the colonists had suffered the worst drought they had yet experienced. The soil turned to dust; temperatures of 129 degrees in the shade were recorded. "It almost appeared as if the Australian sky were never to be again traversed by a cloud," Sturt noted in his journal. Land watered by rivers rather than by unpredictable rains had to be found.

Sturt and seven companions set out from Sydney on the first of the truly epic journeys of Australian exploration. Their plan was to trace the Murrumbidgee and Murray river system. After four months of appalling difficulties they found themselves stranded near the mouth of the Murray. Their only chance of survival was to return the way they had come—a thousand miles of rowing, this time *against* the current.

They started back, said Sturt, "without hopes of our eventual safety." Most of the original provisions, calculated initially for only a single journey, had been consumed or lost in accidents or spoiled by the intense heat. They rowed for six weeks, from dawn to seven or nine at night, and one day for 11 hours without a break to escape harassment by Aborigines. Their hands were raw with running sores, their backs and legs rigid with pain; they were hardly alive at all.

Incredibly, they survived. When the party was at last within striking distance of its starting point, two men were still strong enough to volunteer

for a 90-mile trek overland in search of help. A relief party arrived just as Sturt was handing out the last round of the meagre flour ration to his men.

Sturt had discovered and charted a great river system, and it had a dramatic effect on the colony's development. As a direct result of his glowing reports, the British province of South Australia was founded in 1834 as an experimental free colony without convict settlers. Sturt's reports received further confirmation when Major Thomas Mitchell explored the rich western regions of Victoria in 1836. "The Major's Route" threw Victoria open to the land-hungry of New South Wales.

With the immediate needs of the colonists satisfied, the attention of the explorers turned once again to the "ghastly blank," this time more because of its mystery than its potential.

First off the mark was 24-year-old Edward John Eyre, an immigrant from Yorkshire, who in 1840 headed the first direct expedition to the heart of Australia. His most prized possession was a Union Jack sewn by the ladies of Adelaide and presented to him by Sturt with instructions "to carry it to the centre of the mighty continent, there to leave it as a sign to the savage that the footsteps of civilised men had penetrated so far."

For three months the party floundered in the arid wastes 400 miles north of Adelaide between two great shallow swampy lakes, Lake Torrens and what was later named Lake Eyre. The land was barren and seemed to be demonically enchanted by mirages. The names Eyre left behind, such as Mount Deception and Mount Hopeless, indicate the weight of his despair. Finally, he called a halt. Determined to find a way of "making amends for past failure," he would find a crossing to the west rather than to the north: a thousand miles along the southern coast from Fowler's Bay to Albany at the tip of Western Australia.

After suffering so many mishaps that the expedition became a nightmare without meaning, Eyre managed to hail a passing whaling ship. After rest and replenishment he went on to

his goal. The young Yorkshireman became a hero to the young country. It was his courage that was celebrated; his failure to penetrate the north and the negative reports on the country he had crossed on his trek lost significance.

Charles Sturt had never abandoned his dream of finding an Australian Caspian. In 1844 he led an expedition north from Adelaide, pushing farther inland than any man previously. He did not find his inland sea, but he did locate Cooper's Creek, running from Queensland south-west towards Lake Eyre, a water course that was to prove a vital lifeline for future explorers. Sturt returned to England in 1853, where his journals of discovery had made him famous. When he died there in 1869 he was the most respected Australian explorer.

Meanwhile, Ludwig Leichhardt, a German botanist, crossed the tropical northern tip of the continent, effectively opening up the future state of Queensland. In 1848 he set out again to cross from the east coast to Perth in Western Australia. He was never heard of again.

During the 1860s two men, Robert O'Hara Burke and John McDouall Stuart, filled in the remaining vital gaps. They were greatly encouraged by a £2,000 prize put up by the South Australian government for the first crossing of the continent south to north.

Burke, a charming but wild Irishman, left Melbourne on August 21, 1860, with the best organized and equipped expedition ever to challenge the Australian desert. They laboured northward to Cooper's Creek. Leaving the rest of the party there, Burke and two companions pushed on and successfully completed the crossing. When they staggered back to Cooper's Creek on April 21, 1861, however, the camp was deserted. The rearguard had left that very morning—Burke and his party missed them by ten hours. Without good horses, equipment, or food, they had to stay at the creek in the hope that a rescue expedition might find them. Burke and one companion died, leaving the last man, John King, alone with a small group of Aborigines. Somehow they managed to keep him alive until, weeks later, a search party reached the creek. The triumph of this first crossing of the continent thus ended in tragedy, but Burke and the men who died with him have become legends in the opening-up of Australia.

While they had been pressing north from Melbourne to the Gulf of Carpentaria, John McDouall Stuart was making a similar bid from Adelaide to cross the very heart of the continent. Two years in succession he was forced to turn back, but in 1862 he finally reached the shores of the Indian Ocean near Darwin. The route he pioneered was of prime importance; within ten years the first telegraph line went striding along it across the desert from Port Augusta to Darwin, where it was soon hooked into the cable coming down through South-East Asia. Australia and London were linked.

Behind the explorers came the settlers, determined to expand their sheep stations or establish cattle ranches in the "outback." Their sprawling stations were often the size of an English county. Complex irrigation systems and artesian wells transformed tracts of semi-desert into excellent grazing land. The sheep population flourished. In 1861 there were 21 million; a decade later, 40 million; by 1893, 106 million. Wool gradually ousted gold as Australia's prime export, and before the end of the century three-quarters of the mother country's wool was arriving from down under.

With the opening of the outback, a vast continent stood at the feet of anyone who cared to travel it. It was the railroad, however, that really opened up the country. Before 1871 there had been a mere 1,000 miles of track, none of it reaching more than 180 miles inland. New impetus for railway building was stirred up by Sir Hercules Robinson, appointed Governor of New South Wales in 1875. He proposed that the colony should set a target of 50 miles of new track each year. The other colonies followed suit, and 3,000 miles were laid before 1880. By the turn of the century the continent's rail network exceeded 13,500 miles.

Railway expansion ushered in an economic boom. The railways provided the vital framework for industrial development and for speeding increasing amounts of wool, meat, and wheat to the ports for export. In South Australia, the major wheat-growing colony, new track took the grain harvest down to Spencer Gulf, where the tall clipper ships loaded for the grain races to England. In 1872 South Australia sent 367,000 bushels of wheat to Britain; the following year, 3,495,000. In each of the colonies new wheat-growing land was opened up in belts about 30 miles wide along the railway lines.

The prosperity developing in tandem with the railways received further impetus in November, 1879, when the *Strathleven* sailed from Sydney bound for London with the first

cargo of frozen Australian meat for British markets. Meat exports were soon worth £1 million a year.

Suddenly Australia was leaping ahead like a bushfire out of control. Prosperity on the farm was matched by a new mining boom. Gold was discovered in several areas of Queensland. Then came a rush to Broken Hill in New South Wales, which yielded nearly £2,500,000 worth of silver and lead in the years 1885–89. British investors were finding Australia a most attractive prospect, and the expansion was nourished by over £200 million of British capital.

Cities like Melbourne and Sydney blossomed. Melbourne, with a population of half a million, staged an International Exhibition in 1879 at which there were 30,000 exhibits. Although the city grew apace, officials were careful to prescribe that no building be higher than 132 feet, so that the look of the city would not be spoiled. The streets were broad and large spaces were given over for public gardens. Anthony Trollope, for one, was impressed: "There is perhaps no town in the world where the ordinary working man can do better for himself and his family than he can in Melbourne."

Sydney was less disciplined. "The most unpleasant feature about Sydney is that there is a thoroughly untidy look about the place," complained a contemporary critic. "It is in a perennial state of deshabillé; whereas Melbourne nearly always has its dress clothes on." Nevertheless, Sydney was booming. "The overflow of bricks and mortar has spread like a lava-flood," wrote a visitor in 1886. "The invasion of construction has bridged the harbour and laid out innumerable streets."

The mood of the cities was all-important in Australia. Each colony had one major city-port, the centre of trade and population and the mainspring of all political, social, and economic life. The great sheep stations and wheat farms of the interior employed a relatively small amount of labour; more than a third of the population lived in the major cities—Sydney, Melbourne, Adelaide, Brisbane. It was there that the radical working-class movement emerged that was to help propel Australia towards nationhood.

The boom of the 1870s and 1880s fostered a strong labour movement. Initially unions concentrated on improving working conditions and wages, but once they began to campaign beyond the framework of the individual colonies they became a powerful political force. Union leaders became convinced of the value of united action. "Federated, the numerical and moral power of the working classes would be irresistible," reported an 1884 trade unions congress.

The outstanding union organizer was William Guthrie Spence. He had emigrated with his family to Australia from the Orkney Islands when he was seven. As a young man he became the first professional union official in Australia, secretary of the Amalgamated Miners' Association of Victoria. He believed passionately that "unionism is a new religion bringing salvation from years of tyranny." Spence's aim was "to unite all miners—gold, silver, copper and coal—in one body, with an intercolonial council to deal with large issues." Within a decade the association not only had branches in every colony but in New Zealand as well. When the sheep shearers formed their union in 1886 Spence was a natural choice for president. The union, he said, "must be intercolonial—must ignore political boundaries—and every member must carry his rights and privileges with him." Five years later his efforts were capped by the creation of the Australian Labour Federation.

At a banquet at Tenterfield, New South Wales, in 1889, Sir Henry Parkes, then in his fifth term as Premier of New South Wales and the grand old man of Australian politics, observed that "Australia now has a population of three and a half million. The American people numbered only three or four millions when they formed the great commonwealth of the United States. . . . Surely what the Americans have done by war, the Australians can bring about in peace without breaking the ties that hold them to the Mother Country. . . . The

Waltzing Matilda

Waltzing Matilda is Australia's unofficial national anthem—understandably, for it tells a tale of assertive individuality in typically Australian vocabulary. Yet its appeal is much wider. The swinging tune has made it one of the world's great folk songs.

The story is that of a "swagman," an odd-job worker at sheep stations in the outback. He camps with his "swag," or bundle of worldly goods, by a "billabong," a water hole only connected with a river in the rainy season (*billa* is Aborigine for "water," *bong* for "dead"), under a "coolibah tree," a kind of eucalyptus. As he waits for water to boil in his "billy," a miner's bully-beef can, a sheep ("jumbuck") appears. The swagman seizes his chance, kills it, and stuffs it into his "tucker-bag," an old sugar sack. Up rides a "squatter," the owner of both the land and the sheep, with three "troopers" (policemen). To escape being taken alive, the swagman leaps into the billabong.

The derivation of the chorus, *Who'll come a-waltzing Matilda with me,* is more obscure. To "waltz Matilda" meant to pick up your swag and travel on. It probably came in with German settlers, for *walzen* is German tramp-slang for "to travel around." As for "Matilda," tramps everywhere give prize possessions female names.

In 1895 the Australian poet "Banjo" Paterson was visiting a sheep station in Queensland and its owner told him the swagman story. Paterson adapted the tale to a tune probably derived from the Scottish air *Thou Bonnie Banks of Craigielia*—and a young country had its folk song.

Australia's "white gold mines" were its sheep-shearing sheds; one shown here in action near the turn of the century was painted by Tom Roberts.

time is close at hand to set about creating a great national government for all Australians."

The idea of a federal Australia was not new; it had been the topic of after-dinner speeches for years. But Parkes sensed that the mood of the country was now definitely winging away from the parochialism that had always bedevilled it. By the 1880s Australia had a history of its own. Seventy-five per cent of the population had been born there and had developed their own distinctive character. "Australian nationalism," remarked one observer, "was an optimistic faith, brash and assertive perhaps, rejecting the way of life of the old world, affirming that here in the new a society was coming into being free of the lumbering tyrannies from which Australian immigrants had escaped when they left Europe."

The artificial frontiers between the colonies had been increasingly breached by the boom of the 1870s and 1880s, but the movement towards federation was precipitated even faster by another development: a supposed threat to Australia's sovereignty by French and German expansion in the Pacific. The French had already claimed New Caledonia in the 1850s; then, in 1884, the Germans annexed part of New Guinea. Australia urged the British government to gain control of all the islands of the Pacific, but London was not interested. Queensland thereupon forced the issue by annexing part of New Guinea as its own. The colonists were being drawn together in mutual plans for defence.

Defence was one of the major issues debated at the first Colonial Conference convened in London in 1887. The Australian delegates agreed with New Zealand to contribute £126,000 a year to the cost of an Australian squadron for local defence. Once co-operation had reached this level, federation was not far away. Arthur Deakin, the Victoria delegate at the London conference, returned to Melbourne convinced of the necessity of federation

The railroad became the steel lifeline of Australia's economy, swiftly carrying perishable exports of wheat and meat to such terminals as this one in Sydney.

and thereafter dedicated all his energies to that goal. Federation became known as "Deakin's Dream."

Then in the early thirties, Deakin was already well established as one of the brightest, most progressive of Victoria's politicians. He had studied law at the University of Melbourne and entered the legislative assembly there when he was only 23. He quickly gained a reputation as a liberal by supporting factory acts and minimum-wage legislation. Deakin was convinced that federation was essential, not only for reasons of defence, but to preserve Australia intact as a "white" nation. "No motive power," he wrote, "operated more universally . . . and more powerfully in dissolving the technical and arbitrary political divisions which previously separated us than did the desire that we should be one race and remain one people without the mixture of other races."

The threat to "Australia for Australians" was seen in the steady influx of Chinese and Pacific islanders. The Chinese had first come by the thousands to New South Wales and Victoria in the gold rush days; later the main traffic was to Queensland, where they formed a pool of cheap labour for the sugar-cane industry. The Pacific islanders came in a stream, some drawn by Australia's growing prosperity, some lured away—even kid-

napped—from their homes into conditions of near-slavery, a system that came to be known as "blackbirding."

The "white Australia" movement's hostility increased until, in 1888, demonstrators blocked a shipload of Chinese who tried to land at Sydney and Melbourne. The New South Wales legislature quickly passed a Chinese Restriction Act, and by 1890 all the other colonies had enacted similar legislation.

The imperial government in London opposed the "White Australia" policy, but the colonies took no notice. This opposition, combined with London's seeming lack of interest in checking French and German expansion in the Pacific, gave the six colonies added incentive to merge into a strong and independent federation that would be capable of looking after itself. The first draft of a federal constitution for a commonwealth was drawn up at a convention in Sydney in 1891. The proposals were passed, without much enthusiasm, by several colonial legislatures, but New South Wales rejected them. Sir Henry Parkes, that ardent federalist, was no longer Premier there, and his successor opposed federalism.

Then in 1892 and 1893, in the wake of a recession in Europe, came a grave economic crisis. Banks suspended payments, prices of farm produce

were halved, land prices fell. The crisis punched home the lesson that the complexity of the Australian economy demanded national policies. The colonial premiers duly agreed that a convention should be held to draft a new constitution. Fifty delegates met in Adelaide, Sydney, and Melbourne over the next three years, hammering out an acceptable formula.

They proposed the creation of a Commonwealth of Australia in which each of the six colonies would become a state. A House of Representatives would be elected by universal franchise (women already had the vote in several colonies), while each state would choose six representatives for the Senate. Free trade would exist between the states, with the Commonwealth responsible for trade, taxation, banking, mail and telegraph, immigration, and external affairs. The states would retain control of education, health, and railways.

Each colony held a referendum to approve these terms. At first New South Wales rejected them, but was later appeased by an amendment siting the planned federal capital of Canberra within her territory. Stiffer opposition came from Western Australia, which had been the lame duck of the colonies until the discovery of gold in 1892 started a rush almost on the scale of the original stampede

to Victoria. Western Australia had achieved self-government only in 1890, and was naturally reluctant to relinquish so soon powers for which it had fought so long. Moreover, it was most unwilling to lose the customs revenue created by the gold rush. The diggers, however, held the balance, and they needed the telegraph and a transcontinental railway. When Western Australia held her referendum on federation in 1900, the gold fields voted almost unanimously "yes" and carried the day. The last hurdle was removed.

In London the House of Commons was already debating the Commonwealth Bill that would give the new federation its independence. The bill was duly passed and in July, 1900, just a few months before her death, Queen Victoria gave the royal assent.

On the morning of January 1, 1901, a great crowd gathered in Centennial Park, Sydney, to watch the swearing-in of Lord Hopetoun as the first Governor-General of Australia and Edmund Barton, a Liberal from New South Wales, as her first Prime Minister. A choir sang the *Te Deum*, a little fitfully in the midsummer heat, guns boomed out, and the new Commonwealth flag was ceremoniously raised. Australia, one orator predicted, "would dominate the Southern Seas" and be "a permanent glory

to the British Empire." Most of his countrymen, seeing their new nation as the land of the future, heartily agreed.

Meanwhile, what of the new Commonwealth's neighbour to the east, New Zealand? Was it, as its boosters liked to say, well on the way to becoming "God's Own Country"?

The advertisements of the colonizing companies had proclaimed New Zealand "the Britain of the South," and there were similarities. In the absence of native mammals, the settlers brought in their own sheep and cattle, grasses and fruit trees. Gradually they built churches and schools. By 1854 they had a central parliament, provincial assemblies, and in the main towns, local government. They had their regattas, their dances, their newspapers.

But the differences from home were marked. The great plains, the mountains, the ever-green forest (the "bush") had no parallels in Britain. Nor did the houses and buildings seem English; they looked more like the sets for a Hollywood Western. And New Zealanders were already noted for a definite national character. Many visitors noticed a great degree of social equality. Most settlers were intolerant and resentful of class distinction, "mightily republican" as one shocked newcomer described them. They said that Jack was not only as good as his master, but better. The settlers wanted to live like the people at home—but better off. By and large, they succeeded.

In 1870, as the Maori wars were drawing to a close, colonial treasurer Julius Vogel put forward proposals for a major scheme of borrowing for economic development. Vogel was a Londoner of flamboyant character and expensive tastes who had abandoned business at home to try his luck in the Australian gold rush. From Victoria he hurried to a short-lived strike in the South Island, then started a daily newspaper, then entered politics. Under Vogel's ambitious scheme, £10,000,000 was to be raised in Britain to build roads, railways, and encourage immigration. Forests and lands opened up by new communications and settled by new immigrants

would yield the increased production needed to repay the loans and their interest charges. Borrowing proved catching. Successive governments in the 1870s borrowed twice as much as Vogel proposed, but failed to establish the reserves he had deemed prudent.

For a decade, however, the borrowing programme stimulated prosperity and expansion. The population doubled. Over a thousand miles of railways were laid. Roads and telegraph lines went up. The area under pasture quadrupled. The introduction of American reapers and binders led to a boom in wheat farming.

By the mid-1870s, however, with the expansion of American and Australian agriculture, overseas wheat and wool prices were falling. At first this was a warning ignored. Then in 1879 the Bank of New Zealand panicked and cut its loans back. It was the start of a long depression. Traders were ruined. The land boom collapsed. Prices for wool and wheat plummeted, and unemployment climbed. Immigrants found a sad contrast between their hopes and reality, and during the late 1880s departures exceeded arrivals—"the Exodus," it was called.

Poverty bred dissent and protest. Soon the old politics was challenged by a popular radicalism that focused on two major issues.

One was land tenure. In 1882 the first shipload of refrigerated New Zealand meat reached England. This technological advance seemed to offer a real future to New Zealand's small farmers. Food could now be shipped to great overseas markets. But much of the land was "locked up" in huge estates. There arose a widespread demand either that this land be nationalized or that it be taxed so heavily that the owners would be forced to subdivide and sell. The second issue was labour reform. Unemployment meant that labour was cheap. "Sweated" labour conditions existed and women and children were increasingly employed. The evils of the Old World were springing up down under. Trade union members, their organizations given legal recognition in 1878, took up the fight for reform.

In 1890 a radical Liberal government, led by the modest and courteous John Ballance, swept into power. The rule of the early colonial gentry, with their public-school background and their refined speech and their

clubs, was over. From now on politicians cultivated the common touch. For a time, New Zealand became the most radical state in the world.

Most of the Liberals believed in some degree of public ownership as a means of achieving equality. They introduced a graduated land tax and the income tax. They began to repurchase great estates and subdivide them for closer settlement. Small farmers began to prosper again. In 1893 the women of New Zealand, preceded throughout the world only by their sisters in Wyoming, joined their menfolk on the voting rolls. (It was only four years since all men had received it.) An extensive code of factory legislation, including compulsory arbitration of labour disputes, was introduced.

Ballance's successor, Richard John Seddon, a huge man who had been a publican in the South Island gold fields, introduced old-age pensions. There was strong opposition, but in 1898 he wore out his opponents after

At right, below, Richard Seddon, New Zealand's forceful Prime Minister, known as "King Dick," addresses a 1906 rally. The frontier town of Carterton (opposite) reflects a solid prosperity in 1910.

a lengthy battle in Parliament that included an exhausting 90-hour sitting.

By the turn of the century New Zealand had one of the highest standards of living in the world. There was far less of a contrast between rich and poor than in other Western nations. To many travellers the country seemed too good to be true. Americans especially were ready to concur in "King Dick" Seddon's judgement that New Zealand was "God's Own Country."

Most Europeans now living in New Zealand had been born there. They were proud of the country's development. Its practical and undoctrinaire radical legislation had won wide international acclaim. Herbert Asquith, Britain's future Liberal Prime Minister, acknowledged the world's debt when he described New Zealand as "a laboratory in which social and political experiments are every day made for the information and instruction of older countries."

New Zealand's relations with the outside world seemed securely based on an unswerving loyalty to Britain. When imperialism was at its height at the end of the century, no country was as jingoistic. Gordon's death in Khartoum produced a flood of sentimental and obstreperous verse. At Victoria's Diamond Jubilee in 1897 Seddon gave unstinting support to Joseph Chamberlain's policy of an imperial federation. No other colony had such a reputation for adoring the security offered by maternal Britain.

It was an unfair judgement. New Zealand's "more-English-than-the-English" attitudes were, strangely, the result of her attempts to establish the greatest possible independence without losing the security offered by the Empire in an increasingly militaristic world.

The key to New Zealand's pro-British policy lies in Seddon's remark that by helping to bear the burdens of Empire, New Zealand would build up a case for having a voice in imperial government. The Liberals were not content simply to follow Britain's lead: they wanted to influence it, and thus hold the key to their own future. It was this attitude which lay behind the decision in 1907 to "raise the status" of New Zealand by declaring it a Dominion. This underlined the general feeling that the country was moving along the right lines, that the foundations of the new nation had been well laid.

To some extent the Maoris shared in the nation's new prosperity—if they happened to be employed by Europeans, or if they sold them food. Yet they continued to find the process of adapting to a European-dominated world a painful one. Many clearly did not want to be "integrated" into white New Zealand. In the 1890s new-style Maori leaders began to appear, highly educated and successful in European society, yet able to move freely among their own people. Such men, who were collectively called "the Young Maori Party," fervently desired to improve the condition of their people, whether by health reforms or by introducing better farming techniques. Three of them entered Parliament and became cabinet ministers.

Despite these occasional, if dramatic, success stories, most Maoris still lived in their own settlements in rural areas. Few Europeans saw many Maoris, and few Maoris saw many Europeans. Indeed it is not unfair to say that up to the Second World War the two races lived apart. Perhaps that period of separation contributed to better race relations in the future. There was time for the old wounds of war to heal. There was time for the two races to reach an understanding of how to adapt to one another.

—*Timothy S. Green, Keith Sinclair*

III. A Remote Elite

After the shock of the great Mutiny of 1857, the British in India withdrew more and more into a world of their own. Never again would an Indian—Hindu or Muslim—really be trusted; their loyalty had been taken so much for granted that their officers had faith in it right up to the moment they were shot down by their own men.

The armed forces were completely reorganized so that the firepower was controlled by white troops. In the civil service even the most Westernized Indians were barred from the upper levels, despite Victoria's proclamation of 1858 that all her subjects should be "impartially admitted to Offices in Our Service." Most of the British in post-Mutiny India approved of such discrimination. For the first time in the history of their rule, *all* the British—administrators and soldiers, businessmen and planters—felt an overwhelming sense of racial solidarity, of belonging to a caste which was (it went without saying) the highest caste of all. The high-minded self-righteousness of India's official guardians; the blatant prejudices of the business community; the continual need (especially by the memsahibs) to escape from the India of inefficient servants and depressing heat; and the small, introverted social world that evolved as a result—all this created a widening gap between rulers and ruled.

Government administrators might be imbued by a sense of caste, but it was tempered by dedication to duty. The Mutiny, the British decided, had caught them by surprise because they had been out of touch with the people. A more personal and direct system of administration was needed.

Gone was the belief that British civilization should be the model for India. The great reforms, the militant Christianity, had led only to revolt. The administrators saw their Christian duty in a new light. Their aim was to keep the peace, maintain law and order, bring India some of the material blessings of Europe—and not worry about Indian family life or private morals. Nothing was expected in return except "the blame of those ye better, the hate of those ye guard." This

was quite acceptable. Duty was a hard taskmaster, and satisfaction lay in the approval of one's own kind.

This stern appraisal of the British purpose was not shared by the non-official community whose feelings were more coarsely straightforward. In the 1860s a flood of Englishmen arrived in India—to plant coffee and tea, to build railways and cotton mills —and they brought with them attitudes influenced by the wave of anti-Indian feeling that had swept over Britain at the time of the Mutiny. Generally speaking, these new men, and particularly their wives, viewed India only as a place to make money. They had no interest in learning anything about Indians, who were to them simply dangerous and dirty. They demanded from the government laws with which to coerce those they employed, packed juries, and patronized an English-language Press virulently racialistic. In some areas the behaviour of European planters was almost an incitement to rebellion. Fortunately, the planters were mainly confined to the indigo-growing areas of Bengal and Bihar, the coffee-growing districts in south India, and the tea-gardens of Assam.

Elsewhere the European did not penetrate the countryside, and the District Officer was almost on his own, as described by the historian George Trevelyan:

"Here is Tom, in his thirty-first year, in charge of a population as numerous as that of England in the reign of Elizabeth." Tom's day is a very full one. "He rises at daybreak, and goes straight from his bed to the saddle. Then off he gallops across fields bright with dew to visit the scene of the late *dacoit* [bandit] robbery; or to see with his own eyes whether the crops of the *zemindar* [landlord] who is so unpunctual with his assessment have really failed; or to watch with fond parental care the progress of his pet embankment."

Two or three times a month the routine is broken by a run with the "hounds," a motley pack made up of dogs of assorted breeds or of no breed at all. But this is only the curtain-raiser to the real business of the day. After a quick bath and a meal of tea

and toast, the administration of the Empire must be attended to. Seated on the veranda of his bungalow, Tom "works through the contents of one despatch box . . . after another; signing orders, and passing them on . . . dashing through drafts, to be filled up by his subordinates; writing reports, minutes, digests, letters of explanation, of remonstrance, of warning, of commendation."

During the cool season the District Officer would take his tents and tour his domain. After "examining schools, and inspecting infirmaries, and quarrelling about the sites of bridges with the superintending engineer in the Public Works department," he would ride out with his gun to get a bird for the pot while his servants moved the tents to the next camping place. How pleasant it was to "reach the rendezvous in the gloaming, rather tired and dusty, to find your tents pitched and your soap and curry within a few minutes of perfection, and your servant with a bottle of lemonade. . . ."

The Mutiny had taught that a rebellion fed on discontent. It was not enough simply to stop interfering in religious matters. A contented peasantry was the best safeguard, and there seemed no better way to ensure this than by bringing material benefits to as many people as possible.

At first it was thought sufficient to build bridges, keep roads in reasonable repair, and erect vast irrigation works, the most likely agents for agricultural prosperity. Digging canals took time, however, and not every part of the vast country could be served by them. For most of the second half of the 19th Century the majority of India's peasants were dependent on the fickle monsoon rains.

In India nine-tenths of the annual rainfall comes in the months of July, August, and September, when the south-west and south-east monsoons strike the coasts and move slowly cross-country to meet each other. In a good year, when the two monsoons meet in the centre of the country, everyone has rain, the land bursts into life, and two crops can be harvested. But if the monsoons fail to meet, central and northern India turn slowly into a desert. With difficulty the peas-

Text Continued on Page 288

OUR LIFE IN INDIA

Leaves from a Victorian album . . .

The Guardians at Ease

"Duty and red tape, picnics and adultery" – this was how one cynical writer summed up the social world of the British in India. There was certainly a feeling in some remote districts that the feverish social life in the larger Anglo-Indian centres, especially in hill stations like Poona and Simla, was less proper than it looked. There, away from the cares of day-to-day work, the usual Society pastimes multiplied. Balls and picnics, badminton and croquet, amateurish art exhibitions and the Dramatic Club – especially the Dramatic Club – were all fertile soil for scandal.

Affairs there may have been, but for most people life was more prosaic. One civil servant wrote – perhaps with a tinge of regret – that Simla ladies were "most of them pretty and all of them good."

Field-Marshal Lord Roberts of Kandahar (centre), like his subordinates, enjoyed donning period costume for theatricals.

Picnics were a popular pastime, though the formality assumed for the benefit of the cameraman was often upset by plagues of ants, flies and mosquitoes.

An amateur dramatic group indulges a taste for melodrama with a stage version of Sir Walter Scott's story, *The Talisman.*

British guests leave a maharajah's magnificent lakeside palace for a brief trip in a steam-powered launch.

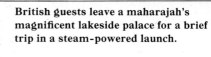

With heavy clothing, retinues of servants, elephants and lavish tables, quite ordinary people could in India assume an aristocratic way of life impossible at home.

Ladies and gentlemen displaying a wide variety of headgear exchange local gossip at an afternoon fête of parade and sport.

Polo-players compete avidly in an inter-regimental match. For most young officers, polo, in Churchill's words, was "the serious purpose of life."

Members of the Peshawar Vale Hunt, in traditional fox-hunting costume, assemble in a handsome estate for the start of a day's sport.

A Sporting Life

Sport played a great part in a social life often lacking in variety. For men, sport had wider significance: it developed the steady nerve and grit a man needed in his work. Pig-sticking, in particular, demanded the horsemanship, judgement and determination needed in times of crisis. Polo, too, was popular, especially in the Army, but it could add ruinously to the expenses of social life.

Every station had its racecourse, perhaps only a dingy ring of beaten earth with a few wooden stands for the loyal women spectators. The ladies joined the men for tennis, and for everyone there was the hunt, often in small stations a motley pack of different breeds.

A fashionably dressed horsewoman poses outside her bungalow.

...is- and badminton-players, complete with suits and hats, look up dutifully as the camera snaps this record of two favourite pastimes.

Officers of the 93rd Highlanders in the Deccan proudly show off some hunting trophies and some new-found pets. The wealth

...he gave Englishmen an opportunity to display a contradictory pride in themselves both as animal-killers and animal-lovers.

ants might survive in near-starvation one year's crop failures. But two lean years meant famine in the land.

Before 1858 the British had attacked famine with economic theories and charity. They believed in the law of supply and demand: if there was a shortage in one place, the natural process of profit-making would move food from somewhere else. But where there was no adequate means of transportation, supply and demand failed to operate. Even where transport existed, merchants had a distressing habit of hoarding their stocks in the hope that prices would rise.

During a serious famine in 1866–67, the government moved to end hoarding and artificial shortages, but too late, and over a million died. When another famine the following year was faced more successfully, the principle was accepted that the need to prevent starvation must guide official action.

Though action was delayed by the fear that relief might "check the growth of thrift and self-reliance among the people," by 1880 the government had decided to establish some kind of machinery for dealing with famine. This was not only a matter of common humanity but sound policy as well. The result was the Famine Code, the first acknowledgement by any modern state of responsibility for the welfare of those it ruled.

Railways were built that had little possibility of commercial profit but that could transport supplies of food to places of shortage. Plans were drawn up for relief work that would pay fixed wages and at which food would be sold at fixed prices. At work sites there were to be hospitals and doctors and simple accommodations for the worker and his family. In addition, the Code provided for the remission of land-taxes and the free distribution of seed for the next planting.

With the help of the Famine Code and other acts designed to protect the peasant, the government hoped to exact from the masses, if not loyalty, at least neutrality in any conflict between it and the Indian middle classes. It would have been difficult to find anyone in the British community in India, official or non-official, to take

exception to the opinion of the middle classes expressed in 1877 by a Viceroy (as the Governor-General was known after the British take-over), Lord Lytton: "The only political representatives of native opinion are the Baboos, whom we have educated to write semi-seditious articles in the native Press, and who really represent nothing but the social anomaly of their own position."

The basically inoffensive word "Baboo" had achieved a special place in the vocabulary of racialism. Originally it had been a term of respect, and then it became a name for a native clerk who spoke English. But with the expansion of schools and universities after the Mutiny, it was applied indiscriminately to any educated Indian. The Baboo's malapropisms rising out of his struggle with English were the butt of much cruel Anglo-Indian humour.

Behind the laughter lurked dislike and even fear. The usual British image of a "good" Indian was that of a somewhat wayward child, in need of an occasional fatherly correction to keep him on the right path. He understood his place in the scheme of things, and humbly tugged his forelock when his master passed. The educated Indian, however, would not keep his place. He was always questioning the decisions of his betters, that "race whom God has destined to govern and subdue."

With India now the direct responsibility of the Crown, that meant supervision by Parliament. Members of Parliament frequently travelled out to India, especially after the opening of the Suez Canal, making themselves a nuisance while they were there and even more so when they returned home and aired their ignorant views in the House of Commons—that, at any rate, was how the Anglo-Indians saw them. "Mr. Cox, the member of parliament?" one wrote bitterly. "A little red-haired fellow was he, who wrote a book about India on the back of his two-monthly return ticket?"

These travelling M.P.'s were always asking why the Baboo was not employed on the higher levels of the civil service. Victoria's proclamation of 1858 had made it quite clear that

there was to be no racial discrimination in her Empire. No one objected to the employment of Indians in the lower ranks of the administration—in fact, without them the British would have been unable to govern—but it was generally felt that the Queen's generosity did not reach as far as the sacred ranks of the Indian Civil Service. Indians were not excluded outright from taking the competitive examination, but they could only take it in London, which meant a costly voyage. When four Indians did pass in 1869 and seven candidates turned up in the following year, the government decided to make things even more difficult for them by reducing the maximum age from 21 to 19. In 1880 there were only two qualified Indian candidates.

Even those Indians who made the I.C.S. found themselves treated very differently from their British colleagues. In 1874 Surendranath Banerjea, one of the first Indians to join the service, was dismissed for an action which would have meant no more than a departmental reprimand for one of his white colleagues. Banerjea was convinced that "the personal wrong to me was an illustration of the impotency of our people." He dedicated the rest of his life to "redressing our wrongs and protecting our rights, personal and collective."

Such activists were particularly resented by the British business community. It was feared that the least concession to educated Indians meant the erosion of those many socio-economic privileges the British had so painstakingly built up and so carefully preserved.

The Mecca of Anglo-Indian society was the administrative capital, Calcutta. In spite of the discomforts of the climate and the presence of deadly diseases, the British resident in Calcutta generally enjoyed a far better standard of living than he could have hoped for at home. The wealthy lived in great houses built at the end of the 18th Century, Palladian mansions requiring an army of servants. Those not so well off lived in bungalows, while the bachelors usually shared a house and its servants. The men—lawyers, merchants, bankers—in the main spent busy days at their offices, but there was always plenty of time for that social round which is the cement binding a small expatriate community together.

It was the custom for the English to take the air in the evening in Eden Gardens, perhaps to listen to the music of a regimental band, but mainly to see and be seen. In the cool weather when the Viceroy was in residence and the Calcutta season in full swing, there were balls and dances almost every night. Such occasions were rarely meetings together of equals, for the British in India had their strict class divisions. Indeed, the government published a "warrant of precedence" with the Viceroy at the top and the Sub-Deputy Opium Agent at the bottom. The position of non-governmental people was not defined, but considered low.

During the hot season the Viceroy and his higher officials made their way to the hill station of Simla. Only the most important of the business and trading community followed the Viceroy to the summer capital of the Raj; the commercial or professional Englishman preferred the company of his own kind at other hill stations. But regardless of where they went, as many Englishmen as possible tried to get away, emphasizing the remoteness of the élite that ruled India.

The whole decision-making apparatus was concentrated on a ridge in the Himalayas during the hot season. Simla was linked to the plains by 50 miles of indifferent road, and frequently the telegraph lines were broken by landslides. Other hill stations were even more isolated. Indeed, this remoteness was an important element in the attraction of such places. Not only was the climate clean and bracing after the muggy heat of the plains, but in the hills the British could pretend they were not in India at all. Simla, it was said, looked like parts of Surrey with a touch of Tibet. In the hills the British could forget they were imperialists and enjoy themselves.

Not everyone spent the whole of the hot season in the cool hills. The Viceroy could, of course, and so could senior members of the government

and many of the women and children, but most of the men, whether in the services or not, could only afford a short time away from their everyday work.

In the hot weather, particularly in a city as unhealthy as Calcutta, cholera made its annual visitation and took its toll. Even in the best of circumstances tempers frayed to the breaking point. Inside the houses the air would press down heavily, stirred fitfully by punkahs, the swinging fans attached to the ceiling and pulled by servants who were always nodding off to sleep. In the morning there would be a short stay at the office. By noon it was time for a siesta. Outside in the streets the white sunlight laid upon the roads "so palpable a heat that it might be peeled off: the bare, blinding walls, surcharged with heat, refuse to soak in more, and reject upon the air the fervour beating down upon them. In the dusty hollows of the roadside the pariah dogs lie sweltering. . . . Beneath the trees sit the crows, their beaks agape. . . . Not a human being is abroad of his own will."

In these gruelling conditions the British made their exile comfortable by the erection of ghettoes of both the mind and the body and thus created the apartheid of colonialism. They sustained their sense of superiority with prejudices essentially racial in origin. After the necessary contact with the real world they ruled, the administrators could retire into the security of an expatriate society, into a simulation of Home. The distinctive features of this particular Englishman's castle—and of the view from it's battlements—were to a large extent the creation of memsahib.

The memsahib's India was a very small country, confined mainly to the European quarter of the larger cities and, elsewhere, to what were known as the "Civil Lines" or the "Military Cantonment." The frontiers of this special nation were defended as strongly as possible by the barbed-wire of prejudice. In the course of their imperial business the men claimed friendship with rajahs and landowners, and many cultivated paternal feelings for the hard-working

peasant, but there was little or no social mixing. The women did not approve of it, and after the Mutiny few of the men did either. "Your ladies," said one Indian indignantly, "look upon me as something of a wild beast, and you yourself perhaps grow a little brutal after your third glass of sherry." The memsahib's opinion of Indians was almost entirely the product of sexual fears, highly coloured interpretations of Indian religious and social practices, and the regrettably unavoidable task of dealing with servants.

Memsahib soon learned from experienced friends and from books specially written to advise her that the trouble with Indian servants was that "laziness, dishonesty, falsehood, with a host of other vices, seem to be inherent in them." This was, of course, not surprising considering how "they have been brought up." Firmness and no toleration of impertinence were essential, "for an Indian household can no more be governed peacefully without dignity and prestige, than an Indian Empire." The paternalism of the imperialist's home was the paternalism, writ small, of the Empire he ruled.

A properly run household of 14 indoor and outdoor servants (the minimum, as no Indian servant would do another's traditional task) took up only an hour or two of the memsahib's day. That being so, what was left to occupy her time? In big cities with large British communities, hierarchies of senior civil servants, military officers, and Government House, social life could be as involving as anyone could wish. But in the hundreds of lonely stations where five or six men and women made up Society, there was often literally nothing to do. There the memsahib fought her "daily battles against heat, dust, cholera, and that insidious inertia of soul and body that is the moral microbe of the East."

The pressures of life in India were real and they fell most heavily upon the women. The men, after all, could point to achievement—a bridge built, a famine relieved, or even occasionally an injustice righted. The memsahib had no such outlets against which to reckon success. Yet her influence

Text Continued on Page 292

POSH

Port Out, Starboard Home.

The opening of the Suez Canal revolutionized travel to the Eastern Empire. Gone was the tedious four-month voyage via Cape Town: now for the same £100 fare administrators and merchants could be in India in under three weeks, and travel First Class into the bargain. The most affluent reserved north-facing cabins on both legs of the journey – "port out, starboard home" – to avoid the Equatorial sun, and the happy coincidence of letters – P.O.S.H. – used to locate these cabins gave the word "posh," originally slang for "money," a new and lasting meaning. The well-to-do ordered meals from lavish menus, drank free wines and spirits, entertained each other with concerts and devised shipboard games galore. But, as these sketches by a passenger in the 1890s show, even "posh" travellers could not totally escape the rigours of Biscay storms or Red Sea heat.

The Captain sets a breakfast guest at ease.

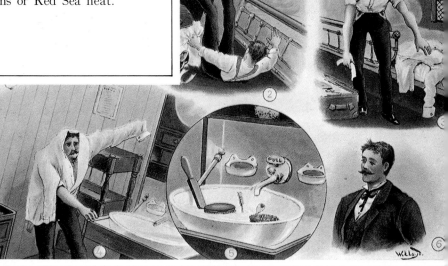

Pitched about by a choppy sea, an aspiring young bachelor utterly fails to master shirt, collar, tie, hair-brushes and soap.

Journey's start at Tilbury: the latest arrival checks his cabin with the steward amidst bustling preparations for departure.

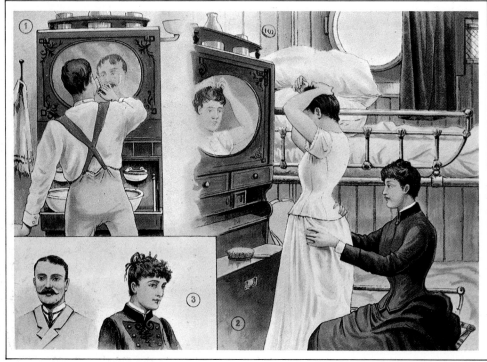

Even a still day – and, for madam, a maid's steadying hand – cannot guarantee a gash-free shave or an unruffled hair-do.

A shipboard Sunday: the saloon's whist, bezique, cigars and drink give way to the universal ritual of Victorian piety.

A musical evening adds a touch of home.

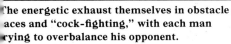

The energetic exhaust themselves in obstacle races and "cock-fighting," with each man trying to overbalance his opponent.

A fielder retrieves the ball-on-a-string during a vigorous game of deck cricket.

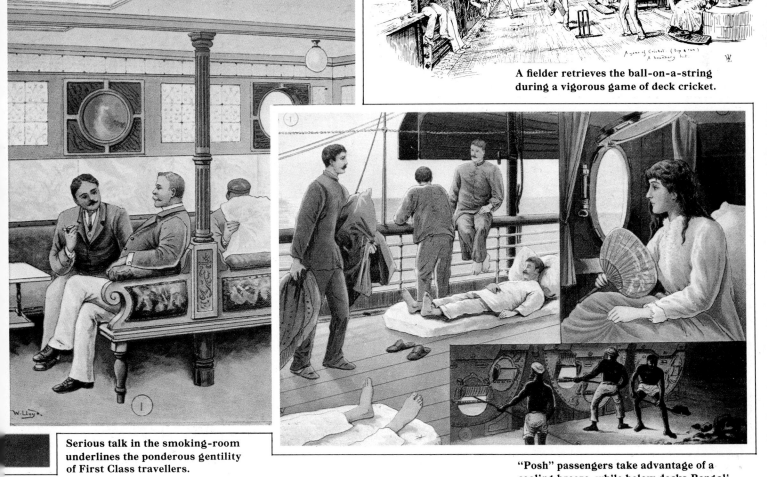

Serious talk in the smoking-room underlines the ponderous gentility of First Class travellers.

"Posh" passengers take advantage of a cooling breeze, while below decks Bengali firemen stoke the blistering furnaces.

was all-pervasive. She projected upon the great world of the subcontinent not only her experience as a minor employer of Indian labour but her fears of sexual contamination. In the typical Anglo-Indian novel one of the recurring themes is of some loathsome fakir, personifying all the moral and emotional anarchy of India, confronting a young and innocent white woman, defiling her by his very presence—and threatening much worse.

In 1901 the historian James Bryce summed up the Raj in these words: "Three things the career of the English in India has proved. One is, that it is possible for a European to rule a subject race on principles of strict justice. . . . The second is that a relatively small body of European civilians, supported by a relatively small armed force, can maintain peace and order in an immense population on a lower plane of civilisation. . . . The

third fact is that the existence of a system securing these benefits is compatible with an absolute separation between the rulers and the ruled."

Such statements were applauded by Anglo-Indians. Though the qualities of the men were perhaps disguised behind a "surface of muteness and officialdom," and those of the women behind complaints about prices and servants, the British community was convinced of its remarkable character. Its self-proclaimed virtues, displayed like a peacock's tail, were those of duty and sacrifice, "the sturdy self-control, the patient persistent driving force that have made the country what it is today."

At the pinnacle of the Anglo-Indian pyramid was, of course, the Raj; and for splendid imperial bearing no Raj ever quite matched George Nathaniel Curzon, who became Viceroy in 1899.

When Curzon arrived at Govern-

ment House in Calcutta to take up his duties, he could be forgiven if he felt a sense of fulfilled romance. The great Palladian-style mansion he was entering was modelled directly upon his own family home at Kedleston in Derbyshire. He was not yet 40; only Lord Dalhousie, a half-century earlier, had been appointed to rule India at an earlier age. Whereas most Viceroys had been selected for their general good judgement and capacity more than for their knowledge of the East, Curzon had prepared himself for the post from his boyhood at Eton through his undergraduate career at Oxford.

He confessed to having been haunted by a passion for India from the time when a visiting speaker, the redoubtable Anglo-Indian administrator Sir James Stephen, told the Literary Society at Eton of an empire in the East more populous, more beneficent, and more amazing than that of Rome. Even before he left Oxford, Curzon had a high reputation as a debater, as a leader of young Conservative opinion, and as a scholar. "He was at twenty-two," recalled Winston Churchill many years later, "notorious as The Coming Man." Welcome in Society for his high spirits, charm, and wit, Curzon already displayed that natural taste for the magnificent and the stately that made him the subject of a famous Oxford rhyme:

My name is George Nathaniel Curzon,
I am a most superior person.
My cheek is pink, my hair is sleek,
I dine at Blenheim once a week.

The phrase "a most superior person" clung to Curzon. His public manner gave colour to the description, and those who felt the sharp edge of his tongue, or who envied his gifts, repeated it.

He entered Parliament for Southport in 1886 and attended assiduously to his many duties in the constituency and the House, laying the foundations of a successful political career. But he never intended to devote himself solely to that. His overriding interest lay in foreign affairs, particularly in Asia.

Asia possessed attractions that, for him, no other part of the world could

Lord and Lady Curzon pose with their trophy after a big game hunt in Hyderabad, an entertainment traditionally arranged by Indian princes for honoured guests.

match. It was, he used to say, a university in which the scholar never took his degree. In a series of journeys between 1887 and 1894, he visited Persia, central Asia, Afghanistan, and India itself. The man who did not know the East, he said, was not fit for statesmanship.

He became Under-Secretary at the India Office in 1891 and Under-Secretary at the Foreign Office in 1895. Curzon was clearly establishing himself as one of the principal authorities on Asiatic questions. "I believe a very great work can be done in India by an English Viceroy who is young and active and intensely absorbed in his work," he wrote to Lord Salisbury, the Prime Minister. "A good deal of energy and application would be wanted and—what very few men take to India—a great love of the country and pride in the imperial aspect of its possession." In 1898, when the time was drawing near for Salisbury to make a decision on the appointment of a new Viceroy, he continued his campaign: "It may be thought that I am too young—yet I am in my fortieth year; or too ardent—yet nothing considerable has ever been done without enthusiasm. . . . For 12 years I have worked and studied and thought, with a view—should the chance ever arise—to fitting myself for the position." The man and the job seemed made for each other.

The viceroyalty that Curzon took up had no parallel in any other part of the British Empire. It combined the functions of a president, a monarch, a prime minister, and a foreign secretary. The government of India was arranged in a pyramidal fashion, with the Viceroy himself, as Dalhousie used to complain, the final authority in every matter from a sea-wall at Tumlick to a plunge-bath at Peshawar. He was expected to entertain on a grand scale; in Curzon's first month no fewer than 3,500 meals were served to viceregal guests at Government House.

Immeasurably fortified by his knowledge of India and never lacking self-confidence, Curzon looked upon all those features which made the government of the country so problematical—its vast area, its extremes of climate, the turbulence of the North-West Frontier, the ancestral rivalries of the communities, the presence of so small a number of Britons governing an area the size of Europe, "a speck of foam upon a dark and unfathomable ocean"—as increasing the opportunities for imaginative administration. He probed into questions relentlessly, settling issues that had been dragging about the offices for years, in some instances for decades. He never dealt with a case of importance without scrutinizing its history and asking himself what would be the results of alternative courses. He made it his business not only to know the machine as it was but to fettle it up.

He found the Indian Civil Service, although generally honest and incorruptible, deficient in initiative and ideas at the senior levels. Precedent had become a fetish instead of a guide. What was needed, he judged, was stimulus, encouragement, example, and incentive from the top. The I.C.S. resembled, he once wrote, a gigantic quagmire, into which every question that came along either sank or was sucked down, "and unless you stick a peg with a label over the spot at which it disappeared, and from time to time go round and dig out the relics, you will never see anything of them again."

On the face of it, India when Curzon assumed the viceroyalty looked little different from the India of, say, 15 years before. Except for the outbreaks on the North-West Frontier, there had been 40 years of peace since the Mutiny. Trade and revenue were increasing. There was no sign of substantial discontent with British rule and no obvious racial friction. The British were, to outward appearances, in secure control.

Curzon soon concluded that appearances were misleading. He was conscious of a growing, though still small, force of nationalism, which he hoped to tame or deflect. He believed that many of the most vital questions had been shelved for too long and that reform was urgently necessary.

To initiate change in complex land through a highly developed, almost Byzantine bureaucracy was no easy task. Though his appetite for files

The Great Game

In the second half of the 19th Century it seemed that the Russian bear and the British lion were destined to meet head-on. For a century Russia had expanded steadily south and east, and Britain was determined to stop her before India's North-West Frontier was threatened. This was "The Great Game."

Seeking to turn Afghanistan into a pliant buffer state, the British won the short, sharp Second Afghan War in 1879. But peace was illusionary. The British mission in Kabul was massacred and the garrison at Kandahar trapped by Afghan rebels.

On August 11, 1880, General Sir Frederick Roberts set out to relieve the Kandahar garrison. It was a remarkable march. In just 21 days Roberts's force marched 313 mountainous miles under appalling conditions. At night it was freezing, at noon the temperature soared to 110 degrees. Dust storms raged and delays forced a cut in rations. As the troops approached Kandahar, Roberts, weak with fever, mounted his horse to lead the way. A tenth of his men were sick and exhausted and unfit for duty, yet after relieving the Kandahar garrison he went forward to do battle.

On September 1 Roberts smashed the Afghans by skilful deployment of his cavalry and artillery. "I went to each regiment and battery separately," he wrote his wife. "They cheered me again and again, I felt very proud." The march and the brilliant victory became an enduring imperial legend, and "Bobs" was later raised to the peerage as Lord Roberts of Kandahar.

and papers was legendary, he confessed to his secretary in 1902 that he sometimes felt as if he were going mad. The method Curzon followed in instituting reform was simple but effective. Within his first four months as Viceroy he had identified a dozen main subjects calling for urgent attention. When deficiencies were detected, expert investigation by a small commission, or sometimes by a single individual, followed. Then legislation or administrative action would be taken on the basis of the report.

He laid down four general principles upon which the governance of India was to be conducted henceforth. First, there must be an end to drift; every branch of the administration must have a policy laid down in clear language. Second, the administration of India must be devoted above all to the welfare of the peasantry that constituted nearly 90 per cent of the population. Third, the government must take the people into open confidence as to its intentions and never mystify or deceive. Finally, and most important, it must look ahead not just for a year or two but with an eye to the more distant future.

Many measures—the reform of the rules governing land revenues, the encouragement of commerce and industry, the liberalization of the Famine Code, the increase of railway mileage by more than a quarter—could be put through promptly, despite occasional opposition from the India Office in London. Measures involving large sums of public money or with political overtones, however, were not so easily instituted—a great increase in the irrigated area, the reform of the educational system, the partition of the vast province of Bengal.

There is probably no feature of his viceroyalty for which Curzon is more gratefully remembered today than his loving attention to India's architectural heritage. From the time of his first visits to Asia he had found the Indo-Saracenic style the most satisfying and artistic of all. The Taj Mahal, he exclaimed after his first glimpse of it in 1888, was "incomparable, designed like a palace and finished like a jewel . . . perfect and unutterably lovely." In 1899 the government was spending £7,000 a year on the preservation of priceless buildings and historic fabrics. By the time Curzon left, the figure had reached £40,000 a year. Nearly £50,000 was spent at Agra, "an offering of reverence to the past and a gift of recovered beauty to the future."

Curzon gave short shrift to the thesis that a Christian government had no duty to preserve the monuments and sanctuaries of other faiths. Art and beauty and the reverence owed to everything that has evoked human genius or inspired faith, he explained, are independent of creeds: "What is beautiful, what is historic, what tears the mask off the face of the past, and helps us read its riddles, and look it in the eyes—these, and not the dogmas of a combative theology, are the principal criteria to which we must look."

Apart from official visits, Curzon, like other Viceroys of his day, had little continuous contact with distinguished Indians. Many were, of course, entertained formally at Calcutta, and among some who admired his high ideals, industry, and deep love of India he aroused admiration. Among many others, who took his attempted reforms as deliberate attacks on developing national feeling in India, he provoked reactions of anger and hostility.

In foreign affairs the Viceroy was no less active. When playing the Great Game of diplomatic sparring with Russia he generally favoured a firmer line than London wished to adopt, and this made him enemies at home. Opposition also rose, in Press and Parliament, to some of his actions and some of his reforms; this was perhaps inevitable in a situation where a strong-willed executive runs head-on into an entrenched social order and an ingrown bureaucracy.

Curzon's viceregal career came to an abrupt end in a clash with another strong-willed figure of towering reputation—Lord Kitchener, the hero of Omdurman. Kitchener had been brought in to reform and reinvigorate the Indian Army—at Curzon's insistence, ironically. Soon the two men were in sharp disagreement over military administration, sides were taken in Cabinet, and Curzon considered his position undercut. He resigned in August, 1905.

For all his realization that the new wine of national consciousness was beginning to ferment in the country, Curzon never suggested that British government of India should be brought to an end in the foreseeable future. By his insistence on strict and impartial justice, by making the government more efficient, far-sighted, and responsive, Curzon hoped to perpetuate and strengthen the foundations of British power, to cause it to be regarded as indispensable, a state of affairs which he sincerely believed to be in India's best interests.

On balance Britain did not send his superior to India in the 90 years that separated the Mutiny and independence. In a farewell speech he spoke eloquently of his conception of Britain's duty as an imperial power, of his conviction that her work was righteous and enduring:

"A hundred times in India have I said to myself, 'Oh that to every Englishman in this country, as he ends his work, might be truthfully applied the phrase "Thou hast loved righteousness and hated iniquity."' No man has, I believe, ever served India faithfully of whom that could not be said. All other triumphs are tinsel and sham. Perhaps there are few of us who make anything but a poor approximation to that ideal. But let it be our ideal all the same . . . to remember that the Almighty has placed your hand on the greatest of his ploughs, in whose furrow the nations of the future are germinating and taking shape, to drive the blade a little forward in your time, and to feel that somewhere among these millions you have left a little justice or happiness or prosperity, a sense of manliness or moral dignity, a spring of patriotism, a dawn of intellectual enlightenment or a stirring of duty where it did not exist before— that is enough, that is the Englishman's justification in India. It is good enough for his watchword while he is here, for his epitaph when he is gone. I have worked for no other aim. Let India be my judge."

—*Michael Edwardes, David Dilks*

IV. The Mystique of Empire

During the last three decades of the Victorian Age Britons became conscious as never before of their imperial role. Where once the very word "imperialism" carried an unpleasant (and un-English) taint of military despotism, it was now acclaimed—by such as Lord Curzon—as the expression of an ennobling ideal.

This imperial mystique took many forms and operated on many levels. At the higher altitudes were historians, philosophers, and politicians who, speaking to their equals, propagandized for Empire for the most practical of reasons—to insure its health and survival. The 1870s saw the birth of the imperial federation movement. In the course of the next two decades a large number of schemes were put forward, mostly by the Liberals, for binding the white colonies—Canada, South Africa, Australia, New Zealand—much more closely to the motherland by means of a federal system before they went their own way and were beyond recall. It was widely believed that such a system was a practical possibility now that distance had been "abolished" by the steamship and the telegraph.

The federationist case found its most forceful expression in *The Expansion of England* (1883), a set of lectures originally delivered to Cambridge undergraduates by Professor of Modern History Sir John Seeley, and in the writings of James Anthony Froude, notably in *Oceana* (1886). Like many federationists, Seeley took pains to dissociate himself from what he termed the "bombastic" school of imperialism. His conclusions, he claimed, were based on a sober analysis of the facts, yet he had little to say about the concrete difficulties facing his scheme—he left out of account, for instance, the growth of nationalism that was operating so strongly in the older colonies. His talk of imperial unity was simply an expression of faith in England's continuing worldwide mission and as such it was extremely influential.

Froude was, unlike Seeley, much preoccupied with race and with the transmission of rugged "Saxon" virtues. Among other things, this made him a determined advocate of white supremacy, so much so that while visiting South Africa he frequently took the part of the racialist Boers against the British.

It was, of course, generally true that imperialism rested on racialist assumptions, and there were those who elevated these assumptions into an ideology based on Darwin's *Origin of Species*. The theory of evolution through natural selection and the survival of the fittest provided a rationale for the claim that the very existence of the Empire proved that the British were selected by Nature to rule. Others saw British superiority as something sacred to be preserved at all costs in the face of threats from inferior races. In *National Life and Character,* Australian C. H. Pearson argued that coloured men—especially Asiatics—could insidiously undercut and undersell white labour, which should therefore be carefully protected. Pearson's views were largely responsible for the adoption of the "White Australia" policy barring non-white immigration.

Less systematic racial doctrines obtained an ever more widespread hearing. From the time of Sir Charles Dilke's *Greater Britain* (1868), for example, it was increasingly argued that the English-speaking peoples, if they worked in unison, had it in their power to inherit the earth. Occasionally the Germans were allowed to join the club—it was not just a private whim that led Cecil Rhodes to set aside a number of Rhodes scholarships for them.

Many prophets of imperialism, notably Seeley and Froude, transferred to the idea of Empire emotions which they would otherwise probably have invested in religion. In both men, imperialism came to be as much a substitute for Christianity as a means of promoting it. And in a man like Kipling, descended on both sides of his family from Methodist ministers, it is not hard to see an Evangelical sensibility still at work after it had been almost completely severed from orthodox religious belief. Kipling's God, whoever and wherever He may be, imposes a stern and often thankless code of Duty on His Children, and in running an Empire they are essentially carrying out the Law of a quasi-religious morality. Such a doctrine was no less powerful for being vague. At its best, it pointed to an authentic tradition of devotion and service; at its worst the portentous capital letters suggested a rhetorical smoke screen, and the Law could sound ominously like the law of the jungle—or the law of natural selection.

The men who actually ran the Empire also contributed to the development of the mystique. The late Victorian and early 20th-Century imperial proconsuls—Cromer, Curzon, and scores of lesser lights—had a lofty sense of their own calling. This was particularly true of the Indian administration. Though sons still followed their fathers into the civil service, suitable connections alone were no longer enough. Brains, and an ability to do well in examinations, were also necessary.

The all-important preliminary examination for the Indian Civil Service was a stiff one covering a wide range of standard subjects, from natural sciences to ancient history. The "competition wallah," as the old East India Company hands dubbed him, usually had a classical training, as often as not at Oxford. The actual details of administration they mostly learned as they went along, but from their elitist education they had imbibed, almost without thinking about it, a picture of themselves as a superior caste, charged with the duty of preserving civilization in India and uniquely well qualified for the task. They were "the Guardians," as the author and former Indian Civil Service official Philip Woodruff calls them, borrowing the term from Plato's account of his ideal, self-perpetuating aristocracy.

The Colonial Civil Service, which supplied officials to imperial areas outside India, was a much less august, much less tightly organized affair. There were no qualifying examinations, and candidates were selected by interview, with a premium on "soundness" rather than academic prowess. It was the proconsuls of the I.C.S., therefore, who were the vanguard of the imperial ethic. They wrote copiously, and they presented themselves as guardians of a sacred trust, master-builders of civilization. The very word "proconsul" reinforced echoes of Roman grandeur that were meant to be stirred by the official language of imperialism, and comparisons between Britain and Rome were commonplace throughout the late Victorian period.

The imperial mystique was kept going by its own momentum. Education, propaganda, and popular culture drummed in the message, colouring attitudes from early childhood onwards and ensuring the correct responses.

A special part in this was reserved for the public schools, a prime function of which was the shaping of an administrative caste. Not that this had any very direct effect on what they taught or the way they were run. Future administrators prepared themselves for their qualifying examinations later, at the university or at a crammer. It was a question, rather, of the whole public-school ethos as it had evolved by the late Victorian period, with its emphasis on manliness (where an earlier generation had stressed godliness), on character (as opposed, all too often, to intellectual ability), and on sport, on submission, on authority. As an Old Boy, the former pupil inherited a set of enduring loyalties. The values of the public-school code constituted the working philosophy of most servants of the Empire; as E. M. Forster says in *A Passage to India*, they were designed never to go bad, "even in the tropics." Despite the official trappings and insignia, the most potent emblems of the imperial creed were the stiff upper lip, the straight bat, and the old school tie.

The public schools, though intended to turn out gentlemen in general rather than Empire-builders in particular, helped form the imperial outlook and the Empire in turn increasingly gave them their rationale. Headmasters tended to make a cult of patriotism for, although the chapel and the sermon were still an essential part of school routine, religion was no longer the driving force that it once had been.

Distinguished visitors, too, waxed eloquent on the imperial theme. It was an address given to the boys at Eton by Sir James Stephen that first kindled in the ambitious young Curzon a sense of his own destiny. Half a century after the Canadian imperialist George Parkin lectured at Harrow, Winston Churchill and Leopold Amery could both recall word for word his appeal to the English sense of duty as he compared the rallying cry of imperial federation with Nelson's signal at Trafalgar.

The literature of public-school life enshrined the same fierce conviction. In Horace Annesley Vachell's *The Hill* (1905), a classic specimen of the public-school story, the exemplary Desmond is first licked into shape by Harrow and then, after enlisting in the army, goes off to lay down his life on the South African veld. There were poets, too, anxious to celebrate the link between school and Empire. The best known of them, Sir Henry Newbolt, often wrote as though the most fundamental purpose of a public-school education was to prepare boys, if necessary, for the supreme sacrifice. In *He Fell Among Thieves*, the young officer who is about to be killed by marauding tribesmen recalls "the School Close, sunny and green" and his early athletic triumphs, while in the dire situation described in *Vitaï Lampada*—

> The sand of the desert is sodden
> and red . . .
> The Gatling's jammed and the
> Colonel dead

—the broken ranks are rallied by a boyish cry of

Play up! play up! and play the game!

Even at the time, and even among the ranks of professed imperialists, there must have been many who found it hard to keep a straight face. Yet Newbolt's melodramatics, however lurid, do point to an authentic aspect of the imperial outlook, the quality that made Anglo-Indians talk of the power-struggle for mastery in central Asia as "the Great Game," or which led the American philosopher George Santayana to describe the 19th-Century Englishman as "the schoolboy master of the world."

Such works are examples of the late 19th-Century infusion of imperial sentiment into popular culture, in which the real flavour of Empire at home is to be found: in music-hall songs, advertisements, memorials, mementoes, and, more lastingly, in prose; boys' papers, and verse.

The interest of the British public as a whole in Empire was generated by the less respectable branches of literature. In the popular imagination, adventure stories, most of them now unreadable, and poetry, some of it the most appalling doggerel, counted for more than academic treatises. The *Boy's Own Paper*, Haggard, Henty, Kipling: these loomed large in the public mind as the Empire reached apogee.

The way for the novel of specifically imperial adventure was paved in 1883 by Robert Louis Stevenson's *Treasure Island*. It established a vogue for a new kind of writing: the adventure novel written for boys, but also offering easy, enjoyable reading for adults. The Education Act of 1870, which established state schools for children up to 13, had created a newly literate generation eager for light reading. Public library returns show that by the 1880s, when over three-quarters of the books borrowed were novels, readers seldom called on Henry James and Thomas Hardy, but on the "sun-drenched, blood-stained prose" of the imperial adventure writers.

Penny weekly papers and boys' magazines, too, show the movement towards imperial thinking. The prime example was the *Boy's Own Paper*. From its birth in 1879 until its demise in 1967, the *B.O.P.* provided entertainment and practical advice for generations of middle-class British schoolboys. It was considered by parents to be "safe" reading; did it not carry fiction and articles by clergymen, headmasters, and baronets as well as a clutch of popular authors?

One of the *B.O.P.*'s most prolific contributors was Dr. William Gordon Stables, whose habit of wearing full Highland dress, complete with kilt and sporran, made him a well-known figure in Fleet Street. Stables specialized in tracing the arduous but inevitably triumphant climb of an ordi-

The imperial thrillers in the *Boy's Own Paper* were fair game for *Punch* in an 1882 satire: Wet Bob of Eton nearly becoming a "half-eaten" boy.

nary lad to the top of his profession. He was the author of such *B.O.P.* serials as *For England Home and Beauty, Frank Hardinge: Adventures from Torrid Zones to Regions of Perpetual Snow,* and *From the Slums to the Quarter Deck.* Stables also wrote a regular advice column, which appeared to be chiefly devoted to recommending cold baths as a universal panacea.

The *B.O.P.* was only the most popular of a wave of publications—including *Boys of England, The Union Jack, Chums, Sons of Britannia, The Young Englishman,* and *The Captain*—that specialized in bloody, naturalistic, and heroic tales of adventure set in the wilder parts of the British Empire. In today's terms all these boys' magazines broadcasted amazingly naive and offensive views on race. Negroes were usually allowed to play only two basic roles: comic buffoons or screaming savages. In stories, jokes, and il-

lustrations they were singled out for pain, death, and humiliation. Chinese were also favourite subjects of racial stereotype, stock figures for brutal, sadistic treatment at the hands of English public schoolboys, "reptiles" to be strung up by their pigtails.

These sentiments could not be termed consciously vindictive; they were more a reflection of a common attitude, attempts to express differences of culture and colour in terms that had been unquestioned for generations. Such stories were meant to be enjoyed, not to win converts, and it would be misguided to take them too solemnly. At the same time, who can say how much they did to shape their readers' underlying picture of the world as a place to be dominated by the British and their Empire?

The growing Victorian public schoolboy would probably, after abandoning the *B.O.P.,* have gradu-

ated to the two supreme imperialist novelists, Rider Haggard and G. A. Henty.

Though the two are often mentioned in the same breath, Haggard's books are the richer and more complex. He had a deep knowledge of Zulu history and folklore, for example, which he acquired from his career as a colonial civil servant in South Africa. After the Zulu War of 1879 and the British defeat by the Boers at Majuba Hill in 1881, Haggard decided to leave Natal and return to England to pursue a legal career. His version of the events leading up to these wars—which is highly critical of the Gladstone government's abandonment of the Transvaal to the despised Boers—can be found in his first book, *Cetewayo and his White Neighbours,* published in 1882.

In 1885 Haggard, then 28, was called to the Bar and went to London. Soon

MY STRUGGLE WITH A TIGER.

By Charles Jamrach,
St. George's-in-the-East.

IT is now a good many years ago, when one morning a van-load of wild beasts, which I had bought the previous day from a captain in the London Docks, who brought them from the East Indies, arrived at my repository in Bett Street, St. George's-in-the-East. I myself superintended the unloading of the animals, and had given directions to my men to place a den containing a very ferocious full-grown Bengal tiger, with its iron-barred front close against the wall.

They were proceeding to take down a den with leopards, when all of a sudden I heard a crash, and to my horror found the big tiger had pushed out the back part of his den with his hind-quarters, and was walking down the yard into the street, which was then full of people watching the arrival of this curious merchandise. The tiger, in putting his forepaws against the iron bars in front of the den, had exerted his full strength to push with his back against the boards behind, and had thus succeeded in gaining his liberty.

As soon as he got into the street, a boy of about nine years of age put out his hand to stroke the beast's back, when the tiger seized him by the shoulder and run down the street with the lad hanging on his jaws. This was done in less time than it takes me to relate; but when I saw the boy being carried off in this manner, and witnessed the panic that had seized hold of the people, without further thought I dashed after the brute, and got hold of him by the loose skin of the back of his neck. I was then of a more vigorous frame than now, and had plenty of pluck and dash in me.

I tried thus to stop his further progress, but he was too strong for me, and dragged

OUR BOYS' NOVELIST.

BEING STORIES OF WILD SPORT AND STIRRING ADVENTURE, FOR THE AMUSEMENT AND INSTRUCTION OF THE YOUTHS OF ALL NATIONS.

WET BOB, ON HIS WAY BACK TO ETON, SURPRISED BY THE FOREST KINGS.

WET BOB;
OR,

THE ADVENTURES OF A LITTLE ETON BOY AMONGST THE HOTWHATA CANNIBALS.

(By the Author of "*The Three Young Benchers, and How they all Got the Woolsack,*" "*From Back Yard to Yard-arm,*" &c., &c.)

CHAP. XXXIV.* (*Continued.*)

The jungle grew denser at every step. Bob, however, was still heading the party; his keen, clear, penetrating youthful vision

* Editor to Author of Wet Bob.—The last chapter was numbered IV. Why is this XXXIV.? Some mistake?
Author of Wet Bob to Editor.—All right, and no mistake. It's a sensational story calculated to make you jump. The effect was so powerful even on myself, that I jumped from IV. to XXXIV. Every nautical Novel-reader, or Skipper, will be able to understand this. I'll fill up the interval if you like. Say the word.
Editor to Author of Wet Bob.—Oh, no. Quite understand. Admirable finish! Never was so

flashing sun-signals into the deepest recesses of the gloomy forest. At one time he would stir up a flock of wild mongeese; at another as suddenly bring out an opera-buffalo; and the startled creature would look for a moment as if it intended to run. But nothing ever came of it.

"It's all my eye," said Bob, and they pressed on again.

Then the Provost halted.

It was now three years since he had—when travelling in Central Africa, with a circular ticket, in search of his daughter—been captured by the Hotwhata Cannibals and forced to join their band. He had to adopt their savage dress. This, at least, was a feather in his cap.

But he determined to escape.

Tortured every morning, he was allowed the privilege of lounging about on his own hook. At last he got off it. He escaped, and here his knowledge as an Algebraist materially assisted him, as, while wandering about, he contrived to subsist on the square roots he himself extracted. Then he turned to history, and lived on dates. Such are some of the advantages of a good education! The figures came readily enough to hand, but the diet soon cost him his own.

afterwards, on a train journey, he suggested to one of his brothers that Stevenson's *Treasure Island* did not deserve the high praise it had received. His brother promptly offered to bet him a shilling that he could not do anything as good himself. Rider took the wager and that very evening sat down and began to write a tale of adventure for boys. He completed it in six weeks. When *King Solomon's Mines* was published in 1885, Haggard's fortune was made; more than 650,000 copies in one form or another were printed in his lifetime.

King Solomon's Mines is an astonishing adventure story. The first to exploit an African setting, it has excitement, suspense, and massacres on almost every page. The heroic tale it told of Allan Quatermain, Sir Henry Curtis, Captain John Good, and the mysterious witch Gagool had a huge appeal. It enchanted and thrilled critics and readers alike. Allan Quatermain, the hero of 18 of Haggard's 58 volumes, is the Englishman of Empire, the imperial crusader carrying the White Man's Burden of Anglo-Saxon justice to the far corners of the earth. Through him, Haggard cast the medieval romances of Sir Walter Scott in an imperial Victorian mould and inaugurated a new school of romantic fiction.

Haggard was heavily influenced by Darwin's theory of evolution, but not in a glib way. Unlike many of his contemporaries (including Henty), he did not deduce from Darwin's theory that the British were racially superior simply because they were politically dominant. For him, different races—European, African, Chinese—could each be superior in their own way, and he often lauds the achievements and potential of African society to the detriment of Western civilization.

It is difficult, however, to completely exculpate Rider Haggard from the charge of over-stressing violence. *The Quarterly Review* accused him of fill-

A typical Rider Haggard novel began with "Into the Unknown" (top). Later a loyal Zulu saves our hero. Then it was into a volcano via underground river.

ing his pages with "blood and barbarism." The *Pall Mall Budget* wrote off *Nada the Lily* as "drenched, sodden, dripping with blood." There are indeed gory passages galore: arms severed, blood gushing from arteries, beheadings and battles without quarter.

His audience was not overly concerned, and sales continued to spiral throughout the 1890s. By propagating a concept of adventure inextricably tied to the Dark Continent, Haggard helped cloak British imperialism in Africa with imaginative innocence, drawing a veil of romance and high adventure over a part of the world that became the scene of some distinctly sordid transactions.

George Alfred Henty's appeal, unlike that of his contemporary Haggard, was almost entirely restricted to a juvenile audience. Henty's major claim to attention rests upon the 80-odd historical adventure stories he wrote for boys between 1870 and his death in 1902. About a quarter of these deal with the British Empire.

Henty himself led an adventurous life mainly as a foreign correspondent, which took in the Crimean War, the campaigns of Garibaldi, and the Paris Commune as well as various imperial excursions. Without preaching any high-flown political lessons, he implied that the Empire was the most natural setting for displays of manly valour.

The very titles of his books constitute a miniature imperial gazetteer, punctuated by appropriate battle-cries: *With Clive in India, St. George for England, Maori and Settler, By Right of Conquest, With Wolfe in Canada, The Dash for Khartoum.* A Henty hero might expect to find himself *On the Irrawaddy* or *Under Wellington's Command.* In *For Name and Fame* he accompanies Roberts to Kabul; and although one of his many imitators was the first off the mark *With Roberts to Kandahar,* Henty regained his customary lead *With Roberts to Pretoria* and *With Buller in Natal.* Henty stuck, almost literally, to his guns. He was preoccupied with the deeds that won the Empire rather than the men who administered it, and needless to say neither he nor his readers were great-

ly concerned with the more mundane underpinnings of imperialism. As one critic has observed, "he never took a hopeful lad *With Barnato to the Diamond Diggings* or celebrated *A Venture in Argentine Rails.*"

With their stereotyped heroes and mechanical plots, Henty believed that his books helped to foster in the young "the imperial spirit"—a combination of the will to rule, heroism, and the moral code of the British Christian gentleman. If popularity is any guide, he accomplished his purpose. According to one of his publishers, for many years Henty's books enjoyed a circulation of from 150,000 to 250,000 copies a year in Britain and 50,000 in America. By the 1890s he dominated the field of juvenile literature: school libraries limited boys to three Hentys a week, so popular had they become.

Henty provided a contribution to the mythology of the British Empire that was very much his own: the bovine public schoolboy hero. The Henty hero is the product of an assembly-line process that produced characters like Yorke Harberton, a "typical public school boy," who had the good fortune to go *With Roberts to Pretoria.* He was above all else "a good specimen of the class by which Britain has been built up, her colonies formed, and her battle-fields won—a class in point of energy, fearlessness, and the spirit of adventure, and a readiness to face and overcome all difficulties unmatched in the world." He was athletic, manly, and a believer in the "open-air life." Rather than a personality he was an abstraction of all the virtues of the Victorian belief in "character."

Despite the popularity of the low-grade works produced by Haggard and Henty, the British Empire could occasionally be the setting for literary creations of real insight and imagination. This is most evident in the case of Rudyard Kipling.

Kipling was born in Bombay in 1865 and—like most Anglo-Indian children —was sent back to England for education. As a young man he worked in the 1880s on Anglo-Indian newspapers in Lahore, Simla, and Allahabad. In 1888 he published *Plain Tales From*

the Hills, which established his reputation as a writer on the British in India. In *Kim,* written over a decade after he left India, Kipling tellingly displayed his fascination with the multitudinous variety of races, creeds, and religions scattered over the subcontinent.

Kipling's ballads, too, brought him immense fame. His *Barrack Room Ballads,* which owe much in technique and content to music-hall songs, were published when Kipling was only 23 and made him the most talked-about figure on the London literary scene. In 1897, having spent four years in America, he settled down in his beloved Sussex. Apart from the Boer War, the seminal experiences that were to determine the shape of his art were already in the past. He was only 32.

For Kipling the Empire brought with it moral responsibility as well as an awareness of grandeur and achievement. The concept of the sense of responsibility and its values are served up in his concept of the Law. The Law is central to nearly everything he wrote and the key to an understanding of his imperialism. The concept implied a certain code of conduct and a hierarchy of values transcending individual cultures. Set out in the poem "McAndrew's Hymn" (1893) the code, within a generalized Christian framework, involved Law, Order, Duty, Restraint, Obedience, and Discipline. The forces of social control imposed a code of behaviour, a standard of conduct that the administrative class in India, which Kipling so much admired, was expected to uphold in order to sustain its moral integrity in an unceasing conflict with the alien environment.

The Law also symbolized the hope of a better arrangement of life for the subjects of the British Empire, to be brought about through the paternalistic instrument of imperialism. Peace, Order, Public Works (the fruits of imperial rule in India), Progress, and Civilization followed in their wake as a natural corollary of imperialism.

Kipling's command to the imperialists, as he put it in "A Song of the English" in 1893, was basically quite simple:

The wickedly ironical Max Beerbohm drew a jingoistic Rudyard Kipling on an outing "along with Britannia, 'is gurl."

*Keep ye the Law—be swift in all
    obedience—
Clear the land of evil, drive the
    road and bridge the ford.
Make ye sure to each his own
That he reap where he hath sown;
By the peace among Our peoples let
    men know we serve the Lord!*

The men who obeyed the Law in whatever age, engineers, railway-builders, administrators—the "doers" —were the men who compelled Kipling's admiration.

From being one of the finest and earliest short-story writers about Anglo-Indian life, Kipling developed into a prophet of imperialism. But his imperialism is highly moral and should not be lightly dismissed. Kipling preached the doctrines of imperialism in the interests of good government. The oft-quoted "Recessional" (1897) urges a Britain "drunk with sight of power" that holds domain "over palm and pine" to be careful lest, without adherence to the Law, "all our pomp of yesterday" becomes "one with Nineveh and Tyre!" The famous reference to "lesser breeds without the Law" draws a distinction between those imperial nations who submit in all humility to the Law and the more arrogant "breeds," like the Belgians in the Congo, who refused to observe its imperative demands and are thus outside the pale of civilization.

"The White Man's Burden," written in 1899, is another Kipling poem calling the imperialist power—in this case America about to take over the Philippines—to a sense of the duties and responsibilities, as well as the economic rewards, that possession of an empire imposes on the rulers as well as the ruled:

*Take up the White Man's burden—
Send forth the best ye breed—
To bind your sons to exile
To serve your captive's need;
To wait in heavy harness
On fluttered folk and wild—
Your new caught, sullen peoples,
Half devil and half child.*

Kipling's imperialism was based on his profound conviction that the sacrifices and responsibilities that ruling imposed on the rulers helped to form the character of the British élite. This led in turn to less admirable political implications. Faith in the British Empire and in the corps of disciplined hierarchical, dedicated, and hard-working officials he had met as a journalist in the India of the 1880s convinced him of the British right to rule and strengthened him in his opposition in later life to modern, urbanized, democratic, liberal society.

No individual author, however widely read, could hope to compete in influence with the Press, which in the 1890s fanned the flames of the New Imperialism. The first great penny daily, the *Daily Telegraph,* had as its pundit on policies affecting India Sir Edwin Arnold, a staunch imperialist. The *Telegraph* also made a specialty of subsidizing expeditions into Darkest Africa, making a regular contributor out of the explorer Henry Stanley.

By the 1880s the more garish possibilities of popular journalism were also being enlarged by W. T. Stead in the *Pall Mall Gazette.* Stead combined high-mindedness with prurience and a flair for the sensational that persisted to the end; he died appropriately in the sinking of the *Titanic.* Personal conviction and editorial astuteness alike led him to promote the imperial cause with vigour. He played an important part in building up Cecil Rhodes's reputation as a colossus. "If you could imagine an emperor of old Rome," he wrote, "crossed with one of Cromwell's Ironsides, and the result brought up at the feet of Ignatius Loyola, you would have an amalgam not unlike that which men call Cecil Rhodes."

Although Stead and others like him had helped to lay the ground, the outstanding single landmark in the rise of mass journalism remains indisputably the founding of the *Daily Mail* by Alfred Harmsworth in 1896. Selling at a half-penny, proclaiming itself on the front page "The Busy Man's Paper," by 1900 the *Mail* had achieved the unprecedented circulation of a million. Its readers were left in no doubt where its political sympathies lay. It stood, Harmsworth wrote, "for the power, supremacy and greatness of the British Empire"; it was above all "the embodiment and mouthpiece of the imperial idea." Here, as nowhere else, the voice of the New Imperialism could be heard in its full brashness.

The Diamond Jubilee of 1897 was commemorated in a special number printed throughout in gold ink. The British reconquest of the Sudan was covered by the paper's star correspondent, G. W. Steevens, and Kitchener was put on a pedestal from which a later generation of statesmen found him hard to dislodge. The Boer War called forth further spectacular efforts. When Harmsworth—soon to become Lord Northcliffe—started the *Overseas Daily Mail* in 1904 he was interested "in establishing it as a bond of empire, a newspaper connection between the mother country and the scattered hundreds of thousands of Britons in the far corners of the world."

It would be a mistake to assume, as the Press lords themselves discovered, that the popular Press had a political influence commensurate with its sales. The ruling classes still paid much closer attention to the papers and periodicals that catered to educated opinion, and at this level, too, the various brands of imperialist thought found their dedicated spokesmen. Above all there was the voluble J. L. Garvin, editor of the *Observer*, best connected of imperialist leader-writers and, in his later years, official biographer of Colonial Secretary Joseph Chamberlain. The public served by such men was the one that counted politically, and also one that tended to look askance at the antics of the new popular Press.

Another element in the popular, turn-of-the-century imperialist feeling was provided by the music halls. It was there, during a threatened imperial conflict with Russia, that "jingoism" was introduced as a term for patriotic, imperialist xenophobia:

We don't want to fight,
But by Jingo! if we do
We've got the ships, we've got the men
And got the money too!

There were innumerable songs about sons of the sea and Soldiers of the Queen, and countless "descriptive vocalists" who kept alive the legends of Lucknow. One popular performer, Leo Dryden, was known as "the Kipling of the Halls" on account of such colonial-cum-patriotic numbers as *The Great White Mother* and *The Gallant Gordon Highlanders*. The Boer War produced a spate of topical songs—*For England's Bit of Bunting, The Boers Have Got My Daddy*, and dozens of others like them.

Stories, poems, the Press, songs: all no doubt had a cumulative effect. But a note of caution is necessary before concluding that large sections of the populace were in the grip of an unprecedented chauvinism. The whole question of whether or not imperialism had a genuine mass following remains a vexed one. It is hard to say how much influence all the publicity had in practice, or to what extent this is a question of momentary enthusiasms as against rooted convictions. When we consider imperialist sentiment as a whole it is worth bearing in mind George Orwell's comment that "'What Have I done for You, England, my England?' is essen-

Victoria's crest as Queen-Empress of India hangs in the House of Lords.

tially a middle-class query; almost any working man would follow it up with What has England done for Me?'"

For most Englishmen, imperialism was something in the air rather than a systematic set of beliefs, and the Empire was not so much a direct concern as part of the general décor against which they lived their everyday lives. They might be reminded of it at any time in a hundred different ways—by a street name, a pub sign, a bit of slang, a travel poster, a war memorial, a box of toy soldiers, the fashion for ostrich feathers or cashmere shawls or the kind of gaudy bric-a-brac which can still be found in the dustier corners of any antique shop. Schoolboys learned the finer points of imperial geography from stamp-collecting; Piccadilly Circus was the "Hub of the Empire"; in some quarters, Sir Edward Elgar's melody from *Pomp and Circumstance* set to words by A. C. Benson as *Land of Hope and*

Glory, with its promise of limitless expansion ("Wider still and wider shall thy bounds be set . . ."), virtually assumed the status of a second national anthem. Advertisers in particular exploited imperial motifs for all they were worth.

Some of these reminders of Empire were explicit, others indirect or vague, but all of them reinforced a sense of exotic grandeur and power. The imperial mood at the high noon of Empire defies easy generalizations. It was compounded of many factors, among them earnestness and frivolity, greed and self-sacrifice, complacency and instability. Much of what passed for an imperial mystique was rationalization or whitewash. Yet without a mystique there might well have been less willingness to recognize that power entailed responsibility, and the Empire would probably have been a harsher place than it was.

—*John Gross, J. O. Springhall*

Chapter Eight

WELLSPRINGS OF POWER

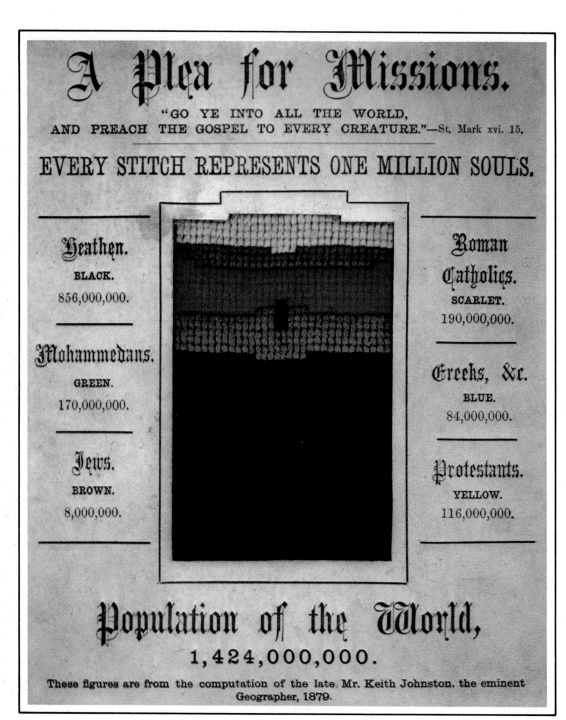

One of the motive forces behind imperialism was the urge to spread the Gospel among the heathen, and this fund-raising advertisement presented a vivid picture of the enormity of the missionaries' task.

I. The Missionary Impulse

In the Victorians' pantheon of heroes and heroines, few ranked so high as the missionaries. In pursuit of their evangelical work brave men and women were decimated by malaria and yellow fever in Africa, boiled and eaten in the Pacific islands, tarred and feathered in the Caribbean, massacred in India during the Mutiny of 1857 and in China during the Boxer Rebellion of 1900. None of these disasters deterred them, and the newly dedicated were always ready to fill the ranks of the fallen. In its heyday the missionary movement was one of the cutting edges of Empire. It provided much of the Christian civilization in the overseas colonies for which politicians in England smugly took credit; an estimated 90 per cent of the educational and health services in the Afro-Asian Empire were staffed by missionaries and financed by their supporters at home.

The missionary movement was hardly a flicker in the darkness before the end of the 18th Century. Throughout the period of Empire which ended with American independence, very little was done to take Christianity to the unconverted world overseas. The Anglican chaplains and missionaries dispatched to India, America, and the West Indies were primarily concerned with the moral and spiritual health of settlers and officials who were already Christians rather than with making converts among the natives.

The figure most responsible for the dramatic end-of-the-century change was John Wesley. Wesley spent two frustrating years in the 1730s as an Anglican cleric in the American colony of Georgia. He converted not a single soul to Christianity, and ended his stay in the New World with doubts about his own beliefs. In England,

however, he found the certainty he was searching for. Like St. Paul in biblical Palestine, he saw the Truth in a sudden flash of inspiration. Armed with a new, unshakable faith, he began an astonishing career that brought a dramatic religious revival to Britain and a new, forceful approach to the unconverted in foreign parts.

The faith that Wesley found was Evangelical Puritanism, whose key concept was the literal truth of the Bible. If the Bible was the Word of God, he argued, every Briton was doomed unless he repented. The force of this clear, urgent message was electric. Preaching in halls and prisons and fields among the toiling, uneducated masses, Wesley was soon drawing hysterical crowds of up to 80,000.

The British Establishment was shocked and disgusted at this emotional Puritanism. It challenged the prevailing ethos, the tolerant scepticism and pleasant hendonism of the Age of Enlightenment. It looked like a revolution and the ruling classes treated it as such. The demagogic fury released by the French Revolution helped to change their minds. It seemed as if frighteningly egalitarian slogans from France would contaminate the English working classes. Suddenly Wesleyan doctrines began to appear a positive godsend to British political and social stability. For Wesleyanism—known as Methodism after its adherents' resolution to conduct their lives by "rule and method"—was a gospel that sanctified the values of the new bourgeoisie: thrift, hard work, temperance, discreet ambition, respect for authority. Buoyed up by the prestige of a few conversions among the upper classes, the new religion spread like wildfire, building up a faithful home constituency that

provided lasting support for the missionary movement overseas.

Lady Huntington, one of Wesley's adherents, once told him: "Attempt nothing less than all mankind." He could hardly have imagined to what extent that message would come true. Wesley died in 1791, but the Evangelical Revolution he started did not stop short at the British Isles. Countless converts prepared to obey literally Christ's command set down in the Bible: "Go ye into all the world and preach the Gospel to every creature."

Almost providentially, new and fertile fields for missionary endeavour presented themselves. The discoveries of Captain Cook, the victories during the Napoleonic Wars that brought new acquisitions of territory to the Empire, the anti-slave-trade campaign headed by William Wilberforce—all offered fresh challenges to the variety of Protestant churches that became part of the Evangelical movement. In swift succession the major organizations for preaching to the heathen overseas were founded: in 1792 the Baptist Missionary Society, in 1795 the Congregationalist-sponsored London Missionary Society, in 1799 the Anglican Church Missionary Society, in 1804 the inter-denominational British and Foreign Bible Society.

The foot soldiers of the Evangelical Revolution sallied forth to do battle wherever the enemy was to be found. It made no difference to these warriors whether they fought sophisticated higher religions such as Islam, Buddhism, or Hinduism in Africa and Asia, or pure primitive worship in Australasia, the South Seas, and Canada. Like all impatient revolutionaries, they were convinced they had to be cruel to be kind, that they had to clear away a lot of rubbish in

The mass baptism of slaves in Jamaica caused an uproar among planters, and in 1791 the missionaries responsible were arrested.

order to bring the light of Christianity, that even if their work initially created a spiritual desert, so be it. The uprooting was essential if true religion was to be securely planted.

Until the 1860s few missionaries were ordained. Very few had received secondary, let alone higher, education. For example, the London Missionary Society task force that landed at Matavai Bay, Tahiti, in 1797 included only four ordained clergymen. The rest were butchers, carpenters, weavers, tailors, harness-makers, bricklayers, and shopkeepers. Together with some wives and children they formed a model Christian community that would set an example to the idle, sensual, blood-thirsty islanders of the Pacific. Robert Moffat, the great L.M.S. missionary who went in 1816 to the Bechuana people in South Africa, among whom he laboured for nearly 50 years, had little education and no formal theological training. Mary Slessor, whose work in Africa won her the name "the white Queen of Okoyong," sailed for Old Calabar in 1876 with but three months of instruction from a Presbyterian clergyman.

These keen, fearless evangelists got small wages: £20 a year plus seeds, some livestock, and agricultural implements in New Zealand, £60 a year for Mary Slessor as a "female agent." Yet often they were, as one of them put it, "little Protestant Popes . . . forced by self-imposed isolation to be prophet, priest and king rolled into one." Unofficial (and sometimes, like David Livingstone and Mary Slessor, official) British consuls, they made peace between warring tribes, legislated for their "subjects," and came home to enthrall big audiences with accounts of witch doctors, cannibal feasts, human sacrifices, harems, and the inexorable but hard-fought advance of Christian decency.

In India the missionaries faced stiff opposition from the all-powerful East India Company. The Company was dead set against missionary work among the Indians on the ground that it would cause civil disturbance. When William Carey, a Baptist village pastor, arrived in Bengal in 1793, he was treated as an illegal immigrant. The Company forced him and his com-

panions, Joshua Marshman, a schoolteacher, and William Ward, a printer, to seek refuge in the Danish colony of Serampore, near Calcutta.

The "Serampore Trio" toiled for 30 years translating the Bible into Bengali, Sanskrit, Marathi, and ten other languages. They also ran a college "for the instruction of Asiatic, Christian and other youth in Eastern Literature and European Science." Carey's study of classical Hindu texts triggered a Hindu literary renaissance.

For his scholarly efforts poor Carey reaped a harvest of criticism from both friend and foe. His sponsors frowned on his Bible translations, believing it unwise to open Protestant principles to the scrutiny of converts whose adherence to Christianity might be questionable. Charles Marsh, a former Madras barrister speaking for those who wanted India to remain "unspoiled," prophesied the likely outcome of missionary activity there: "I leave to those who are versed in moral calculations to decide . . . whether predestination and gin would be a compensation for the changes which will overcome Indian habits, morals, and religion."

For the Evangelicals, however, final success came in 1833 when, after a debate on the renewal of the Company's charter, India was opened to any missionaries who wished to go there.

Yet arguments about political disruption never lost their force with the rulers of India, even after control passed from Company to Crown. The missionaries were reckoned by the administration to have been largely responsible for the Indian Mutiny. Right up to the time of independence in 1947, despite most missionaries' hostility to the nationalist movement, the administration remained suspicious of them.

In the West Indies the missionaries were regarded as agents of the hated abolitionists. Even though the missionaries were carefully briefed before leaving England that "You are not sent to relieve the slaves from their servile condition but to offer them the consolations of religion," their mere presence was provocative. To slaveowners the pretense that the Negroes

would resign themselves to a purely spiritual equality—in itself an offensive notion to white colonials—was considered naive to the point of hypocrisy.

When missionary John Smith arrived in British Guiana in 1817, he was bluntly told by the Governor, "If you ever teach a negro to read and write and I hear of it, I will banish you from the colony immediately." Held responsible for a slave revolt in 1823, Smith was arrested, sentenced to death by court martial, and died in a cell in Colony House, Demerara, while awaiting confirmation of his sentence from London. His martyrdom was the subject of a heated Parliamentary debate and provided excellent emancipationist propaganda. Only after the abolition of slavery in 1833 did the attitude towards missionaries in the West Indies improve.

In Australia the first missionaries were free from government interference since the Governor, Arthur Phillip, was a thoroughgoing sceptic perfectly willing to make any use of Christianity if it could help insure a peaceful community. But they found other serious obstacles in their way. Richard Johnson, a graduate of Cambridge and therefore a notable exception to the general run of humble, artisan missionaries, began one of the toughest assignments in missionary history when he accompanied the first consignment of convicts to Botany Bay. Johnson's rough fellow passengers greeted him with ribald and violent hostility. But he had the help of the Rev. Samuel Marsden, a robust and persistent Puritan. Together Johnson and Marsden weathered the storm. In 1814 Marsden went on to found the first mission in New Zealand.

As the missionary movement became stronger so did opposition at home and abroad. Anti-imperialist "Little Englanders," agnostics who opposed conversion of the natives to any religion, humanists who argued that indigenous religious practices should be respected, anthropologists aghast at the suppression of long-established ways of life—all had criticisms to make of missionary work.

True believers in the lower echelons of the movement simply brushed aside the objections of these annoying people, but those who held positions of power in the missionary societies were less hasty. They were political realists who knew that only through clever manipulation of the techniques of persuasion could they ensure their freedom to work the overseas vineyards. To woo the rising middle classes, the backbone of Victorian society, their propaganda stressed the missionary role in multiplying commercial outlets (all those savages to be clothed and raised towards Western living standards) and inculcating the heathen with the gospel of hard work. To overcome government opposition, missionaries pointed out that their efforts produced political docility in the newly acquired territories.

Missionaries on furlough lost no chance to paint the "dark" side of native life in order to attract funds. Missionary meetings, with their tales of physical and moral squalor in Asia and Africa, were relished as edifying entertainments. Missionary magazines, depicting noble lives and self-sacrificing deaths, thrilled a huge pious-patriotic readership.

It was John Williams of the London Missionary Society who devised the indivisible trinity—Christianity, Commerce, Civilization—as justification for "meddling" in India and the Pacific. In *A Narrative of Missionary Enterprise in the South Sea Islands,* Williams bluntly stated that missionaries "in presenting the one great object to which their lives are consecrated . . . will keep in view whatever may promote the Commerce and Science as well as the Religious Glory of their beloved Country." To this end, Williams introduced the banana to Pacific islands where hitherto it had been unknown, and Anglican missionaries pioneered the planting of wheat in New Zealand.

In these efforts to convince the British people of the value of their work, the missionaries were remarkably successful. Most of them were peculiarly representative of their time, faithfully reflecting that mixture of pious self-righteousness and hard-headed pragmatism that characterized the Victorian era, and they had no difficulty amassing a vast group of supporters. In the 19th Century the missionary lobby in Britain headed a pressure group so large and so powerful that it became a kind of evangelical state within the state—often the bane of statesmen, diplomats, colonial administrators, and businessmen.

It was over Africa that the missionaries and their supporters became most baneful. Africa was the most important theatre of missionary operations, and having within their grasp an entire dark continent to be illuminated with the light of Christian civilization, the evangelists made every effort to prevent so exciting a project from being sabotaged. But

their task—to transform whole savage nations and peoples into model Victorians—was so vast that their own resources were inadequate. Consequently, they had to compromise in ways which proved most uncomfortable. For their own ends they became the allies of colonial authorities and even on occasion the instigators of imperial expansion, and so tarred themselves, in the view of later generations, with the brush of imperialism.

The missionaries realized that they alone could not protect their converts or their investments from the rival patriotic-religious attempts of other European powers or from undesirable commercial elements. Nor did they have sufficient prestige to win over African rulers. So they went cap in hand to the government. To maintain their shaky ascendancy in Sierra Leone, for example, they used all their influence to ensure an official British presence in the form of a naval squadron that patrolled the coast. During the African Scramble of the late 1880s, when the European powers disputed who was to have what part of Africa, Evangelical groups claimed that more than £200,000 had been spent in Nyasaland alone to "create a Christian nation" and pointed out that it would be a disgraceful waste to abandon this socio-economic investment. Such arguments were successful in helping convince Whitehall to take over sections of Africa.

It was during this period of Empire in Africa that missionaries proved their nuisance value. They were not content merely to pull strings in Whitehall. After a naval bombardment razed Old Calabar, the missionaries made rebuilding conditional upon the chief's full acceptance of missionary civilization. Delighted with their success in this instance, the missionaries then began to look with favour upon armed expeditions into the interior. By the 1890s these forays had become almost continuous, and with the aid of Maxims and repeating rifles the hinterlands were opened to missionary—and imperial—activity.

The availability of troops was a temptation to missionaries who for a long time had had to make diplo-matic concessions to Satan, acquiescing through weakness to un-Christian practices. They were soon tempted to go too far. Relying on the presence of colonial troops near by, Herbert Tugwell, the fiery C.M.S. Bishop of Equatorial West Africa, led a missionary commando force into Northern Nigeria where he was ignominiously halted by a native army. Frederick Lugard, the British administrator of Northern Nigeria, felt obliged to send a face-saving detachment of his already over-extended West African Frontier Force to rescue Tugwell.

From that moment on, missionary activity was severely restricted in the Muslim strongholds of Egypt, the Sudan, and the northern territories of West Africa. In non-Muslim areas, too, missionaries were now carefully watched by administrators who, like the traders, often saw them as troublesome fanatics. Colonialism had come to the side of the missionary, but it proved an often untrustworthy ally.

Compared with their pioneering days, the missionaries found themselves bound hand and foot by the colonial regimes they had asked to shore up their enterprises. A period of uneasy co-existence began. Many imperial bureaucrats openly preferred Islam to Christianity because there was no nonsense about democracy nor any attempt to produce bumptious "savvy boys," their contemptuous phrase for mission-educated African intellectuals. Officials conceded that there had to be some kind of Western schooling, if only to provide the necessary quota of clerks for commerce and the lower ranks of the civil service, so the missionary schools were allowed to continue to operate.

There was another change in missionary life as well—no longer were the living conditions so primitive. In their increasingly congenial stations the missionaries began to copy the living standards and segregationist ideology of colonial government—"equality in things spiritual, agreed divergence in things physical and material," as Lugard phrased it. Officials and businessmen were willing to put in an appearance at church for example's sake, but only if they did not have to worship with the natives. The separate churches which resulted were a symbol of racial apartness.

In the Pacific and the Far East the missionaries needed government help and protection just as they did in Africa. And here also their relations with government were uneasy. One minute the missionaries were pushing, the next they were pulling; one minute they were urging government intervention, the next they were demanding freedom from government interference.

In the South Sea islands the combination of dedicated missionary activity and heavy government protection produced astonishingly rapid results. In a short time the first Evangelical arrivals succeeded in demolishing age-old traditions, and in their place several generations of missionaries grimly substituted a semblance of Puritan life. But once this was achieved thoughtful missionaries began to have serious second thoughts about the value of Crown control.

In truth, force was still necessary to protect the islands against the threat of assorted riff-raff—the traders who sold guns and liquor, the "blackbirders" who kidnapped islanders to work as near-slaves on plantations and in pearl-diving ventures. The islanders murdered 30 innocent missionaries, the only scapegoats at hand, in reprisal for these blackbirding raids. Eventually London was pestered into passing the Pacific Islands Protection Act in 1872. It then had to be cajoled into implementing it and shown how to administer it.

One such persuader was the Reverend James Chalmers, whose chosen field was New Guinea. Chalmers was noted for his refusal to wear the top hat and funereal garments that made so many of his colleagues look like undertakers. He refused to condemn work on the Sabbath and he refused to Anglicize the New Guineans. "Christ," he said, "will receive them without adopting English customs." He was quite prepared to call for government protection when he thought it necessary, as when he summoned a British man-of-war to Port Moresby in 1878 to prevent Australian gold prospectors from ruthlessly pushing tribes-

A United Society for the Propagation of the Gospel dispensary in Africa in the 1890s featured an impressive array of medicines and even a microscope.

Mary Slessor

A working-class background and first-hand experience of poverty, hunger, and disease helped Mary Slessor to adapt with remarkable ease to missionary life in West Africa. Like most missionaries, she had experienced a dramatic conversion, a blinding revelation of God's purpose. Her calling was Africa.

She had common sense and an unshakable conviction in her cause. She lived with her people and ate their food, and she was free of the wide-spread missionary neurosis about clothes. She saw no sense in braving the tropical sun in the heavy, clumsy clothes Victorians thought essential for their health and reputations. As often as not she went about hatless and barefoot.

Mary's service on the Niger coast lasted nearly ten years, sandwiched around a term back home lecturing (which she found a torture) and teaching (at which she excelled). In 1888 she moved inland to work with the Okoyong, a tribe so wild that most missionaries considered them beyond redemption. Without fuss she devoted her energies to "daily mixing with the people," tackling every problem as it rose —teaching, treating the sick, nursing orphaned children, giving religious instruction. She was made British Vice-Consul in Okoyong. Her health failing, she went on to dispense her own brand of unorthodox justice among the Ibo and Ibibio.

When Mary Slessor died in 1915 she was granted a magnificent London funeral, with flags at half-mast and schools and offices closed—a fuss that would have appalled this blunt Scotswoman who hated ceremony.

men off their land. When he thought government help was not necessary, he resolutely refused it. With legendary bravery he went unarmed among head-hunting tribes famous for their savagery. His success as a peacemaker was such that the administrators of British New Guinea, annexed in 1884, did not need a single soldier to assist them.

China was a special case. The Celestial Empire was not a colony, nor even within the sphere of influence of any one European power. The missionaries' task was therefore a delicate one, beset with political complications.

Beginning in the mid-19th Century several of the Evangelical organizations sent pioneer groups to sell Christianity to this vast market of souls. The most picturesque and daring organization was the China Inland Mission, founded in 1865 by the Baptist James Hudson Taylor. The C.I.M. stressed the priority of "pure" (preaching) as opposed to "welfare" (classroom and hospital ward) evangelism. Hudson Taylor ruled his enormous empire with skill and tact—from China, not from London. But though his missionaries were ordered to keep clear of consular officials and "win their way by love alone," they inevitably caused bellicose incidents. In 1868 gunboats were ordered up the Yangtze to Hangchow, where the lives of the Taylors were said to be in danger.

Sir Rutherford Alcock, the British representative in Peking, was highly annoyed by the incident and suggested that "it would be decidedly for the peace of China if Christianity and its missionaries were, for the present at least, excluded altogether." His despatches drove the Foreign Secretary to complain in the House of Lords that "we are always on the brink of war, not on account of the violation of any British rights or of any injury to commerce, but on account of good but imprudent men." Yet in China missionaries were found indispensable as interpreters, in the widest sense, and political consultants. Even the Boxer uprising of 1900, during which more than 100 Protestant missionaries were killed, did not deter any of the societies.

Many critics have attacked the mis-

sionaries for their involvement with imperialism. They accuse them of being the forerunners of imperial expansion and, on occasion, its instigators, meddling in politics when they should have been concerned solely with religion. To what extent is this indictment justified?

It is true that missionaries often asked the government to intervene in native affairs. They summoned gunboats, they called in colonial troops, they demanded annexation. On the face of it, they behaved just like imperialists. They also tended to think like imperialists, for they were affected by the imperialist ethic that swept European society in the latter part of the 19th Century. Soon the missionary lobby in Britain openly admitted that the missions were implicated in the activities of commercial and political interests.

Eventually, it was hard to decide whether the missionaries were influencing the imperialists, or the imperialists influencing the missionaries. Joseph Chamberlain's aggressive speeches, Rudyard Kipling's exultant imperialist mystique borrowing missionary ideals and arguments, seemed to more excitable evangelists to contain the heart of the matter. It was exhilarating to feel part of a grand imperial mission, gratifying to be lauded as the fearless exponents of all that was healthiest and most virile in the national character—and a relief to find some common ground with the colonial authorities.

Since the missionaries were men of their own time, their heads were turned by the arrogance of the era. They felt they were bringing to the non-white, non-Christian world the unquestionably superior civilization of their own society and, like imperialists imposing upon natives the manifold advantages of colonial rule, they forced down their throats the manifold advantages of Western thinking. The Pax Britannica had bred in many missionaries a heavily paternalist tone towards their "children."

All this was true, but it was not the whole truth. Only a hopelessly over-simplified hindsight can classify all missionaries as agents or cat's-paws of imperialism. As in any human group, there are those for and those against: missionaries who opposed Empire as well as missionaries who welcomed it.

C. C. Newton, a Baptist missionary in Nigeria, welcomed an 1892 punitive expedition: "Thousands of slaves will rejoice to see the Union Jack waving above their masters' heads. . . . A sword of steel often goes before a sword of the spirit." To Newton, freeing slaves was a humanitarian act made possible only by British intervention with armed force. There were missionaries who supported opposite viewpoints with equal trenchancy. One of the earliest superintendents of the London Missionary Society missions in Cape Colony, John Philip, openly expressed his conviction that, given equal opportunities, the African would disprove the theory of innate European superiority.

The missionaries often asserted their right to oppose the government —or at least to circumvent its decisions—whenever they felt that they were in the right. It is surprising how often they got their way. But then so many of them were not the sort to be content with less. They were individualists, sometimes to the point of eccentricity. C. T. Studd, for example, had a "cricket-pitch church," 22 yards long and wide, built in the Congo jungle, and in his sixties imagined that St. Paul was urging him to "go in for a slog!" Francis McDougall, the first Bishop of Borneo, fought off pirates with a double-barrelled rifle. Bishop MacKenzie engaged in gunfights with Arab slave-raiders along the Zambezi. Mary Slessor, as a vice-consul and justice of the peace in Africa, sometimes whacked obstructive chiefs with her umbrella. People of this stamp were not likely to be awed by official disapproval of their methods. Indeed, by many of their actions the missionaries can reasonably claim to have been the conscience of the British Empire, not its unthinking agents.

Missionary achievement was almost bound to fall short of the original aims of the movement, for those aims were too ambitious to take account of reality. Nevertheless, the missionary onslaught left a considerable mark on indigenous societies all over the world, considerable enough to generate a hot controversy about its good or bad effects.

There is no doubt that the missionaries caused great disruption of traditional systems: social disintegration that made "every man a chief," the breaking down of tribal, caste, and kinship orders that were part and parcel of their activity. One reason why colonial governments were keen to curtail the power of the missionaries was that they found their activities creating a kind of anarchy: the setting of slaves against their master, of Christian children against their heathen parents, of "savvy boys" against the ignorant masses as well as their British mentors.

A further destabilizing influence was the fact that the missionaries' job was only half done. Limited resources prevented them from expanding their educational programme much beyond the elementary level, particularly in tropical Africa. Through no fault of their own, the evangelists overseas did much to create a situation where old and new social forms existing side by side led to conflict.

However, the effects of missionary activity were not all bad. Historians now admit that they preserved as well as destroyed. They defended, for example, teaching in the local vernac-

A pair of stalwart Victorian lady missionaries—or "female agents," as they were often called—posed for a photographer before setting off through the African bush.

ular languages against the wishes of colonial governments in West Africa; they shielded the Aborigines of Australia; and they often created the very possibility of an indigenous cultural heritage. There were a number of indisputable humanitarian gains. The suppression of suttee and other manifestations of a decadent, oppressive Hinduism, the attacks on cannibalism, ritual murder, and trial by poison, and the victorious anti-slavery campaign were forward steps which no one would wish to retrace. It also has to be recognized that the missionaries persistently and courageously worked to protect indigenous peoples against land-grabbing and labour exploitation. Mission hospitals, treating patients of all creeds, made a profound impression on native populations by showing the impartial compassion as well as the efficiency of the White God's Magic.

The British missionary movement emerges finally as one of the most remarkable, adaptable, and sustained outbursts of humanitarian zeal in modern history. Its influence on world history has been considerable. In particular, the doctrine that all men are spiritually equal gave a strong impetus to egalitarianism in many forms. This set off an anti-colonial chain reaction whose effects are still being felt.

—*David Mitchell*

II. The Imperial Machine

The powerhouse of the British Empire was London, the Rome of the modern world. By the end of the 19th Century London complacently felt itself to be, as the bards of the 1897 Diamond Jubilee called it, "the hub of the world." With its contrasts of patrician glitter and fetid slum, its hugger-mugger mixture of pathos and parade, its humour, its boisterous and libidinous night life, its glorious parks and its glowering smoke-filled skies; with the murky old Thames rolling grandly through its centre, and the millennium of history that flowed through its very soul; with all its quirks, splendours, and disgraces, London possessed a universal, Shakespearian quality that every perceptive visitor remarked. Here were the shrines, symbols, and the mechanisms of the greatest empire ever known to history.

In the centre of the metropolis, loftily above St. James's Park, stood the headquarters of the whole imperial organization, built in Italian style by George Gilbert Scott. The building had been the subject of a famous architectural controversy of the 1850s. Scott wanted to build it in the Gothic style, but Gothic had come to be identified with Toryism, and when the Whigs returned to power in 1857 Palmerston insisted on Renaissance. The result was a not very inspired building—a heavy towered block decorated with sculpted representations of imperial races, Indian rivers, or dead Colonial Secretaries—but it housed both the Colonial Office and the India Office, beneath whose dual authority lived nearly 400 million people.

The Colonial Office administered a gallimaufry of overseas possessions, from infinitesimal tropic islands to unexplored immensities of Africa. It was run with gentlemanly assurance by a handful of civil servants. Clublike, secluded, aloof but traditionally humane, it was only now being rejuvenated with electric lights and typewriters by the energetic new Colonial Secretary, Joseph Chamberlain. Nonetheless, it retained its dark mahogany and deep leather furnishings, its smoky coal fires and high narrow corridors. It possessed the fireplace, taken from the waiting room of its old premises, before which Nelson and Wellington had warmed themselves during the course of their only meeting.

At the India Office next door was stacked all the knowledge, experience, and self-esteem acquired during two centuries of British presence in India. India was, in fact, ruled from Calcutta, its practical executive the Viceroy. But the India Office, his link with the imperial government, was an alter ego of the Raj. All the departments of Indian government had their microcosms here in Whitehall. The men who ran the India Office were clever and dedicated careerists, and their methods were nothing if not deliberate— "stately, solemn, sure, and slow," as Lord Curzon put it. The Office was old, sombre, powerful, and legalistic, with a daunting reputation.

Conveniently close were the offices of military power, the scaffolding of Empire. If one left the Colonial Office through St. James's Park and strolled past the shining lake where the pelicans gravely meditated upon their rocks and the spanking little water fowl bobbed beneath the suspension-bridge, then up the Duke of York's Steps past the German Embassy and round the corner past the Athenaeum and the Travellers' Club, presently one would discover, opposite the Army and Navy Club on the south side of Pall Mall, the sprawling premises of the War Office.

Ponderous architecturally, the War Office was overweight professionally too, despite successive reforms in the latter half of the century. It was, nevertheless, alarmingly powerful in the world of the 1890s. It had a finger in the pie from Canada to Singapore, forts and barracks and military hospitals everywhere, 72,000 men in India, 23 battalions in Ireland, cavalry regiments in Egypt and South Africa. Its regiments with their scarlet jackets, kilts, bugle-calls, and Maxim guns had struck a bewildered terror into the hearts of enemies as variously formidable as the Zulus, the Egyptians, and the Métis of Manitoba.

Walk up Whitehall and you would soon reach a very different institution, the headquarters of Her Majesty's Board of Admiralty. With its exquisite 18th-Century boardroom above the courtyard, its ancient traditions of victory and insouciance, its flair for the showy and the eccentric, its marvellous uniforms and its highly individual officers, the Admiralty controlled easily the biggest of fleets and enjoyed a prestige altogether unique. The world feared, admired, and copied the Royal Navy, and there was to those elegant premises, behind the Tuscan columns of Robert Adam's Admiralty Screen, an air of unshakable and aristocratic assurance.

Often one would see, striding between these several offices of state, tanned or pallid men of Empire, dressed in clothes a little out of fashion and carrying around them, like a nimbus, a lofty suggestion of far responsibility.

London was the fulcrum of Empire, allegorically situated, if one consulted the right map projection, at the centre of civilization. All roads led to the New Rome. Here were the offices of the cable companies, whose lines had woven a web round the Empire—lines across the Atlantic, down both coasts of Africa, to India, Singapore, and Hong Kong, boldly across the Australian outback, tentatively (and unprofitably) to minuscule outposts of Empire like the Cocos or St. Vincent. Here too were the headquarters of the imperial shipping companies that dominated the world's sea traffic— Peninsular & Oriental, Orient Royal Mail, Castle Mail Packets, British India Steam Navigation Company.

To the east, within the mystic square mile of the City of London, was the financial clearing house of Empire. Clustered round the Bank of England, in a rich maze of medieval lanes and cobbled courts, were the private banks and investment companies that provided capital for world-wide enterprise. Railways in India, copra plantations in the Caribbean, iron mines in Australia, gold mines in South Africa depended upon their skills. Through their accounts passed in turn much of the profit of the overseas Empire, to be transmuted into family wealth, distributed in dividends, or reinvested elsewhere. The economy of Empire was built upon the resources of these modestly opulent premises, along whose corridors the bank messengers hurried in their tall hats and frock-coats and the omniscient financiers moved from boardroom to boardroom to discuss the future of Sarawak, the mineral resources of British Columbia, or whether or not Mr. Rhodes should be encouraged in his campaign against the Matabele.

Sundry other establishments, monuments, or mere memories reminded the citizen of London that his was the capital of a quarter of the world. There were foundations like the Royal Colonial Institute, the Imperial Institute, or the Ladies' Imperial Club. There were the offices of the colonial travel specialists ("Portmanteaux Shipped Direct to Bombay"), the colonial wine merchants ("Manager, Lieut.-Colonel Haskett-Smith, Late of the Cameron Highlanders"), the shops selling tropical medicines, Camp Beds for Colonial Climes, mosquito nets, patent field cookers, leather-bound trunks, the Shikaree Tropical Hat or the Jungra Shooting Suit.

There were statues, here and there across the grimy old city, to viceroys and imperial conquerors. Richard Burton, the African explorer, slept beneath his marble Arab tent in the Catholic cemetery at Mortlake. In the nave of Westminster Abbey lay the incomparable Livingstone.

Sometimes the Londoner might catch a glimpse of living imperial functionaries. He might, for instance, observe the judges of the Judicial Committee of the Privy Council, the ultimate tribunal of the British Empire, assembling in their dowdy Whitehall premises to discuss a tribal dispute from Malaya, a tort from Manitoba, or the disposal of temple properties in the Punjab. He might see the Speaker of the House of Commons, an assembly whose writ ran in one degree or another throughout the British possessions and whose approval was theoretically required for every stutter of a Maxim gun. He might see the 95th Archbishop of Canterbury, head of a church whose 96 bishoprics spanned the entire Empire, emerging in splendid canonicals from his official home at Lambeth Palace.

Or he might set eyes on the Queen of England. She often came to London from her castle at Windsor, and her carriage might be seen on its way from the railway station to Buckingham Palace or clattering through the palace gates between her saluting Guardsmen. To the end of her reign, though her political power was oblique rather than direct, she remained the most significant person in the land. Her presence exemplified all that the Empire meant to the British nation—beyond politics, beyond gunboats, beyond even the deliberations of those financiers in the City. She was Victoria the Good, the Great White Queen, the Raj personified.

The Empire over which the Queen presided was a vast and complex structure, made up of a multiplicity of races and countries differing in customs, law, religion, and language. There were the self-governing colonies of Canada, Australia, New Zealand; the Indian subcontinent, Ceylon, and Burma; tropical protectorates and dependencies; and a mass of smaller territories and bases.

No single, monolithic bureaucratic machine ran the collective imperial domain in the sense of a board of directors running a business. The Crown, Parliament, the Colonial and India Offices, colonial governments, the legal system: all were axles on which the machine ran, yet they were not linked together by any coherent mechanism. There was an enormous variety of political, diplomatic, social, and economic problems to face. An Empire of such disparate elements could not possibly operate as a monolithic system.

There was, for example, no uniform legal system. India had a penal code devised by Thomas Babington Macaulay. Quebec kept a civil law derived from France, and Mauritius and the Seychelles had the Napoleonic Code. South Africa and Ceylon used mainly Roman-Dutch law, and Malta maintained Sicilian law. Colonies of British settlement naturally leaned heavily on English experience for their statute law, following English textbooks, borrowing English interpretations, and benefiting from English draftsmanship. It was the supreme court of appeal, the Judicial Committee of the Privy Council, that provided a sense

Both whim and local architecture inspired the builders of the Government Houses scattered across the Empire. From top: a more or less French Renaissance Government House in Rangoon; a Moorish delight in East Africa; and a sturdy, practical structure in the bleak Falkland Islands.

of unity at the apex of the Empire's complex legal structure.

In theory, all imperial power was exercised in the name of the Crown, whose symbolic significance was immense. The Queen was the highest constitutional authority in every part of the Empire: she was the executive head of each government, her assent was required for legislation to become effective, and her refusal to give assent negated a bill. The mystically remote figure who sat on the imperial throne in London was the font of imperial authority.

The Queen's representatives in every colonial government shared something of her god-like aura, particularly her representative in India. The Viceroy enjoyed the most coveted, magnificent, and resplendent of all posts in the overseas administration. In other colonies the Queen's representative was the Governor, who also enjoyed the aura of royalty, although on a less glamourous scale. The Governor's power derived from letters patent issued under the great seal. He wrote his minutes and signed his initials in red ink. He usually lived in an imposing Government House where the Union Jack flew every day from sunrise to sunset. He was addressed as "His Excellency" and his appearance on a public occasion was the signal for the national anthem to be played.

The Governor exercised the royal prerogative of mercy and carried out "royal" instructions. His functions, however, were in practice carried out under the direction not of the Queen but of the Secretary of State for the Colonies in London. He addressed his dispatches to that worthy, who in turn sent him the instructions on which he was expected to act. He was required to consult his executive council on all matters related to the exercise of his powers, although he might reject his council's advice.

Colonial governors in the middle of the 19th Century had come mostly from the senior ranks of the army or navy, and were men with an upper middle-class background. Governing a colony was then regarded as a natural extension of an officer's job, but later in the century an increasing number of governors were men who had made the colonial service their whole career. Governors moved from one territory to another in a succession of appointments, thus building up their experience. Sir Henry Barkly, the son of a West Indian merchant, was successively Governor in British Guiana, Jamaica, Victoria (Australia), Mauritius, and Cape Colony between 1848 and 1877. Sir Arthur Gordon was Lieutenant-Governor in New Brunswick and Governor in Trinidad, Mauritius, Fiji, New Zealand, and Ceylon between 1861 and 1890. Sir George Grey was Governor in South Australia, New Zealand, and Cape Colony between 1841 and 1868. The quality of the 19th-Century governors was generally good, yet there were those who deserved the epithets "wind bag" and "pompous donkey" applied by irritated officials in Whitehall.

The Governor, like the Queen, was not only the head of government but also the pinnacle of social life. A well-ordered social consciousness lubricated the machinery of imperial administration, and the Governor and his wife were expected to maintain and foster it. A colonial Governor was required to observe the niceties of social protocol just as the Queen and her advisers observed them in London. He and his wife organized balls, dinners, bazaars, polo, horse-racing, and fox-hunts, and their presence at any function was deemed an honour to it. They always had to find time in their programme to drink tea under the trees in the garden with the social élite of their community.

Next to the Crown in the pyramid of imperial authority emanating from the New Rome was Parliament. The Parliament at Westminster was the supreme legislative institution of the Empire. However, it contained few members with any interest in imperial problems. It was interested in Ireland, but Ireland was seen more as a domestic than an imperial problem. As there were no votes to be gained from colonial issues, they were of little consequence to the parties. Parliament was kept in the dark most of the time about imperial problems; even debates on India—the showpiece of Empire—were sparsely attended.

Imperial policy was left to the jealous care of the ministers whose responsibility it was.

The principal political figures concerned with the Empire were the Secretaries of State—one for India and one for the other colonies. They were responsible to Parliament and to their colleagues in the Cabinet, and across their desks came practically all imperial matters. Nevertheless, the post of Secretary of State for the Colonies was not regarded as an onerous one and ambitious politicians did not value it except as a stepping-stone to higher office. No established political figure until Joseph Chamberlain actually sought the appointment. The Secretary of State was not influential in the Cabinet, where colonial affairs were regarded an unimportant.

Under such circumstances it is surprising that the calibre of Secretaries of State was so high. The only one in the 19th Century who was demonstrably incompetent was Sir Edward Bulwer Lytton, who held the office for only a year.

The Secretary of State for India controlled the India Office, the communications channel between the Raj and London. The India Office had inherited from the East India Company a collection of oriental manuscripts and printed works and records which formed the basis of an excellent library and the major repository of publications on Indian subjects. The India Office itself, however, was regarded as a depressing place to work. Possibly its sheer wealth of fine pictures, furnishings, woodwork, and sculpture was overwhelming, emphasizing the heavy burden of responsibility imposed by the affairs of India.

The India Office recruited the officials to govern India. Successful applicants to the superior Indian Civil Service were originally appointed under a "covenant" with the Secretary of State to executive, judicial, and specialized posts. They were distinct from the "uncovenanted" service recruited largely among Indians and Anglo-Indians domiciled in India, whose members were appointed to subordinate positions.

This domination of the I.C.S. by British appointees caused growing

Text Continued on Page 316

313

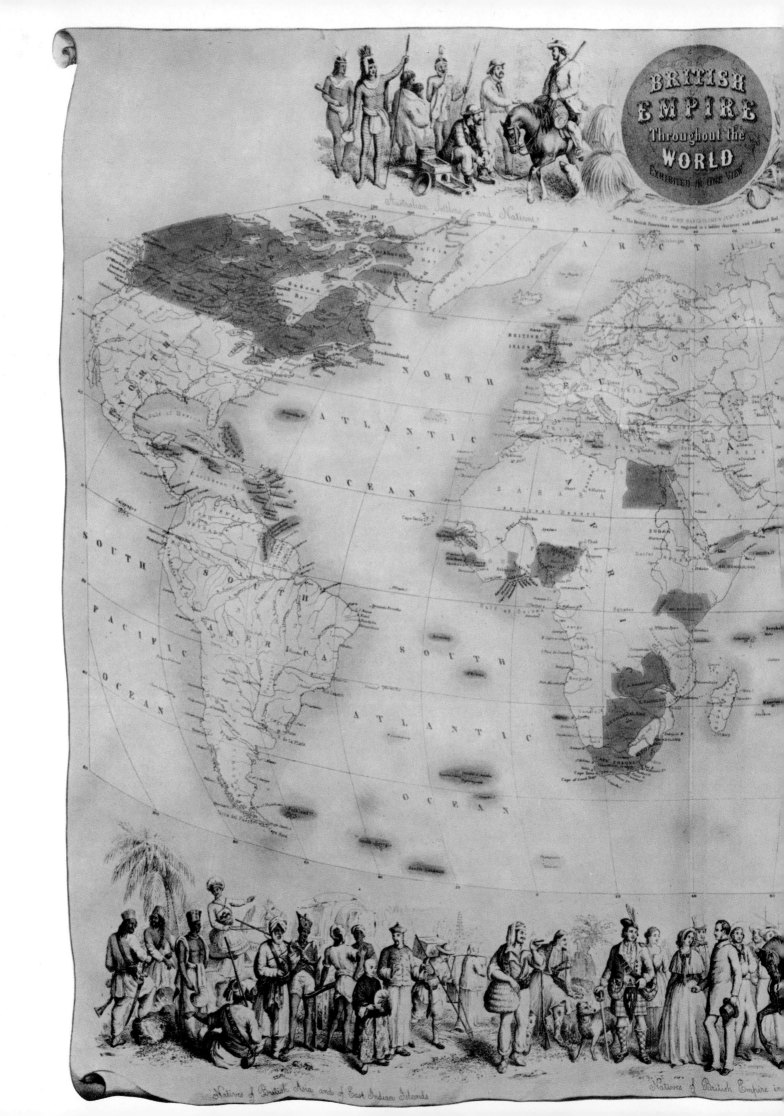

BRITISH EMPIRE Throughout the WORLD EXHIBITED IN ONE VIEW

Australian Settlers and Natives

Natives of British Asia and of East Indian Islands

Natives of British Empire

THE BRITISH EMPIRE 1897

EUROPE

Great Britain, Cyprus, Gibraltar, Malta.

Area : 157,500 square miles.

Population : 43,210,000.

The British Isles were, correctly, the United Kingdom of Great Britain and Ireland. But everyday terms were looser : "Great Britain," "Britain" or even - to the dismay of Scots, Welsh and Irish - simply "England."

AFRICA

Basutoland, Bechuanaland, British East Africa, British Somaliland, Cape Colony, Egypt, Gambia, Gold Coast, Natal, Nigeria, Northern Rhodesia, Nyasaland, Sierra Leone, Southern Rhodesia, Swaziland, Transvaal, Uganda, Walvis Bay.

Area : 2,150,000 square miles.

Population : 37,900,000.

AMERICA

Antigua, Bahamas, Barbados, Barbuda, Bermuda, British Guiana, British Honduras, Canada, Grand Cayman, Grenada, Jamaica, Montserrat, Nevis, Newfoundland, St. Christopher, St. Lucia, St. Vincent, Tobago, Trinidad, Virgin Islands and other small islands.

Area : 3,094,000 square miles.

Population : 6,898,000.

ASIA

Aden, Brunei, Ceylon, Hong Kong, India, Labuan Island, Malay Federated States, North Borneo, Papua, Sarawak, Singapore.

Area : 1,700,000 square miles.

Population : 296,500,000.

AUSTRALASIA

New South Wales, New Zealand, Northern Territory, Queensland, South Australia, Tasmania, Victoria, Western Australia.

Area : 3,100,000 square miles.

Population : 4,000,000.

ATLANTIC OCEAN

Ascension, Falkland Islands, Gough Island, St. Helena, South Georgia, South Sandwich, Tristan da Cunha and other small islands.

Area : 8,670 square miles.

Population : 6,200.

INDIAN OCEAN

Amirante Islands, Andaman Islands, Chagos Islands, Christmas Island, Cocos (Keeling) Islands, Kuria Muria Islands, Laccadive Islands, Maldive Islands, Mauritius, Nicobar Islands, Seychelles Islands, Socotra, Zanzibar and other small islands.

Area : 1,200 square miles.

Population : 400,000.

PACIFIC OCEAN

Antipodes Island, Bounty Islands, Campbell Island, Chatham Island, Ellice Islands, Fiji Islands*, Gilbert Islands, Kermadec Islands, Lord Howe Island, Norfolk Island, Pitcairn*, Southern Solomons and other island groups.

Area : 7,500 square miles.

Population : 150,000.

GRAND TOTAL

Area : 10,200,000 square miles.

Population : 387,400,000.

NOTE : There were many different forms of imperial rule and it was not always clear whether a territory was in or out of the Empire. For example, Transvaal in 1897 was only debatably part of the Empire - as an autonomous republic whose foreign affairs were under British control; Egypt was under British military occupation, but not yet formally annexed ; and Cyprus was nominally under Turkish sovereignty, although administered by Britain.

Figures for area and population are approximate.

*This mid-Victorian map has been updated to 1897 but does not show certain islands in the Pacific.

Many of the Old Boys of the Indian Civil Service came out of Haileybury, the East India Company's college. When Haileybury lads like those at left grew up, they typically appeared in formal group portraits such as the one at right—Lord and Lady Curzon posing with the Nizam of Hyderabad, the richest man in the world, in 1902.

criticism in India and led in 1886 to the setting up of a commission to inquire into the employment of Indians. The commission's proposals were accepted by the government, and civil officials were divided into three classes: the Indian Civil Service, recruited in Britain; provincial services, recruited in India; and subordinate services of lowlier officials such as postal messengers and police constables. By the end of the century Lord Curzon, the grandest of Viceroys, was warning of "the extreme danger of the system under which every year an increasing number of the 900 and odd higher posts that were meant, and ought to have been exclusively and specially reserved, for Europeans, are being filched away by the superior wits of the native. . . . I believe it to be the greatest peril with which our administration is confronted." At that time, less than five per cent of the Service were Indians.

The men who ruled India operated an efficient, incorruptible, impartial, and impersonal machine. It was so efficient and inflexible, as Curzon

ruefully discovered, that individual initiative and any enterprise in the direction of change were stifled. There was little or no vision of what India might become, and little or no concern with solving its problems. The Anglo-Indians would not be hurried into letting the Indian people assume more political responsibility than was good for them, and were imbued with the notion that British rule was not only efficient and incorruptible, which it was, but also a privilege and a boon for the ruled, which was less certain.

The responsibilities of the India Office in London and the Indian Civil Service were manifold and complex, but at least they were largely confined to one recognizable geographical area. The responsibilities of the Colonial Office encompassed all corners of the globe. The old Colonial Office premises had been at No. 14 Downing Street, which grew so dilapidated that in 1837 they were condemned. For decades the staff laboured in "temporary" quarters where the roof leaked, doors would not close, corridors were draughty, faulty chimneys

belched smoke, and cracks in the walls and ceilings added to the general atmosphere of decay.

Finally the Colonial Office moved into the new block of buildings designed by George Scott. The Crown Agents, who provided for the wants of colonial governments, occupied the basement and ground floor; the Secretary of State was on the first floor; the library was on the second; and clerks worked on the second and third floors.

The Secretary of State's room was large and stylish. At one end was a globe that turned on its axis and remained a feature well into the new century. It is difficult to believe, remarks Sir Cosmo Parkinson, a Colonial Office veteran, that Secretaries in the Victorian era "can have resisted the temptation to pose for their portraits with one hand resting upon this symbol of world-wide imperial sway." The room was also distinguished by a portrait of George Washington, a salutary reminder of the consequences that might flow from a misguided colonial policy.

316

As the volume of business increased, however, the new premises became as inadequate as the old. An unreliable lift was a source of nervous anxiety, and when stoppages occurred it was customary to ask the Admiralty for help. Until Chamberlain's day the rooms were dimly lit by candlesticks and poorly maintained gas lights. There was nowhere to store the mounting accumulation of records and files, which were frequently left lying about the corridors. It is surprising that efficiency and devotion remained prominent characteristics of the staff.

All official communications to and from the colonies passed through the Colonial Office, whose business routine was founded on the circulation of paper. It was customary for the more senior officials to arrive at about 11 in the morning. Subordinate clerks arrived earlier and prepared the day's business for their seniors, who stayed later in the afternoon or evening until the work was completed. On the whole the office exuded a dignified and leisurely calm.

Incoming communications arrived in white sealed canvas bags and were numbered and registered with related correspondence by clerks in the registry. From this beginning the filing system developed, with all its anomalies. Cosmo Parkinson recalled a search for papers about a maternity hospital in one of the West African colonies: "No trace of them could be found in the 'Medical' cutting of the register; only after prolonged search was it discovered that a clerk had entered them in the 'Labour' cutting."

A communication was passed from the lower division clerks to the second class clerks for minuting. In some instances a précis might also be made. It was then forwarded to a first-class clerk or departmental head for his comment, and perhaps a suggestion of a suitable reply. The matter would then be passed through the senior secretariat to the assistant under-secretary or the permanent under-secretary for further comment, then to the parliamentary under-secretary and, finally, the Secretary of State, for decision. It returned through the same channels, where the senior clerk or his assistant composed a draft reply. This went back up the ladder for approval and down again for copying. The finished copy was then sent to the departmental head or under-secretary for signature, and on to the second-class clerks who indexed it and prepared it for mailing. Although it was laborious even by 19th-Century standards, this procedure ensured that all the expertise in the office was brought to bear on a matter, and it had the virtue of being systematic.

Those who had business with the Colonial Office often became impatient about delays, but it was other departments that were very often to blame. Colonial laws were examined by the Board of Trade, which knew little and cared less about the majority of them, then confirmed by the Privy Council, which met infrequently. All overseas expenditures were examined by the Treasury, whose approval could never be taken for granted and was seldom quick. The Colonial Office once had to wait two years for the Treasury to supply its answer on a question involving Tasmania.

Such delays were sometimes the Treasury's way of discouraging unnecessary requests, thus keeping the British taxpayers' financial responsibility for the Empire to a minimum.

By the 1870s the Colonial Office was becoming progressively less able to cope with the mounting paper work. In the year 1870 about 26,000 letters, dispatches, and telegrams entered or left the premises, and three-quarters of these were seen by the Secretary of State personally, who had to authorize instructions and decisions. Sir William Molesworth had made sarcastic play on this in a speech years before: "One day the Colonial Secretary is in Ceylon, a financial and a religious reformer, promoting the interests of the coffee planter and casting discredit on the tooth and religion of Buddha; the next day he is in the West Indies, teaching the economical manufacture of sugar; or in Van Diemen's Land, striving to reform the fiends whom he has transported to that pandemonium. Now he is in Canada, discussing the Indemnity Bill and the war of races; anon he is at the Cape of Good Hope, dancing a war dance with Sir Harry Smith and his Kaffir subjects; or in New Zealand, an unsuccessful Lycurgus, coping with Honi Heki; or at Natal treating with Panda, King of the Zulus; or in Labuan, digging coal and warring with pirates; or in the midst of South Africa, defeating Pretorius and his rebel Boers. . . ."

A subsequent streamlining of the paperwork system helped, but the work load remained heavy, especially when the "scramble for Africa" accelerated towards the end of the century. The staff was engaged in all kinds of subjects, from postal regulations to health problems, public works, colonial appointments, extradition of criminals, trade exhibitions, and economic, political, and diplomatic questions of varying degrees of importance. The more senior clerks, especially, found themselves working on Sundays, foregoing holidays, and keeping longer hours.

Staff organization revolved round the geographical departments, each of which dealt with a particular area of the Empire. A general department, presided over by the chief clerk, dealt with office procedure and matters affecting the Empire as a whole. Entry into the ranks of the upper division clerks was, in practice, restricted largely to public-school and university men, especially the classics scholar who found his enjoyment in reading Greek or Latin. These men, with their privileged upbringing and education, were all of a recognizable mould. One of the Colonial Office staff remembered "a beloved senior who always kept a Greek or Latin classic open on his desk, so that he could refresh his mind between files. He would even stop in the middle of a tiresome minute to read a few lines of Homer or titivate his personal translation of an epigram by Simonides."

At the apex of the staff structure was the permanent under-secretary, who was responsible for the functioning of the office routine. He was crucial to the whole policy-making process and the Secretary of State depended heavily on him for advice. Among those who filled this position were Frederic Rogers, holder of a "double first" in classics and mathematics at Oxford, and Herman Merivale, who read Latin before he was five, took a first-class degree in classics at Oxford, and became a professor of political economy at the university.

The Colonial Office was a marvelous source of patronage, especially for drop-outs—Members of Parliament who had lost their seats, aristocrats who had fallen on bad times, politicians whose removal was thought desirable. Positions in the colonial civil service were mostly patronage posts, and candidates were selected for character as much as for intelligence. Since there was no job training and they had to learn by trial and error, successful candidates were expected to be adaptable all-rounders, with an ability to lead and decide. These were qualities commonly regarded as being exclusive to the products of the public schools and the universities. The examiner who described a candidate as a good type of "English Public School man" was ensuring that he would be looked upon with a sympathetic eye. "He rowed in the Cambridge eight" was considered an important qualification in the 1880s.

Salaries in the colonial services were lower than in the Indian Civil Service, even in West Africa, which inflated salaries to help compensate for its reputation as "the White Man's Grave." Recruitment standards for some colonies were much lower than for others. An army officer who lost his commission as a result of a canteen brawl was accepted in the Gold Coast constabulary; another who absconded with regimental funds became a customs collector in British Guiana. Yet the duties in the less favoured territories were the most onerous and exacting.

Most colonial territories were, in practice, left to be governed by the men on the spot. The Colonial Office decided the general principles and sought to dampen down any excesses that might creep into the day-to-day administration. Sometimes there was much to dampen. Sir John Pope-Hennessy, one of the more exasperating colonial governors, habitually disobeyed or ignored instructions with which he disagreed and locked unwelcome dispatches in a drawer, unanswered. But even with governors like Pope-Hennessy the Colonial Office felt obliged to support the man on the spot.

There was considerable pressure on the colonial Governor, not the least of which was adapting to life in a strange environment—something the Colonial Office knew nothing about. In the African territories they were generally obliged to surrender family life, or even the prospect of it. There were psychological strains involved in living a life away from home amidst alien, if often beautiful, surroundings. The Governor and his wife were under a special social responsibility. Margaret Brooke, the wife of the "White Rajah" of Sarawak, held a tea for her English friends every Tuesday afternoon. The conversation, she confessed, was not very exciting, but it possessed one remarkable characteristic: "they would wax quite enthusiastic when someone would announce, how, with a great good fortune, he had induced a small half-ripe strawberry to appear on a plant

Text Continued on Page 326

318

THE CROWN AGENTS

More than law-books and soldiers were needed to run the colonies. Somebody had to organize the supply of paper-clips, desks, railways – and even the inevitable red tape. The Crown Agents were appointed in 1833 to do just that. Ever since, though their wide-ranging, non-profit-making activities are little publicized, they have played a vital part in providing developing countries with everything they could possibly need.

The Crown Agents no longer act only for colonial administrations, and they have stopped using their coat of arms with its royal crest (above), to emphasize their political impartiality to the many public authorities, international bodies (like the U.N.) and governments – many in former colonies – that they now serve.

Suppliers to Empire

Until 1833, a senior clerk at the Colonial Office could look contentedly forward to a sinecure as agent for one of the colonies. He would arrange loans and supplies for a colonial government at a handsome profit. But by the early 1830s, complaints from the colonies about the inefficiency and dishonesty of the system were becoming too vociferous to be ignored. In 1833 two Colonial Office men, styled "Joint Agents General for Crown Colonies," were made responsible by Parliament for the needs of the 13 Crown Colonies that then existed. Slowly, the agents began to build up the reputation they enjoy today for integrity and efficiency.

From the 1860s, Crown Agents were generally recruited from outside the Colonial Office and detailed instructions for their guidance were issued by the Treasury. A parliamentary committee of 1908 defined their position as "officers of the Colonial Governments serving in England under the ultimate control of the Secretary of State." As their abilities became more and more obvious and overseas governments increasingly demanded their services, so that "ultimate control" became looser and looser.

Sir Maurice Cameron served as junior and senior Crown Agent from 1895 to 1920. Once a military engineer, he quickly saw the colonies' need for technical assistance and built up the present engineering division.

TENDER.

Affix Postage Stamp Here.

THE CROWN AGENTS FOR THE COLONIES,

Whitehall Gardens,

LONDON,

S.W.

Tenders have always been put out by the Crown Agents for the goods they buy. For the really big contracts, the tenders are opened in public.

22

SUPPLIES.

PROCURING AND FORWARDING TO THE COLONIES THE FOLLOWING ARTICLES.

Anchors and Chains
Asphalte
Arms, Rifles, Swords and Pistols, &c.
Agricultural Implements
Books — Printed and Account
Bank Notes
Bricks
Coals
Chemicals of all kinds
Clothing, Local Corps, Police, Prison, Hospital, and Asylum
Cloth, and Materials for making clothing
Cement
Canvas
Copper Coins
Cranes
Dredging Vessels
Dies and Crests for Public Bodies

Distilling Apparatus
Diving   ditto
Engines, Steam, &c.
Engineers' Tools
Fire Engines
Glass of all kinds
Gunpowder
Hemp
Hardwares
Iron of all kinds
„ Bridges
„ Buildings
„ Boats
„ Gates and Railings
„ Vessels
Ironmongery, general
Lead
Leather
Life Boats, and apparatus for saving life
Light House apparatus and Lanterns
Lathes, Duplex, &c.

23

Metals of all kinds
Medicines
Machinery of all kinds
Mathematical Instruments
Meat, Salt, Navy
Meats preserved
Moorings for Ships
Oils, Lighthouse and Linseed
Paints
Pitch
Plant for Railways, Gas, and Water Works
Plates for Debentures, Bonds, Bank Notes, and Postage Stamps
Paper
Postage Stamps
Photographic Apparatus

Police equi
Rope of al
Stationery
Saddlery ;
    for mo
Slates an
Surgical
Sub-Mar
    Cable
Steam V
Timber,
„ C
Tools,
    actin
Telegr
Tin sh
Tallow
Tar
Vesse
Zinc

INCIDENTAL D

Custom House duties of all kin
Warehousing Goods
Securing Freights
Insurances, Marine and Fire
Instituting enquiries respecting persons and property in the Colonies.

[TURN OVER]

TREASURY INSTRUCTIONS

FOR

THE GUIDANCE OF

THE

AGENTS-GENERAL FOR CROWN COLONIES

5TH MARCH, 1860

Pages (left) from the Treasury Instructions (above), issued to guide the Crown Agents in their work, show the variety of goods supplied as early as 1860.

The office in Whitehall Gardens, where the Crown Agents moved in 1903, was the last stop before they moved into their own building at Millbank.

Ten "lady clerks" pose in the Downing Street offices of the Crown Agents, conscious of their role as the emancipated, working women of the 1890s.

This 2s. 3d. duty stamp, supplied by the General Agents was affixed to every firkin of Tasmanian beer, consumed throughout Australia.

Licence to Print Money

The Crown Agents organize and supervise the printing under tight security of colonial stamps, banknotes and pre-paid mail from the moment the paper is made until the finished products are safely in the strong rooms of the ship carrying them to their destination.

The Crown Agents' vaults in London hold three priceless stamp albums containing a copy of every stamp issued for the British colonies since 1860 and also a comprehensive collection of banknote specimens. A selection of these are shown here.

Rolls of paper for the stamps are made under the scrutiny of the Crown Agent inspector. Any mistake in the printing – a collector's delight – means a court of inquiry for the inspector. He watches especially closely to ensure that the watermark is incorporated. From the mills the paper goes to the printer to be impressed with the correct design. If the design incorporates the monarch's head, then it has to be approved by Buckingham Palace. King George V, a famous philatelist in his own right, even chose the two colours for the Silver Jubilee issue of 1935. After printing, the stamps are stored in the Crown Agents' own vaults. Finally, the Crown Agents organize transportation overseas.

The Crown Agents' stamp-making activities do more than bring money into Britain: they often prove an investment for the client, for stamp sales to collectors are often a vital source of revenue for small countries. A commemorative issue of 1950 for the Cayman Islands paid for radios for many of the inhabitants.

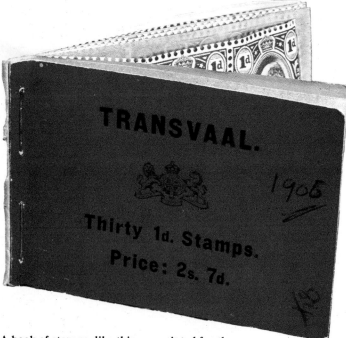

A book of stamps, like this one printed for the Transvaal in 1906, was available from the Crown Agents for a charge of 1d. over the cost of the stamps.

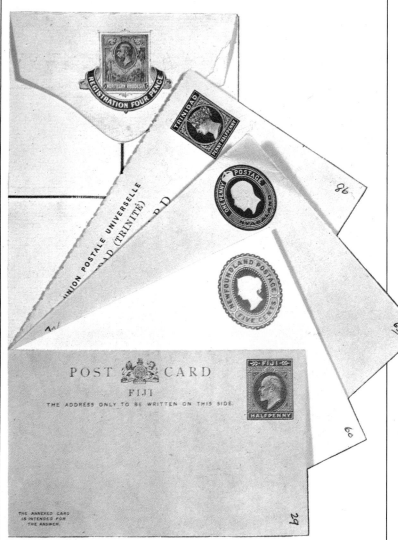

This coronation stamp was a second proof, made after a small error was discovered in the size of the lettering on the original.

Every kind of pre-printed mail, from postcards to registered letters, was supplied by the versatile Crown Agents.

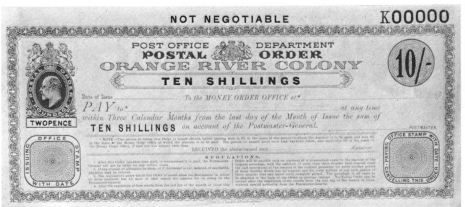

Orange River Colony's postal orders had a specially designed border of orange blossoms.

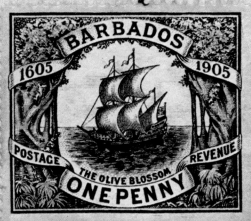

Three commemorative stamps for Barbados illustrate the skill of the engraver. The top two show Nelson's statue in Barbados, and the lower depicts the supposed arrival of English settlers in 1605. In fact the story is based on an historical error: no settlers arrived until 1627.

The toucan in this banknote would have been fully checked at the Natural History Museum.

The four languages on the Straits Settlements banknote are English, Chinese, Malay and Hindi, the most common languages used in Singapore.

![sewing machine illustration]

This particular sewing machine was designed not to mend the petticoats of the Governor's wife, but for sewing and repairing sails and tarpaulins. In remote island colonies, it was a valuable commodity.

![portable writing case illustration]

Many a harassed colonial official must have been grateful for this portable case to hold papers ready for signing in spare moments.

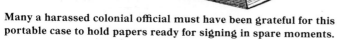

An elegant tent of striped cloth was ideal to protect the ladies from the tropical sun as they watched a game of tennis on the Governor's lawns.

From Saddles to Sewing Machines

When the Governor of a colony left Government House, travelled to the Courts, attended a garden party or signed papers, his every action was surrounded by reminders of the Crown Agents: the bed he left, the carpet he walked on, the carriage he travelled in, the desk he sat at and the ink he wrote with – each one of these items was furnished on request by the Crown Agents, who kept catalogues galore to assist him in his search for any colonial requirement, large or small. Some items from the catalogues are shown on this page.

To acquire an item, the Governor would send an indent to the Crown Agents who passed it on to the Colonial Office for authorization. Eventually the indent returned and the goods were bought. This cumbersome system was altered in the late 19th Century to allow the Crown Agents complete responsibility for purchases under £100. Finally, in 1903, the Crown Agents were given complete autonomy in dealing with their principals.

This bizarre spring-clip with its lacquered and bronzed hand was more likely to be used personally by the Governor than by his subordinate secretaries and clerks.

A perambulator lined with American leather-cloth came in two sizes, single and double. It was well sprung, in readiness for rough, unmade roads in out-of-the-way places.

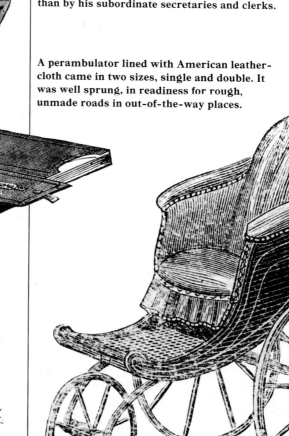

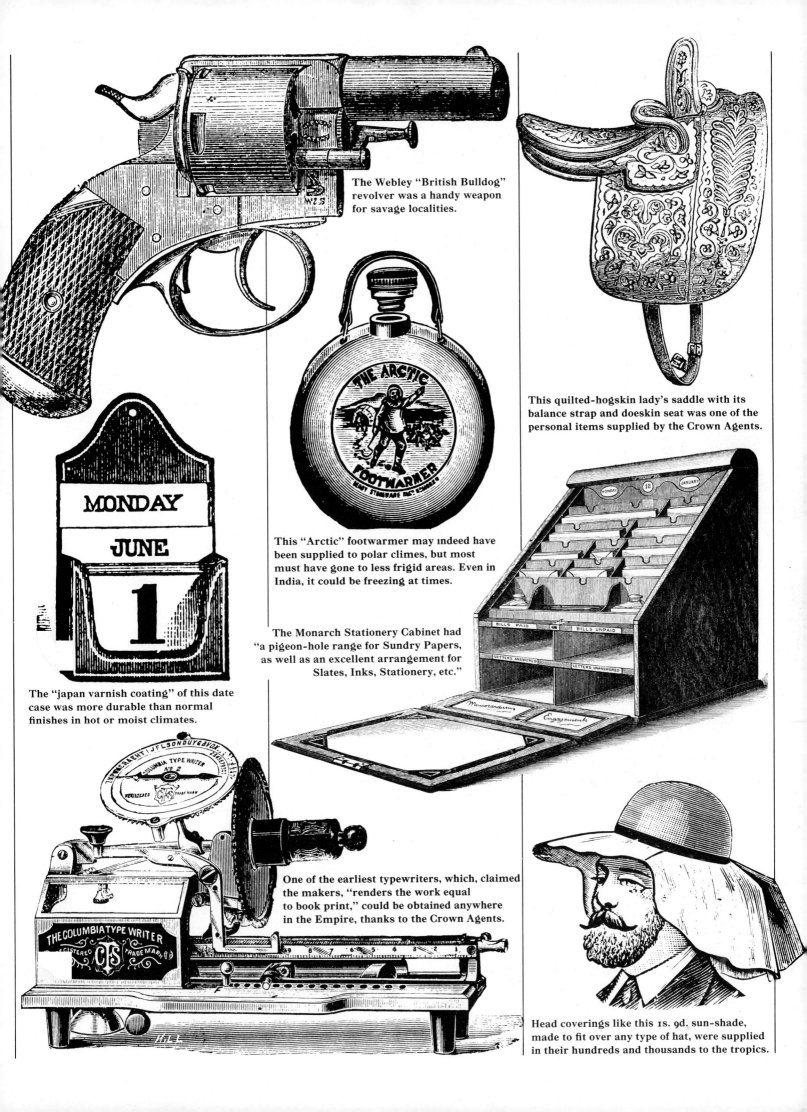

The Webley "British Bulldog" revolver was a handy weapon for savage localities.

This quilted-hogskin lady's saddle with its balance strap and doeskin seat was one of the personal items supplied by the Crown Agents.

This "Arctic" footwarmer may indeed have been supplied to polar climes, but most must have gone to less frigid areas. Even in India, it could be freezing at times.

The Monarch Stationery Cabinet had "a pigeon-hole range for Sundry Papers, as well as an excellent arrangement for Slates, Inks, Stationery, etc."

The "japan varnish coating" of this date case was more durable than normal finishes in hot or moist climates.

One of the earliest typewriters, which, claimed the makers, "renders the work equal to book print," could be obtained anywhere in the Empire, thanks to the Crown Agents.

Head coverings like this 1s. 9d. sun-shade, made to fit over any type of hat, were supplied in their hundreds and thousands to the tropics.

he had brought from England!... This in the midst of the exquisite prodigality of the tropics. They all wanted to be oh, so English."

Next to the Governor in the chain of command was the colonial secretary or chief secretary. He was the Governor's principal lieutenant, ran the administration in his absence, headed the local bureaucracy, and led the legislative council. As a permanent holder of office he supplied useful experience as well as a sense of continuity.

The man in immediate contact with the subject peoples, however, was the district officer. He needed to be exceptionally adaptable. This meant, by the criteria of the exclusive Colonial Office circles, that he had been to a public school and probably to a university, institutions which, in the view of the celebrated proconsul Lord Lugard, "produced an English gentleman with an almost passionate conception of fair play, of protection of the weak, and of 'playing the game.'" He was expected to have personal initiative and resourcefulness. One district officer had to execute seven men and marry five couples in one and the same day. "In an isolated station," wrote Lugard, "he may have to discharge the functions of all the departments—postal, customs, police and engineering—in addition to his normal work.... To him alike the missionary, the trader and the miner look for assistance and advice. The leper and the slave find in him a protector."

In many areas, of course, it was physically impossible to administer to great masses of people directly through British officers. A solution to this problem was the concept of indirect rule, which had its classical exposition under Lugard in Nigeria but was also influential in other British territories in Africa and in the Malay States and New Guinea. The imperial officials retained power to interfere when necessary, but in general the people and their tribal authorities were expected to conduct their own administration. It was a cheap method of administering a colonial territory and, it was argued, had the advantage of giving the natives the experience of governing themselves. On occasion it was also corrupt, venal, and tyrannical.

For all its stresses and tribulations the imperial machine of the New Rome worked effectively. No one actually ran the Empire, but the team that operated the machinery, from the Secretary of State and his staff in Whitehall to the Viceroy in India to the district officers and tribal chiefs in Nigeria, gave the Empire a style of administration that had much to recommend it. Nevertheless, the inclusion of native peoples in the upper ranks of the machine had scarcely begun by 1900, and British rule was regarded as being, for all practical purposes, permanent. "Localization" was not yet a word imperial administrators used freely.

The assumption that the European was inherently superior was not easily modified. But in the 20th Century there was a growing awareness that the possession of colonies in underdeveloped parts of the world carried duties and responsibilities to native populations, whose interest should be paramount, and that the Empire was not merely a vehicle for uplifting British racial pride or for extending British territorial and economic power.

The imperial order in the 19th Century was not devoid of humanity—nor was it rich in it. It was pragmatic and impersonal. It gave its subjects security, justice, impartiality, and peace. It did not offer prosperity and it did not furnish rapid constitutional, social, and political advance to its subject peoples.

—*James Morris, Trevor Reese*

III. Guardians of the Pax Britannica

Contemplating her burgeoning Empire, Queen Victoria once jotted down, in her peculiarly emphatic style, a pointed summation of its burdens. "If we are to *maintain* our position as a *first-rate* Power," she wrote, "we must, with our Indian Empire and large Colonies, be *Prepared* for *attacks* and *wars, somewhere* or *other,* CONTINUALLY." The instruments of such a policy were those twin supports of the Pax Britannica, the Queen's Army and the Royal Navy.

The story of the British Army in the 19th Century is the story of imperial wars. The army fought Chinese and Afghans, Abyssinians and Maoris, Zulus and Sudanese, Boers and Canadians. Its Victorian battle-honours are nothing less than a roll-call of Empire, or more prosaically, a gazetteer of Africa, the Near East, and Asia. Indeed, the British professional army owes its very existence to the growth of the British Empire.

Until the 18th Century the English were consumed with a violent hatred and suspicion of professional standing armies, which they regarded as obedient instruments of royal tyrants for the destruction of Parliamentary government and political liberty. The traditional militia, being merely English society with a weapon in its hand, presented no such political dangers. Indeed, it was seen to be a safeguard of national liberties against potentially absolute kings. And militarily it was perfectly adequate for the home defence of an island kingdom with a strong navy—adequate, that is, in the simple era of the longbow for tasks like repelling the Scots or putting down local rebellion.

The English Civil War, however, demonstrated that for a long war, even at home, the militia was obsolete. Then the rapid succession of wars and internal emergencies from 1661, after the restoration of Charles II, until the Treaty of Utrecht in 1713, gradually led to the establishment of a standing professional army—much against the wish of Parliament, which continued to pretend that the army was just an emergency creation that could be abolished once normal times returned.

"Normal times" never did return. In the 18th Century there were not only four more great conflicts with the French but also a steady expansion of the British Empire: in India, in North America, in the Caribbean. It was these foreign wars and colonial conquests that finally forced a permanent professional army down the throat of the British. And the colonial conquests, once made, required garrisons, a function beyond the compass of part-time citizen forces whose members disliked leaving their own country, let alone spending ten years in some fever-stricken Caribbean sugar island.

So it was that the British in the 18th Century, like the ancient Greeks and Romans before them, discovered that the acquisition of an empire brought with it the creation of a regular army made up of professionals. By the late 18th Century the army had been grudgingly accepted as a permanent feature of national life.

It was already in effect an imperial army. Though the American colonies were lost in 1783, by then India was ready to replace America as Britain's greatest imperial possession, with some 6,000 troops of the Crown as part of its garrison. Ireland, Britain's oldest and most disaffected colony, demanded 12,000, the other parts of the Empire drew in another 15,000. In England, Scotland, and Wales there were no more than some 17,000.

Wellington's victory at Waterloo in 1815 ended the need for an army capable of serving as a field force in major European wars. The prestige of his triumph gave British diplomacy an unbeatable leverage that lasted until the creation of a united Germany in 1871. The British Empire, on the other hand, kept on expanding by a self-perpetuating process that governments seemed powerless to stop. By the time of the haphazard imperial expansion in the Victorian Age it was the army rather than the navy which became the most active instrument of British power.

The heroics of the Soldiers of the Queen inspired patriotic songwriters. This example celebrates Wolseley's 1882 victory at Tel-el-Kebir in Egypt.

Thanks to this professional volunteer army scattered across the globe, the Victorians as a whole never felt the burdens of world power. The middle classes in their prosperous suburbs were not called upon to furnish officers to die in China, the Gold Coast, or Egypt; the respectable lower middle classes in their neat red-brick streets were not called upon to furnish non-commissioned officers or privates to expire of enteric fever, cholera, or heat-stroke in the Sudan, India, or southern Africa.

If the British citizenry in general had been obliged to go and fight the small colonial wars, or endure tedious years in hot garrison stations, it may well be doubted whether Britain would ever have acquired the Empire at all, let alone held on to it. For the statesmen, too, war was a noise far away, demanding little and leading them to believe that general peace in Europe could be preserved through diplomacy. It was thus the professional army that enabled the Empire to come into existence and to become a source of popular pride rather than an unpopular burden.

The army's imperial role moulded more than attitudes to Empire: it moulded the character of the army itself. For one thing, its organization was totally unlike that of 19th-Century Continental armies. It hardly existed as an "army" in the sense of a large field force organized into divisions and corps, under a single chain of command headed by a general staff. Instead it was scattered far and wide. Where a battalion might be in a remote coaling station, a couple of battalions elsewhere pacifying some dissidents, a brigade would be engaged thousands of miles away on some punitive expedition.

The personal qualities demanded of the officers and men were likewise a product of Empire-wide responsibilities. The scattering of forces in penny packets threw emphasis on the regiment as a closed family and the framework of military life. Small-scale wars against ill-armed and ill-organized natives fostered the "regimental" military qualities as the principal ingredients of military success—discipline, personal bravery, boldness in combat. At the same time, the regimental approach led to the relative neglect of the intellectual and organizational requirements necessary for the conduct of modern war. The Sikhs of India, for example, were among the most disciplined and formidable enemies the British met during the Victorian Age, yet to beat them did not call for any of the tactical and technical skills needed for success in combating a European army.

Of the victory over the Sikhs at the Battle of Gujerat in 1849 an observer wrote: "The right brigade of cavalry was ordered to charge, which they did in splendid style, cutting the enemy down in all directions, and driving them back in disorder. By this time, the fighting had become general along the whole line: roll after roll of musketry rent the air, and clouds of smoke rose high and thick, while death was dealt out without mercy; now was heard the well-known cry of 'Victory!' With levelled bayonets we charged; but they could not stand the shock of cold steel. They gave way in all directions."

Nearly 50 years later, in the Sudan campaign of 1898, little had changed in the British Army's style of fighting, despite the invention of the machine gun, quick-firing field artillery, the bolt-action magazine rifle, and smokeless powder. Drawn up at Omdurman in lines as at Waterloo, the army destroyed the Dervishes with formal volleys. Yet European armies, led by Germany, had long abandoned such parade-ground tactics in favour of small dispersed groups of men making the best possible use of cover and firing individually.

How hopelessly out of touch with modern tactical developments the imperial role had left the British Army was shown during the first stages of the Boer War in 1899, when all the courage and discipline of the British line could not avail against the accurate, long-range rifle fire of the almost invisible Boers, lying prone in the folds of the veld. The British soldiers' mindless obedience was defeated by the intelligence and initiative of the Afrikaners.

In higher leadership and field organization, too, the imperial role caused British military outlook and method to diverge further and further from those of other great powers. After 1870 especially, European military chiefs became concerned with a single professional task: the perfecting of the swift mobilization and deployment of a mass army for a great Continental war. The British continued to concentrate on how to meet a succession of essentially minor emergencies in different parts of the world.

Whereas the European armies' tasks required scientific study, deep technical knowledge, and high managerial skill, the British Army came to depend on last-moment improvisation. Whereas all European armies developed a general staff as the collective brains of what had become a "big business," the British depended on the personal resourcefulness of individual commanders—men who became Victorian heroes, like Lord Roberts of Kandahar, Lord Kitchener of Khartoum, and Sir Garnet Wolseley.

When Wolseley marched to Kumasi in 1873–74 to crush the Ashanti, he had to organize his own field force and all its logistics on the spot, besides constructing his own road and bridges through the Gold Coast jungle. His much greater expedition to Egypt in 1882, leading to the defeat of Arabi Pasha at Tel-el-Kebir, was yet another improvisation. At first it worked well, when 40,000 troops and 41,000 tons of supplies were conveyed without hitch to Egypt. However, his supply and transport arrangements later broke down, holding up his advance on Cairo. Wolseley's attempt to relieve Gordon in 1884–85 in Khartoum failed because even his remarkable energy and resourcefulness could not solve the problems of marshalling transport and supply in time. Lord Roberts, who created all his own supply and transport arrangements for his famous march to relieve the British garrison in Kandahar during the Second Afghan War in 1879, became a hero at home, but the campaign would not have impressed any of the European powers' general staffs.

Kitchener, who in 1898 organized and led the expedition that recaptured Khartoum and destroyed the Dervish power in the Sudan, was a supreme example of the British faith in a man instead of a system. Kitchener was an intense and secretive egotist who communicated his plans to no one. His office methods were absolutely chaotic; everything was in his head. There could be no greater contrast to the intricate and complex methods then prevailing in the German and French armies. In the event, Kitchener was successful in his improvisation. Nevertheless, the fact remained that his command numbered only some 15,000 men and his enemies were savage tribesmen armed with antique weapons. His final victory at Omdurman was won at the minuscule cost of fewer than 50 casualties.

Thus while the British Army adequately met the demands of its 19th-Century imperial role—despite the occasional disaster—it became less and less fit to fight a modern war against a great power. At the same time, since few of the army's imperial foes took advantage of its want of professionalism, colonial victories created a dangerous impression at home that wars were distant and exotic adventure stories, combats to be won by a hero, all essentially painless to the nation as a whole. Like the British Army itself, the Victorian public lost its sense of proportion. The defence of Rorke's Drift by less than 100 men against the Zulus in 1879 became the work of a Wellington. The miniature victories won by Kitchener or Roberts or Wolseley were hailed as the triumphs of a Marlborough.

The professional army, since it bore the burden of Empire easily, was not a primary object of national care. Several traditions had combined to remove it as an institution from the main stream of British life. There was the inveterate suspicion, dating from the time of the Stuarts, of the political dangers of an efficient army. There was the vicious circle of low pay, appalling conditions of service, and brutal discipline which by the early 19th Century had rendered military service hardly less of a disgrace than prison to the "respectable" work-

ing and lower middle classes. There was the imperial role itself, which took the army away from the heart of the nation, a role differing radically from that vital task of national preservation enjoyed by European armies. For all these reasons the Victorian army was an institution on which Parliament and the people resented spending money.

Financial stringency coupled with the army's low prestige among the lower classes as a career, coloured the whole of military life. But the army still attracted its officers from the apex of the Victorian social pyramid. Wellington as commander-in-chief sought officers who were landed gentlemen of substance as a safeguard against the political dangers he believed inherent in a professional officer corps. Officers' pay since the days of Cromwell was never sufficient to live on. They always had to be able to dip into their own pockets to support them-

selves, and many went farther and used their own funds to clothe and equip their regiments above regulation scale.

The paramount position of the wealthy upper class among the officer corps was assured by the peculiar institution of purchase. It was a survival of a custom universal throughout Europe in the 17th Century, though the Prussian and French armies had long since ended it. Commissions and the commands of regiments were bought and sold—for anything up to £14,000—until the abolition of purchase in 1872. Even then the hold of the rich and well-born was only barely relaxed; there remained the need for a private income to maintain a lavish social life, especially in the fashionable regiments that dominated the life and higher posts of the army, and this effectively kept out all but a few middle-class career officers.

The combination of rich upper-

That staple tactic of imperial warfare, the classic infantry square, was put to devastating use in the Battle of Ulundi in 1879 during the Zulu War. In this view, one side of the square has opened up to allow the cavalry to charge out and complete the victory.

class origins with the limited professional horizon of the regiment produced an officer with high natural qualities of leadership, ideal for commanding the simple type of men in the rank and file: brave and hardy in the field and adequate to the demands of the unsophisticated, small-scale warfare of imperial conquest. However, the British officer was largely lacking in intellectual curiosity, in the wider study and understanding of war. Too much of his time and attention was occupied with the social aspects of army life: hunting, polo, dinners, and balls.

The officer entered the army in one of three ways: by direct recommendation from a well-connected family friend to the colonel of a regiment; as a step up from service in the militia; or via the two army colleges—the Royal Military College, Sandhurst, for cavalry and infantry, and the Royal Military Academy, Woolwich, for engineers and gunners. There was little formal training for those who entered a regiment directly; the officer picked up the rudiments as he went along. The course at Woolwich was narrowly technical, that at Sandhurst a polite farce.

After the frightful muddle in the Crimean War exposed the inadequacy of methods and training good enough to beat Sikhs, what had been the Senior Department at Sandhurst burgeoned forth in 1857 as the Staff College. However, the courses were in general limited and technical, devoted to matters like fortification and surveying rather than to the managerial and strategic handling of great armies as taught to officers in the French and German staff colleges.

Throughout the 19th Century the recruits for the rank and file came from the very lowest level of British society. The army depended largely upon the supply of destitute Irish peasants until the famines of the 1840s drove vast numbers out of Ireland to America. Up to 1847 men enlisted for life, and between 1847 and 1870 for ten years, with the option of going on for 21 years to qualify for a pension. As in the 18th Century the recruits were found in pubs, slums, and villages. Recruiting parties persuaded the unfortunate or misguided to take the Queen's shilling by a combination of flattery, tales of glory, free drinks, and the offer of a lump-sum bounty upon joining the colours, usually

spent instantly on drink. In the 1850s and 1860s, however, when the reservoir of Irish recruits had dried up, an acute recruiting problem arose. Few "respectable" or intelligent members of society were likely to join the army for a shilling a day if they could emigrate to America or the colonies where there were opportunities to better themselves.

In the early Victorian period army life in the home islands was rough and brutal in the extreme. Soldiers in their barracks enjoyed less space than convicts in prison, and their mortality rates were double those of civilians. There were no cookhouses, but simply two copper kettles issued to each mess, in which to boil up three-quarters of a pound of meat per man which, together with a pound of bread, was the extent of the daily rations provided by the nation. Recreation consisted of wet canteens where the troops could buy liquor and "swipes," the watered-down beer supplied by rascally contractors.

In late Victorian times, however, the building of new barracks and the provision of cookhouses made the army healthy, if still tough and austere. Weedy recruits from slum homes began to find themselves better housed, better fed, and better exercised than they had ever been, and their physique and bearing improved enormously. At the same time, army discipline instilled regular habits into men who had never had any. Even on the eve of the First World War the army was still the only complete social rescue service provided by the state.

The military day consisted of parades, fatigues, and guard duty. Training hardly went beyond drill and gymnastics. Field-Marshal Sir William Robertson, one of the very few ever to rise from private soldier to field-marshal, wrote of cavalry training in the 1870s: "Antiquated and useless forms of drill, blind obedience to orders, ramrodlike rigidity on parade, and similar time-honoured practices were the chief qualifications by which a regiment was judged." Field-days, the nearest thing to the large-scale and realistic manœuvres of European armies, took place some

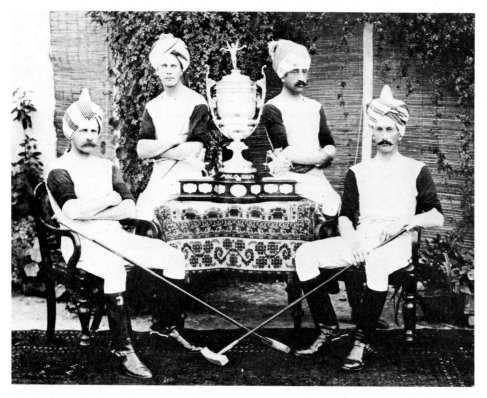

Nothing added more to the social prestige of a crack regiment stationed in India than winning a polo cup. This team of the 18th Bengal Lancers did just that in 1896.

six times a year. Right up to the Boer War, such field-days were a ritual re-enactment of the tactics of the Battle of Waterloo.

The months between October and March made up the trooping season, when fresh drafts left England for India or other imperial stations and time-expired units due for home-posting returned. Long voyages by troopships were an essential part of the experience of the imperial army. At the end of a three-week voyage through the Mediterranean, the oven-hot Red Sea, and the Indian Ocean lay Bombay, the fetid gateway to India, the British Army's second—perhaps its first—home. For generations of British soldiers right down to the Second World War, the first acquaintance with India was made in the vast transit camp at Deolali. From there the new drafts proceeded to their garrisons in slow, suffocatingly dusty, cockroach-ridden trains, moving by night and resting in camps during the day.

Despite the ferocious heat in summer, life in India—celebrated in the verses of Kipling—was good for the rank and file. Each battalion had its native bazaar to supply it with cheap food and every necessity. Even the privates had servants to wait upon them: boys to clean the bungalows, punkah-wallahs to keep the large fans or punkahs in motion without pause during the hot season, water carriers, sweepers, latrine-wallahs, cooks, laundrymen, and cleaning-boys to polish boots, brass, and equipment. In the winter there was plenty of sport, especially football and boxing.

Officers in India enjoyed a life of leisured splendour. "If you like to be waited on and relieved of home worries," wrote Winston Churchill of his service with the 4th Hussars, "India was perfection. All you had to do was hand over all your uniform and clothes to the dressing boy, and your ponies to the syce [groom], and your money to the butler, and you never need trouble any more."

Unless on active service, the duties of an officer's military day in India were not exacting: parade of the battalion or regiment at six in the morning, an hour and a half's drill or manœuvre, breakfast and orderly-room parade at which defaulters and prisoners were dealt with, then prolonged refuge from the fierce heat of the day until five in the afternoon, finally polo and, as Churchill described, "hot baths, rest, and at eight o'clock dinner, to the strains of the regimental band and the clinking of ice in well-filled glasses."

The bill for the leisure and luxuries was submitted when the army was called on to back the police in quelling communal disturbances in the close, crowded, stinking cities, or when it marched on punitive expeditions up the valleys of the North-West Frontier where enemy sharp-shooters swiftly disposed of the unskilled or unwary.

For it was to keep the internal peace of the Indian Empire and to guard it from foreign invasions that about one-half the British Army's infantry was always stationed in India. However, this was only one element of the British military strength in the subcontinent. The other was the Indian Army, made up of sepoys commanded by British officers.

The Mutiny of 1857 cast a long shadow, and the British military system in India in the late Victorian and Edwardian eras was founded on distrust of the Indian troops. From the Mutiny until the eve of the Second World War, the Indian Army was provided with no artillery of its own except mountain batteries, while its equipment and weapons were deliberately kept less modern than the British Army's. Finally, there was always one British battalion stationed with two Indian battalions in any brigade.

A myth arose and long persisted that the Indian Army was the grand source of the strategic power of the British Empire, so far as land forces were concerned. In support of this belief, historians have glibly listed all the imperial campaigns in which Indian troops were supposed to have taken part during the 19th Century. The fact was that India was an immense source of strategic weakness to Britain.

The use of Indian forces in these various campaigns far from made up for the 50 British battalions that had to be stationed permanently in India. In addition, there were the other British troops protecting the route to India from stations in Cyprus, Egypt and the Sudan, Somaliland, and Aden. The possession of India involved Britain in rivalry with other great powers, especially France and Russia, from the Mediterranean to the border between Burma and French Indo-China. Whatever India's economic value, she never constituted a net military asset, for her military contribution never began to compensate for the strategic drain she imposed on British strength or for the risks of embroilment with other powers.

The problem of finding troops for the Empire, and above all for India, dominated reforms of the organization of the army in the period between the Crimean War and the First World War. Edward Cardwell, Secretary of State for War from 1868 to 1874, brought home some 20,000 British soldiers from "white" colonies such as Canada and New Zealand, having turned over the problem of local defence to locally raised forces. He further tried to ease the problems of recruitment and reserves by new, shorter terms of service and better conditions. The difficulty was that the home battalions were in no way organized and ready to act as a field force, either in defence of Britain or in Europe.

In 1906, when Richard Haldane became War Minister, the danger posed by increasingly aggressive German ambitions was grimly apparent. This, and the improvement of relations with France, Britain's traditional enemy, opened the way to unofficial contacts between the British and French general staffs. Haldane had now urgently to reconcile the demands of the Empire, most of all India, with the need to find troops for the military support of France.

There was another and more complex problem for Haldane and his advisers to solve: the British Army's unfitness to meet a European enemy in the field. The setbacks that shocked Britain during the Boer War demonstrated how almost a century of impe-

The Road to Magdala

Robert Napier's 1868 march against the Emperor of Abyssinia was a classic of imperial campaigning. Reacting to a supposed slight from the Foreign Office, the paranoid Emperor Theodore had imprisoned the British consul and 58 other Europeans in his rocky eyrie at Magdala. Napier mounted a massive rescue operation: 13,000 British and Indian troops, an array of artillery, and 32,000 pack animals, including 44 elephants. Between his Red Sea staging area and Magdala lay 400 miles of hostile desert and mountain.

The route passed over sheer slopes and yawning chasms, yet Napier maintained a steady ten miles a day advance. On the Arogi plain before Magdala Theodore attacked. Napier was ready, and a hail of fire from his breech-loaders tore into the advancing mass. The Emperor's hordes fled.

After the crushing defeat, Theodore released his hostages. But Napier was determined on punitive measures—he would sweep the Emperor from his rock fortress. The attack began with a furious artillery bombardment, then assault troops rushed up a narrow path and burst into the fort. Theodore killed himself with a pistol Queen Victoria had given him. Napier set fire to the bastion and marched away. At home he was greeted by ecstatic crowds; to the man in the street he had showed that the lion's tail could not be tweaked with impunity. It had cost £8,600,000, but the country was consoled by the boldness of Napier's winning gamble. No one was going to quibble over the stakes.

rial warfare had led to amateurism, to narrowness of mind, to professional neglect, to wholly outdated tactics and methods—the shortcomings of an army accustomed to easy campaigns against native irregulars. Nor was it easy for the minority of keen officers to train their men, whether in England or abroad, because of the general way of life of the "imperial" army. As a Committee of Inquiry put it:

"Under the existing system the officer rarely sees the men for whose military efficiency he is responsible. They are largely employed in non-military duties, such as waiting in canteens and regimental institutes, the charge of cricket and tennis grounds . . . in addition to the large number constantly required for fatigues." And it went on to reflect upon the uneducated and frequently unintelligent men who made up the army.

The lack of education and intelligence among the rank and file pervaded the whole question of military discipline and tactics. Such men could blindly and doggedly obey their officers and N.C.O.s in parade-ground battles against natives; but against intelligent, cunning foes like the Boer farmers they were helpless.

It is to the abiding credit of Haldane and his advisers that in a few short years they succeeded in remaking the British Army from top to bottom. The War Office was reorganized and for the first time there was set up a general staff on the European pattern, with a clear division of duties. The parade-ground line and volley-firing of imperial warfare disappeared. The Staff College acquired a sense of purpose it had never enjoyed before. The war game, complete with full dummy orders and schedules, was introduced. The cavalry learned to fight on foot with rifles, to act as the eyes of the commander-in-chief instead of charging with lance or sabre. New quick-firing field guns were introduced. The British were equipped with machine guns on the scale of two per battalion, the same as in the German army. The mobilization and movement of the British Expeditionary Force to northern France was worked out down to the last comma.

As a result of all these innovations, on the outbreak of war in 1914 the army moved with a precision, efficiency, speed, and on a scale never approached by the improvised expeditions of the Victorian imperial army. Not only did it outfight its German opponents in the campaign of 1914, but it was able to act as the framework for the creation of huge citizen armies representing a cross-section of the nation, with all its talents and skills, in the four years of war that followed.

While the army was squeezing into one century a remarkably varied assortment of imperial brushfire wars, the same century witnessed a military phenomenon. From the moment in 1815 when Napoleon Bonaparte was escorted aboard the British man-of-war *Bellerophon* for transit to exile in St. Helena there began a century unique in the history of the sea—99 years, to be precise, when the prestige of the Royal Navy stood so high that sea warfare entirely ceased.

When the 19th Century began the navy was fighting its greatest war and had reached a higher peak of efficiency than any navy had ever achieved before—as Napoleon learned to his chagrin. His ambition for conquest had been world-wide, but at Trafalgar Nelson drove him off the seas and confined him to the mainland of Europe and the western edge of Asia. Ironically, in the course of his campaigns Napoleon suppressed all the former rivals of the British Navy or dragged them down with him, creating a vacuum of power at sea which only the Royal Navy could fill. The way was cleared for the British to expand and cement their Empire.

That, of course, was one use the British made of their century of sea supremacy. But it was not the only one. They also used it to make the sea safe and free for the trade of every nation, including their recent enemies. The Royal Navy put an end to piracy and almost all the slave-trade. It studied the sciences of the sea, surveyed all the coasts and oceans of the world, and published its findings for the use of every seafarer. On the day

Napoleon surrendered, the role of the navy abruptly began to change, from fighter to peace-keeper, from conqueror to policeman and scientist.

The navy's new role was the only thing that remained the same: every other aspect of seafaring changed completely in that century. It started with wooden sailing ships that had scarcely altered since they fought the Spanish Armada. It ended with steamships, steel armour, explosive shells and long-range guns, torpedoes, mines, and submarines. Looking back on it now, historians are apt to say the navy was far too slow in accepting all these inventions, that it was too self-satisfied and rested too much on its Nelsonian reputation.

There is some truth in this accusation. The great inventions of steam power and iron ships were only accepted with open reluctance by the Royal Navy. Advances in armament were mostly made by other nations, especially the French in the latter part of the century; British advances were mostly made in defence against some novelty the French had introduced. But again looking back, there is one answer to this criticism—the navy succeeded completely, all through the century, in the role the national policy had given it. And there were arguable reasons at the time for resisting change for the better.

One reason was that the fighting ships of Nelson's day had existed so long. Two hundred years of thought had gone into perfecting every detail of their building and design and the technique of sailing and fighting them. They had been tested in war after war, and in the early part of the century it was hard to imagine they could be much improved. Admiral Collingwood, Nelson's second in command at Trafalgar, always took acorns in his pocket when he went for country walks at home, scattering them in the hedges to grow into oaks for building warships a century later. That was not mere eccentricity. To everyone the wooden navy seemed eternal. It was logical enough in 1815 to think the ships that had won world-wide command of the sea were the best ships to keep it.

The navy's new work needed far fewer ships and men. In 1815 there were over 700 ships in commission, and 140,000 men; three years later there were only 130 ships and 19,000 men. Those who remained in the navy were volunteers, and that fact made a basic difference in the sailor's life. The press gangs came to an end in 1815 and were never used again. So did the system of sending minor criminals to the ships instead of prison. Now a man knew all his shipmates were there because, for one reason or another, they wanted to be. The comradeship and pride of life at sea began anew.

Slowly—sometimes ever so slowly—conditions of life aboard ship began to improve. Flogging, running the gauntlet, and other such customary punishments began to decline. Captains began to grant shore-leave, and if most of the men came back dead drunk, they did at least come back rather than deserting. And increasing numbers of trusted seamen were allowed to take their wives to sea; the Admiralty order merely said that no ship was to be "too much pestered" with wives.

Food, too, began to improve. It had always been plentiful—there was far more to eat in the navy than most people could afford ashore. It may have been true that the meat could sometimes be carved and polished like mahogany, and that buttons made of naval cheese wore better than metal or bone. Still, the weekly ration was filling: seven pounds of biscuit, six pounds of pork and beef, 12 ounces of cheese, three pints of oatmeal, two pints of peas, six ounces of butter, six ounces of sugar, and, on the one day in the week when meat was not issued, the makings of an enormous plum duff. At this time, too, came the greatest of all improvements in seamen's food—the invention of bully beef in tins. This was a French idea; its name was the British sailor's version of *boeuf bouilli*.

But the central part of naval life was still the working of the ship, and that was as tough as it had always been—four hours on watch and four off, month after month, working aloft in storm and rain and snow, living below in every climate of the world on incredibly crowded decks with no heating and little ventilation. The only thing that had gone from the sailor's job with the end of war was the chance of a battle, and life was duller without it.

Men often looked back on the war with nostalgia, calling it the "Shooting Season." For battle, after all, had not been so dangerous as it looked: at least ten times more men had died of disease and accident in the war at sea than had ever been killed in battle. And battle had brought with it the glorious gamble of prize-money, paid to any ship's company that captured an enemy and brought it home. The seaman's proportion had been very small: a lucky fight could make a captain rich for the rest of his life, yet only give each seaman enough cash to get drunk on. Still, every seaman in wartime had the excitement of hoping to win a fortune. They never forgot the occasion when two British frigates happened to capture a ship laden with treasure, and each seaman's share came to nearly £500—much more than a lifetime's pay—and the glorious party in Portsmouth afterwards when men celebrated by buying gold watches and frying them. Nothing quite so good could happen in peacetime.

If life in peace was dull for the seamen, it was duller still for the officers. Seamen had been paid off at the end of the war and they signed on again if they wanted to. But officers had started at sea when they were ten or 11 to make a life's career of the navy, and there was no way to make them retire. Three years after the war the navy still had nearly 6,000 commissioned officers. Four out of five were living ashore on half pay with nothing to do and very little chance of getting a ship again.

A favourite wardroom toast was "Bloody war and quick promotion." Now there was no war and no promotion. The upper ranks became clogged with aging men. It was a situation that grew depressing, inefficient, and finally fantastic, but the only people who could have changed it were the officers themselves, and they were not likely to suggest a reform that would lose them their easy living. Un-

Britannia poses with her traditional symbols of strength: shield, lion—and the Royal Navy. From a songsheet cover.

less an officer had exceptional private influence, promotion was entirely a matter of seniority, of waiting for older men to die. Half-way through the century there were lieutenants more than 60 years old, and a man could suddenly be promoted captain or admiral when he had not been to sea in 30 years.

These were the men who had had to drag the navy into the Age of Steam: no wonder they were slow. Steam had already started before Trafalgar; the first steam tug, the *Charlotte Dundas*, was towing barges on the Forth and Clyde Canal in 1801. Others followed during the war, in Britain, France, and America, and within a couple of years after Napoleon's downfall a steam passenger service was started from Brighton to Le Havre. But the thought of using steam in a warship was a very different matter.

This was not quite so reactionary

as it looks in retrospect. There were arguments against steam. It was still much less reliable than the wind. Paddle-wheels were vulnerable and would get in the way of the broadside of a fighting ship. If the navy, with its world-wide mission, relied on steam, it would have to set up world-wide coaling stations and defend them. Finally, the navy had a fleet of sailing ships far more powerful than anyone else's, so why should it encourage a new idea that might make its own ships obsolete?

None of these arguments could stand against technical progress. The screw propeller, for example, was fitted with great success in the early 1840s to the passenger liner *Great Britain*, and the Admiralty had to admit that a warship with a propeller could carry the traditional broadside armament. By 1851, exactly half a century after the *Charlotte Dundas*, the

navy had given up its opposition to steam. New warships were designed with engines, and some of the old ones fitted with them. But still they were sailing-ships; the engines were only used in leaving harbour and, as a last resort, when the wind fell calm.

It took a war to change naval doctrine. In the Crimean War in the 1850s there was no naval opposition, but the ships with propellers were far more useful than the ones without; steamers were more manœuvrable while supporting the army ashore, and they could keep out of the way of shore batteries. And the conflict taught another unwelcome lesson—great ships of the line, impressive though they were, were not of much tactical use when no other navy had them. Their draught was too deep. There were many shores and harbours they could not approach, and small vessels could escape them by making for shallow water. And so a new naval concept was born: the small steam-powered gunboat. For the next 50 years, "Send a gunboat" became a well-worn phrase in British diplomacy.

There have always been naval officers who prefer small ships, from Francis Drake down to the commanders of modern motor torpedoboats. In the Victorian navy the gunboat gave that kind of officer his chance. At last, after 40 years of stagnation, young men had the prospect of independent adventure and command. They made the best of it.

Gunboats were seldom offensive weapons, although they sometimes supported the army on its campaigns—on the Nile, for example, or up the rivers of China. For the most part they were the equivalent of the policeman on his beat, and all over the world people in alarming situations asked for their help and protection. British traders caught up in riots or revolutions in distant lands sent urgent requests for gunboats; so did missionaries, colonial governors, consuls, and foreign rulers. Even the British Museum and the Archbishop of Canterbury asked for gunboats—the first to protect an archaeological dig in Cyrene, the second to look after missionaries in trouble in Borneo.

In the year 1858, for example, requests came from New Zealand (to help fight the Maoris), Panama, the Kuria Muria Islands (to protect the guano trade), Honduras (a border dispute), Siam, Brazil (a slave revolt), Sarawak (to fight pirates), Alexandria, Vancouver (to police a gold rush), Vera Cruz, Morocco, and the fishing-grounds off Newfoundland. Every one of these requests was granted.

Gunboats were effective simply because they could turn up wherever there was trouble. They seldom opened fire. The mere sight of a gunboat flying the British ensign steaming into a roadstead or a river mouth with a conscious air of nonchalant rectitude was enough to discourage most troublemakers. It was a threat, or a promise, of power, a reminder that the British were keeping an eye on things. It was the growl of the lion.

The young men who commanded the gunboats were often thousands of miles away from their senior officers, and British policy put great responsibility on them. They had to weigh a local situation, judge who was right and who was wrong, and decide whether tact or a salvo of shells was needed. The power they carried did not seem to worry the young lieutenants, but it did worry the Admiralty and the Foreign Office, and gunboat commanders were told not to exceed their orders and not to involve themselves in politics—which was easier said than done.

Very occasionally, things went badly wrong. In Jamaica in 1865 the British Governor, Edward Eyre, declared martial law in a riot and appointed a gunboat commander, Herbert Brand, as president of a court martial. Brand was only 26, had no books of law on board and nobody to advise him, and broke all the rules of the administration of justice by condemning 177 civilian blacks to be hanged.

But that was an exception. Gunboat diplomacy on the whole, in its 50 years of life, unquestionably did more good than harm. Of course, it put British interests first—not principally British conquests, but British trade. But it often went far beyond that to sort out troubles where Britain was scarcely involved at all—to sup-

port a local ruler whose regime was peaceful, to oppose a movement that offended British ideas of law or morality, to protect a lawful person against lawlessness whatever his nationality. Perhaps it was arrogant, but to most Britons at the time it seemed a duty, one of the obligations of wealth and power. And although other nations sometimes resented it, especially France and the United States, most of the world appeared to be content to let the Royal Navy carry on with its laborious and almost thankless chore, and to reap the benefits of it.

To confer world-wide benefits no less than to protect the freedom and safety of the sea: that was the primary British interest, and also the interest of all sea-going nations. The policy that the sea should be safe meant more than suppressing such malefactors as pirates and slave-traders. It also meant helping ships to avoid natural hazards. British naval survey ships produced charts and sailing directions (pilots) for all the seas of the world that were far better than any others, even where others existed. It was a huge undertaking, so expensive that nobody else could have done it, and the resulting fund of information might well have been treated as a naval secret—in war it would have been priceless.

But war at sea seemed inconceivable, and British Admiralty charts and pilots were published for anyone to use. They still are. Some other nations since then have made their own, but the original British surveys are hard to beat. Many of today's charts are based on those drawn by Victorian officers. These men crossed and recrossed every ocean under sail or in primitive steamships, observed the sun and stars, sounded with lead and line, landed with infinite patience on every rock and reef, and rowed into every creek and harbour.

Seafarers are now safe from pirates, slavers, uncharted rocks, and unpredicted currents. It is taken for granted that ships of every nation, in times of peace, can go unmolested wherever they wish. But that is not an ancient freedom. It is a legacy of the century when the British said it should be so.

In the second half of the 19th Cen-

tury the British began to take a romantic pride in the Royal Navy, to show a sentimental affection for it the army never shared in quite the same degree. It was a great age for naval songs and poems. "The Old Superb," "Drake's Drum," "Admirals All," "Land of Hope and Glory," "Rule Britannia": gentlemen sang them at musical evenings in drawing rooms, and humbler men in pubs, and everyone joined in choruses that brought tears to the eye.

In sober fact, however, the British were beginning to delude themselves about their navy—to think the British, in some special way, had the sea in their blood, that British sailors were by nature the best in the world, and always had been. Britannia seemed to have ruled the waves so long that they came to believe she had always ruled them in the past, and always would in the future:

> When Britain first, at Heaven's
>   command,
> Arose from out the azure main,
> This was the charter of the land,
> And guardian angels sung this strain:
> "Rule, Britannia, rule the waves;
>   Britons never will be slaves."

It was an old verse, but they gave it a new lease on life. It was a call to greatness, but it was taken as a statement of historical fact. As such, it was nonsense. Britain in fact had been a late starter as a maritime power; her prowess at sea only dated back to the defeat of the Spanish Armada, and between the Armada and Napoleon's downfall that power was often challenged. Historically, Britannia's self-appointed task did not go back far.

And as for the future, it was dangerous nonsense. The British began to have blind faith in the navy's invincibility, and the blind faith infected the navy, too. It seemed unthinkable that the navy of Nelson could ever be defeated. But towards the end of the century the navy's supremacy rested more and more on bluff, a hollow self-confidence with no real power, or not enough power, behind it. It is the nature of a bluff that somebody sooner or later will call it.

It was not in the quality of its seamen or its officers that the Royal Navy

Spithead Review

The royal review of the fleet at Spithead in 1897 took place four days after the Jubilee procession. It was a less imperial occasion than the great parade to St. Paul's, but it was a far more explicit statement of intent.

The Royal Navy was insular, introspective, proud, and at Spithead it deliberately struck its grimmest and gaudiest pose. The review was said to be the largest assembly of warships ever gathered at anchorage, and it must have been one of the most brilliant. In lines seven miles long were 170 ships, including 50 battleships.

Most were ablaze with brass and bunting, and not one of them (it was carefully publicized) had been specially withdrawn from foreign station. They were war machines of formidable silhouette: painted white and yellow, cluttered with barbettes, torpedo booms, and conning towers, some with funnels side by side, some with enormous turrets like fortresses; their crews spotless in white along the rails, their officers on the bridges in postures of unapproachable swagger. As the Prince of Wales and his guests inspected the fleet in a convoy of elegant yachts there was a touch of Nelsonian impertinence. Quite unannounced appeared the fastest ship afloat, the experimental *Turbinia,* belching flame from her funnel as she weaved exuberantly among the giants.

Yet beneath the glitter was a hollowness. None of these ships had ever fought a battle. They were stronger in numbers than in fighting power. Most were out of date. A Goliath was standing guard over the Pax Britannica.

lagged behind—it was in the design of its ships and armament. That was not surprising. For generations the navy had been designed to keep the peace, and the peace looked everlasting. It could not give all its attention to that and still be prepared for war. British seamen may not have had quite the heaven-sent skill of the patriotic songs, but they were certainly good, and there was something peculiarly British about the finer arts of naval seamanship. But seamanship could not win if a hostile power appeared on the sea with faster ships and guns of longer range, and that was what was happening.

The French were the principal pacesetters in design, with the United States sometimes taking a part when she was not too preoccupied with her own westward expansion. The competition with France went back as far as 1848, when the French launched the first line-of-battle ship that was designed for a steam engine. She was ominously named the *Napoleon.* The British made their counter-move two years later with the *Agamemnon.* But the *Napoleon* could make voyages under steam alone, and reached a speed of nearly 14 knots. The *Agamemnon* was no more than a sailing ship with a small auxiliary engine.

The next move was in the late 1850s, when the French replaced solid cannon-balls with explosive shells for naval guns, and also built the obvious corollary—an armour-plated ship, the *Gloire,* that could withstand them. Both navies started breech-loading guns at about the same time, but the French mechanism worked and the British one did not; it so often burst and injured or killed its crew that the British went back to muzzle-loading for another 20 years.

Larger guns had longer range and far more hitting power, so that a few large guns became better than a mass of small ones. That meant putting them in revolving mountings on the centre-line of the ship instead of in the broadside gunports that had been used since Henry VIII. That in turn meant that the masts and rigging of a sailing ship restricted the arcs of fire. The daring answer to this was to get rid of the rigging and rely on

steam alone. The United States took this step with the *Monitor* in 1862. The British ironclad *Devastation* of 1873 was a product of fierce controversy, and a rather more orthodox rival, the *Captain,* was launched the same year. She had armour, steam, centre-line guns—and a full rig of sail. But she also had the low freeboard that the heavy guns demanded, and she capsized and sank in a storm in the Bay of Biscay. That disaster was the final end, after so many centuries, of the battleship under sail.

So it went on: the French first made steel armour instead of iron, followed ten years later by the British. In retrospect, one would think the British lacking in inventiveness. But that was certainly not the trouble. Britain led the world in mechanical invention, even at sea, with the single exception of developments in warships. The trouble was that the Admiralty still behaved, with all these new ideas, exactly as it had with steam: it wanted to shut its eyes to anything that threatened to make its huge fleet obsolete.

The most striking case of this attitude was the submarine. The early submarines were American, and they began—under manpower—as early as 1776. In 1804, a year before Trafalgar, one was offered to the British by the American inventor Robert Fulton. The First Lord of the Admiralty rejected it—not because it would not work but because it might. Submarines continued to exist, but the Admiralty continued for nearly a century to pretend they did not, until the French built one in 1899 that could make ocean passages.

The torpedo was another weapon the British would gladly have discouraged. In various elementary forms they also dated back to the War of Independence, but the first that could steer itself under its own power was invented by Robert Whitehead in 1867. Whitehead was a Scotsman, but his invention was inopportune for Britain. It could be fired by a very small ship to sink a very big one—and Britain owned most of the big naval ships in the world. France, Germany, Russia, and Japan all equipped themselves with fleets of small fast torpedo boats. The British had to fit their battleships with small defensive guns as anti-torpedo boat armament and with cumbersome torpedo nets to be rigged round the ships at anchor.

In the 1880s and 1890s new ideas and inventions were coming so fast that a warship could be obsolete before it was launched. Britain had formed a policy of maintaining a navy at least as large as any other two navies in the world. But other navies grew, and a race in sheer numbers began. British yards turned out new battleships and cruisers at hectic speed. But they had an inherent weakness. Most were designed to counterbalance some specific threat—a new arrangement of armour, for instance, to stop a new kind of shell. They were not designed as a coherent fleet to fit a strategic plan. There were far too many different kinds of ships, and of machinery, guns, and ammunition. Training, store-keeping, and maintenance grew impossibly complex.

The naval review arrayed at Spit-head for Victoria's Diamond Jubilee in 1897 was a splendid spectacle and a source of pride to the nation. But something was terribly wrong, and a few people knew it. The truth was that if any other nation started from scratch and built a modern, smaller, more coherent fleet, most of the British ships would be useless against it. And in 1898 another nation began to do so—not one of Britain's traditional rivals, but a naval upstart: Germany.

What the navy needed was a man who was clear-headed and perfectly ruthless, and luckily it produced one: Admiral Sir John Fisher. In 1901 "Jacky" Fisher became Second Sea Lord and instantly began to show his power. The appointment made him responsible for personnel, and within two years he totally changed the navy's training. He disregarded or trampled on opposition (of which there was a great deal), founded the colleges for officers at Osborne and Dartmouth, extended officer training from 18 months to four years, scrapped the ancient training ships for seamen and replaced them with schools ashore.

For a year after that he was commander-in-chief Portsmouth. Then, in 1904, he came back to the Admiralty as First Sea Lord, which gave him the chance to be equally ruthless about the navy's ships. "Scrap the lot" was his best-remembered phrase; he wrote it across a list of 154 ships, including 17 battleships. Then he produced world-wide strategic plans for the navy's disposition, no longer as a police force, but in readiness for the war at sea that the Germans were seen to be planning. A new battleship was planned with ten 12-inch guns and turbine engines, and the first of the class was built from start to finish in a year and a day—the famous *Dreadnought.*

The storms he raised blew away a century's dust and cobwebs. It was just in time to meet the challenge of 1914.

—*Correlli Barnett, David Howarth*

The design of H.M.S. *Dreadnought*, shown here at her launch in February, 1906, symbolized Jacky Fisher's recasting of the Royal Navy to meet the new challenges of the 20th Century. She was the largest, fastest, most powerful battleship of her day.

Chapter Nine
THE BUSINESS OF EMPIRE

The commercial links and advantages of Empire were frequently cited arguments in support of imperialism. This Peninsular & Oriental steamship line travel poster suggests these links while at the same time sounding the alluring call of exotic places.

I. Trade and Capital: the Other Empire

As Britain's Empire grew through the 19th Century into the vast mosaic of Victoria's realms, a second edifice grew up beside it. It had its roots in the onset of technical innovation and large-scale industry. Transforming the soil of the homeland, eventually sweeping sail from the seas, it mushroomed into a great parallel structure built on trade and capital—the "Other Empire." For many years the two empires—the Queen's Empire of fleets and armies, proconsuls and officials, and the Other Empire ruled by increasingly powerful manufacturers, bankers, and investors—were largely independent of each other. And though towards the close of the 19th Century their spheres of interest increasingly merged, they never completely coincided.

An empire of imperial trade had existed in embryo since the days of the first British overseas possessions. The colonies sent home whatever their pioneers produced. Canada supplied English shipyards with masts from her splendid pine forests and furs for the well-to-do. Sugar and tobacco from the West Indies and America flooded into Britain, and light, comfortable Indian cottons displaced cruder homespuns. Tea, coffee, and chocolate soon appeared on English tables.

In exchange, British farmers supplemented the colonial diet and cottage-based spinners and weavers sent clothing and fabrics. Scotland dispatched her pots and pans and linens, Manchester her fustians. And for the mother country the trading balance was augmented by revenues from India: the spoils of conquest and annexation, the interest on loans floated in Calcutta, the profits brought home from the East by retired Nabobs.

Lest the national interest be endangered, however, all British trade was fenced about with a host of restrictions. To keep imports within bounds, duties—many of them prohibitive—were levied against nearly a thousand articles and commodities, and the export of materials considered vital to Britain's livelihood or security was virtually forbidden. At the same time, the Navigation Laws, dating back to medieval times and reinforced by Cromwell in the 17th Century, still laid down that, by and large, British trade be carried in British ships.

The restrictions buttressed a system managed by a ruling landed aristocracy more concerned with political stability in Britain than with economic opportunity. British trade beyond Europe gained little ground during this era.

Yet beneath the placid surface of this 18th-Century Georgian Golden Age, forces of profound change were gathering momentum. Population was increasing. Interest in science was spreading. It was clear that below the broad acres of farm and park lay thick seams of coal and rich deposits of iron ore. And Adam Smith, in *The Wealth of Nations* published in 1776, launched the first serious attack on trade restriction, urging instead the benefits of exchange based on specialization.

All these stirrings were brought together by men of technical genius: by Abraham Darby and Henry Cort applying coal to the smelting of iron; by Thomas Newcomen, James Watt, and John Wilkinson developing the steam engine; by George Stephenson and Henry Bell setting the engine on rails and in the hull of a boat; by James Hargreaves, Richard Arkwright, and Samuel Crompton introducing machines to spin cotton; by Matthew Boulton, Robert Owen, and Josiah Wedgwood organizing technology into business. They and their associates not only released productive power on an unheard-of-scale, but spread a new attitude to its proceeds.

For the most part, ironmasters, engine-wrights, inventors, and proprietors were men of humble urban origin, the antithesis of the landed gentry with their comfortable inherited rent-rolls. Self-made, thrifty, they knew the creative value of money and were well aware of the vital importance of ploughing back profits, thus amassing capital to perpetuate and expand the cycle of production and distribution.

Two industries in particular—the manufacture of cotton and woollen clothing—leaped ahead as a result of the new productivity. Their demands for raw materials quickly affected the old patterns of overseas trade. By 1810 the hand-spinners of cotton, who had drawn most of their supplies from the eastern Mediterranean, were extinct. The new Lancashire mills were importing growing quantities of cheaper, better-quality cotton from the slave plantations of the American South. And Yorkshire, previously working with wool from flocks in Spain, Saxony, Silesia, and England, was turning to a source within the Empire.

In the 1790s the tempestuous Australian John Macarthur had started to breed sheep experimentally on his farm near Sydney, basing his flock on five pure Merino rams purchased from the royal stud at Kew. Soon Macarthur was declaring that beyond the Blue Mountains "lay tracts of land adapted for pasture so boundless that no limit can be set to the fine-woolled sheep which can be raised." Their imagination fired, free settlers and ex-convicts began their surge inland, buying up every head of sheep they could afford. Wool imports from Australia rose with extraordinary rapidity.

The main encouragement for the burgeoning British economy came from Napoleon. The great wars with France at the turn of the century created demand for every kind of manufacture, while at the same time they conveniently disabled European competition. And as a result of Britain's role as purveyor to the armies of her allies, wartime dealings vastly increased the experience of British merchants in international trade. Mexican silver arriving in London from the sale of calico in Spain had to be changed into other currencies to meet military pay rolls falling due in Flanders; uniforms from Bradford, sabres and muskets from Birmingham, saddlery from Norwich, horses from Ireland, needed to be assembled and delivered to Trieste for a campaign in Austria. Only British firms had the chance to master such intricate operations and to make them matters of everyday routine.

Equally valuable, the struggle against Napoleon increased the quantity of capital in Britain available for investment. It was, first of all, accumulating rapidly from industrial expansion at home. The banking system of deposits, of loans, of notes and credit to speed and multiply money was getting into its headlong stride. And the French Wars brought in refugee funds. Led by the wealthy financiers of Amsterdam, bankers from all over Europe, eager to find safe outlets for their capital, transferred great sums to Britain. With all these funds at hand, with profits and savings accruing beyond the needs of home industry, the search began for fields abroad where the surpluses could be rewardingly invested.

In the early 1820s, the first years of peace the 19th Century knew, very little of the world understood the rules of capitalism. In the eyes of the London money-market the imperialists certainly did not: the Empire was seen as a collection either of sparsely populated white colonies or of primitive native territories. Only Europe and the Americas offered responsible and hopeful fields for investment. "The confidence of capitalists flies by the law of its nature from barbarism and anarchy to follow civilisation and order": thus, somewhat pompously, spoke the historian Thomas Babington Macaulay. But as a rough yardstick it was true. So the first major outward movement of British capital took its course across the Channel and the Atlantic.

Loans from London underpinned the reconstruction of Europe. The peerage conferred on Nathan Rothschild for his prominence in floating them set his merchant-banking house on the road to power. And a City firm headed by Alexander Baring, "a heavy-looking young man with a hesitant manner," quickly rose to fame by lending to the Continent. There were now, it was whispered, six great powers in Europe: Britain, France, Russia, Austria, Prussia—and the Baring Brothers.

At the same time, an institution that had evolved from Jonathan's Coffee House in London's Change Alley, now known as the Stock Exchange, began to display a lively interest in Latin America. Here was a group of young countries manfully throwing off the yoke of Spain and Portugal. To help them on their way would combine British ideals of freedom with the prospect of future trade. Such was the rush to finance Chile, Colombia, Peru, and Brazil that when a joking broker proposed an issue for the non-existent "Republic of Poyais on the Mosquito Coast" it was heavily over-subscribed by eager investors.

Much more important was the first quiet interest shown by far-sighted investors in the young United States, where canals were criss-crossing the East and Midwest and cotton-planters were extending their fields towards the Gulf of Mexico.

This first wave of British overseas investment came largely from the big men of the City, for the small investor had scarcely appeared. Much of the investment, especially the loans to Latin America, turned out badly. But it raised London's eyes permanently to the world scene. It increased foreign purchasing power and so created new markets for British goods. It advertised, to all nations eager for progress, Britain's new role as trader and money-lender.

And it did next to nothing for the British Empire. To the leaders of the growing empire of trade, the Empire of the Union Jack meant little. Indeed, many businessmen actively disliked the whole imperial idea. They saw the British possessions merely as costly liabilities, and to judge from the experience with the American colonies, transitory liabilities at that. Their sights were set on the wider world. For this reason they found increasingly irksome the old labyrinth of restrictions that strait-jacketed the movement of goods. Did the well-being of powerful progressive Britain really hinge on continuing the ancient rules that severely limited the import of bulrushes, canaries, fossils, and manna? Was it rational to retain long lists of dutiable articles when just 17 of them produced nine-tenths of the entire Customs revenue? The Corn Law, enacted in 1815 at the insistence of the landowners to exclude cheap foreign cereals, was anathema to industrialists; to them cheap food meant cheap labour.

Year by year Manchester, with its ever-swelling export of cotton goods, was growing more influential. Its foremost men—wealthy spinners like the tireless James Turner, the acid-tongued Hugh Mason, the fox-hunting Quaker Edmund Ashworth—were increasingly powerful. Britain, they argued, had nothing to fear from foreign competition. Let her sell to all, buy from all, as market opportunity dictated. Let her take the lead in freeing trade. Others, with needs to satisfy and goods to offer, would follow suit.

"Free Trade," industrialist Richard Cobden proclaimed, "is God's diplomacy." Free trade was based on the concept of non-interference or *laissez-faire* (literally, "let-do," i.e., "let people do as *they like*"). This, it was thought, was the only certain way of binding nations together in peace. Ensure that other peoples, be they subjects of the Queen or not, could earn the wherewithal to buy from Britain: then British merchandise, "carrying the seeds of intelligence" abroad, would be able to perform its task of civilizing and uplifting.

At Westminster free trade found a less idealistic but very practical champion in Lord Palmerston, Foreign Secretary in the 1830s. Aware that some nations might not immediately perceive its advantages, he declared it was government's duty "to open and secure the roads for the merchant" —and if the occasion demanded, with the help of the guns of the Royal Navy.

One such nation was China. The Chinese had always strictly controlled their trade with the outside world. British merchants and their Western colleagues were permitted to trade only at Canton. Moreover, though the demand for teas and silks in England was high and growing, the Chinese would admit few British products in exchange. The one commodity they were prepared to accept without limit was silver, and the readiest way for the British merchants to obtain silver was through the illegal sale, in China, of Indian opium.

When Peking, alarmed at the toll the drug was taking, tried to halt the trade, the resulting Opium War was a resounding British "victory." By the Treaty of Nanking (1842) Hong Kong was ceded to Britain to become the great clearing-house of British Pacific trade, and five ports along the coast were opened to foreign commerce. The Other Empire had forced the gates of the Celestial Empire.

In England the free trade movement was becoming irresistible. The customs lists shortened, the duties on industry's staple materials shrank. The Great Hunger caused by the Irish potato famine of 1845 sounded the knell of the Corn Law. Four years later the Navigation Acts disappeared. The world, selling to Britain, catalysed by London's overseas investments, rushed to order a wide variety of British goods.

Around the damp foggy sprawl of Manchester in Lancashire the cotton towns moved to specialization as production escalated, Bolton, Chorley, and Preston concentrating on the finer cloths, Oldham on mediums, Burnley on ordinary printings, and Blackburn on *dhotis*, the long, universally worn loin-cloths for the Indian trade. Neighbouring Yorkshire spewed forth the woollens and worsteds of Bradford, Huddersfield, and Barnsley. Now producing more than two-thirds of all British exports, the two counties enjoyed perpetual markets, for all clothes need replacing eventually.

Over the forges and machine shops of the Black Country Dickens recalled that "as far as the eye could see tall chimneys crowding on each other, poured out their plague of smoke." Along the Clyde the shapes of furnaces and foundries blotted out the hills. From the mines of Tyne and Tees, the Midlands and South Wales, came top-grade coal to fire British-built boilers. From Birmingham came edged tools, harness, bedsteads, trinkets; from the Potteries, Leeds, Sheffield, Nottingham, from a hundred shapeless sooty towns, came the china, glass, cutlery, footwear, and ornaments that tempted the throngs in far-off bazaars with the vision of a new way of living.

And the imports, freed from all restrictions save moderate revenue-earning tariffs, came pouring in to the docks of London and Liverpool. Shawled Lancashire girls were now dependent for three-quarters of their raw cotton on the "peculiar institution" of slavery in the Southern United States. Yorkshire weavers relied on the sing-song chants of the wool-auctioneers 13,000 miles away in Sydney, where a squatter's entire clip—after his long fight against drought, wild dogs, and land agents —would be bought in a split second by the movement of a hat or the waggle of a beard. Foodstuffs too, like grain and pork, were beginning to come in.

Selling abroad had its setbacks. With China now open, "the heads of staid Lancashire manufacturers were turned by the prospect of 300 million customers waiting to buy their shirtings." China accepted the shirtings —on a modest scale, so it seemed, for her size—but she stopped short at more "primitive" British goods. A Sheffield firm shipped a huge batch of knives and forks to test the market, "declaring themselves ready to supply all China with cutlery." On the spot, however, gowned impassive merchants politely pointed out that the subjects of the Celestial Empire had abandoned such crude implements on becoming civilized centuries before. For years Sheffield's finest products, fashioned into knick-knacks, were hawked round Hong Kong at knockdown prices.

But most other countries were greedy for the products of British factories. "High output, low cost" was the order of the day in Great Britain. It took its toll. "In the midst of plethoric plenty the people perish; amid gold walls and full barns no man feels safe or satisfied." This protest by the historian Thomas Carlyle, like the poet William Blake's rage against the dark satanic mills, marked the murkier aspect of the Other Empire's foundations. Low wages, long hours, child labour, slums—"abodes of men o'er which the smoke of unremitting fires hangs permanent"— these were the cost of the first phase of "God's diplomacy," of ploughing back profits relentlessly into expansion at home and development of markets overseas.

In 1851, when Victoria and Albert opened the Great Exhibition in Hyde Park, doubts about the booming economy could be set aside. For here, in the most original and sumptuous of trade fairs, stood the embodiment of free trade's triumph. Here was enshrined Britain's lightning passage from the age of soil and sail to the era of steam and capital; from the closed trading estate to the open world market. Here she displayed everything her new productivity could offer, from tankards and carpets to machine-looms and hydraulic presses. Here she showed the welcome she now extended to the wares of other nations: to Tunisian dresses, Austrian musical boxes, Indian jewellery; to the raw cottons, fleeces, jutes, oils, hides, that her manufacturing economy required. And beneath Sir Joseph Paxton's glittering naves of glass, Britain's capitalists, traders, workmen, and their foreign guests celebrated their country's dazzling success by consuming 900,000 Bath buns

Text Continued on Page 349

THE GREAT EXHIBITION

"We shall probably have to give up the whole Exhibition," Prince Albert gloomily wrote in July, 1850, for the public was outraged by his Royal Commission's plan to build a squat exposition hall in Hyde Park. Then Joseph Paxton came forward with a brilliant design for a vast, imaginative glass structure, and Britain's "Exhibition fever" rose as rapidly as the building. For the opening on May 1, 1851, fully half a million people thronged the park, many taking to boats on the Serpentine for a better view of the Crystal Palace (below). And the "Great Exhibition of the Works of Industry of all Nations" – shown in the contemporary watercolours on these pages – was an unprecedented success from the start.

Victoria found the sight "magic and impressive" as she mounted the sun-drenched dais beneath the great glass arch of the transept to open the Exhibition, her "dearest Albert" at her side. A 27-foot-high crystal fountain lifted a sparkling lacework of spray above the dignitaries, while a giant leafy elm lent the proceedings a cool, green aura.

Problems had threatened the Exhibition up to the last minute. China had sent so few exhibits that Commissioners had to rush round borrowing from English collectors to fill the Celestial Empire's stands. The Russian exhibits were still at sea. But all problems were submerged in the flourish of trumpets and 100-gun salute that answered Lord Breadalbane's stentorian pronouncement: "Her Majesty commands me to declare this Exhibition open." It was, said the Queen, "a day to live for ever."

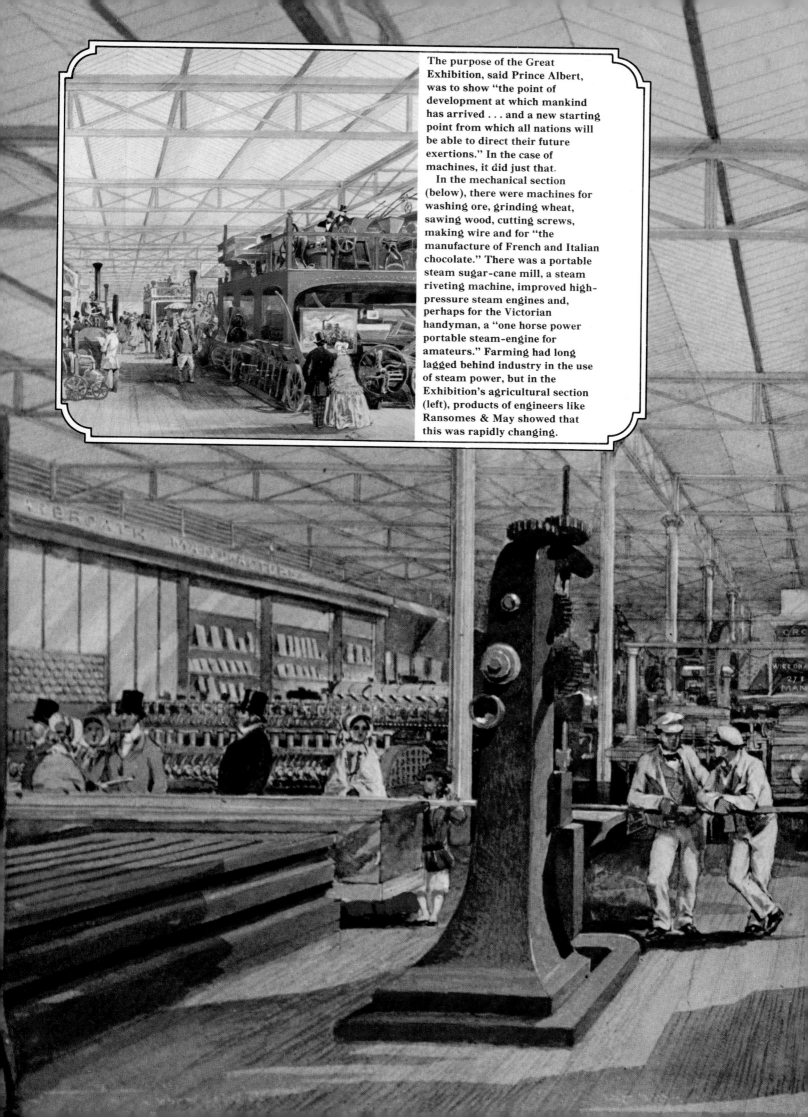

The purpose of the Great Exhibition, said Prince Albert, was to show "the point of development at which mankind has arrived . . . and a new starting point from which all nations will be able to direct their future exertions." In the case of machines, it did just that.

In the mechanical section (below), there were machines for washing ore, grinding wheat, sawing wood, cutting screws, making wire and for "the manufacture of French and Italian chocolate." There was a portable steam sugar-cane mill, a steam riveting machine, improved high-pressure steam engines and, perhaps for the Victorian handyman, a "one horse power portable steam-engine for amateurs." Farming had long lagged behind industry in the use of steam power, but in the Exhibition's agricultural section (left), products of engineers like Ransomes & May showed that this was rapidly changing.

The Great Exhibition was much more than a trade fair; it was a national experience. Merchants took a keen interest in seemingly prosaic displays like the woollen fabrics seen here, surmounted by banners bearing the arms of the great textile-manufacturing cities. Workers could find products from their own factories, a symbol of their involvement in the Industrial Revolution.

This sense of participation drew people of all classes from every part of Britain, many making their first-ever railway journeys on cheap excursions for the Exhibition's "shilling days." But many returned again and again, and attendance soared. Among the most faithful visitors was the Queen herself, who toured the Crystal Palace more than 40 times and professed that "it has taught me so much that I never knew before."

and over a million bottles of assorted soft drinks.

High output, low cost. It was the secret of the ever-steepening curve that was to multiply Britain's exports ten times over in the course of the 19th Century, from £58,000,000 to nearly £500,000,000; to increase her overseas investment of capital from a mere £10,000,000 in 1816 to over £700,000,000 in 1870. Yet even at the time of the Great Exhibition Britain was already importing more than she was exporting. In only three years between 1816 and 1913 did her sales abroad exceed her purchases. But her unfavourable trading balance was more than compensated in the sums earned by the services she was rendering to the world. The greatest of these was shipping.

This began, of course, in the age of sail. The fantastic growth of British trade is, by and large, a sober chronicle of careful businessmen. Risks were accepted, if the possibility of profit was great enough, but the leading merchants and manufacturers and financiers of the era were rarely romantic where their money was at stake.

There was, however, one glorious and relatively short-lived exception to this sensible approach—the tea trade with China that was carried halfway round the world in the now-legendary clipper ships.

In the 1860s the Pagoda anchorage at Foochow was a renowned place. For it was from here, near the southern tip of Lo-sing Island, that the annual tea-races from China to England started. The teas of China were both valuable and perishable. If kept too long at sea they lost the subtlety of their fragrance. So the first shipments of each season's crop to reach the London docks invariably fetched the highest prices. The faster ships of the tea fleet commanded a freight rate of up to £7 a ton, and for the vessel that outpaced her rivals an additional premium was waiting. Big money was at stake, too, in betting on the winner, for the races had become a sporting as well as a commercial event. Bewhiskered wagerers in West End clubs engaged in furious arguments on the merits of hulls, rigs, and can-

vas; office-boys in the City gave each other black eyes. And it was taken for granted that the only ships that stood a chance of a place were the clippers.

The clippers were the fastest and loveliest sailing ships the world ever saw. They were loosely described as "any sort of square-rigger that carries just as much sail as the traffic will bear, including the captain's shirt." Their design had originated in the genius of American shipbuilders. They could trace their ancestry back to the nimble 18th-Century pilot-boats of Chesapeake Bay and the ranging privateers of the War of 1812.

By the 1840s and 1850s there was a rising demand for ships that combined extreme speed with adequate carrying capacity. The sea trade from the Orient was growing. The gold rushes in California and Australia had sent seasick hopefuls scurrying by the thousands across stormy seas. Irish emigrants were clamouring for passage to New York. Wherever there were passengers or light, high-value cargoes to be moved, ships of the clipper type—with their long fine hulls, concave bows, clean-run sterns, and their huge spread of sail—were among the most profitable vessels afloat.

Using softwood hulls, the Americans evolved ever-larger ships with towering masts and tremendous spars. From America, in 1845, came *Rainbow*, first of the true Yankee Clippers. So hollow did her lines appear that old salts, gathered round the cracker-barrel, swore she looked as though she was constructed inside out; they were convinced she could never survive a real sea. The next year *Sea Witch* began a skein of record-breaking never matched by a sailing ship of her size. Then came *Oriental*, making the London docks only 97 days after leaving Canton, the first ship under the Stars and Stripes to land a cargo of prime tea in England. In that one voyage she netted freight money that covered three-quarters of her building cost.

American clippers were capturing the tea trade, and for the British worse was to follow. Donald McKay of Boston, greatest of the clipper designers, entered the lists. From

Cutty Sark

The most celebrated British clipper, *Cutty Sark*, only achieved fame late in her career, when at last she got the master she deserved. It was Captain Richard Woodget who coaxed the extra knots needed to beat all comers on the Australia-to-England run.

Launched at Dumbarton on the Clyde in 1869, *Cutty Sark* was small by clipper standards —921 tons, half the displacement of McKay's great Yankee Clippers. But the sleek lines of her copper-clad teak hull and the 32,000 square feet of canvas she carried meant speed (she was capable of over 17 knots) under a driving captain. But for the first 16 years of her life, only second-raters commanded her.

When Woodget took her helm in 1885, however, *Cutty Sark* seemed to take flight. A 49-year-old Norfolk farmer's son, he had sailed the seven seas as seaman, steward, cook, and mate; he was an intuitive sailor and a born leader, able to get the best from both ship and crew at any time and in any weather. *Cutty Sark* began a dazzling series of record-breaking voyages, speeding Australian wool from Sydney to Britain in 77 days as against the 100 or so for most of her rivals.

These glory days were brief. In the mid-1890s, no longer able to compete with steamships, she was sold to a Portuguese firm. For almost three decades she roamed the sea lanes as the *Ferreira*, all but forgotten. Then Captain Wilfred Dowman bought the careworn vessel and restored her to her former glory. Today *Cutty Sark* is berthed at Greenwich, the sole surviving example of the breathtakingly beautiful clippers.

The *Cutty Sark* enjoyed the proudest moment of her life on July 26, 1889, when she swept past the P. & O. steamer *Britannia* off eastern Australia. The crack mail ship had overtaken the clipper on the previous day, but with a freshening wind the *Cutty Sark* caught her up off Sydney and stormed past at 17 knots. The clipper had been anchored for a full hour in Sydney Harbour when the *Britannia* steamed in, her passengers and crew lining the rails to give the remarkable sailing-ship a resounding cheer.

Brunel

Isambard Kingdom Brunel, the greatest engineer of the 19th Century—perhaps of any century—revolutionized every field he touched. His tunnels and bridges were not only innovative but their portals and towers were pleasing to the eye. Crack trains on his Great Western Railway averaged nearly a mile a minute —in the 1850s.

But it is as a shipbuilder that Brunel is best remembered. He had an iron determination to excel and an imagination that was breathtaking. His first vessel, the *Great Western*, was not only the largest steamship of its day but furnished conclusive proof that transatlantic steam navigation was practical. The *Great Britain* that followed seven years later was the first iron-hulled, screwdriven liner.

But it was with the *Great Eastern*, this third and last ship, that Brunel outdid himself. Launched in 1858, she was four times the displacement of any vessel afloat; a larger ship was not built for half a century.

Brunel died in 1859 and was thus spared knowing the sad fate of the *Great Eastern*. For once his vision had exceeded the technology of his time, and the huge vessel's engines were insufficient for their task. And bad luck dogged the leviathan from the start. She ended her nautical career as a cable-layer in the Atlantic and the Far East. The *Great Eastern* may have been a failure, but she was a magnificent one. "The commercial world thought him extravagant," a friend wrote of Brunel, "and although he was so, great things are not done by those who sit and count the cost of every thought and act."

1850 on he produced a series of speeding monsters of 2,000 tons or more: *Lightning, Champion of the Seas, James Baines,* and—as her owners gratefully called her—the *Donald McKay.* These were among the few sailing ships ever to run 400 sea miles in 24 hours, distances not to be achieved until the advent of modern liners. Down the American ways went *Flying Cloud, Witch of the Wave, Winged Racer, Tornado, Romance of the Seas:* glorious ships with glorious names, slamming round Cape Horn to the Golden Gate or surging across to Melbourne via the Cape of Good Hope—"running their eastings down," as it was called.

The British, building with hardwood—oak and teak—concentrated on smaller, lighter craft. As the building race developed, Aberdeen vied with the Clyde, Liverpool with the Thames, to win back the laurels for Britain. From English and Scottish yards came *Sir Lancelot, Titania, Forward Ho,* and later *Cutty Sark, Leander, Thermopylae, Black Prince.*

The clipper captains were as celebrated as champion jockeys. The American masters were often men of education and social standing. Their British rivals, by contrast, were a rougher-hewn lot. There was the brawny, fiery Dick Robinson from Cumberland, and James "Bully" Forbes, who once sailed *Marco Polo* into Liverpool bearing on a huge pennant the instantly disputed statement that she was "The fastest ship in the world." There was an illustrious roster of Scots captains, for many of the finest ships came from Aberdeen: Maxton, a "very skeely skipper," Mackinnon, Innes, and the wry Keay, wise in the ways of the dreaded typhoons of the China Sea.

Such men milked the wind. When prudent captains shortened sail, they piled it on into the teeth of a rising gale. They strained canvas and cordage to breaking-point. Total wrecks were not infrequent. But most of the chances they took paid off. Speed was money.

Then, for the Americans, came crushing misfortune in the form of the financial depression of the late 1850s, followed by the devastation of

the clipper fleet by Confederate commerce raiders in the Civil War. After that the British virtually had the seas to themselves. And the greatest prize that returned to them was dominance of the China sea trade.

In the late spring of 1866 some 16 of the most famous British clippers lay at the Pagoda anchorage taking on tea. *Ariel*'s cargo was completed first. Her captain was Keay, and his cabin was piled so high with tea chests that he had to sleep on the chart room settee throughout the voyage. He got his ship away on May 28, but that night he had trouble crossing the Foochow harbour bar and had to let go his anchor again. Next morning he saw to his dismay that *Taeping,* as well as *Fiery Cross* and *Serica,* were all at sea ahead of him.

Threading the pirate-infested islands of the South China Sea, tested by erratic currents and scarcely charted shoals, through the misty rainfall and tumbling waves of the monsoon, the four clippers raced westward across the globe. At Mauritius in the Indian Ocean *Fiery Cross* and *Ariel* were in the lead, *Taeping* was lying 12 hours astern, and *Serica* was a long three days behind. Rounding the Cape and heading into the Atlantic, *Ariel* and *Taeping* drew level with *Fiery Cross.* By St. Helena *Serica,* lucky with her winds, was closing up.

Though out of sight of each other, the three leading ships crossed the Equator almost simultaneously. Then came trouble for *Fiery Cross.* The north-east trades were poor that year, and she was becalmed for a crucial 24 hours. At the Cape Verde Islands *Ariel* was ahead, with the others bunched up a day behind her.

But now the uncertain weather gave way to fresh westerly breezes. Each captain "cracked on the dimity," supplementing every stitch of canvas he could send aloft with strange unorthodox sails—ringtails, save-alls, Jamie Greens, watersails, moonsails— thought up by himself or his colleagues. Pounding into the approaches to the Channel, *Ariel* sighted Bishop Light on the reefs of the Scillies in the small hours of September 5. But dawn broke to reveal a ship on her starboard quarter. It was Mackinnon in *Taeping.*

Brunel's *Great Eastern* in 1857, before launching. The massive ship had a propeller as well as paddlewheels. The chain windlass was used at the launch.

By noon both ships were hoisting their identification numbers for the benefit of watchers on Start Point, Devon. At midnight Beachy Head was abeam, and still the two surged on neck and neck. At Deal, within a few cables' lengths of each other, they signalled for their tugs. All the way round the North Foreland and into the Thames the battle continued, the stokers on the tugs sweating at their shovels, the water churning below the straining hawsers. At 9 p.m. that evening *Ariel* was outside the gates of the East India Dock and it seemed a foregone conclusion that she had won. But *Taeping*, hot on her heels,

drew less water. On the rising tide she was able to get through the lock-gates first—and she docked just 20 minutes before *Ariel*. An hour later *Serica*, lying third, was berthed. It had taken 99 days for all three ships to cover some 14,000 miles.

Such feats of seamanship were common in the heyday of the clippers. With gunwales awash, making 18 knots and more, they were driven, canvas tearing, stunsail booms snapping, to the limit of the stresses their hulls could stand. To achieve such performances the well-paid, superbly fit young crewmen might be sent reeling into the scuppers by the captain's boot, laid on their backs for weeks by the mate's belaying-pin, ordered to the masthead for "malingering" in weather so foul that any misstep meant certain death.

These wooden ships, flayed through the seas by iron men, stood for a supremely romantic moment in the saga of British ocean trade. But it was a brief moment, for the clippers and their kind were fighting for survival. In the long run their builders and owners, Yankee and Limey alike, had backed a losing horse. The steamship, with her grimy smokestacks, was slowly but remorselessly pushing the clippers from the seas.

In a wider sense, as well, the majestic greyhounds of the 1860s symbolized an older order. They were vestiges of the era of soil and sail from which the British Empire had sprung. For it was the soil at home that had provided the country gentlemen, the yeomen, the artisans who had gone as governors and settlers to America, as merchants and soldiers

353

to India. And it was sail at sea that had fought off rival imperial powers and borne the first peaceable traffic between the motherland and the colonies.

The lead Britain's technology had given her ashore spread to the seas. Iron hulls, screw propellers, and improved engines were transforming plodding little coastal paddle-steamers into swift ocean-going giants. The be-funnelled brain-children of Isambard Kingdom Brunel, the liners of the driving, tight-lipped Samuel Cunard, were spanning the Atlantic. The lively Peninsular group added Oriental to their name and scheduled mail services to Alexandria to connect with India. William Mackinnon's British India Steam Navigation Company was drawing its strands round the East.

The British merchant marine was the largest and most up-to-date afloat. Shipping agents everywhere sought the efficiency, regularity, and lower rates offered beneath the Red Duster, taking advantage of the insurance and brokerage services that went with it.

The Other Empire was adding the high seas to its dominions.

Before 1850 Britain's commerce with her colonies never exceeded a third of her total trade. Now came the first signs of a change of emphasis. At mid-century she was forging another instrument that was to extend her economic web across the world's land surfaces as her ships were stretching it across the seas. That instrument was the railway.

In the 1840s, inspired by engineers of the calibre of the Stephensons and by financiers of the flash of George Hudson, a vast quantity of national savings had been poured into railway-building all over the British Isles. By 1847, when the bubble of the mania burst at home, the railway fever was jumping the Channel, releasing across Belgium, France, and more distant Europe another tide of British energy. Even the Pope was badgered by British railway promoters into agreeing to the linking of the Papal States.

Kings of this new field of endeavour were the big contractors: self-reliant

stalwarts of enterprise whose names—Thomas Brassey, Mackenzie, Peto, Fox—became magic on the London Stock Exchange and on exchanges across the Continent. To support their phalanxes of beef-eating navvies working abroad, British industry massively increased its output of rails, locomotives, signalling equipment, rolling stock. Soon, in the rush to build railways overseas, English directors were sitting on the boards of 19 French companies, and across the Atlantic the bulk of the shares in railroads like the New York and Erie, the Illinois Central, and the Baltimore and Ohio were English-owned.

Amid the thunderous prospectuses of the fabled contractors, a little event passed almost unnoticed: the completion of a modest railway in the 1840s by the sugar planters of Jamaica for their own use. Probably the first colonial line to be financed through the London stock market, it was significant. For if British-pioneered railways were a source of dividends in themselves, they could also serve

another purpose. They could open up the further continents as sources of the raw materials Britain's growing industries required. It was this realization that first directed capital and skill on a major scale to the Queen's Empire.

In India, though it still continued to trade there, the East India Company's monopoly had ended in 1813. The passing of its grip had not been regretted by the newer business community. "Its very name so stinks in the nostrils," the Manchester *Examiner* roared, "that no prospect of gain is sufficient to tempt enterprise within its borders." Since then, independent commerce had increased until India held first place in the trade of the British possessions. Coffee and indigo raising had expanded. The mills of Dundee had abandoned Russian hemp in favour of Indian jute. Tea-planting, encouraged by the palate of the British worker, had begun to expand in earnest.

In at least one respect the *Examiner*'s onslaught was justified. Under the old regime little had been done for transport: the East India Company and the bullock-cart had gone hand in hand. Merchants and planters were now demanding improvement, and Manchester, anxious for an alternative source of cotton in case of a slave rebellion in the United States, was adding its powerful voice. The meetings to urge action grew more numerous, the exhortatory speeches longer, but little happened until James Andrew Brown Ramsay, tenth Earl of Dalhousie, was appointed India's Governor-General in 1848.

Dalhousie had been President of the Board of Trade. He understood the vital role of communications in developing economies, and he quickly became the most dynamic of India's rulers since Warren Hastings. Under him the Ganges Canal and the Grand Trunk Road strode to completion, telegraph lines began their march between cities. But his main aim was a network of railways across the great subcontinent. "Great tracts are teeming with produce they cannot dispose of," he wrote. Moreover, railways in India "would enable the Government to bring its military strength to bear" in days rather than months.

Scarcely had the first lines been tentatively laid when the 1857 Mutiny broke out—and proved Dalhousie triumphantly right. At a moment of dire crisis the few hundred miles of new railways sped reinforcements from Calcutta and brought relief to scattered commands.

But the Mutiny did much more. Its outcome convinced British investors that the Raj was there to stay. And it fired their imaginations with that compound of good intention and commercial hope that frequently guided their choice of securities. Free trade had already shown itself a promoter of peace through prosperity. Here was an opportunity to apply that beneficent aim to an imperial domain. A great transport network in India would pacify and civilize, and yield rewards to all concerned.

Dalhousie wanted his railways, but did not want the Indian government to build them. It would be better done by private enterprise—with the supervision necessary to prevent a mania like that which had swept Britain a decade earlier. Accordingly, to attract capital he offered a 5 per cent government guarantee on Indian railway stocks while simultaneously imposing government control of plans and routes. Some 50,000 British savers took up the offer. But the control in India proved inexpert: too many railways spread across the dusty plains and unprofitable lines fell back on the guarantee.

The experiment thus both failed and succeeded. Stockholders, thankful for their 5 per cent, did not ask by whom it was so regularly produced. In fact, the golden egg came from the Indian taxpayer, who for years to come faced a drain of interest payments without receiving goods or services in return. Manchester, moreover, never got its cotton. The quality remained poor, and the Indian administration, fearing for law and order, refused to allow the changes in traditional cultivation methods that Lancashire urged. But the Indian railway system—to this day one of the finest in the world—paid other dividends. It reduced the impact of famines, started the welding of diverse societies into a nation, and brought that nation into the world market. By the 1870s £150,000,000 of new British capital was at work in Indian industry and commerce.

The Empire of the Queen and the Other Empire of trade and capital were beginning to draw together. Both had their seats of power in London. The centre of the former lay at Westminster. The hub of the Other Empire—the "Informal Empire" as some called it—was the City.

It was a sunless smoky square mile at the heart of the metropolis, loud with the clop of hoofs and pungent with the smell of horse dung. Its narrow streets and alleys—Eastcheap, Cornhill, Mincing Lane, St. Mary Axe, Old Jewry—lay squat beneath the soaring fingers of Wren's steeples, clustered in a crowded patternless huddle round the Old Lady of Threadneedle Street.

It was a hive of pale clerks on high stools, bent over massive ledgers in counting rooms where gaslights hissed during the day. It was a maze of paper indited in flowing Victorian copperplate—bills, bonds, and certificates—circulating in the pouches of top-hatted brass-buttoned messengers. It was a rendezvous for all in search of cash or credit: ministers of foreign governments, agents of British colonies, directors of companies from every continent. It was a smooth-running, almost unfathomably intricate machine for buying and selling money.

In carved and panelled offices, on a nod and a quiet word, the great merchant-banking houses clinched their loans to foreign countries. Hambro's specialized in Italian issues, Frühling and Goschen's in Egyptian, Morgan's in Chilean, Schroeder's in Peruvian, Raphael's in Hungarian, Baring's competing with Rothschild's for the honour (and profit) of financing the Tsar, Oppenheim's, Bamberger's, Bischofheim's—all lending to governments eager for progress and without inordinate concern for their taxpayers. Advancing the funds for public buildings and stately boulevards, for street lighting and water mains, irrigation and sewerage; for

Growing and exporting Ceylon tea was a British monopoly by the late 1800s, dominated by the vast holdings of ex-Glasgow grocer Thomas Lipton.

armaments and the symbols of prestige; for (who cared, given adequate security) the greasing of political palms in distant government offices.

Behind drab façades finance companies opened accounts for all who wanted to purchase shares, undertaking on behalf of the small man and woman "such operations as an experienced capitalist might effect with a capital of millions." Investment firms baited their prospectuses to attract the growing public who now had money to spare: aristocrats, professional men, successful shopkeepers, prudent widows; the affluent with thousands behind them, the careful with a few pounds put by. One such company might promote debentures to enable the great Brassey to build a railway in the Danubian Principalities. Another might assure its depositors that it could "ally the demand of India for capital at ten per cent with the English demand for investment at four or five." Cheques from comfortable bank balances, sovereigns from socks beneath the bed: money for railways, harbours, bridges, factories, for sober certainties and glittering gambles.

At street corners pennies were held out for the papers that trumpeted the opportunities of the moment: the *Financier*, the *Money Market Review*, the *Bullionist*, the *Bondholder's Register*. There was a hot sale for the *Railway News*, backed by the fabled James McHenry who was himself engaged in the acrobatic feat of building a railway in America without contributing a penny of his own money. And it was said to have been a financial journalist—Frederick Greenwood of the *Pall Mall Gazette*—who, at one of the celebrated daily luncheons given by the Rothschilds, first suggested that Disraeli would do well to buy for Britain the Suez Canal shares owned by the bankrupt Khedive of Egypt. It was an idea that was to net Rothschild's a commission of over £250,000 in return for finding four millions overnight.

Close by, shipowners and their superintendents passed in and out of Lloyd's, arbiter of ocean traffic, with its individual underwriters sharing the risks on vessels and cargoes tra-

versing the seven seas, with its minutely informed agents in every major port, its signal-stations running up their bunting on the headlands. In the halls of the Livery Companies— wealthy fraternities of Goldsmiths, Fishmongers, Mercers, Vintners, all descending from the trade guilds of the Middle Ages—stewards and toast-masters oversaw the setting out of plate and table linen and glass, many-branching candlesticks of solid silver, rich-wrought golden loving-cups and embossed illuminated menus for gargantuan banquets.

And all the time the Stock Exchange ticked over in its shadowy dimness, reacting like a barometer to the fluctuating pressures of world trade.

The ablest note of the Foreign Secretary, it was said, spoke with feeble force compared with a Stock Exchange list. Here the two empires overlapped. Some prominent City men belonged to both, alternating directorships with ministerial posts as governments rose and fell. Banking firms often had more partners in the House of Commons than on the Court of the Bank of England. Yet between Westminster and the City a chilly gulf was fixed. Repeatedly, officials in Whitehall penned austere minutes: "Her Majesty's Government do not feel justified in seeking the sanction of Parliament to adopt coercive measures." Although Palmerston's growls might once have backed up British merchants on the spot, now Lombard Street could look after itself.

The City was adventurous, optimistic, young in spirit. It said "Yes" almost as often as "No." However unknown and tongue-tied you might be, if your proposals to expand an Indian tea-property made sense, if you could prove your Uruguayan mining concession genuine, sooner or later you would find someone in the City to listen. British capital moved quickly, freely, boldly. And once put up, it stayed put up—patiently awaiting its reward, often through thick and thin. Governments might default, land companies overreach themselves, railroads go bankrupt, booms and crises alternate. Swings and roundabouts: the City was constantly renewing itself, absorbing the losses or

passing them on, reinvesting the profits in a new scheme.

Above all, London reflected the brash go-getting confidence of the Midlands and the North: of the manufacturers, contractors, merchants, shippers, men of rough tongue and hard head, who were clothing the continents, setting them on rolling wheels, creating new needs and desires in populations from the Ganges to the Plate. And this confidence it passed on, heightened and strengthened, to that new Lord of Creation, the British investor. In the 20 years from 1860 on, the City was able to coax from the public some £320,000,000 in loans to foreign governments, £480,000,000 for India and other Empire countries, £230,000,000 for companies engaged in engineering works abroad, and additional millions to swell the capital of wholly foreign concerns.

In effect, the dingy square mile hugging the north bank of the Thames was collecting Britain's savings and channelling a large part overseas— there to build a world in Britain's image, materially and mentally equipped to trade with her.

Then, in the 1870s, the whole structure of Britain's overseas economy began to change. Hitherto, except in India, the Empire of Westminster and the Other Empire of the City had had but a nodding acquaintance with each other. But development in India paved the way for a new interest in the British possessions as a whole. Now the two empires were increasingly to merge.

For Britain the 1870s were a time of reckoning. It was the moment of realization that by financing other energetic countries, by exporting to them her manufacturing know-how, she had been building up competition for herself. The younger industries of Germany and America, formerly eager markets for British capital goods, were now equipping themselves. The factories of France and Belgium were getting under way; India, Brazil, Japan, often with the help of British machinery and expertise, were beginning to clothe themselves. Britain's markets were under attack. She must find new ones, redouble her export efforts.

It was the moment, too, when the underlying effects of the Industrial Revolution became starkly apparent at home. The point of balance between industry and agriculture had been passed. The urban population, and its expectations, had been steadily rising, but until recently, Britain still grew four-fifths of her own food. Suddenly, within a few years, that proportion dropped to scarcely a half. Home farming, faced with larger imports of cereals, meat, and wool, cut back on the old staples and began specializing instead on perishables like milk and vegetables. Yet the population was still rising by 10 per cent a year. Henceforth Britain would need greatly increased supplies of food for her work force and similar increases in raw materials to step up her exports against the accelerating competition. These imports, and the new markets to pay for them, could only come from the opening up of hitherto virgin areas.

America, though her eastern seaboard was already industrialized, had not yet filled her inner spaces. Nor had Argentina. Equally important, there was a huge untapped potential within the British Empire proper: in Canada, Australia, New Zealand, Africa, the Far East.

The dawning of these new perspectives coincided with a crisis in the City. Unstable foreign governments, especially in Latin America, were defaulting on their loans, suspending interest payments. A Parliamentary committee, set up to investigate, revealed a fetid London money-market: there had been too many doubtful loan transactions, too many fat commissions. A recession in stock prices began to react back on industry and commerce.

With such worries piling up, it seemed to the British investor that the wide-open spaces were a healthier field for his money, especially the spaces of the temperate latitudes where white populations had been settling. Colonists of British and European stock were hard-working and responsible. True, earlier in the century their countries had been but frontier territories, fluid and risky, but now they were becoming stable

In an 1889 cartoon from an American pictorial weekly, Uncle Sam threatens to start a second War of Independence, this one against John Bull's colonialism by capital.

and experienced nations. Investment in them would help kith and kin. It would ensure Britain's own future. It would yield a surer return.

Events conspired to heighten the attractions of the "areas of recent settlement." The opening of the Suez Canal had suddenly brought Australia closer to the British Isles. Diamonds had just been discovered in South Africa. In New Zealand Julius Vogel, gold-prospector turned journalist turned statesman, was advancing far-reaching schemes for investment in industry. The Canadian Pacific Railway was opening the Dominion's vast western prairies.

As the dust of the City's crisis settled, an entirely new picture became clear. British capital was leaving its old haunts in Europe and else-

where and heading out to develop the far-flung plains and valleys of the Queen's Empire, of the American West, of the Argentine. And with it flowed a fresh tide of emigration— trained, skilled, enterprising people confident of prosperity ahead. Simultaneously, British industry began to find the new markets it urgently needed. The last 30 years of the century saw a second giant boom in railway-building as new lines drove into the interior of new continents. And along them, with the immigrants, went the infinite range of hardware required to start whole new economies, most of it made in Britain and despatched in British ships: structural steel and galvanized iron, intricate mechanical mining equipment, telegraph line and submarine cable, tubes for artesian bores, agricultural machinery, mile upon mile of fencing for fields and ranches, and a myriad of domestic articles to ease life under new skies.

So, as the yields of food and materials from overseas began to mount, the Other Empire began to overlap Victoria's Empire. Here was the empire of Poet Laureate John Masefield's rusty British coaster butting down-Channel with the humdrum wares of Birmingham; of Kipling's big steamers bringing back the eggs, apples, and cheese. Of the plough-teams criss-crossing the prairies as they turned the black soil, and the elevators of the wheat co-operatives rearing their gaunt frames above switching-yards and flat horizons. Of the boundary-riders ranging the Australian outback beneath the shimmering gum trees, and the crack of a stock-whip across boundless stations owned by wealthy grazing families and served by ubiquitous firms of specialized agent-brokers. Of the green carpets of sheep pasture spreading down from New Zealand's Tararua Range to the Pacific, and the long mountains of yellow slag rising round Johannesburg above the pay-streaks of the Rand, and the sarong-girded labourers cupping the latex in the deep shade of Malayan rubber groves. Of British banks and credit-houses shuttling from the tropics to the icy north the paper of a trading world based on the unquestioned solidity of the pound sterling.

It was a productive, extractive, creative empire. But the great shift of capital, the new quest for materials and markets, had its uglier aspects—particularly Europe's scramble to carve up Africa. It was, at root, an economic scramble. "Colonies," declared a French minister in 1885, "are for rich countries one of the most lucrative methods of investing capital."

To Britain, as the leading imperial power, it seemed impossible to stand aside. But the British government would not itself face the responsibility or the cost. Instead, a long-dead practice was revived: granting total privileges to chartered companies, allowing, in effect, profit-seeking businessmen to usurp the functions hitherto reserved to government officials. Accordingly, agents of powerful financial groups penetrated the African interior, negotiating treaties with unsuspecting native chiefs. By these treaties all rights to develop vast tracts of land were handed over, often in return for trivial gifts.

In this way George Goldie's Royal Niger Company acquired control over some 300 native-ruled areas in West Africa, and the Imperial British East Africa Company of William Mackinnon came into possession of a realm of 200,000 square miles and four million Africans. The most notorious was the British South Africa Company of Cecil Rhodes. Appropriating lands described as "the pick of central Africa on both sides of the Zambezi," buying out rival mining concerns, fighting off Boer resentment and native hostility, Rhodes made what was probably the greatest fortune ever amassed in imperial adventure. It was a time of triumph for economic freebooters.

By the eve of the Great War the extent of British world trade and investment was not only far vaster than it had been 50 years before but entirely different in pattern. Some £4 billion of British capital was at work overseas. Of this, no less than half was invested in the Empire proper. Of the other half, £1,500,000,000 was lodged in the Americas and only about £500,000,000 remained in Europe and elsewhere. Since 1896 the total value of British exports had surged up by 120 per cent. To Canada they had increased fourfold, to Australia threefold, to New Zealand and India they had doubled. And as she was supreme among the trading nations, so too was she on the seas between them: Britain owned nearly half the world's shipping tonnage, carried half its goods, was building more ships than the rest of the world together.

Through the bustle of the commodity exchanges, the roar of the furnaces, the yelping of the tugs among the swinging cranes, it was possible to trace a series of unguided yet strangely logical steps by which Britain had climbed to this peak of economic power. She had first generated surpluses through the produc-

tivity created by her industrial pioneers and through her lucky position in the Napoleonic Wars. She had launched and multiplied her overseas trade by investing these surpluses in the countries—mainly in Europe and America—which then offered adequate safety and reward. At a critical point in her destiny she had shifted the bulk of her ever-swelling capital and resources to the support of the newer countries—most of them within her own imperial domains—whose now maturing energy could meet her changing, growing needs.

Yet a process of erosion was already under way. Britain had equipped much of the world for the Industrial Age, and its leading nations, now in fierce competition with her, were protectionist in trend. Despite the calls for tariff reform led by the crusader for imperial preference, Colonial Secretary Joseph Chamberlain—he lambasted his critics for denying that "a system accepted in 1846 could possibly require modification in 1903"—Britain remained true to her free trade principles. But she was finding it more difficult to keep old customers and obtain new ones.

If free trade had worked Britain's economic miracle, it was in some respects beginning to work against her. Before her rivals began to catch up with her, she had enjoyed easy markets abroad and in some fields of manufacture this had not been conducive to a constant search for improvement in quality and performance. The onset of competition now exposed failures wherever they occurred in her industrial system: conventional design, slipshod workmanship, late delivery. Britain was still living by her traditional exports: textiles, railways, "classical" engineering products, coal.

But a second Industrial Revolution was in the making. Demand was rising for electrical equipment, scientific instruments, chemicals, artificial fabrics. In these she lagged behind—and even found her home market invaded by new lines she could well have turned out herself.

Moreover, the main lines of world trade were altering, becoming disparate. Trade between Brazil, Argentina, and the U.S. was rising. India was evolving her own connections in the East. Australia was shopping around. German and Italian immigrants in Canada preferred consumer goods imported from their old homes. Japan was creating a commercial network in the Pacific. Trade was no longer running along a few established routes that mostly radiated from Britain. It was weaving a series of regional skeins, and those skeins were becoming interlocked in a complex multilateral web that was increasingly difficult to dominate from a single point.

The sins of Britain's Other Empire during its heyday are still hurled against its memory. It is held that at home it created a *rentier* class which, typified by Galsworthy's Forsyte family, lived on the fruits of investments and came to identify the national and imperial interest with its own; and that by the same token it excluded the vast majority of the British people from a share in the country's growing wealth. It is said that, overseas, it extinguished valued traditional patterns of livelihood in the older possessions like India and imposed upon

the new lands specialized unbalanced economies; that it favoured the more experienced white countries of the world and did little for the less; and that in its latter phase it shamelessly disregarded native interests—an opinion which was powerfully developed by Lenin in his attack on economic imperialism.

In all such accusations there is truth, but in calmer retrospect other factors emerge. Nothing like Britain's building of a global system of trade and capital lay within the world's previous experience. The sheer scale and dynamism involved were unique, and perhaps the only comparable achievement since has been the take-off of the American economy—which, in its earlier phases, was directly catalysed by Britain. In creating the first universal economic order Britain herself was inexperienced, working pragmatically from the only cardinal rule the leaders of the nascent Other Empire knew: the hope of gain.

Rigging, killing, and cornering of markets in pursuit of that hope certainly occurred. But in the main the dividends came from fixed-interest securities rather than from shares.

Few got rich quickly; it took time to reap the benefits of securities offering a steady 5 per cent. It was their continuity and their constant reinvestment, rather than their size, that swelled the compound total. And for the greater part of the 19th Century the management of British trade and money was the reverse of imperialistic. It was cosmopolitan rather than national. It willingly admitted others to its enterprises, if only to share the risk. And though in the long run it took much, it was often on the side of small business and of liberal regimes.

In its century of dominance the Other British Empire—with its passionate belief in *laissez-faire*, free trade, open competition—laid the economic foundations and raised the physical infrastructure of the free world of today, and of part of the Communist world as well. It is arguable that had the inevitable industrialization of the world been launched by other doctrines and by other hands, it might well have been more artificial, more disruptive—and on balance undertaken with far less humanity.

—*Stuart Legg*

II. The Imperial Engineers

Arthur Cotton's name will be venerated by millions yet unborn when many who now occupy a much larger place in the public view will be forgotten." That was the opinion confidently voiced by Sir Charles Trevelyan, Governor of Madras, in 1858.

He could not have been more wrong. Far from venerating General Sir Arthur Cotton, very few have ever heard of him. A single paragraph in the *Encyclopaedia Britannica* is sufficient to satisfy posterity's interest in this Victorian Englishman. Yet Trevelyan's prediction was as justified as it was unprophetic. For by his work Cotton saved millions of lives.

Arthur Cotton was an engineer. In India he built dams and dug irrigation canals that made oases out of

deserts and transformed agriculture. During one of the subcontinent's many famines, in which four million people died, Cotton's works were credited not only with saving all the inhabitants of his district but in addition providing enough extra food to keep three million alive elsewhere.

His deeds were remarkable, but not unique. Cotton was but one of a special breed of 19th-Century Englishmen who worked wonders so regularly, and with such apparent ease, that the world came to accept their miracles as commonplace. Like him, most are now forgotten. They did their work, took their scattering of knighthoods and lesser honours, and disappeared into yellowed old Parliamentary reports and dusty company files.

But these engineers of the British Empire transformed the world.

They carried the Industrial Revolution to the limits of Empire and beyond. They built railways in lands that did not use the wheel and strung their telegraph lines between jungle villages just emerging from the Stone Age. They curbed rivers that had terrorized man from the beginning of time and used them to make deserts bloom. They built harbours that turned rude villages into thriving international ports and installed sanitary systems that drove disease from cities notorious for pestilence. To those whose power was the ox, they introduced the marvel of machines.

In a century of furious activity they created for Britain's subject peoples the substructures of modern life, the

British bridge builders at work in South Africa in 1885; from an engineering journal.

very foundations upon which today's nations function. Some believe the price these nations paid in British domination was too dear. But they cannot devalue what they received from the imperial engineers.

These were the Englishmen who joined mad dogs in the noonday sun. They helped give Great Britain a national superiority complex, hardly surprising when Victorians read over their breakfast tables stories like this one from the *Daily Mail*, describing the engineer William Willcocks's work on the Great Nile Dam, completed in 1902:

"A knot of sheiks and reis [boat captains] greet him with the courtly Eastern salaam. Bedouin and fellaheen work like ants, and dark-skinned, smiling, good-natured Sudanese ram home the concrete, as if they took the whole thing as a huge joke. Here and there, under broad sun

helmets, may be found a wily Greek or excitable Italian, acting as a useful lieutenant to the solitary Englishman perched yonder on an elevation of masonry, apparently an idle spectator, and yet seeing all."

Each evening, said the *Mail*'s correspondent, the workmen headed for the bazaar to "indulge in the nightly fantasia and the everlasting tap of the tom-toms," but not our stalwart engineer. If one peeped into his window, "one would see a picturesque group of gaily dressed Arab sheiks and reis standing around one man of a foreign race, making reports and receiving them till midnight strikes, when this representative of the Dominant Power encloses himself within his mosquito curtains, and the dam has risen two feet within the last twenty-four hours."

Whatever they thought in London, life for a British engineer abroad was

hardly a matter of striking arrogantly casual poses for journalists. "They mostly cursed their work," said Kipling, "yet carried it through to the end, in difficult surroundings, without help or acknowledgement." Deprived of their families or even worse, seeing them suffer the same gruelling hardships, they struggled against disease, sudden death, hostile climates, and frequently hostile populations.

Arthur Cotton suffered devastating fevers which again and again forced him temporarily to abandon India and his work. Alex Taylor, who built the Punjab section of the Grand Trunk Road across northern India, was blind for months on end—a common affliction for engineers in the Indian sun. They were drowned in floods, maimed in construction accidents, and over the years more than a few of their bodies were found mutilated at the farthest reach of a telegraph line or at a lonely railhead miles from civilization.

Yet they stuck to their jobs, inspired more often than not by the selfless motivation of service to mankind. As Carlyle said, History itself had assigned Englishmen "the grand industrial task of conquering half or more of this terraquaceous planet for the use of man." And of course it was true, since Britain was the world's first industrialized nation. For a time she was the world's only workshop, the world's only massive trading power, the world's only foreign investor. The exhilaration of conquering nature was hers alone, and her engineers were the missionary pioneers of modern civilization. In their hands they held the power to transform continents. Their job was of world importance, and they took it seriously.

"There was a glow of work about us in the Punjab such as I have never felt before or since," wrote Alex Taylor. "I well remember the feeling when I went on furlough to England; the want of pressure of any kind, the self-seeking, the dulling and dwarfing of high aims."

Nowhere were the engineers more successful than in India. The Victorians, in their enthusiasm, called that country "the greatest achievement of the English race." The achievement was actually that of a very few men, most of them from a single school, the East India Company's college at Addiscombe, near Croydon. In 52 years Addiscombe trained some 3,600 cadets for Indian service. Of those, about 500 were engineers.

One of those graduates was Arthur Cotton. Had Galsworthy wished to portray the other archetypal Victorian family—one as devoted to public service as were his Forsytes to property—he need have looked no further than the Cottons. Arthur Cotton was the tenth son of the tenth son of a fourth baronet—a nice pedigree, but one which puts one a long way from the money, which may be why his family worked so hard. Among his brothers were two more generals—one an engineer like himself, the other a fighting soldier; a colonel in the Royal Engineers; a member of the Indian Civil Service; and the family representative in the Anglican Church.

Arthur was born in 1803 and spent his childhood—or so his family recalled later—making canals with his bread and milk. At 15 he went to Addiscombe to study war and engineering and by 23 had considerable practice in both. He found the First Burmese War of 1824–26 "a very melancholy business, inconceivably mismanaged" (throughout his life he maintained a healthy disrespect for his superiors' abilities), but made a name for himself by leading seven storming-parties against enemy fortresses.

Besides bravery, Cotton demonstrated other qualities which distinguished him as an exemplary Victorian: priggishness and Evangelical religion. Having gambled away £20, which he lost to a superior officer, he announced that he abhorred card-playing and thereafter would not allow a pack in his house. He made no secret of his religious beliefs either. On a voyage to India he amused and annoyed fellow officers by inquiring in the gin-soaked saloon if anyone had a Bible he could borrow.

Soon his facility for handling great watercourses was recognized and he was put to work on the Cauveri, the largest river in southern India.

Enough of its water escaped unused into the sea to irrigate ten times as much grain as the area was producing. Cotton had a scheme for capturing this flow, and nothing like it had ever been seen, not even in Europe. It involved two major dams and canal systems. According to an official, the province considered it "the greatest blessing that had ever been conferred on it." His employers, who measured blessings by a different standard than did Indian farmers, were equally pleased. Water charges and navigation fees on one of the systems were soon returning 69 per cent annually on capital invested, the other 100 per cent.

In 1838 Cotton left India for sick-leave in Australia. There he indulged his engineer's passion for machinery, designing a centrifugal steam engine much like later steam turbines. It was not entirely successful. He wrote to a friend: "the boiler burst and injured both my legs, taking off the flesh of one of them, but I succeeded in getting 150 revolutions a minute." He also indulged another passion, Elizabeth Learmonth. "If God would give me so great a gift," he exclaimed, "I would marry that girl." After another visit in 1841 he took her back to India as his bride.

Jackals prowled outside the young wife's door and snakes plopped from the rafters into her babies' cradles. She was always near her husband's work—he was able to rush home one day to shoot a cobra that had taken over the nursery—but proximity also had disadvantages. Almost every day she had to call the children indoors so blasting could begin. Stones showered the roof, walls split, and more snakes slithered into the house to escape from Cotton pounding nature. One day an unexpected flood washed through the home. Cotton expected his family to suffer such calamities without complaint, and to work hard. "If you want rest," he told his children when they were growing up, "vary your employment."

He also instilled in them those other cherished Victorian virtues: religion and patriotism. He led church services at six each morning—any later would have been too hot. Patri-

otism was an equally serious matter. His daughter told of the family once standing on the deck of a ship in Mauritius Harbour, tears in their eyes, while "to our loyal and devoted ears came the welcome strains of God Save the Queen." Wherever they travelled they believed they were secure in Empire's protective bosom.

In 1844 Cotton took on India's third biggest river, the Godavari, and his biggest job. The area south of Madras through which it flowed was one of the most poverty-stricken in the subcontinent. Famines littered the roads with corpses. Peasants sold their daughters to strangers for a few days' supply of food. Wagons bringing relief supplies of grain needed armed escorts. Cotton was called in to assess the problem. "I could not help seeing what it wanted," he said, "which was simply everything."

It mainly wanted irrigation from the Godavari, but damming the river would be a monumental task. Its flow was one and a half million cubic feet per second, three times that of the Nile at Cairo, 200 times that of the Thames at Staines. He asked for six officers and eight sappers to assist in a detailed survey and was alloted by the tight-fisted Company a staff of "one young hand to teach and two apprentice surveyors."

The project took eight years to complete. Much of the time Cotton was ill, but he did not allow that to slow the work. The main dam was two and a quarter miles long, and he daringly built it of rubble encased in masonry rather than of solid stone. His colleagues jibed that he was "founding the cheapest school of engineering in the world," but the Company directors in London were delighted. The low cost meant the project would pay 30 per cent a year on capital invested.

It irrigated 364,000 new acres, created 340 miles of navigable channel, insured millions of people against starvation, and was called "the noblest feat of engineering skill which has yet been accomplished in British India." Cotton hoped it might increase India's "appreciation of a Christian Government."

Cotton retired in 1860 and returned to England and a knighthood. It was

This huge 100-horsepower road steamer went into service on India's Grand Trunk Road in 1872. Hitched at the end of its train of wagons is a passenger coach.

small enough reward, but as he told a House of Commons committee some years later, "I have never asked for an appointment, or for anything else, except to be allowed to irrigate India."

Even before Cotton retired, other engineers were surpassing his great works with larger and bolder projects. When the 530-mile Ganges Canal opened in 1854 it was the biggest work of engineering in the world. It was built by Sir Percy Cautley, another Addiscombe graduate, who was given such a meagre budget that he had to do his own surveying. Even so, he found time to make himself one of the great Victorian amateurs of science, in palaeontology. He wrote numerous papers with titles like *On a Sivalik Ruminant Allied to the Giraffidae* and eventually presented to the British Museum his collection of fossils—all 40 tons of them.

In the spectacular Periyar project in southern India British engineers outdid themselves. They dammed a river with a flood as great as Niagara Falls, drove it through a mountain in a mile-long tunnel, and made it flow down the other side of the subcontinent. It took eight years. For half of each year it rained four out of every five days. Floods washed away the foundations several times. First malaria, then cholera swept through the community of engineers and workers, requiring them to burn one camp and later move the new one. Tigers prowled the surrounding jungles. Elephants knocked down tents and houses. Herds of bison stampeded the workmen. But on October 10, 1895, the Periyar River began flowing towards an ocean it had never seen before and 100,000 acres of barren land were brought to life.

The engineers would try anything. They carried canals over rivers and, when necessary, carried rivers over canals. Two rivers cross the Ganges Canal on super-passages, one of them 300 feet wide. Not all these wonders were mechanically created. Some of

them proved cheaper to build by labour-intensive methods. The most important equipment employed on the Sirhind Canal in the Punjab was three jails, housing convicts who removed 900 million cubic feet of earth in baskets on their heads.

It would be wrong to say that Britain "gave" India water—or anything else. The dams were viewed as commercial propositions, and in fact paid an average of 7 to 8 per cent, an excellent return on capital in a period of consistently low interest rates. Non-paying works were often undertaken because they directly benefited the British themselves. In Lahore, a filthy place "full of stagnant water," malaria was killing too many British troops. For this reason the streets were paved and a modern drainage system installed, and "the most malodorous of native capitals" gained repute for its cleanliness. In building roads—and later, railways—a primary purpose was to facilitate troop movements.

The greatest road-building achieve-

ment of the British—perhaps the greatest the world had seen since the Roman Empire—was the Grand Trunk Road that ran from Calcutta to Delhi and was later extended across the Punjab to Peshawar on the borders of Afghanistan. "The Grand Trunk Road," wrote Kipling, "is a wonderful spectacle; a stately corridor; all India spread out to left and right. It runs straight, bearing, without crowding, India's traffic for fifteen hundred miles—such a river of life as nowhere else exists in the world."

It was a mammoth task and took 40 years, on and off, to complete. In one 264-mile section, between Lahore and Peshawar, engineers had to build 103 major bridges, 459 smaller ones, tunnel through six chains of mountains, and erect immense embankments to carry the road over two great river beds. It was a job for exceptional men —men like Alex Taylor, who at the age of 24 was supervising the work of 60,000 labourers over an area four times as large as Scotland. In tempera-

tures that hovered near 120 degrees he lived on horseback, commuting between the seven separate sections under his control.

Sometimes it seemed that nature resented the engineers' efforts. James "Buster" Browne, building a bridge on Taylor's part of the Grand Trunk Road, was awakened by shouting one night. "I saw the river coming down in a huge wave, about 200 feet wide: one wall of roaring water." His most precious machine, a giant pile-driving engine, broke from its moorings. Browne and four others plunged into the flood and chained the engine to a ram, a great piece of iron held between two floating wooden beams. A carpenter swam out with an axe and they chopped away at the beams. Five miles downstream the iron ram, freed of its timbers, finally sank and anchored the pile-driver, five minutes short of a waterfall. "The worst part of it was I had to walk five miles without my shoes," said Browne, "in my nightshirt."

A turning point in India's history was the coming of railways. "Railways may do for India," wrote Sir Edwin Arnold in 1865, "what dynasties have never done—what . . . Akbar the Magnificent could not effect by government nor . . . Tipoo Sahib by violence—they may make India a nation."

Until the Mutiny in 1857, the Indian government was not very interested in railways. Thereafter it viewed them as a military investment. "After all," Arnold wrote, "the first condition of improving India is to hold it."

To build railways, the British had to build harbours where they could land heavy equipment: rails, ties, locomotives, bricks. Madras was an open roadstead where cargo was landed through the surf; Calcutta was a few jetties 100 miles upriver. Skilled labour was non-existent. "Our ballasting and wagon work," an engineer told a government inquiry, "is conducted and managed by men who never in their lives before saw a wag-

on. Our bridges with scarcely an exception are superintended by men who do not know a brick from a stone."

Rebels and bandits harried the crews. Two engineers, surveying for a new line in 1859, were murdered. Nor did India's endemic diseases do railway-builders any favours. In the autumn of the same year a cholera epidemic in one district killed 10 per cent of the work force per week. Four thousand died before it was finished.

Yet the railways were built. By 1869 4,000 miles of track were in operation. The social and economic consequences were enormous. Soon Thomas Cook & Son were running package pilgrimages to Mecca from India and branch railways to Hindu shrines were showing a big profit. "The chances of a god doing a large and increasing business," one Englishman observed, "are greatly improved by a railway station." Internal trade flourished and, able to move her products to ports, India became

363

an exporter. During famines large amounts of food were transported quickly. And in a wild land without communications the railway had a unifying, civilizing effect. Matthew Arnold called it the "most persuasive missionary that ever preached in the east."

Not all the great builders of the Empire were, strictly speaking, engineers. Sir William O'Shaughnessey was a physician, pathologist, professor of chemistry, and Deputy Assay-Master to the Mint who just happened to have an insatiable interest in the telegraph. His first experiments showed it simply would not function in India. If the fierce winds failed to blow down the poles, white ants ate them hollow or bandicoots uprooted them. But the telegraph's greatest enemy was the atmosphere itself. Thunderstorms poured such heavy charges of natural energy into the wires that the magnetic polarity of the instrument was deranged.

"I was driven step by step to discard every screw and lever and pivot, and foot of wire, and framework, and dial, without which it was practicable to work," wrote O'Shaughnessy. "I successively tried and dismissed the English vertical astatic needle telegraph, the American dotter, and several contrivances of my own invention." In 1851, "when almost driven to despair," he devised "the little single needle horizontal telegraph" which would work without interruption in all weathers. An experimental line was strung from Calcutta to near-by Diamond Harbour on bamboo posts; these would bend with the wind and hold up through hurricanes that destroyed brick houses and drove steamships ashore.

Impressed, the Company approved a plan to connect Calcutta, Agra, Bombay, Peshawar, and Madras by wire. O'Shaughnessy was appointed Director-General of Telegraphs and work began in 1853. He worked fast. The 800-mile line to Agra was opened within six months. In another year 3,050 miles were operating; by 1856 the entire 4,000-mile system was completed—just in time for the Mutiny. "The telegraph," declared Lord Lawrence, "saved India." A mutineer

on his way to execution agreed, calling it "the wire that strangles us." News of the uprising was flashed instantaneously across thousands of miles and enabled the British to concentrate their troops where they were most needed.

The man who kept the wires functioning against all odds during the Mutiny was Lieutenant-Colonel Patrick Stewart, who succeeded O'Shaughnessy in 1856. Another Addiscombe boy, Stewart had been working for two others from the school, Percy Cautley on the Ganges Canal and Alex Taylor on the Grand Trunk Road. (Stewart wrote home that he hoped to finish his road section within 12 weeks, but still had 20 bridges to build.)

He was 24 when he took up the telegraph appointment. He re-strung the wires as fast as the rebels could pull them down. He was the first to lay telegraph wire under fire through hostile territory. Wherever the commander pitched his tent, Stewart was near by, setting up a makeshift station. The Governor-General allowed him to participate in the relief of Lucknow, but told the commander that Colonel Stewart "was, if possible, not to be killed."

In 1862, when Britain was just starting to lay an international cable system, Stewart was assigned the job of connecting India to Britain by telegraph. He worked westward, laying the cable under the Persian Gulf, and then went to Turkey to negotiate for that section. There, in 1865, he fell ill and died. In such cases there was little interest in the precise cause; it was explanation enough that he was a British engineer working in the tropics. Stewart was 32 years old.

After Stewart's death the work was carried on by yet another Addiscombe graduate, John Underwood Bateman-Champain, who was then in Teheran wrangling over the construction of the Persian section. The Persians insisted that they would build it themselves and would permit only one English officer to enter the country to direct the work. They were enraged at the "cool impudence" of the 30-year-old engineer when he arrived with three officers, 12 NCOs, and six civilians—

but they gave him five months to complete the 1,250-mile line. Bateman-Champain could have as easily been a diplomat as an engineer. He charmed the Shah into giving the project his support, thus insuring its completion. In St. Petersburg, negotiating for the line through Russia, he became a favourite of the Tsar. The concession was granted, and by 1869 messages that had previously taken three months were passing from England to India in twelve hours.

There was one field in which an engineer, if he was lucky, could grow rich: mining. Many of the men who sailed from Great Britain to seek gold in South Africa or copper in Australia were not qualified engineers, of course. Until late in the 19th Century mining was less a science than a trade—or a gamble. The miner did not need a degree, but he required a large amount of fortitude.

South Africa owes its position as the world's richest gold-producer to a Glasgow man, J. S. MacArthur. In 1889, only three years after the rush began, the gold mines of the Rand hit a pyritic zone. This meant trouble. The processing mills were unable to extract enough gold from the pyrites and began closing down. One-third of the houses in Johannesburg were soon on the market and the town square was jammed with second-hand furniture for sale. The boom appeared to be over.

In 1890 MacArthur came to town with his new cyanide process. Watched by the industry's representatives "to make sure there was no humbug," he fussed with his vats and pipes and a sample of ore for two days and nights, until a gold ingot emerged from his little portable furnace. He had achieved 98 per cent extraction. The Rand was saved.

Britons were just as important to Australian mining. Cornishmen flocked down under, and their Cornish boilers, Cornish pumping engines, and years of experience transformed the haphazard diggings into a rational industry. They were not always welcomed. At Ballarat one had to defend his steam-pump with firearms because other miners thought it gave him an "unfair" advantage.

Text Continued on Page 372

POWER TO MOVE MOUNTAINS

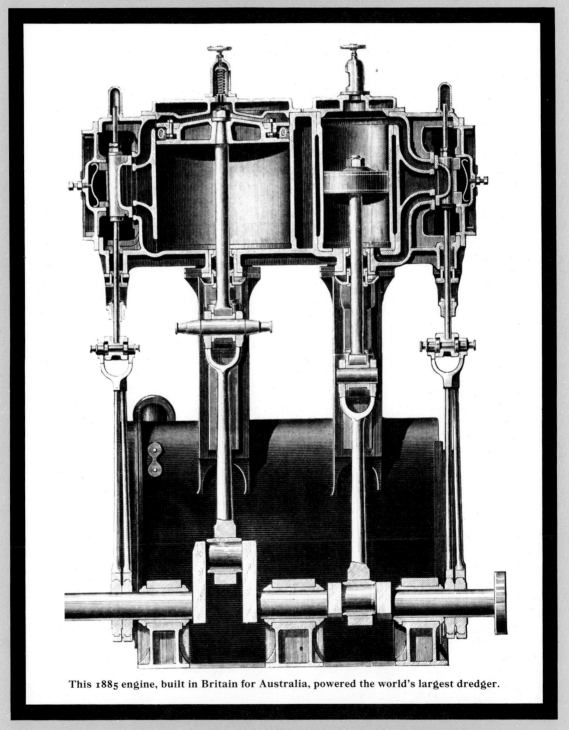

This 1885 engine, built in Britain for Australia, powered the world's largest dredger.

Between 1880 and 1900, the worth of Britain's machine exports doubled to £20,000,000. To the Victorians, this was heady stuff, further proof that Britain was the world's leader in mastering nature. But it was a superficial judgement. The engines that scraped, dredged, puffed and clanked their way so effectively across the Empire and the whole wide world merely served to conceal Britain's increasing weakness. For they supplied other nations with the means to build rival economies.

Changing the Face of the Earth

There was no limit to the optimism the Early Victorians felt for the God-like powers they seemingly held in their hands. They were, in the words of Sir Humphry Davy, "powers which may be almost called creative." Canals, mines, deep-water harbours: these proved that progress was possible, that hard work produced lasting results for the general good. "God helps those who help themselves," wrote Samuel Smiles, the biographer whose faith in this dictum led him to make heroes of Britain's engineers.

Many of his heroes lived in the 18th Century, and it was an 18th-Century optimism that bore up the Early Victorian engineers. Railways and canals had knitted a diverse country together, brought mobility to millions, shown how the application of steam could perhaps lay the foundations of Utopia in Britain.

Now, in the latter part of the century, she could do the same thing all over again with the Empire, a raw estate ready for the hand of the developer. Starving millions awaited dams, canals and railways. British settlers awaited water-pumps, winders and presses. The mother country had helped herself at home and God had rewarded her with a great Empire. It was now her duty to ensure the same rewards for her imperial children.

The sonorously named combined excavator and steam crane which ran on rails was used for quarrying, for ditching and dredging waterways and for excavating canals.

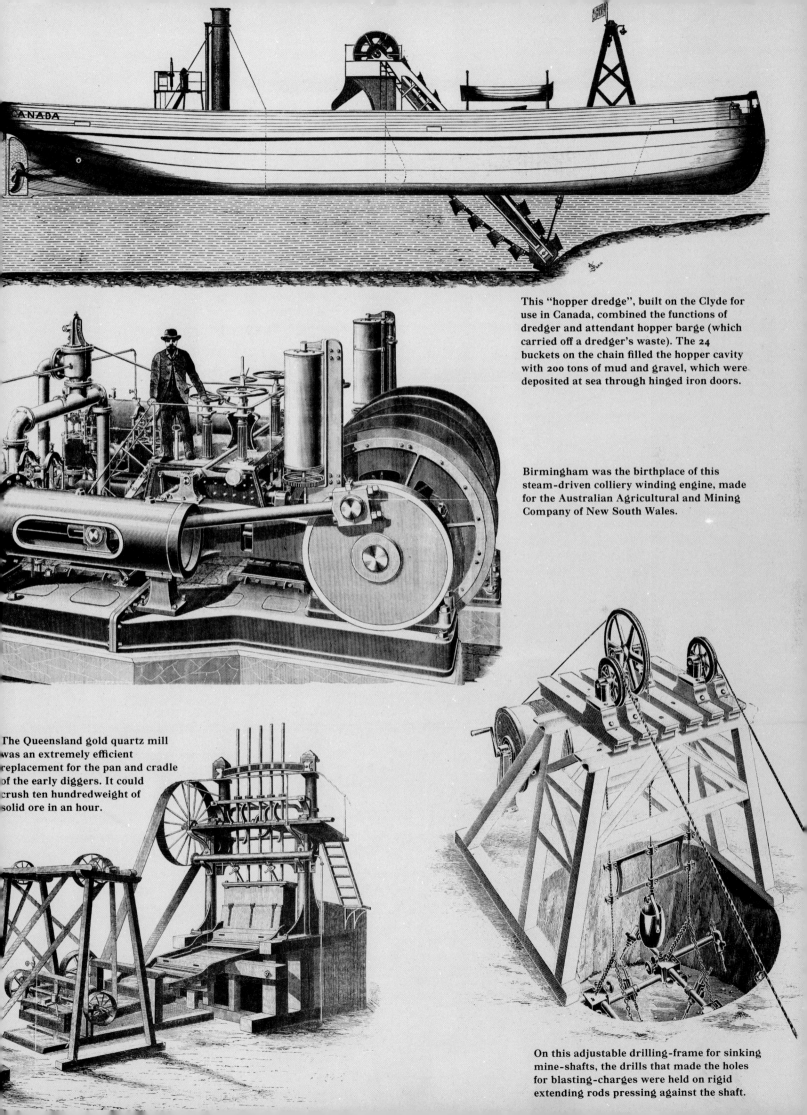

This "hopper dredge", built on the Clyde for use in Canada, combined the functions of dredger and attendant hopper barge (which carried off a dredger's waste). The 24 buckets on the chain filled the hopper cavity with 200 tons of mud and gravel, which were deposited at sea through hinged iron doors.

Birmingham was the birthplace of this steam-driven colliery winding engine, made for the Australian Agricultural and Mining Company of New South Wales.

The Queensland gold quartz mill was an extremely efficient replacement for the pan and cradle of the early diggers. It could crush ten hundredweight of solid ore in an hour.

On this adjustable drilling-frame for sinking mine-shafts, the drills that made the holes for blasting-charges were held on rigid extending rods pressing against the shaft.

Muscles of Iron

The most fascinating products of Victorian factories were the railways and the traction-engines – steam-powered, self-propelled tractors. At home, these monsters – they weighed anything up to ten tons – were limited by law and climate. To ensure the safety of open-mouthed on-lookers, the Red Flag Act of 1865 laid down a maximum speed of 4 m.p.h. for traction-engines and an accompanying team of four men, one of whom bore a red flag. And traction-engines, widely used as a stationary power source, tended to bog down in damp ground.

But in imperial lands there were no such restrictions, and these solid, ungainly machines – the familiar Baroque creations of twisted brass columns were made only for English fairgrounds – were in constant demand. They rumbled their way along India's Grand Trunk Road, hauling impressive trainloads of goods. In the Boer War, solicitously groomed by "steam sappers," they kept troops supplied with equipment. And during the construction of the Uganda Railway in 1898, when the human supply line proved too susceptible to fever, heat and lions, materials were lugged to the railhead by eight ton tractors, "the dense bush presenting to them as much difficulty as a well-mown field to a bicycle."

This fire-engine with a steam-powered water-jet was used in locations as far apart as Chile, India and Singapore. Just eight and a half minutes after lighting the fire, a working pressure was raised and water could be thrown 250 feet.

This traction-engine was designed for use in India to bale cotton into one-seventh of its original bulk and so cut out the danger of its catching fire during transit. Uncompressed cotton destroyed in this way cost one railway £30,000 during one year alone.

Designed to travel at "high speed" – 8 m.p.h. – on wheels cushioned by coil springs this engine, built in Leeds for passenger service in India, could pull three tons.

Gadgets Galore

Huge band-saws that sliced through the forests of Canada, stone-crushers that hammered out the gold from the Rand and Australia, lighthouses that glimmered along the sea-routes of the world: to the British public, such devices proved that British expertise was paramount.

It was true. But there was another side to the coin. Because of the swift success of Britain's technical engineers, there had grown up a split between pure science and engineering that was eventually disastrous for British technological leadership. In the 1860s, an eminent civil engineer could dismiss scientific formulae on the proportions of retaining-walls in a mine-shaft as "having the same practical value as the weather forecasts for the year in *Old Moore's Almanac.*"

But while technicians and scientists derided each other – convinced nevertheless of British supremacy – and gentlemen recoiled from trade, German, French and American scientists were busy building the future – on the basis of British-pioneered techniques. Britain's success in transforming her Empire merely allowed the old complacency to live on until Britain was more the world's industrial museum than its workshop.

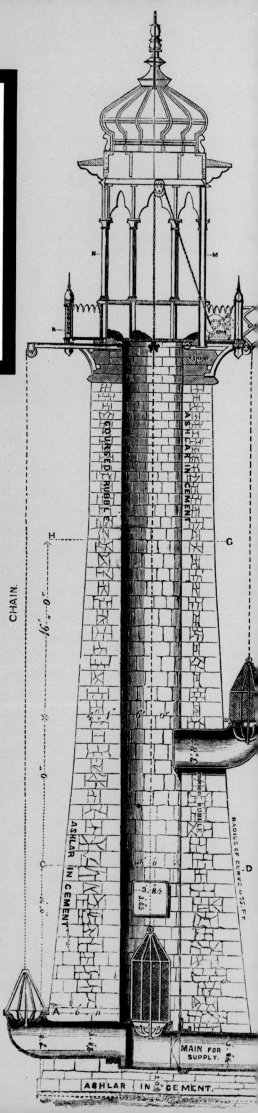

The growth of the timber industry meant new inventions in sawing machinery. This eight-inch endless band-saw kept turning while the log travelled on moving tables.

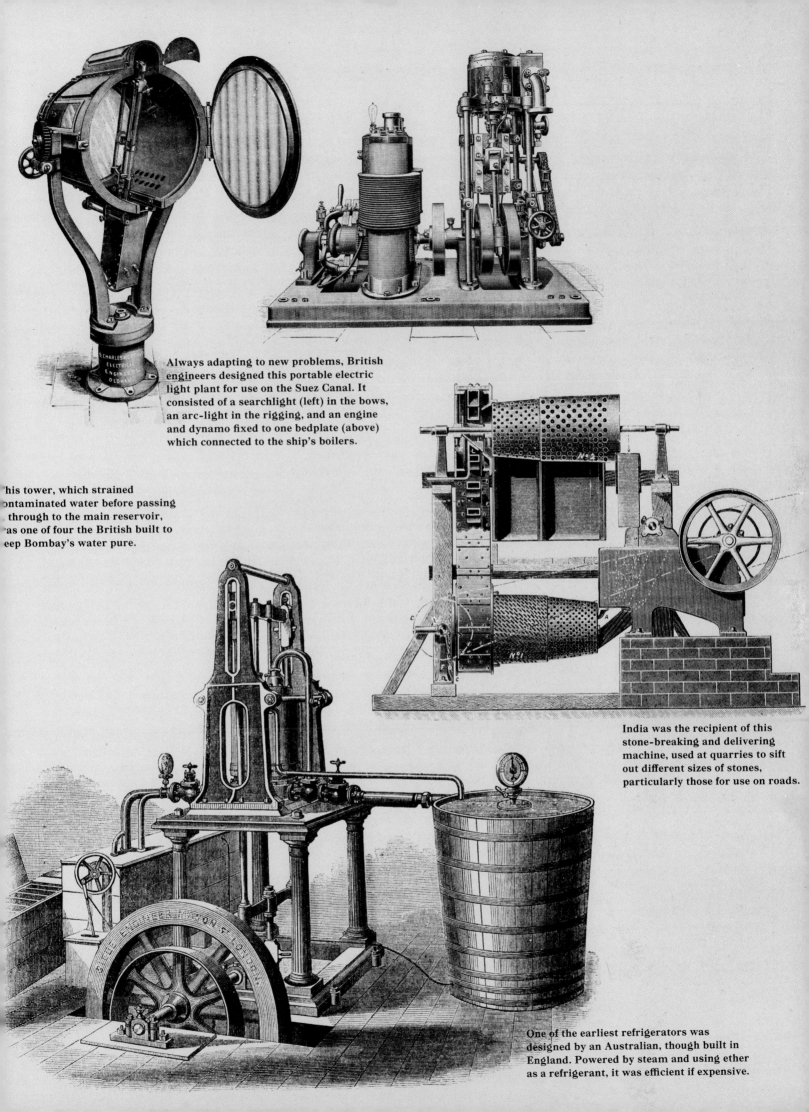

Always adapting to new problems, British engineers designed this portable electric light plant for use on the Suez Canal. It consisted of a searchlight (left) in the bows, an arc-light in the rigging, and an engine and dynamo fixed to one bedplate (above) which connected to the ship's boilers.

This tower, which strained contaminated water before passing through to the main reservoir, was one of four the British built to keep Bombay's water pure.

India was the recipient of this stone-breaking and delivering machine, used at quarries to sift out different sizes of stones, particularly those for use on roads.

One of the earliest refrigerators was designed by an Australian, though built in England. Powered by steam and using ether as a refrigerant, it was efficient if expensive.

Cleopatra's Needle

One of the most dramatic engineering feats performed by the Victorians was the removal of the pink granite obelisk known as "Cleopatra's Needle" from Egypt to Britain in 1878. The monolith, 70 feet high and weighing nearly 200 tons, had been presented to the British people in 1819 in gratitude for Britain's expulsion of Napoleon from Egypt.

The Needle had led an errant life. Fashioned in 1460 B.C., it was erected outside the Temple of the Sun at Heliopolis. Centuries later, traditionally on the orders of Cleopatra, it was uprooted and carried off to the Palace of the Caesars at Alexandria.

In 1875 General Sir James Alexander, distinguished soldier and explorer, went to Egypt to bring it home for the nation. An engineer convinced him that the Needle could be cocooned in a round iron hull, rolled into the sea, and towed to Britain. The craft assembled with the precious monolith inside was named *Cleopatra*.

In September, 1877, with a steamer towing her, *Cleopatra* forged out into the Mediterranean. All went well until they ran into a cyclone in the Bay of Biscay. *Cleopatra's* ballast of rails shifted, causing her to list dangerously, and the tow rope had to be slipped. *Cleopatra* disappeared. It was only after some days that a Glasgow steamer found and rescued the abandoned vessel. Finally, in January, 1878, the Needle arrived in London and, after months of furious debate over the siting, was erected on the Embankment beside the Thames.

Richard Henry Hancock migrated to Australia in 1859 and became manager of its largest mine. His innovations made it the most mechanized and progressive in the industry. "Captain" Hancock became a legend. He was a religious man and a reformer, compelling his illiterate miners to attend four sessions of night-school each week before he would let them work the following week.

Often, engineers' work was the most important event in the current history of the country involved. Such was the Great Nile Dam at Aswan—not the one recently built by engineers from that other, newer empire, the Soviet Union, but the first one, which was completed in 1902.

To gain a foothold in the Nile, William Willcocks tried lowering four-ton stones into the stream. The water, which he said "rushed at a pace exceeding the fastest University crew," tumbled them away like children's blocks. He wired several stones together, but even these could not withstand the torrent. Finally he lashed them onto railway tracks, 50 tons at a time, and shot them down an incline into the river. They lodged.

When the one-and-a-quarter-mile-long dam was finished, it formed a lake stretching the same distance as London to Nottingham and sufficient to provide the entire population of Great Britain with water for a year. It gave Egypt 8 million irrigated acres and made that country prosperous for more than a decade—until the population caught up with the improvement. It was called the Eighth Wonder of the World.

Thanks to British engineers, the world was getting a surfeit of Eighth Wonders. Another was the Victoria Bridge, which opened in 1859. Built by Alexander M. Ross, it carried a Canadian railway across the St. Lawrence at a point where the river was two miles wide, an alarming distance to bridge in those days. American engineers hooted at Ross's scheme, saying blocked ice would topple the bridge the first winter. It consisted of a huge rectangular tube resting on masonry piers. The ironwork was made in England in numbered sections and shipped to the assembly

site. The Prince of Wales, later Edward VII, opened it, and the ice did not bring it down. In fact, 25 years later other engineers found it perfectly capable of carrying a roadbed twice as wide as the original one. Their only complaint was the durability of Ross's work; they said it was easier to build the new part than to cut away the old.

Railways, with their bridges and tunnels, were the British speciality. They built them everywhere they were allowed to, and some places where they were not. Napier took a complete railway with him when he marched on Magdala in Abyssinia in 1868; Kitchener, himself an engineer, laid one on his way to Khartoum. Cecil Rhodes's most pressing imperial dream was to link up with that line from the other end of the continent, a dream he never realized.

British engineers had a knack for getting round small budgets with ingenious improvisation. Building a railway in New South Wales, John Whitton had to negotiate a steep precipice. Tunnelling would have solved the problem, but the Governor disallowed funds for that, suggesting instead that Whitton lay tracks on the existing highways and have horses pull the railway cars. That, needless to say, was no answer for a railway man. Instead he built a gigantic zig-zag. The train ran forward down one incline, stopped while a switch was thrown behind it, ran backwards down the next incline, stopped, and so on, traversing three miles of zig-zag track to drop 600 feet, a gradient of 1 in 26.

The British railway-builder was ubiquitous. Richard Trevithick, in South America on a mining venture, planned a line from Lima to Callao as early as 1817. Had he been able to raise the money, the world's first public steam railway would have been built in Peru rather than in Britain. British engineers tried to get permission to build the Trans-Siberian Railway, but the Russians insisted on waiting until they were capable of doing it themselves.

As the 19th Century rolled towards the 20th, British engineers faced stronger and stronger competition. They had not lost their expertise, but its exclusiveness began to slip as knowledge and technique spread. In Australia Cornish miners were being replaced by graduates of Australian mining schools and by Americans. Even a London consulting firm sent American engineers to work there: one was a future President, Herbert Hoover. Building a railway in Burma, the British turned to an American firm for the most difficult task, the fantastic Gokteik viaduct spanning a deep, half-mile-wide gorge. The construction of one of Empire's greatest triumphs, the Canadian Pacific Railway, was directed by American engineer William Van Horne. Now, it seemed, there were Arthur Cottons all over the world dreaming up canals at breakfast time.

The old pioneer himself was still busy trying to convince the British government to build more dams and canals in India and fewer railways. The famines which kept recurring there seemed to substantiate his argument. "A patient is bleeding to death," he wrote in one of his many pamphets, "and a spectator begins a long discourse on the best mode of treating him so as to restore his strength, but another says, 'Stop a minute, let us first stay the bleeding.'" In fact, the bleeding was being stayed. Before Sir Arthur died, India had 55,202 miles of canals, and by 1947, when it became independent, there were 70 million acres under irrigation.

Towards the end of his life the man most responsible for this great achievement lapsed into another of those 19th-Century Victorian roles he performed so well: tinkering with inventions. Cotton's strange experiments with a brass canoe made his family frantic with worry. And on the roads around Woodcot, his home near Dorking, he terrorized passersby with a man-sized tricycle he was trying to perfect.

"Now you just watch me" he told one stranger, "and tell me how many turns this wheel makes in a minute." With that, the 70-year-old engineer wobbled down a hill, hit an embankment, and flew over the handlebars into a hedge. The concerned stranger ran to his aid, but Cotton waved him away. "Look after the machine," he said. "I can take care of myself." When his wife begged him to get rid of it, he told her, "Rome was not built in a day. It will take me a long time to complete my patent brake." Learning of a missionary who lacked transport, Cotton made the noble sacrifice and sent him his tricycle. The missionary returned it, after breaking an arm.

Sir Arthur made his last public utterance in the letter columns of *The Times*. It was another condemnation of the government for "giving India iron instead of water." He died a few days later, June 14, 1899. In his lifetime he and others like him had linked the past and future with technology. In a coffin draped with the Union Jack he was lowered into the soil of a very different world than the one he had been born into, a new world he and other engineers of Empire had helped create.

—Jim Hicks

III. The Indefatigable Tourist

On weekday mornings in the 1890s a dapper little Londoner with a small beard would arrive punctually at the headquarters of Thomas Cook's, the world's most famous travel agency, in Ludgate Circus. He was John Mason Cook, the son who completed the name "Cook & Son." Before passing briskly through the portals to begin the day's work, he always paused purposefully to inspect the posters on the outside, checking for splashes of mud from the horse-drawn traffic clattering round the corner. The posters had to be kept spotless, as spotless as the reputation of Cook's itself.

The son's pride was entirely natural. Cook's was the pioneer of modern tourism and already the name had become a household word in many languages. By the end of the 19th Century Britain had spanned the globe with railways, steamship lines, postal services, telegraphs, and cables like a parcel tied up with string. This network of modern communications, which linked the distant business and administrative centres of the Empire, also provided a magic carpet of travel for pleasure. Britons set out to see the world, especially the imperial parts of it, and Cook's built a great tourist industry, an empire within the Empire.

Since his father's death in 1892, Cook had taken into his hands the reins of an astonishing power. From his office in the grandiose building at Ludgate Circus he directed the movement of travellers throughout the world. He could accommodate a thousand tourists in Victorian luxury under canvas in the Holy Land, or convey Eastern princes across oceans and continents with all their panoply of servants, elephants, and tame tigers. He could lay on a boat trip round the world, a trans-Canadian railway journey, a steamship cruise to the Azores, or a meeting with a chieftain in Darkest Africa.

The age of world tourism had its roots in the beginnings of the Empire itself. At the same time as Elizabethan explorers sailed out into the unknown in search of Eastern riches, new worlds, and national glory, the nobility began to cross the Channel in search of the latest and best in European culture. Thus was invented a new form of travel, that peculiarly English institution called the Grand Tour.

The early practitioners of the Grand Tour—from which the word "tourism" derives—went with the entirely serious intent of completing their education by acquiring a gloss of Renaissance culture from Italy and the international language of diplomacy from France. They were concerned with art, science, and politics, and regarded the Continent as a finishing school. But as larger numbers of aristocrats went abroad, the Continent came to be regarded more as a playground. Their spending was lavish, their pleasure extravagant. A duke might spend as much as £25,000 over five years.

This kind of tour was long the privilege of a tiny élite. By the late 18th Century the social and economic changes that were overtaking Britain enabled a few successful merchants and professional men to creep in at the bottom. The newcomers to travel paid £100 or £150 for a shortened, less grand tour lasting for perhaps a season. But far more radical change was required before tourism could come within the reach of ordinary men. That change came on the heels of the Industrial Revolution that by 1800 was beginning to alter radically the way of life in Britain.

Popular tourism was a British invention, for tourism was inextricably linked with technological advance—with railways and steamships. At the start of the 19th Century man could travel no faster than a horse at the gallop. Then, in 1825, George Stephenson opened the world's first steam railway. Five years later the Manchester to Liverpool railway became the first regular passenger line. In its first year of operation it carried 445,000 passengers—almost 4 per cent of the population of Britain. Travel was becoming a mass movement.

By the late 1830s, with the railways stretching their iron fingers across Britain and industrialization creating a new class of working men eager for fresh air and new sights, the material and social conditions for popular tourism were firmly established. The time was ripe for an entrepreneur who would build a business on this foundation by offering special outings at reduced fares for instruction and pleasure. The hour awaited the man. By the vagaries of chance and circumstance, Thomas Cook stepped forward—chosen, as he liked to believe, by Providence—to become the pioneer of modern tourism. He made travel not just a movement of people but a people's movement.

Cook's background placed him in the right social station to lead such a movement. He was born in a humble cottage in Melbourne in the Midlands. At the age of ten financial problems at home forced him to leave school and become a penny-a-day farm labourer and then, at 14, an indentured wood-turner. The formative influence on his life was his mother, daughter of a Bible-thumping Baptist minister. She brought him up in the stern, religious mould of Evangelicalism, and to the grave he remained a God-fearing, serious man.

Throughout his life Thomas Cook—who lacked the single-minded business approach later possessed by his son—was a fervent supporter of good causes. For more than three years he was a full-time village missionary, trudging the Midlands countryside for the Baptist church, eking out a living by publishing religious tracts and pamphlets. As late as the 1850s he personally organized a 15,000-gallon nightly free "soup-run" and retailed potatoes at cost to the poor of Leicester. But the cause to which he was most firmly committed was temperance. In this role he built temperance hotels and later formed—with laudable but purblind idealism—a teetotal club for Fleet Street newspapermen.

It was as secretary of the Harborough Temperance Society that in 1841 Cook organized a round trip between Leicester and Loughborough so that a party of abstainers might attend a temperance meeting. In nine open railway carriages 570 people were carried 11 miles, entertained with a band, harangued for three hours about the "monster intemperance," and carried back without mishap—all for one shilling apiece. This type of special trip at reduced price was called an "excursion." Cook was not the first to organize one (there had been a similar outing in 1838 to a public execution), but his personal supervision of the trip was a genuine pioneering feature.

The success of the venture encouraged him to attempt "a wider and more circuitous range" in the future: what he called "tours." Cook applied to his tours the same dogged Evangelical determination that he put into his other good works. At first travel arrangements occupied him only during the summer months. But by the

A Canadian Pacific parlour car (right) was, exclaimed a tourist, "a marvel of elegance." The dining car (opposite) was no less elegant. Such cars cost the line more than its locomotives.

1850s he was beginning to take tourism more seriously, seeing his work as a social crusade to bring ordinary people the educational advantages of travel.

Early tourism was a very serious business. Cook's continental travellers—"Cookites" they were called— were a source of upper-class amusement and disdain. Cook clients were "tradesmen and their wives, merchants, clerks away for a week's holiday, smart mechanics and a Cockney element," reported a journalist. These humble people had the high-minded outlook characteristic of the Evangelical Revival; in his publication *Physical, Moral and Social Aspects of Excursions or Tours,* Cook endorsed the idea that the chief value of tourism was to "unite man to man, and man to God." Many of Cook's competitors began their enterprises with similar attitudes. John Frame demanded strict temperance from all his clients; Dean and Dawson began with do-gooding factory outings for the proletariat of Stockport; Sir Henry Lunn started his continental tours mainly for clergymen and their families.

In the 1850s Cook's horizons widened. He invented the package tour by incorporating numerous diverse items in the overall price of his tours— travel by rail, ship, horse, and coach over different national networks; beds, food, cabs, and sightseeing; and even drink in his later, less fervent years. And as the railways expanded, he extended his operations to take in all the British Isles, then Europe, and finally the world.

About the same time, steam began to conquer the oceans, thus opening up the world to modern cheap tourism. Until the steamship came into regular use, sea voyages were prohibitively expensive as well as unbearably long and hopelessly unscheduled. The passage to India in the late 18th Century, for example, could take anything up to nine months, depending on the weather. Steam travel on the high seas became reliable and efficient thanks to those two British innovations, iron hulls and screw propellers. After that, and with the opening of the Suez Canal in 1869 (appropriately, Thomas Cook attended the opening ceremonies), journey times to India dropped to 17 days and second-class fares to £50. The flowering of Victorian world tourism could begin.

A change was also occurring in the social complexion of tourism. The serious, pioneering period of travel passed and the earnest attitudes of the early Victorian era began to fade. They were replaced by more straightforward, worldly ideas of recreation and enjoyment.

Cook's new projects clearly reflected this process of rapid expansion and decreasing seriousness. In 1864, less than ten years after his first continental tour, Thomas Cook was taking groups to Italy. The following year, when the American Civil War ended, he reconnoitred the United States. In 1869 he began his tours up the Nile, the first step towards making Egypt a favourite winter holiday resort of Victorian Britain. In 1872 he made a much-publicized world tour to discover "with perfect accuracy the best way round the globe" for large numbers of people. A Scottish newspaperman christened him "Field-Marshal" Cook, manœuvrer of massed bodies of eager travellers.

In 1870 he gave his son, John Mason Cook, full control of the London office. The younger Cook was very much a late Victorian, unencumbered by his father's Evangelical preoccupations. As he took an increasing part in running the business a change of emphasis occurred. Cook's ceased to be associated with philanthropy and became a byword for comfort and middle-class respectability. Late Victorians wallowed in a leisurely and luxurious style of tourism. They also drew themselves up with pride, for there was an element in their travel that had been absent from the European Grand Tour: Empire.

At the height of Empire, British domination of the sea lanes, postal services, submarine telegraph lines, coaling stations, the growing network of railways, were a boon to the tourist. The ubiquitous figure of the Englishman, upright in the panelled dining car of an express train, supine in the deck chair of a steamship, peering at the sights from Canada to Australia, from Jerusalem to Hong Kong, introduced natives everywhere to the customs and quirks of the most powerful nation in the world.

When people went abroad as tourists in those days, they travelled almost as conquerors. Supplied with Cook's amenities, they could look down with easy disdain on less civilized peoples, convinced of their own immense superiority. There was much

talk of "annihilating distance," a military metaphor in keeping with the time. Every railway bridge, every culvert, every viaduct soaring above river or canyon was seen as a monument to British power.

At his death in 1892, Thomas Cook was a quasi-imperial figure. In Egypt he had his own fleet cruising the Nile, his own shipyard at Boulac, his own luxury hotels at Luxor, his own army of Arab employees. Along the Nile peasants grew produce to feed tourists from Tunbridge Wells or Cheltenham, who devoured country-house breakfasts on board Cook's paddle steamers. In the reading-rooms the newspapers arrived with the faultless regularity expected at a Pall Mall club. Battalions of Arabs waited ashore, ready to convey sedan-borne expeditions into the desert; aboard, more Arabs in white robes served Huntley & Palmer's biscuits for tea under awnings.

Cook's pilgrims proceeded through the Middle East with enough tents, horses, and servants for royalty. Every morning the whole movable hotel—iron bedsteads, wool mattresses, carpeted floors—was struck, transported on baggage animals, and at sundown pitched again so expertly that each person found his own numbered napkin from breakfast laid beside his dinner plate. "Grand Hotel service" all over the world—that was what the British enjoyed.

In the Far East Cook & Son charges investigated the teeming streets of Singapore or took passage to marvel at the unique flora and fauna of Australia and New Zealand. After the opening of Cook's offices in Bombay and Calcutta, sightseers were soon bowling across the subcontinent in first-class railway carriages or the earliest motor cars, with *Murray's Handbook* on their knees and plenty of Scotch and soda in their tiffin baskets.

Few experiences were more romantic than a tour via the Canadian Pacific. At an average speed of 28 m.p.h., including stops, it took a week to cross the continent. For the leisurely, frock-coated tourist of the 1890s, it was delightful to saunter through carriages beautifully inlaid with rare woods, recline in a cloud of cigar smoke in the smoking room or sip iced water in a stateroom as the prairies and mountains of virgin Canada slipped by the window. It was bracing to feel impe-

rial pride in "this Canada of ours," as one British traveller put it, on those mighty steel rails "beneath our Northern skies."

The same imperial pride continued after the First World War. In the 1930s, the era of the great liners, the national power complex was expressed in international duels to capture the Blue Riband, the coveted award for the fastest ocean crossings. Tourists could browse with patriotic pride through thick little handbooks crammed with impressive statistics of British shipping tonnage and sectional plans of such monarchs of the seas as the *Aquitania* and the *Queen Mary*.

Until the Second World War, world tourism remained a middle-class idyll. The whole drama of British tourism from 1870 to 1939 was a period piece in which the proud attitudes of the golden years at the turn of the century continued hardly without alteration. British tourists set out with Empire in their hearts and minds, and wherever they went, whether the Union Jack happened to be flying there or not, Empire went along with them.

—*Simon Rigge*

A pyramid climb was de rigueur for the Victorian visitor to Egypt. Above, a Cook's Nile steamer lies moored at the Temple of Abu Simbel in 1907.

Chapter Ten
THE CRACKED FACADE

The Boer War was instrumental in bursting the bubble of imperial euphoria that surrounded the British in the 1890s. A remarkably symbolic view of that conflict is this portrait of three generations of rough and ready Boer warriors.

I. Behind the Pomp and Circumstance

Within a month of the 1897 Diamond Jubilee celebrations, even before the last bunting had been removed, a disturbing poem was published in *The Times*, traditionally the organ of the British ruling classes and currently as hotly imperialist as the most sensational of its penny competitors. It was by Rudyard Kipling, the acknowledged laureate of the imperial idea. Kipling more than anyone had succeeded in equating Empire with duty, honour, national pride, and opportunity, and he might have been expected to crown the triumph of Jubilee with some culminating paean.

The following, though, is what *The Times* published that morning of July 17:

God of our fathers, known of old,
  Lord of our far-flung battle-line,
Beneath whose awful Hand we hold
  Dominion over palm and pine—
Lord God of Hosts, be with us yet,
Lest we forget—lest we forget!

The tumult and the shouting dies;
  The Captains and the Kings depart:
Still stands Thine ancient sacrifice,
  An humble and a contrite heart.
Lord God of Hosts, be with us yet,
Lest we forget—lest we forget!

Far-called our navies melt away;
  On dune and headland sinks the fire:
Lo, all our pomp of yesterday
  Is one with Nineveh and Tyre!
Judge of the Nations, spare us yet,
Lest we forget—lest we forget!

If, drunk with sight of power, we loose
  Wild tongues that have not Thee in awe,
Such boastings as the Gentiles use,
  Or lesser breeds without the Law—
Lord God of Hosts, be with us yet,
Lest we forget—lest we forget!

For heathen heart that puts her trust
  In reeking tube and iron shard,
All valiant dust that builds on dust,
  And guarding, calls not Thee to guard,
For frantic boast and foolish word—
Thy mercy on Thy people, Lord!

This noble poem, "Recessional," referred at one level directly to the Jubilee itself. The visiting captains of the colonial forces were at that moment returning to their stations, the vast fleet assembled for the Spithead Review was dispersed to its separate squadrons. Only the ashes were left of the beacons which, on dune and headland across Britain, had blazed the meaning of Jubilee.

But in a deeper sense Kipling had in mind the profounder act of sacrament which was Empire itself—the ritual imposition of British values, like a laying on of hands, upon so many alien races, speaking so many different tongues and honouring such diverse religions. "Recessional" was a warning against the degradation of this ethic. It was a reproof to a newly bombastic people. It hinted at unresolved doubts about the moral nature of imperialism. And, disconcertingly, it suggested that British supremacy in the world was not so inevitable, not so divinely ordained as it seemed.

As Kipling sensed in premonition, the imperial glory was skin-deep. It was a veneer. The craze for Empire was new-born and would be short-lived; London was really far more an island capital that an imperial capital. Those statues of Empire worthies, though they had assumed a transient prominence in 1897, were rightly overshadowed by memorials to all the statesmen, artists, scientists, and men of war who had, during a thousand years of history, given the kingdom

a more durable greatness. The frenzy of those super-imperialist jingos was camouflage for an underlying insecurity. The power of the British Empire was partly illusion, and the disarming grandiloquence of the Diamond Jubilee, so sentimental, so brassy, disguised a growing sense of unease.

The exuberance of Empire was genuine enough, and much of the self-adulation was deserved, but the truth was that London, Hub of the Universe, was already passing the peak of its supremacy. Some of the very soldiers who lined the Queen's route on Jubilee Day, and many of the children who skipped and sang in the streets in celebration of Empire, would live to see the dismantling of the whole imperial edifice, like a stage-set when the play is over.

Economists knew that the industrial momentum of British progress, the basis of imperial expansion, was already slackening. Other powers were catching up. Germany and the United States were already greater producers of steel. France, Italy, Japan, and Russia were industrial powers too, and Britain no longer set the pace in invention, production techniques, or distribution. The fiery salesmanship of earlier times had decayed into complacency. "The usual story," reported a foreign correspondent of the 1890s, home from the Far East, "foreigners content with smaller profits, excessive rates of interest charged by English agents, inelastic terms of credit, incompetent travellers." In absolute terms Britain was still the greatest of foreign traders, but her rate of growth was less than others' and her dynamism was perceptibly fading.

Diplomatically, too, the old command had weakened. The "splendid

Colonial Secretary Joseph Chamberlain advocated positive imperialism. "Our Joe's Dream" has the Australian kangaroo, Indian tiger, South African ostrich, and Canadian moose joining the British lion to carry Chamberlain in imperial unity towards the premiership.

isolation" that had gone into the language was not really so splendid. Britain, the most consistent of the great·nations, was threatened by the rising force of more volatile and restless powers. The United States was recognizably the super-power of the future. Commercially the Americans were already challenging the British in markets everywhere; politically Britain and America repeatedly clashed, notably over interpretations of the Monroe Doctrine by which the U.S. claimed the right to protect all independent states of the Americas from foreign intervention. London was always careful, however, not to press the majesty of the Pax Britannica so resolutely as to go to war with her former colony.

France, too, as the only other major colonial power, was often at odds with Britain over frontiers or spheres of influence. Even as the Jubilee celebrations proceeded, Captain Marchand was tramping across Equatorial Africa to plant the Tricolour on the Upper Nile, and his confrontation with Kitchener at Fashoda the following year almost led to war. France had a technically progressive navy, and so persistent were the old antipathies between Wellington's people and Napoleon's that in Malta the British were building a hefty new defence line specifically to keep out the French. Although the two powers would eventually make common cause in international affairs, the imperial rivalry remained.

The threat from Russia was more legendary than real, but the fear of a Russian invasion of India was an old perennial of British strategy—as the Tsar once said, all he had to do to paralyse British policy was to send a telegram mobilizing his forces in Turkestan.

But in 1897 the most real threat was from Germany—cock-a-hoop, ambi-tious, presided over by Victoria's flashy and unpredictable grandson, Kaiser Wilhelm. The Germans were frank challengers. They had started an empire of their own in direct imitation of the British. Though Lord Salisbury had achieved a peaceful division of spoils between the two empires in Africa, still everyone knew that the rivalry was intense and possibly perilous. The Germans were building a powerful new fleet. Their diplomacy seemed designed to exclude Britain from the affairs of the Continent. Their industry, already in some respects more advanced than Britain's, was expanding faster from more modern foundations.

British foreign policy had traditionally been based upon two fundamentals: a fleet more powerful than the combination of any two potential enemy navies, and a balance of power in Europe to prevent the emergence of a single super-state across the

Channel. The rise of Germany put both these principles at risk. The Germans were clearly bent upon the hegemony of Europe, and the Royal Navy, though numerically unchallenged, was hardly Nelson's incomparable fleet of old. As an instrument of imperial parade it was still superb; as a weapon of national policy it was considerably less formidable than it seemed.

The ebullient Diamond Jubilee celebrations, which had turned London into an exhibition of imperial grandeur, were partly intended to mask these weaknesses. Superficially Britain seemed supremely sure of herself, but thoughtful Britons, like Kipling, were already half-conscious of the cracks in the facade and haunted by visions of their country becoming one day a second-class power. More significant still, a small minority of citizens was already beginning to wonder if Empire was such a good thing after all.

The common sense of the imperial idea, like its morality, usually went unquestioned by the general public. It was assumed that the Empire was the basis of British power and prosperity, and most people thought that the nation had a perfect right to acquire underdeveloped overseas possessions—even a duty. A few seers, however, thought otherwise. Some economists doubted if the expansion of the Empire really benefited the British economically: capital invested overseas, they argued, could better be used to improve conditions at home. Some strategists, disturbed by the dispersion of British power across the seas and continents, believed that Empire was a source of weakness rather than strength: Britain's real enemies, bristling with modern warships and well-drilled conscript armies, were marshalled close to home, not waving assegais in Zululand or aiming flintlocks in the Khyber Pass. Some people were simply repelled by the aesthetics of Empire: its bluster, its sanctimony, its coarse self-satisfaction.

And there were a few visionaries, even at that arrogant time, who wondered whether imperialism was really *right*. Was it right, for instance, that a kingdom dedicated to the ideal of personal freedom should rule its dependencies as absolute autocracies? Was it right to impose Western culture upon peoples with ancient civilizations of their own? Were the coloured races of the Empire getting their fair share of progress, or were they merely being exploited? Was the bullying of Empire justifiable, was its inevitable militarism worthy of England? Was it all, to use a favourite value-judgement of Victorian England, *fair*?

The imperial theorists were tortured by the contradictions of it all, and their principal difficulty was the dual standard of Empire: one standard for Britons, one for the rest. The glory of England lay in her free institutions, now extended so successfully to her white colonies; but the whole coloured Empire was governed as a benevolent despotism. The British could flatter themselves that they were guiding a score of less-advanced nations towards democratic independence. Realists knew that this was a meretricious picture.

These were debilitating self-doubts, rare though they were, and confined to fastidious moralists and radicals. They were a portent of declining conviction.

When the Queen's Jubilee procession passed the Parliamentary stands at Westminster, to the boisterous greetings of the House of Commons, one tier of seats was seen to be ostentatiously empty. These were the places reserved for the Irish Members. Since the formal union of their country with England in 1800, they had represented their constituents at Westminster, spending most of their time arguing for Irish independence and making themselves the curse of each successive government.

The nearest dependency of Britain was also the most fractious. It so happened that 1897 was a quiet time in Ireland, between storms, but even so the temper of the people was ominously unreliable. In that green and impoverished sister isle, so near and yet so foreign, there smouldered the passion of nationalism that was to ignite half the world in the coming century.

The Diamond Jubilee was marked

in Dublin by riots, mock funerals, looted shops, and fused illuminations. A black flag flew at half-mast above city hall, and the celebrated nationalist agitator Miss Maude Gonne cried from her rostrum in Phoenix Park that the Irish would never get justice from Britain until they were able to wrench it from her "in some hour of danger or defeat, which pray God may come soon." The ultimate threat to imperial supremacy—the threat of rebellion—was suggested more clearly in Ireland than anywhere. Patriotic Irishmen saw liberty and imperialism as incompatibles: one of their favourite slogans was "Live Ireland—Perish the Empire!"

There were other potential subversives among the subject peoples of

Staunch imperialists had little use for Gladstone; here he has sold off India to Russia as Uncle Sam bids for the next choice parcel.

Empire. In Canada the introspective French-Canadians considered themselves a nation apart, survivors of pre-Revolutionary French civilization in the country they still liked to call Nouvelle France. In South Africa a rather similar people were the Boers—primitive Calvinists in religion, ethnically descendants of Dutch, Huguenot, and German emigrants, and so long away from Europe that they had developed habits and values altogether their own. The Boer nation was essentially a tribe of white Africans, and it chafed against the sophisticated and alien interference of London's civil servants.

Like the Irish and the *Quebecois*, the Boers felt they were victimized by the British. Wherever they wandered over

the high veld of South Africa, redcoats, missionaries, and administrators were sure to follow, to corrupt the Boers' biblical folkways, mollycoddle their black retainers, exploit their resources, and ultimately shatter their independence. Most had been forced, by the pressure of imperial expansion, into a front of resentful nationalism, and were only biding their time to humiliate the British in return.

Among most of the coloured peoples, nationalism was either bludgeoned into impotence or had not yet been aroused. The stalwart Zulu nation, which had inflicted the terrible defeat of Isandhlwana upon the British Army in 1879, had been reduced to vassaldom at last. The Ashanti of West Africa were temporarily subdued. The Canadian Indians were quiescent. The Maoris of New Zealand were co-operative. All the tributary monarchs of Empire, the sultans and nizams and rajahs and paramount chieftains and hereditary khans, had been persuaded into postures of loyal respect.

Even among those vast and docile subject nations, though, there were tremors of dissent. The British were well aware that this Empire was held together by coercion, and the Indian Mutiny had shattered any illusions they may have had about the perpetual loyalty of grateful subjects. The sepoys seemed content enough in 1897, but India was politically astir. Though the country was ruled despotically by the British, it enjoyed almost complete freedom of speech, and many of the vernacular newspapers were furiously critical of Empire. Religious militants preached a return to older Indian ways. Intellectual activists, especially in Bengal, argued for racial equality and demanded political opportunity.

The Indian National Congress, which had been founded (by a Scot) as a moderate body of political commitment, was turning into a fiercely nationalist force. On the very day of the Diamond Jubilee two British officers were murdered in Poona. The British papers, in exalted mood, scarcely noticed the event, but in India it was seen as an omen—an earnest of the blood that would one day flow when agitation gave birth to revolution. "It may be," wrote the nationalist Gopal Krishna Gokhale, "that the history of the world does not furnish an instance where a subject race has risen by agitation. If so, we shall supply that example for the first time. . . ."

Parallel texts awaited their authors in many another corner of Empire. In the commercial enclaves clinging to China's coast the representatives of imperial trade sensed that perhaps they were sitting on a volcano about to erupt. The Sinhalese had lately been excited by Buddhist revivals of a distinctly nationalist tinge. Educated West Africans protested against discrimination in jobs and social standing. In Egypt the educated classes were almost unanimously hostile to the British occupation.

Even the self-governing white colonies had complaints, emotionally devoted though they were to flag and mother country. The Australians resented British restraints in the Pacific, the Canadians negotiated directly with Washington, the Rhodesians did their best to evade what they called with distaste "the imperial factor." Many a hard-pressed colonist viewed with tired contempt the efforts of the Colonial Office to prove that blacks and whites were equal before Queen as before God. The movement in England for a federation of Empire, starting with economic union, was enthusiastic, and Colonial Secretary "Pushful Joe" Chamberlain tried to harness the emotions of Jubilee to this end. But the colonials would have none of it. They preferred to be their own economic masters, and were not ambitious to share more equably the financial burden of imperial defence. They felt themselves to be nations on their own now, at liberty to decree their own tariffs and even pursue their own foreign policies. Such attitudes were disconcerting to the British: no imperial theorist could ever forget 1776 when British colonists of an earlier vintage had broken an earlier British Empire.

Still, there was no immediate danger in 1897. For the moment all was safe. No foreign country dared assault

An 1896 American cartoon has the big powers eyeing John Bull covetously, wondering how long he can hold his tasty possessions.

the British Empire yet, and no disgruntled subject peoples were yet in a position to rebel. All these several symptoms were no more than early warnings—straws in a fine fresh wind or clouds upon an azure horizon—and of them all the most truly prophetic was the flicker of doubt that played in the minds of Britons themselves and was given such startling expression, that summer morning in July, by Kipling's grave "Recessional."

Such then was the zenith of the Pax Britannica: a muddled and contradictory climax, its motives tangled, its brag partly bluff, its assurance tempered by gentle hearts, its arrogance by homely sentiment. The British Empire in 1897 was tainted with vulgar opportunism and vainglory, but on the whole, as empires go through history, its intentions were not dishonourable.

A Briton surveying the Jubilee setting from the vantage-point of Queen Victoria's accession 60 years before would have been astonished at its scale and ostentation. That Trafalgar and Waterloo (that "near run thing") should have led to this! That the tight little island of 1837, only beginning to

feel its strength, should have so flexed its muscles as to rule a quarter of the world! That the whole nation, rich or poor, gentry or pleb, should be so fired by the exotic notion of overseas dominion! That little Victoria, the virgin queen of 1837, should have matured into the ruler of the most powerful nation the world had ever seen!

For us, looking back, different emotions are evoked, and we see a poignancy to that gaudy triumph. The thick woollen uniforms look fusty, the campaign ribbons commemorate wars long forgotten or discredited, the field-marshals on their chargers look like little men dressed up to shine. Even the Queen herself is only a mortal old lady after all, soon to join her husband beneath the dome of his Frogmore mausoleum. We know now how insubstantial was the pageant. We can see what tragedies and disillusions are to come in the near future. The silvery note of the trumpets, echoing to us still across the generations, rings with a sweet sadness now from the lost forts and frontiers of Victoria's Empire.

—*James Morris*

II. Bitter Victory: The Boer War

Within 24 months of Victoria's Jubilee, Britain and the two independent Boer republics in South Africa, the Transvaal and the Orange Free State, hovered on the brink of war. It was more than 40 years since the Crimea, and the thought of war did not alarm the British people. There was no reason why it should. Less than 100,000 Boers would be pitted against the rest of the Empire—nearly 400 million people. It seemed hardly fair; it certainly would not take long.

The situation was not unexpected. The minor war with the Transvaal 18 years before, in which the British had been humiliated at Majuba Hill, had settled nothing. The Boers had gained confidence by it, and the British— most dangerous, this—had been shamed.

South Africa in the 1890s had become a cauldron of political unrest, thanks in large measure to the machinations of Cecil Rhodes. At the beginning of the decade the Colossus, his coffers overflowing with Kimberley diamonds and Rand gold, cast his eyes northward beyond the Boer republics—"my north," he liked to call it—towards the native kingdom of Matabeleland. For this vast land, reputedly the site of King Solomon's fabled mines, he had a multiple vision: as a counterweight to the troublesome Boers, as another imperial square in an all-British southern Africa, and as a key link in his dream of a mighty Cape-to-Cairo railway.

The instrument for achieving this goal was the royally chartered British South Africa Company. The Matabele resisted stubbornly, but they were no match for Rhodes's Maxims. Thus an area eight times the size of the British Isles came into the Empire—named, appropriately enough, Rhodesia.

Cecil Rhodes was not content just having a country named for him. His new goal was the overthrow of the Transvaal. It was clear that if he wanted the annoying Boer republic to fall, he would have to engineer it himself. Time was short: he was suffering from a weak heart and knew he had not long to fulfill his ambitions.

He was aware that the foreigners in the Transvaal, the *uitlanders*, objected strongly to the limitations on their rights by the Boers. It seemed to him unreasonable and grotesque that they, constituting about half the Transvaal's population and largely responsible for its wealth, should be subjected to Boer discrimination. With this in mind, Rhodes planned direct action against the Transvaal: a coup, to be sprung by the anti-Boer *uitlanders* supported from without by Rhodes's own men, and clinched by the arrival from the Cape of the British High Commissioner to declare the Transvaal British. With a friendly government in power and no trade restrictions, all South Africa would, he thought, rapidly become the English-speaking federation of which he dreamed.

The supposed hotbed of discontent was Johannesburg, where hordes of foreign-born gold miners chaffed at Boer rule. In 1895 Rhodes's agent, Leander Starr Jameson, stationed himself with a body of troops on the Transvaal border, ready to assist when the revolt simmering in Johannesburg broke out. As it happened, Rhodes misjudged Johannesburg's revolutionary spirit. There was no rebellion— but the impatient Jameson decided to ride in and start one, certain that his act would win wide approval.

The raid was a fiasco. There were no stores, no fresh horses, no support from within Johannesburg, and positive rejection by the imperial government. Due to a bungled attempt to cut telegraph lines at the border, Paul Kruger, the Boer President, knew of the invasion at once. Reputedly quoting the 69th Psalm—"Let thy wrathful anger take hold of them"—he ordered out his commandos.

At Krugersdorp, 30 miles short of Johannesburg, the Boers prepared an ambush. A melodramatic charge on the well-ensconced, sharpshooting Boers led only to the death or injury of some 30 of Jameson's men. Seeking to escape, Jameson ran into a second ambush, this time an inescapable one in a ravine. Running up a white apron borrowed from an old Hottentot woman, the raiders surrendered. The next day, as Boer police swooped on the would-be revolutionaries in Johannesburg, Jameson and the other in-vaders were marched into the Pretoria jail, singing with forced gaiety "After the Ball is Over." A petty event in itself, the Jameson Raid had momentous effects. It rallied Boer opinion solidly against the British. Equally important, once more the British had been shamed.

Demands on the Boers became more vociferous than ever. A principal grievance was that the foreigners (mostly British) in the rapidly developing gold-mining area of the Rand were denied the vote. Rhodes claimed that the capital being invested in Johannesburg was too great to be left to the mercies of what he called an inefficient and corrupt administration. Colonial Secretary Chamberlain was inclined to agree. Paul Kruger was equally firm: if he gave the vote to the *uitlanders* they would take over his country. Anyway, he asserted, the internal affairs of the Transvaal were no concern of the British.

What made war even more likely was the presence of Cape Colony's High Commissioner, Sir Alfred Milner. Until recently Britain's leading tax expert, Milner was a fervent imperialist who saw his mission as getting all southern Africa under the umbrella of Empire. He believed that if war was inevitable, it was better to have it sooner than later. This policy, however, ignored one important consideration: there were hardly any British troops in South Africa.

The commander-in-chief in Cape Colony was General Sir William Butler, a tall, genial man with an Irish brogue. He happened to believe that war was not only unnecessary but also avoidable, and he said so, forcibly and as often as he could. This did not endear Butler to High Commissioner Milner, but Sir William would not be silent. "Present policy, in my opinion," he said, "can only end, if persisted in, in producing a war of races— a conflict the ultimate consequences of which no one could adequately estimate. . . . I believe war between white races would be the greatest calamity that ever occurred in South Africa." Butler was promptly recalled.

The British government, however, did little to reinforce the South African garrison. One of the few things that

The Matabele of Rhodesia were not easily pacified. This sketch by newspaper "special artist" Melton Prior shows the citizens of the Rhodesian town of Buluwayo taking shelter during a bloody tribal uprising in 1896; in the background troops mobilize.

it did do was to send out in 1899 Colonel Robert Baden-Powell, an ambitious, balding, slightly-built officer of 42. His orders were to raise a force to patrol the Rhodesian-Transvaal border and repel any Boer attacks. An insignificant township called Mafeking, on Rhodes's railway from the Cape to Rhodesia, was named in his orders as "the place with the nearest friendly force," a contingent of police. His superiors in Cape Town refused to give him permission to enter the town, but he went in none the less. Baden-Powell was risking a court martial, but he was a protégé of Lord Wolseley, the commander-in-chief of the British Army, and he was a long way from authority. Instead of keeping himself mobile, as had been intended, the only measure he took against Boer attack was to prepare for a siege.

The Boers prepared for action. Their army consisted of irregulars organized into hard-riding commandos. The burghers in each of the 40 electoral districts in the two republics were obliged to raise a commando. These military units were unlike any others in the world. The commandant of each was elected, often more for political reasons than for any military expertise. Discipline was virtually unknown; a Boer could be compelled by law to serve in the local commando, but no one could compel him to obey any orders. But every one was a patriot with a cause to fight for. Kruger ordered mobilization on September 27, 1899.

Two Boer forces began concentrating near the borders of British South Africa, one near Mafeking and one on the other side of the Transvaal near Natal. Kruger believed that the railways would be the key to the coming war. In the east, on the Natal front, the important railway junction was Ladysmith; in the west it was the "diamond city" of Kimberley.

On October 8 Kruger issued an ultimatum demanding, among other things, the withdrawal of all British forces from the Boer borders. War was imminent. The single "enemy" force near the Boer borders was the hodgepodge of police, regular officers, and half-trained civilians—a mere 1,200 men—that Baden-Powell had dug in at Mafeking. The British were in a precarious situation.

Kruger's ultimatum became effective at 5 p.m. on October 11 and Britain found herself at war with the Boer republics. That day Boer patrols crossed the border of Cape Colony near Mafeking, and late in the evening a second Boer force rode into the province of Natal. The next day the telephone line to Mafeking went dead, and two days later the line to Kimberley was cut while the commander of the small garrison there, Colonel R. G. Kekewich, was talking to Cape Town. Silence enveloped the north.

The relaxed Boers above, photographed during the siege of Ladysmith, are a study in contrast with the spick-and-span Coldstream Guards below. Most Boer riflemen had the clip-loading German Mauser, far superior to the single-shot English Lee-Metfords.

In Natal 14,000 Boers under Commandant-General Piet Joubert rode through the mountains that formed a natural barrier between the Transvaal and Natal, then down into the plains past Majuba Hill, symbol of British humiliation. "As far as the eye could see," one of them wrote, "the plain was alive with horsemen, guns, and cattle, all steadily going forward." To their amazement, there was no opposition. Passes were unmined, bridges were still standing, the railway was intact.

The British commander in Natal was General Sir George White, who had won the Victoria Cross in the Afghan War of 1879. Having just arrived in South Africa, he knew next to nothing of the Boers or their tactics. After two weeks of skirmishing and five fierce little engagements, about a quarter of the colony was in Boer hands. White, bewildered by the rapidity and ferocity of the Boer movements, decided to concentrate his 13,500-man force at Ladysmith. The Boers, whose strategy was to keep themselves mobile and the enemy immobile, gratefully put him under leisurely but effective siege.

There was a strange lull in the war while the world waited with intense interest to see what would happen. Nothing happened. The towns of Ladysmith and Kimberley and the outpost of Mafeking were besieged—after a fashion. No attempt was made to encircle the towns with troops. The Boers remained in their camps, mostly out of sight. It was as if they were frightened by the immensity of the prizes that lay waiting for them. All Natal and Cape Colony, virtually defenceless, were at their mercy. In the Cape, Boer sympathizers were waiting to rise in revolt. But Kruger's men continued to laze around Ladysmith, Kimberley, and Mafeking.

It was a fatal error. An army was being hurriedly assembled in Britain. The late Victorians prided themselves on being imperturbable, but a slight air of frenzy could be detected. The thought of any of the besieged towns falling to the arrogant enemy, an army which did not even have a uniform, was not an attractive one.

Reservists and volunteers rushed to the colours. Most were marched through the streets of London before embarkation so that the public could get a good look at the kind of men who were going to deal with Kruger. "The troops were of splendid physique," noted one observer with satisfaction. "Their conduct was sober, steady, and irreproachable." The Queen felt "quite a lump in my throat" for her departing soldiers. As the Brigade of Guards marched to Waterloo Station, "women hung sobbing to the arms of husbands and sweethearts," the *Daily Mail* reported. "Relatives and even total strangers, carried away by the enthusiasm, broke into the ranks and insisted on carrying rifles, kit-bags." A cartoon in *Punch* depicted one Cockney urchin confiding to another: "The Boers 'll cop it now. Farver's gone to South Africa, *an' tooken 'is strap*."

Well ought the naughty Boers quail. The British saw themselves as normally patient, but firm when righteously aroused. Jingoism was at its peak. The country was aware of Empire as never before, and there were constant comparisons with the Romans. Most Britons were determined not to allow a lot of irritating Boers to disturb imperial rule. It would be embarrassing in other places—especially in India—if the word spread that a few thousand armed farmers could shake the British Empire.

Garnet Wolseley gave command of the force now assembling to General Sir Redvers Buller. An Etonian from Devon, Sir Redvers was known to the public for his outstanding gallantry (he had won the Victoria Cross in the Zulu War) and to the army for his prodigious alcoholic capacity. Buller decided to split his force in two: half to Natal to join up with White at Ladysmith, and half to march to Kimberley. He himself would command in the Natal sector. The relief column for Kimberley was to be commanded by Lieutenant-General Lord Methuen. For one of high rank Methuen's experience of war had been minimal, but like Buller he was a Wolseley protégé.

Buller, against his inclinations, was forced to treat the relief of Kimberley as an urgent matter. Cecil Rhodes was on the scene and, ignoring the authority of the military commander, Colonel Kekewich, had been sending messages claiming that the town was on the verge of being taken. "Boers oozing around on every side," he told High Commissioner Milner, and predicted a "terrible disaster." He even managed to contact the London Rothchilds, who had financed him in the first place, and the Rothchilds exerted pressure on the Cabinet.

There was real alarm: Rhodes was the most famous man in Africa, a Privy Councillor, and presumably he knew what he was talking about. Kimberley covered some of the richest few square miles in the world, and its loss would have sensational consequences.

In fact, as Kekewich's dispatches insisted the defence of Kimberley was progressing without the slightest trouble. Rhodes had grossly exaggerated the situation. There had been no attempt to storm the town. The enemy was seldom seen. There were few shortages and life continued much as usual. However, Rhodes was worried, not only about his mines and his dividends, but about the route from the Cape to his beloved Rhodesia, which passed through both Kimberley and Mafeking. He was used to getting his own way, used to moving about Africa where and when he pleased. Above all, he had no time for military regulations. From the start the relationship between Rhodes and Kekewich was frigid.

Rhodes sent off a message to Baden-Powell urging him to exaggerate the situation at Mafeking, as he himself had exaggerated matters at Kimberley. "Do not be foolhardy and pretend you can hold out for months. My theory is, if you make out you are all right they will not bother." This, however, was not Baden-Powell's style. Unlike Rhodes, he was enjoying himself. A chirpy, jolly little man, he sent back cheery reports about the real state of affairs. The Boer bombardment was so inefficient it was a joke. With the stocks of British commissary stores the population was in some respects better off than it had been before the siege began.

Baden-Powell's first message to reach London had said: "All well.

Citizen Generals

To the British, whose military leaders came from the apex of society, the rough-hewn Boer generals were all but indistinguishable from the ragged farmers they led. In fact, there were two groups of generals, a generation apart in character.

When the war began the Boers were led by old men. The lawyer Piet Joubert, commanding on the Natal front, was 68. Careful and unaggressive, he was determined to avoid casualties.

Joubert died in 1900, adding to the gloom cast by the fate of General Piet Cronje. Old "Honest Piet" shared Joubert's distaste for decisive action and was content to besiege Mafeking. In February, 1900, Roberts captured him and his 4,000 men.

Cronje's surrender and Joubert's death hit the Boers hard, but they cleared the way for younger, more aggressive commanders—Louis Botha, Koos de la Rey, Christiaan de Wet. Although the military balance had shifted, they effectively used their thin resources in a guerrilla campaign.

Botha, a 38-year-old farmer, was the youngest and best of these new leaders. He personified the Boers' unorthodox approach to warfare. He used no maps and propounded no theories and was happiest playing the accordian, but the British were sufficiently dismayed by his military operations to offer him an annuity of £10,000 if he would give up. Botha relied upon personal magnetism to rally his hard-pressed followers. "Never mind," he told them, "let's keep up our courage and do our duty." It was a spirit that was to survive defeat.

Four hours' bombardment. One dog killed. Baden-Powell." It was received with delight as a classic example of British understatement of the kind that Wellington had made famous. Who was this man Baden-Powell? Clearly he had true British grit. The public could not hear enough from and about him.

The heroic Baden-Powell in which the public believed did not exist. The real man was quite different: showy, artistic, thoroughly unbellicose (in 1907 he would found the Boy Scouts). He had always been the life of every party and he had never had such an excellent party as this. He designed currency for use in the town and issued stamps with his own portrait on them. He organized camp concerts in which he played a prominent part, sometimes a frenzied portrayal of Paderewski at the piano, sometimes a mad impersonation of a high-pitched prima-donna. It kept the Mafeking garrison, some of whom were restless for military activity, fairly content.

The only pressure that was, in fact, severe was at Ladysmith. The Boer commander there, Piet Joubert, had made a better job of his siege. But, as at Kimberley and Mafeking, it was a matter of starving the town out rather than rushing it. There were about 22,000 people inside the perimeter. Since he had more artillery and over ten times more troops than at the other two defending towns, Sir George White was able to construct a sophisticated system of defence, with forts and posts linked by telephone. The Boers, with more than 20,000 men, also dug in. Their bombardment, utilizing two 94-pounder "Long Tom" siege guns, was no joke.

Away in Cape Colony, Lord Methuen had assembled his 8,000-man column for the relief of Kimberley and Mafeking. Methuen was schooled in traditional methods and relied on the invincibility of British infantry. They would march up the railway to Kimberley, brushing the unskilled opposition aside. The Boers, appreciating Methuen's reliance on the railway, were preparing themselves at a number of strongpoints on the way.

As it progressed across the grassy plain under a burning sun, the column

was a magnificent sight. Shrieks of command drifted across the veld; sometimes whistling and singing could be heard. Row upon row of dun-coloured helmets steadily advanced with rifles and brasses gleaming through clouds of dust. Boer scouts on the distant heights kept it under constant observation.

At Belmont, a steep escarpment, the Boers barred the way. A staff officer asked Lord Methuen whether he was going round them. "My dear fellow," said Methuen, "I intend to put the fear of God into these people." His troops succeeded in taking the ridge, but not without heavy casualties. The troops, undismayed by the first action, proceeded to the next enemy position, a ridge of hills at Enslin.

As they advanced in the brightness of the morning in perfect order they were mown down. As they clawed their way up the side of the hills they were picked off by sharpshooters above. Nearly half the attacking force was killed or wounded before the Boers withdrew.

At the Modder River Methuen at last decided on a turning movement. But he lost control of the battle, going up to the front himself and giving commands to small parties. Although some of his men, showing great courage, got across the river, the main Boer position remained inviolate. But, next morning, the Boers were found to have pulled out during the night. Once again British casualties had been heavy. Methuen had lost about one-seventh of his strength since he had started out. On the other hand, he had successfully taken three strong Boer positions and had made rapid progress towards Kimberley. The column marched on, still sure of its invincibility. Reinforcements had arrived, including the famous Highland Brigade which contained such legendary regiments as the Black Watch, the Gordon Highlanders, the Seaforth Highlanders, and the Highland Light Infantry.

Only one obstacle remained before Kimberley—a low ridge known as Magersfontein. With hardly any mounted troops, Methuen had no alternative but to take it as he had taken the previous ridges. This time the

Highland Brigade would comprise the storming force. Their attack was due to begin at dawn on December 11. In command was Major-General "Andy" Wauchope, one of the best-known and most popular personalities in the army.

The brigade formed up in drizzling rain. It advanced slowly, kept in tightly packed formation by men on the flanks holding ropes. At 4 a.m. Magersfontein was just discernible. Suddenly, unexpectedly, there was a shattering volley of Boer rifle fire. Then another. Then steady, remorseless firing without cease. The brigade shuddered: men fell, some charged blindly ahead, others turned about. Consternation turned to panic. A horrible truth dawned on every man. The

Boers were not, as they had always been before, at the top of the ridge; they were entrenched at its foot, where they could fire with their eyes shut and hardly miss.

Wauchope was one of the few who kept calm, but within seconds he fell, muttering as he died, "What a pity." Panic brought a wild stampede to the rear. Fallen men, including the commander of the Highland Light Infantry, were trampled underfoot. As one of them admitted later, "It was like a flock of sheep running for dear life." Magersfontein, a word not popular in Scotland to this day, was one of the most appalling reverses that British arms had suffered in any war since the American Revolution. The remnant of the brigade did not stop its

flight until it reached the Modder River.

There was also disaster for the British in Natal. While still maintaining the siege of Ladysmith, a Boer column 4,000 strong under Louis Botha pressed on into Natal. It collided with Buller, slowly advancing to the relief of Ladysmith, at Colenso on the Tugela River. Although displaying his usual personal courage Buller made a terrible mess of his attack. His attempted flanking movement became trapped in a loop of the river, and his artillery opened up within a few yards of unsuspected enemy trenches. As a result ten guns were lost. "A very trying day," Sir Redvers commented. Like Methuen, he was nonplussed and unable to decide what to do next; he

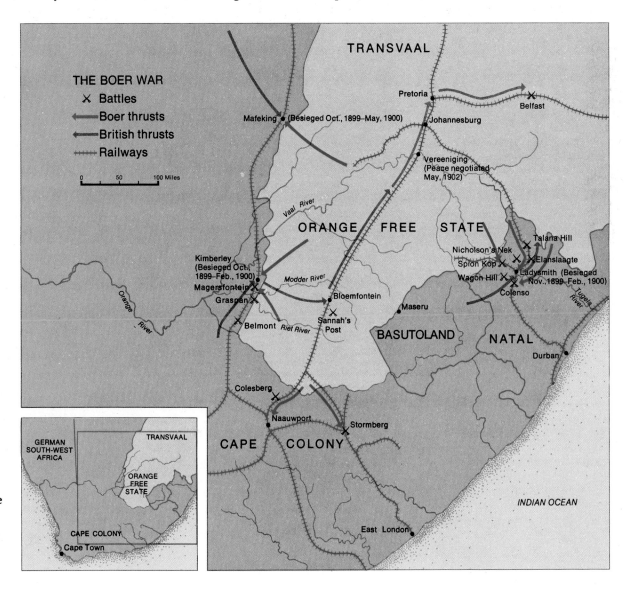

As shown here, the campaigns of the Boer War centred on the Kimberley, Mafeking, and Ladysmith sieges.

HOW I ESCAPED
FROM PRETORIA.

By Winston Churchill.

THE *Morning Post* has received the following telegram from Mr. Winston Spencer Churchill, its war correspondent, who was taken prisoner by the Boers and escaped from Pretoria.

LOURENCO MARQUES, December 21st, 10 p.m.

I was concealed in a railway truck under great sacks.

I had a small store of good water with me.

I remained hidden, chancing discovery.

The Boers searched the train at Komati Poort, but did not search deep enough, so after sixty hours of misery I came safely here.

I am very weak, but I am free.

I have lost many pounds weight, but I am lighter in heart.

I shall also avail myself of every opportunity from this moment to urge with earnestness an unflinching and uncompromising prosecution of the war.

On the afternoon of the 12th the Transvaal Government's Secretary for War informed me that there was little chance of my release.

I therefore resolved to escape the same night, and left the State Schools Prison at Pretoria by climbing the wall when the sentries' backs were turned momentarily.

I walked through the streets of the town without any disguise, meeting many burghers, but I was not challenged in the crowd.

I got through the pickets of the Town Guard, and struck the Delagoa Bay Railroad.

I walked along it, evading the watchers at the bridges and culverts.

I waited for a train beyond the first station.

The one 11.10 goods train from Pretoria arrived, and before it had reached full speed I boarded with great difficulty, and hid myself under coal sacks.

I jumped from the train before dawn, and sheltered during the day in a small wood, in company with a huge vulture, who displayed a lively interest in me.

I walked on at dusk.

There were no more trains that night.

The danger of meeting the guards of the railway line continued; but I was obliged to follow it, as I had no compass or map.

I had to make wide *détours* to avoid the bridges, stations, and huts.

My progress was very slow, and chocolate is not a satisfying food.

The outlook was gloomy, but I persevered, with God's help, for five days.

The food I had to have was very precarious.

I was lying up at daylight, and walking on at night time, and, meanwhile, my escape had been discovered and my description telegraphed everywhere.

All the trains were searched.

Everyone was on the watch for me.

Four wrong people were arrested.

But on the sixth day I managed to board a train beyond Middleburg, whence there is a direct service to Delagoa.

Churchill's own account of his spectacular escape appeared in a telegram to his home paper. Six months later the now-famous correspondent ran for Parliament and won.

even suggested the capitulation of Ladysmith.

Meanwhile, a small British column under Lieutenant-General Sir William Gatacre had been advancing up the railway from East London towards the Transvaal. Attempting a surprise night attack near Stormberg, the column got lost, was itself surprised by the Boers and forced to withdraw with heavy losses.

These three humiliating defeats—Magersfontein, Colenso, Stormberg—occurred within a single week. It became known as "Black Week": a dreadful, almost unbearable hurt to the pride of the British people. The Empire had been utterly defeated in the field by the two nearly bankrupt Boer republics. This was not an incident in imperial policing; it had turned into a major war.

The British government acted with unaccustomed speed. Wolseley's protégés had wasted their chance. There was only one figure in the British Army equal in prestige to Wolseley: Field-Marshal Lord Roberts of Kandahar, V.C., beloved of the nation and known to all as "Bobs." Roberts, now in Ireland on the verge of retirement, had spent nearly all his long career in India. He had lost his only son at Colenso. Now he was given the command in South Africa, with Major-General Lord Kitchener of Khartoum as his chief of staff. A small, trim, unhappy-looking figure with a darkly tanned leathery face, Roberts left Southampton on a bleak day before a silent crowd. With him went the hopes of all those who cherished the Empire.

There was one piece of good news to cheer the public. It concerned a well-known newspaper correspondent named Winston Churchill. Although only 25, Churchill had already seen a great deal of action: in the Cuban revolution of 1895, in the North-West Frontier campaign of 1897–98, and at Omdurman, where he had charged with the 21st Lancers. Now, in the thick of the war, he had been captured by Louis Botha's guerrillas.

Churchill insisted that as a war correspondent he should be released; the Boers, with some justification, insisted that he had acted as a combatant and would be treated as such. But Churchill escaped from the prisoner-of-war camp in Pretoria by scaling a ten-foot wall while two sentries chatted with their backs towards him, and reached neutral Portuguese territory by jumping aboard a train. Barely a month after he had been taken prisoner he returned to cover Buller's operations. The public was delighted with this display of daring and defiance. As Churchill put it, "I became for the time quite famous."

The British public had assumed the war would be a short one, over by Christmas. But now it seemed the war had hardly begun. Both armies celebrated Christmas as best they could. At Ladysmith the Boers thoughtfully sent plum puddings into the town. At Kimberley there were also plum puddings, a gift from Rhodes. Rationing was in force, although hardly severe: four ounces of meat, sometimes horse, and 12 ounces of bread per day. Rhodes was as agitated as ever. Explosive rows with Kekewich were commonplace, and the Colossus started to talk of surrendering the town. His bluff worked. Roberts, who had advanced from Cape Town, began to prepare an immediate relief column.

Mafeking, on the other hand, was still the most pleasant place to be in this war. At the Mafeking Hotel there was a special Christmas menu of 28 items. Baden-Powell attended a private party: turkey, plum pudding, wines, and brandy. After more than two months of siege Mafeking had suffered less than a dozen casualties from the ineffective Boer bombardment. Only the Africans in the native quarter of the town were feeling the effects of the siege.

Meanwhile, in January, 1900, Buller was battering away at the approaches to Ladysmith, the fall of which, as the Queen herself had said, was "too awful to contemplate." The town was only 20 miles away, but the range of hills along the northern bank of the Tugela River posed a major obstacle to Buller, who was saddled with a vast supply train of baggage and impedimenta. Again opposing him was Louis Botha.

Buller decided that the best path through the ridge that blocked him was at a hill called Spion Kop. It was to be the site of the costliest battle of Buller's campaign, which is saying a good deal.

After a heavy, sustained artillery barrage, the British scrambled courageously to the top of the hill, but they were unable to dig more than a foot or so into the rocky surface of the exposed plateau. Three thousand men, crowded into an area of some three acres, came under a furious fire. Breastworks of corpses were built to protect the living. An officer of the 2nd Middlesex wrote, "We lay prone and could only venture a volley now and again, firing independently at times when the shower of bullets seemed to fall away, and the shells did not appear likely to land especially amongst us. Everywhere, it was practically the same deadly smash of shells mangling and killing all about." Winston Churchill reached the top of Spion Kop, passing on the way streams of returning wounded: "Men were staggering along, alone or supported by comrades, or crawling on hands and knees, or carried on stretchers. Corpses lay here and there. There was a small but steady leakage of unwounded men of all corps. Some of them cursed and swore. Others were utterly exhausted, and fell on the hillside in stupor."

After a day of hell, the order to withdraw was given. Left behind in the shallow trenches were more than 700 dead.

At home there was an uproar over the heavy casualties at Spion Kop. The Liberal Opposition demanded and got a debate in the House of Commons deploring "the want of knowledge, foresight and judgement displayed by Her Majesty's Ministers." The debate turned into a bitter discussion, not so much on strategy, but on whether the war was necessary at all. Joseph Chamberlain was presented as a callous warmonger.

When at last Buller bludgeoned his way into Ladysmith, he had suffered casualties totalling more than the entire force opposing him. Roberts, rounding Magersfontein with a mounted column, had already relieved Kimberley without difficulty. (In Kimberley, Rhodes may well have fatally injured his health by his apoplectic behaviour during the siege; he died two years later, aged 49.) With Ladysmith and Kimberley safe from the Boers, only Mafeking remained.

The defence of this remote place had gripped the public as nothing else in the war. It seemed to symbolize British pride during a miserable time. But Roberts thought that less than 1,500 men were sufficient to relieve

the town. They rode north from Kimberley with a posse of newspaper correspondents, all anxious to see the now world-famous Baden-Powell and to observe for themselves the plight of the town. After a brief skirmish, the Boers raised the siege and the advance party entered Mafeking on May 17, 1900. They were surprised at the lack of interest shown in their arrival. Most people in Mafeking seemed more concerned with the final of the billiards tournament which was being held that day.

The relief of Mafeking unleashed delirious, unbridled rejoicing in England that not even the Armistice in 1918 or V.E. Day in 1945 were to equal. As word spread that the siege of the distant African town under the indomitable command of Colonel Baden-Powell had been raised after 217 days, the whole country exploded in a frenzied celebration that lasted five days.

London went mad. "Women absolutely wept for joy," the *Daily Mail* reported, "and men threw their arms about each other's necks—strangers' necks for the most part; but that made no difference, for Mafeking was relieved." Theatres announced the news in mid-play and audiences stood in

uproar. Restaurants were in chaos. In the streets crowds were thick and frenzied, waving flags and pictures of Baden-Powell, which had been prepared for the event, and singing and dancing. Express trains from the capital progressed through the countryside with whistles in constant shrill acclaim, announcing the news to village and town. The sky was alight with rockets and bonfires.

There was a genuine and immense feeling of relief. Mafeking had been built up as a place that would never fall to the Boers, no matter what it had to suffer, and fall it had not. The mild, unwarlike Baden-Powell had become a strong, calm soldier given to superb understatement, the greatest hero since Wellington or Nelson. Everyone was overjoyed at his brave defiance of the insufferable Boers. It was the same all over the Empire. In Canada a correspondent reported that "every town and village went wild with patriotic fervour." In Melbourne guns were fired, bells rang all day, and crowds packed the streets.

In Mafeking itself there was some tension among the relievers, who were infuriated to find the besieged better fed and more comfortable than they

A Boer cartoon portrays John Bull caught in an Afrikaner web while France, America, Russia, and Germany (right, threatening Britannia's rule of the sea) look on.

themselves. Certainly Baden-Powell did nothing to disillusion the public. In his official report he claimed he had been surrounded by 8,000 enemy, although in his general orders at the start of the siege he had put the figure at "5,000 to 6,000." The figure went up nearly every time he wrote of the siege, which was not infrequently, reaching 12,000 by the final account. But probably it was too late for anyone involved to explain that the siege had been one of the most comfortable in all history.

After the relief of Ladysmith, Kimberley, and Mafeking, and the capture of Bloemfontein, capital of the Orange Free State, Roberts marched on Pretoria in the Transvaal. On June 5, 1900, a silk Union Jack, given to the commander-in-chief by his wife for the purpose, was run up a flagpole in the city centre. Roberts, with sound generalship and an overwhelming superiority in arms, had, it seemed, won the war without any difficulty at all, whereas poor Buller had been able to do nothing right. "Bobs" had not let the country down. He returned home to an earldom, the Garter, an award of £100,000, and the gratitude of the public.

But was the war really over? There were no more battles, but Boer forces were still at large, moving about much as they pleased. They mingled with the population, or disappeared into the vastness of the veld, to reappear suddenly and unexpectedly to attack an isolated strongpoint or an unwary column. The new British commander-in-chief was Kitchener, who prided himself on cool efficiency. "People here do not seem to look upon the war sufficiently seriously," he said of his officers. "They consider it too much like a game of polo with intervals for afternoon tea." Being a practical man, he believed the only way to combat the Boer commandos was by cutting up the country into sections, using wire fences guarded by some 8,000 blockhouses, then sweeping across each section. Kitchener, who had never before been engaged against Europeans, was an engineer by training, and it was an engineer's decision. But it was not by any means an unqualified success.

It was an expensive policy, largely responsible for an increase in taxes at home. It turned public opinion against the war, and public opinion, as the relief of Mafeking had shown, was making itself more vocal than ever before. The public also reacted to the inhuman consequences. Farms owned by Boers who were said to have fought against the British were burned, often indiscriminately. The thousands left homeless were herded into a new sort of institution—what were officially called "concentration camps."

Conditions in these camps, which eventually contained 60,000 Boers, were the subject of bitter controversy. Kitchener, who seldom saw one, said they were all right, but an Australian reporter wrote of "criminal neglect of the most simple laws of sanitation." At one time in 1901 the death rate in the 46 camps reached 34 per cent. The majority of the dead were children, many of them from measles; in Bloemfontein camp their death rate was 50 per cent. When the news of conditions in the camps trickled home, there was a surge of outrage against this new horror.

Quaker Emily Hobhouse ("that bloody woman," Kitchener called her) saw the camps for herself and agitated against the government to such effect that a committee, composed entirely of women, was sent out to investigate. Lloyd George declared that "A barrier of dead children's bodies will rise up between the British and Boer races in South Africa." Liberal leader Sir Henry Campbell-Bannerman described the policy as one of "barbarism." Kitchener, however, remained totally unmoved and unrepentant.

Early in 1902, a year and a half after the capture of Pretoria, sporadic fighting still continued. Christiaan de Wet, a potato farmer, and Jan Christiaan Smuts, a Cambridge-educated lawyer who had left his home in the Cape in disgust after the Jameson Raid, led commando attacks even against Cape Colony. In March Lord Methuen returned to the news. His large column, engaged in "sweeping" operations, was surprised, panicked, and fled, and Methuen was taken prisoner. Kitchener was appalled at the disgrace of a

defeat and of a general being captured at a time the war was supposed to be virtually over. He went to bed for 36 hours, "gone all to pieces," as he said. However, his tribulations were not to last much longer.

The Boers were near the end; Kitchener's policy had at last taken effect. There was, as they now realized, no chance of help from abroad, and the "bitter-enders," as they were called, had lost support among their own people. In April Kitchener met President Schalk Burger, Kruger's successor (Kruger had fled to Holland). Negotiations were begun and another conference was held at Vereeniging a month later, when the British government was represented by Milner and Kitchener. At first the British were prepared to concede little, but Kitchener, anxious to get away from South Africa, shrewdly pointed out that the pro-Boer Liberals were almost bound to win the next British election, and then the Boers would be likely to get some of their independence back anyway. The peace treaty was signed shortly before midnight, May 31, 1902, on Kitchener's dining-room table.

Over 400,000 British troops had been engaged in the war, including contingents from Canada, Australia, and New Zealand, against a Boer army less than a quarter of that number. Twenty-two thousand British troops were dead, the majority from disease. Some 28,000 Boers died in the concentration camps, 22,000 of them children. The war shocked the British as nothing had done since Napoleon's day. Imperial confidence was never quite the same again.

The Boers did not do badly in defeat. Under the terms of the Treaty of Vereeniging, the Dutch language was to be retained in schools and law courts, £3,000,000 was granted to restore farms, and a civil administration leading to self-government within the Empire was set up. After the election of the Liberals, the Transvaal became a self-governing colony in 1906 and the Orange Free State followed in 1907. The new leaders in South Africa, Louis Botha and Smuts, recognized that Boer interests would be best served by co-operation with the British, and the two Boer colonies

"Our boys" adopt standard once-more-into-the-breach postures for mothers back home.

General White successfully resisted War Office pressure to abandon Ladysmith.

Field-Marshal Lord Roberts holds the place of honour among his colleagues.

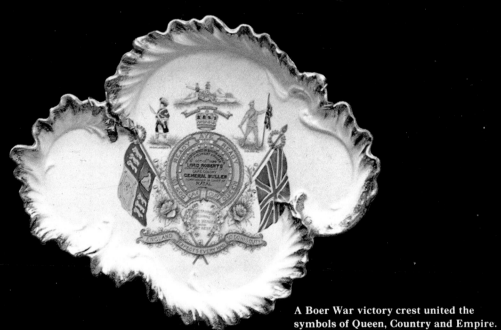

A Boer War victory crest united the symbols of Queen, Country and Empire.

The Boer General, Piet Cronje, surrenders to Lord Roberts at Paardeberg.

BRITAIN'S SOLDIER-HEROES in South Africa were depicted on plates that were welcomed by housewives at home. Wishing to impress neighbours with their patriotic zeal, they could display generals on the dresser or battles under the tea-buns.

joined the Cape and Natal in 1910 to become the Union of South Africa. The enemy, it seemed, had been absorbed in the imperial ideal.

But Afrikaner nationalism was to prove far too strong for that. The constitutions for the two Boer provinces had enfranchised only white men, since the Liberal government had given way on this point to the Boers. Winston Churchill, a Liberal at that time, was Under-Secretary of State for the Colonies. He told critics in the House of Commons that the Boers had shown their customary stubbornness: "I think we could not do more." What in fact the Boers had done was play on the sensibilities of the Liberals, reminding them of their promises to grant autonomy. As a result, the British, having won the war, lost the peace.

After the Act of Union, the franchise of the non-whites in the Cape was whittled away by Pretoria, the administrative capital of the Union. The bitterness of the Boers over British interference in their affairs, far from being solved by the Boer War, had become even more intense. In South Africa's subsequent history, Afrikaner nationalism kept alight the views and prejudices that had inspired the Great Trek away from the Cape over 70 years before.

—*John Man, Brian Gardner*

III. Rising in the Celestial Empire

Our hatred is already at white heat.... You English barbarians have formed the habits of wolves.... If we do not completely exterminate you pigs and dogs, we will no longer be manly Chinese able to support the sky on our heads and stand firmly on the earth."

Such bloodthirsty threats were repeatedly hurled at British merchants and traders in China in the years following the 1842 Treaty of Nanking that ended the Opium War. The spoils of victory had made Hong Kong a British colony and forcefully opened five Chinese ports to foreign trade. It also opened six decades of rising tension between the Celestial Empire and the "Foreign Devils." Western nations grabbed territory and wrung leases for trading ports from a government unable to withstand the commercial and military onslaught of more advanced societies. The Chinese responded with a virulent xenophobia. The result was a fresh imperial crisis for the British even as they struggled to subdue the Boers.

The peace that followed the Opium War lasted less than 20 years. In 1859–60 Britain and France undertook a grand expedition to Peking to force China to ratify the highly advantageous Treaty of Tientsin, itself forced upon local Chinese officials the previous year by the allied seizure of the forts guarding the capital. The central government had refused to approve the treaty, so the two powers set out to compel compliance.

Again the forts were taken and the advance on Peking begun. The allied mood of buoyant optimism evaporated when a British negotiating team was snatched from under its flag of truce and taken hostage. In retaliation, the Emperor's Summer Palace just outside the city was seized and its fabulous collections of jewels, silver, porcelain, and silk were looted, smashed, burned, or hawked on street corners by troops drunk with the sight of such undefended treasure. After killing 16 of the hostages in revenge, the Chinese surrendered Peking's main gate to the "barbarians." British envoy James Bruce, Lord Elgin, felt that the murder of the prisoners demanded a "solemn act of retribution," and completed the cycle of atrocities by ordering the destruction of the looted Summer Palace—an act with which the French refused to be associated. The buildings burned for two days, darkening Peking with a pall of ash and smoke.

A week later, with vengeance successfully exacted, Lord Elgin made a state entry into the capital to sign the Convention of Peking confirming and extending the Treaty of Tientsin. China's humiliation was all but complete.

The years that followed saw Britain lead the way in sharing out the "Chinese melon." Chinese satellites were lost: northern Burma to Britain, Vietnam to France. In China itself Russia obtained land leases and railway concessions in the north, France acquired mining and trading rights in the south, and Germany used the murder of a missionary as an excuse to send troops into Shantung, winning commercial rights in the hinterland. Towards the turn of the century Japan defeated China in war, wrested numerous islands, including Formosa, from her, and forcefully opened several Chinese ports to Japanese trade.

The British were determined to have their full share of any concessions that could be wrung from the Chinese. They obtained a lease on the port of Weihaiwei, were granted further territories in Kwangtung inland from Kowloon, and enforced the opening of yet more ports to British trade. The Other Empire of capital and trade was as active as ever.

The appearance of these trading ports was soon transformed by the arrival of European merchants and officials with their families. The British, in particular, succeeded remarkably well in maintaining the way of life they were accustomed to at home.

Passengers sailing into one of the harbours, pleasurably anticipating their first sight of the "Flowery Kingdom," must have been astonished by the spectacle that greeted them. The Chinese houses were overawed by European-style villas with white-painted façades and shaded balconies, English rectilinear flowerbeds and neatly mown lawns. Behind the villas were row upon row of storehouses and workshops with roofs of galvanized zinc, and along the waterfront

The Treaty of Vereeniging that brought the Boer War to an end was greeted jubilantly by Britons. These are celebrants in London's Ludgate Circus.

and on the rivers were steamboats and cranes hooting and cranking against the background of cargo-crowded wharfs. In the larger ports there were offices and banks, European clubs with billiard rooms and libraries, and first-class hotels with European cuisine.

Reacting against this wholesale Westernization and the voracious commercial appetites of the foreigners, Chinese reformers urged the modernization of the Celestial Empire as the only means of combating them. The young Emperor, Kuang-hsü, supported the progressives and embarked on a sudden, cataclysmic programme of reform. But he was no match for his formidable aunt, the Empress Dowager, who was the real power behind the Manchu throne. Strongly disapproving of his radical measures, she came storming to his room in a terrifying rage and forced him to kneel down in submission at her feet.

The Empress Dowager had ideas of her own as to how the foreigner could be defeated. She rested her hopes on a secret society, formed on the eve of the turn of the century, whose banners proclaimed the welcome summons: "Support the Manchus! Exterminate the Foreigners!" The members of this society practised a kind of shadow-boxing, Taoist in origin, that was known as *Shen Ch'üan*, "Spirit Boxing." Taking note of their addiction to this exercise, a missionary gave them the name by which they became known throughout the world: the Boxers.

The Boxers, fanatically xenophobic and anti-Christian, were subjected to the severest discipline by their commanders: no meat, no tea, no contact with women. They were encouraged to practise strange rites and exercises in addition to their shadow-boxing, and to work themselves into states of such nervous exaltation that they induced fits, spasms, and trances that made them appear immune to fear and pain.

To the Empress Dowager it seemed that in the strange power of the Boxers might be the salvation of China and the Manchu dynasty. When reports came of their attacks on missionaries

and Chinese Christian converts, she did not disguise her satisfaction.

Up till now the British minister in Peking, Sir Claude MacDonald, had viewed the Boxers without much concern. He assured London that there was "little to confirm the gloomy anticipation" that the ministers of other countries were voicing. There was good reason, however, for their gloom. The French minister had been informed by the Vicar-Apostolic of Peking, early in 1900, that the lives not only of missionaries but of all Europeans were in danger. "The Boxers' accomplices await them in Peking," he warned. "They mean to attack the churches first, then the Legations."

The French minister urged Mac-Donald and the other foreign diplomats to pressure the Chinese government to outlaw the Boxers—which at present they showed no inclination to do—by bringing an international guard into Peking to protect the legations. But MacDonald still doubted there was any real danger. He allowed his two little daughters to leave Peking for the cool of the British legation bungalow in the Western Hills.

Even when the railway station at Fengtai, south of Peking, was attacked by Boxers and set afire and the houses of several Europeans farther down the line burned, Sir Claude was satisfied that a guard of sailors and marines from the warships anchored at the mouth of the Peiho River would answer all purposes. The legations, he assured the naval commander, would be the "last place attacked."

As the stiflingly hot month of June, 1900, progressed, however, Mac-Donald was forced to change his mind. The anti-foreign violence was spreading beyond the ranks of Boxers to imperial troops from Kansu province. The chancellor of the Japanese legation, while on his way to the railway station, was dragged from his cart by Kansu troops who took violent exception to the sight of his Oriental features beneath a bowler hat. They slashed him apart with their swords and cut out his heart.

The Boxers themselves went on a wild rampage through Peking, swinging swords and spears above their

heads, shouting their war-cry, "*Sha! Sha!*" (Kill! Kill!), looting shops and houses, setting fire to missions and other foreign buildings, and cutting down anyone they suspected of being Christian. A patrol of marines that went out to find any Chinese converts who might have escaped the slaughter came upon fearful sights, including many women and children hacked to pieces. At about the same time, the German minister was murdered.

Kansu troops shared in the atrocities. They rushed through the streets massacring countless people accused of being spies for the prime enemy—foreigners—or for "Secondary Devils," as Christians were called. A witness, who was afterwards told that a quarter of a million people lost their lives in Peking that summer, remembered "the shrieks of the women and children whom they were butchering. . . . Their swords and clothes were dripping with blood, as if they had come from a slaughter-house."

As yet the legation quarter had been immune from attack, but after a meeting of the Chinese Imperial Council on June 17, when the Empress Dowager announced her intention of declaring war upon the Western world, the foreigners knew they would not be spared much longer. They were right. The siege began three days later.

No one supposed they could hold out for long. The legation guards were limited to 20 officers, 389 men of eight different nationalities, and four pieces of light artillery. The British legation, being the largest and least exposed of the compounds, became the general headquarters. It also became the refuge for scores of American and European missionaries, lecturers, engineers, customs officials, hundreds of Chinese Christian converts, and the staffs of the other legations, with their wives and families. When the most vulnerable of the legations were abandoned, there was what *The Times* correspondent called "a veritable stampede" into the British compound. By the end of the month the foreigners were, as the Empress Dowager contentedly wrote, "like fish in the stew-pan."

In proper panoply, troops of the International Relief Force take possession of Peking in 1900. U.S. soldiers form the honour guard.

Her more moderate advisers persuaded her to hold back from ordering an immediate general massacre, and day by day the defenders took fresh heart. They had little ammunition, but there was a plentiful supply of water, food was abundant, and spirits were high. MacDonald, who had been an infantry officer in his youth, assumed responsibility for the defence, and the besieged made frequent offensive sorties.

While the men were fighting, the wives made sandbags out of the legations' expensive furnishings and silks, or formed lines with their children to put out fires, passing buckets, basins, jugs, and chamber-pots from hand to hand. It was believed that each had pledged to shoot herself and the girls in her care should the defences fail.

Help was on the way at last. A so-called International Relief Force of 20,000 men was assembling in Tientsin. An earlier attempt by a far smaller force to get through to Peking had been thwarted by massive numbers of Boxers and Kansu cavalry, and doubt was felt that even this larger force would be able to get to Peking before the legations were captured. On August 4 it lumbered forward, but it was not until the arrival in Tientsin of the energetic General Alfred Gaselee, commander of the British contingent, that its lethargic pace was speeded up. By August 11 the pace-setters, the Japanese, American, Russian, and British contingents, had reached Chang-chiawan, within striking distance of Peking.

Two days later, while the defenders of the legations were fighting off a thunderous and determined Boxer assault on the British compound, the Relief Force raced towards the gates of Peking. One by one the gates fell, and at half past two on the afternoon of August 14, the fifty-fifth day of the siege, General Gaselee, smiling broadly and with tears in his eyes, was standing in the British compound shaking hands with its defenders.

An American view of the Western powers and Japan descending on China after the Boxer Rebellion is captioned, "The real trouble will come with the wake."

Sixty-six foreigners had been killed and over 150 wounded. Beyond the line of defences lay uncounted rotting Boxer corpses. Towards the end, the Chinese converts had been reduced to eating the leaves and bark of the trees in the legation grounds. Yet in the best tradition of the British Empire, the white survivors soon appeared looking fresh and unconcerned, as though nothing particularly untoward had happened. "The ladies," according to one eyewitness, "were quite 'got up,'" and the men "had speckless linen on."

Already the looting of Peking by Relief Force troops had begun, and continued for days until the city was thoroughly ransacked. When the looters were done, yet another harsh treaty was imposed upon the Chinese government. An indemnity of no less then $450,000,000 was required, the forts defending the city were to be demolished, foreign troops would be stationed between Tientsin and Peking, and China was to import no more armaments.

The treaty was signed on September 17, 1901, and China once more relapsed into an uneasy acceptance of foreign domination. But subservience was brief. The seeds of revolution had been sown.

As for the imperial ethic, it had received another dent. Although few Britons were willing to condone the atrocities of the fanatic Boxers, the more thoughtful were ready to raise questions about the morality of propping up trade and commercial monopoly in a foreign land by means of the Soldiers of the Queen and the ships of the Royal Navy.

—*Christopher Hibbert*

IV. The Other Island

The symbol of Britain's long presence in Ireland can be found by walking up Cork Hill in Dublin, a steep little street twisting up above the River Liffey. Suddenly one comes upon a gloomy castle, almost hidden by the surrounding buildings. The entrance is a sombre stone gateway surmounted by the figure of Justice. Within are two medium-sized courtyards boxed in by a haphazard variety of buildings in Classical, Gothic, and Queen Anne styles; all round, rows of glowering windows hide minor government offices. This is Dublin Castle. It is a structure without plan or unity. Through its long history it has been almost constantly under repair.

For over seven centuries this grim pile was the palace of the Viceroys of Ireland, who fulfilled all the functions of royal government on behalf of the King of England. Known usually by the innocuous title of Lord Lieutenant—"Lord Leff*nent*" in the brogue— they were in fact "vice-kings" with most of the powers of a king and prime minister combined. Not only did they perform the ceremonial functions of head of state—"drowning the shamrock" on St. Patrick's Day, attending horse shows, bestowing the viceregal kiss on the debutantes— but they also summoned or prorogued Irish parliaments, served usually as commander-in-chief of the army, and

from their dirty and badly furnished offices in Upper Castle Yard directed the whole Irish administration.

Dublin Castle is a fitting symbol of the British presence in Ireland. Like it, British rule was ramshackle, without plan, almost constantly in disrepair. The twin pillars on which it rested—conquest and colonization— were never wholly sound. Almost the entire sweep of Ireland's colonial history, 750 years, is a chronicle of Britain's failure to win complete control. Across three great swathes of time— four centuries of conquest, two centuries of Protestant colonization, and the 19th-Century age of nationalism— this theme remained constant. The result was an endemic state of upheaval which the bewildered Victorians christened the Irish Question. It was a question to which they had no answer.

The explanation for Ireland's chaos lay in her chameleon nature, for during her long and tortuous history she was constantly changing her colours: at one moment she was a European nation proud of her ancient traditions; at another, a colony in the British Empire; at yet another, an integral part of the United Kingdom. Her geographical position across the Irish Sea placed her too far away for complete integration, and too close for complete independence. Ireland became a country with a split personality, half-nation

and half-colony, and that is why she ended in a state of war with herself and with the mother country.

It was a consequence of her close proximity to the mainland that Ireland became Britain's first colony. In 1167, a mere century after the Norman victory at Hastings, an expedition of Anglo-Norman barons crossed the Irish Sea with visions of rich lands in their heads, a mandate from Henry II in their hands, and the blessing of the Pope in their souls. Their mission was to conquer Ireland. They took Dublin and the kingdom of Leinster, and four years later Henry arrived with an army of 4,000 and finished the conquest. Pope Alexander III promptly recognized the King of England as Lord of Ireland. The invaders began to settle in.

But very soon things began to go wrong. On an Easter Monday hardly more than 30 years after the arrival of the first conquerors there was a sanguinary warning. Five hundred citizens of Bristol, to which city Henry had "presented" Dublin, crossed over to view their property. As they were enjoying a little sightseeing, a horde of wild, dispossessed Irishmen descended on them from the hills. What happened none of the Bristol holiday makers lived to tell. As a result, in 1205 Dublin Castle was begun.

The Irish, as the English had discovered to their cost, were a warlike people and, despite their chronic disunity and internecine feuds, they proved remarkably resistant to effective conquest. Their own way of life, their language, their laws, their bardic folklore did not easily wither at the touch of Norman feudalism. Their leaders—princes, abbots, scribes—continued to cultivate "wisdom and knowledge and booklore," as a contemporary writer put it. They looked back to their Gaelic traditions, to the Golden Age of the mid-9th Century when Irish learning was admired throughout Europe. Through all the vicissitudes of Ireland's troubled history, this Gaelic heritage never faded completely, and to Irish patriots centuries later it became a badge of national identity to be worn with pride and emotion.

So resilient were the Irish that over the next two centuries the Anglo-Norman conquest became a shadow. English power resided at Dublin Castle and nominally extended to the whole of Ireland, but in practice the King's writ did not run beyond walled towns and a narrow strip of land on the east coast centred on Dublin. This area was known as "the obedient shires" or "the English Pale."

Worse still, the Norman colonists, on whom the Crown depended for the control of Ireland—the de Burghs, the Butlers, the Fitzgeralds—were going native, becoming more Irish than the Irish themselves. In 1366, in a parliament summoned at Kilkenny, the Lord Lieutenant passed a total of 35 statutes that prohibited the colonists from wearing Irish dress, following Irish customs, marrying Irish heiresses, or even entertaining Irish minstrels or poets or storytellers. These Statutes of Kilkenny were an admission that the conquest of Ireland had failed. They were also totally ineffective. By the middle of the 15th Century English control had almost vanished. Ireland was governed by the great Anglo-Norman family of Fitzgerald, Earls of Kildare, which passed the all-powerful office of Viceroy from father to son like a royal dynasty. The Irish Sea might have been an ocean, so far apart did England and Ireland drift.

Not until the Tudors came to power in 1485 did the English Crown tackle the problem of regaining control in Ireland. There was no easy solution. Direct rule from England, through English officials backed by English troops, would be expensive. Indirect rule, through Hibernicized Anglo-Normans like the powerful Earl of Kildare, might allow Ireland to drift completely out of English control.

Henry VII opted for indirect rule, but his domineering son, Henry VIII, took the other course. He antagonized the Kildare family. He broke with Rome. And he provoked the Pope's allies, chiefly France and Spain, into probing at one of Protestant England's weaknesses—staunchly Roman Catholic Ireland.

In 1534 a full-scale rebellion broke out, led by the Kildares, hailed by the friars as a holy war against the heretic Henry, and encouraged by Spanish agents. Henry crushed it with unparalleled severity. By 1540 the House of Kildare was shattered. An Irish parliament obediently enacted the ecclesiastical legislation of the English Reformation and "most willingly and joyously" conferred on Henry the title King of Ireland. But it was only a paper victory. Beyond the Pale the magnates, both native Irish and Anglo-Norman, remained all-powerful and now nurtured the hope of foreign aid.

For her own safety, England could no longer risk the two countries drifting apart.

The pattern of Irish history had been set. There could be no going back. With the House of Kildare broken and no one to take its place, indirect rule—rule on the cheap—was impossible. In the future Ireland would have to be ruled by an Englishman backed by an English army. And that would be prohibitively expensive. Out of this dilemma was born a fatally ineffective policy of coercion and conciliation: coercion to put down rebellion, conciliation to cut costs.

As an immediate consequence, Henry's daughter Elizabeth was threatened by four Irish rebellions, all involving the risk and two the reality of foreign intervention. Regarded as illegitimate by Catholics who wished to see her deposed, desperately insecure on her throne, Elizabeth crushed them all, the last in 1603.

So ended the first period of Anglo-Irish history. At last the conquest seemed complete. The country that a 16th-Century Irish poet called a "sword-land" was united under the English civil government of Dublin Castle. The wartime devastation faded and the old Ireland "abounding with all the sustenance of Life" soon reap-

A design for the Great Seal of Ireland (1595), with Elizabeth the central figure. But the Irish remained unpacified and it was never executed.

peared, phoenix-like, from the ashes.

More lasting were the social and political problems. Despite Elizabeth's tough coercive measures, the conquest of Ireland was only partial. Though the old Gaelic order had received a mortal blow, the native population was no less hostile, no less England's "Irish enemies" than before. To men of the time there was a simple solution: replace the disloyal natives by loyal settlers; establish "plantations" or colonies. Ireland would not be safe or happy until the people, as Sir John Davies of the Irish administration put it, "in tongue and heart and everyway else become English, so as there will be no difference or distinction but the Irish Sea betwixt us."

The estates of expatriate rebel leaders were declared forfeit to the Crown and Ulster opened to colonization. The bulk of the lands were assigned to contractors, known as "undertakers," who were required to bring over English and Scottish settlers and "plant" them in Ulster in easily defended, solidly built villages or towns.

The undertakers had difficulty finding sufficient numbers of settlers and, anxious for quick profits, accepted Irish tenants instead. Rather than forming compact, easily defended islands of Britishness, the settlers were scattered piecemeal through a mainly Gaelic population. To revitalize the programme, the City of London was invited to plant colonies in the county of Coleraine and rebuild its two main towns, Coleraine and Derry. In 1610 a joint-stock company was formed. Derry was renamed Londonderry and gave its name to the whole county; other towns were named after the City companies which founded them: Draperstown and Salterstown, for example, survive as a permanent monument to the plantation policy of the early British Empire. Scots made up a large proportion of the tenants. They brought with them livestock, new towns, new prosperity, new customs, and their own Presbyterian religion.

However, the plantations were not enough to create another Britain, and in 1615 lands were confiscated for colonization all over Ireland. Tough measures of this sort only doubled the problems of government, for they

hastened the division of the country into two nations, one native and Catholic, the other Anglo-Scottish and Protestant. Thus land and religion became burning questions in Ireland. The confiscation of land naturally alarmed existing landholders, who included not only the mass of the Gaelic people but also the "Old English" of the Pale. Both groups had remained Catholic almost to a man after Henry VIII's break with Rome. Any attempt to step up the plantations policy and any campaign to enforce the reformed faith, Anglicanism, could have the disastrous consequence of uniting them against the Dublin Castle government.

The difficulties of trying to rule two nations was quickly apparent. To conciliate the one aroused the anger of the other. In 1641 the enforcement of extreme Protestant policies demonstrated how dangerous the division had become. Puritan administrators halted all semblance of conciliation towards "Papists and rebels" and Ireland was plunged into religious war. The Ulster Rising of insurrectionary native Irish spread rapidly. Many Protestant settlers were slaughtered in the first heat, others taken prisoner and then murdered. Thousands were driven from their homes. After some hesitation, the Old English joined their fellow Catholics in revolt.

In 1649, after the execution of Charles I and the establishment of the Commonwealth, Oliver Cromwell landed in Ireland with 3,000 of his Ironsides to complete mopping-up operations against his enemies, whether Catholic or royalist. He took Dublin and on September 11, in one of the most notorious events of Irish history, he stormed and sacked the town of Drogheda, about 30 miles north of the capital. Most of the royalist garrison and all Catholic clergy who could be found were massacred, and many townspeople perished also. It was called retribution for the Irish massacres of 1641.

By the early 1650s, the Cromwellian reconquest was almost complete. Ireland lay helpless in the power of the Puritan Parliament. Once again the country was desolate; once again the shaky structure of British rule had to

be repaired. According to the conventional wisdom, the solution was to create more plantations.

The Act of Settlement of 1652 outlined the plan. All rebels—"delinquents" they were termed—lost their lands outright. All the best land, i.e., east of the Shannon, went to Protestant settlers, mostly discharged Cromwellian soldiers or "adventurers" who had advanced money to Parliament on the promise of later repayment in confiscated Irish estates. On the eve of the Ulster Rising the Catholics had held about three-fifths of the land of Ireland. A decade later they owned about one-fifth. A landed ruling class, English and Scottish in origin and Protestant in religion, had been set up to dominate a population that was mainly Irish in origin and Catholic in religion.

The pillars on which English rule rested—conquest and colonization—had been repaired and reinforced by Cromwell's coercive settlement. For over 30 years, right through the Restoration, Ireland remained quiet. Then, in 1685, James II came out with what he called his "Catholic design," a policy to secure freedom of worship for the downtrodden "papists." "To the astonishment of all sober men," recorded a diarist, he appointed a co-religionist, the Earl of Tyrconnell, as Lord Lieutenant. Tyrconnell filled the army, the administration, and the judiciary with Catholics and appointed Catholic sheriffs to most counties.

Then Tyrconnell sent his newly constituted Catholic army to support James, and Englishmen trembled for their Protestant constitution. An invitation was dispatched to William of Orange to come over and save England from Catholic tyranny. William accepted and landed at Torbay in November, 1688, and in December James fled to France. The "Glorious Revolution" was over.

But what hope was there for a similarly bloodless revolution in Ireland, where the Lord Lieutenant still held out for Catholic James? James himself soon arrived from France to continue by force of arms the struggle he had given up in England. In Dublin a "patriot parliament," almost entirely Catholic and predominantly Old English in membership, drew up a programme to extirpate the Protestant settlement interests from Ireland.

In the spring of 1689 James and his Jacobite army laid siege to Londonderry, the Protestant stronghold of the north. For 15 weeks the city held out. Thousands died of starvation before an English fleet broke through, forcing the disheartened Jacobites to retreat.

The decisive battle of modern Irish history was fought a year later. William of Orange, now William III of England, had arrived to re-establish the Protestant kingdom of Ireland. James, reinforced by 7,000 French troops sent by Louis XIV, decided to defend the line of the River Boyne that flows into the Irish Sea at Drogheda, on the old northern boundary of the English Pale. On July 1, 1690, the two armies met. It was not a hard-fought struggle. After a heavy bombardment William's forces managed to cross the river. Although James's cavalry fought well, his infantry did not, and quickly broke and fled. By the end of the day it was all over.

Though militarily a petty event, the Battle of the Boyne was a crucial turningpoint. The strength of the Catholic nobles and gentry, both Irish and Old English, that had managed to survive the Elizabethan and Cromwellian "settlements," was at last doomed. Nearly one million acres of rebel-owned land were confiscated. Over 10,000 defeated Irish troops sailed away into exile on the Continent. It marked the collapse of Catholic resistance for over a century.

Although, like all other English kings to date, William III was prepared to offer the Catholics a measure of toleration, he was outflanked by the hard-line Irish Protestants. Having narrowly escaped two determined assaults on their power and property within one century, they were in no mood for toleration. In their view they had been "delivered out of the hands of their enemies" and were far too nervous to entrust Jacobite hands with any sort of power again.

Their answer to toleration was an anti-Catholic penal code of great severity. Between 1692 and the 1720s, laws were passed in the Irish parliament that forbade Catholics to sit in the chamber or vote in parliamentary elections; to join the bar, the bench, Ireland's one university (Trinity College, Dublin), the navy, or any public bodies; to run a school or send their children for a Catholic education abroad; to bear arms; to marry a Protestant; to buy, inherit, or in any way receive land; or even to own a horse worth more than £5. Special privileges were given to any Catholic who turned Protestant. To convert a Protestant to Catholicism, on the other hand, was a capital offence. Senior Catholic clergy were banished; if they returned they could be hanged, drawn, and quartered.

Britain was now dependent for control of Ireland on a fearful, arrogant minority group whose religious apartheid she distrusted but whose power as a colonial garrison she dared not challenge. This tight ruling class, which became known as the Protestant Ascendancy, survived more or less intact for two centuries. Right into the Victorian age the history of Ireland is the history of the Protestant Ascendancy.

Their wealth and power rested upon land, the green and fertile soil of Ireland. Land paid tithes to the church, taxes to the government, and rent to the landlord. In 18th-Century Ireland, six out of seven landlords were Protestants. The English landed classes who owned the largest blocks of Irish land regarded Ireland as a savage, uncivilized country. Most of them preferred to live at home, letting out their Irish estates to middlemen and drawing the rent. The middlemen subdivided what they had obtained wholesale, so to speak, and sublet at retail prices until the actual tiller of the soil supported a great top-heavy system of idlers and skivers, paid a crippling rent, and had almost no security of tenure. The Irish peasantry lived in harsh poverty.

Yet the condition of Ireland was not just the fault of improvident, rapacious landlords. The evils of the system were greatly increased by the distorted development of the Irish economy. Apart from linen manufacturing in the north, the only industry that did really well was the export of cattle products and, to a lesser extent, the wool trade. This led to a great expansion of pastureland, which was disastrous for the ordinary tenant farmers. They were squeezed into an area of land that grew smaller and smaller. To make matters worse, the population almost doubled in the 18th Century. An ever-increasing number of the Irish people sank to subsistence level, existing on potatoes and buttermilk, with a salt herring or a piece of bacon on rare occasions.

By the 1760s agrarian violence was beginning to disturb the Irish nights as bands of desperate men roamed the countryside, destroying property, killing cattle, and torturing the victims of their displeasure. These men represented the mass of the Irish people, the hidden Ireland of Gaelic folklore and legend, suppressed but not destroyed by the Protestant Ascendancy, inspired by memories of past struggles and dreaming of a resurrection for their vanished glories.

At least some of the blame for this dangerous state of affairs rested with Britain. Ireland lacked the capital, skilled labour, and resources for economic development, and British trade restrictions made these disabilities hard to overcome. Powerful British interests jealous of Irish competition lobbied to prohibit Irish exports to Britain or even to any country. Irish wool had to be smuggled out to France or not exported at all.

In addition, the Crown used Dublin Castle as a political dustbin. The first two Georges off-loaded their mistresses, bastards, and German relations and dependants on the Irish pension list, and used Irish sinecure offices to bribe or reward English politicians, who discharged no duties of office beyond drawing a salary. By the 1770s pensioners and sinecure holders were costing Ireland about ten per cent of its annual revenue.

Even the Protestant Ascendancy rebelled against these restrictions, creating a nucleus of opposition to the policies of Dublin Castle. Its members were known as the Patriots. Though loyal to the English Crown, they demanded parliamentary autonomy as a means of removing trade restrictions and other abuses. The Patriots won the support of the growing Protestant middle class and even of Catholics; since trade was one of the few activities from which they were not barred by the penal laws, Catholic merchant interests were keen to see the last of the trade restrictions.

The outbreak of the American Revolution gave the Patriots a great opportunity. The parallel between the two countries was too close to be ignored. The British government could not afford another America just across the Irish Sea. The Protestants were firmly united behind the Patriots and now possessed a citizen army, the Volunteers, which had a potential muster of 50,000 armed men.

Rather than risk a confrontation, the Crown made large concessions. In 1783 Britain conceded the sole right of the Irish parliament to legislate for Ireland. A blow had been struck, a link broken in the chains with which Britain bound her colony. To Irishmen of every political hue, of every religious sect, it was a stirring moment.

The Protestant Ascendancy, confident and secure, was becoming a very considerable institution. It claimed some of the greatest literary names of the 18th Century—Burke, Swift, Sheridan, Goldsmith—and its capital, Dublin, was taking on the distinctive appearance of one of the finest cities in Europe. For a time it seemed that Protestant rule might bring peace and unity. The penal code had been relaxed in practice, if not in law, as the bitter memories of the Battle of the Boyne grew dimmer.

But it was all a mirage, soon to be whipped away by the breath of the modern world blowing in from Europe. The all-too-familiar landscape of Irish politics would reappear: sectarian divisions, poverty, agrarian violence.

Modern Europe was born in the French Revolution, and so was modern Ireland. The egalitarian ideas unleashed by the Revolution split the Protestant Ascendancy along class lines. The first Irish revolutionary cell was established by middle-class Protestants in Ulster, by then the most economically advanced part of Ireland. If the aristocratic landowners inside the Irish parliament would not open the doors to them by parliamentary reform, they were prepared to force an entrance.

The first blow was struck by a 28-year-old Protestant barrister, Theobald Wolfe Tone. He was the leading light in the Society of United Irishmen, founded in Belfast in 1791. Wolfe Tone had a grand vision of Ireland—an independent republic, united above religious divisions, inspired by the French Revolution and taking its national identity from the old Gaelic tradition. Despite his commitment to a united Ireland, however, Tone was prepared, for expediency's sake, to play Catholic against Protestant.

In 1795 events played into his hands. Sectarian strife broke out in the countryside between Catholic militants calling themselves the Defenders and the Protestant Orange Society (later known as the Orange Order), named for their deliverer, William of Orange. Orangemen subjected Catholics in Ulster to a persecution so violent that thousands fled south. Catholic peasants flocked to join the Defenders, and by playing on their fears Wolfe Tone managed to attach a large body of them to his United Irishmen.

The government of Dublin Castle was alarmed, for the old danger of foreign intervention was now very real. Revolutionary France fully intended to support an Irish revolution. The Castle launched a counter-revolutionary campaign, and Wolfe Tone was forced to flee to Paris. Late in 1796 an invasion fleet carrying 15,000 Frenchmen sailed for Ireland and part of it, accompanied by Tone himself, actually entered Bantry Bay. But bad weather and bad leadership prevented a landing, and after a few days the would-be invaders sailed away again.

Nevertheless, the United Irishmen were immensely encouraged and armed themselves for the overthrow of the state. Dublin Castle in turn stepped up its counter-revolutionary campaign. In Belfast the troops acted savagely, burning houses, flogging or torturing suspects, and sending hundreds to the fleet as pressed men. The Castle went on to extend military coercion to the rest of the country. The Defenders were by now openly practising military manœuvres and were firmly behind Tone's United Irishmen. Ireland, gripped by the two rival terrors of government coercion and revolutionary intimidation, drifted into anarchy.

Under the pressures of martial law, the United Irishmen felt they had to act at once, or not at all. So it was that the Insurrection of 1798, the most celebrated of Irish rebellions, broke out on May 23. There was no effective leadership. There was no idea of when French help could be expected. And there was no plan of action. In Ulster the rebellion lasted a mere ten days, and only in County Wexford was there any real threat to the government. There it took the form, not of republicanism, but of a religious war.

"The boys of Wexford," as the rebels were remembered in Irish legend, rose in rebellion under the leadership of a Roman Catholic priest, Father John Murphy. Goaded into fury by months of military coercion, they struck out with uncontrolled savagery, plundering Protestant property, attacking and slaughtering innocent citizens simply because they were Protestants. The troops struck back with equal savagery. They burned houses, executed the inhabitants on the merest suspicion of harbouring fugitives, and laid waste wide areas of the country. No one's life or property was safe as all the deep, burning hatreds of divided Ireland came boiling to the surface.

The end came quickly. The rebels attacked the town of New Ross and were repulsed by government troops with great slaughter. Only a month after the rising began, their stronghold at Vinegar Hill was captured, and by the end of June the rebellion was petering out.

Foreign help, so often Ireland's hope and so often her disappointment, arrived too late. Not until August did a French invasion force reach Connaught, and it consisted of only three ships with 1,100 men. Although it fought courageously, it was defeated. A month later a second French expedition, accompanied by the tireless Wolfe Tone, was intercepted by a naval squadron. Tone was taken prisoner and sent to Dublin. To avoid the disgrace of hanging he committed suicide.

It was all over. Wolfe Tone's vision of a republican Ireland united above religious animosities had proved ephemeral. The Insurrection of 1798 turned out to be not a struggle of Irishmen against Britain, but of Irishmen against Irishmen, and 30,000 of them were dead. The old configuration of two nations, Protestant against Catholic, came once again to dominate Ireland.

One thing remained as a memorial to the United Irishmen: the tradition of revolutionary nationalism. Wolfe Tone's ideals were enshrined and the Insurrection was remembered, and later idealized by Irish nationalists, not for what it was but for what Tone hoped it would be.

Virtually no British troops had been employed in suppressing the Insurrection—the work had been done by irregular troops raised by the landlords—but in British eyes the Protestant Ascendancy had failed. The Ulster Protestants had shown themselves unreliable. With French intervention still threatening, Prime Minister William Pitt decided to take away the Protestants' proud constitution and replace it with a stronger safeguard for Britain.

Pitt's solution was to amalgamate the two countries and neutralize Catholic discontent by returning to them the right, lost in the 17th Century, of sitting in the English Parliament—Catholic Emancipation, as it was now known. In 1800 the Dublin parliament, the pride of Ireland, was persuaded to accomplish the extraordinary feat of voting for its own extinction, and the United Kingdom of Great Britain and Ireland came into existence. Over £1,240,000 was paid in bribes and compensation to key members of the landed classes. But the fundamental reason for this oddest of events was that the gentlemen of Ireland believed the Protestant Ascendancy was doomed without British support. If the price of that support was the abolition of their own parliament, they must pay it. From now on, 100 Irish M.P.s would sit in the House of Commons and 32 Irish peers in the House of Lords.

The second part of Pitt's plan, Catholic Emancipation, proved more difficult. Anti-Catholic prejudice was still strong in Britain, and when the Cabinet split on the question in 1801 Pitt resigned. The new ministry shelved the issue. Britain was left still ruling Ireland through only one section of society, the weakened, frightened, but nevertheless tough-knuckled Protestant Ascendancy.

Pitt's failure to carry Catholic Emancipation was disaster for the future

George Cruikshank did this savage and highly partisan drawing of the martyrdom of Protestant prisoners murdered by Wexford rebels in the Insurrection of 1798. The chief weapon of the rebellion was the pike, easily forged, easily hidden, and very deadly.

The Great Famine

Potato blight, *Phytophthora infestans*, reduces potatoes to a stinking slime. When it first appeared in Ireland in 1845 the disaster was not immediately apparent and there was hope for a plentiful harvest the following year. But in 1846 the blight struck again, and again the next three years. "I beheld with sorrow one wide waste of putrefying vegetation," wrote a priest. "Wretched people were seated on the fences of their decaying gardens, wringing their hands and bewailing bitterly the destruction that had left them foodless." It was the most horrific disaster in the British Isles since the Black Death of 1349.

Pleasants desperately combed the black, blighted fields for rotting potatoes while their children screamed with hunger. Bands of walking skeletons, lice-ridden, filthy, staggered into the towns howling at doors for food. Weakened by famine, the Irish were struck by disease—typhus and relapsing fever, dysentery, scurvy, famine dropsy. They died in the lanes, in doorways, in their homes, confronting horrified relief workers with visions of the Apocalypse.

Landlords, facing bankruptcy as their incomes dried up, began a massive campaign of eviction. Police and troops dragged families from their homes, and "crowbar brigades" demolished the huts to prevent their return. Women, half-naked children, tottering grandparents, were turned out in all weathers and left to crouch in shallow holes roofed with sticks and turf in the countryside. The Great Famine killed 1.5 million; the survivors would never forget.

stability of Ireland. By giving the Catholics a burning grievance, it reinforced the religious division of the country and kept alive a will to resist that later threatened the peace of Britain herself. For the first 20 years after the creation of the United Kingdom, Irish politics almost ceased to exist. For almost half a century, there was only one Irish politician of stature, Daniel O'Connell. It was Catholic Emancipation that he made his platform.

O'Connell was a leader of immense energy and resourcefulness. He soon became known for his extraordinary command over large crowds, and he created a mass political movement designed to wrest Catholic objectives from Britain by constitutional means. In 1826 O'Connell displayed his power in the countryside by getting himself elected to the House of Commons. He then refused to take the Oath of Supremacy—which by acknowledging the King of England as the supreme head of the church would technically have converted him to Anglicanism—and was refused entry to Parliament. All over Ireland Catholics staged semimilitary demonstrations of protest, and the British government, fearing civil war, felt it best to yield. In 1829 Catholic Emancipation became a reality.

O'Connell's campaign for emancipation had been a symbolic crusade against the Protestant Ascendancy. And because Britain had allied herself with the Protestants, it was implicitly a crusade against the 1800 Act of Union. The Catholic cause and the cause of national independence had become intimately linked. The stage was set for the next century of Irish history.

Although his first campaign had ended in success, O'Connell's second—for repeal of the Act of Union—was a flat failure. The way was left open for new leadership, this time of a more extreme kind. It was already in existence, a group known as Young Ireland. Its members took their cue from Wolfe Tone: like the United Irishmen of 1798, they had a vision of an Irish nation united above religious differences. Unlike O'Connell, whose movement was strictly constitutional, they were prepared to use force. In

Europe's revolutionary year, 1848, Young Ireland staged a minor rebellion in Munster. It was easily suppressed, but the revolutionary tradition laid down by Tone in 1798 had been picked up and preserved.

A revolutionary programme could not succeed without deep-seated economic and social grievances, and the mass of the Irish people had them. Four-fifths of the population was dependent on the land still held by the Protestant Ascendancy. In the mid-19th Century they were even more impoverished than they had been in the mid-18th. The population had continued to grow, from about five million in 1800 to well over eight million in the 1840s. Holdings had been divided and subdivided, and half of all tenant farmers were reduced to cultivating the potato as their only crop. When the potato harvest failed—as it often did on a local level—they starved.

But in 1845 blight ruined the potato crop over the whole country, and the blight was repeated in successive years from 1845 to 1849. This was the Great Famine.

As millions faced the prospect of starvation, various government relief measures were suggested and tried: £100,000 worth of Indian corn, public works to provide employment, relief committees set up to raise funds and distribute donated food. Such methods might have worked in England, but in Ireland they were doomed to failure. There the peasant rarely handled money and virtually never used it to buy food: he paid his rent by his labour and fed himself and his family on his own potatoes. No one had the slightest idea how to mill and cook bullet-hard Indian corn. There was no way of turning wages into food, no system of retail distribution, no village shop where food could be bought.

The prevailing *laissez-faire* doctrine of political economy inhibited effective government direct aid. Even more inhibiting was the British attitude to Ireland—and it is this that has impressed itself most deeply on the Irish memory. Britain was only interested in Ireland when she became a threat to British security. The Great Famine was no such threat. The average Brit-

The French comment at left on the Irish Question has Victoria seeing nothing untoward on a tour of the island. In another French satire (below), dating from 1870, Britain is a fusty Victorian spinster preoccupied with her recalcitrant Irish "pet" as the Continent seethes with change.

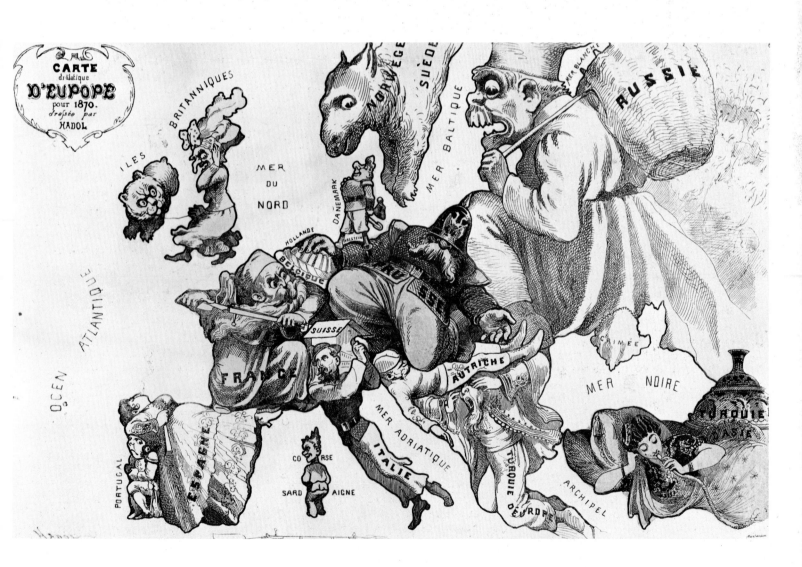

ish politician persisted in jealously opposing any proposal for wasting British taxpayer's money on an Irish population that not only seemed alien and far away, but also seditious.

There was a hysterical rush to escape the "doomed and starving island," and thousands of panic-stricken refugees put to sea for the United States and British North America. They crowded into any hulks that were to be found, which came to be known as "coffin ships." Of the emigrants sailing from Cork, one in nine died on the voyage, more than on many 18th-Century slave ships. By 1851 Irish emigration had risen to a quarter of a million a year and remained very high for the rest of the century.

The catastrophe of the Great Famine left a legacy of bitter hatred towards Britain. Though voluntary organizations had done much to mitigate the suffering, Irishmen could not but feel that British government policy dis-

played a callous disregard for Ireland. That was the crux of the problem. Despite the Act of Union, Ireland was still being treated as an alien dependency. Dublin Castle was still the centre of administration, still the court of a Lord Lieutenant—a sign of continuing colonial status. After the Great Famine, thoughtful Britons began to wonder about the value of a union that condemned Ireland to such unnatural suffering. The Irish Question became a hot political issue. At last the inherent injustice of the Protestant Ascendancy came to be questioned.

In Ireland the dispute was argued for the next 20 years by the usual methods of agrarian outrage. Only now there was a new determination and direction. In 1858 James Stephens and John O'Mahoney set up a Catholic secret society dedicated to the forceful overthrow of British power in Ireland. Significantly it had two branches. In Ireland it was christened the Irish Republican Brotherhood and in Amer-

ica the Fenian Brotherhood. Both branches were usually called Fenians.

After two ineffective insurrections, the Fenians began to sortie into Britain. In 1867 they rescued two Fenian prisoners from Manchester, killing an English policeman in the process, and the next year, during a similar rescue attempt at Clerkenwell, they exploded a bomb that killed 20 people. There was a wave of public horror and fury in Britain, but it was followed by the realization that there must be something fundamentally unhealthy about Irish politics.

With the new awareness of Irish troubles went a willingness to consider the bold remedies that were necessary. At long last the figure of Justice presiding over the gateway to Dublin Castle was to become the symbol not just of Britain's own national aspirations, but of her goodwill towards Ireland. The man who took the initiative was William Gladstone, who became Liberal Prime Minister for the first

Riding his Home Rule nag, Gladstone carries Britannia towards the abyss of National Disaster. Fenian vultures, both Irish and American varieties, await a feast. Gladstone's introduction of his first Home Rule Bill in 1886 inspired this bitter Tory attack.

time in 1868. The Irish Question had long been one of his deepest concerns, and his first comment on receiving his summons from the Queen was: "My mission is to pacify Ireland."

In 1869 Gladstone disestablished the Anglican Church of Ireland. The legal connection between church and state was severed, and the Church of Ireland became a voluntary body and its property was confiscated. This made little practical difference to the Irish people, who continued to pay tithes to the state, but it was a highly important symbolic gesture. With very little fuss, a totem of the old Protestant Ascendancy had been torn down.

The following year Gladstone steered through Parliament the most radical land act that he could expect an assembly still largely consisting of landowners to pass. It gave tenant farmers the right to compensation for unfair eviction, and offered government loans to those who wished to buy their holdings from the landlords. But it fell far short of true reform. Irishmen were still not convinced that their interests could be safely entrusted to British parliamentarians, however well-meaning.

There was only one solution to the economic ills of Ireland: to abolish both the Protestant Ascendancy and the land settlement on which it rested. The political animosities built up by long Protestant domination had also to be abolished. How much would Britain have to concede: self-government, or perhaps complete independence? After Gladstone's failure to go fast enough in 1869 and 1870, two traditions, one constitutional, the other revolutionary, ran side by side so closely that in the end they came under the umbrella of a single political movement.

The moderate wing was founded in 1870 by Isaac Butt, son of a Church of Ireland parson, a successful barrister and, in politics, a conservative. Butt believed a Fenian revolution would be a disaster and that the best guarantee against it would be the government of Ireland by her natural rulers: the nobility, the gentry, the wealthy middle classes. To win popular support, however, Butt had to widen his programme to include land reform and denominational education for Catholics. Calling itself the Home Rule League, the movement won a major election victory in 1874 when 59 of its members were elected as M.P.s to Westminster. This Home Rule party represented Ireland in the imperial Parliament for the next 40 years.

The extremist wing of the Home Rule movement began as the Land League, founded in 1878–79 by two Fenians, Michael Davitt and John Devoy. Like the Fenians, it had both an Irish and an American branch and was financed by American money. The Land League combined mass meetings with a subtle and highly effective policy of organized ostracism. Selecting estates with bad records for rack-renting and eviction, it proceeded to make everyday life impossible for the landlord or his agent. It was one such campaign against a certain Captain Charles Boycott, agent for an estate in County Mayo, that gave the word "boycotting" to the language.

The two wings of the movement, the Land League and the Home Rule League, were first linked in the remarkable person of an Anglo-Irishman, Charles Stewart Parnell. In 1879 Parnell became president of the Land League and in the following year, after Isaac Butt's death, chairman of the Home Rule party. It was a remarkable achievement for a man of 34 who was a Protestant and a landlord.

It was Parnell's family background that engendered in him the radicalism of a patriot. His great-grandfather and grandfather had both opposed parliamentary union with Britain, and his mother was an American with a strong antipathy towards Britain (her father had fought in the War of 1812). Parnell grew up with that ambiguous mixture of jealousy and contempt with which many colonists regarded their mother country.

Ambiguity marked everything Parnell did. To win a popular following he had to strike the extreme attitudes of revolutionary Irish nationalism: that was his Land League personality. But he had no intention of leading an armed rebellion, and worked for the maximum independence possible by constitutional methods: that was his Home Rule personality. For ten years

American Fenians

The American branch of the Irish Republican Brotherhood missed no chance to strike at Great Britain. Not content with raising money ("the pennies of Irish serving-girls," their enemies said) for the cause of Irish independence, the American Fenians began hatching bizzare plots.

Having founded an "Irish Republic" in New York, in 1866 they sought to enlarge it dramatically—by invading British Canada. From there they planned to wage an undefined but glorious campaign against England. The Fenians won a brief scuffle with Canadian volunteers, then fled back across the Niagara River when reinforcements arrived. It was highly inglorious, and when several other invasion attempts also fizzled out, they began to look for ways to reinvigorate their cause.

The man they turned to was an Irish-American named John Holland, the "Father of the Modern Submarine." The Fenians' plan was to conceal small submarines in a freighter, sail it into a Royal Navy anchorage, release the subs through a secret sea door, and watch as the unsuspecting warships were picked off one by one. Holland, who was getting nowhere trying to interest the U.S. Navy in his experiments, welcomed their backing. He built two submarines for the Irishmen. The second one, the *Fenian Ram* (1881) was a remarkably efficient craft capable of firing projectiles while submerged. But by this time, fortunately for the Royal Navy, the American Fenians were in collapse. However slight their other accomplishments, they did advance the development of the submarine.

Parnell performed this balancing act.

In 1881, during his second ministry, Gladstone shepherded a stronger Land Act through Parliament. It conceded the "three Fs" which would at last make Irish tenant farming viable: fair rent, fixity of tenure, and freedom to sell the right of occupancy. Landlords were reduced to mere receivers of rent. Parnell, caught between extremists, temporized, neither condemning nor applauding the Act. The hard-line Lord Lieutenant, William Forster, believed he was deliberately trying to wreck the Act, and imprisoned him in Kilmainham gaol and proscribed the Land League.

This solved Parnell's dilemma. His prestige among the peasantry soared. Parnell and Gladstone came to an informal arrangement, known as the "Kilmainham treaty," by which Parnell was released to continue his moderate policies and thus calm the country.

Gladstone, determined to create a true reconciliation between Britain and Ireland, decided to back Home Rule. Had he succeeded in carrying such a bill through Parliament, Ireland might well have been satisfied with self-government within the Empire. His first attempt in 1886 split his party and brought the Tories back to office. But he was prepared to try again, and by 1890 a Liberal return to power and a second Home Rule Bill seemed possible.

Then, unaccountably and perversely, the course of Irish history was altered by what was in itself a quite insignificant event. In 1890 Parnell was cited as co-respondent in a divorce action by one Captain W. H. O'Shea. Parnell had indeed been living with Captain O'Shea's wife and actually had two children by her. He offered no defence, and the verdict was given against him. Utter confusion followed. Gladstone, though not censorious himself, felt it impossible to continue his alliance with the Parnell-led Home Rule party. Parnell's followers were in a dilemma: whether to lose Gladstone and keep Parnell, or vice versa. The result was a split—43 walked out, 27 remained under Parnell's leadership.

Parnell reacted wildly. In a "mani-

A pamphlet attacking Parnell, published by disillusioned American Catholics.

festo to the Irish people" he turned his back on his previous moderate policy, denounced Gladstone's Home Rule proposals as hopelessly inadequate, and repudiated the idea of alliance with any British political party. The strain broke his health. Within a year he was dead. He was just 45. The man who had spent his whole political career working for a moderate, constitutional solution to Ireland's troubles went down in Irish memories as the "lost leader" of 1891. He became the hero of the Fenians, not the parliamentarians, and joined the pantheon of Ireland's revolutionary liberators.

Parnell had been fighting for two objectives: the demolition of the Protestant Ascendancy, which meant giving the land of Ireland to the peasant farmers; and Home Rule, which meant reopening the Dublin parliament. On the first count he had partially succeeded; on the second he had completely failed. After his death, Gladstone returned briefly to power, an old man now of 83, and introduced his long-planned second Home Rule Bill in 1893. But it was rejected by the House of Lords and he resigned for the last time. From 1895 until 1906 the fortunes of Ireland were entrusted to the Tories.

Home Rule became impossible. The Conservative party represented the most politically cautious, staunchly Protestant, imperialistic sections of British society. It declared its intention to oppose implacably any threat to the Union of 1800 or to the integrity of the Empire.

The man now faced with the task of ruling strife-torn Ireland was Arthur Balfour, Chief Secretary in Dublin Castle. He adopted a well-worn policy: coercion and conciliation. To suppress agrarian violence he would use coercion; to win over the mass of the Irish people, conciliation. He was prepared to go very far in conciliation. Balfour sought to dismantle what remained of the Protestant Ascendancy by encouraging farmers to buy out their landlords with the aid of government loans. In 1903 the Irish Land Act was passed. Its success was dramatic. That year there were over 500,000 tenant farmers in Ireland; by 1909, 270,000 had bought and 46,000 more were negotiating to buy their estates; ten years later Irish peasant farmers at last owned the soil they tilled. Britain had bought out the very landlords she had sent over two centuries before as settlers.

Balfour's conciliation was very far-reaching, but it was too late and not enough to alter the trend of Irish history. He was remembered by Irish Catholics not as "kind Balfour" but "bloody Balfour" the coercionist. Any policy aimed at keeping Irish M.P.s at Westminster at the expense of Home Rule could never have succeeded, however much "kindness" accompanied it. The centuries-old legacy of bitterness built up against the Protestant Ascendancy was too strong.

There was another legacy of the 17th Century that Balfour could not alter: Protestant Ulster. There the settlers had established not just a landed oligarchy but a homogeneous, prosperous community. In Ulster the idea of implanting a new nation had worked. It is possible to buy out landlords, but very difficult to buy out a whole nation.

Ulstermen had undergone a sea change since the revolutionary nationalism of Wolfe Tone's United Irishmen in the 1790s. Above all, they were influenced by the old sectarian fears. The bald fact that the Catholic population of Ireland was overwhelming always inclined Protestants against a total break with Britain. Home Rule because Catholics were for it must mean "Rome Rule." The Ulster attitude was summed up in the blunt slogan "We will not have Home Rule."

The death of Parnell and the failure of Gladstone's second Home Rule Bill had deflated popular Catholic enthusiasm for constitutional methods and encouraged revolutionary nationalism. This seemed more romantic, more Catholic, more Gaelic.

It was an extremist outlook, born of long hatred and misery. The Gaelic League, a militant cultural society, made de-Anglicization into an Irish crusade. Everything English was to be cast aside, including "such foreign and fantastic field sports as lawn tennis, polo, croquet, cricket and the like." At the Abbey Theatre, opened in 1904, writers of first-rank stature, including Yeats, Synge, and Joyce, greatly strengthened the new cultural nationalism by creating a powerful form of drama evocatively Irish in spirit.

How irrevocably divided Ireland had become was demonstrated after the return of the Liberals to power. With their majority reduced in the election of 1910, they found themselves dependent on the votes of the Irish M.P.s under Parnell's successor, John Redmond. Redmond's price was a third Home Rule Bill. In January, 1913, it was passed by the Commons but rejected by the Lords. Nevertheless, under the terms of the 1911 Parliament Act, the Lords' veto lasted only two years and the bill would automatically become law at the end of 1914. It seemed like a victory for Redmond, who received congratulations from the Dominions of Canada, South Africa, and Australia. Even though the Bill conceded less than Dominion status, the vast majority of Irishmen were in favour of it.

In fact it was the end of the road for constitutional methods. Presbyterian Ulster had already sworn, with religious determination, "to defeat the present conspiracy to set up a Home Rule parliament in Ireland." Under the determined leadership of a Tory lawyer, Edward Carson, and with the open support of the Conservative party under Bonar Law, Ulster began drilling its own citizen army, the Ulster Volunteers, to defy Parliament by force of arms. Senior British Army officers took an enthusiastic interest in the movement and in March, 1914, 57 cavalry officers stationed at Irish military headquarters declared they would resign rather than fight the Volunteers. The following month a large consignment of arms was illegally landed with the connivance of the British authorities.

In Catholic southern Ireland events quickly took a similar course. The delay to the Home Rule Bill played into the hands of the extremists. The Irish Republican Brotherhood (the Fenians) sponsored the formation of a counterpart to the Ulster Volunteers, the Irish Volunteers. Hundreds of recruits came from among the ranks of those tired of waiting for Home Rule. In July, 1914, the Irish Volunteers staged their own arms landing at Howth—in broad daylight. Dublin Castle tried to seize the arms, and in the ensuing commotion three civilians were shot by troops. Ireland was on the verge of civil war when the First World War broke out.

Reviving the ancient adage "England's difficulty, Ireland's opportunity," the Republican Brotherhood decided to try once again the old idea of insurrection aided by Continental allies—this time Germany. They felt, much as the rebels of 1798, that they must strike at once or not at all if the flame of Irish nationalism was to be kept burning. They struck in Dublin on Easter Monday, 1916.

The Easter Rising, like the Insurrection of 1798, was bungled. As so often before, no foreign help came—except a German submarine to return Sir Roger Casement, an Irish nationalist who had had a distinguished career in the British consular service, from his unsuccessful mission to enlist aid in Berlin. He was quickly arrested.

The British were taken by surprise. Dublin Castle was occupied. The rebels seized and held the General Post Office and from the steps proclaimed the establishment of the first Irish Republic: "In the name of God and of the dead generations from which she receives her old tradition of nationhood, Ireland, through us, summons her children to her flag and strikes for her freedom." By nightfall almost the whole city centre was in rebel hands.

But it was hopeless. Dublin Castle was relieved within hours. On Tuesday British reinforcements arrived and artillery was brought into play. The General Post Office was gutted. On Saturday the rebels surrendered unconditionally. Fifteen of the leaders were executed after secret courts martial, and Casement was later tried and hanged. As each day brought a new curt official announcement of the executions, Irish opinion all over the world turned to sympathy with the rebels, then to anger.

The revolutionary tradition, which had been kept alive by the most tenuous of threads since 1798, was stained into the consciousness of the nation. Home Rule could never satisfy Irish nationalists now. For the honour of the martyred dead the objective had to be total independence: Dublin Castle, captured only for a few hours in seven centuries of British rule, had to be seized for good. In the words of Yeats, Ireland had passed under "the tyranny of the dead."

For Britain, the Easter Rising was the day of reckoning. At the least, Ireland could no longer be denied Home Rule: that was finally accomplished. But neither could Ulster be denied continuing integration in the United Kingdom. An Ireland of "West Britons" was no longer possible; a united Irish republic was no longer possible. The consequence of partial conquest and partial colonization at last became clear. All that was possible was a partial solution—a partitioned Ireland, half-nation and half-colony; an Ireland tortured by disunity and division; an Ireland where the struggle has still to be decided.

—*Simon Rigge*

Chapter Eleven
WAR AND COMMONWEALTH

A last glimpse of the old order: George V (right) and Germany's Kaiser Wilhelm in full imperial panoply, decked out on the occasion of the wedding of Wilhelm's daughter in Potsdam in 1913. The two cousins never met again.

I. The Empire at War

In England it was Bank Holiday Monday, a warm, sultry August afternoon. Straw-hatted men punted on the Thames while their girls lazed under parasols. Racing drivers hurled their roaring cars round the track at Brooklands. Bathing-machines trundled on the crowded beaches. Gin was 6*d.* a double and cigarettes 5½*d.* for 20. It was August 3, 1914.

Britain was at the moment the greatest power the world had ever known—greater than Rome, greater than the Mongol hordes. Her Empire covered a quarter of the earth's land surface, her influence reached to every corner of the globe. It was a time of British self-confidence and superiority. There was talk of war, but it was a prospect that filled people with enthusiasm rather than dismay. They could not know that the First World War heralded the end of their Empire and their world.

The Cabinet had met that morning, and during the afternoon the House of Commons was in special session. At 5:03 p.m. the Aldershot Command received a one-word telegram: "Mobilize."

Next day, August 4, was another fine warm day over most of Europe. The French Army, following a master defence plan perfected over many years, moved towards the German frontier. The French plan was acknowledged to be foolproof, and the main worry at the War Office was whether there would be time for the British Expeditionary Force to get across the Channel before the fighting was over. Crowds waving British and Empire flags gathered at Westminster.

At 2 p.m. a Belgian lieutenant named Picard, peering through his field glasses, saw enemy cavalry crossing the German-Belgian frontier. Britain had a treaty dating back to 1839 that guaranteed Belgian neutrality, and accordingly London demanded that the German advance end by midnight or it would mean war. During the evening ministers waited in the Cabinet Room at 10 Downing Street. No word of a German withdrawal came. In fact, a grey mass of Uhlans was already sweeping across the fields of Belgium on a journey that would change the face of Europe forever. Fifteen minutes after midnight, Berlin time, the German Ambassador was handed Britain's declaration of war.

The British Empire was something of a mystery to many Europeans, who were inquisitive as to just how strong the oft-mentioned "family ties" really were between the self-governing Dominions and the mother country. Although Britain's declaration of war was legally binding on all her dependencies, there was no reason whatever why countries such as Canada and Australia should actively participate in a contest against a country that posed no real threat to them. Indeed, London had not even consulted with the Dominions before going to war. Many thought that the far-flung colonials would show little loyalty.

The answer to this uncertainty was given with a speed and force that astonished all Europe. It is the most remarkable demonstration in imperial history of the loyalty that did exist in the Empire.

In Australia the Labour Prime Minister, Andrew Fisher, declared, "Our duty is quite clear: to gird up our loins and remember that we are Britons." He promised to fight "to our last man and our last shilling." His Minister of Defence said, "Australia wants the rest of the Empire to know that . . . all she possesses, to the last ear of corn and drop of blood, is freely offered to maintain the glory and greatness of the Empire, and to battle in the righteous cause wherein she is engaged."

New Zealand was considered to be the most socialist state in the world at the time. Prime Minister Richard Seddon was regarded as positively revolutionary in some quarters, yet he proved himself a staunch imperialist. As a history of New Zealand at war put it, "Telegrams passed to and from the Imperial Government, the Dominion offering, the Mother Country accepting, no unnecessary questions being asked, no stipulations being made: in time of common danger the Empire does not bargain." The first New Zealand troops, nearly 8,000 strong, left only ten days after the outbreak of war.

Australia and New Zealand at least had some personal interest because of the presence of German colonies in the Pacific, at which both Dominions had long looked askance. Such considerations did not exist in Canada. But the Prime Minister, Sir Robert Borden, had already cabled London three days before the outbreak of war promising support and inviting suggestions as to how Canada could best help. A division of 22,000 men was offered and accepted, the first portion of Canada's massive war-time assistance. In 1916 she promised to raise half a million men. Canada, said Borden, was "united in a common resolve"

The other "white Dominion" was South Africa. There the scars of the Boer War were still unhealed. Could the old enemy be expected to join forces with Britain only a decade and a half after the bitterest of wars? The Prime Minister was an old Boer War opponent, Louis Botha. But he and his right-hand man, Jan Christiaan Smuts, had become firm believers in the Empire, mainly out of pragmatism. In the eyes of many diehard Afrikaner nationalists they had become "more British than the British." Botha declared South African support for Britain, and promised to take the neighbouring German colony of South-West Africa and to assist in the taking of German East Africa. But he did not have all his countrymen with him, and there was even talk of rebellion.

German East Africa was by far the richest German overseas colony, and its conquest seemed the obvious responsibility of the Indian Army. That army, with its magnificent uniforms, its spectacle and display, was considered one of the most powerful weapons available to the Empire. The response from India was encouraging: politicians suspended their controversies, princes made lavish offers of help, and thousands of Indians, though involved in a war about which they knew nothing, swarmed to the colours.

Inevitably, as the Dominions knew well, the major part of the war would be fought in Europe. Germany concentrated about 1,500,000 men on the Western Front, relying on Austria to deal with the Russians. After four weeks of war, the German plan seemed to be achieving spectacular success.

The British Expeditionary Force reached the front in time to delay the German advance. But it was soon obliged to fall back before the fury of the onslaught, which was only halted at the Battle of the Marne in September. The Germans retired, and by the end of the year the Western Front had settled down into a complex line of barbed wire and trenches from the Belgian coast to the Swiss frontier. It was a line that would remain substantially unaltered for nearly four years, although occasionally dented by great offensives known as "pushes." The Western Front, on which much of a generation of British, French, and German men died, was to haunt Europe for half a century.

The war of movement that both sides had planned had become a stalemate, a war of attrition. The generals and their staffs could think of no other way. As the months passed the casualty figures mounted with awful inevitability, neither side seeming to have gained anything except sometimes a few acres of shell-powdered soil or corpse-filled mud. Between pushes little or nothing happened. The poet Edmund Blunden characterized it as "the imbecile, narrow, bullet-beaten, but tranquil front line."

Overseas, the German Empire was beginning to fall. Scattered between West, South-West, and East Africa, the Pacific, and the China coast, it depended for its security on command of the seas. With this in mind, Germany had developed a powerful navy, but thanks to Jacky Fisher the Royal Navy was prepared.

The Pacific was primarily the responsbility of Australia and New Zealand. Germany held the Bismarck Archipelago, German New Guinea, the Carolines, north Solomons, Marshalls, Samoa, and some smaller islands, a total of nearly 100,000 square miles. German raiders, including the cruisers *Scharnhorst, Gneisenau,* and *Emden,* were operating in the Pacific. Since Samoa was the main objective of the Royal Australian Navy, the German squadron was able to sail for the Atlantic unmolested, where it was eventually destroyed in the Battle of the Falkland Islands. The *Emden* did not accompany the fleet to the Atlantic; she left for the Indian Ocean where with the *Königsberg* she caused much destruction among British merchant shipping. The *Emden* met her death under the guns of the Australian cruiser *Sydney.* The *Königsberg,* last of the raiders, was found sheltering in an East African river and was pounded to pieces. These victories and the neutralization of the German High Seas Fleet at Jutland in 1916 left the Royal Navy in control of the oceans.

The invasion of Samoa, aided by the Australian Navy, was undertaken by a New Zealand force of 1,400 men. The expedition appeared unexpectedly, and the island yielded without bloodshed. The remaining German possessions in the Pacific and the Far East were taken by Australia and by Japan, which had entered the war on the Allied side. These conquests were of great assistance to Britain, destroying the German outposts in the East and freeing the Royal Navy for duties in the Atlantic and the North Sea.

Meanwhile, large expeditionary forces were being assembled in Australia and New Zealand. The intention was for this force to join the Canadians training in Britain. However, at the last minute it was decided that the Australians and New Zealanders, who were already in the Red Sea, should disembark in Egypt, where they could train and then go direct to the Western Front. The presence of this force in the Near East, some 28,000 strong, was to have vital bearing on the Empire's part in the war.

Turkey, as an old foe of Russia, had joined the war against the Allies. The British felt that the Russians, who were taking a fearful battering, needed support, and a naval demonstration against the Dardanelles, the straits connecting the Black Sea with the Mediterranean, was suggested. If a fleet could pass through the straits, Constantinople would be at the mercy of the Allies. The project was enthusiastically championed by Winston Churchill, First Lord of the Admiralty. Frustrated and appalled by the deadlock in the West, he knew that the plan would give a prominent role to the Royal Navy. David Lloyd George, the Chancellor of the Exchequer, was also a firm advocate; he wanted to rally the Balkan states against Austria and Turkey. The project received the assent of the War Minister, Lord Kitchener.

In the early months of 1915 an Anglo-French squadron that attempted to force the Dardanelles ran into difficulties under heavy Turkish bombardment. An amphibious assault would be required. It was decided that the Australian and New Zealand Army Corps (the Anzacs) in Egypt was well placed for the task, and should form the bulk of the invasion force. All this was planned without consultation with the Australian and New Zealand governments.

At dawn on April 25 the Anzacs, supported by two British divisions, struggled ashore on the Gallipoli peninsula overlooking the straits. The brass hats could hardly have chosen

In Norman Wilkinson's painting, the Allied Suvla Bay beachhead at Gallipoli, established in August, 1915, comes under Turkish fire.

worse terrain for an invasion. Gallipoli's narrow beaches were dominated by fortified heights from which the Turks directed a murderous fire. Bungling distinguished the whole operation. The British, usually so efficient, not only rushed troops and supplies to Gallipoli without any coherent military plan but even without regard for basic common sense.

The two beachheads were hardly more than footholds. Both sides resorted to suicidal frontal attacks. Some 10,000 Turks were shot down in a massive nine-hour attempt to throw the Anzacs back into the sea. British officers were no more imaginative. Attempting a raid on machine-gun nests, 400 Australians were lost in 15 minutes; on another occasion, British troops managed a gain of 500 yards in return for 17,000 casualties.

For eight months the stalemate dragged on under appalling conditions. Sentiment at home was mounting against the operation and pressure

was rising for evacuation. Finally Lord Kitchener, the War Minister, visited the scene and advocated withdrawal. Gallipoli's final irony, after so much futile heroism and sacrifice, was the tactical brilliance of the evacuation. Yet this could not conceal the fact that it was the most humiliating defeat of the war. Casualties had exceeded a quarter-million. While censorship disguised the worst blunders, enough became known of the mistakes made by British politicians and generals to generate in Australia and New Zealand a demand for participation in major decisions involving Dominion troops.

The failure at Gallipoli meant a renewal of the offensive on the Western Front. Nothing was achieved except the lengthening of the casualty lists—60,000 fell on the first day of the big summer push along the Somme in 1916, for example—and the widening of imperial rifts. A South African division decimated in one abortive at-

tack was darkly bitter, believing that British troops would have been relieved earlier. Many of them thought that Empire troops got the dirty jobs because their British commanders would not have to answer to Dominion politicians. There was also mistrust between British and Empire commanders. Sir Douglas Haig, British commander-in-chief on the Western Front, confided to his diary that "Some of the divisional generals are so ignorant and (like many Colonials) so conceited, that they cannot be trusted to work out unaided the plans of attack."

While the Dominion troops were learning how to cope with the siege warfare of Europe, the war elsewhere was teaching similarly hard lessons.

The Indian Army, the pride of the Empire, was thought to be one of Britain's trump cards, but there was a reluctance to commit Indian troops to European conditions. It was decided they would be used mainly against the Turkish forces in the Middle East and against German East Africa across the Indian Ocean.

Brigadier-General A. E. Aitken was put in command of an Indian expeditionary force to seize the port of Tanga in German East Africa. In command of the German forces, mostly native troops, was a remarkable officer, Paul von Lettow-Vorbeck. He made careful preparations to meet the much-vaunted Indian Army.

The landing was made in November, 1914. General Aitken took personal control of the advance through the thick scrub. The 13th Rajputs were to the fore, and as soon as the enemy opened fire they broke and began to withdraw. "They were all jibbering like terrified monkeys and were clearly not for it at any price," an English officer wrote. He had to shoot an Indian officer who drew his sword on him when he attempted to stop the rout. Confusion and panic were losing the battle after only a few minutes of action. The unhappy truth was that the Indian troops, expert in ceremonial drill, were completely nonplussed by a kind of warfare for which they had received no training whatever. General Aitken, seeing his career and reputation crumbling, himself charged into the fray with his staff, but to no avail. By nightfall it was obvious that the expedition had been completely defeated. Evacuation was haphazard and undisciplined.

When the cable announcing the failure reached London, it was a bitter shock to the government. Strict censorship was imposed, and news of the defeat was not released. Lettow-Vorbeck remained in control of German East Africa, although cut off from the Fatherland. With intelligence and resource he created a siege economy that kept the colony going until the next Allied offensive, in 1916.

The other theatre outside Europe that engaged the Indian Army was Turkish-controlled Mesopotamia (now Iraq). In charge of a probe up the valley of the Tigris towards Baghdad was Major-General Charles Townshend, an eccentric who regaled his front-line troops with violin music. Disease was rampant. There was a shortage of medical staff and a chaotic muddle over medical equipment and stores. The sufferings of the sick and wounded became national scandals in both Britain and in India.

Townshend reached the fly-ridden port of Kut with the 6th Indian Division, but could get no farther. Having lost nearly one-third of his force, he prepared for siege in Kut. The relieving force was strengthened by the arrival from war-torn France of the 3rd and 7th Indian Divisions, but all efforts to relieve Kut were thrust back. In April, 1916, after five months, Townshend surrendered.

Command in Mesopotamia passed to the enterprising Lieutenant-General F. S. Maude, who had 107,000 Indian troops under him. A steady advance was made, and by October, 1918, the Turks asked for an armistice. Nearly 16,000 imperial troops were killed in battle in Mesopotamia, and almost 13,000 died from disease.

Across the continent from German East Africa was the sister colony of German South-West Africa. When war started, its conquest was undertaken by the Union of South Africa, with General Botha, the old Boer commander, in charge. The campaign was delayed by internal problems in the Union, however. Many of the Boers were loath to support Britain in the war, and several veteran Boer commanders assembled a 10,000-man force to defy the Union government. Using German South-West Africa as a base and refuge, the rebels attempted to set up a provisional government. They were not supported, and after three months' fierce fighting the rebellion broke up. The feeling against Britain was strong enough to ensure light sentences for what was in fact treason in time of war, and within two years all the rebel Afrikaner prisoners had been released.

The invasion of German South-West Africa now proceeded. Botha used Boer tactics and cut off the German retreat into Angola. At the same time, Jan Christiaan Smuts advanced on the capital. Another column of 3,000 men marched nearly 500 miles from Kimberley across the Kalahari Desert, one of the most remarkable feats of the war. In July, 1915, the Germans surrendered. The next year the Camer-

oons fell to a force that included Indian and West Indian troops.

South Africa was now free to take on Lettow-Vorbeck in German East Africa. Smuts was put in command of the Union expeditionary force being readied in Kenya. His three divisions consisted of South African, East African, Indian, Rhodesian, and British troops.

Smuts soon discovered that Lettow-Vorbeck, hopelessly outnumbered, did not want an open battle that might end the campaign in one stroke. Brilliantly, the German harassed the invading force as it pushed forward. Smuts's main problem was disease. The capital, Dar-es-Salaam, was not occupied until September, 1916. Soon afterwards Smuts declared the campaign over, much to the chagrin of his successor. Lettow-Vorbeck was still very much in the field. He had been pushed out of his own colony, but by the time of the Armistice his still undefeated army, the last German force to surrender in the war, was deep in Rhodesia and threatening Salisbury. Nevertheless, thanks largely to imperial forces, the German overseas empire had ceased to exist.

As illustrated on the following pages, Dominion forces continued to play important roles in the great battles of attrition on the Western Front right up to the last shot. It was the most terrible war in history. Over 8,500,000 were dead; the British Empire had lost 908,371, the flower of a generation. The war had been won by overwhelming manpower and economic strength, especially after America's entry.

The fine phrases of the Empire premiers in 1914 seemed a long way off, and although common experiences in the struggle strengthened bonds of loyalty on a personal level, the end of the war heralded a new age for the Empire. Now the Dominions were battle-scarred veterans, wearing the honours of a major war. After their sacrifices they believed themselves to be the equals of Britain. The Empire appeared to be more powerful than ever before, but its senior members would never be subordinate to Westminster again.

—*Brian Gardner*

WESTERN FRONT

UNITED FOR FREEDOM AGAINST GERMAN MILITARY OPPRESSION

THE EMPIRE'S STURDY SONS WILL NOT SHOW THE

WHEN KING AND COUNTRY NEED THEM TO BEAT THE GERMANS BACKWARD HOME

From all across the Empire they came by the thousands—
Canadians, New Zealanders, Australians, Rhodesians, Indians,
South Africans—to fight an enemy that represented only
the most remote threat to their own security.
Unhesitatingly they adopted Britain's cause as their own, fighting
in flooded trenches and dying in shell-blasted no-man's-land
to hold the thinly stretched lines of the Western Front.

Exploiting a breakthrough by British tanks, cavalry of 9th Hodson's Horse (otherwise known as 4th Duke of Cambridge's Own Lancers) attack under fire near Cambrai in November, 1917.

BUY
WAR LOAN BONDS

THEY WILL HELP US TO
BEAT THE GERMANS
AND SAFEGUARD INDIA

Indians in the Front Line

Among the battles fought by Indians on the Western Front was a cavalry action at the town of Cambrai, in northern France. Barbed-wire entanglements on the front usually denied cavalry much chance of action, but here special circumstances gave the Indian cavalry a fine opportunity to show its battle skill.

On November 20, 1917, British tanks cut great lanes in enemy wire, infantry broke through across a front four miles wide and, in the wide open spaces so created, the Indian cavalry made a dash for Cambrai – a dramatic though brief advance: the Germans blew up a canal bridge, stalled the attacks and forced the British and Indian troops to fall back. Ten days later, when the British line had been broken by a German counter-attack, the Indian Ambala Brigade – including Hodson's Horse, a unit formed in 1857 during the Indian Mutiny – scattered the Germans in a sharp engagement and subsequently, fighting on foot, took 300 prisoners in an action with the 1st Guards Brigade. For this valuable support, they were presented with a Guards' bugle by the grateful British.

Indian infantry, wearing an early type of gas-mask to protect them from lethal yellow clouds of chlorine gas, stand ready to repel an enemy attack on a forward trench.

Canadian Calvary

Passchendaele, a village lying on a ridge in western Belgium, near Ypres, has a particular place in Canadian memories. During October and November, 1917, 16,000 Canadian troops were killed in the battle to take it and the two surrounding square miles of flooded shell-craters.

For three years, German guns had pounded the Allied trenches there, but on October 9, 1917, a major Anzac-British-French attack began. After a week, four fresh Canadian divisions were brought in to relieve the Anzacs, who had suffered serious casualties. Under heavy fire, these 20,000 men inched their way from shell-crater to shell-crater, and on October 30, with two British divisions, they began the assault on Passchendaele itself. They gained the ruined outskirts of the village during a violent rainstorm and for five days they held on grimly, often waist-deep in mud and exposed to a hail of jagged iron from German shelling. By November 6, when reinforcements arrived, four-fifths of them were dead. Passchendaele had become a Canadian Calvary.

Canadian troops with fixed bayonets leave their trench to charge the enemy near the Belgian town of Menin, during the Flanders offensive of October, 1916. A bullet stops the soldier on the right.

A solitary Canadian officer inspects the flooded Passchendaele battlefield on November 14, 1917, a week after the Canadians had won this ghastly wilderness.

Scottish-Canadian troops in a reserve trench use a pause in operations to clean their Lewis gun at Menin in November, 1917.

FORWARD!
TO VICTORY WITH
THE
245

In Command:
Lt. Col. C.C. Ballantyne.
→ Recruiting Base ←
GRENADIER GUARDS ARMOURY,
ESPLANADE AVENUE, - MONTREAL.

MEN OF Princess Patricia's Canadian
Light Infantry repel a fierce German attack
at St. Eloi, near Ypres, in March, 1915.

Wollen
1915

Australians at the Somme

In the last two years of the war, Australians took part in some of the heaviest fighting on the Western Front, as the Allies inched the Germans back across France and Belgium at extravagant cost in human life.

Their worst experiences came on the Somme sector of the front in 1916. Unending rain flooded the battlefield, trenches oozed yellow, waist-high mud and the front line was cut off from the rear by swamps and lagoons. On November 5, the Australians together with the British and their fellow New Zealanders in 1st Anzac Corps, attacked the town of Bapaume, 76 miles north-east of Paris. It was the appalling weather as much as enemy action which cost them heavy casualties. Supply lorries foundered, so that the guns had no shells. As the troops slithered and fell through a sea of mud, many found their rifles and machine-guns clogged and became easy prey to enemy fire. Others drowned in flooded shell-craters. The attack came to a halt, and after the costly failure of a further attack a week later, the Australian survivors were left to endure a long, bitter winter in the shattered battlefield.

An Australian soldier sleeps in a buttressed front-line trench in June, 1916, with a caged canary beside him. The birds died at the first trace of poison gas and thus warned the troops to don their gas-masks.

Australian machine-gunners fire at enemy aircraft during Anzac attacks in the Somme sector in May, 1917. An officer with binoculars watches the aircraft for hits.

Australian troops take cover on November 6, 1917, in shattered terrain 70 miles north of the River Somme where they joined the battle for Passchendaele, taken by Canadians that day.

Australian signallers pass up a communication trench to lay field telephones on a southern sector of the front in May, 1917, while advancing cavalry cross above them.

New Zealand Makes History

The New Zealanders, including native Maoris whose submission to white civilization had begun barely 100 years before, made a forceful impact on the Western Front. On their first day's fighting – September 15, 1916 – they took part in the world's first tank action. Joining an attack made by the British 4th Army in the Somme battle area, they advanced with the great steel monsters lumbering beside them. When they were held up by wire and machine-gun fire at the second line of enemy trenches, two tanks broke through and knocked out the guns. The New Zealanders went in with bayonets and seized the objective, laughing as the Germans fell back in consternation before the rumbling armour.

ONWARD!

A butcher of the Maori Pioneer Battalion prepares the meat ration near Fricourt, on the Somme, in September, 1916. These Pioneers were famed for their doggedness.

Horse transport of the New Zealand Division's supply column, including a pet donkey, advances up the Albert–Amiens road in September, 1916, while enemy shells scream overhead.

New Zealanders rest beside their loaded lorries while advancing to hold a sector of the Somme battlefield in September, 1916.

New Zealanders receive their rum ration in May, 1916, at Fleurbaix in northern France, a quiet part of the line.

South Africans' Sacrifice

South African troops fought on the Western Front from the early part of the war, but they made their most significant contribution in its last year, during the German spring offensive of 1918. On March 21 the Germans launched a mass attack with 47 divisions and 7,000 guns on a critical part of the British line at Marrières Wood. The British defences were smashed and part of the 5th Army fell back; but its South African Brigade held on grimly until the ammunition ran out, and all but 100 men out of 3,000 were killed or wounded. It was a sacrifice that blunted the enemy advance and saved the tottering British front.

A South African sentry watches wind vanes that signalled the dangers of gas attacks on the Western Front.

II. Birthpangs of Commonwealth

When they left the mother country and established new communities overseas, free-born Englishmen took their rights with them, and it was this simple doctrine that shaped the British Empire from the beginning. Elaborated later under the pressure of events, it ultimately transformed an empire into a commonwealth—an outcome perhaps surprising to the colonists and certainly accepted reluctantly by London. The principle proved irresistible with the march of time, and what had been originally an association of free individuals became an association of free communities.

In the 17th Century the rights Englishmen took with them to the New World were private rights: the rights to English law and to assemblies for their local affairs. These colonial assemblies have been compared to the corporations of the City of London—bodies clearly with rights but clearly also not sovereign. There was no conflict here so long as the Crown rather than Parliament was regarded as the seat of sovereignty. But in the 18th Century sovereignty passed from the Crown to the Crown in Parliament. Parliament claimed an overriding authority to legislate for the colonies just as it did for any chartered institution in Great Britain. This claim led to the American Revolution: the American colonies were willing to recognize the sovereignty of the King, but they were not prepared to recognize the sovereignty of Parliament.

Although the American colonies were lost, the doctrine of Parliamentary sovereignty was not abandoned. It provoked little trouble in the days when Canada was the only remaining colony apart from the West Indies. But in 1837 Canada, too, became restless. British statesmen reluctantly accepted the principle of responsible government propounded by Lord Durham, surrendering the conduct of domestic affairs to a colonial government responsible to its legislature rather than subordinate to the Colonial Office. This concession was made first to Canada and then to the other British communities growing up overseas: Australia, New Zealand, South Africa. The change took place without

any legislative enactment. It was merely a change of practice on the part of the Colonial Office, and was meant to apply only to domestic affairs. As seen by the outer world the British Empire remained a united structure, its policy determined solely by the British Cabinet and its defence provided solely by the British taxpayer.

Another concession soon followed. The colonies claimed the right to impose duties on imported goods, even if they came from Great Britain. The British government was taken aback. It protested, then acquiesced. The economic unity of the Empire was dissolved.

At the end of the 19th Century Joseph Chamberlain attempted to restore it. He proposed an imperial customs union that would lay down a single economic policy for the entire Empire. Underlying this was a mercantilist doctrine outmoded even in the 18th Century: that Great Britain should be the manufacturing centre of the Empire while the colonies should be content to produce foodstuffs and raw materials. The colonies were determined to promote their own industries and to defend their fiscal autonomy. They offered only imperial preference—voluntary concessions on British goods. Chamberlain's ambitious plan was laid aside.

The British government continued to assert exclusive control over foreign affairs. Occasionally a colonial representative was allowed to take part in negotiations when colonial interests were involved, between Canada and the United States, for example, but British diplomats exercised the formal authority. With the approaching threat of a major war, the British government hastened to secure the co-operation of the Dominions, not merely their acquiescence. At the Imperial Conference of 1911 the Dominion representatives heard a disquisition on foreign policy from Sir Edward Grey, the Foreign Secretary, and were invited to contribute to the Royal Navy and to pool their military resources.

The Dominions would agree only to co-operation without any formal system. Some made voluntary contributions to the navy. All of them agreed to work for uniformity in naval and

military equipment. But they refused to surrender a scrap of their independent authority. There was to be no imperial army or navy. The Committee of Imperial Defence might advise; it could not control. At the same time, the Dominions refused to "encroach" on British independence and insisted that foreign policy remain a purely British affair.

Hence in August, 1914, the British government declared war on Germany without seeking the agreement of the Dominions or even consulting them. Each Governor-General proclaimed a state of war on the instructions of the Colonial Office. In Canada the Dominion parliament subsequently expressed its approval. The other Dominions accepted without debate the principle: "When Great Britain is at war, we are at war." In practice they were at war as independent communities.

The naval forces of Canada, Australia, and New Zealand were placed under the direction of the British Admiralty for the duration, but only for the duration. The Dominion land forces remained independent, though usually coming under a British commander-in-chief when serving in the field. The commanding general of the Canadian army corps in France was a British officer, furnished by the British government at Canadian request; but when he fell out with his subordinates, Douglas Haig removed him, again at Canadian request, and appointed another who met with Canadian approval. In this transaction Ottawa ignored the Colonial Office and negotiated directly with Haig by means of its own military representative. Australian and New Zealand forces served similarly under British command at Gallipoli and later in Mesopotamia and Palestine. Before the war ended the Australians in France had their own commander, Sir John Monash, probably the ablest general the war produced. In East Africa it was the other way round, with imperial forces serving under the South African Smuts.

There were other signs of Dominion independence. The emergency measures of Parliament were carefully drawn so that they did not apply to

Imperial statesmen of World War I bespeak unity in James Guthrie's canvas. Prime Minister Asquith sits at right; his successor, Lloyd George, sits third from left. Arthur Balfour discourses. Full-face at centre is Churchill; close behind him is Canada's Borden.

the Dominions, and when the British government attempted to requisition Canadian ships, Canadian Prime Minister Robert Borden reminded them that, while this might be legal, it was not in accordance with evolving constitutional practice. The ships were not requisitioned.

Despite the co-operation there was no co-ordination of military policy. The Dominion governments sometimes complained over the conduct of operations—as Australia and New Zealand complained over Gallipoli—but they had no share in determining what these operations should be. In 1915 Borden was invited to attend meetings of the Cabinet when he visited England, but this was a gesture without real significance.

There was a dramatic transformation when David Lloyd George became Prime Minister at the end of 1916. He was convinced that the war would be lost unless the military effort of the Allies and of the Empire was brought under a single direction. With the Allies he aspired to establish a Supreme War Council, with the Dominions he sought an Imperial War Cabinet.

The Supreme War Council of the Allies was not formed until November, 1917, and did not become effective until the following year. The Imperial War Cabinet was easier to establish. Lloyd George had already replaced the traditional Cabinet with a War Cabinet of five men, mostly without departmental responsibilities, who exercised supreme power at his invitation. He had only to invite the Dominion prime ministers also and the Imperial War Cabinet was in existence. There was one startling newcomer. Hitherto co-operation had been only with the self-governing Dominions, for it was assumed that they, with their background of British traditions, were alone equipped for the tasks at hand. Now an Indian representative appeared. With India making such a large contribution to the war effort, it was impossible to ignore her. It is true that the Indian representative was merely the Secretary of State for India, a British Cabinet minister; but the fact remained that the admission of India was an advance

South Africa's Smuts (left) and Canada's Borden championed Dominion independence.

payment on account, anticipating a time when India, too, would achieve responsible government. Here was the decisive acknowledgement, however delayed in application, that the Commonwealth would not ultimately be limited to people of British stock.

The Imperial War Cabinet met in March, 1917. Lloyd George claimed that an imperial executive had come into existence. The Dominions were not caught so easily. Borden was a determined protagonist of Canadian independence and he had defended that independence against the United States; he would defend it equally against the imperial government. Smuts seconded him. Although his people had lost the Boer War, Smuts was determined that they should secure virtual independence.

Borden insisted that the essence of cabinet government was responsible government. If Lloyd George chose to bring in Dominion prime ministers as additional members that was his affair, but they were responsible solely to their own parliaments—as the British War Cabinet was responsible to the Parliament at Westminster—and nothing the Imperial War Cabinet decided could be allowed to infringe this responsibility. In Borden's view they were simply a group of friends meeting for discussion, not an execu-

tive. Far from strengthening the authority of London over the Empire, the Imperial War Cabinet seemed to assert the authority of the Dominions over London. The Dominions claimed "an adequate voice in foreign policy and foreign relations" and demanded effective arrangements for continuous consultation on all important matters. Thus London, not the Dominions, was forfeiting autonomy. At the time the dispute did not come into the open. All agreed that the war must be won, and the Dominion prime ministers were ready to second Lloyd George in winning it.

The Dominions certainly expected to be consulted before hostilities were concluded. No such consultation took place. Lloyd George claimed that there was no time, though he managed to consult Greece and Portugal. The Dominions were committed, whether they liked it or not, to the Armistice and to the acceptance, with certain reservations, of Wilson's Fourteen Points as the basis of the peace treaty. Subsequently they insisted on independent representation at the peace conference. The War Cabinet had planned a British Empire delegation of five—four Cabinet members and one Dominion Prime Minister. The Dominions answered that they had made greater sacrifices than any but the major contestants and greater than the United States. The result was a curious compromise that must have baffled foreigners. The British Empire delegation survived, but in addition Australia, Canada, India, and South Africa received two delegates apiece, and New Zealand one.

This would have given the British Empire 14 votes if the peace conference had ever decided anything by voting. In the outcome it did not. Lloyd George, Clemenceau, and Wilson decided every important question at private meetings and the other powers merely acquiesced. Even so, the Dominions played some part. Smuts and Borden became chairmen of committees that settled minor questions, and Smuts acted as the delegate of the Big Three in their abortive negotiations with Bolshevik Hungary. Moreover, the Dominions secured mandates in their own names and became independent members of the League of Nations.

The British Empire thus came out of the First World War with its greatness apparently much enhanced. It had been the chief of the victorious powers. A new Empire, disguised as mandates, came into existence from Egypt to India. Against this, the Dominions had acquired a degree of independence and international recognition that would have been inconceivable before 1914. There were further sources of imperial weakness. India had been promised responsible government in some remote future. But when the National Congress party, led by Gandhi, demanded fulfilment of this promise, the imperial government answered with repression, and the massacre at Amritsar in 1919 set an indelible river of blood between the Indian people and their rulers.

The Dominions did not care much about India, but they were deeply involved over Ireland. Irishmen were active in Australian politics; they were an important element of the Canadian population; and the Boers of South Africa saw a close parallel between the Irish position and their own. Yet in the immediate post-war years the British government resisted Irish claims to independence by violent means.

At the end of the war the Irish set up their own parliament and proclaimed a republic. The British relied on their military garrison and, when this proved inadequate, brought in reinforcements of irregular troops who instituted rule by terror. Civil war raged. Lloyd George and his government insisted that Ireland was a purely domestic question: though willing to grant Home Rule, it must remain within the United Kingdom. The Dominions could not see why the position granted them could not be granted the Irish as well. At bottom they regarded Ireland as a distinct nation like themselves rather than an integral part of the U. K.

By 1921 Irish affairs had reached deadlock. The Irish could not expel the British; the British could not subdue the Irish. An Imperial Conference again met in London, and Smuts, now South Africa's Prime Minister, became the agent for conciliation. Having himself accepted Dominion status for South Africa instead of fighting a war of independence, he was the tame elephant who would lure the wild Irish elephants into the Commonwealth corral. Smuts assured Eamon de Valera, head of the Irish Republic, that Dominion status was actually preferable to independence: while it gave the Dominions complete control over their own affairs, it compelled the imperial government to serve Dominion interests, giving all the advantages, without the burdens, of greatness. De Valera was not convinced, but he agreed to negotiate. He left the actual negotiations to other Irish leaders, Arthur Griffith and Michael Collins, and they were won over by the mixture of conciliation and threats that Lloyd George offered.

In December, 1921, a treaty ended the conflict between Great Britain and the Irish rebels. Twenty-six counties of southern Ireland became the Irish Free State. There was still an oath of loyalty to the King and Britain kept control of three Irish ports; otherwise the Irish Free State received Dominion status in the same measure as Canada. Underlying this was a basic difference, however. Canada, having received virtual independence, now wished to preserve the Commonwealth. The

Splitting the Emerald Isle

The first attempt to set up a revolutionary republic in southern Ireland, the Easter Rising of 1916, was quickly suppressed by Britain. The second was more serious. Led by the most extreme republicans in Sinn Fein ("Ourselves Alone"), its military arm was the Irish Volunteer Force, forerunner of the I.R.A. Commanded by Michael Collins and armed with stolen or smuggled rifles, this citizen army launched a guerrilla war against the Royal Irish Constabulary in early 1919.

Britain reacted by adding two para-military wings to the Constabulary: the "Black and Tans," who wore khaki with black police caps and belts, and the similarly dressed Auxiliary Division, the "Auxis." Rebel outrages and the undisciplined reprisals of these Crown irregulars fed upon each other and plunged Ireland into anarchy.

In Britain voices from the Left and the churches demanded any settlement to end the war. In July, 1921, a truce was declared, and five months of peace negotiations began.

In the early hours of December 6, 1921, a treaty was signed creating the Irish Free State and ending the most fratricidal guerrilla war ever fought in the Empire.

"Peace for Ireland," exclaimed the newspapers; "Vision of a free and happy Ireland." It was an illusion. Britain had stopped the fighting and saved the prestige of Empire for the time being. For the future, she had stored up a conflict that would still torment her a half-century later when the Empire was only a memory.

Above: A great crowd packs College Green in Dublin in March, 1922, to hear Michael Collins (on the speakers' stand) proclaim the Irish Free State. Eamon de Valera (right) led the die-hard Irish republicans in refusing to accept the treaty settlement with Britain, and soon southern Ireland was rent by civil war. Below, a Free State soldier takes aim at the headquarters of I.R.A. Irregulars in Dublin in June, 1922.

Irish had had Dominion status forced on them, and many still meant to shake it off.

At the time it seemed that the Commonwealth was actually growing stronger. When the Imperial Conference met in 1921, Lloyd George announced that an Imperial Cabinet had come into existence. The Dominion prime ministers were less enthusiastic. Smuts said that the meeting was "no Cabinet. . . . It has no executive functions . . . merely a consultative body." The result, as often happened with Lloyd George, was equivocal. It was agreed that the Imperial Cabinet should meet again. In fact it never did. It was agreed that there should be a single foreign policy conducted by the British government and that the means of communication and discussion with the Dominions should be improved. No improvements were made, and the Dominions therefore quietly forgot their acceptance of a single foreign policy.

Events further weakened imperial ties. In a crisis in Turkey in 1922, Britain acted first and sought Dominion help later. All the Dominions, particularly Canada, were indignant at having been kept in the dark. They were no longer willing to accept a British foreign policy blindfolded, and they faced, however reluctantly, a situation where Great Britain could be at war while some of the Dominions held aloof. Imperial unity was shattered.

This was evident at the Imperial Conference of 1923. No attempt was made to provide the consultation promised in 1921 and then so conspicuously neglected. No suggestion was made for regular meetings in the future. The Imperial Cabinet was not merely buried; it was implied that no such idea had ever existed. Moreover the Dominions insisted that, just as Great Britain could make international agreements without consulting them, they could do the same without consulting her, thus taking a further step towards complete independence in the international field. The Dominions also expressed approval of imperial preference, by which they meant that Great Britain should tax foodstuffs imported from non-Empire countries in exchange for the Dominions' prom-ise not to increase their taxes on British manufactured goods while raising them against everyone else. This was not an attractive bargain for Britain. It carried with it the dreaded shadow of "stomach taxes," which the electorate had repeatedly rejected, and London passed over the offer in silence.

Imperial relations were now thoroughly in a muddle. It was clear that the Dominions were no longer prepared to accept rule from London even in international affairs. Yet no one had thought of an alternative. Indeed the British government went on behaving in the old fashion, apparently hoping no one would notice. In 1924 the Labour government recognized Soviet Russia without warning the Dominions and then, despite their protests, went on to arrange an international conference on German reparations without providing for their participation. London explained that it had forgotten Dominion claims to independent representation until too late.

Ultimately Britain drew a moral from these developments. In 1925 she took the lead in promoting the conciliation of Germany, and the Treaty of Locarno included a guarantee by Britain and Italy of the Franco-German frontier. The Dominions were not invited to the conference which preceded the treaty and they were not told what was going on until the conference was concluded. Then they received surprising news: the guarantee was given solely by Great Britain. The Dominions were not involved. Where previously they had asserted their independence of London, London now apparently asserted its independence of them. Here certainly was the end of Empire. If the terms of Locarno really meant what they said, Britain was not merely admitting that the Dominions might remain neutral in a future war, it was assuming that this would happen.

The Dominions could not believe it. They thought it must be some subtle trap, and expected trouble. But there was no trouble. The British government had abandoned any idea of imposing its authority on the Dominions. British statesmen, themselves bewildered, were anxious to remove Dominion grievances and make the situation clear. In 1926 the elderly Arthur Balfour produced a miraculous formula. It defined the members of the Commonwealth as autonomous communities within the British Empire, equal in status, in no way subordinate to one another in any aspect of their domestic or external affairs, united by a common allegiance to the Crown, and freely associated as members of the British Commonwealth of Nations.

Of course this definition had been true in practice for a long time, but neither the Dominions nor London had realized it. Balfour, by putting it on paper, removed the corpse of Empire and substituted a living Commonwealth.

In the course of the next few years there was much tidying up of the constitutional system in order to confirm the definition of 1926. The Governor-General of a Dominion ceased to be the agent of the imperial government and became a constitutional figurehead. Relations between London and the Dominions were now conducted by high commissioners, who were ambassadors under another name. The Dominions gained complete freedom of action in international affairs, negotiating with foreign countries and concluding treaties almost as though the Commonwealth did not exist. In 1931, by the Statute of Westminster, Parliament formally renounced its shadowy right to legislate for the Dominions and acknowledged their right to change their constitutions, regardless of former imperial restrictions.

What remained of the Commonwealth? In appearance almost nothing except for the common allegiance to the Crown, and even that was not much more than a form of words. Outwardly, the Commonwealth seemed to be a slightly more intimate League of Nations, the members of which were on friendly terms and extremely unlikely to go to war with each other.

Under the surface, however, there was a good deal more to the Commonwealth than legalistic phrases. It was still unmistakably British. All the Dominions had a political and legal system derived from Great Britain's, and all had the ideas of civil liberty that went along with these principles. In all of them English was still the prevailing language and the social system was British, except for the lack of an aristocracy. They were all nominally Christian and predominantly Protestant. An Englishman would feel more at home in a Dominion than anywhere else; a man from any Dominion would feel more at home in England than anywhere else.

But even this underlying unity of sentiment began to change in the years following the Statute of Westminster. In the earlier period of conflict the Dominions had displayed a nationality that was in effect a new expression of their British character. Now nationality in the older sense raised its head. This was clearest with Ireland.

The Irish no longer accepted the idea of a common British nationality, whatever they may have done in the past. Coached by de Valera, who held power throughout the 1930s, the Irish firmly regarded Great Britain as a foreign country. De Valera used the new freedom bestowed by the Statute of Westminster to get rid of the 1921 Anglo-Irish treaty, change the constitution, and transform the Irish Free State into Eire, a virtually independent country. The Governor-General disappeared. The oath of loyalty to the King disappeared, and in 1936 de Valera used the opportunity of the Abdication crisis to eliminate all mention of the British Crown except as an anonymous "organ" for international relations. In an effort to appease de Valera, London surrendered control of the three Irish ports it had kept under the 1921 treaty. Ireland had the legal appearance of a foreign country.

There were nationalist conflicts elsewhere. The French of Quebec were increasingly vocal against English superiority, and there was a persistent attempt to reduce the British character of Canada. But since the French were equally distrustful of American predominance, they did not turn openly against the Commonwealth; this national question remained a domestic affair. It was otherwise in South Africa, where the Boers worked relentlessly to establish the superiority they had failed to win in the Anglo-Boer War. The British there

were transformed into a tolerated minority and compelled to go along with the Boers. South Africa lost much of its British character, particularly when it adopted the Boer principle of treating the coloured inhabitants as an inferior race. South Africa's separation from the Commonwealth became only a matter of time.

The British Empire and the Commonwealth after it were legal structures. They were also economic organizations, at first for the advantage of Great Britain, later as a partnership for common benefit. Canada could stand on her own feet, drawing the capital for her economic advance largely from her own resources. Australia and New Zealand were financed from London on favourable terms and derived much of their prosperity from supplying Great Britain with foodstuffs and raw materials. The association could grow no closer as long as Great Britain stuck to free trade. But suppose Great Britain abandoned free trade and turned the Commonwealth into a closed economic area?

This was the purpose of the so-called Empire Crusade which Lord Beaverbrook launched in 1930. Its slogan was "Empire Free Trade." Great Britain was to impose duties on foreign foodstuffs for the benefit of the Dominions, and they would repay her by opening their doors to her manufactures. This programme was out-of-date even when Joseph Chamberlain had first proposed it; it certainly ran against insuperable obstacles in 1930. The British people were still against stomach taxes and the Dominions were unwilling to endanger the development of their own industries; nor indeed was Great Britain capable of becoming the workshop of the Dominions.

Yet Beaverbrook's Empire Crusade, though unsuccessful, left its mark. The Dominions were quite willing to accept favourable terms for the import of their foodstuffs into Great Britain, especially as the great depression of 1929–33 was striking hardest at the primary producers. The Imperial Conference of 1930 expressed a strong desire for imperial preference, though London did not respond.

But in 1931 the depression struck

Great Britain also. London was forced to abandon the gold standard, and this strengthened the Commonwealth, for Australia, New Zealand, and Ireland joined the sterling area. Moreover, the economic crisis destroyed Britain's traditional allegiance to free trade. In 1932 she adopted protective tariffs. Joseph Chamberlain's son, Neville, was the agent of this change and so far forgot the legacy of his imperialist father that he even intended to impose duties on Commonwealth goods. An urgent plea from Ottawa caused him to relent and Commonwealth goods were temporarily exempted. Instead there was to be a gallant attempt to resurrect the economic unity of the Empire.

The result was a Commonwealth meeting at Ottawa in the summer of 1932. This was the only Imperial Conference ever held outside London—a striking gesture of imperial sentiment. The great gathering was a failure, the end of a dream. The Dominions were as much concerned to protect their industries as to benefit their farmers. The British ministers were still frightened of stomach taxes. In the end there was no economic charter of Empire, only 12 individual agreements over details of preference between Great Britain and the Dominions and between the Dominions themselves.

All the same, Ottawa had some effect. Tariffs and preferences helped to shift British trade away from foreign countries to the Dominions. And the dependent colonies were brought within the imperial system. Hitherto Great Britain had claimed to administer these colonies as a sacred trust; now she treated them as an undeveloped estate. They were "invited" to give preferences to British goods and had no choice but to do so. The result was exactly as it had been with the original British Empire of the 18th Century: colonies accepted British suzerainty when it brought them security and good government, but they grew restless when it made the goods in their shops more expensive. The closed economic system which London imposed provoked an answering demand for colonial freedom.

Economically, the immediate benefit went to Great Britain. Between 1931 and 1937 British imports from the Dominions, India, and the dependent colonies increased from 24 per cent to 37 per cent of her total overseas trade, and her exports to them increased from 32 to 39 per cent of the total. There were benefits overseas as well, but there was also more discontent. Great Britain was in fact no longer powerful enough and advanced enough economically to make the imperial partnership a reality, and the strains of a new war would complete its dissolution.

The one remaining element of Empire was security. This was the ultimate benefit Britain had bestowed on her colonies and Dominions throughout the 19th Century. The Royal Navy had ruled the waves, solely at the expense of the British taxpayer, and he still bore most of the burden.

Canada was wealthy enough to provide for her own defence and in any case could assume that any threat to the New World would be resisted by the might of the United States. Australia and New Zealand, on the other hand, still counted on British protection, particularly against Japan, and looked confidently to the great base at Singapore as the lynchpin of imperial defence in the Far East. South Africa felt in no danger except perhaps from her own coloured people, and tolerated the British naval base at Simonstown mainly as a further guarantee of Boer independence. Eire was the strangest case. She was a small country, unable to defend herself against any resolute aggressor. De Valera accepted the protection of the Royal Navy, yet asserted Eire's neutrality as firmly against Great Britain as against any other power.

As the international scene grew darker in the late 1930s, Great Britain alone seemed to be in trouble, and the Dominions would have liked to hold aloof. The Imperial Conference of 1937—the last of the old sort ever held—insisted that Germany's march to European hegemony was a purely Continental affair and that Britain should keep out of the quarrel. New Zealand and Australia had their own anxiety over Japan, and this made them especially emphatic for British detachment from Europe. Prompting from the Dominions contributed largely to the policy of appeasement towards Germany that Neville Chamberlain followed, and the Munich Agreement was welcomed enthusiastically by the Dominions. If war had broken out in 1938, Eire and South Africa certainly, and Canada probably, would have remained neutral; Australia and New Zealand would have followed Great Britain with reluctance.

Astonishingly, a year later an almost united Commonwealth went to war. Eire remained neutral and South Africa declared war only after a change of government, but the other Dominions entered the war without hesitation or equivocation. All the assertions about Dominion independence, all the reservations about their not being committed by British obligations, were swept aside. Great Britain and her Dominions were the only Allied countries that went through both world wars from first to last. Despite all the constitutional changes, public opinion in the Dominions responded to the call of British sentiment. Their peoples did not stop to ask whether they themselves were in danger; they did not contemplate for one moment the policy of benevolent neutrality which the United States followed until forced into war by attack from Japan. The Dominions acknowledged their solidarity with Great Britain and recognized, even more strongly than in 1914, that the mother country was defending the principles of freedom and toleration in which they themselves believed.

Britain and the Dominions fought the Second World War with unparalleled mutual generosity. Posterity may wonder that this generally unselfish partnership, so marvellously displayed in wartime, was after the war so casually and completely dispelled. The words Churchill addressed to the British people on June 18, 1940, applied with equal force to the peoples of the Commonwealth: "If the British Empire and its Commonwealth last for a thousand years, men will still say, This was their finest hour.'" The British Commonwealth is gone. The memory of its last achievement will endure forever.

—*A. J. P. Taylor*

III. The Threatened Raj

On June 22, 1897, all across India the British were celebrating Queen Victoria's Diamond Jubilee with military parades, dances, and champagne dinners. At Poona, the summer seat of the Governor of Bombay, the festivities were particularly glittering, climaxed by a dinner party at Government House. As the guests left in their carriages, they were startled by the sound of firing. A woman's screams brought guests and guards to two of the carriages. Lieutenant Walter Rand lay dying in one of them; in the other his aide Charles Ayerst was dead.

The authorities reacted with surprise, then angry panic. Was the murder of Englishmen a signal for a popular uprising? The area was indeed in turmoil. A serious famine in western India had been followed by the outbreak of bubonic plague. Doctors knew no treatment for this scourge, and in Bombay alone 20,000 people died. In Poona the plague officer was the martinet Walter Rand, who adopted brutal methods to prevent the spread of the disease. British troops destroyed property believed contaminated, and men, women, and children from supposedly infected areas were segregated in special plague camps. The troops were not gentle. They damaged religious shrines, looted, and often sent to the camps people who were in fact free of infection. To the inhabitants of Poona, Rand appeared to be carrying out a reign of terror.

Their answer was assassination. Terrorism had appeared on the Indian political scene.

As the 19th Century moved to its close, Indian nationalism was on the rise. The reluctance of the government to share its powers with educated Indians and the unquestioning belief by the British in their racial superiority pushed the middle classes into political action. It also split them into two camps.

One camp, clustered round the Indian National Congress founded in 1885, clung to its belief in British institutions, in liberal democracy, in law and justice. Members of the Congress had no desire for independence. On the contrary, they believed that the British had brought many blessings to India, and that being part of the Empire was not only a gift of Providence but good fortune as well. The leader of the Congress, Gopal Krishna Gokhale, typified middle-class Indians of this persuasion. He had many friends among the British and had visited England. He believed that the inequalities and inadequacies of Hindu society were the only reason for India's political subordination to her foreign rulers. He wanted India to progress gradually in partnership with "the genius of the British people."

But there were others of similar background who did not share this faith and hope and innocence. Most of them were also Western-educated, but this had brought them only unease and unemployment. In British India there were only a limited number of outlets for the educated. The unemployed found themselves without a place in Westernized society or in that society from which their education had cut them off. Had they become bastard Englishmen? To these educated unemployed, the appeal of a revived Hindu religious nationalism offered a refuge, a chance of identity with something greater than themselves.

It was the province of Bombay that this looking backwards in order to see the shape of the future first took the form of positive political action. The man who gave it that form was Bal Gangadhar Tilak. The British, Tilak was convinced, would never give India its freedom, and any political power they granted would only be to those most in sympathy with their rule. This would simply mean exchanging one set of alien rulers for a partnership of two. Tilak turned to the organization of grass-roots action, quickly assuming leadership of the Hindu masses in western India. The British did not fear the moderates of the National Congress, but they had every reason to fear a popular uprising—and was not assassination a weapon of revolution? Tilak was arrested.

When the police could find no connection between Tilak and the murders at Poona, he was charged with sedition, convicted, and sentenced to 18 months' imprisonment. The news of the sentence spread his fame—and his ideas. Young activists began to think that their future lay in manipulation of the masses and the use of violence. The moderates, with their obsequious flattery of alien ideas and their feeble requests for a slice of the cake, had failed them.

As yet, however, this remained a localized feeling. Elsewhere in India the Raj seemed as immutable—and as beneficent—as ever. Tilak had worked only in Bombay, his success fertilized by local fears and feelings. In Bengal there was a sense of unease but no focus for protest. In the Punjab there were mutterings but no one to give them shape. As for the British, despite momentary panic they did not feel that their rule was really menaced.

The impatient young men of India, organizing themselves into secret societies, reading about European revolutionary terrorism, had to wait eight years for an event that would make them the spearhead of mass protest. The British supplied it in 1905 with the high-handed decision to divide the province of Bengal. The province was proving too large to be administered as a single unit; it was to be split into Hindu and Muslim halves.

Here was tinder to spark the flame of Hindu nationalism: not only was the unity of the motherland threatened but so were the economic privileges of the Bengali Hindus who dominated the professional and business life of the entire province. Violent agitators stressed the helplessness of Indians before the arbitrary decisions of the British. Two weapons of protest emerged—an economic boycott of British goods, and terrorist bombs.

Violence spread throughout Bengal. New secret societies were formed and bomb "factories" set up. The government assumed special security powers. Leaders were deported without trial, political organizations were declared illegal, many arrests were made and sentences of flogging imposed. In 1907, the 50th anniversary year of the Mutiny, two attempts were made on the life of Sir Andrew Fraser, Lieutenant-Governor of Bengal. A magistrate was assassinated. In 1908 two Englishwomen aboard a train were killed when a bomb intended for a magistrate was planted by mistake in their compartment. In reprisal, newspapers hitherto free were prosecuted for sedition, many people were deported without trial, and public meetings were severely restricted.

These methods appeared to work. An attempt by young activists to capture the leadership of the Congress party failed. The extremists, out of the party, suffered two further setbacks: in 1908 they lost their leader, Tilak, sentenced to eight years' imprisonment for inflammatory comments on the murder of the two Englishwomen; and in 1911, when the partition of Bengal was revoked, they lost that source of popular discontent.

The government sought to assist the moderates by doling out a measure of reform. This was the work of the Viceroy, Lord Minto, and the cautious Secretary of State for India, John Morley. The believed that small concessions would encourage those Indians who were loyal to Britain and help insure that India's future would remain firmly in British hands. The moderates welcomed these reforms because, they said, the *next* lot could only move further towards responsible government. The reforms were also well received by the Muslim minority, concerned by the growing strength of Hindu nationalism.

The uneasy alliance between the National Congress and the Raj lasted well into the First World War. The war initially produced an outburst of enthusiasm in India that in the light of subsequent events seems almost incomprehensible. Over a million men volunteered for the armed forces, messages of support came in from every level of Indian life, and there were large cash contributions to war loans. The British were agreeably surprised and leapt to the conclusion that their fears of violence and terrorism had been exaggerated. Politicians seemed ready to see Indian nationalism in a new light. "It is clear," the Under-Secretary of State for India told the House of Commons, "that India claims to be not a mere dependent but a partner in the Empire, and her partnership with us in spirit and on battlefields cannot but alter the angle from which we shall henceforward look at the problems of the government of India."

But as the war lengthened and the battles dragged on, Indians noted that the tone of statements about India in Parliament became more and more restrained. The extremists again emerged to voice popular aspirations, and Tilak (now released from prison) and his followers were readmitted to the Congress in 1916. Indian Muslims, too, alienated by the fact that their spiritual overlord, the Caliph of Turkey, was at war with their temporal master, the King of England, were no longer so pro-British. Their organization, the Muslim League, established ties with the Congress party, and Britain was once again faced with a united Indian opposition.

London, worried by the course of the war in Europe and the confusion that might result on the North-West Frontier if its ally, Tsarist Russia, collapsed, began to fear trouble in India. There could be no question of repression for there were just not enough British troops available. Instead, bribery seemed to be called for: the announcement of further reforms.

But conditions in India and the world had changed radically since the reforms of 1909, and both Muslims and Hindus were not so ready to accept bounty meekly from their overlords. In 1919 subject peoples all over the world were looking for the right to determine their own futures, free from interference by the major powers, and Indians were no exception.

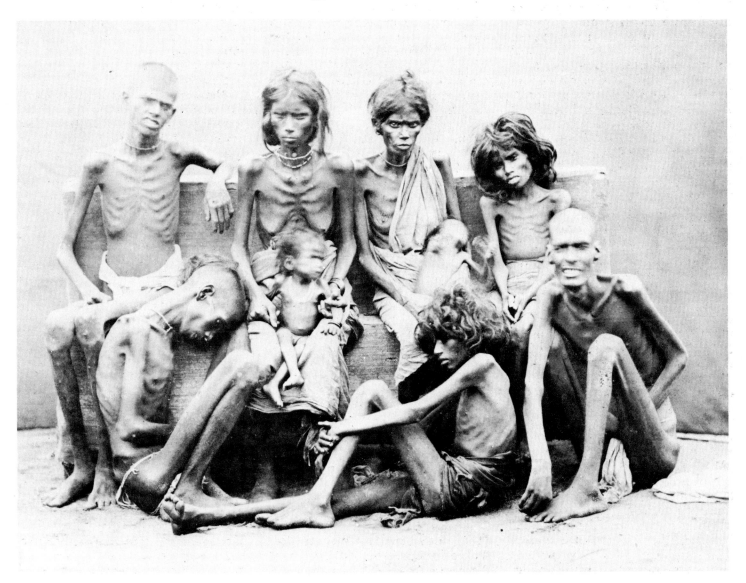

The severe famine of 1896–97, the worst of the century, was followed by bubonic plague, creating great social turmoil in India.

The British proceeded to dissipate their remaining good will by one of the more unimaginative and ill-timed moves in their long history of rule in the subcontinent. At the same time as the Secretary of State for India, Edwin Montagu, arrived to talk with Indian leaders and the Viceroy, Lord Chelmsford, about the reforms, a committee under Mr. Justice Rowlatt was sitting to "investigate and report on the nature and extent of the criminal conspiracies connected with the revolutionary movement in India" and to advise measures "necessary to enable Government to deal with them." The existence of the Rowlatt Committee guaranteed that Indian nationalists would be suspicious of any proposed reforms.

These new reforms—the Montagu-Chelmsford Reforms—were in fact quite radical, even by the changed standards of the time. The British government not only accepted the principle of self-government for India but actually prepared for it. Some government departments were to be handed over to elected Indian ministers. The electoral rolls were to be considerably enlarged. There was also a promise that the working of the reforms would be examined after ten years when, it was implied, the next stage forward would be decided upon.

Indian nationalists were on the whole ready to give the reforms a try. In Britain, except for a few right-wing diehards, all parties supported the programme. Politicians welcomed the expressions of loyalty which flowed from the Congress. Even the demands for a declaration of the rights of the Indian people used the words "as British citizens" and "Indian subjects of His Majesty"; if this was opposition, it was surely a "loyal" one. All seemed set for a new honeymoon in Indo-British relations.

But almost simultaneously with the announcement of the reforms early in 1919 (they would come into force three years hence) the Rowlatt Committee was heard from. Two bills incorporating its security recommendations were introduced in Delhi. These harsh measures placed unlimited power in the hands of the executive and police to decide who was conspiring against the government and called for the rapid trial of the accused, who was denied counsel, a jury, or an appeal. To Indian nationalists it was plain that while Westminster might be giving up some of its powers to Indians, the government in Delhi was taking them away. This was the turning point in the growth of nationalistic fervour in India. In an atmosphere of tension and indignation that united the political classes and the people as never before, a new leader sprang up who was to become to all the world the symbol of India—Mohandas Karamchand Gandhi.

A 49-year-old lawyer, Gandhi had only recently returned from South Africa, where he had spent almost the whole of his adult life. There he had made his name as the leader of the Indian community in its fight against discrimination by the South African government, using his own method of protest he called *satyagraha,* or "soul force." At first sight it seemed no more than passive resistance, but in fact it was something much more positive. To draw suffering on oneself and thus shame one's opponent into a change of heart, to die—but not to kill—for the truth: this was the essence of *satyagraha.*

When Gandhi returned to India in 1915 he spent a year or two travelling to find out what the people thought. His views had always been those of the moderates, and no one really considered him as either the spokesman or potential leader of Indian nationalism. He was a supporter of the British and had even taken part in recruiting campaigns for the Indian Army. But he became convinced by experiments in passive resistance in India that there was a place for his kind of moral and non-violent approach to political action.

He was right. Gandhi's moral condemnation of the Rowlatt security laws struck a chord in the hearts of all classes. By using religion he made the political movement widely acceptable. He proposed a traditional Hindu method of protest—the *hartal,* a closing of all shops and places of business as a sign of mourning. All over India people responded to the call, perhaps because it had never been made before. A *hartal* was not just a negative act but a positive rededication of the spirit. But such action needs discipline, and the tensions of the time were too great. In many places the *hartal* led to violent rioting. Horrified, Gandhi tried to call off the strike, but it was like reasoning with a whirlwind. It merely grew more violent, especially in the Punjab.

Tensions there ran particularly high. Thousands of demobilized soldiers had returned with little hope for the future. An influenza epidemic had killed hundreds of thousands in this province alone (throughout India more than 12 million died). The British in the Punjab, who had a long tradition of action first and questions afterwards, believed the *hartal* was a cloak for rebellion and determined to suppress any signs of revolt. The explosion took place on April 13, 1919, in the town of Amritsar.

Amritsar was a holy city, the centre of the faith of the Sikhs, tough farmers and fighting men who had been the last of the great Indian kingdoms to submit to British rule. The causes of the April disturbances were rooted in economic distress, but Bolshevik-inspired sedition seems to have been the chief fear of the government officials. Their overstretched nerves were tautened by rioting on April 10. Following the arrest of two nationalist leaders, banks were attacked and five Europeans murdered. The railway station was set on fire and a woman missionary was beaten and left for dead in the street.

Putting a martinet like Brigadier-General Reginald Dyer in charge of restoring order in Amritsar was almost a guarantee of trouble. Face to face with what he took to be a hostile mob acting in what he assumed was deliberate violation of his orders, Dyer could see only humiliation and ridicule in a withdrawal. He would not face that prospect, and gave the order to shoot. Over 1,600 rounds were fired, by his own admission, and nearly 400 Sikhs died.

Dyer went away thinking that his action had saved the Punjab from anarchy. Two days later he declared martial law. Public floggings were imposed for such offences as "the contravention of the curfew order, failure to salaam to a commissioned officer, for disrespect to a European, or refusal to sell milk."

A few months after the massacre, a young Indian named Jawaharlal Nehru was travelling by the night train from Amritsar to Delhi and overheard some of his fellow passengers talking. "One of them was holding forth in an aggressive and triumphant tone," Nehru recalled, "and I soon discovered he was Dyer, the hero of Jallianwala Bagh, and he was describing his Amritsar experiences. He pointed out how he had the whole town at his mercy and he had felt like reducing the rebellious city to a heap of ashes but he took pity on it and refrained. I was greatly shocked," Nehru added, "to hear his conversation and to observe his callous manner."

So were many others who, like Nehru, had been only lukewarm supporters of the Indian National Congress. Nehru became a close associate of Gandhi. The young Jawaharlal was captivated by the Mahatma ("The Great Soul") and his beliefs. His father, Motilal, a rich and successful lawyer whose politics had gradually been moving to the left, soon joined his beloved son in Gandhi's movement. Foreign journalists dubbed the three "Father, Son, and Holy Ghost."

Political attitudes in the 1920s were polarizing. Though Dyer was dismissed from the army, he arrived in London to a hero's welcome, a large public subscription, and a vote of thanks in the House of Lords. Gandhi, the one-time supporter of the British, condemned any further co-operation "with this satanic government." Instead, there must be open and widespread non-co-operation. He felt he could speak not only to those who had been inflamed by the Amritsar Massacre but to those Muslims who had been shocked by the British treatment of defeated Turkey and its ruler, the Caliph of Islam. However, as Gandhi's reputation grew among the Hindu masses, Muslims began once more to see the spectre of Hindu domination. As some kind of parliamentary system was about to be introduced into India, they feared the

tyranny of the majority would be endorsed by the ballot box.

In 1921 Gandhi, now in control of the Congress party, called a non-co-operation movement, rashly promising freedom for India within a year. The sheer force of his personality persuaded the Muslims to work with the Hindus, but they did so "making it clear that they did so as a policy only and not a creed." As in 1919, Gandhi's plea for non-violence was ignored. The Muslims of Malabar murdered as many Hindu moneylenders as they could before the army arrived. In Bombay, in riots following a demonstration against the arrival of the Prince of Wales, 53 died and 400 were wounded. A village mob murdered 21 policemen. This incident was the last straw for Gandhi, and on February 12, 1922, he called off the non-co-operation movement. He was imprisoned for sedition.

The young men of the Congress party, radical-thinking and anxious for revolution, were frustrated by Gandhi's unwillingness to use his growing power with the masses. After his release from prison in 1924 on grounds of ill health, Gandhi turned away from politics altogether and settled down to campaign for the hand-spinning of cloth to end reliance on foreign cottons. His attitude seemed to be both reactionary and weak.

While the political life of India was stagnating, tensions between the two communities, Hindu and Muslim, were increasing. A pattern of bloody conflict was being established that was to become a regular feature of Indian life. Campaigns of insult and harassment were carried on daily. Self-seeking politicians, whose places depended on divided electorates, incited the two communities to further hate.

In late 1927 *The Times of India* could write of the "completeness of the Congress collapse, the utter futility of the Congress creed, and total absence among Congress supporters of a single political idea." Yet three years later everything had changed once again.

The Conservative government in London, fearing that Labour would

The depth of nationalist sentiment in India was brought home to many Britons in 1921 when leaflets like this triggered the ostracizing of the visiting Prince of Wales.

win the next elections, decided in 1927 to bring forward the review of the 1919 reforms by two years. It sent a commission headed by Sir John Simon and staffed entirely by Englishmen to investigate their workings. Congress suddenly revived and its leaders refused to meet the commission. Realizing Gandhi's importance, the Viceroy, Lord Irwin, opened up negotiations with him—and was condemned by Anglo-Indians for "taking tea with treason." Winston Churchill, spokesman of the diehards, pictured Gandhi as "a seditious Middle Temple lawyer, now posing as a fakir of a type well known in the East, striding half-naked up the steps of the vice-regal palace . . . to parley on equal terms with the representative of the King-Emperor." But Irwin had a better sense of the realities than Churchill, for Gandhi was about to demonstrate anew his control over the Indian masses.

The Labour party did win the elections of 1929, but both Conservative fears and Indian hopes were to be confounded. Despite Labour's support for Indian self-government when out of office, in power it became cautious and its statements vague. Congress leaders decided to demand not self-government but independence. On January 26, 1930, at gatherings all over India, the Congress flag was raised and a declaration of independence was read out.

It was all but a non-event. The government of India took no action. The mass of the people did not understand what it was all about. Something both commonplace and dramatic was needed to activate them; flags and declarations were meaningless.

Gandhi decided upon salt. It was a weird idea, but typical of his immensely astute use of publicity. Everyone in India used salt; in tropical countries men die without it. Salt was a government monopoly. No one was allowed to make his own and in effect every pound bought was a tax paid to the government. Gandhi declared that he would lead a march to the sea and there make illicit salt. He even sent a letter to the Viceroy to tell him what he proposed to do. Irwin, equally courteous, wrote back gently regretting Gandhi's decision to break the law. On March 12, 1930, with 79 followers, the Mahatma set out from his retreat near the town of Ahmedabad.

The 79 soon became a crowd of many thousands. At their head strode the little figure, half naked in the simple clothing of the Indian peasant. In his hand was a large iron-tipped staff. Before him the people threw down green leaves as if he were a conqueror. Gandhi expected to be arrested before he reached the sea—and was taking a roundabout way of getting there in order to give the government time to act. But non-co-operation is a game two can play. The government refused to move, and Gandhi continued unimpeded. Every day brought a rising excitement. News of the march was spreading across India and beyond, for the foreign Press had sent its correspondents and newsreel cameras. The image of a 61-year-old man marching along the dusty roads of India to do battle with the majesty of the British Empire began suddenly to appear more heroic than ridiculous. By the time he arrived at the seashore, after walking 241 miles in 24 days, Gandhi had become a world figure.

After a night of prayer, Gandhi walked into the sea as a ritual act of purification. Then he picked up a lump of natural salt from the beach. That was all. There were no policemen and, except for a woman's cry of "Hail Deliverer!" the anti-climax was complete. But within a week it seemed that all India was making salt. Away from the sea coasts no one was quite sure how to go about it, and the Congress was compelled to issue explanatory leaflets. Nehru recalled that after considerable trouble "we ultimately succeeded in producing some unwholesome stuff." But it did not really matter whether the product was edible or not; it was the act of breaking the law that counted.

If a pinch of salt was enough to inspire enthusiasm, it was not, however, sufficient to maintain it for long. The government continued to ignore Gandhi and the salt-makers.

Two events unconnected with Gandhi changed the government's mind. In Bengal a band of terrorists raided an arsenal and murdered six people. On the other side of India near the North-West Frontier, the city of Peshawar exploded into a violent week-long riot. The government decided it could no longer tolerate defiance of the laws, including the salt law. Gandhi was arrested and detained without trial, and more than 60,000 others joined him in jails and special camps. Sentences were punitive—five years for failing to give information to the police, seven years and a heavy fine for carrying a Congress flag. Nehru got six months for breaking the salt laws.

It was hardly the way to persuade the Congress to join in a so-called Round Table "peace conference" being called in London. The initiative was taken by the Viceroy, who released Gandhi and the other Congress leaders early in 1931. Gandhi, always anxious for a peaceful solution, promised to approach the whole situation with an unbiased mind. "I am hungering for peace," he said, "if it can be had with honour." Together, Gandhi and Irwin worked out a truce. The government would release political prisoners, Congress would call off the

civil disobedience campaign, and Gandhi would attend the conference.

Gandhi turned out to be a poor negotiator. He did not impress English politicians and antagonized the other Indians at the conference by maintaining that they represented only themselves and that the Congress alone spoke for India. When he arrived back in India in December, 1931, having achieved nothing, he found that a new Viceroy had rearrested most of the Congress leaders. "Christmas gifts from Lord Willingdon, our Christian viceroy," he commented bitterly.

Gandhi began another civil disobedience campaign. The Viceroy, fully backed by a new Conservative-dominated government in London, answered with severe repression. Gandhi was arrested once more. There were some isolated acts of terrorism, but

the mass of the people had grown tired of constant disturbances. By the middle of 1932 a sullen peace had descended on the subcontinent. Gandhi had apparently once more lost interest in the freedom struggle, and in prison concerned himself only with the social disabilities of outcaste Hindus. In Britain the Secretary of State for India remarked smugly: "The interest of many Congress leaders has now been diverted from self-government to Mr. Gandhi's campaign against Untouchability."

In London, however, things were moving, though with the characteristic slowness of the British legislative process made even slower by the determination of Winston Churchill and others to hold up new reforms. Finally, in 1935, a new Government of India Act was passed by Parliament. It seemed to contain something for

Gandhi and a few followers set out on the Salt March in 1930. Within a day the procession was swollen to a length of two miles.

In David Low's 1933 cartoon, die-hard imperialist Winston Churchill bawls out "Yah, Untouchable!" to fellow Tory Stanley Baldwin, author of a progressive Indian policy.

everyone, except the most radical Congress activists. Nehru, now publicly acknowledged as Gandhi's political heir, described it as a "new charter of bondage," but for all the criticisms that can be levelled against it, the act was a blueprint for freedom. Dominion status—that is, complete self-government—was clearly stated to be the goal, a federal system that would unite all the diverse political interests was to be the framework, and parliamentary institutions the form of government.

The most important part of the act called for almost complete parliamentary government by elected ministers in the provinces. Muslims, who had been divided amongst themselves for many years, began to find a focus in the Muslim League as reactivated under a new leader, Muhammad Ali Jinnah. They prepared to defend politically the rights of the minority.

When the elections took place in 1937, the Congress party won clear majorities in five of the eleven provinces and was the largest party in another three. The Muslim League, which won no majorities but expected to join coalition governments with the Congress, was told that any such

agreement was null and void. In the arrogance of their overwhelming victory at the polls, Congress leaders could ignore Jinnah. "There are only two forces in India today," said Nehru, "British imperialism and Indian nationalism as represented by the Congress."

This was too much for Jinnah. He decided to take nationalism to the Muslim masses, just as Gandhi had done to the Hindus. The propaganda of the League reiterated the threat to Islam from the Hindu Congress, and this call to faith was answered. Even the Congress began to worry about the trend towards religious polarization. If the League, as Jinnah was claiming, was accepted as the spokesman for Muslim Indians, Congress would lose its claim to speak for all Indians. Attempts to open negotiations were unsuccessful; Jinnah's new sense of power and Nehru's hatred of religion in politics would allow no compromise. Thus were the seeds of Indian partition nourished.

The Congress itself was not without its internal troubles. Once in office, it was difficult to reconcile the conflicting demands of its supporters. How could the peasants be given re-

forms without antagonizing the landlords? How could legislation be passed to help the worker without threatening business? An attempt by the radical Subhas Bose to turn the Congress towards a positive revolutionary stance was fought off by Gandhi. In 1939 Bose was forced to resign as president of the Congress party, but it was by no means the last India was to hear of him.

There is no knowing what might have happened if it had not been for the outbreak of World War II. On September 3, 1939, the Viceroy declared India at war with Germany. It was his right to do so; the King of England was also Emperor of India. But it seemed to underline once again the essential powerlessness of Indians who, even in matters of life and death, did not count very much and had no right to be consulted. The Congress promptly demanded that Britain state her war aims and their meaning for India. If they included a promise of independence after the war and participation in the central government in the meantime, then the Congress would co-operate against the common enemy. But the British had watched the growth of the Muslim League and other groups that disputed the Congress's claim to speak for all India. The Congress's demands were not taken seriously and were replied to only in the vaguest of terms. The party's leadership then made the fateful decision to order all its ministries to resign.

The Viceroy, Lord Linlithgow, was pleased. He had always considered the Congress a "movement of Hindu hooliganism" and he now looked, with such enthusiasm as his cold nature could muster, with favour on the Muslim League. Jinnah celebrated his triumph by fixing December 22, 1939, as a "day of deliverance and thanksgiving" to be observed by all Muslims in gratitude for their release from the "tyranny, oppression and injustice" of the Congress Raj. Chances of a compromise between the two nationalist movements evaporated. India was set upon the road that would end in freedom from British rule—and also on the road to internal rupture.

—*Michael Edwardes*

IV. Middle East Tinderbox

Complacency and over-confidence were common, highly visible hallmarks of the British Empire at its apogee. When these characteristics were applied to the British presence in the inflammable Middle East, trouble was bound to result.

In the early years of the new century Lord Cromer, that prototype proconsul, had reason to feel complacent about Britain's position in Egypt. Operating with the powers of pharaoh behind the screen of his modest title of Consul-General, he had restored bankrupt Egypt to fiscal integrity, transformed its economy, cleansed its bureaucracy, and lightened the burdens of its peasants.

Cromer was so convinced that the benefits of British rule must be apparent to any right-minded Egyptian that he was apt to dismiss anyone who opposed it as a hooligan or scoundrel whose opinions were not worth bothering about. He tolerated a free Press because he did not regard it as important, ignoring the violent denunciations of the British occupation that frequently filled its pages. His heaviest contempt was reserved for what he called the "Gallicized Egyptians"—those who had managed to acquire some higher education in Europe or at the French-controlled law school in Cairo.

His complacency blinded him to reality. Sometimes these bright young lawyers and journalists were indeed superficial and irresponsible, yet they represented a real and growing opposition to British rule. The chief reason they lacked the wisdom of experience was simply that Cromer denied them any share of political power.

The political situation was an odd one. Both for constitutional and political reasons, Egypt was most unlikely to become part of the British Empire. Theoretically it remained a part of the Ottoman Empire, with the Khedive in Cairo ruling on behalf of the Sultan in Constantinople. And other European powers, who had many long-standing privileges granted by the Sultan, were determined that Britain should not annex Egypt or threaten their rights there.

In any case, the home government did not want to take on more imperial responsibilities. Liberals and Conservatives alike were anxious to withdraw from Egypt. But they could only do so if this vital link with the Indian Empire was secure. But it never was. The British could neither relinquish control nor seize it outright. Thus Cromer's "Veiled Protectorate." From time to time British ministers would respect the assurances first made by Gladstone in 1882 that Britain did not contemplate an indefinite occupation. (By one estimate, the promise of an early withdrawal was made 72 times between 1882 and 1907.) But there was always some good reason why the withdrawal had to be postponed.

By the time Cromer retired, in 1907, a nationalist movement had gained a foothold in Egypt. During the four-year reign of his liberal successor, Sir Eldon Gorst, ill-starred attempts at reform only increased the popular discontent. Disturbed by the rising nationalist feeling, London now decided that a firm hand was required. The man chosen for the task was Lord Kitchener of Khartoum.

Kitchener was at the height of his prestige. Omdurman was a name that still sparkled on the army's role of imperial victories. In 1905, as commander-in-chief of the Indian Army, he had emerged victorious from a blazing row with the Viceroy, Lord Curzon. His vision of Empire matched his prestige. He shared Cecil Rhodes's dream of an all-red route the length of Africa. He dreamed of ending Turkey's suzerainty over Egypt and of creating a viceroyalty of Egypt and the Sudan, with himself as Viceroy.

In pursuit of this vision, he reversed Gorst's liberal policies. His style was flamboyant; with his aura of prestige he established himself as an archetypal oriental potentate, accepting petitions from the humble and proceeding from time to time through the countryside to observe how the peasantry was faring. He snubbed the "wicked little Khedive," as he referred to him in his private letters, and appointed more Englishmen to senior positions in the administration. He employed special powers to suppress the nationalists so that their leaders were either imprisoned or went into exile.

Then, in 1914 the slowly-developing struggle between Egyptian nationalists and Britain was put in sudden abeyance by the outbreak of war. Kitchener's reign was cut short by his appointment as Secretary for War. Meetings were barred, the Press muzzled, and the legislative council closed indefinitely.

From the British point of view there were good strategic reasons for such stringent controls. Turkey had thrown in with the Central Powers, making Egypt, technically, enemy territory. After some debate between Whitehall and Cairo, in which outright annexation was considered, a British Protectorate over Egypt was declared, replacing Cromer's Veiled Protectorate, and the British Consul was re-titled High Commissioner.

Egypt was not formally incorporated into the Empire; its people remained subjects of the Egyptian Sultan (as the Khedive was renamed), not of George V. But Egyptians could be forgiven for failing to see the difference. Martial law was declared and British and Indian troops arrived to defend the Suez Canal against possible Turkish attack. With the launching of the Gallipoli campaign in 1915, Egypt became a huge military transit and hospital camp. Thousands of Anzac troops, free spirits all, thronged the bars and brothels of Cairo and Alexandria.

British military authorities were too busy with the conduct of the war to be aware of a powerful undercurrent of discontent in Egypt. The nationalist movement was not dead; it had merely gone underground. The students in the cities were as rebellious as ever while the fellaheen in the countryside became increasingly resentful at such war measures as the requisitioning of their draft animals (more precious to them than their children) and the reintroduction of forced labour. Wartime profiteering by landowners inflicted fearful hardship on the towns and led to an outright famine in 1918.

Even then, very few Britons in Egypt were aware of the country's explosive mood. It came as a considerable shock when, two days after the Armistice, Saad Zaghlul, the leading figure in the nationalist movement, presented himself at the head of a delegation in the office of High Commissioner Sir Reginald Wingate to inform him that the Egyptian people wanted their complete independence and that he planned to lead his delegation to London to negotiate with the British government.

He had good reason for confidence. Declarations by the Allies had promised self-determination to the former subject peoples of Turkish rule. Already the Arabians, whom Egyptians regarded as far more backward than themselves, were looking forward to independence and preparing to send a delegate to the Paris Peace Conference. But British imperial interests in Egypt were as great as ever. The Foreign Minister, Arthur Balfour, curtly replied that "no useful purpose" would be served by Zaghlul's visit.

Thereafter, Anglo-Egyptian relations deteriorated rapidly. Zaghlul called upon the country to protest; the British authorities, making use

of the martial law still in force, exiled him and three of his colleagues to Malta. In consequence, there occurred what Egyptians refer to as the 1919 Revolution. Beginning with violent student demonstrations and strikes, the protest spread first to civil servants and professionals and then—to the astonishment of Anglo-Egyptians who believed the fellaheen were impervious to student agitation—to the countryside. Telegraph wires were cut, railway tracks torn up, and stations burned. Englishmen were murdered, the worst incident being the killing and mutilation of seven unarmed soldiers and a civilian by a frenzied mob on the train from Luxor to Cairo.

The British commandant mobilized all the troops available, issued stern warnings to Egyptian government officials, and dispatched mobile columns to the trouble spots. Planes bombed suspicious gatherings and armoured cars fired on suspect groups

near roads or railways. Gradually the country relapsed into a resentful peace.

News of these events was as unwelcome as it was unexpected to the Lloyd George government, which was heavily involved in the affairs of the Peace Conference. It was decided to give full military and civil powers to General Edmund Allenby, who in 1917 had taken Jerusalem and then forced the capitulation of Turkey, to restore law and order in Egypt.

The result was an odd reversal of policy. Despite Allenby's reputation and formidable military bearing, he had strong liberal instincts. He quickly reached the conclusion that many of the Egyptians' grievances were entirely justified. He also believed strongly that they be allowed to administer themselves as far as possible. He persuaded a reluctant British government to release and return to Egypt Zaghlul and his colleagues.

Egypt went wild with joy, but Allenby's hopes that the country

Egyptians mount a demonstration alongside the Nile in 1919 in support of their first prominent nationalist, Saad Zaghlul.

would be pacified were disappointed. The nationalists continued their protests against the Protectorate; strikes, demonstrations, and occasional assassinations of British officials continued. In this tense atmosphere London sent out a high-powered Commission of Enquiry under Lord Milner, a celebrated proconsul and arch-imperialist. Milner had already served in Egypt and written a justification for British intervention there, and he had been the most powerful advocate of war against the Boers in 1899. But now, almost 70, he had mellowed. After a bleak and hostile visit to Egypt—the nationalists boycotted him and the moderates were afraid to offer their co-operation—Milner reached the same conclusion as Allenby: the Protectorate would have to go.

It was not, of course, as simple as that. Egypt was still the vital link with India and the Far East. It was also (with the Sudan) a key to Africa, where Britain's colonial holdings had recently been enlarged through the break-up of the German Empire.

On Milner's return in 1920, he recommended that Britain sign a treaty recognizing Egypt as an independent constitutional monarchy but—to safeguard British interests—with its independence qualified in a number of respects, the most important of which was the establishment of a permanent military alliance. Such a plan was hopeless: no Egyptian political figure would voluntarily agree to terms which implied so many limitations to Egypt's sovereignty, particularly in the face of Zaghlul's opposition. On the British side, several Cabinet members, led by Winston Churchill, Secretary of State for the Colonies, strongly opposed accepting even limited Egyptian independence.

Nearly two years passed in fruitless discussions as the strikes and sporadic violence in Egypt continued. Allenby in exasperation sent Zaghlul into a second exile, this time to the Seychelles. The agitation died down, but he knew he had only a temporary respite. He decided to act. In February, 1922, he arrived in London with an ultimatum for the Lloyd George government: either it declare Egypt's independence or accept his resignation—which would leave him free to make an influential attack on the government in the House of Lords. The Prime Minister twisted and turned, but finally capitulated.

Britain's unilateral declaration of Egypt's independence was made on February 28, 1922. Sultan Fuad became King Fuad I, with considerable powers deriving from a parliamentary constitution. But independence was severely qualified, for Britain reserved rights on four key matters until bilateral agreement could be reached at some future date: the security of imperial communications in Egypt, the defence of the country, the protection of foreign interests and minorities, and control of the Sudan. British officials remained, though their numbers were to be steadily reduced, and Allenby retained the title of High Commissioner.

Despite these qualifications, there was no denying that Britain's influence was severely reduced. Instead of the British residency in Cairo being the only real power centre in the country, it was now one of three, alongside the Palace and Zaghlul's party, the Wafd. Their three-cornered struggle lasted with varying intensity for the next 30 years.

Zaghlul returned from exile in 1923 to triumph the following year in Egypt's first parliamentary election, from which he emerged as Prime Minister. But his hopes of reaching a settlement on the four reserved points with Ramsay MacDonald's newly-elected Labour government were soon dashed. Labour showed itself as mindful of imperial interests as the Tories.

Agitation increased. In late 1924 the Governor-General of the Sudan was murdered in Cairo by Egyptian terrorists. Allenby's reaction revealed the limits on Egypt's sovereignty. Without awaiting Foreign Office instructions he issued an ultimatum that included, apart from punishment of the criminals, the payment of a £500,000 fine and the banning of all political demonstrations, the withdrawal from the Sudan of all Egyptian officers and troops, and the affirmation of Britain's wishes concerning the protection of foreign interests in Egypt. When Zaghlul's government rejected several

Francis Dodd sketched Edmund Allenby in 1917 during his Palestine campaign.

terms of the ultimatum, the British expressed their determination to enforce them, occupying a customs post at Alexandria to prove it. Helpless, Zaghlul resigned.

Nothing, however, changed. Lord Lloyd, the enthusiastic imperialist and close friend of Winston Churchill who succeeded Allenby as High Commissioner, put his finger on the anomaly of Britain's role in Egypt in a letter to a friend. "Our present position is impossible," he wrote. "We cannot carry on much longer as we are. We have magnitude without position; power without authority; responsibility without control. I must insure that no foreign power intervenes in education, aviation, wireless communications, railways or army (where all seek to do so) and I must achieve this without upsetting the parliamentary regime which we forced upon the country in the face of the king's wishes; without weakening the power or alienating the loyalty of the monarchy which we set up, and without displaying the military power which

Farouk

When the 16-year-old Farouk arrived in Cairo in May, 1936, to succeed his late father, King Fuad, vast crowds gave him a tumultuous reception. He was their idol—handsome, self-assured, impressive, apparently a leader to generate Egypt's national rebirth. He would, his people hoped, end the endemic corruption, eliminate near-feudalism and forced labour from the social system, and drive away the British.

Farouk was like-minded. "I declare it is my duty to work with you for the good of our beloved Egypt," he said in a radio broadcast. "With all my will I shall seek to reform the country." The well-meaning young king would be cast in a different and less alluring role, however.

Farouk's image remained bright until well into the Second World War, but all was not well. An emotionally deprived childhood, a poor education, a glandular problem that retarded his sexual development and blighted his marriage: all caused deep flaws in his character. Adversity worsened them. In 1942 the British, backed by tanks, offered him the choice of abdicating or installing a puppet government. He remained king, but under the shock of his political humiliation he deteriorated with startling rapidity. He grew grossly fat, aged prematurely, and became partial to graft, gambling, and the pursuit of a reputation (spurious) for sexual athleticism. It was a disastrous combination of vices. In 1952 he was ousted. Thirteen years later, in exile, after one of his gluttonous meals, he suffered a thrombosis and died, largely unmourned.

is in fact our sole remaining effective argument. I must maintain and respect Egyptian independence and yet justify our army of occupation."

It *was* an impossible situation, rendered many times more complex by the British need to cope with both King Fuad and the Wafd, and by the struggle between these two. Fuad (and his son Farouk, who succeeded him in 1936) saw the Wafd rather than Britain as his chief enemy. Whenever elections were held under the 1923 constitution the Wafd, as the only party with mass popular support, always won a sweeping victory. The King would bide his time until the Wafd committed some act of folly (as it invariably did) which enabled him to suspend or amend the constitution to rig the elections, send the Wafd into opposition, and rule through some independent of his own choosing. Popular pressure would then build up until he was obliged to restore the constitution and allow the Wafd to return to power.

Fuad's longest period of quasi-dictatorship, five years, ended in 1936 when the Wafd returned to power. In a sudden reversal of policy, the new government signed the treaty suggested under the terms for independence 14 years before. There were good reasons for signing. After the chastening experience of many years out of office, the Wafd had come to realize the disadvantage of fighting both the Palace and the British at the same time. And they were thoroughly alarmed at Mussolini's imperial ambitions in Africa, against which Egypt would be virtually defenceless without Britain as an ally.

The treaty, under which Britain retained a dominant if diminished influence, was to run for 20 years; both parties were committed to negotiating a further alliance in 1956. The British occupation of Egypt was formally ended, though British troops would remain in some areas. As Egypt's self-defence capability improved, they would be withdrawn to the Canal Zone and Sinai, where their numbers would be limited to 10,000. Britain reserved the right of reoccupation in the event of war.

It was a definite advance towards total independence. For the first time since 1882 Egypt gained control over its own security forces. The British High Commissioner became an ambassador. The Egyptian Army named its own inspector-general and military intelligence was Egyptianized. The number of Europeans in the police was to be reduced by 20 per cent a year, and the nation obtained full rights of jurisdiction and taxation over all residents. Britain sponsored Egypt's entry into the League of Nations. Both the treaty and the new King, the handsome, outgoing 16-year-old Farouk, were wildly popular. A new and hopeful era seemed to have opened.

The heady mood of optimism did not last. Farouk, although not unintelligent, was spoiled and wilful. With astonishing speed the golden boy-king declined morally and physically into a corrupt and frivolous premature middle age, becoming an object of ridicule. Then, in 1939, practically all the advantages Egypt had gained by the treaty were destroyed by the outbreak of war. Once again it was occupied by a huge imperial army.

Italy's entry into the war in June, 1940, transformed the situation. Many Egyptians hoped for an Axis victory, not out of sympathy with fascism but because they believed it would finally rid Egypt of the British. Churchill, who had never shown much sympathy for Egyptian nationalism, declared it intolerable that Cairo should be a "nest of Hun spies" and gave orders for the dismissal of the pro-Axis Egyptian chief of staff and the removal of all Egyptian troops from the combat zone.

Matters came to a head in 1942, when Erwin Rommel's German Afrika Korps smashed into Egypt from Libya and his name was chanted in the streets of Cairo. Farouk was thought to be on the point of appointing a new Prime Minister with anti-British and pro-Axis sympathies. The Palace was surrounded by British tanks and the towering figure of Ambassador Sir Miles Lampson forced his way into Farouk's presence to present him with a choice between abdication or forming a pro-British Wafd government. The King gave way and for the

Farouk as the teen-age idol of Egypt.

rest of the war the Wafd fulfilled Britain's wishes. The inevitable reckoning would be postponed.

The other highly volatile area in the Middle East in this period was Palestine. Like Egypt, it was not technically part of the British Empire, yet during the years from 1920 to the establishment of the state of Israel it looked as if it was. Palestine was a Mandate, its sovereign the League of Nations (while it lasted) and then the United Nations. Up until 1939 "the Mandatory," the British government, reported every year on the stewardship of its "sacred trust" to the League.

The Mandate system was devised at the Paris Peace Conference with the avowed purpose of preparing politically inexperienced people for independence and to rescue them from previous misrule. It was applied only to the colonial possessions of Germany in Africa and the subject provinces of the Ottoman Turks in Asia. The powers who accepted Mandate responsibilities were instructed to rule in their territories as they thought best.

Skeptics and enemies declared (and still declare) that the Mandate system was a piece of imperialist cunning. Certainly the character of the French regime in Syria and the British in Palestine strongly evidenced imperialism. But the skeptics overlooked a main reason for the imperial style: there was simply no precedent for overseas rule other than imperialism. There was a great measure of sincerity in the establishment of the Mandate

system. Proof of this came when in 1931 the British Mandate in Iraq was withdrawn and replaced by a treaty with the newly independent country.

British rule was in fact instituted in Palestine in 1917 with Allenby's conquest of Jerusalem. At the end of the war few British authorities foresaw any great complications in the new undertaking. That there were contradictions in the British promises to the former Palestinian subjects, both Jewish and Arab, of the Ottoman Empire was apparent only to men on the spot. This does not mean that the British leaders were blind or stupid; what it does mean is that they were complacent and over-influenced by theory.

In the early documents conveying Britain's support of Arab nationalism, Palestine was not mentioned. There was good reason for this. Until 1920 there was no such place, politically speaking. It was reasonably argued that without a nation you cannot have nationalism—certainly not a nationalist problem. The area called Palestine was a conglomeration of imperial Turkish provinces without any unified authority and containing large and influential minorities who enjoyed special privileges. The most ancient of these minorities was the Jewish one. The Jewish community of perhaps 60,000 represented less than 10 per cent of the Palestinian population, of whom the great majority were Arabic-speaking Muslims.

Under the influence of Prime Minister Lloyd George and Foreign Secretary Arthur Balfour, the government had added a further complication. It is known to history as the Balfour Declaration. It took the form of a letter written by Balfour to Lord Rothschild in November, 1917:

"I have much pleasure in conveying to you, on behalf of His Majesty's Government, the following declaration of sympathy with Jewish Zionist aspirations which has been submitted to, and approved by, the Cabinet:

'His Majesty's Government view with favour the establishment in Palestine of a national home for the Jewish people, and will use their best endeavours to facilitate the achievement of this object, it being clearly

understood that nothing shall be done which may prejudice the civil and religious rights of the existing non-Jewish communities in Palestine, or the rights and political status enjoyed by Jews in any other country.'

I should be grateful if you would bring this declaration to the knowledge of the Zionist Federation.
Yours sincerely,
Arthur Balfour."

These often-quoted words made surprisingly little stir at the time. In the House of Commons the Declaration was the subject of some forgotten questions and answers. The French government had already accepted a pro-Zionist policy with little argument and little perception of what it implied. In fact, the loudest clamour (never very loud) against the Declaration came from British Jews who feared that it would force all Jews into divided loyalties. The United States expressed no objections to the new policy.

Why did the British government make this declaration? No one has found a wholly satisfactory answer to that question. Contemporary documents show plainly enough that in British military and political minds there was a great desire to take Palestine into the British sphere of influence to counter French imperial ambitions in the Near East. Since the time of Napoleon British governments had been obsessed with fears that a French establishment of power in the eastern Mediterranean would block the way to India, and the wartime alliance had done little to lessen that anxiety.

From this an imperialist view naturally developed: let Britain, under the guise of Mandate or whatever, take Palestine into the Empire (temporarily or permanently) by acting as the guardian of Zionism. This idea was widespread in the second rank of government service but less so at the ministerial level. And its motives were positively opposed by Arthur Balfour.

Balfour was certainly averse to a French regime in Palestine, but he was equally averse to a British one. He wanted the United States to accept a Mandate for the country and tried

Arthur Balfour (left) and Chaim Weizmann, proponents of a Zionist state in Palestine.

hard for this at the Peace Conference. President Wilson seemed receptive and assured Balfour that he shared his hopes and could get American acceptance. The matter of course fell out differently.

Of the reasons prompting those who conceived the Declaration, only those of Balfour and the Zionist leadership can be known with certainty. Both were idealistic, believing that the establishment of a territorial Jewish state would redeem the Jews from the habits of mind towards which centuries of ill-treatment had contributed. Balfour, Zionist leader Dr. Chaim Weizmann, and other Zionists took a very gloomy view of the effects of segregation and anti-Semitism on Jewish character. Balfour, for example, believed (and persuaded his colleagues in the government) that the Bolshevik revolutionaries in Russia were Jewish. One reason why the Balfour Declaration was made when it was lay in his hope that it would detach Jews from Lenin (whom Balfour wrongly believed to be a Jew), emasculating his party and keeping Russia in the war on the Allied side. It is hard to find a greater political miscalculation.

From 1917 on, the military regime in Palestine, the Occupied Enemy Territory Administration (OETA), was in great difficulties. On OETA fell the full weight of the contradictions in British policy. It was discovered that there was such a thing as Palestinian nationalism after all, in the sense that most of the Arab population shared the ideas and emotions of the Arab national movement. The task of OETA was not made easier by the presence on the scene of a Zionist Commission intent on establishing its rights. This activity, of course, further stimulated Arab Palestinian nationalism.

Of the two political forces in the country, nascent Arab nationalism and nascent Jewish nationalism, OETA found the former easier to deal with. The Arabs had a clear case, easy to understand sympathetically, while the Zionist cause was more complex and sophisticated. OETA faced a formidable political problem but it had no politician of outstanding ability to give it advice; under the circumstances, it is not surprising that it made many mistakes. The most absurd was its suppression of the text of the Balfour Declaration in the hope that by this act of censorship it might be forgotten and tranquility restored. As nearly every Jew and many Arabs had a copy, the hope was peculiarly empty.

Anti-Zionism increased in OETA and most of its officials became openly pro-Arab. The reason was not far to seek. Palestinian Arabs were welcoming British rule because it was a great improvement on Turkish rule. On the other hand, when Zionist immigrants discovered that the Balfour Declaration was no guarantee of a pro-Zionist British administration, they became disillusioned and distrustful and difficult to manage.

OETA stumbled on. Exasperated at the meddling of the Zionist Commission, OETA's Lieutenant-General Sir Louis Bols wrote to the Foreign Secretary, Lord Curzon, to ask that the Commission be abolished. It was a classic case of poor timing. Curzon was at the time attending the Conference of San Remo with Lloyd George and Arthur Balfour, the strongest Zionist sympathizers in the Cabinet. When he consulted them about Bols's dispatch, they were both incensed at what they saw as OETA's incompetence, bias, and disloyalty. The Conference was then discussing the partitioning of the former Turkish provinces; the text of the Balfour Declaration was promptly included in the terms of the Mandate for Palestine. Sir Herbert Samuel, an eminent British Jew and a Zionist, accepted the post of High Commissioner. OETA was abolished. It was a great triumph for Zionism.

These decisions took effect on July 1, 1920, when Samuel arrived in Palestine. The Jews received him with acclaim, believing that the wrongs of many centuries would now be cancelled in the building of a new Jewish state. The Arabs received him with gloom, dreading reduction to servitude under new masters. Both soon found they were mistaken.

The most prominent feature of Herbert Samuel's character was fairness. He made his aims very clear to his secretary: "You know my policy with regard to the non-Jewish population—not only to treat them with absolute justice and every consideration for their interests in matters relating to the establishment of the Jewish National Home, but also to adopt active measures to promote their well-being." Such fairness was of little interest to either Jews or Arabs.

The former wanted not fairness but the New Jerusalem; the latter wanted only to expel the Jews. Samuel wanted an equitable adjustment of Jewish and Arab claims on the basis of adequate representation. He remained loyal to a moderate Zionism that took no account of Jewish statehood in the foreseeable future. Only an extremely able man, as Samuel was, could have survived the unpopularity which his attitude brought on him from both sides.

After the San Remo Conference responsibility for the Palestine Mandate passed from the Foreign Office to the Colonial Office, then under Winston Churchill. Churchill had had no part in the original negotiations leading to the existing position in Palestine, and he could start fresh. In 1921 he convened in Cairo a conference on Middle East questions. With the Arab world in turmoil, the gravity of the Palestine situation seems to have gone unremarked, and it was low on the Cairo Conference agenda. Churchill achieved little or nothing new to solve the Palestine problem, but he did what he could. Without much hope of success he and Samuel urged on all parties the desirability of an elected legislative council and the erection of a constitution to replace the High Commission's arbitrary rule.

The Jews accepted the proposition though they saw the considerable danger to themselves. With inconceivable folly the Arabs rejected the institution of a legislative council so effectively that the High Commission had to abandon the whole enterprise.

The Arab argument was that by taking part in the elections they would be admitting the legality of the Balfour Declaration and of the Zionist endeavour in Palestine. This was quite true. What they overlooked, and continued to overlook, was that by co-operating in a legislative council they would have had the Zionists at a permanent disadvantage through holding a permanent working majority. It is hard to see how, if the council had been accepted by the Arabs, a state of Israel could ever have come into being. But the parliamentary game has never suited Arab temperaments;

they preferred to go a more heroical and, as it turned out, suicidal way.

In 1920 there had been bloodshed between Jews and Arabs. In 1921, after the Cairo Conference, there were worse clashes with more loss of life. To pessimists it seemed that the Mandate could only lead to a long period of lethal Jewish-Arab conflict.

From 1921 to 1929, however, there was peace in Palestine—difficult and often broken peace, but peace nevertheless. The credit is due largely to the remarkable characters of the first two High Commissioners. Unpopular as Samuel was with Jewish and Arab politicians he commanded respect, and the honesty of his approach to his impossibly difficult task was apparent to everyone in Palestine. His successor in 1925 was Field Marshal Lord Plumer, dissimilar from Samuel in superficial respects but his equal in uprightness and determination.

Plumer was the typical British senior officer of his time. He wore large white moustaches and was severely correct in the discharge of his official duties. All this disguised an acute political sense. When asked what was his policy, he replied in his sharpest military manner: "I have no policy. I am here to carry out that of His Majesty's Government." He looked unintelligent but had much perception; he looked a martinet, but he was a tolerant man with a broad sense of humour. Older residents of what was formerly Palestine and Transjordan, both Arabs and Jews, still remember Plumer with affection.

In the mid-1920s there was a sizable immigration of Jews into Palestine, reaching a peak in 1925 when more than 34,000 arrived. Here surely was a most dangerous situation, yet nothing happened. None of the newly formed Palestine Arab parties were moved to action. No protest came from surrounding Arab states. The peace remains difficult to explain, but it certainly owes something to the remarkable British public servants on the spot.

Lord Plumer, suddenly overcome by ill-health, asked to be relieved of his post in 1928. The new High Commissioner, Sir John Chancellor, was a man of great administrative ability but

lacking in the political flair of his predecessors. Tensions rose between Arabs and Jews and incidents multiplied. In 1929 the peace broke down completely. In the last week of August Arab attacks on Jews spread throughout the country. Several Jewish settlements were laid waste. The worst of the atrocities took place at Hebron, where 60 Jews, including children, were murdered, and at Safed, where 23 were killed. Before British reinforcements arrived from Egypt, 133 Jews were killed and 339 wounded.

After the events of 1929 there was again an uneasy peace in Palestine. Jewish immigration, which had slumped off after 1925, completely changed character in the 1930s and became the cause for new anxieties and redirections of policy. In 1933, as the menace of Hitler and Nazism became grimly apparent, over 30,000 Jews entered Palestine; in 1934 there were 42,359; in 1935, 61,854. Inevitably this radical change in the population figures affected Arab nationalist elements. It was clear that Palestine alone could not solve the problem caused by

Palestine High Commissioner Plumer was three years on the Western Front.

451

Hitler's anti-Jewish mania. The only way to relieve the strain was to open doors elsewhere, and Great Britain could in fact have absorbed the whole German Jewish population. But to open the doors to any such large foreign immigration would not have been a popular political move; it would likely have added to the already large unemployment figures. British authorities never sent Jewish refugees back to Germany, but they made no public move to encourage their immigration. The burden continued to fall on Palestine. The number of visas was cut; illegal immigration increased.

The expected trouble broke out in 1936. An immediate cause was the constitutional issue. The Arabs were finally willing to accept the principle of a legislative council, but this time the Zionist leadership emphatically rejected it. This inevitably drew ill-will and suspicion; the Arab leadership felt encouraged to take a strong line. The result was the Arab Rebellion.

Casualties were severe (the highest number being Arabs killed by rebels as collaborationists) and the rising continued for seven months. It was only called off on the promise of the British government to send out a Royal Commission to enquire into the causes of unrest.

The Commission was led by Lord Peel and had a distinguished membership. Although it failed in its attempt at solution (as all these Commissions did) it is historically important because it ultimately influenced events. Its main recommendation was for a partition of Palestine into Jewish-ruled and Arab-ruled polities. From then on the notion of a solution by partition was ever-present in the Jewish and Gentile minds concerned.

Before submission to the League of Nations, the Peel recommendations needed to be approved by the Houses of Parliament. The commissioners' work was defended feebly, but the man who actually killed the recommendations was Viscount Samuel, the former High Commissioner. In a brilliant speech in the House of Lords Samuel pointed out the disconcerting fact that in a time of peace it is literally impossible to move populations except by force and with an accompani-

ment of cruelty that would revolt world opinion, and that the Jewish population of Palestine was neither concentrated enough nor large enough for the proposed partition to be put into effect by any other means. His argument proved irresistible, and the government put Lord Peel's proposals aside.

In the summer of 1937 the Arab Rebellion flared up again and persisted for two years. Early in 1939 Prime Minister Neville Chamberlain and his Colonial Secretary, Malcolm Macdonald, summoned a conference in London that was attended by both Palestinian Arab and Jewish delegations, plus other delegations from the Arabic-speaking world. Since the Arabs refused to meet the Jews it was held as two conferences: Anglo-Arab and Anglo-Jewish. Though the army was slowly mastering the Arab Rebellion, the Palestine Arabs were in a strong position. The neighbouring Arab countries were large suppliers of oil, which would be essential if war came. The Jews had no oil. It would have been madness for a British government in 1939 to open a serious quarrel with the Arab world.

The government still believed that reason would prevail if only there could be frank discussion. It was in vain; faith and hope the government had, but it found it impossible to practice charity. After the abortive conference, London imposed its own solution in what Zionists called "the infamous White Paper." This was in mid-May, 1939.

The White Paper distressed not only the Zionist party but all Jews, especially in the English-speaking world. What most exasperated opponents was the rigid limits set on Jewish immigration to Palestine: 10,000 immigrants a year for the next five years, with an additional immediate immigration of 25,000. Later immigration would be with Arab agreement, and that meant none. The proposed figures, sizable by former standards, were minute in contrast with the numbers victimized by Nazi Germany and her anti-Semitic followers elsewhere. It was psychologically impossible for a Jew to accept the White Paper of 1939.

The Jews were in a helpless position. They protested vigorously, but they could do no more than protest. It was impossible for them to take the anti-British side in the manifestly approaching war with Germany. The Arabs had no such inhibitions and tended to look with admiration on Hitler. In fact the White Paper achieved its immediate political aim. The incentive for the Arab Rebellion weakened and it slowly ceased. Oil supplies to the British Middle East Command were not interrupted. But the dubious morality of this appeasement had later to be paid for.

The outbreak of the war postponed any resolution of the problems in Palestine just as it did in Egypt. But even in wartime the issues remained very much alive. In 1940 and 1941 there was great Zionist bitterness at London's insistence on sticking to the Palestine immigration quotas laid down in the 1939 White Paper. (Immigrants arriving in excess of the quotas were not sent back but given asylum in British overseas territories, sometimes in extremely uncomfortable conditions.) But by 1942 the matter of quotas was moot; as Hitler's "Final Solution" moved into high gear the flow of immigrants seeking entry to Palestine became a pitiful trickle.

Chaim Weizmann and the Zionist leaders wanted above all things to form a Jewish army to fight Nazism. Churchill was in full sympathy, but the Mandate administration and the Middle East High Command vigorously opposed the proposition, believing that the Zionists would use such an army for political ends. Not until late in 1944 did the Zionists obtain official sanction—and then only for a brigade group. It went into action under its own standards bearing the Star of David. However, thousands of Palestinian Jews found their way into the fight against Nazism by the simple course of joining the British Army.

When international peace came at last in 1945, it was the ironic signal for turning Palestine into a battlefield. Britain would now face new and even more daunting problems in trying to administer its "sacred trust."

—Peter Mansfield, Christopher Sykes

The Arab Rebellion that wracked Palestine in the late thirties tested the British Army. The soldiers at left conduct a weapons search, while those below inspect a train ambushed near Haifa by an Arab terrorist band.

Chapter Twelve
SUNSET OF EMPIRE

Queen Elizabeth is seen on a 1961 tour of Ghana, the former Gold Coast and the first of Great Britain's African colonies to gain independence. With her is Ghana's Prime Minister, Kwame Nkrumah.

I. Global War

It is a truism of history that in war are the seeds of destruction of empires—just as empires in their prime wax and grow in war. There is no clearer illustration of this than in the performance of the British Empire in the two world wars of this century.

In August, 1914, King George V had declared war on behalf of the whole Empire. The threat from growing German sea power and the imperial ambitions of the Hohenzollerns was clear and menacing. Four years later the British Empire emerged greatly enlarged, both by mandate and direct annexation.

But in 1939, with the Dominions and India far more independent than in 1914, the entry into war, like the policies that preceded it, was a much more ragged affair. The ultimatum to Hitler expired on September 3, and Britain's declaration of war applied to the Crown colonies as well. The governments of Australia and New Zealand followed the British example at once without consulting their parliaments. In South Africa James Hertzog, the Prime Minister, wished to remain neutral, but the Governor-General refused him a dissolution. Smuts became Prime Minister and declared war on September 6. The Canadian government waited for its parliament to declare war on September 10. In Delhi the Viceroy declared war on behalf of India. The Congress party was affronted. Constitutionally it was impotent, but a statement was issued: "If co-operation is desired in a worthy cause, this cannot be obtained by compulsion and imposition." Only Ireland managed to stand aside from the conflict.

What was the Empire fighting for? Residual loyalties and memories of 1914 played their part (although they were later to affect imperial strategy in a less welcome manner). Also, the ties of blood and tradition made it politically impossible for the Dominion parliaments to stay out. But in strategic terms it was hard to identify any direct threat from Germany to the imperial territories.

Indeed, involvement in the European theatre would be a positive disadvantage for Australia and New Zealand, who were increasingly apprehensive of Japanese influence in the Far East. Even in Canada, to whom war would bring obvious industrial benefits, it was not easy to resist the isolationist case when no military aircraft could fly the Atlantic non-stop and when Germany possessed few battleships and no aircraft carriers.

These uncertainties had been reflected in the attitude and policies of the Cabinet in London in the late 1930s. There was, first of all, confusion over whether Russia or Germany was to be regarded as the main enemy. The majority of the prewar Conservative party (from which that Cabinet was selected) regarded Soviet communism as the primary long-term threat to the country's security. In addition, Germany's territorial ambitions were eastward; she offered, indeed, "the best defence against communism." It was this view—not cowardice (although that came into it) and not military unpreparedness (although that cramped his style)—that underlay Neville Chamberlain's appeasing attitude to Hitler.

In the months after Munich, public opinion, stimulated by the repeated warnings of Winston Churchill, forced a change. Resentment grew at the country's repeated humiliations and the Nazis' bad faith. War—"Hitler must be stopped"—came to be regarded as inevitable. After the Nazis broke their word and humiliated British diplomats yet again by annexing what remained of Czechoslovakia in the spring of 1939, British leaders cast about desperately for new policies. Military guarantees were scattered through the Balkans and forced on Poland. But the only power capable of giving substance to these guarantees was the Soviet Union, and here the British still dragged their feet. When they sent a military mission to Russia it went by the slowest route, through the Baltic.

Hitler abruptly pre-empted the whole British strategy of containment by concluding a non-aggression pact with the Soviets on August 21, 1939. The Chamberlain government's vacillations in foreign policy and its muddled efforts to distinguish between the two ideologies of fascism and communism had finally come home to roost, and the hours of the old Western order were numbered.

The defection of Russia made it militarily impossible for Britain to discharge successfully any of the guarantees she had given Poland and the Balkan countries. But by now prestige and fear were running in harness, hauling the band wagon to inevitable war. Prestige: the British could not tolerate a further humiliation, either at a domestic political level or worldwide, in the eyes of the United States, the Empire, and the Dominions. Fear: the British saw that at each stage where they had bought off the aggressor they had been better placed to fight him than at the stage which followed. Any further delay might bring greater disaster.

British leaders expected a repeat of the First World War, with Germany fighting on two fronts. As it was, the

Germans, having swallowed Czechoslovakia and neutralized Russia, now demolished Poland in three weeks. The war on two fronts seemed to be eliminated as a strategic possibility.

The Allies had now to consider how—if at all—the war was to be prosecuted. Germany was militarily stronger, both numerically and (though this was not admitted even in Cabinet) in terms of quality. The British Chiefs of Staff had originally planned on a stalemate in western Europe, where the twin fortified positions of the Maginot and Siegfried lines were assumed to balance each other, and to direct their surplus strength against Italy in the Mediterranean, scooping up the Italian African colonies at the same time as they made the Suez Canal and the route to India secure. This had led to a good deal of preparatory work, but in 1939, with Mussolini a cautious neutral, the plan was still-born.

All that could be hoped for was that the Germans might make a frontal assault on the Maginot Line and exhaust themselves. Most military men on the Allied side still thought in terms of the First World War, where defence had always asserted itself after a few days and where the real damage to Germany had been inflicted by blockading its ports and starving its population. This theory ignored the fact that the blockade was incomparably less complete in 1939 than it had been during the First World War. This time Germany's back door into the granaries and oil fields of eastern Europe was wide open.

There was very little the Western Allies could do except sit still and hope Hitler would go away. Indeed, there is evidence that some members of the Cabinet hoped that this would actually happen and that after a decent interval of time, in which memories might blur, the Germans would once again turn eastward and a peace patched together in the West.

Such wishful thinking went up in the smoke of the Nazi blitzkrieg in the spring of 1940. The collapse of Denmark and Norway was followed by the spectacular German drive through the Low Countries and France. It was readily and painfully apparent that German military technique, particularly the skill and vigour with which armour and air power were combined, was many years ahead of Allied practice. France, which had stood steadfast through four years of conflict in the First World War, was crushed in six weeks. The heroic evacuation of the British Expeditionary Force from Dunkirk was the single bright spot of the campaign.

Dunkirk galvanized the British into demanding a deep commitment from the Empire. Far from resigning themselves to imperial isolationism, even after the French surrender, they proposed instead to concentrate the whole of the Empire's energies on securing a European victory. Churchill, now in power, composed a message to all the Dominion prime ministers, explaining that Britain's resolve to continue to struggle alone "was not based upon mere obstinacy or desperation" but upon an assessment of "the real strength of our position."

Churchill's assertions of confidence and power got a mixed reception in the Empire. Canada, New Zealand, and Australia made congratulatory response—although the two Pacific Dominions were deeply uneasy at the naval implications of British strategy and of their own vulnerability.

In South Africa the attitude of some was harsher. Hertzog's assessment of Britain's predicament differed radically from Churchill's: "England today stands...defeated and threatened, with nearly all her armaments, munitions and other war material in the hands of the enemy ... her population of some 50 million in a spirit strongly permeated by despair." His motion in the House of Assembly advocating that South Africa conclude a separate peace with Germany and Italy was defeated, but the figures reflected a substantial weakening of Smuts's position. In India Nehru was less brutal, but just as firmly set against involvement: "England's difficulty is not India's opportunity, but it is no use asking India to come to the rescue of a tottering Imperialism."

In the last days of June, 1940, Mussolini had brought Italy into the war so as to get in on the victory parade. This gave the British the opportunity they had planned for, and with amazing strategic *sang-froid* they immediately committed over half their remaining tank strength to the water, sending them in a fast convoy on the two-month journey round the Cape to Egypt.

Meanwhile, one of the critical battles in the history of civilization was being fought out in the skies over the mother country. The British had rejected Hitler's peace overtures, made after the French surrender, and the Führer was determined to invade. The German General Staff, exceedingly apprehensive, insisted on total air superiority over south-east England as a prerequisite to the movement of troops across the Channel.

Those few pilots and air crew from the Dominions who had managed to get into the RAF in time played a vital part in blunting the cutting edge of the Luftwaffe in the Battle of Britain. In equipment and numbers (considering the short range of the German fighters) there was virtual parity. In morale there was a direct collision between two rival indoctrinations— the short, intense, crude philosophy of the *Herrenvolk,* and the 200-year-old tradition of imperial education in the public schools: the high-minded toughness, the conditioned certainty strengthened by childhood reading of Kipling and Henty that one must never give up, that Right was on our side, that "Britain always won the last battle."

And win it she did. By October the Germans' attack had run down and they, too, had to accept stalemate in Europe, turning their attention to the south and east.

Here the British were already busy. The arrival of an Australian and an Indian division had given Britain's Middle East commander, Archibald Wavell, the strength he needed to face the Italian army in North Africa. Although still outnumbered ten to one, the arrival of the tank convoy from Britain assured Wavell a technical superiority.

In December, 1940, the Western Desert Force advanced from Egypt into Cyrenaica, the coastal bulge of

Anthony Gross sketched the arrival in North Africa of a party of imperial troops who eluded capture on Crete and made good their escape in a small boat.

Libya. Making skilled use of tanks to prise open fixed defences and the 4th Indian Division to cut up the enemy infantry, the desert army made a shambles of the Italians' front. Wavell then ordered the Indian division south to the Sudan, where it repeated its performance and pursued an Italian army deep into East Africa. The 6th Australian Division took the Indians' place in Cyrenaica and rapidly finished off the campaign. By February, 1941, the Western Desert Force, whose strength never exceeded 30,000 men, had bagged over 130,000 Italian prisoners and seized all of Cyrenaica. Wavell's casualties were less than 2,000. Over a thousand miles to the south-east, South African and Indian troops were fast reducing the Duke of Aosta's army in East Africa and opening the Red Sea to British shipping. Here the bag of prisoners exceeded 200,000.

These astonishing victories marked the final point of strategic balance for the British Empire in its old form. The equilibrium was upset almost immediately by the extension of the war

to the Balkans and by the emergence of differences in the Empire countries.

Churchill had a private obsession with the Balkan theatre, where (as he believed) his own plans for victory had been thwarted at Gallipoli in 1915. Now he welcomed the chance to move the victorious desert army into Greece, threatened in the spring of 1941 with German invasion.

Tactically speaking, an Allied defeat was a foregone conclusion. The Greeks were already exhausted by months of heroic battling against Mussolini's legions, while the British sent in to support them were without proper air support or logistic backing. But strategically the outcome was equally catastrophic for both Britain and Germany. For the Germans it entailed the postponement by one month of their attack on Russia, for which they would pay a terrible price in the coming winter. As for the British, they uncovered their North African flank just when total victory there was within their grasp. With Erwin Rommel and his Afrika Korps now on the scene to shore up the battered Italians, this lapse was to be very costly.

The consequences of diverting imperial troops to Greece were equally serious. By committing Australian

and New Zealand forces to a purely European venture that had no possible relevance to the Dominions' own security and was anyway doomed to failure, the British brought to a head divisions and uncertainties over imperial strategic policy. The issue was sharpened when these troops, after evacuation from Greece, suffered further losses in a gallant but fruitless defence of the island of Crete.

The Royal Navy, which suffered heavy losses in the battle for Crete, was in jeopardy elsewhere as well. The 45,000-ton German battleship *Bismarck* had broken out into the North Atlantic, and before being hunted down and sunk had destroyed the battle cruiser *Hood*, the finest ship in the Royal Navy. Far from being able to reinforce the Far East stations, it was becoming necessary to withdraw ships from there.

On land, too, the position had worsened to such an extent that Churchill was trying to draw additional Dominion forces out of the Far East to North Africa. In April, 1941, Rommel led the Afrika Korps on a rampage. Retaking all of Cyrenaica, he isolated and bypassed an Australian division in Tobruk and halted only when he reached the Egyptian frontier.

Yet even as the pendulum was

swinging back in the Germans' favour, imperial strength in the Near East continued to grow. At Churchill's prompting, Wavell occupied the whole of Iraq and attacked and reduced the Vichy French colony in Syria. By June 15, 1941, the bounds of the British Empire—that area of the globe that could legitimately be coloured red—were at the widest extent they ever attained. Seven days later occurred the first of the events which within a decade would reduce the imperial concept to a nullity.

Hitler's invasion of the Soviet Union, launched on June 22, 1941, immediately ended the European stalemate. This attack carried a general though somewhat remote threat to the whole British position in Asia Minor, but its most important effect on strategy was to free the Japanese from concern over a major land battle on their own eastern frontiers. They were now convinced that the time had come to strike in the Pacific—a chance, the Japanese Foreign Minister observed, "that may come only once in a thousand years."

During the first 18 months of the war Britain had drawn enormous benefits out of what was, effectively, a one-way traffic of material aid flowing in from the colonies and Dominions. But from here on the imperial possessions were to be serious liabilities.

The RAF had become increasingly dependent for its expansion on the influx of air crew pledged under the Empire training scheme; the forces in the Middle East—the only theatre where Britain was actively engaged on land—were predominantly imperial. In addition, British investment was greatly stimulating manufacturing industries in the Dominions and India, thereby lightening the load on munitions factories at home. But once the Far East became a theatre of war, or was even threatened by conflict, the balance would be disastrously upset.

British leaders, however, continued their attempts to focus imperial resources on achieving victory in the European theatre despite the fact that, with the German attack on Russia, the threat to Britain had subsided. The precious months when a redeployment of force might have changed the

After sinking H.M.S. *Hood* in May, 1941, the German battleship *Bismarck* was spotted by the RAF (as painted by Norman Wilkinson) and the Royal Navy soon took its revenge.

balance in the Far East were allowed to slip by.

In August, 1941, Churchill and President Roosevelt had their first meeting at Placentia Bay, Newfoundland. The British were anxious to discuss joint strategy and, in particular, to gain American assurances of cover for their Far Eastern possessions. But Roosevelt would not be drawn. In two respects the conference left the British worse off. Roosevelt was determined to send help to Stalin. The result was that spare items of military equipment were allocated to Russia, where the difference they made at the time was marginal at best, instead of going to the Far East, where the difference they might have made was critical.

Equally unfortunate, at least in its aftermath, was the joint "Declaration of Principle" which came to be known as the Atlantic Charter. It contained a number of high-sounding references to "the right of all people to choose the form of government under which they will live." This was in decided contrast to the declaration made by Lord Linlithgow, the Viceroy of India, that "it is no part of our policy, I take it . . . gratuitously to hurry the handing over of controls to Indian hands at any pace faster than we regard as best calculated, on a long view, to hold India to the Empire." Churchill, when questioned, was forced to declare that the Atlantic Charter was intended to apply to Europe and in no way altered policy towards India, Burma, or "other parts" of the Empire.

The British possessions in the Far East were in double jeopardy. The strategy for their defence had been superseded by the march of events and their military resources neglected. But in the last resort it was solely on British military power that their security rested, for any possibility of getting the possessions to assume some responsibility for their own defence by encouraging nationalist aspirations to independence was excluded by Churchill's pronouncements.

The Australians and New Zealanders, being nearer the threat, saw these dangers more clearly than the British. Throughout the second half of 1941 there were persistent but unavailing pleas to Churchill from the Dominion prime ministers urging a grouping of their troops in a unified force under the command of one of their fellow countrymen, a step that would have made their deployment under the direct orders of their own governments very much easier. Churchill also failed to give the Far Eastern forces the technical reinforcement they required. He had become obsessed with the figure of Rommel, and that summer squandered enormous masses of matériel in attempts to defeat him. There was nothing left to send elsewhere.

It was not until late in the year that intelligence reports convinced the Cabinet that a Japanese attack was inevitable. Even then it was hoped that a "show of force" might deter them. The Admiralty, in common with other Western defence organizations at the time, held Japanese military efficiency in some contempt, and concluded that it would be safe to show the flag with two battleships, *Prince of Wales* and *Repulse,* sailing unescorted. They arrived at Singapore on December 2, 1941.

In numerical terms, substantial imperial forces garrisoned Malaya and the Singapore fortress, but their equipment was largely obsolete. And the attitude of mind that pervaded the military hierarchy—a kind of mental arrogance, essential to the administrative pattern of Empire, that assumed the inferiority of the subject races—led to a fatal complacence. Within 24 hours of the attack on Pearl Harbour and the first landings in Malaya on December 7, the two battleships had weighed anchor, their crews eager to get at the Japanese fleet whose gunnery, so they confidently believed, would be affected by the fact that "all Japanese men wear glasses." They never sighted a Japanese warship and instead on December 10 sailed directly into an attack by 86 torpedo bombers that put both ships at the bottom of the sea within three hours, with the loss of a thousand men.

With the American Pacific fleet crippled by the Pearl Harbour attack, the whole of the Far East was now open to the aggressor. The Dominions of Australia and New Zealand were without the protection of the Crown for the first time in their history. Most significant, for the first time an Asiatic race had shown itself technologically superior to a country of the West, and had defeated its élite military force in a direct trial of strength.

From the fall of France until Pearl Harbour, the British Empire had conducted war against Germany and Italy on its own. But with the entry of Russia, which was to engage the bulk of the German Army, and the United States, which possessed the greatest material power, British influence over the course of the war gradually declined. And Britain found, paradoxically, that though she had acquired new allies, she could not both fight in Europe and fight to preserve the Empire.

The Eastern Empire was, it appeared, to be no more than "maintained." Churchill declared that "although we cannot afford to accept indefinite defeat from Japan, we are still bound to regard her as a secondary enemy in comparison with Germany." Since Japan's "chief value to the Axis," he said, lay "in her power to draw away to the Pacific the forces now accumulating in Europe and the Middle East . . . it is in our interest to resist that pull as much as possible."

As a result, the Far East received minimal support. With every hour that passed, the state of the forces there deteriorated. They had lost control of the sea and the air, and these critical handicaps were compounded by a divided command, poor morale, and the difficulty of establishing communications among the various commands—the British in Malaya, the Americans in the Philippines, the Dutch in Java, the Australians in Darwin.

The defence of Malaya, as originally envisaged, was primarily a matter for the RAF with the army providing protection for the airfields. But, although new airfields had been built, the required first-line aircraft never arrived. There were no modern fighters, no torpedo bombers, no adequate attack aircraft.

On Christmas Day, Churchill could proudly announce the capture of Benghazi in Libya and elaborate on his plans for a seizure of the whole North African coast. But the impending collapse in Malaya and the reaction in Australia was of far greater significance for the future of the British Empire. John Curtin, the new Prime Minister, was bombarding London with cables urging decisive action—a joint Anglo-American fleet should be formed by taking vessels out of the Atlantic; 500 aircraft from Bomber Command should be dispatched immediately to Australia; Russia should be induced to declare war on Japan by the immediate acceptance of Soviet claims to the Baltic states. On December 28 Curtin published a highly combative article in the Melbourne *Herald* in which he asserted that "Australia looks to America, free of any pangs as to our traditional link or kinship with the United Kingdom."

By now the disintegration of the front in Malaya was painfully apparent in London and a hideous possibility opened. Could it be that the fortress of Singapore, one of the very few strongpoints which had been maintained even through the years of depression and appeasement, was not in fact impregnable? Once the idea took root, its unhappy corollary immediately followed. If there was a danger that the fortress would fall, then plainly it was madness to waste meagre resources by reinforcing it. However, any weakening of resolve to hold Singapore would have immediate and catastrophic effects on imperial prestige and on the morale of the Pacific Dominions. Their governments sent daily exhortations to London for extravagant action to save the position. Partly in response to these, partly from sheer inertia, the stream of reinforcements continued to flow into Singapore in spite of the tacit acknowledgement that this made no sense militarily.

By January 21, 1942, as the Japanese drove unchecked down the Malayan Peninsula, the question of evacuation was being openly discussed. The reaction from Australia and New Zealand to any possible withdrawal was immediate and violent. "After all the assurances given in the past," Curtin cabled, "the evacuation of Singapore would be regarded, not in Australia alone, as an inexcusable betrayal." There was no evacuation. Indeed, fresh troops were still disembarking less than three days before the final collapse. Allied morale simply collapsed completely. Of higher leadership and inspiration there was none. Despite their own numerical superiority, the Allied soldiers on the spot regarded the Japanese as invincible. On February 15, 1942, the 70,000 Empire troops in Singapore laid down their arms.

Without doubt, the surrender of Singapore was the worst disaster for British arms since the surrender of Cornwallis at Yorktown signalled the loss of the American colonies. Nor was it much less significant. The losses were more than just military and territorial, catastrophic though these were. The prestige of the white man, his *ethos* of superiority that allowed a single District Officer to rule and administer enormous, populous regions, was shattered.

The spring of 1942 was a dark and cloudy season for the British Empire: Singapore gone, Burma threatened, India in turmoil, Rommel again on the rampage in North Africa. The Empire gritted its teeth and waited for the whirlwind to descend. Remarkably, it passed by.

The monsoon in Burma ended the immediate threat of an invasion of India. American carrier units blunted the Imperial Japanese Navy's offensive capacity. In North Africa Rommel's advance finally ground to a halt, starved by the Fuhrer's determination to concentrate German resources on the conquest of Russia.

Such reprieves, however, brought little comfort to Churchill. His physician, Lord Moran, has written: "My diary for 1942 has the same backcloth to every scene: Winston's conviction that his life as Prime Minister could be saved only by victory in the field." For the sake of imperial prestige, he was determined to see that victory came from the Eighth Army in its contest with the Afrika Korps. But he found himself facing increasingly vocal and widespread public support for a "Second Front," a frontal assault on the French Channel coast. The performance of the Red Army, fighting more or less single-handedly against the Germans had aroused universal admiration in Britain. Press lords who had once sounded stentorian warnings about the "Red Menace" now vied with Communist shop stewards in clamouring for swift action to support the Russians.

Churchill could hardly give a detailed account in public of the Allies' lack of resources. It was tough enough for him in private to convince the Americans that a landing in France was as yet beyond their joint capacity. He was able to convince Roosevelt, however, and an Anglo-American landing in North Africa—Operation Torch—was agreed upon.

As planning for the enterprise began, the Allies received grim evidence of what a premature attack in Europe would involve. During the previous two years, small-scale raids had been made on the German-held coastline by highly trained specialist units. Taking the enemy by surprise and forcing a considerable dispersal of the German defence, they had been relatively successful. In the spring of 1942 the idea took root for another operation of the same kind, but mounted on such a scale that it might appear to the Germans as the forerunner of a major invasion attempt. The target would be Dieppe.

Since the Canadian government refused to allow their forces to be used in the Middle East, it was decided to allocate the Canadian division based in England for the assault. The risks could be expected to be great, which made the choice of the Canadians somewhat unfortunate in the light of previous sacrifices by individual Dominion contingents: Australians in Greece, New Zealanders in Crete, South Africans and Indians in North Africa. In the event, Dieppe was a planning fiasco and a tactical disaster. Over 60 per cent of the Canadian division was killed or captured; none of its soldiers penetrated beyond the foreshore or the seawall. One of the finest units in the imperial army had been crippled at a single stroke.

The failure of the Dieppe Raid convinced the senior British military staff—in particular Sir Alan Brooke, Chief of the Imperial General Staff—that an ill-considered frontal assault on the German-held coastline would be an act of pointless butchery. Most of these men had been young subalterns in the First World War. Now the echoes of those terrible mass attacks across no-man's-land that had crippled the Empire for 20 years returned to haunt them. As an American official observed, British military deliberations were conducted beneath the "shadows of Passchendaele."

The Americans had no such memories and, therefore, no such inhibitions. Their military leaders treated every British diversion to the Mediterranean with suspicion and continued, even after the bloody lesson of Dieppe, to press for a frontal assault across the Channel or a complete switch of their resources to the Pacific. The British got their way, largely because of Churchill's prestige, backed by longer experience and more skilful arguments and by the fact that, in the late summer of 1942, British and imperial military strength still gave the appearance of superiority. The fledgling U.S. air effort could not yet compare with the strikes of RAF Bomber Command. And on November 4, after 12 days of savage battle, Bernard Montgomery's Eighth Army broke the Afrika Korps at El Alamein. Three days later, the Allies landed in French North Africa in Operation Torch.

Churchill finally had the major victory he had so long desired, and he felt the time had come to pronounce against the critics of British imperialism, in America as well as at home. "I have not become the King's First Minister," he declared, "in order to preside over the liquidation of the British Empire."

Underlying this sentiment was the idea that the imperial government could still pursue its own course while laying claim to complete equality of power with America. But as 1943 wore on such thinking was shown to be an illusion. In South Afri-

Officers of the Singapore garrison are escorted to Japanese headquarters to surrender the colony on February 15, 1942. The "Gibraltar of the East" held out just 15 days.

ca political considerations, and in India and Australasia military ones, led to the withdrawal of the bulk of their military contingents from the Middle East and the diminution of their governments' interest in the European conflict. Even the flow of trained air crew from the Dominions, which had been sustaining Bomber Command, began to slow down as new recruits took the option of flying in defence of their own homelands.

Economically, Britain also faced problems. Her industrial and economic capacity was already stretched to the absolute limit, and except for Canada the Dominions were unable to satisfy the new demands. For a whole range of necessary items, civilian and military, Britain could look to only one source—the United States. By 1943 it had become clear, therefore, that the end of British strategic independence was near.

Britain also faced other troubles on the home front. The labour force declined by 150,000 as the population aged and the low between-the-wars birth-rate—itself a product of the casualties of the First World War—took effect. The passing of immediate danger and humiliation still left "total" victory depressingly remote. The number of strikes increased dramatically and a mood of disenchantment among the civilian population was apparent. The last thing in most people's minds was the Empire. It no longer yielded any visible benefit and in Britain there was a dim but pervasive impression that resources which might speed the end of the war (to the British people, the "war" meant the fight against Germany) were being needlessly diverted.

The time had now come for the Allies to resolve their plans for the Second Front. Many on the British side still doubted the wisdom of gambling everything on a frontal assault against the daily increasing strength of the German Atlantic Wall. But against this a new, unspoken, but widely shared feeling began to make itself felt. The Russians had smashed the Germans at Stalingrad in February, 1943, and again in the summer at Kursk. It was only a matter of time before the Red Army moved towards western Europe.

War artist Richard Eurich's panoramic canvas shows a portion of the enormous Allied invasion armada on the eve of D-Day. Landing craft take aboard supplies and armour.

The Germans would be unable to stop them; the only thing that might would be an inter-Allied agreement backed up by an Anglo-American army moving from the opposite direction. The wheel had come full circle: once considered essential to avert Russia's defeat, an Allied landing in France had now become the vital means of preventing the Soviet victory from being too complete and too menacing.

The landing, on June 6, 1944, came not a moment too soon. For Germany, though hard-pressed by the Russians, was by no means finished. Her war production was increasing and a whole new range of sophisticated weapons—"Schnorkel" U-boats, jet and rocket aircraft, two different kinds of ballistic missile—were on the point of becoming operational. If the D-Day landings had been as ill-prepared as the Dieppe Raid, the Western Alliance and the British Empire would have been exposed to perils even greater than those of 1942. But the costly lesson of Dieppe had been learned, the lodgement was quickly secured, and preparations for the inevitable break-out proceeded. The Battle of France was quickly won.

In September Churchill met Roosevelt in Quebec. An early end to the war in Europe seemed possible and the Prime Minister was anxious to concert plans for future operations in the Far East. In August, 1943, a major Allied offensive to recover Burma had started and was entering its final phase in March, 1944, when the Japanese, supported by the so-called Indian National Army, had suddenly invaded Assam to begin their long-heralded "March on Delhi." In June they had been defeated at Imphal, inside the Indian border, and Britain now looked forward to recovering all her lost imperial territories in Asia. The Americans, however, were more interested in pursuing their own successful campaign against the Japanese in the Central Pacific, and this raised two immensely difficult problems for Churchill.

He warned his colleagues that if the United States alone was responsible for driving the Japanese from Malaya and the East Indies, she might demand "a dominating say in their

One of Churchill's great moments was stepping ashore on the Rhine's east bank in March of 1945. At the right is Field Marshal Montgomery.

head of the new Labour government.

A major question of imperial policy remained to be settled. Were the economic wealth and trading potential of Britain's enormous possessions in the Far East worth the strain of the major military effort that was (it seemed) necessary to wrest them from the Japanese? In the event, the matter was decided at Hiroshima and the British returned to their Far Eastern Empire by courtesy of American power. The business-as-usual sign flickered on again at the Colonial Office, but there were few who were any longer interested in buying the goods.

The reputation of the British government—indeed, of all colonial governments—had been severely shaken, not only by the inability of imperial leaders and military commanders to withstand the onslaught of a great Asian power but by their apparent acceptance of outdated notions of Western superiority. Had the British returned on the tide of a military victory of their own making, they might at least have won the respect of their subjects. As it was, they provoked outright hostility or mere indifference.

At home, the British people, who for the most part had supposed the Empire to be founded firmly upon the loyalty of the indigenous inhabitants, were in no mood for gunboats and glory when they found it was not. Hugh Dalton, Labour Chancellor of the Exchequer, summed up the mood of his fellow countrymen with prosaic but forceful clarity: "If you are in a place where you are not wanted and where you have not got the force to squash those who don't want you, the only thing to do is to come out."

The self-governing Dominions had also acquired new international status and assertiveness. They had stood as free and equal nations with Britain from first to last against the Axis powers. If the days of colonialism were seemingly numbered, the idea of Commonwealth had acquired new significance. It remained to be seen how far the idea could by trade, tariff, or defence agreements be given real substance in the turbulent time of peace.

—*Alan Clark*

future" and gain control of their oil. Above all, the Prime Minister was concerned that if the Americans pursued an independent campaign against the Japanese they might end the Lend-Lease arrangements without which Britain could neither sustain operations in the Far East nor manage the transition of her economy from war to peace. Churchill therefore considered it vital to secure a major Pacific role for the Royal Navy.

Roosevelt accepted the offer, and also promised American support for the campaign in Burma. Further Lend-Lease worth $3.5 billion was secured for the war against Japan plus a credit for $3 billion for non-military purposes. It was one of Churchill's last diplomatic triumphs.

In the last months of the war the British people turned in on themselves. They thought mainly of social security, housing, full employment. The armed forces were permeated by

"discussion" groups whose spokesmen, drawn from the Left, aired popular grievances in a kind of socio-economic jargon that at the time seemed fresh and inspiring. The old concepts of Empire and the flag, with which Kipling and Henty had sustained national self-esteem, were no longer mentioned except as objects of ridicule on account of their association with "privilege" and the old order.

By 1945, then, Britain's status (as distinct from her prestige) as a world power rested largely on bluff. She had no economic assets, her armed forces were over-stretched, and what leverage she could exert depended on the diplomatic skill of her political leaders. These changed abruptly in the middle of the Potsdam Conference in July when the general election results were declared and the Tories were turned out. Clement Attlee, Churchill's wartime deputy, became

II. The Lost Jewel

The Second World War came at a critical moment in India's history. It exposed two great questions: how much longer would Britain be able to hold on to the sub-continent, and if forced to relinquish "the brightest jewel in the British Crown," how would she leave it—united, or driven by religious and political animosities into civil war?

Between the wars, the rising nationalistic fervour in India had been predominantly Hindu, drawing pride and strength from Hindu history; the Congress party claimed to speak for all Indians, and Gandhi's charisma overshadowed rival nationalist figures. His disciple Nehru, though more practical in approach, was no less passionate in his concern for India's freedom.

In 1935, however, Muhammed Ali Jinnah was persuaded to return from his London law practice to lead those Muslims who feared domination by the Hindus. He revitalized the moribund Muslim League party. A cold, impassive man who could not even speak Urdu, the language of the peasants, Jinnah planned his strategy carefully and executed it ruthlessly. Branches of the League were opened in the remotest villages and the membership fee was reduced to a minimum. In hundreds of pamphlets, speeches, and meetings, alleged Hindu atrocities were reported; peasants were told that their daughters would be sent to Hindu temples as dancing girls. Any means was exploited towards the end of uniting the Muslims into a cohesive force.

Lord Linlithgow, a most cautious Viceroy in time of peace, became positively unbending after the declaration of war in 1939. He could not believe that the British Raj would ever come to an end. When the Congress presented him with its demands—a promise of postwar independence and a role in wartime administration—he chose not to take them seriously. "The same old game is played again," Nehru wrote bitterly to Gandhi. "The background is the same, the various epithets are the same and the actors are the same and the results must be the same." The Congress condemned the Viceroy's attitude and called upon its ministries in the various provinces to resign in protest.

Jinnah had already rejected Nehru's plea that the Muslim League join the protest. Now he went much further. At a meeting of the League in Lahore in March, 1940, he startled not only the British and the Hindus but also those Muslims who were not part of his inner circle. Out of the blue, in a statement that later became famous as the "Pakistan Resolution," Jinnah declared: "Muslims are a nation according to any definition of a nation, and they must have their homelands, their territory and their State." This state was to be known as Pakistan, a name coined by a Muslim idealist at Cambridge during the 1930s. It included the initial letters of Punjab, Afghan, Kashmir, and Sind, and added up to "Land of the Pure."

The reaction of Hindus and non-League Muslims was immediate and contemptuous. Gandhi dismissed the concept of two nations with the strongest reproach he knew, calling it "an untruth." Muslim leader Abul Kalam Azad described it as "meaningless and absurd," and Nehru said angrily, "There is no question of settlement or negotiations now." Jinnah's concept certainly appeared "meaningless and absurd" in 1940. Even he himself did not really think it would materialize; the vaguely-worded resolution was designed more as a bargaining weapon and a rallying point. Yet Linlithgow was delighted to encourage any development that undermined the Congress party's attempts to act as a unifying opposition to British rule. He assured Jinnah that no constitution for India would be enforced by the British government without the approval and consent of the Muslims.

Linlithgow, however, did go so far as to recommend to London that India be conceded Dominion status a year after the war, but that implacable enemy of Indian independence, Winston Churchill, considered the suggestion far too revolutionary. The result was the so-called Linlithgow Offer of August 8, 1940. Though it stated that Dominion status for India was the objective of the British government, it referred to neither date nor method of accomplishment. All the Viceroy was prepared to do was to invite "representative Indians" to join his executive council and to set up a War Advisory Board. Only Jinnah got something precise: the British would not contemplate transferring power to a Congress-dominated national government, the authority of which was "denied by large and powerful elements in India's national life." The chimera of Pakistan began to take on some substance.

As the Japanese Far Eastern blitzkrieg gathered speed in early 1942, it began to look as if nothing could stop their forces from threatening India itself. It was no longer a time for non-violence, nor for its spokesman, Gandhi. The Mahatma stood down in favour of Nehru, who felt no moral objection to warfare.

After the fall of Singapore and Rangoon, both China and the United States began to show increasing anxiety about affairs in India. The British felt compelled to make some gesture if only to satisfy their allies. It was announced that a Cabinet minister, Sir Stafford Cripps, would go to India with new proposals.

Cripps, the Labour leader of the House of Commons in the wartime coalition government, had long been deeply interested in the problems of India. As soon as he arrived, however, he discovered that India was more deeply divided than he had imagined. Nehru, eager for a compromise, was hopeful. Gandhi was not. Jinnah seemed to think that the only real enemy was the Congress. Extremist Hindu parties defied the Muslims to come out into the streets and fight. Sikhs threatened anyone, Hindu or Muslim, who sought to divide their homeland. And there were many who saw in the growing threat to India good reason not to negotiate with the British for less than they might receive from negotiations with the victorious Japanese.

In the end, the Cripps proposals amounted to little more than the Linlithgow Offer of 1940. Churchill was not going to let India go easily. Cripps offered full Dominion status after the war, but the British, he emphasized, would not hand power over to a government which was unacceptable to large minorities. Again, the possibility of a separate Muslim state was given official recognition. All parties rejected the plan because it stated that no constitutional demands would be granted immediately. As Gandhi was reported to have said, "Why accept a post-dated cheque on a bank that is obviously failing?" Though the Cripps Mission came to nothing, Jinnah was well pleased with his tactical gains.

Nehru's anti-British attitude did not mean that he condoned Japan's aggression. As he assured President Roosevelt, "We, who have struggled so long for freedom and against an old aggression, would prefer to perish rather than submit to a new invader." While most Indians inclined to this view, the once-influential nationalist leader, Subhas Bose, was assuring his countrymen from a radio station in Germany that "Japan has no designs on India. Japan is our ally, our helper. Co-operate with the Japanese in order to eliminate British domination and establish a new order!"

Bose, once a leader of the Congress party, had always been a revolutionary. Indian support for Britain in her hour of need disgusted him, for he believed that India's liberation could be achieved only with outside aid. He seized his opportunity when the Japanese menaced South-East Asia, and in 1943 he arrived in Tokyo to organize the Indian National Army, largely recruited from prisoners-of-war. He continued to make eloquent appeals over the radio for Indians to cross the border and join him, but with little success. Only one combat division of some 14,000 Indians actually went into action, fighting alongside the Japanese in Burma.

On the other hand, despite the Congress party's refusal to co-operate in the war effort, more than two million Indians volunteered for military service in the Allied cause by 1945, the largest voluntary recruitment in history. From the conquest of Italian East Africa to the defeat of the Japanese in Burma, where 700,000 of the one million Allied troops were provided by the Indian Army, Indians were at the forefront of the battle.

Unfortunately, their enthusiasm and courage provided no resolution to the political stalemate at home.

The Congress was frustrated and confused. Every attempt to find a solution seemed only to push Hindus, Muslims, and British farther apart. In this mood, the Congress looked once again to the Mahatma for guidance. His answer was to mean the party's eclipse for the rest of the war and the enhancement of Jinnah and the Muslim League.

In Gandhi's famous "Quit India" resolution of July 6, 1942, the Congress called on the British to "purify themselves by surrendering power in India." It was obvious that Gandhi expected no response from the British. If they remained obdurate, there must be mass civil disobedience. "Even if the whole of India tells me I am wrong," he declared, "even then I will go ahead, not for India's sake alone, but for the sake of the whole world. . . . I cannot wait any longer for Indian freedom. . . . If I wait any longer God will punish me. This is the last struggle of my life." A month later he told the All-India Congress Committee, "We shall either free India or die in the attempt."

The government could hardly remain inactive in the face of a call for open rebellion. Early in the morning of August 9, 1942, Gandhi and the whole of the Congress leadership were quietly arrested. Mass demonstrations immediately took place in all the principal cities. The protests were spontaneous and, initially, nonviolent. Crowds of students and workers, shopkeepers and housewives, emerged from the bazaars, singing nationalist songs and demanding the immediate release of the Congress leaders. The regular police were overwhelmed. As tension grew, the army fired upon the angry crowds. As the violence continued, the British, believing themselves faced with the gravest threat to their rule since the 1857 Mutiny, replied harshly with mass arrests and the machine-gunning of rioting mobs from the air.

The campaign was vicious but short-lived. The government announced at the end of November that just over a thousand people had been killed and

about three times as many seriously injured. Almost certainly these figures are low. Over 100,000 nationalists were jailed, some for the duration of the war. India was finally quiescent.

With the Congress impotent, Jinnah set about building the Muslim League into a powerful mass party whose demands for the establishment of Pakistan would be irresistible when the time of final reckoning came. In April, 1943, the League captured the government of Bengal and, a month later, that of the North-West Frontier province. With all the Muslim-dominated provinces except the Punjab under Jinnah's control, the concept of a separate Muslim state was turning into a reality.

A few months later, Lord Linlithgow was succeeded as Viceroy by General Lord Wavell, formerly Commander-in-Chief Middle East and currently Commander-in-Chief India. Wavell considered himself to be a simple soldier and his approach to Indian problems was straightforward and honest. Probably his biggest fault as ruler of India at a time of endless discussion, manœuvre, and argument was his inability to talk easily; his long silences were legendary in the British Army. Yet he believed that the end of the British Raj was in sight and was determined to bring Indians into the central government and to work out the problems of independence.

In the fall of 1944 Gandhi (who had been released from prison on medical grounds) met Jinnah in Bombay and offered the Muslim leader a postwar plebiscite in Muslim areas on the question of separation from the rest of India. Essentially, it was an acceptance of the principle of Pakistan—but not in so many words. Jinnah demanded the exact words be said. Gandhi refused and the talks broke down. Jinnah, however, had greatly strengthened his own position and that of the League. The most influential member of the Congress had been seen to negotiate with him on equal terms as the leader of all the Muslims.

After the breakdown of the Gandhi-Jinnah talks, Wavell thought it was time for the British government to take a fresh initiative. In June, 1945, the Viceroy broadcast new proposals and invited Indian political leaders—all those in jail had now been released—to a meeting at the hill station of Simla, the historic summer home of the Viceroys.

The proposals were those of 1942 with the addition that the Viceroy's council was to be immediately reconstituted to consist entirely of Indian members except for the Viceroy himself and the commander-in-chief. Council representation, however, was to be dictated by *religious* rather than political criteria: there were to be equal proportions of Hindus and Muslims.

Jinnah and the Churchill government promptly made it impossible for the Congress to accept the Wavell formula. Jinnah insisted that the Muslim League alone had the right to nominate the Muslim members of the council and he was discreetly supported by the Tories in London and by at least one member of Wavell's staff, without Wavell's knowledge. The Congress, which since its inception had claimed to represent all Indians and not just Hindus, could not accept this. It was stalemate again.

With the failure of the Simla Conference, events moved like a landslide. Labour, which came into office in July, 1945, was committed to the cause of Indian independence. Unlike the Churchill government, it sympathized with the Congress as India's representative body of national and progressive forces. The Attlee government's first move, following Japan's surrender, was to declare a general election in India for the winter of 1945–46. As expected, the Congress won nearly all the seats in the Hindu-majority provinces. The Muslim League, though it captured outright only Bengal of the provinces Jinnah claimed for Pakistan, did much better than in the last general election, in 1937.

Trouble began sooner than anyone had anticipated. The Indian government decided it could not allow members of Bose's Japanese-sponsored Indian National Army to return home without punishment, lest the morale of the loyal Indian forces be ruined. (Bose himself, fleeing to Tokyo, had been killed in a plane crash at the war's end.) It decided to court-martial the I.N.A.'s leaders for "waging war against the King-Emperor." The Congress—which had still not recognized that the Muslim League, not the British, was now its real enemy—seized on the trials as a stick with which to beat the Empire.

The trials proceeded in a blaze of nationalist rhetoric, which intensified when the defendants were found guilty. When their sentences were later remitted on the grounds that they would become martyrs, it was too late. The accused and their supporters claimed victory. The outcome had an unsettling effect on Indians in the armed forces. If Bose and his men had been on the side of right and justice, then those who fought for the British must obviously be in the wrong. The logic was confused, but the tensions were very real. There were violent demonstrations.

In February, 1946, a warning was served on the British government that it would find it difficult, if not impossible, to keep the peace. Units of the Royal Indian Navy went "on strike" against low pay, bad food, and racial discrimination in Bombay and other ports, backing up their demands by training their guns shoreward. Recognizing the danger signs, Congress leaders helped to end the mutiny in Bombay (after the mutineers had refused to obey their British officers), but at Karachi the British military commander opened fire on the ships with artillery, causing heavy casualties. India was sliding into anarchy.

The British government seemed to realize this, and Attlee announced that a delegation of Cabinet ministers

A wartime Japanese propaganda leaflet depicts the British Army taking its pound of Indian flesh to feed Churchill's imperial appetite.

would visit India. The highest powered mission in the history of the British Raj was to set up a constitution-making body and a representative Viceroy's executive council.

In April, 1946, the Cabinet Mission arrived in India. It was headed by Lord Pethick-Lawrence, Secretary of State for India, a warm, emotional man who appealed to both Hindu and Muslim with his obvious and genuine love for India. He was accompanied by Sir Stafford Cripps, whose "cold-water logic" was a balance to Pethick-Lawrence's emotionalism.

Though Cripps had announced optimistically before leaving that "the gulf between these two points of view [of the Congress and the League] is by no means unbridgeable," the mission discovered it was as wide as the Indian Ocean. The Congress would agree to nothing that opened the door to Pakistan, the League to nothing that would shut it against Muslim demands. It was left to Cripps, a lawyer, to produce a solution, a complex

three-tiered federal system, that was beautifully logical and a superb exercise in academic planning—and doomed to failure. It promised to preserve Indian unity, allay Muslim fears of Hindu domination, and remove the Congress's fears of the splintering or "Balkanization" of India. But the plan, workable or not, was given no chance to prove itself. Both sides claimed contradictory rights on the composition of an interim government. It was back to the familiar stalemate.

The Cabinet Mission did achieve one thing: it convinced Indian leaders that the British were actually serious about handing over power. This meant that there was no longer an incentive for the Congress and the League to search for a compromise. Since there was now no need to fight the British for independence, the way was clear for a fight over the inheritance—a war of succession. The issues would be settled not around the table but in the streets.

Elections for a constituent assem-

bly took place in July, 1946, and proved dramatically that the Congress represented the majority of Hindus and the League the majority of Muslims. The Congress gained an absolute majority—205 seats to the Muslim League's 73. Nehru then made the astonishing declaration that Congress was "not bound by a single thing" and immediately outlined plans that went against the principles of the Cabinet Mission's proposals. The last chance for compromise had gone.

The Muslim League declared August 16, 1946, Direct Action Day, a silent statement of protest against both the British and the Congress. In most places there were only marches and the waving of black flags. But in Calcutta, seat of the League government of Bengal, demonstrations mushroomed into bloody rioting. Muslim mobs waited for Hindu shopkeepers to arrive at their businesses, then cold-bloodedly cut them down and looted their shops. Hindu mobs retaliated by maiming and killing

Below are the major figures in turbulent postwar India: Muhammed Ali Jinnah (left), "Father of Pakistan," and Jawaharlal Nehru (with imperial envoy Stafford Cripps). Opposite, club-wielding police battle rioters in Bombay in 1946; ten died in the flare-up.

Muslim old men, women, and children. The historic city of 2.5 million people was given over to four days of terror and death.

Sobered by these terrible events, Congress leaders accepted an invitation from the Viceroy to join the interim government. The Muslim League, in fear of being isolated, followed a month later, but with no intention of co-operating with the Congress. The League's next step was to boycott the constituent assembly. Against such tactics the Viceroy was helpless. As the fruitless discussions dragged on, the normally placid Wavell was exasperated beyond endurance. "This is lawyer's talk!" he exclaimed. "Talk to me in plain English, I am a soldier and you confuse me with the legalistic arguments." "We cannot help it if we are lawyers," Nehru replied, "No," said Wavell, "but you can talk to me like honest men who are interested in India's future and welfare!"

In desperation, Wavell produced "Operation Ebb-Tide," a scheme to withdraw British troops and administrators province by province, to force the Indians to co-operate with one another. Both Churchill and Attlee condemned the plan. On February 19, 1947, Wavell received his recall.

Next day Attlee announced that the British would leave India not later than June, 1948, and that Admiral Lord Louis Mountbatten would replace Wavell as Viceroy to prepare a plan for the transfer of power. The last act in the drama of India's fight for freedom had begun.

Four men dominated the stage, though the cast included 94 million Muslims and 295 million Hindus. There was Lord Mountbatten, cousin of the King-Emperor, his already impressive personality subtly enhanced by the aura of royalty. He had been a dynamic war leader, supreme commander of Allied forces in South-East Asia. Utterly self-confident, he radiated forcefulness, decisiveness, and above all, a sense of urgency. In contrast, like someone from another planet, there was Mahatma Gandhi—enigmatic, inconsistent in his attitude to Partition, but firmly unequivocal in his desire to bring peace and reconciliation to the riot-stricken area. Jawaharlal Nehru, Gandhi's succes-

sor and soon to be the first President of India, was emotional and unpredictable, particularly when the times called for patience and understanding. Finally there was Muhammad Ali Jinnah, in his elegant Bond Street clothes, with an inflexible will and a power to inspire loyalty almost as intense as that of Gandhi. His determination to achieve the creation of Pakistan as quickly as possible was reinforced by the knowledge—a secret carefully guarded—that he was dying of cancer.

The scene in which these men met to end an empire was dark with blood and anarchy. Time was running out. The Punjab was in virtual civil war. Bengal, after an uneasy quiet, seemed again on the edge of chaos. Despite Mountbatten's attempt to leave a united India behind the departing British, he was faced with the choice of Partition or collapse, Pakistan or civil war. Gandhi withdrew and concentrated his efforts on bringing about reconciliation between Muslims and Hindus in Bengal. He was not even to attend the independence celebrations.

On June 3, 1947, Mountbatten pro-

duced a plan for Partition. The British would transfer power to two new states—India and Pakistan—at midnight on August 14, 1947. A boundary commission would mark the lines of Partition.

The boundary commission was headed by Sir Cyril Radcliffe, a judge experienced in arbitration and with the additional "advantage" that he had never been to India and could not be accused of bias. He had just five weeks to divide the subcontinent. The four judges chosen to assist him (two Hindu and two Muslim) politely informed him that they were not going to risk their careers or indeed their lives by sitting on the commission. Completely unaided, working from outdated maps, Radcliffe accomplished his task in the allotted time. "People sometimes ask me whether I would like to go back and see India as it really is," he said later. "God forbid. Not even if they asked me. I suspect they'd shoot me out of hand—both sides."

In the rush to dismantle the Indian Empire, many errors were made that contributed to civil war, the deaths of 600,000 people, and the creation of some 14 million refugees. The warlike Sikhs of the Punjab, finding their homeland and their sacred places divided between India and Pakistan, reacted with fury. But it was not only the Sikhs who were involved in the slaughter. After Partition it became common for trains to arrive in Pakistan packed with hundreds of dead Muslim refugees and painted with the crude message "A present from India." Dead Hindus filled the returning trains.

One of the thorny problems was the status of the princely states within the two new countries. Mountbatten was of royal blood, but he had no sympathy for his Indian counterparts, privately calling them "a bunch of nitwits." A scheme was evolved under which accession to India would leave the states virtually independent except for external affairs, defence, and communications. The plan was put to Mountbatten, who enthusiastically agreed to use his influence to persuade the princes to accept.

By the time of Partition, all except three had agreed with varying degrees of reluctance. Two of the three holdouts were rulers of the most important states in India: the Muslim Nizam of the huge state of Hyderabad in the centre of India whose subjects were nearly all Hindus, and the Hindu Maharajah of the overwhelmingly Muslim state of Kashmir. The third was the tiny coastal state of Junagadh, 240 miles south of West Pakistan.

The Muslim Nawab of Junagadh, whose chief passion was breeding his 150 dogs, was persuaded to join Pakistan. It was a ludicrous choice, and when India became independent her army marched in to occupy the state to a rapturous welcome from the populace. Pakistan claimed the right to do exactly the same to Kashmir, should the Maharajah decide to opt for India. Dithering over his decision, he nearly caused a war between the two new countries in 1947. Nineteen years later that war was fought, and today the problem of Kashmir remains unsolved. The fabulously wealthy Nizam of Hyderabad thought he could go it alone and, in fact, managed to survive until India occupied his territory in 1949.

By then the long rule of the British was over. As the Indian Empire faded into the history books, it was left to Jawaharlal Nehru, on August 14, 1947, to pronounce the end of the struggle for independence: "Long years ago we made a tryst with destiny, and now the time comes when we shall redeem our pledge, not wholly or in full measure, but very substantially. At the stroke of the midnight hour, when the world sleeps, India will awake to life and freedom."

In Karachi, the capital of the new state of Pakistan, Muhammed Ali, who was to be the state's first Governor-General, made a less literary speech. But even its formality could not disguise his feeling of triumph. As he entered the parliament building, Jinnah made a revealing remark to his aide-de-camp. "Do you know," he said, "I never expected to see Pakistan in my lifetime. We have to be very grateful to God for what we have achieved."

Along with London's decision on India went parallel decisions on the rest of the Far East. In a matter of months after India's independence, both Burma and Ceylon took the same road. Later the Malay States, after a fierce bout with communist insurgency, became part of the new state of Malaysia. The sun set swiftly on the Eastern Empire.

As Partition became a reality, the soldiers and administrators who symbolized and maintained British supremacy in India, a supremacy that reached back nearly two centuries to Clive's victory at Plassey, packed their bags and returned home. It was difficult for many of them to believe. The Indian Civil Service had been recruiting young men to dedicate their lives to the service of the subcontinent as late as 1946. A few remained in the service of the new nations. Mountbatten, the last of the Viceroys, became the first Governor-General of free India, and British generals for a time commanded the armies of both countries.

But these were personal commitments. For Britain, "the brightest jewel in the British Crown" was lost forever. Perhaps two million Britons had left their bones in forgotten cemeteries scattered across the subcontinent. The rest was memory, nostalgia, the stuff of history books.

A small ceremony symbolized the historic change. On the evening of August 13, 1947, a small party of British officers made their way to the ruins of the Residency at Lucknow, scene of the heroic defence against the rebellious sepoys during the 1857 Mutiny. Since that year a Union Jack had flown day and night from the tower. The officers watched as the flag was hauled down and carefully folded. The flagstaff and its base were then demolished by British sappers. The flag was sent to the commander-in-chief. On the day of India's independence, George VI—no longer King-Emperor—received in audience his last Secretary of State for India. The King had only one personal request—that the Lucknow flag be given to him to hang at Windsor alongside the other historic banners of an Empire that had now lost its cornerstone.

—Michael Edwardes

III. Exit from the Middle East

In any reckoning of the trouble spots that plagued imperial Britain in the postwar years, none matches the bitter, tragic, crisis-ridden story of the Middle East. Nationalism vs. imperialism, Arab vs. Jew, the economics of oil vs. the politics of justice—through this tangled maze Britain tried to pick her way, and she is not entirely free of it yet.

The year 1945 saw the end of the war, Labour in power, and the surviving Jews of Europe demanding the right to go to Palestine. The British there faced manifold problems. One was Labour's rash commitment to unlimited Jewish immigration and the transfer of the bulk of the Arab population to neighbouring countries. There was the revival of Arab nationalism following a serious British miscalculation: sponsorship of the Arab League. The League had been encouraged by Britain to try to divert Arab preoccupations from Palestine; in fact it was united on very little else except anti-Zionism. Finally, U.S. interest in the Middle East was revived by the enormous proven reserves of oil in Saudi Arabia. Like his predecessor, President Truman was genuinely grieved at the suffering of European Jewry, yet the success of his treasured Marshall Plan for European recovery depended on the availability of oil in great quantity. Like the British in 1939, the U.S. could not afford a serious quarrel with the Arab world.

In 1945 Truman sent a personal emmissary to Europe to ascertain the situation of the Jews. The Jewish Agency had made earlier enquiries. Both reached the same conclusion: 100,000 Jews stood in immediate need of emigration. David Ben-Gurion, a rising figure in Zionist circles, led a delegation to the Colonial Office and demanded sanction for a Jewish immigration of 100,000 and the recognition of Palestine as a Jewish state. Truman urged Prime Minister Attlee to accept the immigration request. Both representations met emphatic refusal from British authorities; the old quotas would stand. That winter an "Anglo-American Committee of Enquiry" went to Europe and Palestine. In April, 1946, its unanimous report recommended the continuance of the British Mandate and the admission of 100,000 Jews. The Labour government, at odds after all over Middle East policy, rejected the report. Truman publicly welcomed it.

Palestine meanwhile was moving into a state of civil war among three combatants: Jews, Arabs, and British. Jewish terrorists, who had achieved notoriety in 1944 with the murder in Cairo of Lord Moyne, the British Minister of State, stepped up their activities. As sabotage and atrocities increased, the High Commission in desperation arrested Zionist leaders. In July, 1946, the Jewish terrorist Irgun group blew up the wing of the King David Hotel in Jerusalem that housed British military headquarters, killing 91 people, including British, Arabs, and Jews. Britain retaliated with increasingly violent attempts to stamp out the terrorists. The Arab League began to band together for an invasion of Palestine.

The last eighteen months of the British Mandate is a record of confusion, complication, inconsistency, loss of direction, and loss of nerve. Irresolution seemed infectious; everyone who attempted a solution lost his way before long. Perhaps the problem always had been insoluble—except by war.

Early in 1947 Ernest Bevin of the Foreign Office declared that Great Britain would hand back the trusteeship to the United Nations in its role as successor to the League of Nations. Yet the United Nations was frustrated at every turn by the High Commission. British political behaviour at this time seemed hardly sane, probably attributable to the nation's general postwar demoralization.

The UN made a bold but unavailing attempt to solve the problem by partition through its Special Committee on Palestine (UNSCOP). In the midst of the UNSCOP investigations, and certainly affecting them, there occurred the celebrated *Exodus* incident.

Since the war numerous attempts had been made by refugee ships to run the Royal Navy's blockade of Palestine. Few succeeded, but the publicity harvest for the Zionist cause was

The battered refugee ship *Exodus*, photographed at Haifa in 1947 after running the Royal Navy's blockade. The 4,500 German Jews aboard were refused entry to Palestine.

great. In June, 1947, the *Exodus* challenged the blockade and reached Haifa with some 4,500 German Jews on board. The refusal of British authorities to allow the passengers to land led to wild scenes of protest in Haifa and Jerusalem. The government, alarmed at rising anti-Semitism in Britain sparked by Jewish terrorist activities in Palestine, eventually routed the *Exodus* to Hamburg, where its passengers were given asylum in the British zone of Occupied Germany. Refugees from Nazi Germany, barred from their Promised Land, returned to Germany (of all places), forcibly disembarked by British troops—given the chance, Zionist propagandists could hardly have staged it better. World opinion was outraged. In the bright blaze of publicity Jewish terrorist atrocities like the blowing up of the King David Hotel faded and were all but forgotten.

In November, 1947, the UNSCOP plan for partitioning Palestine was approved by the United Nations. The British Mandate would end in eight months. Zionist leadership, accepting the notion of compromise, agreed to the plan and Jews danced in the streets. Their celebration was short-lived. Palestinian Arabs attacked at once, determined to alter the partition plan by force.

Over the next few months Arab assaults along the roads and on isolated settlements intensified. British military opinion anticipated a swift Arab victory. But the Jews struck back with equal venom. Both sides had been amassing illegal weapons under the noses of the British, and both were geared for war. At the end of March, 1948, the Zionist forces secretly received a massive supply of arms from Czechoslovakia. The Czech interest seems to have been only mercenary; they sold equal quantities of arms to the Arabs, but Zionist agents organized the theft of these shipments and redirected them to the Jewish fighting force.

Though Zionist troops were compelled to surrender almost the whole Jewish quarter of the old city of Jerusalem, a most bitter sacrifice, they were able at the beginning of April to fight a long battle with decisive success west of Jerusalem. This victory enabled them to keep the road to the coast open and, with great difficulty, to retain the new part of Jerusalem. Before this battle was concluded, terrorists on both sides were guilty of ghastly atrocities.

Since January there had been an increasing flight of Arab refugees from the contested areas; as panic grew, the fleeing thousands turned to tens of thousands and then hundreds of thousands. The British had lost the will and now the capacity to impose order. As helpless spectators they watched a policy undertaken with rash idealism go down amid hate and bloodshed.

Arab forces from neighbouring countries began to mass along Palestine's borders, waiting for the British to leave, and London decided to withdraw two months ahead of schedule. On May 14, 1948, the British Mandate ended and the High Commissioner departed Jerusalem.

That same day, in a ceremony at the Tel Aviv airport, David Ben-Gurion proclaimed the state of Israel. Israel's first act was to swing open the gates to the refugees who languished in British internment camps and to hundreds of thousands more from Europe and the Arab countries. Jews who had once lost all hope flooded into the Promised Land. By a secret agreement with Chaim Weizmann, President Truman immediately signified American recognition of the new state. Stalin soon announced Soviet recognition. Before such a combination Great Britain had no choice and finally recognized the new state on January 29, 1949.

Palestine's last High Commissioner had predicted that Britain's departure would unleash "misery, distress and chaos." The war that raged for the next seven months was far more terrible than even he had envisaged. Jews and Arabs strove alike in bitter combat, each to hold what the United Nations had accorded, each to seize from the other what it had been denied. The fighting ranged from the stark arid Negev Desert to the gentle hills of Galilee, from the shrine of old Jerusalem to the docks of Haifa.

Hostilities finally ended in a grudg-

David Ben-Gurion reads a declaration proclaiming the state of Israel in 1948.

ing series of armistice agreements between Israel and the Arab nations. Egypt occupied the Gaza Strip and Jordan annexed Judea, Samaria, and the old city of Jerusalem. But it was a peace in name only. Sporadic outbursts continued and broke into open warfare again in 1956 when Israeli units routed Egyptian forces east of the Suez Canal. In 1967, in the "Six-Day War," Israel seized all of Jerusalem, the Gaza Strip, the Sinai, the West Bank of the Jordan, and Syria's Golan Heights.

So the enmity between Arab and Jew continues. Britain had faced one of the most tragic and intractable dilemmas in her imperial history—and found it insoluble.

In Egypt in the postwar period there was a similar gap between high British principles and confused British actions. Humiliation was the result.

The Egyptian government believed that its fulfilment of treaty obligations during the war gave it the right to generous treatment from Britain. The decision had anyway been taken to grant independence to India, removing the chief historical reason for the continued occupation of Egypt. In 1946 Britain accepted the principle of total evacuation—but once again failed to reach firm agreement on terms, refusing to surrender sovereignty over the Sudan. In the Suez Canal Zone there remained 80,000 British troops, eight times as many as stipulated by the 1936 treaty and a constant affront to Egyptian pride.

The nationalists, incensed by King Farouk's feeble wartime capitulation and the Wafd's collaboration with Britain, accumulated additional grievances. In the army an organization called the Free Officers, formed by a brilliant young officer, Gamal Abdul Nasser, plotted the overthrow of the monarchy.

The regime tottered from crisis to crisis. In 1948 its ill-trained and ill-equipped army suffered humiliating defeat at the hands of Israel. In 1950 Farouk turned in despair to his old enemies, the Wafd. Anxious to cleanse their soiled nationalist credentials, the Wafd stepped up the anti-British campaign, denounced the 1936 treaty unilaterally, and launched a sabotage and guerrilla campaign against the Suez Canal Zone. This ended disastrously.

The country was now virtually ungovernable. In July, 1952, Nasser's Free Officers were able to overthrow the monarchy and the parliamentary regime with astonishing ease. The British made no attempt to intervene.

At first all went well with the new government. Whatever Britain's doubts about the ability of a band of young colonels to govern Egypt, they seemed to be capable of maintaining order and protecting foreign interests. They showed political sagacity by announcing their willingness to separate the Sudan question from that of the Suez Canal Zone occupation—a move that could have solved Anglo-Egyptian difficulties at a stroke.

It also seemed an astute move to oust Britain from the Sudan and preserve Egyptian influence there. Over the years of Anglo-Egyptian deadlock since 1936, Britain had acted unilaterally to establish the Sudan as an independent, pro-British entity. In 1948 an elected legislative assembly was formed representing the whole country, and London proceeded with plans for Sudanese self-government under a British Governor-General. The situation was entirely changed by the Nasser coup. His new regime formally accepted the right of the Sudanese to self-determination and therefore to the choice of independence. The Free Officers thought they were calling Britain's bluff, believing that once they were given a free choice the majority of Sudanese would opt for union with Egypt.

Having accepted the principle of self-determination, both Britain and Egypt had to run the risk that at the coming elections the Sudanese would choose full independence. To Britain's dismay, the elections were won by a coalition of groups that stood for union with Egypt. To Egypt's dismay, the Sudanese nationalist parties at once about-faced and expressed their desire for complete independence. The assembly passed a resolution demanding the evacuation of both British and Egyptian forces from the Sudan. On January 1, 1956, the flag of the Sudanese Republic was raised and the 57-year life of Lord Cromer's curious brainchild, the Anglo-Egyptian Condominium, came to an end.

The Sudanese settlement did not improve relations between Egypt and Britain, but it did open the way towards an agreement on a British evacuation of Egypt—the principal goal of the Free Officers. Negotiations were prolonged and difficult, but on October 18, 1954, final agreement was signed in Cairo. On March 31, 1956, some three months earlier than provided for in the agreement, the last British troops left Port Said.

"A new era of friendly relations based on mutual trust, confidence and cooperation exists between Egypt and Britain and the Western countries," Nasser said at the time of the signing of the 1954 agreement. "We want to get rid of the hatred in our hearts and start building up our relations with Britain on a solid basis of mutual trust and confidence which has been lacking for the past seventy years."

It was not to be. The antagonisms engendered during the negotiations over the Sudan and the Canal Zone occupation grew into something much worse. Nasser began to look beyond Egypt's borders towards the creation of a neutral and independent Arab bloc under Egyptian leadership allied to other nations in Africa and Asia. The British government, still inclined to patronize Egypt as a natural Western satellite, soon came to regard the revolutionary regime as a mortal danger to British interests in the Arab world. Prime Minister Anthony Eden developed an almost pathological hatred of Nasser, whom he regarded as the source of all Britain's troubles in the Middle East. Eden once shouted at Anthony Nutting of the Foreign Office, "But what's all this nonsense about isolating Nasser, of 'neutralizing' him, as you call it? I want him destroyed, can't you understand?"

The consequence of this hysterical rage was folly. In July, 1956, four months after the last British soldiers left Port Said, Nasser nationalized the French- and British-owned Suez Canal. Seeing this as so serious a threat to British interests that it justified the use of force, Eden secretly initiated plans for an Anglo-French invasion. The two countries prepared for joint operations by air, land, and sea and invited Israel, long angered by Egypt's support of Palestine guerrillas, to strike at the same time. On October 29 the Israelis attacked, giving Britain and France the excuse to invade Egypt in the guise of peacemakers and protectors of the Canal.

World opinion was not deceived. The British and French were assailed from every quarter for their blatant cynicism. Russia threatened rocket attack, the UN called for a cease-fire, and even the United States, upon whom Eden had relied for support, condemned the attack. The pound plummeted throughout the world and Arab countries stopped the flow of oil. President Eisenhower refused the British credit to buy American oil unless there was an immediate cease-fire and evacuation. Eden had no choice but to surrender and endure the humiliation of a withdrawal.

In Victorian days the British (and the French, too) would have protected what they regarded as their vital interests with an immediate strike and not waited three months. They would have marched in boldly and not hidden behind an invented subterfuge. And they would have ignored the plaints of world opinion. But this was a new age, an age of Cold War, and the international balance of power had

Above, British commandos prepare for a dawn assault on Port Said, Mediterranean terminus of the Suez Canal, during the Anglo-French attempt to seize the Canal in 1956. Opposite, troops evacuate Port Said after pressure from the major powers thwarted the venture.

changed drastically. The Suez crisis brought these lessons home. The Empire's last fling had failed.

The third area of imperial concern in the Middle East was that region familiarly known as "east of Suez"—Arabia and the Persian Gulf. The end of British imperialism here was almost anticlimactic. In 1971 the last relics of the Empire in the Middle East slid quietly into history. Almost without knowing it, Britain said good-by to the last, scattered outposts of the Raj.

English involvement in the region went back to the early 17th Century, when Persia was the mistress of the Gulf. In 1619 the Persian Emperor granted the East India Company a monopoly of his country's silk trade. By the second half of the 18th Century, however, Persia was sinking into chaos and threats to the East India Company's supremacy in the Gulf were appearing from all directions. The British response was cautious but consistent. Her primary imperial concern was to protect her trade routes to the East, especially to India. And so for over a century and a half she was led into a steady and, as she believed, defensive extension of imperial con-

trol from the Persian mainland westward to the Arabian shore of the Gulf and thence, by degrees, round the whole Arabian coast until by 1914 a *cordon sanitaire* covered the approaches to India all the way from Teheran to Suez.

The pattern of British activity in this region was also consistent. It had two main features. In the first place, the "British" presence was Indian in origin, control, and style. From Cairo to Constantinople London juggled the intricacies of the Eastern Question; east of Suez the British in India were in command.

In the second place, British control was based on the Pax Britannica: maritime rather than territorial, a girdle of sea power round the eastern extremities of the Arab world. Where territorial control of some kind was deemed essential it was achieved by the traditional British method of indirect influence. The Indian administration simply extended its system of protective overlordships from the native states of the subcontinent to the petty coastal rulers of Arabia and the Gulf. Only in one place, some 75 square miles round the port of Aden

near the entrance to the Red Sea, did the British assume the responsibility of colonial rule. Elsewhere they took some 40 or 50 independent principalities into a variety of treaty relationships that made them what Lord Curzon called "loyal feudatories" of the Crown.

What little more was needed to complete the British cordon round the approaches to India was accomplished in the First World War with the collapse of the Ottoman Empire. When the Mesopotamian Valley was formally included in the British sphere of interest as a postwar League of Nations Mandate, the Empire appeared supreme from the Caspian to Cairo. Yet it was still an empire of influence and custom, as maritime and Indian as ever. The goals remained the protection of British trade and the extension of India's defences.

Yet in that moment of apparently unchallenged supremacy the Raj, in truth, had already passed its peak and in both its Arab and its Persian outposts new revolutionary forces were emerging that would eventually destroy the whole imperial structure. They were those 20th-Century twins

of Middle Eastern politics: nationalism and oil.

The first oil concession, signed by the Shah of Persia, was dated May 21, 1901. Although its terms were to be revised, denounced, broken, and restored many times by many different signatories long before its 60 years were up, it was the foundation of one of the biggest economic operations the world had ever seen and its results inspired political changes more radical than any the Middle East had known for centuries.

The first strikes prompted other countries to seek concessions in the area, and the British hurried to plug possible loopholes in their screen round the Gulf by signing agreements with all the local Arab states, from Bahrain and Kuwait to the Trucial coast and Muscat, giving them the exclusive right to oil concessions in their territories. This was the first sign that Britain would soon switch her policy from maritime containment in the interests of India to territorial engagement for economic gain.

The Empire was meanwhile being forced to come to terms with that other new and challenging phenomenon encouraged by the First World War—nationalism. Like the search for

oil, nationalist rumblings from the Arabian interior forced the British to look to the land in earnest. To leave frontiers unmarked and tribes at war in regions nominally under British protection or control was to place both the new oil concessions and imperial authority in jeopardy.

From Iraq to Aden diplomatic negotiations with the new Arab leaders went hand-in-hand with the pacification of unruly tribesmen and the first attempts at frontier-making. Snarling biplanes of the RAF dropped bombs on rebellious villagers in Kurdestan while Indian officials trekked into the Yemeni mountains to talk to the new Imam. Soldiers, surveyors, and administrators followed them and a wave of explorers penetrated parts of Arabia rarely, if ever, seen before by Europeans. By the mid-1930s the modern map of Arabia was taking shape and a fitful sort of peace was falling upon ancient tribal squabbles.

The new treaties that were signed marked a transfer from the Indian administration's influence to the authority of Whitehall. Increasingly preoccupied by the independence struggle at home, Indian officials no longer had the energy or the interest to spare for the Arabian outposts of

their empire. In 1937 the Colonial Office in London assumed responsibility for the Aden Protectorate and made Aden itself a full-fledged Crown Colony, with the intention of pursuing a "forward policy" of colonial development and defence to safeguard Britain's interests.

But the time was already later than it seemed. The ink was scarcely dry on this scheme when the Second World War began. For the next ten years the war and its aftermath prevented any rapid reforms, and when the postwar demand for oil and the renewed challenge of Arab nationalism forced Britain to intervene more decisively in Arabian affairs, it was too late for any "forward policy" to be effective. The rest of the Empire was by then crumbling and British power was in eclipse.

In a consistent pattern of nationalist challenge and British response, the Empire sought to assert itself all round Arabia. The demands of oil and strategy, the provision of advice and social welfare, the need for economic development, the extension of law and order—in one combination or another all these drew the British on towards new horizons and new responsibilities. Yet, in spite of it all, these territories in which Britain now sank the last of her imperial energy remained in limbo. At heart the Arabian sheikdoms the British were trying to protect were still the same lawless places whose "mania for fighting" had been so striking a century before.

Few of their inhabitants were ever seen without a rifle, a dagger, and a bandolier full of cartridges. Slavery was still endemic to most of them; poverty and isolation seemed inbred. Even in those states where oil discoveries had begun to confer vast riches, the follies of the local ruling families, unused to such wealth, were legendary. Girls were imported en masse from Beirut for their harems, and gold watches and jewelled bracelets were showered upon casual visitors while their own people looked on in mingled wonder and resentment. In Qatar the ruler was reputed to cast aside his Cadillacs when the ash trays were full.

In vain did the British Resident send his agents to remonstrate with such men. The new world was not their world and the treaties their ancestors had signed with the Raj had never required them to listen to British reproaches about the way they should run their own affairs. And so an imperial system constructed for the first half of the 19th Century shambled on uncertainly into the second half of the 20th—an increasingly embarrassing example of British responsibility without power. Of course it could not last. As the 1950s opened, events elsewhere were sweeping Arabia and the Persian Gulf into the mainstream of international politics and forcing the British Empire into one of the last of its many rearguard actions.

In the years of imperial withdrawal after the Second World War, few men so nettled the pride of Britain as Dr. Mohammed Mossadeq, Prime Minister of Iran. Tearful, contumacious, hysterical, stubborn, he seemed preeminently the sort to whom the Empire of old would have given short shrift; when he nationalized the Anglo-Iranian Oil Company in 1951 it was widely assumed that the dispatch of a gunboat, in the good old-fashioned way, would soon bring him to heel.

But though the cruiser *Mauritius* stood by off Abadan with orders to land marines if necessary, Anglo-Iranian stayed nationalized and Mossadeq remained in office. The marines were never landed, the cruiser was withdrawn, and three years later, when the crisis was finally resolved, Britain's exclusive interest in Iranian oil had been reduced to a small joint shareholding with a number of American companies.

The Mossadeq affair was a blow from which British prestige in the region never recovered. Iran, it is true, suffered from a commercial blockade of her oil exports and Mossadeq ultimately lost his job. But he had called the British bluff in the Gulf, and what had once seemed an imposing structure of imperial power was revealed as a rickety façade. In retrospect this outcome seems inevitable. The withdrawal from India and the abandonment of Palestine had already signalled the approaching end of Empire elsewhere and, although postwar nationalism had made only a fitful impact upon the British-protected fringes of Arabia and the Gulf before the Mossadeq crisis, the competition of the new superpowers was being increasingly felt.

In Saudi Arabia the Americans had secured an oil monopoly before the war, and ibn Saud had slid from the protection of the Raj into the more capacious arms of Washington. American oil advisers and State Department officials discreetly penetrated all Britain's commercial strongholds round the Gulf. During the war the United States had taken over Britain's traditional military and political influence in Iran as a result of the great American drive to get war supplies into Russia through the Persian back door. When Mossadeq destroyed the British oil monopoly there, the Americans took over the commercial leadership as well.

The Soviet Union was equally active. The Russian tactic was to encourage incipient nationalist movements throughout the Middle East. Mossadeq himself was spurred on by Russia's Communist allies in Iran, and growing Arab bitterness over the creation of Israel, accompanied by accusations of British and American betrayal, offered Moscow many new revolutionary friends.

By now the proven oil deposits round the Persian Gulf amounted to two-thirds of the free world's resources and, although Britain's share of them had dwindled to only half that of the United States, the profits were vital to Britain's balance of payments and the preservation of the worldwide sterling area. Strategy and finance, therefore, prompted a hard line.

It made for painful dilemmas. One of the justifications for the 1956 Anglo-French attack on Egypt, Anthony Eden said, was the fear that if Nasser "got away" with nationalizing the Suez Canal he might thereafter get his hands on Arab oil, and with Russian approval, strangle Britain's livelihood. In the aftermath as well as the event, everything went wrong. The Canal was blocked, the trans-desert pipelines from Iraq to the Mediterranean were blown up, Saudi Arabia refused to pump oil for British (or French) tankers, and there were riots in Bahrain and explosions in Kuwait. When the final cost was reckoned, it included the destruction of nearly all remaining trust between Britain and the Arab world.

Yet still the British government was unwilling to reverse its imperial policies altogether. The protection of the Gulf's oil was now as much an obsession in Whitehall as the defence of India had been a century earlier, and the troops and aircraft that pulled out of Egypt, Jordan, and Iraq were concentrated afresh upon the last remaining British strongholds in Arabia.

Aden, for so long little more than India's farthest outpost, became Britain's largest overseas military base. The naval units in the Gulf were strengthened, troops were trained in the Oman desert, and the belated "forward policy" of the 1930s became an urgent drive for military security, economic development, and political reform. But the British were running further than ever behind the clock and, paradoxically, the more they tried to catch up, the more events accelerated out of their control.

The nationalist bandwagon was

rolling euphorically onwards in the post-Suez atmosphere of Arab triumph and British defeat. Yemen increased its raids on the Aden Protectorate and appealed to the United Nations for support. Both the Soviet Union and China took their first cautious steps into the quicksands of Arabian politics by aiding Yemen.

Farther east, in Oman, the British were moved to protect their oil interests and to honour old obligations to the Sultan. Three times between 1955 and 1959 small British forces joined the Sultan's men in subduing rebellious chieftains. In 1961 the threadbare forces of a vanishing Empire were dragged into yet another gunboat action, to preserve Kuwait from a takeover by Iraq. Such sorties added to the growing catalogue of imperialist crimes in the folklore of Arab nationalism.

It was in Aden that the British presence seemed most obviously self-defeating. Ostensibly established to defend the Gulf oil fields, this post-Suez base had to devote most of its energies to protecting itself from local unrest. In 1962 a multisided civil war broke out, involving Egyptians and Yemeni rebels, with Russian and Chinese support, against supporters of the old regime, sustained by money and arms from the Saudis, who proclaimed a holy war against communism and Nasserism on the sacred soil of Arabia.

By the end of 1967 it was all over and practically every party to the conflict was a loser—not least the British, who were forced to evacuate Aden. The indignity of their final departure ranked with the retreat from Palestine. There were no friendly ceremonies of independence, only bitterness and the taste of failure. The British High Commissioner had to be lifted out by helicopter under armed guard to a carrier standing well offshore.

Like a golfer scrambling nervously from one bunker to another, the British extricated themselves from the perilous trap of Aden only to land ignominiously in another along the Persian Gulf. To replace the Aden base they created a vast new army camp in the little Trucial state of Sharjah and justified a general increase in

their military forces in the Gulf by the now ritual reference to the need to protect the free world's oil supplies.

By 1968 the Soviet Union had greatly strengthened her influence in Iraq and was maintaining a naval squadron in the Indian Ocean with a boldness that must have made Lord Curzon turn in his grave. China had sent military and technical advisers into the new Marxist state of South Yemen. Rebellion flourished in Muscat.

To withdraw before such threats seemed unthinkable, yet the unthinkable happened. Britain was faced with one of her recurring postwar financial crises. The pound was devalued. In 1968 Labour Prime Minister Harold Wilson announced that the cost of maintaining world-wide military bases had become too great and that the British presence in the Gulf—along with that in Singapore and Malaysia—would have to go by the end of 1971. For the next three years the only real question to be answered was just how big a mess the British would leave behind.

In the end it was not nearly as bad as many people had feared, despite the fact that Britain's withdrawal exposed once more many Gulf conflicts both old and new. Luckily the oil money was now plentiful nearly everywhere and bought off much potential discontent: the traditional rulers were persuaded to modify their former extravagances in the interests of their citizens. So the British departure from the lands east of Suez proceeded.

At last only the seven Trucial states at the mouth of the Persian Gulf remained. December 1, 1971, was set as the date of withdrawal. On the appointed day the British Resident flew down from Bahrain to the Trucial coast for a final farewell tour by car and helicopter of the last appendages of his once-proud estate. To each ruler in his sheikdom the Resident went in turn, with a flowery Arabic speech in one pocket and a formal declaration of British withdrawal in the other.

With the Sheik of Abu Dhabi there was no hitch. He had put his qualms about Britain's departure behind him and, secure in his great wealth, sent

A British armoured car is saluted by a camel-mounted honour guard in an early stage of the imperial withdrawal from Aden in 1967. Later stages saw few such amenities.

the Resident on his way with an Islamic blessing. In Dubai the ruler, too, preferred the British to stay, but since he also was now a wealthy man and vice-president of the new Trucial union, he accepted the inevitable with a wry joke and turned back swiftly to his account books. In Sharjah a crowd of 300 people welcomed the Resident in the ruler's council chamber.

In the Sheikdom of Ajman the aged ruler rose from his prayers to receive the Englishman, saying that what must be done must be done—it was the will of Allah. In Umm al-Qaiwain there was a brief and equally resigned ceremony with the Sheik and his son. There were a few difficult moments in Ras al-Khaimah when Sheik Saqr made a speech about British perfidy and a crowd outside his palace shouted for the Resident's blood. But the Sheik was an honourable man, and

when he faced the crowd and demanded their traditional courtesy towards a guest they fell back shamefacedly and let the ruler lead the Resident, hand-in-hand, to his car.

It was after dark when the Resident returned to the little town of Dubai for the last act. There, in a small suburban villa, he was to meet the seventh of the Trucial rulers, Sheik Mohammed of Fujairah, known to nearly every Briton in the Gulf by the affectionate name of "Fudge." He was an amiable but elderly gentleman of notoriously fallible memory, who had once suggested that the best way for the British to deal with his independence problems was to enroll his little state as a member of the Greater London Council.

As the British car arrived he was nodding, half asleep, and when the Resident began his speech it was soon

apparent that Fudge had forgotten what the meeting was about. He had never agreed that his British friends should leave, he protested. He had never in his life desired such a thing. Patiently Her Majesty's representative reminded him of the unwelcome facts of life, of the announcements and discussions and agreements of the last three years about what must now replace the arrangements of the past century and a half. Mumbling his sorrow and bewilderment, the old man at last gave in. The final instrument of British renunciation was signed, the last Arabic blessings were offered and returned, and the Resident stepped out into the darkness again, freed of all his historical burdens. He had worked himself, as well as the Empire, out of a job.

—Peter Mansfield,
Christopher Sykes, David Holden

IV. The Wind of Change

Early in 1960 the South African parliament was addressed by Britain's Prime Minister, Harold Macmillan. He praised the progress of the Union and expounded on the growing trade between the two countries and Britain's investment in South African industrialization. The nods of approval ended, however, when he proceeded to impressions of his recent visits to Ghana, Nigeria, and the Federation of Rhodesia and Nyasaland.

"In the twentieth century, and especially since the end of the war," Macmillan observed, "we have seen the awakening of national consciousness in people who have for centuries lived in dependence on some other power. Fifteen years ago this movement spread through Asia. . . . Today the same thing is happening in Africa. . . . The wind of change is blowing through this continent, and whether we like it or not, this growth of national consciousness is a political fact. . . ."

The South Africans did not like it. Their Prime Minister, Dr. Hendrik Verwoerd, rose to respond to Mr.

Macmillan on a note of some asperity, in which he included a defence of apartheid as the solution to African tribal (not national) consciousness. What particularly incensed the South Africans was Macmillan's suggestion that their own Afrikaner nationalism was simply the first of the African nationalisms, and they objected to a public statement from such an authority that African nationalism even existed; the admission, they feared, might bring about the Thing itself.

Macmillan only made explicit in Cape Town what had been implicitly accepted in London for some years. But until the late 1950s only a few well-informed and far-seeing people realized quite how rapidly Africa would follow Asia into the era of self-assertive and often anti-Western national states. Most people, even in the Labour party, supposed that the independence of India, Pakistan, Ceylon, Burma, and Malaysia would be followed by a longish pause. It was granted that Africa must be prepared to follow that same road, but it was imagined in London, Brussels, and

Paris that the process would be a leisurely one.

Compared with Asia, Africa was seen as backward, lacking in culture and education and still raw from "savagery." A middle class and an educated elite were needed in numbers sufficient to underpin responsible local government, not just produce a passable imitation of the Indian Civil Service. The notion that Africa could remain colonial while Asia lived independent did not appear inconsistent to British minds. In the early fifties plans were on paper for a huge new Colonial Office building near Parliament Square, and the recruitment of men for the colonial service went on much as before.

To many businessmen, including those with great holdings in Africa, it seemed that for another 20 or 30 years Africa would provide an expanding frontier for European enterprise and energies, a boomland that modern technology would open up as darkest Africa had never been opened up previously. It would be a penetration not just by railways but by highways, airways, hotel and residential developments, mineral extraction, dams and irrigation, and above all by vast agricultural developments springing from new botanical and chemical discoveries. In the late forties the Labour government decided to take Africa by storm with the great Groundnuts Scheme in Tanganyika, which was to show how modern machinery could tame Africa and feed Britons peanuts. The scheme broke down on pests and drought and administrative collapse, giving Round One to Mother Africa. Other great developments, like the Kariba Dam, the Volta River s., Ugandian copper extraction, and the Ripon Falls irrigation plan, went ahead, however. "Eur-Africa" in this sense was a live commercial concept.

The Colonial Office had a broad, if vague, strategy. This was to speed the beneficial spadework of the business tycoons by public investment under the Colonial Development and Welfare Acts (the first was in 1940) and the Commonwealth Development Corporation. The hope was that viable political unions would come into existence, mainly under white leadership, that would thrive economically. The first of these was the federation of Northern and Southern Rhodesia and Nyasaland, which, after several years of gestation, was inaugurated in 1953 without much consultation of African views. It was hoped that there would also emerge an East African grouping (Kenya, Uganda, Zanzibar, Tanganyika), which already had a regional economic customs union with a secretariat to run common services like railways and telecommunications. In West Africa the plan was to bring forward the most advanced and wealthy colony, the Gold Coast, which had prospered on cocoa in wartime, as the nucleus for a union including Gambia, Sierra Leone, and Nigeria. It was a well-meaning dream, promising Colonial Office mandarins years of future employment.

It was a dream blind to realities. It took no account of the pace of independence and nationalism in North Africa, especially in Egypt and the Sudan. The 1956 fiasco of the Anglo-French seizure of the Suez Canal exposed to all Africans able to read or listen to a radio the weakness of their colonial masters. The independence of colonial peoples was on show much nearer than Delhi or Jakarta, built not on ages of apprenticeship but on sheer political determination and the discovery that Britain no longer had the stomach for the use of force. Harold Macmillan, in fact, became Prime Minister because of the failure of Eden's policy of maintaining imperial control over the oil routes. Long before he used the phrase in 1960, "the wind of change" had blown him into office.

The Colonial Office was ordered to review its forward planning, and it was decided that Britain must disengage in Africa—politically—in a matter of years rather than decades. The Tory rank and file, even in the wake of the Suez disaster, still believed Britain led a "British Commonwealth and Empire." They had to be undeceived. This was Macmillan's mission.

By the time of Suez, the men who would take power in Africa and proclaim the end of the continent's European episode were already on the stage. They controlled nationalist parties, newspapers, and public opinion to a degree that doomed even the new Colonial Office timetable. Hardly known to the Briton in the street, they were egregiously underestimated by the colonial administrators who did know them. They would precipitate a "scramble out of Africa."

In West Africa loyalty to British culture (ill-requited as it was) ran high until the 1930s. Nascent nationalism advocated no more than local self-rule under British sovereignty. Even that seemed presumptuous to British officials and traders. Far from accepting that the spread of British education should naturally produce an elite of African leaders capable of working with their white confreres (as happened in the Indian Civil Service), the British looked on them with disfavour, even fear.

But the lid could not be kept on. In 1935 Dr. J. B. Danquah started in Accra the Gold Coast Youth Conference. In Nigeria Herbert Macaulay, with Wallace Johnson of Sierra Leone, formed the Nigerian National Democratic party and vigorously advocated "autonomy within the British Empire." Macaulay dressed as the perfect Englishman, but his newspapers often bitterly criticized the arrogance of the British in Africa. Nigerian political organization really began with the arrival from the United States of Dr. Mnamdi Azikiwe, with his degrees from Howard, Pennsylvania, and Columbia. Azikiwe's paper, the *West African Pilot*, propounded a new and progressive nationalism. H. O. Davies, who had worked under Professor Harold Laski in London, helped to build the new nationalism and start branches of the youth movement.

The influence of these various parties, councils, youth movements, voluntary associations, and above all the nationalist newspapers, was considerable. The British were sublimely unaware how the awe Africans felt for Europeans in the early 1900s had worn off, and that in the prevailing black view the white man was a cunning cheat who used his technical prowess to exploit black people.

These nationalists recognized that European-style education was the key to freedom in the modern world, preferably education abroad, where contact could be made with broader minds than those of missionary teachers and snobbish colonial officials and where democracy could be inspected in action. In the late thirties young Africans flocked abroad in increasing numbers, including Jomo Kenyatta, Hastings Banda, H. O. Davies, Kwame Nkrumah, Obafemi Awolowo, and dozens more who would make their names in the 1950s. In America they met Negro thinkers such as W.E.B. Du Bois. In Britain their Mecca was the London School of Economics, where Laski taught political science with a socialist bent, and where they met many strong anti-Empire figures in the Labour party.

Many were in London and other Western cities during the war years, where they read the Four Freedoms enunciated by Roosevelt and Churchill and felt the upsurge of left-wing thinking that in Britain swept Clement Attlee to power, and they noted the commitment in the United Nations

Kwame Nkrumah (centre) waves to crowds celebrating Ghana's independence in March, 1957. Nine years later he was deposed by his army; he died in exile in 1972.

charter to bring dependencies forward to self-government. Less educated Africans were serving on battlefields across the world. Their eyes were opened to the realities of a life in which whites were not gods always living in superior conditions but who had to take orders and serve often in menial capacities like any black man. Some 50,000 ex-servicemen returned to African villages with new stories to tell of the white man. This development was seminal, for it created the link that had been missing between the African intellectual and the rural masses. In the immensity of Africa they were few—but they were enough.

In 1945 there arrived in London a man destined to bring all these forces for change together. Kwame Nkrumah had already proved, as a schoolmaster in the early 1930s, an impressive speaker on political subjects. He was sent to the United States, where he stayed for ten years and acquired (like Azikiwe) several degrees in

political science. Nkrumah absorbed all the theories, ranging from Marx to Du Bois, from Jefferson to Lincoln, from Gandhi to Hitler. It was as an intellectual of wide background and great personal charm that he made his debut in left-wing London circles.

J. B. Danquah's party, the United Gold Coast Convention, was making good progress, and it was suggested that a full-time secretary-general was needed to make it a popular political movement. It was proposed to Danquah that the young and brilliant Nkrumah should be asked to return to take up the post. Nkrumah had to be persuaded, for he did not see the U.G.C.C. as the tryst with destiny he was waiting for.

With a political flair he hardly knew he possessed, Nkrumah sensed that the political situation would respond to a quite different approach, one he had read of in his books on Lenin. He went directly to the people and spoke of their wrongs and how only an

African government could redress them. When he organized a separate youth wing within the party and started a newspaper to expound his views, other members of the U.G.C.C. began to oppose his rabble-rousing methods. In 1949 the breaking point was reached. The Nkrumah youth section had become a party within a party, and when Danquah reproved him Nkrumah judged the time was ripe to break away. From that day his Convention Peoples party became the mass nationalist movement in the Gold Coast. His C.P.P. plan for "positive action" involved non-violent boycotts, strikes, and demonstrations.

Meanwhile, a more liberal constitution was being drafted under the new Gold Coast Governor, Sir Charles Arden-Clarke, specifically designed for "responsible government"—though still with a timetable of decades in mind. Neither the Governor nor the Colonial Office saw how strong the C.P.P. had become, how late in the day it was. The new constitution gave power to any party that could sweep the board in the limited number of elected seats; when elections were held, the C.P.P. won 34 out of the 38 seats, even though Nkrumah was in jail for sedition. Sir Charles decided to accept the verdict.

He called Nkrumah direct from prison to be "leader of Government business," and a year later Prime Minister. The Gold Coast's approach to its independence as the state of Ghana was slowed by Nkrumah's discovery that administration is more difficult than protest politics, and that his party was not overwhelmingly accepted by the country. Nevertheless, in 1954 came full self-government, the Governor retaining only reserved power over defence and foreign affairs. In that year, despite serious internal corruption, the C.P.P. won 70 per cent of the seats in parliament, and this convinced the British that the time was approaching to transfer power finally.

There then arose in Ghana, as there was to arise in many African states after the cries for freedom had succeeded, a sudden demand for a division-of-power federalism. An opposition group demanded checks on the "creeping dictatorship" of Nkrumah and the C.P.P. The distrust of Nkrumah was suddenly African, not British. Violence swept dissident Ashanti. Whitehall was embarrassed but the government was committed. To defend the new black democracy against overthrow, a form of regional devolution, which entrenched the constitutional amendment procedure, was devised. One mistrustful leader of the opposition was sufficiently satisfied to remark that they had made it very difficult for anyone to establish a dictatorship.

He was to discover how wrong he was. The Colonial Office once again put Ghana through the test of another election, which the C.P.P. duly won. It was a bitter election, where bribery and murder played a part, yet the British raised no objection to the results. The opposition boycotted the chamber when the motion for independence was solemnly moved. London decided to risk it—in any case the risks of delay seemed far greater—and in March, 1957, Kwame Nkrumah was yielded the "political kingdom" in the form of a parliamentary system with safeguards for minority rights.

The C.P.P. immediately began to destroy the paper safeguards. When the opposition was sufficiently weakened, Nkrumah turned on the C.P.P. to weaken it as a possible rival to his own authority. What emerged was Nkrumahism—one-man, rather than one-party, rule. It took just nine years to complete the destruction of all that British officials did in "preparing" Ghana for independence. In 1966 an exasperated army expelled Nkrumah from his dictatorship. But in those nine years the wind of change had blown the rest of British Africa to pieces.

It was Nkrumah who unveiled the "African personality" as a political factor, and introduced the white world to the concept of "neo-colonialism" —the persistence of colonialists who, cast out of an ex-colony's political kingdom, hung on to the economic power and thus obstructed African sovereignty.

In 1958 Nkrumah called the fully independent African states (Ghana, Egypt, Ethiopia, Liberia, Libya, Morocco, Sudan, Tunisia) to Accra to discuss the liberation of the rest of the continent right down to Cape Town. The independence of Ghana was meaningless, he said, if all Africa were not freed from colonial or racialist rule. Ghana, it was made clear, was far more than just a small cocoa republic; it was to become the base for liberating and energizing a new and mighty Africa. Advisers flatteringly opened up even larger vistas. Nkrumah proclaimed his mission on tours of the free African nations and the United States. He visited Nehru, who in the aftermath of Suez shared the same viewpoint: the need to dismantle what remained of British imperial power.

On his return he presided over an even more significant conference: the All-African Peoples Conference, to which nationalist parties and leaders from all over Africa were invited. In attendance were Mboya of Kenya, Kaunda of Northern Rhodesia, Banda of Nyasaland, Lumumba of the Congo, and many others, English, French, and Portuguese-speaking. It was a roll-call of those destined to become presidents, prime ministers, revolutionaries, dictators.

To Nkrumah a "continental government" (to be sited in Accra) could alone prevent the Balkanization of Africa, and this became the basis of his new personality—"Nkrumah of Africa." The further from Ghana, the more impressive was the image; closer to home, the process whereby Ghana's constitution was swept away and total power vested in the President was meeting resistance.

Next door to Ghana, in Nigeria, the solution to the problem of uniting in a single large state diverse tribal and religious traditions was being sought in a federal format, British-designed on the Australian model. In 1947 a reforming British Governor, Sir John Macpherson, decided after consultation with all the Nigerian leaders that a parliamentary federation should be the objective. But vexing questions arose as to the actual division of powers between the states or regions and the central government, as well as the number and size of the regions. It was the overcoming of these problems that delayed Nigerian independence until three years after Ghana's.

Conferences succeeded each other as the British struggled to find compromises between rival Nigerians who imperiously demanded independence but rejected the terms their colleagues put forward for it. On many occasions it seemed Nigeria would be splintered rather than united.

The two dominant parties that emerged proceeded, exactly as in Ghana, to fill party coffers and many of the leaders' pockets by helping themselves to public funds and the resources of exporting companies, which they used to wage political warfare on each other. Initially, this struggle was undertaken with the aim of winning power at the centre in the 1959 federal elections, which Macmillan decided should be the test for handing over final independence. Whitehall assumed that the election would produce a government that would govern and an opposition capable of becoming an alternative government. However, everything that subsequently befell Nigerian democracy could be seen operating in the elections, despite the struggles of British officials—the last act of British rule—to maintain fairness. Bribery, intimidation, and electoral rigging were widespread.

Federal Prime Minister Abubakar Tafawa Balewa set himself to keep peace at the centre, partly by creating an immense government of ministers and so spreading the patronage. Since corruption was not new in Nigeria, British official circles were prone to see in Abubakar an incorruptible black Pitt helping a new country get through its "18th-Century political period." There was no nationalization under Abubakar, and there was general friendliness; Nigeria was praised as a counterpoise to Nkrumahist Ghana.

The real politics of Nigeria took some time to reveal themselves to British observers. They consisted of a ruthless and concerted attempt by the dominant coalition to destroy the opposition. This dragged on until 1966, when the army proceeded to overthrow all the regional and central governments. Prime Minister Abubakar died under a hail of bullets, and there were few survivors among the nationalists who had won Nigeria's independence.

But in 1960 this disaster—and the ensuing succession of Biafra and civil war—were undreamed of in Britain. That year saw a dozen French African colonies become independent as France hastened to put her own empire on a "commonwealth basis." It also saw a real warning of the problems facing post-colonial Africa: the Belgian Congo, which collapsed into civil war and anarchy a few days after King Baudouin handed over sovereignty. The débâcle was ascribed by Nkrumah to neo-colonialist intrigues. The British government primly attributed it to the failure of the Belgians to give the Congo the thorough education in political responsibility given to Britain's West African territories.

To many British politicians and businessmen, West Africa was one thing, East and southern Africa—"white Africa"—quite another. They rationalized the speed with which Ghana and Nigeria attained independence on the grounds that they had been 300 years in contact with the West, producing a long (if thin) line of "professionals." But much of East Africa had been in the Stone Age until the 20th Century; it comfortably followed that what happened in West Africa should be no precedent there.

In East Africa the progress of African nationalism was not related to the number of black university graduates but to the number of white settlers. This was the real hurdle. British policy in the late fifties crystallized round the concept of leading East and Central Africa to independence slowly on a basis of multi-racialism; that is, by evolving constitutions that would balance legislative power between African and European. "One man, one vote," which became the rule in West Africa by 1955 or so, was not to be the rule elsewhere, where the African electorate was to be restricted in size by property or educational qualifications so as not to overwhelm the white community by sheer weight of numbers and voting power. Africans were quick to point out the illogicality of this distinction between East and West, but the Colonial Office believed that the process of "liberalizing" the Africans' franchise could be kept slow while at the same time the white settlers could be "liberalized" in their attitudes towards Africans. It was egregiously wrong on both counts.

As elsewhere in British Africa, Kenya experienced stirrings of nationalism before the Second World War. The main issue was land and labour exploitation as practised by the white settlers, particularly against the Kikuyu people. It was on the person of a Kikuyu named Johnstone Kenyatta that matters came to focus.

In London in the thirties Kenyatta began consciously to prepare for a political future to which he felt destiny called him. He went to summer schools and socialist gatherings and visited Russia. And he wrote a book, *Facing Mount Kenya.*

In anthropology Kenyatta shaped a weapon against colonial rule that fitted the sentiment of the thirties, arguing for an indigenous culture in harmony with nature as against the so-called civilizing method of modern capitalism, of big business masquerading as colonial trusteeship. Boldly he stood up for the validity of the African (that is, the Kikuyu) tribal experience. The Kikuyu, he argued, was not a forest primitive but a man with a valid cultural achievement equal to any in Europe. He stressed the accord of man, land, and nature, and sketched an Eden almost in the image of Rousseau's noble savage. He defended magic, insisting on its medical and psychological powers in the hands of the tribe's approved witch doctor faculty, and he fought against Europeanizing what was of equal worth with anything a crumbling scientific culture could offer the human soul. He took a new name for the title page—Jomo ("Burning Spear"). The book has been called Jomo Kenyatta's "Mein Kampf," but it was perhaps more.

In 1945 he went home to Kenya and discovered his tribe in a state of ferment. Thousands of East Africans had served in the forces, and they found hard to endure the contrast between fighting alongside white troops and being despised and offered menial work by white civilians on their return. Some 200,000 Kikuyu now worked for white farmers. They could see the richness of the land, lovingly built up through two generations of good husbandry. They lusted for it. Lusting for it, they easily convinced themselves that they had owned it, richness and all, before the white man came. It was the classical moment for revolution—the moment when the lot of the underdog is improving and he has the energy to rise against injustices.

At Mombasa, Kenyatta was tumultuously received as the Messiah from overseas who would take charge. It troubled him to find that the emergent nationalism of Kenya was so overwhelmingly Kikuyu. He saw the difficulty of relying entirely on a chosen people: the others must be roused, through newspapers and political organization. The schools indoctrinated their pupils, extolling Kenyatta and warning the people to prepare for a decisive and victorious struggle.

To the white settlers angered at the growth of insubordination among the "kukus," Kenyatta seemed the man responsible. Yet in public Kenyatta was on record with strong homilies calling on the Kikuyu to improve self-discipline, farm better, trade honestly, and abjure corruption and drunkenness. On the other hand, he also said that blood must flow for Africans to win their liberties. Like all politicians he kept his options open.

By 1949 Kikuyu unrest had coalesced into the so-called Mau Mau movement, which burgeoned in white imagination into a secret society plotting against British rule and undermining familiar surroundings. If it had not yet reached those proportions, it was unquestionably growing. Gradually the whole of Nairobi's native quarter was banded together to support the revolution when it came. Stealing arms, money, and equipment for the forest caches was laid on all who had taken the oath.

It was soon demanded of Kenyatta that he denounce the secret oathing and Mau Mau. This he did. He was in continual demand as a speaker. At a huge meeting in Nyeri he demanded African self-determination and made claims for more land, but added, "he who calls us the Mau Mau is not truthful. We know nothing of this thing Mau Mau." But the white settlers were unsatisfied with this performance, especially as it was followed by a spate of murders.

The moderate Governor, Sir Phillip Mitchell, sought a middle course of patience and sensible reform, creating a public opinion for them as he went. But it was too slow. The Kikuyu revolt was developing in a world in which European prestige had collapsed after Japan's wartime victories, India's independence, and the white man's seeming loss of security and purpose. The Kikuyu pressed on with their organization because they knew they had a hope of victory.

Mitchell went into retirement and was replaced in 1952 by Sir Evelyn Baring. The Mau Mau oath-taking and the murders continued and riveted their spell upon the Kikuyu. When Baring arrived the police carefully drove him by a circuitous route to Government House to show how dangerous the situation was. A few weeks later he declared a state of emergency and British troops were brought in. Jomo Kenyatta and the best-known nationalist leaders were arrested. But it was the political leadership, not the militants, that had been removed. After a stunned week, the militants prepared for war. First, two moderate African leaders were killed. Then the first settler died, chopped up on his lonely farm near Naivasha.

The government did not want to make a martyr out of Kenyatta. It was decided to try him for managing Mau Mau and to discredit him with its disgusting aspects, but the trial failed to convince many objective observers that it was fair. It palpably was political. Government witnesses were few and of dubious credibility; it subsequently emerged that the chief witness had perjured himself. Nevertheless, the judge found Kenyatta guilty. He was thus removed from the scene while the war raged and preserved, all unwittingly, as the only leader who would be acceptable to the faction-torn Kikuyu—and the only Kikuyu acceptable to the non-Kikuyu tribes—when peace came.

The British problem was twofold: to find and destroy the units of the "Land and Freedom Army" in the forest, and to cut off their supplies. The Kikuyu initially had the advantage of terrain. The Kenya forest is vast. Attacks on white settlers intensified, but were always sporadic—even if they made up in horror what they lacked in tactical value. The mutilation of humans and animals, however, gave the British what they needed: propaganda material that ensured that "Mau Mau savages" would have no sympathy in the West.

The government made the forest a prohibited area where Africans could be, and were, shot on sight. The Kikuyu were forced to leave their isolated farmsteads and concentrated in fortified villages, where attackers could be held off by the home guard and collaborators neutralized. The security forces combed the forests to force the Mau Mau to fight.

These tactics gradually broke up the coherence of the Land and Freedom Army, which could only be supplied by women with loads on their heads slipping along forest paths or from what it could grow and eat among the trees. The government descended on Nairobi and seized thousands of Kikuyu, who were sent to camps to be screened for Mau Mau affiliations.

The security forces learned to live permanently in the forest, each responsible for a defined area that was combed and patrolled meticulously. Loyalist villagers beat the fringes of the forest and groups of converted Mau Mau fighters helped flush out remaining gangs, which were constantly on the run and frequently starving. In 1956 the Mau Mau "commander-in-chief" was flushed out, wounded, tried, and executed. The war was over, though a few fanatics held out in the depths of the forest for years.

Many settlers now supposed that their world was safe, that Britain would not experiment with African advancement for a long time to come. Exactly the reverse happened. Every dead African in the forest had cost the British taxpayer some £10,000 and the conclusion reached in London was that the settlers were incapable of

Mau Mau

In 1948, as mysterious oathing ceremonies spread among the Kikuyu people of Kenya, the term "Mau Mau" began to be heard. The words are actually meaningless in themselves, and probably arose from whites' mishearing of some Kikuyu phrase; but even Africans adopted it as a convenient name for the resistance (as they saw it) to British repression and for the so-called Land and Freedom Army.

In Kikuyu custom oathing was used to settle questions of fact and guilt or innocence. Its binding power rested on the belief that invoked spirits cannot only effect human life but destroy it. A Mau Mau oath or initiation meant dedication to the overthrow of white rule and white culture. Its object was to create a solid and obedient "passive" nation for militants to use, a base for future insurrection. At the height of the Mau Mau insurrection some 700,000 Kikuyu were so oathed, yet the actual "fighters in the forest" never exceeded 30,000 (perhaps, by other estimates, only 12,000).

The initiate promised never to reveal Mau Mau secrets, to assist its members, and to take anti-European actions that ranged from abjuring English beer to murder. Generally, vowing to kill involved a second and stronger oath ceremony. As the struggle dragged on, new oaths were devised that involved sexual behaviour taboo to the Kikuyu and even cannibalism. Their apparent purpose was to create "unclean" outcasts, killing machines whose only release would be their own deaths. It was a desperate, last-ditch effort, a spiritually bewitched kamikaze corps.

Jomo Kenyatta, Kenya's first head of state and the elder statesman of Africa.

but in Britain the real question by the late fifties was simply one of timing: how long would it take to train enough Africans to play a major role in a stable government?

Iain Macleod, the new Colonial Secretary, yielded a constitution on which Kenya-wide elections could be held. Then the Governor, Sir Patrick Renison, announced that Kenyatta, the "leader to darkness and death," would not be released, thus providing a fervent political issue. An outburst of new oathing frightened the settlers, and there were predictions of tribal warfare and chaos such as existed in the newly-independent Congo. The Governor was forced to back down.

Jomo Kenyatta was approaching his triumph. His trial was now generally regarded as a mistake, its verdict perverse, but he declared he bore no one a grudge. From the day of his emergence he made it plain that on his own terms—leadership of an independent African state—he wanted to collaborate with all.

In 1963 his party triumphed completely at the elections and Kenyatta became Prime Minister. It was clear that a national feeling had emerged and Kenyatta was the focus of it. He formed a multi-tribal cabinet, with white and Asian ministers as well. He was in a position to call for prompt independence, and London agreed. Independence was fixed for the end of 1963.

The white highlands were opened to all, and the great process whereby Britain bought out the settlers and handed the land over to Africans, as well as giving the Indian descendants of Uganda railway coolies the right to become settlers in Britain if the Kenya Africans did not want them, was put in hand. In the hectic preparations for the transfer of power, few knew how enormous the number of applications for British passports, or how well the settlers did out of the deal financially.

On December 12, 1963, came "the greatest day in Kenya's history and the happiest day in my life," as Kenyatta told a vast crowd in the independence stadium. Among the guests were the Duke of Edinburgh, representing the Queen, Secretary of State

Tom Mboya, a Kenyan leader of promise, was assassinated in 1969.

Duncan Sandys, Europeans who had believed in Kenyatta and helped him since his release, and his old friends from London days. In darkness the Union Jack was lowered and the new Kenyan flag broken out.

If Britain had planned to bring into existence in Kenya a moderate government of Africans, led by a moderate and often pro-British African elder statesman, events for the next decade could hardly have worked out better. In Africanization, in racial policy, in the definition of African socialism, Kenyatta chose a moderate path. Money poured into Kenya and, in the main, it was the Kikuyu who administered the state with efficiency. The tribe thus reached its Promised Land in one man's lifetime.

Other remarkable African leaders were breaking other barriers: Nyerere in Tanganyika, Banda in Nyasaland, Kaunda in Northern Rhodesia. They defeated a group of tough Europeans ranged against them; only Ian Smith in Rhodesia defies them—and the rest of the world.

London created the Federation of Northern and Southern Rhodesia and

giving the country leadership. What was needed, in the Colonial Office view, was more sensitive institutions whereby African grievances could be understood and redressed before they produced another explosion: a multiracial regime manned by moderate men of all colours and classes.

The war not only failed to silence Kenyan nationalism, it actually broadened its case. During Kenyatta's detention new leaders came from other tribes, notably the fiery and strident Oginga Odinga and Tom Mboya, whose smooth diction, perfect English, and svelte suitings were in complete contrast to Odinga. Mboya's sophisticated manners did more for the African cause than Odinga's strident extremism, yet both qualities were needed to create the new, inter-tribal movement that arose on the ashes of Mau Mau with a speed that appalled the settlers. Efforts were made to maintain a balance by means of fancy franchises and specially elected members to the Governor's Executive Council to hold off Mboya's relentless drive to overwhelm the settlers at the ballot box,

Nyasaland in 1953 partly to prevent Southern Rhodesia being drawn into the orbit of South Africa, where the Afrikaner nationalists had taken power in 1948, and partly to organize a multi-racial buffer state between the warring blocs of black and white Africa. It was as lopsided a federation as Nigeria. The power lay with Southern Rhodesia, where the whites kept power in their hands by such devices as a franchise with property qualifications too high for most Africans to qualify. It seemed to Africans that in a short time the Federation would obtain independence on the same basis South Africa got self-government—an independence in which blacks had no share.

"Had any of us realized," wrote Harold Macmillan subsequently, "the almost revolutionary way in which the situation would develop, and the rapid growth of African nationalism throughout the whole African continent, I think I should have opposed the putting together of three countries so opposite in their character and so different in their history." By 1959 Nyasaland was in a state of revolt and Northern Rhodesia was going the same way. Unless Britain was to re-press this African protest—the tactics used elsewhere—the Federation had to be dismantled. Sir Roy Welensky, ex-prize fighter and ex-engine driver, was determined to defend it. Banda the ex-medical practitioner and Kaunda the ex-schoolmaster were determined to end it.

Hastings Banda had attracted missionary interest and was sent to the United States for an education. After qualifying in an American medical school, he went to Edinburgh to add British qualifications and started a general practice in London. He was not imbued with African nationalism; indeed until 1953 he believed that benign Colonial Office rule was best for his people until a longish period of development and education prepared them for autonomy within the Empire.

After Federation a group of Nyasa chiefs came to London to protest against being put under white settler rule after their long security as trustees of the Colonial Office. They

were heard but over-ruled, and took their troubles to Dr. Banda's dispensary. He flung himself into the fray but failed. Disgusted with Britain, he went to Ghana to do medical work in Kumasi.

But in Nyasaland a group of young men continued to fight Federation. They had mass backing but lacked a charismatic leader to rouse the people to the fanaticism needed to confront Federation power, with its white troops and white-officered police. They sought out Banda in Kumasi and he finally accepted, and it was as the saviour who had spent 40 years abroad, who understood and practised the white man's medicine, that he returned. At Salisbury, the capital, he was asked what sort of leader he would be. "Moderates have never achieved anything," he said. "It took extremists like Oliver Cromwell and Mrs. Pankhurst to get things done."

Banda's inflammatory speeches against "this stupid federation" soon had the government frightened. Police and informers produced information that a Mau Mau uprising was being planned. The Salisbury government declared a state of emergency and detained Banda and his colleagues. It was exactly the situation (though Roy Welensky failed to see it) of Nkrumah when he was jailed in Ghana.

But the new Colonial Secretary, Iain Macleod, was a man of pronounced liberal views who clearly saw eye to eye privately with Macmillan that the Federation was doomed. Despite Welensky's protests, Macleod held an election that Banda's party won with ease. The result was a state within a state; while Banda could only demand secession, not effect it, he could and did boycott his own capital and refuse to co-operate with its officials. Welensky sent his legal minister to London to fight every British concession.

Sir Roy's strategy, however, turned more upon Northern Rhodesia (his home state) than Nyasaland. He had called Nyasaland "an Imperial slum," and originally the white settlers had tried to keep it out of the Federation; Northern Rhodesia's copper was what they wanted. There were some 75,000 whites in the copper belt and along the railway. For them everything

turned upon a qualified franchise, or they would be swamped by the votes of two million Africans.

But in Northern Rhodesia, too, there had emerged an African leader destined to break white control. Kenneth Kaunda was a tireless organizer who had studied politics in Britain under the aegis of the Labour party. Like Banda, Kaunda knew there was no future in moderation, especially against the whites of Northern Rhodesia. He saw the British government yielding to the pressures exerted by Welensky unless the Africans developed even more persuasive counter-pressures, and this could only be done by threats of riots and violent protest. Kaunda threatened that unless independence was promised in a reasonable time, and secession considered, he would be helpless to stem a popular uprising compared to which the Mau Mau war would be a "child's picnic."

In the 1962 Northern Rhodesia elections the results permitted the Africans to enjoy power. Welensky saw that with the fall of white control in Northern Rhodesia the position of the Federation was hopeless. In the final conference at Victoria Falls in 1964, the only question was the dividing of the Federation's considerable assets. Nyasaland and Northern Rhodesia went their own way, under African rule. The accession to power of Ian Smith meant that Southern Rhodesia would remain white-controlled. Central Africa was finally, fatally divided between white and black.

Nine years after Ghana's independence, the entire British empire in Africa had been dismantled, most of it under the Prime Ministership of Harold Macmillan. He had seen the necessity, and he had brought it about with a minimum of force—but without securing for Britain African goodwill. This was partly because that was never to be expected, partly because the defiance of Southern Rhodesia made it impossible. His was a melancholy role: becoming the Queen's First Minister and finding it his duty to complete the final dissolution of the British Empire.

—*Roy Lewis*

V. A Lasting Presence

Early in the 18th Century a town grew up between the James and York rivers, in the southeastern corner of Virginia. It was planned by Virginia's energetic, choleric Governor, Francis Nicholson, and its layout was to be along "modern" and "substantial" lines. As its buildings rose, contemporary observers commented favourably on them: the Governor's Palace was "the best in all English America," the church was "adorned as the best churches in London," even the gaol was "large and convenient." For some 80 years, while the so-called first British Empire rose to its height, the new town served as the capital of one of the most important American colonies.

Today, repaired and rebuilt through a generation of patient research and loving craftsmanship, Williamsburg stands exactly as it stood two centuries ago: a square mile of stately salmon brick and nestling white clapboard, of graceful ironwork and marching balustrade, of stone beasts and shields emblazoned with the royal arms peeping out from dark topiary and frothing dogwood, of interiors rich with mahogany and walnut, marble and ornamented plaster. And over all, above the towering elms and whispering mulberries, flies the Great Union, forerunner of the Union Jack.

Williamsburg is probably the most generous memorial anywhere to a former mode and a vanished rule. In the days of Empire that presence pervaded not only eastern America but much of the world. For millions upon millions it came to influence the patterns of doing and being, the springs of intercourse, the ordering of belief and behaviour. Moreover, the British did not merely touch the world and pass on. They lastingly transformed it. They offered or imposed their institutions and their attitudes, and many of their subject peoples adopted or adapted them in permanence.

In 1827, in *Blackwood's Magazine*, John Wilson made his famous remark that the sun never sets on the British Empire. Physically, it is setting now. But travel across the globe to Britain's former possessions and everywhere, in the light of the imperial sunset, one finds her image alive and vivid still:

here in the practice of great principles, there in humdrum daily habit, elsewhere in details odd, even ludicrous.

From Williamsburg pass into Canada across the Undefended Frontier: that invisible testament, despite the cynicism of economists, to the common sense of two communities of British stock. Waves of latter-day immigrants have reduced the British element in Canada to a minority, yet at a hundred points in this pluralistic, highly technical society the British past persists. Not so many years ago, the story runs, in the days when Governors-General were still appointed from London, a newly arrived representative of the King came out one morning to take the air on the steps of Rideau Hall in Ottawa. The duty constable of the Royal Canadian Mounted Police snapped to the salute. "Good morning, my man," said the new Governor-General affably, "Tell me, what is the name of your horse?" Perplexed but resourceful, the Mountie pointed to his car parked nearby and read off the figures on the licence plate. The mode of transportation of R.C.M.P. patrols may have changed but the Britishness of that renowned force survives. Their full-dress tunics derive from the lawless frontier days in the North-West when imperial red symbolized a salutary warning. And their Musical Ride, delighting crowds with its fluttering pennons and gold-trimmed saddle-cloths, scarlet forms wheeling on superbly schooled mounts, evokes memories of a crack troop of British lancers.

Nova Scotia remains true to its name. At Caledonian games kilted stalwarts toss the caber, plaids and sporrans swirl to the haunt of the pipes. From Atlantic to Pacific tourists congregate at huge turreted hotels recalling the medieval strongholds of the lairds, reminders that as the English acquired their Empire the Scots often did the work. In Vancouver, set against the white of skyscrapers and the blue of Pacific inlets, is Stanley Park, perhaps the most beautiful public playground in the world. To the English, with their green thumbs, the making of parks came naturally, and their handiwork rings the globe. The Botanical Gardens at Dominica in

the West Indies, at Peradeniya in Ceylon, at Sydney, all possess a flair for combining taste with skill, the wild with the controlled, that amounts to genius.

The city of Victoria is a veritable Little Britain. In former days, when soldiers and officials from India were seeking a haven of retirement, there was much to be said for Vancouver Island. Victoria became an enclave of grizzled heads and white moustaches, carriage-clocks and hot-water bottles, cloth caps and trousers that resembled riding-breeches. Though the Raj and most of its retired servants have gone, Victoria's Englishry has taken root as a profitable industry. The city still wears the gracious air of Tunbridge Wells and Cheltenham. Its more discreet shops reflect the urbane manners of Harrods and the Army and Navy Stores. A trio makes palm-court music amid the tinkle of teacups.

Follow the setting imperial sun into the Pacific, the infinite horizons of sea and sky that Captain Cook reduced to human grasp, to the island chains where Englishmen, voyaging after him, have left indelible impressions of their thought and action. Here are intriguing sidelights on the British presence overseas, reflecting what a pious and powerful section of home opinion wanted its emissaries to achieve at the ends of a savage earth. Sometimes wishful thinking was founded on fact, and in Fiji the results are exemplified today. The Fiji group was once the "Cannibal Isles" of song and story. The aggressive hostility of their inhabitants was notorious, their appetite for human flesh insatiable. Now they are among the most welcoming of Pacific islanders—and the most British-oriented. School playgrounds echo to the thud of rugger balls kicked by barefoot kids, and from almost any family dwelling comes the murmur of the grace that opens and closes every meal. Preaching, teaching, practising, the missionaries effected this extraordinary conversion.

At the Pacific's Asian rim, its peaky outlines restless among the melting hues of cloud and water, stands Hong Kong. And here, with its wealth stacked steeply in white mansions up

The only mounted troop in today's Mounties performs an exercise in its famed Musical Ride.

the hills, its grinding squalor spread below, its four million shouting, sweating, scurrying people clinging to the terraced island and overspilling onto the Chinese mainland, is a full-blown, glass-case British colony.

Here the machinery of colonial administration purrs on, as it once did in possessions round the globe. Britons in Hong Kong have always balanced on a tightrope. The vast bulk of China has ever been uncomfortably close; now it is a Communist monolith that looms across the border. In Hong Kong two worlds watch each other. Yet communist and capitalist banks, cheek by jowl, rear their windows to the sky, and trade with the mainland flourishes in normal times; and British shoulders shrug.

At Kuala Lumpur in Malaysia there is visible a British colonial capital almost exactly as it was early in the present century: its trim official buildings, like a cluster of miniature oriental Oxbridge colleges, set round the green expanse of the Cricket Club, its avenues redolent of high collars above spotless white duck, mutton-chop sleeves at the reins of spanking dogcarts. The railway station is sublime in its Victorian compound of fairy fantasy and strict utility: its bulbous cupolas rise from the tracks, its soaring minarets make a

mosque of booking-hall and waiting-room.

Kipling said of Singapore that though England was supposed to own the island, in fact the Chinese ran it. But even now that it is virtually a Chinese city-state, Singapore retains the stamp set on it by the British. Overlooking the rash of shipping in the harbour, St. Andrew's Cathedral and government offices, side by side, recall the British relationship of church and state. In the old days alcohol at sunset was believed to prevent malaria. Tradition is convenient; at the close of business, characters who might have stepped from Conrad or Maugham congregate at world-famous bars in determined pursuit of pink gin, that standard British tropical prophylactic.

Singapore's position makes it not only an entrepôt of trade but a meeting-place of ideas, a city of conferences. Among the salesmen, strategists, and academes who throng Singapore's hotels are herds of briefcase-laden lawyers. They will have come together from all over the Commonwealth, and beyond it. On their home ground they might wear the robes of barristers or the wigs of judges; others practise in sober gowns or merely in dark suits. But they all serve what has been described as "the

strange amalgam of case-law and statute": the English common law.

To the jurists of the Romano-Germanic system, the other great legal framework of Western civilization, the ways of the English common law often appear puzzling: a curious hodge-podge in which ancient custom and meticulous procedure seem more important than moral concepts, lucid codification, and the expertise of specialized courts. Yet today it governs the lives of, among others, uncounted Africans, West Indians, Americans, Pakistanis, Indians, Irishmen, and Israelis. Its approach to justice is essentially practical and pragmatic, public and oral, single not compartmented. It springs from the conception that no one, however powerful, is above it.

While Romano-Germanic law tends to start from the abstract summit, the common law is rooted in the daily interplay of human circumstance, the realities of everyday life. From this stems its emphasis on precedents as the distillation of accumulating experience, constantly refreshing the law itself and attuning its interpretations to the changing nature of society.

The common law was seldom, if ever, accepted voluntarily in the areas of England's overseas influence. To some the English took it with them, on others they imposed it. But it has shown itself to be one of the most exportable of their major institutions. Parliamentary government may prove a fragile flower; ties of commerce, culture, or sentiment may weaken. But the anchor of the common law holds fast, and its underlying appeal may be a simple one. "We all inherit," said an English judge, "the same sense that individual personality is the unique intrinsic value we know upon this earth."

In the subtle, sweet-and-sour mystique of British and Commonwealth contact, the basic divergence is usually between home stock and offspring. But in the Antipodes today are two neighbouring offspring nations remarkably different from each other.

On the gentle slopes that fringe New Zealand's majestic alpine core live a people so well-ordered and responsible as to approach the ideal of the "reasonable man" beloved of the common law. The foundations of this order are essentially British, for New Zealand, as far away from her origins as the surface of the earth allows, remains in many respects a replica of Britain. Policemen wear helmets. The All-Blacks are respected at Twickenham and Murrayfield. A stream of men clocking in at an Auckland factory could be mistaken for their counterparts in Birmingham. At country shows velvet-capped girls and bowler-hatted judges faithfully mirror Pony Club rallies in the shires. Yet it is a Britain with a difference.

From the first, New Zealand's pioneers sought to establish a community based on British mores, but more encouraging to enterprise and merit. While carefully maintaining her ties, New Zealand has managed to slough off the vestiges of feudality in the British make-up. Earnest and educated, radical yet balanced, she has released her energies in other directions. She was among the earliest of the nations to embrace the concept of the welfare state. The native-white relations finally (and painfully) achieved are the envy of less successful plural societies. She is an active supporter—in works as well as words—of the international order. In many fields of public policy she is

considerably ahead of her prototype.

It is hard to believe that Australia's people, only 1,500 miles away across the Tasman Sea, stem from the same British stock. Here the early British settler was pitting himself against a huge and hostile continent, most of which was proof against his advance. Even now, nearly two centuries later, only its outer seaboard rim has been fully subdued; the great dessicated interior still awaits the quickening touch of fresh technologies.

The Australian of today is not specially noted for the quiet collaborative outlook of his New Zealand neighbour. He tends rather to be a combative, competitive lone wolf. The Australian reaches also for the moon. He takes a chance, gives it a go, preferably on a scale commensurate with his surroundings: the Sydney opera house, with its tremendous ultra-modern shell-backed roofs, is probably the biggest act of faith or folly in the Southern Hemisphere. It is doubtful whether any other country would have welcomed the Pope, as Australia did, on a racecourse. Withal, his code of "mateship" is unique in the unspoken strength of its bonds.

His old ties with Britain are everywhere evident. The billy-can, slung from the stockman's saddle, is the outback version of the English teapot. He is a confirmed, renowned beer-drinker, downing his draughts in an establishment called, befittingly, a pub. Many of his older buildings are decorated with "lace"—the delicate filigreed wrought-ironwork, reminder of a gracious Georgian London, brought out as ballast in returning wool ships. In Newcastle, New South Wales, as in Newcastle-on-Tyne, when a Test match is in progress, assessment of the latest score is as essential a prelude to business as coffee in the Arab world.

But his laconic independence is proverbial. If British seems best he buys it, but he shrewdly shops around. Collectively, he is among Britain's firmest friends, but he demands that each Briton prove himself on his merits, not on his genealogy. "Bloody Pom"—said to derive from the initials P.O.H.M. for Prisoner of His Majesty stencilled on the backs of early con-

victs—applied to a Briton can be a term of pitying endearment or of vicious abuse.

Australia exemplifies the scale and perseverance the British applied to transplanting animals and crops about their Empire. To the vast continent inhabited by marsupial species they imported the entire range of its present domestic livestock: sheep, cattle, pigs, horses, dogs, cats. From Australia went droves of "Walers," the weight-carrying stock-horses that became the favourite mounts of the Indian Army. And as they shunted sugar, tea, tobacco, potatoes, breadfruit, or rubber to and fro across the globe, so the British—in the belief that eucalyptus, like alcohol, was effective against malaria—took the gum tree to India and set it in arching avenues along their trunk roads, in shimmering stands round their compounds and cantonments. At the same time, in Australia, they sowed English grass, vegetables, and cereals, and nurtured there the weeping willow cuttings that, tradition holds, came from Napoleon's tomb on St. Helena.

In the great Indian subcontinent the Viceroys governed an empire within an empire, larger in itself than all the territories ruled by ancient Rome. A memorial to the Indian Civil Service stands intact in the enormous terracotta complex of Sir Edwin Lutyens's New Delhi—combining, in its stretching vistas and austere façades, echoes of both Washington and Whitehall. Nearby, on Independence Day in 1947, the standard of the Indian Republic was raised on the walls of the Red Fort. While Churchill spoke in Westminster of the great ship sinking in the calm sea, the little flag, watched by white-clad multitudes as it climbed from the frowning Mughal bastions, signalled the end of an era the world over.

All along, India fascinated the British with a magic at once magnetic and repellent. In the opening decades of their presence they plundered her with cheerful zest and a measure, between times, of almost friendly intimacy. If the Great Mutiny finally changed their attitude, its outcome renewed British confidence and con-

High quality Crown Agents' issues, such as headgear, set standards round the world. The slouch hat was ordered by Ceylon. For everyday use, the helmet's ceremonial chain strap and spike are replaced by a leather strap and stud.

firmed in British minds the rights and duties of their sovereignty. Thereafter what they did in India was done with posterity in view; what they built was built to last. Now, a generation after their departure, it is hard to move far without encountering the aura of permanence they left.

Here imperial architecture reached its zenith: hill stations with their cozy jumble of church-towers, red-brick lodgings, fretwork balconies; barrack squares, their windows shaded from the sun by heavy fibre matting; English suburban villas—"Acacia Nook," "Windermere," "Rest Haven"—in their tropical guise of bungalows with broad verandahs and rows of potted plants; graceful pavilions, slender-pillared bandstands, ornamented clock-towers. The heart of Bombay is dominated by the domes and pinnacles of gargantuan public buildings, their scale seldom exceeded even in London, their styles ranging from Gothic to classical Italian: secretariat and library, law courts and post office—a herd of elephants frozen in brick and metal. The crowning colossus is the Victoria railway terminus, its approaches be-fountained and be-statued, its ponderous masses towered, columned, rose-windowed.

Indians today tend to smile when complimented on their efficient railway system, for in imperial times its

British originators never tired of singing its praises. And in their glory the Indian railways were indeed a wonder. Uniforms were spick and span, locomotives gleamed, training-schools and sports-grounds were the equal of anything at Crewe or Swindon. Station-masters, drivers, guards, even platelayers, were mostly British, and the impeccable standards of service they pursued perhaps provided, under blazing skies, an outlet for the national love of burnished precision still seen at home whenever Parliament is opened or the Colour trooped. And the railways were but one sector of the physical infrastructure that the British laid from end to end of the subcontinent: roads, dams, canals, telecommunications, power. Insufficient—possibly; built for alien purposes—often. But these foundations, since extended, deepened, multiplied, have done much to equip the modern Indian economy for take-off.

In 1835, when Thomas Babington Macaulay wrote his famous minute urging the teaching "of English literature and science through the medium of the English language," the aim was less philanthropic than political. It was "to form a class of interpreters between us and the natives we govern": to create, in effect, a body of Indian propagandists whose literacy in the British word would help to

strengthen the British Raj. Yet Macaulay might be astonished at the present-day results of what he set in motion. Conversely, the British in India spoke a language that can still be heard. It was a patois of words drawn from native tongues and from those of previous conquerors or settlers—Arab, Mughal, Portuguese, French, Chinese. It was called "Hobson-Jobson," which meant in army slang a confused uproar. *Buggy, bungalow, cheroot, chintz, coolie, curry, jungle, loot, mosquito, paddy, pukka, pyjamas, verandah* (and more) entered English via Hobson-Jobson.

The collision of Britain with India produced bizarre effects, none more so than in the revealing arena of the public notice. British bureaucracy has always had a weakness for this form of communication, ranging from curt warnings to "Keep off the Grass" to elaborately displayed quotations *in extenso* from prosaic bylaws handsomely framed and mounted in wire cages to afford protection against defacing. In India rulers and ruled alike carried the art to great heights. Trudging a century ago along the corridors of Indian hotels one was frequently reminded that "Gentlemen do not strike the Servants." More recently, strollers in a municipal park in Kashmir insist that they have come upon a notice which, in its combination of the didactic with the vague, seems to summarize both the Western and Eastern approaches to authority. It reads, "Do not Urinate near this Notice."

Disraeli said of the British Empire that it represented "the union of those two qualities for which a Roman emperor was deified: Imperium et Libertas." India in her British days saw much of the former quality. Yet modern independent India is among the most liberal of countries, open-minded and experimental. Beset with grievous problems of poverty, corruption, over-population, she seldom seeks to conceal them from outside eyes, and equally seldom complains of their existence. Frank and objective in her assault on them, she acts as something of a beacon to the many, in the advanced as well as the emergent world, concerned with the establishment of new social priorities. If down the years she reached beyond the "imperium" and drew from the British a measure of their "libertas" to add to her own spirit, it surely stands to the credit of both nations.

As the ideas of scientists and settlers suggested the transference of animals and plants across the Empire, so the demands of economic development called for the redistribution of labour among Britain's possessions —sometimes on a considerable scale. These cross-migrations were stimulated by a variety of factors: the abolition of slavery, shortages of local manpower for major construction projects, the simple hope of getting labour cheap.

By far the largest source of migrant labour was India. All round the shores of the Indian Ocean and far beyond, Indians with little hope at home found a living—comfortable or otherwise —in the imperial structure. There were skilled Indian pilots on the St. Lawrence, Indian masons, clerks, and accountants in the Persian Gulf and the Middle East, Indian labourers by the thousand in the cane-fields of the West Indies and the tea-gardens of Ceylon. In East Africa the British presence became to some extent synonymous with the Indian, and there the end of Empire has created a tragic human problem.

To speed the building of the Uganda railway in the 1890s Indian labourers were brought in by the shipload. Many chose to stay on afterwards, and others from the homeland joined them. Intelligent and industrious families grew up, often better equipped than their African neighbours to prosper in the offices and banks, factories and shops of a commercially oriented society. It was perhaps natural that their abilities —and their tendency to remain apart —should come to be resented, and that at independence they should be rejected by African communities struggling to improve their own fortunes. No one now wants India's surplus population—least of all India herself. What these East African Asians saw as a British promise has been but marginally fulfilled.

In West Africa, the White Man's Grave, few Britons passed their lives there who were not essential to the maintenance of government or the conduct of trade. Because Britain's ties with West Africa in imperial days were thus limited, they are now, if anything, stronger than before and rather different from those with other ex-colonial regions. The British presence today is commercial and collaborative, and there is less weight of tradition, less consciousness of a hierarchical past.

On state occasions the mingling of chiefly robes with those of judges and parliamentary officials—grave ebony countenances framed by wigs and bands—perpetuates the pageantry of Westminster. Soldiers wear the berets familiar in Aldershot and officers bear the unmistakable stamp of Sandhurst. Out in the swelter of street and bush, the flavour of Britain is husky, homely, everyday. On market days Africans unload lorries painted with arresting texts—"Jesus Saves!" "Death where is thy Sting?"— that remind of fervent missionary effort. Arrayed in the stalls are staples of the British kitchen-shelf: red-label tea, butter-puff biscuits, sauces by appointment to H.M. At tin-roofed counters, in plastic-seated cafés loud with bleating radios, there is instant coffee, fish and chips, bangers and mash.

Finally, in this quick Cook's tour, there is Ireland, the "green and bitter island." Gladstone called it "that cloud in the west, that coming storm"; and the storm is not yet passed.

Many factors contribute to the present Irish political tragedy, but the immediate roots reach back to the failure of the treaty settlement of 1921, which changed the Irish Question but did not settle it. Union with Great Britain, then membership in the Commonwealth, failed to solve the radical problems of either Anglo-Irish relations or Catholic-Protestant relations.

The treaty settlement supplied few answers to the old question of minorities within minorities. Northern Catholic Nationalists were a minority in Ulster but part of a majority in the whole of Ireland, of which Ulster was but a part, and they were encouraged to see themselves thus by successive Dublin governments. Northern Protestant Unionists were outnumbered by Catholics in the whole of Ireland but were the majority in the north, and they also belonged to the "British" majority in the United Kingdom, of which Northern Ireland was but a part. Thus, Protestants and Catholics were, simultaneously, a majority and a minority, and it was the hopes and fears which this peculiar position implied that made the problem so intractable.

Moreover, the Catholic minority was a substantial one, about one-third of the total population of Northern Ireland and bitterly resentful of a settlement that cut them off from their co-religionists in the south. Their position was different from that of the infinitely smaller Protestant minority left behind in the Irish Free State, which could never hope to reverse the decision of 1921. The Northern Catholic was thus regarded by his Protestant neighbours as a sort of "fifth column," in league with the besieging Catholic majority; there was the constant dread that the gates would be opened by the Catholics in their midst, and the citadel fall to the enemy outside.

A vicious spiral began. Dublin's refusal to abandon its irredentist line increased the grip of the Ulster Unionists in the north. The pressure on Northern Catholics gave Dublin further opportunity to campaign for the end of partition. This anti-partition propaganda further increased Protestant determination to hold what they had. And so on it went.

Events occurred in the immediate postwar years that were to have profound effects on the shaping of modern Ireland. The introduction of welfare services into Northern Ireland during the period of Clement Attlee's Labour government began a slow process by which the north outstripped the south in the standard of living. Ulster was still by no means a prosperous part of the United Kingdom, but she was a good deal better off than the south. There were now even less social and economic grounds for unification than before. In 1948 an ideological barrier was added. Southern Ireland declared itself a republic, severing the last links with the Commonwealth. In the north, Protestant anxiety reached a new fever pitch. The Attlee government responded with the Ireland Act of 1949, guaranteeing that Northern Ireland should never leave the United Kingdom unless she did so voluntarily, with the consent of her parliament. Unity was further away than ever.

By the early 1960s there seemed reason to hope that Northern Ireland was moving towards political stability. The turning point appeared to be the complete failure of the Irish Republican Army's campaign against Ulster in 1956–62. The I.R.A. had never completely disappeared from the scene after its defeat by the forces of the Irish Free State in the south and the Crown forces in the north in the 1920s. In the 1950s it again emerged, seeking to keep the gun as a factor in Irish politics and end partition by force.

It failed. The I.R.A. received little aid and comfort from the Ulster Catholic population. Protestants did not take reprisals on the minority. The Dublin government interned without trial I.R.A. men and their sympathizers. Without support from Catholics in the north, and under pressure from Dublin, Westminster, and Belfast, the campaign fizzled. It was a classic case of how the guerrilla cannot succeed unless he has the support of the civilian population: the fish cannot swim without water.

The prime reason why Northern Ireland Catholics did not support the I.R.A. was because they were, at last, gaining some real benefits from the British connection. The welfare state was having an effect, and poorer sections of the population, Catholic as well as Protestant, were beginning to enjoy greater prosperity, to pay more attention to social and economic issues. Ulster Catholics seemed increasingly prepared to forego demands for unification, at least in the foreseeable future.

But although they were enjoying economic benefits, they remained a politically frustrated minority. There was growing impatience at the lack of effective remedies to their complaints about Protestant discrimination. This involved more than jobs and housing; it sprang from the frustration of a minority that could never hope to gain political power. The Protestant majority remained with the same measure of power, the same amount of control, that it exercised at the beginning of Northern Ireland's existence. To a growing number of Catholics, this was the fundamental problem, and it provided a driving force to Catholic criticism of the regime.

These criticisms came, oddly enough, at a time when Northern Ireland was ruled by the most liberal Prime Minister in her history, Terence O'Neill. O'Neill wanted to do more than rest on slogans like "What We Have We Hold." Catholics were treated to the extraordinary sight of a Unionist Prime Minister visiting Catholic schools, extending the hand of friendship to Catholic citizens. Protestants were treated to the even more extraordinary sight of their leader meeting the Prime Minister of the Republic of Ireland, Sean Lemass, to discuss "possibilities of practical co-operation in economic matters of mutual interest."

In the event, O'Neill was faced with an insurmountable obstacle: if he went too far in his liberalizing tendencies he would alienate large sections of Protestant opinion, ordinarily decent people who had been brought up in the belief that Catholics were the deadly enemies of the state. If he did not go far enough, he would disappoint Catholic hopes and further increase their general frustration. And lurking behind Protestant fear and Catholic impatience were the old sinister political elements in Ireland—the extremists.

The deadly spiral was beginning anew. In 1967 the Northern Ireland Civil Rights Association was founded, with the aim of pressing for reform and redress of Catholic grievances. Such a movement struck a responsive note in many sections of British liberal opinion, and resulted in increasing publicity in Press and Parliament. This raised the fears of the Ulster Protestants, who again felt themselves attacked from all sides. The British, after all, were their friends, their comrades in World War II, like themselves Protestants and loyal to the Crown. Why were they so ready to condemn Ulster? And what was a "Civil Rights Movement"? Was it anything more than a front for the I.R.A.? When the Movement took to the streets in the autumn of 1968, the worst fears of the Protestants seemed to be realized: the fifth column was on the march, ready to join hands with the enemy in the south—with the connivance of the British government. Many, perhaps most, Ulster Protestants were unable to understand a Catholic movement that declared it only aimed at reform within Northern Ireland, for all Catholic movements in the past had aimed at destroying the state altogether. The enemy must be met by force, otherwise there would be a Catholic "takeover." Within a year of the first civil rights marches, the two communities were at each other's throats. Severe rioting broke out in Londonderry, Belfast, and other Ulster towns. People died in the streets, and only the intervention of the British Army prevented a complete collapse into anarchy.

Power was passing from the hands of the moderates to those of the extremists. In 1970 a renewed I.R.A. threat emerged with the formation of the "Provisional Wing" of the movement, differing in important respects from the I.R.A. that had failed so dismally in the 1950s. This new organization drew its strength from the fact that it was recruited from the Ulster Catholic community. The Provisionals declared that they were "traditional Republicans," and this was language that the Northern Catholic (and the Southern Catholic as well) could understand. It was a simple matter of "freeing Ireland" and driving the British into the sea.

The British government found itself, much against its will, more deeply involved in the Ulster crisis than ever before. It was becoming clear that London's hopes of avoiding direct rule were fast disappearing, for no political system, no government, could survive with one-third of the population ranged against it. Yet the dangers of direct rule were apparent. The long-feared Protestant backlash might become a nightmare reality; it might only encourage the I.R.A. to redouble its efforts to overthrow the rule of Westminster; and it would certainly mean a massive increase in England's involvement in the affairs of Ireland, with all its attendant dangers. Perhaps the entry of both the United Kingdom and the Republic of Ireland into the European Economic Community can provide the long-range framework within which these basic problems can be resolved. But one is reminded of the agonized cry of Arthur Griffith during the treaty debates in 1922: "Is there to be no living Irish nation? Is the Irish nation to be the dead past or the prophetic future?" This, perhaps, with hundreds of dead in Ulster since 1969, is the most important "Irish Question" of all.

The journey under the setting sun of Empire is nearly done. One crosses the Irish Sea to the mother country's chalk cliffs and grey skies, to the island landscapes where they speak, in slow broad vowels or swift clipped idiom, the language that has been the cement of so many nations across the globe. It is the language in which Shakespeare dramatized, in *The Tempest*, the shipwreck off Bermuda, one of the first of Britain's overseas settlements; in which Milton prayed to his stern God: "O Thou, who of thy free grace didst build up this Britannick Empire to a glorious and enviable height, with all her daughter islands about her, stay us in this felicitie"; in which the independence of the United States, of India, and of many other former possessions was declared; in which Balfour framed the formula for Commonwealth.

"He seems to me a very foolish man," Alfred the Great wrote in the turmoil of the Dark Ages, "who will not increase his understanding while he is in the world." In recent decades governments of former British colonies, seeking to cut clear of the past, have made attempts to discourage the use of English within their borders. Most have been quietly shelved, for the advantages of a *lingua franca* widespread enough to provide an international medium, poetic enough to crystallize the reaches of the human spirit, sufficiently flexible to convey the concepts of scientific thought, have proved overwhelming. Perhaps the "English-speaking world" will be Britain's most enduring monument to the era of her universal presence.

Examples remain of the architectural cross-fertilization inspired by Empire. The great Victorian pile below was transplanted and flourishes as Bombay's railway terminus. The Royal Pavilion at Brighton (opposite) is an Oriental extravaganza sprouting in Sussex.

If that presence changed the world, the coin has its reverse. Long after the Union Jack has been lowered in the last colony, the face of Britain will surely, as now, reflect the era when she presided over the greatest extent of the earth's surface to be controlled from a single point since the empire of Genghis Khan. Across the green of hill and dale stand palaces and country houses—the Royal Pavilion at Brighton, Sezincote in the Cotswolds—echoing in their styles travel and trade and rule in Orient and Occident, and gardens like Wisley and Hidcote, where rare plants from the Himalayas and the Rockies have been lovingly reared.

London still evokes the impact of the Empire on the city that was its heart: the streets where Gurkhas and Bengal Lancers and Anzacs have marched; the Guildhall's statue of William Pitt the Elder, with its forthright inscription "He made commerce to flourish by war"; the precincts of Westminster, where the abolition of slavery in 1833 made Gladstone sorry for the parliamentarians of later times who would never have a comparable cause to fight for; the magnificent

India Office Library, probably the greatest collection of works on one country ever assembled in the capital of another; the chambers of the Privy Council, where the Judicial Committee sat as the supreme arbiter of the Empire's justice; Kew Gardens, hub of imperial botanical management, with its continuing links to universities and research stations round the globe; the Imperial College of Science and Technology, founded to spread the fruits of British discovery through the colonies; the Albert Hall, where a generation that never saw the Empire in its hope and glory still roars out Elgar's majestic paean of loyalty.

Soldiers, seamen, explorers, merchants, missionaries, governors, viceroys: the great names of Empire have gone, along with the many more unnamed humble men from every part of Britain who executed their orders from the Arctic Circle to the Antipodes. They left a world permanently altered, partly in their material works, partly in the imprint of themselves. And the persistence into our time of that second, intangible legacy seems to suggest that they inspired towards

themselves a love-hate attitude of a kind not seen in history since the decline of Rome.

The hate of conquerors and rulers is easy to understand; and the British could be overbearing, contemptuous, acquisitive, violent, smug, short-sighted, maddening. But they were teachers and guardians as well. Many cared, and with all their faults they were often generous, heroic, efficient, passionate, scholarly, sensitive, amiably eccentric. Their contradictions will in retrospect sort themselves into a balance—a balance, with the passage of time and the onset of judgement, perhaps tilting in their favour.

They had experience, know-how, energy, certainty, qualities of immense importance in the age of their ascendancy and in the lands along their march. And now, amid the perplexities of changing values and the humiliations of dwindled power, there remains Burke's prophetic admonition: "As long as you have the wisdom to keep this country as the sanctuary of liberty, wherever men worship freedom they will turn their faces towards you."

—*Stuart Legg, D. G. Boyce*

Epilogue

A LOOK BACKWARD

Virtually every civilization in recorded history has sought to extend its sway over others. Empires arose first in Egypt and Mesopotamia. The Medes, the Assyrians, the Persians all had their day. Alexander the Great established a short-lived empire that encompassed the known world. The great Roman Empire has left its marks on Europe to the present day. The Chinese Empire overshadowed the Far East for more than 2,000 years. When Europeans broke into the New World they encountered the empires of the Incas and the Aztecs.

All empires were systems of domination, and all began with conquests and rested on superior strength. All, too, had a superior way of life—or so the imperial people believed. Their systems of politics, laws, and religion were supposed to be uniquely inspired, and every empire claimed it was bestowing benefits on those it conquered. In reality the imperial people took most of the benefits for themselves. They acquired power, glory, and wealth: none would have been content with a balance sheet of empire that did not show a clear credit. Much high-flown rhetoric issued from their statesmen, clerics, and historians—chaplains, as they have been called, of the pirate ship—but in fact every imperial people went into empire for the sake of what they could get out of it. They often erred and found ruin where they had sought gain, but the initial calculation was always the same. Throughout history the few have exploited the many, and empires were systems of exploitation more ruthless than most.

The empires of ancient times were land empires, their power resting on armies. Its legions, rather than its

political wisdom, held the Roman Empire together, and it fell when the legions lost their strength. Even the English entered the imperial competition during the Hundred Years' War, attempting to establish an empire in France. This was an antiquated enterprise. Then, during the 15th Century, Europeans on the Atlantic seaboard developed a new form of power by turning to the oceans. This was the beginning of the modern age.

The driving force behind these maritime ventures was economic with a dash of geographical curiosity thrown in. The Portuguese made their way round Africa and crossed the Indian Ocean and as an almost accidental by-product established an overseas empire—the only one, ironically, the relics of which still survive. The Spaniards hoped to reach the Far East directly by crossing the Atlantic. Instead they discovered America and there set up a vast empire richly endowed with gold and silver. Both Portuguese and Spaniards were also missionaries. Roman Catholic Christianity as well as trade followed their flags.

The English were late in entering this imperial competition, for during much of the 16th Century they were hard-pressed to assert their independence from Continental powers. Protestantism was part of this assertion; the English regarded themselves as a Chosen People, authorized by God to override the ordinary laws of civilized behaviour. The sea dogs of Elizabeth's time, so much admired by 19th-Century historians, were in fact pirates, their aim to seize for themselves the loot the Portuguese and Spaniards were deriving from their empires. As this became more difficult, their successors turned more or

less casually to establishing overseas settlements. The richest prizes had, it seemed, gone to others. The English had to make do with North America, where there was no gold or silver, but in their view the pursuit of wealth was a religious duty (especially for the Puritans) and they did not neglect it. At the same time, other Englishmen set up chartered companies to trade with Russia, the Levant, India. The last of these unwittingly led to the greatest overseas empire of all.

Europeans had two great resources when they established their empires. The first was the sea itself. They could move safely across it, fearing no enemy except other Europeans. They could thus inflict on the rest of the world the turmoil the Vikings had once inflicted on them. Their second resource was gunpowder. Their firearms gave them mastery over all other races; for more than 300 years firearms rather than Christianity guaranteed the superiority of European civilization.

The English had one special resource that finally enabled them to win the race for empire. Though European in their origins and culture, they were detached from Europe geographically. When they were wise they used this isolation to keep out of Europe's conflicts. In later times British statesmen pursued a European balance of power in their foreign policy. Having the Continental powers in conflict was a guarantee of their own security, and they were thus free to expand their dominions overseas.

In the 18th Century the British eclipsed all their rivals. Spain was in decay, France was distracted by European ambitions. The British Empire was extended over North America, and another, less formal, empire was

The Viceroy's residence in New Delhi, glimpsed through its imposing gates, was the symbol of British imperial rule over the Indian subcontinent.

495

established in India. The British motive in India was initially entirely economic. They did not seek to impose their way of life on the inhabitants; they wanted peace and security in order to extract wealth and remit it to London. North America, however, was an empire of settlement. There they terminated the native inhabitants to the best of their ability. Why did these Britons overseas emulate Attila and his Huns? Why did they alone of European conquerors practise extermination instead of conversion? It is hard to answer.

This 18th-Century Empire—the first British Empire, as it was often called—was a straightforward institution of plunder. It was "a good thing" for those who profited from it and for no one else. No Nabob pretended that he laboured for the benefit of the Indians; he laboured in order to become a millionaire. Similarly, London did not claim to run the North American colonies for the benefit of the inhabitants, even though they were of British stock. The colonies existed in order to provide cheap raw materials and preferential markets for British goods. No doubt the North Americans believed they were extending the British way of life as they interpreted it. This achievement did not much concern the British government.

One aspect of the colonies concerned the British governing class very much, however, These communities had to be administered, and this meant public offices—jobs for the Old Boys, in the later phrase. All such posts, from governor down to customs officer, were reserved for the British aristocracy and its hangers-on. Needy noblemen were made governors, subservient Members of Parliament were rewarded with colonial appointments for their relatives and dependents. Much the same happened in India, where the administration, nominally still conducted by the East India Company, became a happy hunting ground for the British upper classes. Many a great nobleman added to his prestige, and of course to his wealth, by serving as Governor-General of India. Successful generals, and unsuccessful ones too, received high posts in India instead of pensions.

Hilaire Belloc has immortalized the system:

We had intended you to be
The next Prime Minister but three:
The stocks were sold; the Press
    was squared,
The Middle Class was quite prepared.
But as it is! . . . My language fails!
Go out and govern New South Wales!

Here was a new factor in the imperial drive. The British Empire was increasingly run simply for the sake of those who ran it. In truth, not all were in the game merely for the high salaries they received. Many welcomed power and openings for achievement greater than they could have found in serving as rural magistrates or back-bench Members of Parliament at home. Some had an intellectual curiosity to explore the history or languages of India. Some were glad to escape from boredom. Whatever their motives, the administrators provided an imperial class. The Empire, which provided them with jobs, became for them a mission, a sacred duty. As time passed they came to believe they were extending the virtues of British civilization—and this belief was not without foundation. What had begun as a trading venture turned into a moral cause. The administrators began to consider the interests of those over whom they ruled. They drew the line only at one point: they would do anything for the subject peoples except get off their backs.

The first British Empire of the 18th Century did not last long. The American colonies revolted against exploitation, both mercantilist and bureaucratic; they wanted to run their own economy without restrictions and to lay their own hands on the government jobs. Their independence did not do much damage except to the pride of George III and his ministers. Culturally and economically the United States remained a British dependency until the beginning of the 20th Century. Here was a great discovery, expressed in theory by Adam Smith and reinforced practically by the loss of the American colonies: political overlordship was not essential for economic profit.

There were other reasons for this

development. For much of the 18th Century the West Indies was by far the most profitable part of the British Empire. William Beckford, the richest Englishman of his time, derived his entire wealth from sugar plantations in the West Indies, and he was only one among many. Then towards the end of the century the plantations showed signs of exhaustion from over-cropping. Nature was short-circuiting exploitation.

Simultaneously, there was a significant, rapid change in English economic life. Machines and factories boosted the nation into the foremost industrial community. Some economists have conjectured that the capital necessary for this industrial expansion derived from the exploitation of Empire—primitive accumulation, as Marx called it. Other economists assert that the capital reserves were gradually built up at home, and this is the currently prevailing view. It is a point of not great moment; capitalists had to exploit someone if they were to come into existence at all. The development of industry, which for a time made Great Britain the workshop of the world, was a striking, if negative, event in the history of Empire. For the profits derived from coal and cotton, iron and steel seemed to make Empire unnecessary. British industry did not need protected markets; free trade was implicitly a repudiation of Empire. A free-trade Empire was almost a contradiction in terms—but not quite. Free trade that benefited the British was bestowed on the subject peoples, particularly on India, whether they liked it or not.

The Industrial Revolution that made Empire apparently unnecessary in one way stimulated it in another. Along with the growth of industry went a great increase in the population of Great Britain. We do not know how far the two developments were connected. Possibly the growth of industrial towns made better sanitation and health services essential; possibly industrial workers, though miserably poor, were better fed than agricultural labourers. At any rate, the increased population was there, and it had to go somewhere. Both Australia and New Zealand originated as receptacles for

The traditional 19th-Century nursery of imperial statesmen was the public school. These are Etonians at a 4th of June celebration in 1907.

this surplus. This was a new feature in imperial expansion. Previously men had gone to the colonies in search of gain. Now they went for space and, to some extent, for a freer life. In the mid-19th Century something like a quarter of a million people a year left Great Britain, the majority to the United States but many to the developing British colonies.

In this way British communities complete with British institutions established themselves within a matter of a few decades. The home government exercised little control over them: it had learnt a lesson from the revolt of the American colonies. Canada, then New Zealand and Australia, received "responsible government." This was an unprecedented development in the history of empires. For all practical purposes those colonies with responsible government were no longer under the authority of London. They were bound to Great Britain only by ties of sentiment. They received practical advantages as well, of course. The Royal Navy gave them a painless security until well into the 20th Century. The mother country offered a profitable market for their foodstuffs and raw materials. Later the London capital market was opened to the colonies on advantageous terms. The balance sheet of Empire was reversed: the colonists benefited from the imperial connection and Great Britain drew no great profit from it. Still, the possession of an Empire brought prestige. It still provided agreeable jobs for the

upper classes. Yet British capitalists made most of their wealth by their own activities at home. Great Britain would have been no poorer—perhaps even a little richer—if the colonial empire had not existed.

India was a different matter. Direct exploitation in the old plundering fashion came to an end. The 19th Century saw no more Nabobs as administrators became more powerful than traders. These administrators were now high-minded. Corruption fell out of fashion and public service took its place. Evangelical Christianity played a role in this change, for Victorian England was an intensely religious nation. The British generals and administrators in India saw themselves as Soldiers of God; though they could not actually convert Hindus and Muslims to Christianity, they could impose the Christian virtues.

The rule of the Indian Civil Service brought great benefits to its subjects. India was more peaceful and orderly, more fairly administered and better endowed with hospitals and railways than it could have been without British rule. But there was a heavy debit to be set on the other side. The more efficient and honest the British rulers of India became, the greater grew the cleavage between them and those they ruled. The adventurers of Clive's era had not regarded Indians as different from themselves. They spent many uninterrupted years in India, and it was normal practice for them to marry Indian women. Any servant of the

East India Company who married a Rajah's daughter thought himself in luck's way. Now all was changed. The virtuous administrators of the I.C.S. regarded Indians as inferior: they took bribes, they put the interest of their family before that of the state, they worshipped many gods of a most peculiar sort, they neglected the drains.

The I.C.S. provided the loftiest outlet for the products of the public-school system now flourishing in England. The sons of the gentry and wealthy middle classes were provided with what had previously been an aristocratic education. Those who passed through the public schools were "gentlemen." Having acquired a gentleman's culture, they also needed a gentleman's income. Where were they to acquire it? Not by trade or industry: qualified by their command of Latin and Greek, they were safely immune from any taint of trade and free to discharge their religious mission. The Indian Civil Service was the perfect answer—the life of a gentleman, with a household of 15 or 20 native servants, retirement at an early age on a high pension to England, their sons following the same career.

It is thus easy to conclude who benefited from the Indian Empire. Its administration helped perpetuate the English class system throughout the 19th Century. The benefit for British society is less obvious. The public schools were conservative institutions. Their outlook sapped the spirit

of enterprise and invention that had carried Great Britain forward during the Industrial Revolution. Towards the end of the 19th Century there was increasing speculation about what was "wrong" with Great Britain. Why was her economic growth slowing down? Why did she not predominate in the new industries of electricity and chemicals as she had in coal and cotton? The simplest answer was the public schools. They taught the classics when they should have been teaching the sciences; they sustained an outlook unsuited to a progressive industrial community; and in their turn they were sustained by the Indian Empire.

The Mutiny of 1857 completed the estrangement between the British and their Indian subjects. Henceforth India was ruled as though it was another planet. Any idea of educating the Indians into self-government was postponed to an extremely remote future. Victoria became Empress of India, an imperial title never taken for any other of her dominions. It was in this period that India brought most profit to Great Britain. Internal peace made India a rich market: Lancashire continued to prosper with the Indian demand for cotton goods. India also brought advantages in power. The Indian Army, paid for by Indian taxes but officered by Englishmen, provided Great Britain with military resources. And in addition, about half the British Army was regularly stationed in India, again at Indian expense. Whatever the larger strategic consequences, the Indian Empire was a wonderful device for maintaining armed forces on the cheap.

Until about 1880 the British Empire was the only one of its kind in the world. It encompassed the globe. Its white communities were growing in population and resources. British control of India seemed unshakable. All this rested on command of the seas, the Pax Britannica.

A new epoch opened in the 1880s. Other powers began to covet colonies and turned to Africa, the one continent that had not been seriously penetrated by Europeans. France, Germany, even Belgium and Italy joined in. The British would have preferred to leave Africa alone, and only acquired vast African territories in order to keep others out. There was also a strategic motive. With the Suez Canal now their route to India, they extended rule over much of Africa to make this control more secure.

The imperialism of the late 19th Century has been much discussed by historians. It had many causes, not all of them political. Explorers were eager to chart the Dark Continent and often used patriotic motives as an excuse for purely academic curiosity. Missionaries wished to rescue the Africans from paganism. Philanthropists wished to end the Arab slave trade. On a more practical basis, colonies were supposed to offer profitable markets as they had done in the 18th Century. Further, they were supposed to offer profitable openings for investment. According to the theory propounded by the economist J. A. Hobson and then taken up by Lenin, the yield on capital was diminishing at home as industries became fully developed and production outstripped demand; investment in the undeveloped colonies provided what Lenin called "super-profit." Hence the motive behind this new imperial expansion was the old search for wealth.

This view has been sharply discredited in recent years. It has been shown, for instance, that the direct connection between overseas investment and the New Imperialism, as laid down by Hobson and Lenin, has been grossly exaggerated. British overseas investment certainly increased greatly at this time, but most of it went to South America, the United States, and other independent countries, not to the newly-acquired African colonies. Indeed, few of these colonies "paid" the countries that acquired them. The annual cost to Germany of administering the Cameroons was five times as great as her total trade with that colony, and much the same applied to other imperialist powers. Nor is there any clear evidence that the yield from colonial investments was higher than that from investment at home. On the contrary, the dabbler in overseas shares was far more likely to lose his money. In most every case European countries spent a great deal in acquiring colonies that proved of little economic value.

These arguments, though true, are essentially irrelevant. They treat European countries as communities in which policies were conducted for the benefit of all, much as corporations are conducted (or are supposed to be) for the benefit of their shareholders. This was not the case. If benefit went to the few who determined policy and shaped public opinion, it was irrelevant that this was achieved at great loss to the many. The humourist James Thurber drew extremely ugly women; when told that his women were not attractive, he replied, "They are to my men." Similarly, when we are told that imperialism was not profitable, it can be said, "It was to the imperialists." The humble investor might lose his money, but the corporate promoter did not go away empty-handed even if the company he promoted went bankrupt. Overseas railways often did not pay those who invested in them, but they paid those who built them and those who peddled the shares. The Boer War cost the British taxpayer a great deal of money, but South Africa produced many millionaires. In Edwardian times these millionaires occupied most of the houses in Park Lane. Clearly, imperialism brought economic gain to some people, if not for the imaginary national community.

Economic imperialism was a striking example of conspicuous waste, the doctrine laid down by Thorstein Veblen. According to Veblen, capitalism needs a steady increase in expenditure in order to keep going, and the great problem is to find new excuses for spending money. Imperialism was a splendid way of doing it. If some great nobleman had offered to stay at home instead of becoming Viceroy of India on condition that he be given a rise in the peerage and £200,000, this would have been an excellent bargain for the British taxpayer. But of course no one would have considered it, and the nobleman duly went to India. J. S. Mill said long ago that the Empire was a system of unemployment relief for the British aristocracy. By the late 19th Century it had become a system of unemployment relief for British capitalists too.

Economic imperialism did not last long. The First World War changed the spirit of British imperialism. The supposed strategical danger from the German colonies revived Britain's desire to lay hands on more of the world, and at the end of the war this desire was strengthened by a new alarm over Bolshevik Russia. The British Empire acquired a new empire in the Middle East, stretching from Egypt to India. There was also a change in direction. Germany was deprived of her colonies on the excuse that she had ruled them brutally. The British acquisitions in Africa and Asia were called Mandates, allegedly administered for the good of their inhabitants. The British had to be on their best behaviour, and often they took their high professions seriously.

Yet at this late stage of Empire the British reverted to old ideas of direct exploitation. Free trade no longer brought automatic prosperity. In 1932 Great Britain went over to protection. Lord Beaverbrook preached "Empire Free Trade"—in reality an economic system closed against foreigners—but the Dominions would not accept it. The colonies administered from Whitehall had no choice. In the years before the Second World War these colonies became protected markets for British goods exactly as the American colonies had been in the days of mercantilism. This brought no benefit to the colonies, and most economists now hold that it brought none to Great Britain either. Her principal competitors, the Japanese and the Germans, being excluded from the colonies, merely became fiercer rivals elsewhere.

There was a deeper underlying change. In 1922 the Irish Free State came into existence. It did so by rebellion, not by conciliation and consent; the Sinn Feiners succeeded where the parliamentary Home Rule party had failed. This was an example for other colonial peoples. In India the Congress party led by Gandhi moved from conciliation to resistance— even though on Gandhi's insistence this was non-violent. The British were challenged at their most vulnerable point. They had held their Empire by the possession of superior force. Now the balance of strength was turning against them. During the interwar years they were still strong enough to retain their hold on India and only made concessions that involved no surrender of power. But they were increasingly strained by the mounting challenges from Germany and Japan. In 1939 and then more decisively in 1941 they were plunged into a desperate global struggle for survival.

Though the British entered the war in order to destroy Nazi tyranny in Europe, they fought it in practice mainly as an imperial venture. They fought Germany and Italy in North Africa and the Mediterranean. They fought Japan on the eastern borders of India. Paradoxically, they fought this war for the sake of an Empire they had already decided to relinquish. The Indians were offered their freedom if they would wait until the end of the war and, though they refused the offer, they got their freedom afterwards all the same. Withdrawal from India was really the end of the British Empire. It had been the central point of the whole system and, once it went, there was little point in hanging on to the rest.

The British maintained that they were no longer strong enough to maintain their Empire. It would be truer to say that they no longer believed in it. There is no explaining a loss of belief of this kind. It happened. One day the British believed that they were a great people because they had an Empire. The next day they regarded the Empire as a burden and discarded it without further thought. Now political scientists puzzle over questions about the meaning of Empire and find no convincing answer.

This imperial collapse had an unnecessary and unfortunate accompaniment. The colonies and the Dominions had really little in common though lumped together as British. The Dominions were independent communities, associated with Great Britain through their own free will. As such they were the only allies of Great Britain who went through both world wars from the first day to the last. They imposed no conditions; they asked no reward. They responded instinctively to the call of kith and kin—a phrase now discarded as ridiculously sentimental but once full of meaning. Commonwealth aid in wartime was economic as well as financial. The United States demanded hard terms when providing Lend-Lease. Canada gave Mutual Aid unconditionally. Here was the living reality of Commonwealth feeling. Yet nothing was made of it. Once the Second World War was over, British opinion turned against the Commonwealth as much as it did against the Empire. Admittedly there were some —the French in Canada, the Boers in South Africa—who did not feel the tie of kith and kin. But essentially the Commonwealth was a union of hearts, not a union of interests. The postwar British political leaders deliberately threw it away. By the 1960s Commonwealth citizens, as much British as the inhabitants of Lancashire, were denied free entry into their own homeland. The Commonwealth Immigration Act was the real end of Empire.

It may be debated interminably whether the possession of Empire ever showed a profit to the national community. But such debate is pointless. The British Empire was run for the sake of those who administered it, defended it, and speculated in it.

There remains a final question. Did the British Empire benefit its subject peoples? There is no simple answer. The Empire carried British institutions overseas in the Dominions and made Africans and Indians at least superficially European in their ethics, politics, and customs. If European civilization in its British guise be accepted as a superior form of life, then the British Empire was clearly "a good thing." It all depends on the point of view. Perhaps the subject peoples would have found a way of life more suited to their needs if they had been left to themselves. Perhaps not. In the event, they were given no choice. The British thought that they were discharging a mission of civilization. Probably their real mission was to extract profit for themselves— and it is not certain that they did even this successfully.

—A.J.P. Taylor

Picture Credits

Library of Congress Cataloging in Publication Data
Main entry under title:
The Horizon history of the British Empire.

"Based on material originally produced by Time-Life Books in association with the broadcast of the television series, The British Empire by BBC-TV."

1. Great Britain—Colonies—History. I. Sears, Stephen W., ed. II. Time-Life Books. III. The British Empire.
DA16.H65 325'.342 73-8684
ISBN 0-07-030354-1
ISBN 0-07-030355-X (deluxe)

Index

POPE-HENNESSY, SIR JOHN, 318
PORTUGAL, 15, 177; Africa, 177,
188, 200, 204, 205, 232, 249, 250,
254, 416; Angola, 177, 200, 232,
416; Brazil, 41, 218, 220; commerce
and trade, 15, 17, 19, 22, 44, 161,
177, 188, 249; East Indies, 19, 44;
and Great Britain, 44, 45, 46, 47;
and India, 15, 19, 44, 45, 49; maritime activities, 15, 44, 45, 45, 46,
495; Mozambique, 200, 232, 254;
and the Netherlands, 49
POSTLETHWAYT, MALACHY, 178
POTGIETER, ANDRIES, 191
PRETORIUS, ANDRIES, 192
PRETORIUS, MARTHINUS, 219
PRINCE EDWARD ISLAND, 263,
265, 267
PRIOR, MELTON, 385
PRUSSIA, 89, 177, 249; see also
Germany
PURITANS AND PURITANISM, 34,
36, 37, 38, 47, 303, 402, 495

Q

QATAR, 476
QUAKERS, 38, 179

R

RACIALISM see DISCRIMINATION
AND RACIALISM
RADCLIFFE, SIR CYRIL, 470
RADISSON, PIERRE, 39, 40
RAFFLES, THOMAS STAMFORD,
132, 132, 133
RAILWAYS, 146, 357, 359, 366, 372,
373, 374, 375, 478, 498; Australia,
274, 276, 277, 372; Burma, 373;
Canada, 263-64, 265, 267, 268, 268,
357, 373, 374, 377; China, 395;
France, 354; Great Britain, 348,
352, 354-55, 358, 366, 368, 374;
India, 288, 355, 360, 362, 363-64,
369, 373, 489; New Zealand, 278;
Russia, 372; South Africa, 232, 372,
384, 385, 388; Uganda, 254, 368,
484, 490; United States, 354, 356
RALEIGH, SIR WALTER, 15, 19, 20
21, 33, 34
RAM MOHUN ROY, 145, 147
RAND, LT. WALTER, 437
RANJIT SINGH, 152, 153, 154, 158
RAPHAEL (merchant-banker), 355
RAS AL-KHAIMAH, 478
REBMANN, JOHANN, 200, 210
REDMOND, JOHN, 411
REFORMATION (ENGLAND), 401
REFORM BILL, 180, 263
RENISON, SIR PATRICK, 484
RETIEF, PIET, 191, 192
RHODE ISLAND (Br. colony), 36,
37, 79, 81
RHODES, CECIL, 12, 219-20, 221,
221, 222, 232, 249, 251, 295, 300,

358, 372, 384, 385, 387, 390, 391,
445
RHODES, HERBERT, 219
RHODESIA (NORTHERN RHODE-
SIA AND SOUTHERN RHODE-
SIA), 383, 384, 385, 387, 416, 417
RHODESIA (SOUTHERN RHODE-
SIA; republic), 485
RHODESIA AND NYASALAND,
FEDERATION OF, 478, 479, 484-
85
RICHARDSON, JAMES, 200
RIEL, LOUIS, 266, 267, 268
RIPON FALLS PROJECT, 479
ROANOKE ISLAND COLONY, 21,
21, 34
ROBERTS, GEN. SIR FREDERICK,
9, 282, 293, 328, 329, 388, 390, 391,
392, 393
ROBERTS, TOM, 275
ROBERTSON, FIELD MARSHAL
SIR WILLIAM, 330
ROBINSON, DICK, 352
ROBINSON, SIR HERCULES, 274
ROBINSON, JOSEPH B., 221
ROCKINGHAM, MARQUESS OF, 80
RODNEY, ADM. GEORGE, 86, 87
ROE, SIR THOMAS, 46, 47
ROGERS, FREDERIC, 318
ROMAN CATHOLIC CHURCH:
Canada, 82, 261; England, 15-16,
28, 401, 402, 405; France, 40; Ire-
land, 90, 400-406 passim, 405, 409,
410, 411, 490, 491, 492; Nether-
lands, 22, 24; Portugal and Spain,
15, 19, 22, 24, 27, 33, 495; and
slavery, 178, 179; see also Chris-
tianity (and Missionaries)
ROMMEL, GEN. ERWIN, 448, 457,
459, 460
ROOSEVELT, FRANKLIN D., 466;
World War II, 459, 460, 463, 464,
479
ROOSEVELT, THEODORE, 255
ROSE, SIR HUGH, 172
ROSS, ALEXANDER M., 372
ROSS, MAJ., 115
ROTHSCHILD, BARON LIONEL
DE, 233
ROTHSCHILD, NATHAN, 340
ROTHSCHILD AND SONS, N. M.,
222, 340, 355, 356, 387
ROWLANDSON, THOMAS, 86
ROWLATT, JUSTICE, 440
ROYAL AFRICAN COMPANY, 177,
178
ROYAL GEOGRAPHIC SOCIETY,
205, 210, 212, 214
ROYAL MILITARY ACADEMY
(Woolwich), 330
ROYAL MILITARY COLLEGE
(Sandhurst), 330, 332
ROYAL NAVY see NAVY AND
MARITIME ACTIVITIES (GREAT
BRITAIN)
ROYAL NIGER COMPANY, 252, 358
ROYAL SOCIETY, 97
RUDD, CHARLES, 220, 221
RUM AND MOLASSES TRADE, 42,
43, 79, 118, 178-79
RUSSELL, LORD JOHN, 163, 192,
209

RUSSIA, 232, 336, 372, 379; and
China, 395, 397, 398, 398; Crimean
War, 232, 330, 334; and France,
232, 330, 334; and Great Britain,
11, 16, 90, 151-52, 153, 159, 232,
236, 254, 293, 294, 301, 330, 331,
334, 364, 380, 439, 450, 495; and
Persia, 151, 152, 153; World War
I, 414, 452; see also Soviet Russia

S

SAHARA DESERT, 196, 198, 198
ST. CHRISTOPHER (ST. KITTS),
40, 86, 87; see also British West
Indies
ST. EUSTATIUS, 86
ST. HELENA, 180
ST. LUCIA, 85, 87, 89, 90, 95
ST. VINCENT, 85
SALE, LADY FLORENTINE, 156
SALE, GEN. ROBERT, 158
SALISBURY, LORD, 10, 249, 252,
254, 293, 380
SALT AND SALT TRADE, 22, 39,
44, 136, 159, 442
SAMOA, 414
SAMUEL, SIR HERBERT, 450, 451,
452
SANCHEZ COELLO, ALONSO, 23
SANDERSON, WILLIAM, 17
SAN DOMINGO, 23, 24, 89
SANDWICH, LORD, 82, 83-84
SANDYS, DUNCAN, 484
SANTA CRUZ, MARQUIS OF, 24, 25
SANTAYANA, GEORGE, 296
SAQR, SHEIK, 478
SARAWAK, 133
SARGENT, JOHN SINGER, 237
SAUDI ARABIA, 471, 476, 477
SCHROEDER (merchant-banker), 355
SCHUMACHER, JOHANNES, 189
SCOTT, SIR GEORGE GILBERT, 310,
316
SCOTT, THOMAS, 266
SCOTT, SIR WALTER, 298
SECOND WORLD WAR see WORLD
WAR II
SEDDON, RICHARD, 413
SEDDON, RICHARD JOHN, 278,
278-79
SEELEY, SIR JOHN: The Expansion
of England, 295
SENEGAL, 249
SEVEN YEARS' WAR, 59, 61, 70, 83,
88, 97
SEWARD, WILLIAM H., 265
SEYCHELLES, 95, 311
SHAH ALAM, 71
SHAH SHUJA, 152-56 passim
SHAKESPEARE, WILLIAM, 492
SHARJAH, 477, 478
SHARP, GRANVILLE, 179
SHELTON, BRIG. JOHN, 156
SHERIDAN, RICHARD, 73, 88, 404
SHIPPING see NAVIES AND MARI-
TIME ACTIVITIES; NAVY AND
MARITIME ACTIVITIES (GREAT
BRITAIN)

SHORE, SIR JOHN, 148
SIERRA LEONE, 250, 251, 252, 307,
479
SILK TRADE, 16, 18, 19, 22, 44, 54,
160, 161, 188, 341, 474; see also
Textiles and Textile Trade
SILVER AND SILVER TRADE, 22,
24, 34, 35, 122, 127, 147, 161,
341, 495
SIMON, SIR JOHN, 442
SINGAPORE, 132, 437, 459, 460, 461,
465, 477, 487
SLAVERY AND SLAVE TRADE, 177-
80, 189, 190, 198, 200, 203, 204, 209,
234, 235, 237, 238, 498; Arabia, 476;
France, 177, 179, 180; Great Britain,
22, 23, 36, 38, 42, 79, 142, 144-45,
177-83 passim, 178, 181-86, 185,
186, 249, 251; India, 142, 144-45,
180; Netherlands, 177, 189; opposition to and suppression of, 9, 12,
141, 142, 144-45, 179-83 passim,
181-86, 185, 186, 190, 194, 199, 202,
203, 205, 249, 250, 255, 303, 305,
309, 310, 332, 490, 493, 498; Spain,
22, 23, 24, 177, 178, 179; United
States, 182, 339, 341; West Indies,
22, 23, 40, 42, 43, 177, 178, 179, 180
SLESSOR, MARY, 305, 308, 309
SMILES, SAMUEL, 366
SMITH, ADAM, 496; The Wealth of
Nations, 179, 339
SMITH, IAN, 485
SMITH, JOHN, 305
SMITH, CAPT. JOHN, 34, 35; Gen-
erall Historie, 35
SMITH-DORRIEN, LT. HORACE, 227
SMUTS, JAN CHRISTIAAN, 392,
414, 416, 430, 432, 432, 433, 435,
455, 456
SMYTH, SIR THOMAS, 50, 51
SOCIETY FOR THE ABOLITION OF
THE SLAVE TRADE, 179, 180
SOCIETY ISLANDS, 96, 109
SOLINUS, 195
SOLOMON ISLANDS, 414
SOMALIA, 210, 254
SOMERSET, LORD CHARLES, 190
SOUTH AFRICA AND UNION OF
SOUTH AFRICA, 11, 12, 253, 295,
311, 360, 382, 384-85, 395, 413-14,
416, 430, 432, 433, 436, 437, 478,
485, 498; diamonds, 217-22, 218,
222, 232, 257; gold, 219, 230-32,
364, 384; racialism, 188, 189, 190,
200, 295, 395, 436, 437, 440, 478;
railways, 232, 372, 384, 385, 388;
World War I, 413-17 passim, 428,
429, 430, 432, 433; World War II,
437, 455, 456, 457, 461-62; see also
Boers; Boer War; Cape Colony;
Commonwealth; Griqua and Griqualand; Natal; Orange Free State;
Transvaal Republic; Zulus and
Zululand
SOUTH AMERICA AND LATIN
AMERICA: British, 85, 89, 95, 190,
305, 340, 357, 498; Dutch, 89, 90,
190
SOUTH CAROLINA (Br. colony), 36,
38, 86
SOUTHEY, SIR RICHARD, 217

509

Y

Z